T0215772

Communications in Computer and Information Science 747

Commenced Publication in 2007
Founding and Former Series Editors:
Alfredo Cuzzocrea, Xiaoyong Du, Orhun Kara, Ting Liu, Dominik Ślęzak,
and Xiaokang Yang

More information about this series at http://www.springer.com/series/7899

Liehuang Zhu · Sheng Zhong (Eds.)

Mobile Ad-hoc and Sensor Networks

13th International Conference, MSN 2017
Beijing, China, December 17–20, 2017
Revised Selected Papers

 Springer

Editors
Liehuang Zhu
Beijing Institute of Technology
Beijing
China

Sheng Zhong
Nanjing University
Nanjing
China

ISSN 1865-0929   ISSN 1865-0937 (electronic)
Communications in Computer and Information Science
ISBN 978-981-10-8889-6   ISBN 978-981-10-8890-2 (eBook)
https://doi.org/10.1007/978-981-10-8890-2

Library of Congress Control Number: 2018937392

Printed on acid-free paper

This Springer imprint is published by the registered company Springer Nature Singapore Pte Ltd.
part of Springer Nature
The registered company address is: 152 Beach Road, #21-01/04 Gateway East, Singapore 189721, Singapore

Liehuang Zhu · Sheng Zhong (Eds.)

Mobile Ad-hoc and Sensor Networks

13th International Conference, MSN 2017
Beijing, China, December 17–20, 2017
Revised Selected Papers

 Springer

Editors
Liehuang Zhu
Beijing Institute of Technology
Beijing
China

Sheng Zhong
Nanjing University
Nanjing
China

ISSN 1865-0929   ISSN 1865-0937   (electronic)
Communications in Computer and Information Science
ISBN 978-981-10-8889-6   ISBN 978-981-10-8890-2   (eBook)
https://doi.org/10.1007/978-981-10-8890-2

Library of Congress Control Number: 2018937392

Printed on acid-free paper

This Springer imprint is published by the registered company Springer Nature Singapore Pte Ltd.
part of Springer Nature
The registered company address is: 152 Beach Road, #21-01/04 Gateway East, Singapore 189721, Singapore

Preface

The recent proliferation of sensors and embedded computing devices in daily life, has given rise to sensor networks. Accordingly, mobile ad hoc, and sensor networks have garnered significant attention in recent years. Therefore, the International Conference on Mobile ad hoc and Sensor Networks (MSN) provides a forum for researchers and practitioners to exchange research results and share development experiences in the field of mobile ad hoc and sensor networks every year.

Thanks to the excellent reputation established by past versions of conference, MSN 2017 received 145 quality research submissions. After a thorough reviewing process, only 39 English papers were finally selected for presentation as full papers, with an acceptance rate of 26.90%. This volume contains the papers presented during the main conference. They address challenging issues in multi-hop wireless networks and wireless mesh networks, sensor and actuator networks, vehicle ad hoc networks, delay-tolerant networks and opportunistic networking and cyber physical systems, as well as in Internet of Things, and system modeling and performance analysis.

Additionally, MSN 2017 also included state-of-the-art contributions from keynote speakers Jiannong Cao, Yan Zhang, and Yu Wang, who have made significant contributions to wireless networking.

The high-quality program required significant effort and dedication on the part of many people. We express our sincere appreciation to the authors who chose MSN 2017 as a venue for their publications. We are also very grateful to the Program Committee members and Organizing Committee members, who put a tremendous amount of effort into soliciting and selecting research papers with a balance of high quality, new ideas, and new applications.

We hope that you enjoy reading and benefit from the proceedings of MSN2017.

January 2018   Liehuang Zhu
                                                                              Sheng Zhong

Organization

Organizing Committee

General Co-chairs

Heyan Huang	Beijing Institute of Technology, China
Pengjun Wan	Illinois Institute of Technology, USA
Kui Ren	Zhejiang University, China

TPC Co-chairs

Liehuang Zhu	Beijing Institute of Technology, China
Sheng Zhong	Nanjing University, China

Local Arrangements Co-chairs

Fan Li	Beijing Institute of Technology, China
Zijian Zhang	Beijing Institute of Technology, China

Program Committee

Bang Wang	Huazhong University of Science and Technology, China
Chao Li	Chinese Academy of Sciences, China
Cheng Wang	Tongji University, China
Chao Wang	North China University of Technology, China
Cong Wang	City University of Hong Kong, SAR China
Dongbin Wang	Beijing University of Posts and Telecommunications, China
Fan Li	Beijing Institute of Technology, China
Honghao Gao	Shanghai University, China
Hui Zhu	Xidian University, China
Jia Zhao	Beijing Jiaotong University, China
Jiamou Liu	The University of Auckland, New Zealand
Jingyuan Fan	State University of New York at Buffalo, USA
Kaiping Xue	University of Science and Technology of China, China
Kashif Sharif	Beijing Institute of Technology, China
Kui Ren	Zhejiang University, China
Lan Yao	Northeastern University, China
Li Lu	University of Electronic Science and Technology of China, China
Lianfen Huang	Xiamen University, China
Liehuang Zhu	Beijing Institute of Technology, China
Liran Ma	Texas Christian University, USA
Pengjun Wan	Illinois Institute of Technology, USA
Qi Wang	Chinese Academy of Sciences, China

Qing Cao	University of Tennessee, USA
Ruipeng Gao	Beijing Jiaotong University, China
Ruoyu Chen	Beijing Information Science and Technology University, China
Sheng Zhong	Nanjing University, China
Shui Yu	Deakin University, China
Weili Han	Fudan University, China
Xiaojiang Du	Temple University, USA
Xin Li	Beijing Institute of Technology, China
Yingshu Li	Georgia State University, USA
Yongbin Zhou	Chinese Academy of Sciences, China
Yongjun Xu	Chinese Academy of Sciences, China
Yu Wang	University of North Carolina at Charlotte, USA
Yueming Lu	Beijing University of Posts and Telecommunications, China
Zhan Qin	University of Texas at San Antonio, USA
Zhaoxia Yin	Anhui University, China
Zhipeng Cai	Georgia State University, USA
Zhitao Guan	North China Electric Power University, China
Zhulin An	Chinese Academy of Sciences, China
Zijian Zhang	Beijing Institute of Technology, China

Contents

An Efficient and Secure Range Query Scheme for Encrypted Data in Smart Grid

Xiaoli Zeng[1], Min Hu[1], Nuo Yu[1,2(✉)] [iD], and Xiaohua Jia[1]

[1] Harbin Institute of Technology Shenzhen Graduate School,
Shenzhen 518055, China
yunuohit@gmail.com
[2] School of Electrical Engineering, Anhui Polytechnic University,
Wuhu 241000, China

Abstract. In smart grid information systems, the electricity usage data should be audited by data users, such as the market analysts to finish their tasks. Besides that, electricity company always outsources the data to the cloud server (CS) to release its data management pressure. Since the CS is untrusted and the detailed electricity usage data contains users' privacy, the privacy concern of the data and data users' queries is raised. Although many schemes have been proposed to achieve the encrypted data query in smart grid, they are not applied well due to the numeric attributes in electricity usage data and privacy concern in smart grid application. In this paper, we provide an efficient privacy-preserving scheme for range query in smart grid. Our scheme achieves the range query without disclosing the privacy of the data and queries. And the performance shows that our scheme can reduce the computation cost for both the data owner and data users, and shorten the response time of every query, which is great significance for smart grid application.

Keywords: Smart grid · Privacy-preserving · Range query

1 Introduction

With the rapid development of industrial and economic activities, smart grid has been accepted by more and more people due to its many good features. However, the electricity usage data of customers in smart grid is surging from 10,780 terabytes (TB) in 2010 to over 75,200 TB in 2015 [1]. That is far beyond the electricity company's data management capability. Uploading the electricity usage data into a cloud server is the best way to mitigate this stress. In this approach, electricity company can store the electricity usage data on cloud server and execute computation and queries using the server's computational capabilities.

However, cloud server is often untrusted. It may share the electricity usage data with other parties for profit making. But the electricity usage data contains

© Springer Nature Singapore Pte Ltd. 2018
L. Zhu and S. Zhong (Eds.): MSN 2017, CCIS 747, pp. 1–18, 2018.
https://doi.org/10.1007/978-981-10-8890-2_1

user's private information, e.g., user's name and family address, bank account and telephone number. If the cloud server shares these data with attackers, user's privacy might be compromised. Therefore, our electricity usage data must be stored in encrypted form on the cloud server to protect the data confidentiality and privacy.

In addition, electricity usage data in smart grid information systems should be periodically audited to ensure that the billing and pricing statements are presented fairly [2]. Specially, data users, such as market analysts, are endowed with the task of querying smart grid information systems for auditing, analysis, accounting or tax-related activities [3]. Thus, there is growing need to achieve querying on encrypted data in smart grid.

It is not a trivial issue to query on encrypted data in smart grid at the same time with the following requirements: (1) Confidentiality and privacy of data. The electricity usage data should be protected from being stolen by the untrusted cloud server. (2) Privacy of the query. Since the cloud server is untrusted, it might trace the query results if the query contains sensitive information and make the user's privacy disclosure. Thus, guaranteeing query privacy is also important for smart grid application. (3) Achieving range query. Since the electricity usage data always has the numeric attributes, range query is a common type of queries for the smart grid. (4) Being efficient and low cost. Smart grid is a large-scale system, since the electricity usage data is large and dynamic update in the cloud server, the protocol should be efficient for the query and low cost for both the data owner and data users.

Recently, many protocols were proposed to achieve the query on encrypted data, but they are not suitable to apply for the smart grid. Public key encryption with keyword search (PEKS) is a widely studied approach to achieve querying on encrypted data. Nevertheless, most of the existing schemes (such as [4,5]) about PEKS focus only on the keyword search technique, with little attention to both data and query privacy protection in the scheme. Baek et al. [6] argue that PEKS and data encryption schemes need to be treated as a single scheme to securely provide PEKS service. Qin et al. [7] propose an efficient encryption scheme with one-dimension keyword search (EPPKS) for cloud computing by combining the ideas of partial decipherment with the PEKS. However, it is not quite secure because the partial decipherment will leak partial information of users' data. The Searchable Encryption Scheme for Auction (SESA) [8] in smart grid achieved the security, but it only can be applied for the equality checks.

In this paper, we propose a privacy-preserving range query scheme over encrypted electricity usage data for smart grid, which ensures to secure the data confidentiality, privacy and query privacy in smart grid. We first proposed a range query scheme in smart grid by using the modified Paillier homomorphic cryptosystem. With our scheme, the range query is achieved without disclosing the privacy of the electricity usage data and query context. We then evaluated the performance of our scheme. The results show that our scheme can reduce the computation cost for both the electricity company and data users, and shorten the response time of every range query, which is great significance for smart grid application.

The rest of this paper is organized as follows. Section 2 discusses the related work. Section 3 describes the system model, data query model, security requirements and our design goals. Section 4 introduces the background. Sections 5 and 6 present the modified paillier homomorphic cryptosystem and our scheme respectively. Section 7 discusses how the proposed scheme meets our design goals, and Sect. 8 shows the experiment results. Finally, concluding the paper in Sect. 9.

2 Related Work

Querying encrypted data in smart grid is an important issue that attracts great attention from research communities. But the most existing schemes only can be applied for equality checks. Since the encrypted electricity usage data has many numeric attributes, it is much significant to achieve range query in smart grid.

For the encrypted data query, there are generally four categories of solutions that have been developed for range query: (1) Order preserving encryption (OPE)-based schemes; (2) Predicate encryption-based schemes; (3) Asymmetric scalar-product preserving encryption (ASPE)-based schemes; (4) Bucketization-based schemes.

Order preserving encryption (OPE)-based schemes [9–11] that preserve the relative ordering of data items even after encryption. Agrawal et al. [9] describe the first order preserving encryption scheme for numeric data, followed by [10] which gives a formal security analysis and proposes the Order Preserving Symmetric Encryption (OSPE). Boldyreva et al. [11] revise and improve the security of OPE. The OPE scheme allows direct translation of range predicate from the original domain to the domain of the ciphertext. However, OPE encryption is deterministic and thus it reveals the frequency of each distinct value and is susceptible to statistic attacks.

In predicate encryption-based schemes [12–15] secret keys correspond to predicates and ciphertexts are associated with attributes. The secret key corresponding to a predicate can be used to decrypt a ciphertext only if the attribute satisfies the predicate. Boneh and Waters [12] propose a predicate encryption, named Hidden Vector Encryption (HVE), which can be used for range queries. To improve the search efficiency, tree-based index structures [15,16] were proposed to support multi-dimensional range query [13]. But in those schemes, the cost to compute exponentiation and pairing in group is too high.

Asymmetric scalar-product preserving encryption (ASPE)-based schemes [17,18] that allow the relative distance comparison between two data points under encryption. Given two data points p_1, p_2 and a query point Q, all encrypted, ASPE can determine whether Q is closer to p_1 or p_2. Wang et al. [17] create a hierarchical encrypted index, which first constructs a regular R-tree for a given set of data points and then applies the ASPE to encrypt the minimum bounding box range (MBR) in the R-tree. This tree-based ASPE solution reduces the leakage of sorted information, but it can cause false positives.

The bucketization technique is firstly designed in [19] for query processing in an untrusted environment. In this bucketization-based scheme [19–21], the data owner partitions the whole attribute domain into multiple buckets of varying sizes and assigns a unique bucket tag to each bucket using a collision-free hash function. Pairs of a bucket tag and the encrypted tuples constitute the index, which is maintained on the untrusted server. When a range query is issued by the data owner, it needs to be first determined which tags of buckets intersect the query and then all the tuples indexed by these tags will be returned by the server. Although this scheme is more efficient than the three schemes mentioned before, it always contains some false positives, the data users need to filter the mismatch after decrypting all the results, which is not suitable for application of the smart grid.

Since the schemes presented above all have some shortcomings. In this paper, we aim at providing a privacy-preserving range query scheme for encrypted electricity usage data in smart grid based on the modified paillier homomorphic cryptosystem.

3   System Model

In this section we introduce the system model, data query model, security requirements and our design goals.

3.1   System Model

In the system model, our focus is on how to outsource the users' electricity usage data from the electricity company to cloud server (CS) in encrypted form and how to operate a query over the encrypted electricity usage data in CS by data users. Our system is composed of three components, as shown in Fig. 1: electricity company, data users (such as the market analysts, auditors) and a cloud server (CS).

The electricity company is the data owner, who encrypts the electricity usage data of customers by using cryptosystem before outsourcing the data to CS. And the data user always need to query the electricity usage data for their tasks. CS is honest but curious, it might be interested in users' electricity usage data and data users' queries.

3.2   Data Query Model

Before we discuss the security requirements and our design goals, let us first introduce how the encrypted data is stored at the CS and how data users make queries.

We consider relational databases, where data are represented in the form of tables. Let $R(A_1, A_2 \cdots A_n)$ be a relational table, where $A_1, A_2 \cdots A_n$ are attributes of the table. The encrypted form of the table is as following:

$$R^s(A_1^s, A_2^s \cdots A_n^s),$$

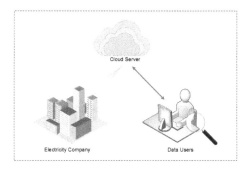

Fig. 1. System model in our scheme.

Table 1. User information table (*UIT*)

ID	Name	Address	Consumption
23	Tom	Maple	40
860	Mary	Main	80
320	John	River	50
875	Jerry	Hopewell	110

where A_1^s, A_2^s $\cdots$ A_n^s are encrypted attributes. For example, consider the *UIT* table below that stores the information of customers (Table 1).

The *UIT* table is mapped to a corresponding *UIT*^{s} table at the CS:

$$R^s(ID^s, Name^s, Address^s, Consumption^s)$$

where ID^s, $Name^s$, $Address^s$, $Consumption^s$ denote encrypted strings of the ID, Name, Address and Consumption respectively. For instance, the following is the encrypted table *UIT*^{s} stored on the CS (Table 2):

Table 2. UIT^s

ID^s	$Name^s$	$Address^s$	$Consumption^s$
1100...	0111...	0001...	0100...
0110...	0011...	0101...	0111...
0010...	1111...	0100...	1000...
1110...	0000...	1001...	1101...

The colunm strings contain the vaules corresponding to the encrypted values in *UIT*. For instance, the first vaule is encrypted to "1100..." that is equal to *encrypt* (23), the second vaule is encrypted to "0111..." that is equal to *encrypt* (Tom).

In this model, data users use the SQL statements to query the encrypted data. For example, data users use:

> **SELECT** Name, Address, Consumption
>
> > **FROM** *UIT* table
> >
> > **WHERE** Consumption>100;

and the client software at userside will translate this SQL query Q into an encrypted form Q^s:

> **SELECT** $Name^s$, $Address^s$, $Consumption^s$
>
> > **FROM** UIT^s table
> >
> > **WHERE** $Consumption^s > 100^s$;

where $Name^s$, $Address^s$, $Consumption^s$, 100^s are the ciphertext of the respective strings. It is then submitted to CS for excution. CS will return encrypted data that satisfy the SQL conditions to the user.

The conditions of the SQL statements can be classified to two categories: (1) Attribute = Value. Such condition is equality query, like consumption = 80; (2) Attribute > Value or Attribute < Value. Such condition is range query. For instance, consumption > 70 or consumption < 60.

Since extensive research has been done on equality condition on encrypted data, we focus on range query in this paper.

3.3   Security Requirements

As mentioned before, in system model, CS might be interested in the electricity usage data. It has the motivation to steal the individual data for its own purpose. In addition, it might trace or analyze the query results, if the query contains sensitive information. Therefore, our scheme should satisfy the following security requirements.

Data Confidentiality: The electricity company should encrypt the electricity usage data before uploading it to the CS, and successfully prevents the CS from stealing the data.

Data privacy: The encrypted electricity usage data should be accessed only by authenticated data users. It means that only the authorized data users can decrypt the encrypted data.

Query privacy: Data users usually prefer to keep their queries from being exposed to others. Thus, the biggest concern is to encrypt the query to protect the query privacy. Otherwise, if the query includes some sensitive information, the CS might trace or analyze the results.

3.4   Design Goals

In this model, our design goal is to develop a privacy-preserving range query scheme over encrypted electricity usage data for smart grid application, and achieves the security and efficiency as follows.

(1) Since the CS is untrusted and the electricity usage data contains the privacy of the user, our scheme should achieve the data confidentiality and data privacy, as well as the query privacy.

(2) In smart grid application, the electricity usage data is large and dynamic update in the cloud. As range query are operated over encrypted electricity usage data, comparing with the existing range query schemes in smart grid, our scheme should reduce the response time of every range query and reduce the computation cost for both the data owner and data users.

4 Background

In this section, we will first introduce the Paillier Homomorphic Cryptosystem which are the based of our scheme.

The Paillier homomorphic cryptosystem is a public key cryptosystem by Paillier [22] based on the "Composite Residuosity Assumption (CRA)". The Paillier cryptosystem is homomorphic, by using a public key, the encryption of the sum $m_1 + m_2$ of two messages m_1 and m_2 can be computed from the encryption of m_1 and m_2. Our scheme is inspired by the Paillier cryptosystem. Hence, we give some preliminaries of the Paillier homomorphic cryptosystem, which consists of three phases as follows.

Key Generation. Set $n = pq$, where p and q are two large prime numbers. Set $\lambda = lcm(p - 1, q - 1)$, i.e., the least common multiple of $p - 1$ and $q - 1$. Define $L(\mu) = \frac{\mu+1}{n}$, and randomly choose g_p, then compute

$$\mu = (L(g_p^\lambda (mod\ n^2)))^{-1}(mod\ n).$$

The public encryption key is a pair (n, g_p). The private decryption key is (λ, μ).

Encryption $E(m, r)$. Given plaintext $m \in \{0, 1, \ldots, n - 1\}$, select a random $r \in \{0, 1, \ldots, n - 1\}$, and encrypt the plaintext m as ciphertext c:

$$c = E(m, r) = g_p^m \cdot r^n\ (mod\ n^2).$$

Decryption $D(c)$

$$D(c) = L(c^\lambda\ (mod\ n^2)) \cdot \mu\ (mod\ n) = m.$$

5 Modified Paillier Cryptosystem

In our scheme, we use the Paillier homomorphic cryptosystem so that CS can perform matching operation without decrypting the electricity usage data and query contexts. In this section, we provide the details of our modified Paillier cryptosystem.

5.1 Making μ Public

Recall that in the Paillier cryptosystem, (λ, μ) is the private key. However, μ can be made public, because it is hard to decrypt an encrypted message by only knowing μ. Hence, we can make μ public while achieving the same security guaranty as the unmodified Paillier cryptosystem.

We take advantage of this operation in order to shift the computation towards encryption and make decryption lightweight.

5.2 Shifting the Computation

With the modification above, the new public key is (n, g_p, μ) and the private key is λ. First, we modify the Paillier homomorphic cryptosystem so that anyone can decrypt using the new public key, but only those holding the private key can encrypt. This is similar to the digital signatures. And the following equations show the modification to the encryption and decryption algorithms:

Encryption:

$$
\begin{aligned}
E'(m, r, \lambda) &= E(m, r)^{\lambda} \\
&= g_p^{m\lambda} \cdot r^{n\lambda} \ (mod \ n^2) \\
&= c.
\end{aligned}
$$

Decryption:

$$
D(c) = L(c \ (mod \ n^2)) \cdot \mu \ (mod \ n) = m.
$$

We can realize that one can perform all the homomorphic operations on our modified Paillier cryptosystem similar to the Paillier cryptosystem.

Note that as we shift the computation towards encryption, the decryption is computationally more efficient than the Paillier decryption. And we also allow the CS to perform certain operations without knowing the private key. Such shifting improves the performance of the range query model, since the Paillier decryption become more efficient.

5.3 Secret Comparisons

With the shift of computation described above, CS can find the difference by simply decrypting each value, which does not assure the privacy of individual values. Therefore, we introduce an additional parameter to the encryption operation in order to allow CS to compute the difference without knowing individual values.

Assume that there are two values x_1 and x_2. We perform the following operation to the encryption so that CS can find the difference $(x_1 - x_2)$ without learning either x_1 or x_2:

$$y_1 = g^t \cdot E'(x_1, r_1) \ (mod \ n^2),$$

$$y_2 = g^{-t} \cdot E'(-x_2, r_2) \ (mod \ n^2).$$

Note that even though μ is known, it can decrypt neither x_1 nor x_2 as they are multiplied with g^t and g^{-t} respectively. Due to the homomorphic property, we can have:

$$y_1 \cdot y_2 = E'(x_1 - x_2, r_3).$$

Anyone can compute the difference as follows using the public key of the modified Paillier cryptosystem:

$$D(y_1 \cdot y_2) = x_1 - x_2.$$

The results $D(y_1 \cdot y_2) > 0, D(y_1 \cdot y_2) < 0$ and $D(y_1 \cdot y_2) = 0$, indicate the cases of $x_1 > x_2$, $x_1 < x_2$ and $x_1 = x_2$, respectively.

For example, if the data user wants to query the users whose electricity consumption is greater than 100, then the x_2 is 100. The CS will return the encrypted data to the user. As we can see, with this method, CS can compare two numeric values, but is unable to know the exact values of them.

6   Privacy Preserving Range Query Scheme

There is three entities in the range query model in smart grid: electricity company, data users and a CS. For each query, the scheme works in the following steps, as shown in Fig. 2:

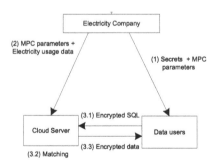

Fig. 2. The steps of range query in our system.

(1) Initialization of the electricity company and the data user.
(2) Electricity company uploads the encrypted electricity usage data to CS.
(3) Data users make queries to CS and get the results.

In the proposed scheme, we aim at providing a privacy-preserving range query scheme in smart grid based on modified Paillier cryptosystem. We will explain each step in details in the following subsections.

6.1 Initialization of Electricity Company and Data Users

When the electricity company initializes, it generates the following values: $E'(r_i)$, $E'(1)$, and $g^t \cdot E'(r_i)$, which are used by the electricity company to encrypt the data before uploading them to the CS.

Besides that, during the initialization, the company checks the identify of the data user. If it is a legal user, electricity company will send the following values to it: $-r_i$, $E'(-1)$, and $g^{-t} \cdot E'(-r_i)$.

Note that these parameters are used by the data user to encrypt the queries and decrypt the results. The electricity company may provide $E'(-1)$ and $-r_i$, and allow the data user to compute $E'(-r_i)$ homomorphically, instead of providing the value directly. In this case, data user can recover neither g^{-t} nor $-t$ from $g^{-t} \cdot E'(-r_i)$.

6.2 Upload the encrypted data to CS by electricity company

When the electricity company wants to upload the data, it frist encrypts the electricity usage data. We illustrate our ideas using examples. Consider the UIT table before, we encrypt one of the columns in the data table as an example. Let one of the consumption values as v_1. It is encrypted to y_1 as following:

$$y_1 = g^t \cdot E'(r_i) \cdot E'(r_i(v_1 - 1))$$
$$= g^t \cdot E'(r_i v_1).$$

The encryption of other attribute values is similar to this example.

Note that $E'(r_i(v_1 - 1))$ is homomorphically computed using $E'(r_i)$. This value can be computed efficiently by using fast multiplication.

After the electricity company encrypts the electricity usage data, it uploads the encrypted data to the CS.

Note that CS cannot decrypt the encrypted data, but our scheme allows the CS to perform privacy preserving matching.

6.3 Secure Data Query by Data Users

When the data user makes a SQL query, the query is encrypted and the encrypted query is sent to the CS.

Considering the following query as an example:
>   **SELECT** Name, Address, Consumption
>   **FROM** UIT table
>   **WHERE** Consumption>100;

The value 100 is encrypted into the form 100^s in the example. We use x_1 to express the value 100 and w_1 expresses the encrypted form 100^s. The operation is as follows:

$$w_1 = g^{-t} \cdot E'(-r_i) \cdot E'(r_i(1 - x_1))$$
$$= g^{-t} \cdot E'(-r_i x_1),$$

When the CS receives the encrypted SQL query:

SELECT $Name^s$, $Address^s$, $Consumption^s$
FROM UIT^s table
WHERE $Consumption^s > 100^s$;

It searches data table UIT (encrypted) and compares each attribute values (encrypted) in consumption column with 100^s. It computes the difference d between each consumption value in the table with 100^s as follows:

$$d = D'(y_1 \cdot w_1)$$
$$= r_i(v_1 - x_1).$$

Since the r_i is greater than 0, CS will return the encrypted data to the data user, which makes the $d > 0$.

Note that, the electricity usage data always contains more than one attribute. If the data user queries the data more than one attribute, CS has to match for a composite range query after evaluating each rang query value.

And after successfully receiving the result, the valid data user can decrypt the encrypted data using the secrets.

7   Security Analysis

In this section, we will explain how our scheme achieves the goals of the data confidentiality, data privacy and query privacy.

7.1   Data Confidentiality

The data confidentiality in our scheme requires that the electricity usage data should be encrypted when it is uploaded to the CS, and prevents the CS from stealing. In our scheme, the electricity usage data is encrypted by Paillier cryptosystem. And as for CS, since it only does homomorphic computing on two encrypted values, it cannot access the electricity usage data. Therefore, the proposed scheme can achieve the data confidentiality.

7.2   Data Privacy

Data privacy in our scheme means that only the authorized data user can decrypt the electricity usage data. Data in our proposed scheme are encrypted by Paillier cryptosystem, so the adversary cannot identify them. But if the adversary fabricates a message and sends it to some entities, it cannot be detected. Hence, we also use the protocol in our scheme, only the data user who is authenticated by the electricity company can get the secrets to decrypt. Therefore, our proposed scheme can achieve the data privacy.

7.3   Query Privacy

The query privacy in our scheme means that the query should be encrypted to keep from being exposed to the CS. In our scheme, queries are also encrypted by the Paillier cryptosystem. When CS wants to do the matching for the electricity usage data, it does not need to know the exact value of the query. It only does homomorphic computing on two encrypted values. Thus, our proposed scheme satisfies the goal of query privacy.

8   Experiment Result

In this section, we evaluate the performance of the proposed scheme in terms of response time of a range query and the computation cost of the data owner and data users.

8.1   Response Time

In smart grid, it is important for data users to know the response time of a range query, which can benefit for them to efficiently schedule their tasks. We analyze the response time of our scheme and compare our scheme with the Bucketization-based scheme.

We implement the proposed scheme and the Bucketization-based scheme respectively in JRE 1.7, eclipse and run it in the computer in Windows 7 OS with the CPU i5 and 4 cores. We test the response time of a range query by those two schemes respectively.

From the Fig. 3, we can see that: when the data records increase in database, the response time of a range query in our scheme changes little. But the change in the Bucketization-based scheme is obvious. We can see from the Fig. 4, which is more precise: when the data records increase, the response time of a rang query in Bucketization-based scheme increases nonlinearly but fast. This is a huge pressure for the data user, because the data uses have a lot of data to be audited in reality.

Therefore, we can conclude that our scheme is efficient enough to meet the requirement of smart grid application. Even the data records are large in database, the response time of our scheme will be small, which is significant for smart grid application.

8.2   Computation Cost

For the computation cost, we give the comparison between our scheme and Bucketization-based scheme too. The experimental environment is the same as the previous subsection and we choose 5000 data records. The computation cost of the data owner and data users will be introduced respectively in following.

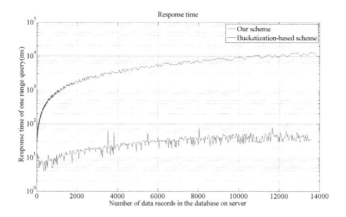

Fig. 3. Response time of our scheme and bucket system.

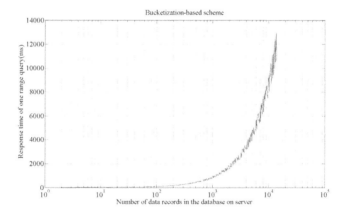

Fig. 4. Response time of the bucketization system when the data records increase.

Computation Cost of the Data Owner. We compare the computation time of the electricity company when the number of users and query dimension changes.

Figure 5 shows the computation time when the number of users in electricity company changes. From the two figures, it can illustrate the linear relationship when the users' size increases no matter what the query dimension is. And from the results, we can see that our scheme incurs less computation cost than the Bucketization-based scheme when coping with large number of users.

In smart grid application, the number of users is very large. From the simulation results, we can estimate that our scheme operates well than the Bucketization-based scheme in smart grid. Therefore, our scheme is very suitable for large-scale smart grid systems.

Figure 6 describes the computation cost of the electricity company with fixed users versus the number of changing query dimension. It is easy to find that our

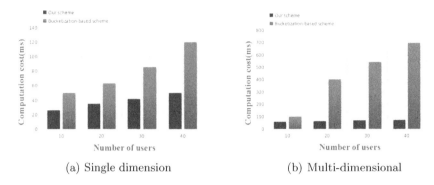

(a) Single dimension   (b) Multi-dimensional

Fig. 5. The computation time of the electricity company when the number of users changes.

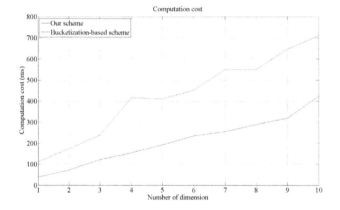

Fig. 6. The computation cost of the electricity company with fixed users versus the number of changing dimensions.

scheme incurs less computation cost than Bucketization-based scheme, especially when the query dimension is large in smart grid.

Computation Cost of Data Users. We compare the computation cost of the data users versus the users' size in Fig. 7 and the number of query dimension in Fig. 8. From the figures, we can see that our scheme is always in lower computation cost no matter what the users' size or the dimension is. Our scheme can greatly reduce the computation cost of data users, which is more important for data users in smart grid.

From the aforementioned analysis, We thus conclude that: (1) Our scheme can shorten the response time for a range query, which is significant for smart grid application. (2) As the users' size and the query dimension increase, the computation cost of the electricity company in our scheme changes little, which is suitable for large-scale smart grid systems. (3) The computation cost in data

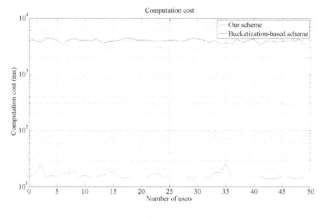

(a) Single dimension

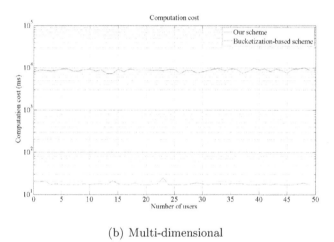

(b) Multi-dimensional

Fig. 7. The computation time of the data users when the users connected to electricity company change.

users' size in our scheme always keep little. This is very important for the data user who need to audit much electricity usage data in real. Therefore, our scheme is efficient enough and suitable for smart grid application.

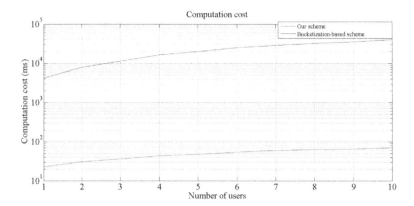

Fig. 8. The computation cost of the data user with fixed users versus the number of changing dimensions.

9 Conclusion

In this paper, we provide an efficient privacy-preserving scheme for range query in smart grid based on the modified Paillier cryptosystem. We achieved the range query in smart grid without disclosing the privacy of the electricity usage data and queries. The performance shows that our scheme can reduce the computation cost for both the data owner and data users, and shorten the response time of every range query, which is great significance for smart grid application.

Acknowledgments. This work was financially supported by National Natural Science Foundation of China with Grant No.61672195 and No. 61732022, National Key Research and Development Program of China with Grant No. 2016YFB0800804 and No. 2017YFB0803002, and Shenzhen Science and Technology Plan with Grant No. JCYJ20160318094336513 and No. JCYJ20160318094101317.

References

1. Wen, M., Lu, R., Zhang, K., Lei, J., Liang, X., Shen, X.: PaRQ: a privacy-preserving range query scheme over encrypted metering data for smart grid. IEEE Trans. Emerg. Top. Comput. **1**(1), 178–191 (2013)
2. Lu, R., Liang, X., Li, X., Lin, X., Shen, X.: Eppa: an efficient and privacy-preserving aggregation scheme for secure smart grid communications. IEEE Trans. Parallel Distrib. Syst. **23**(9), 1621–1631 (2012)
3. Liang, X., Li, X., Lu, R., Lin, X., Shen, X.: UDP: usage-based dynamic pricing with privacy preservation for smart grid. IEEE Trans. Smart Grid **4**(1), 141–150 (2013)
4. Boneh, D., Di Crescenzo, G., Ostrovsky, R., Persiano, G.: Public key encryption with keyword search. In: Cachin, C., Camenisch, J.L. (eds.) EUROCRYPT 2004. LNCS, vol. 3027, pp. 506–522. Springer, Heidelberg (2004). https://doi.org/10.1007/978-3-540-24676-3_30

5. Zhang, B., Zhang, F.: An efficient public key encryption with conjunctive-subset keywords search. J. Netw. Comput. Appl. **34**(1), 262–267 (2011)
6. Baek, J., Safavi-Naini, R., Susilo, W.: On the integration of public key data encryption and public key encryption with keyword search. In: Katsikas, S.K., López, J., Backes, M., Gritzalis, S., Preneel, B. (eds.) ISC 2006. LNCS, vol. 4176, pp. 217–232. Springer, Heidelberg (2006). https://doi.org/10.1007/11836810_16
7. Liu, Q., Wang, G., Wu, J.: An efficient privacy preserving keyword search scheme in cloud computing. In: 2009 International Conference on Computational Science and Engineering, CSE 2009, vol. 2, pp. 715–720. IEEE (2009)
8. Wen, M., Lu, R., Lei, J., Li, H., Liang, X., Sherman Shen, X.: SESA: an efficient searchable encryption scheme for auction in emerging smart grid marketing. Secur. Commun. Netw. **7**(1), 234–244 (2014)
9. Agrawal, R., Kiernan, J., Srikant, R., Xu, Y.: Order preserving encryption for numeric data. In: Proceedings of the 2004 ACM SIGMOD International Conference on Management of Data, pp. 563–574. ACM (2004)
10. Boldyreva, A., Chenette, N., Lee, Y., O'Neill, A.: Order-preserving symmetric encryption. In: Joux, A. (ed.) EUROCRYPT 2009. LNCS, vol. 5479, pp. 224–241. Springer, Heidelberg (2009). https://doi.org/10.1007/978-3-642-01001-9_13
11. Boldyreva, A., Chenette, N., O'Neill, A.: Order-preserving encryption revisited: improved security analysis and alternative solutions. In: Rogaway, P. (ed.) CRYPTO 2011. LNCS, vol. 6841, pp. 578–595. Springer, Heidelberg (2011). https://doi.org/10.1007/978-3-642-22792-9_33
12. Boneh, D., Waters, B.: Conjunctive, Subset, and Range Queries on Encrypted Data. In: Vadhan, S.P. (ed.) TCC 2007. LNCS, vol. 4392, pp. 535–554. Springer, Heidelberg (2007). https://doi.org/10.1007/978-3-540-70936-7_29
13. Shi, E., Bethencourt, J., Chan, T.H.H., Song, D., Perrig, A.: Multi-dimensional range query over encrypted data. In: IEEE Symposium on Security and Privacy, 2007, SP 2007, pp. 350–364. IEEE (2007)
14. Wang, B., Hou, Y., Li, M., Wang, H., Li, H.: Maple: scalable multi-dimensional range search over encrypted cloud data with tree-based index. In: Proceedings of the 9th ACM Symposium on Information, Computer and Communications Security, pp. 111–122. ACM (2014)
15. Lu, Y.: Privacy-preserving logarithmic-time search on encrypted data in cloud. In: NDSS (2012)
16. Wong, W.K., Cheung, D.W., Kao, B., Mamoulis, N.: Secure knn computation on encrypted databases. In: Proceedings of the 2009 ACM SIGMOD International Conference on Management of Data, pp. 139–152. ACM (2009)
17. Wang, P., Ravishankar, C.V.: Secure and efficient range queries on outsourced databases using Rp-trees. In: 2013 IEEE 29th International Conference on Data Engineering (ICDE), pp. 314–325. IEEE (2013)
18. Chi, J., Hong, C., Zhang, M., Zhang, Z.: Privacy-enhancing range query processing over encrypted cloud databases. In: Wang, J., Cellary, W., Wang, D., Wang, H., Chen, S.-C., Li, T., Zhang, Y. (eds.) WISE 2015. LNCS, vol. 9419, pp. 63–77. Springer, Cham (2015). https://doi.org/10.1007/978-3-319-26187-4_5
19. Hacigümüş, H., Iyer, B., Li, C., Mehrotra, S.: Executing SQL over encrypted data in the database-service-provider model. In: Proceedings of the 2002 ACM SIGMOD International Conference on Management of Data, pp. 216–227. ACM (2002)
20. Hore, B., Mehrotra, S., Tsudik, G.: A privacy-preserving index for range queries. In: Thirtieth International Conference on Very Large Data Bases, pp. 720–731 (2004)

21. Hore, B., Mehrotra, S., Canim, M., Kantarcioglu, M.: Secure multidimensional range queries over outsourced data. VLDB J. **21**(3), 333–358 (2012)
22. Paillier, P.: Public-key cryptosystems based on composite degree residuosity classes. In: Stern, J. (ed.) EUROCRYPT 1999. LNCS, vol. 1592, pp. 223–238. Springer, Heidelberg (1999). https://doi.org/10.1007/3-540-48910-X_16

Receive Buffer Pre-division Based Flow Control for MPTCP

Jiangping Han[1,2], Kaiping Xue[1,2(✉)], Hao Yue[3], Peilin Hong[1], Nenghai Yu[1], and Fenghua Li[4]

[1] Department of EEIS, University of Science and Technology of China,
Hefei 230027, Anhui, China
`kpxue@ustc.edu.cn`
[2] Science and Technology on Communication Networks Laboratory,
Shijiazhuang 050081, Hebei, China
[3] Department of Computer Science, San Francisco State University,
San Francisco, CA 94132, USA
[4] State Key Laboratory of Information Security, Institute of Information
Engineering, Chinese Academy of Sciences, Beijing 100093, China

Abstract. Multipath TCP (MPTCP) enables terminals utilizing multiple interfaces for data transmission simultaneously, which provides better performance and brings many benefits. However, using multiple paths brings some new challenges. The asymmetric parameters among different subflows may cause the out-of-order problem and load imbalance problem, especially in wireless network which has more packet loss. Thus it will significantly degrade the performance of MPTCP. In this paper, we propose a Receive Buffer Pre-division based flow control mechanism (RBP) for MPTCP. RBP divides receive buffer according to the prediction of receive buffer occupancy of each subflow, and controls the data transmission on each subflow using the divided buffer and the number of out-of-order packets, which can significantly improve the performance of MPTCP. We use the NS-3 simulations to verify the performance of our scheme, and the simulation results show that RBP algorithm can significantly increase the global throughput of MPTCP.

Keywords: MPTCP · Receive buffer · Pre-division · Flow control
Wireless · Out-of-order

1 Introduction

Nowadays, the Internet is developing rapidly. Various network access technologies have been developed and used, and one terminal is always equipped with multiple network interfaces. However, traditional TCP only makes use of one interface at a time, which neither takes full advantages of the network resources nor meets the increasing demand on data transmission. Researchers have proposed a number of protocols [1–3] that utilize multipath transmission to solve this problem. The solutions on transport layer are hot topics of the discussion [4–6],

© Springer Nature Singapore Pte Ltd. 2018
L. Zhu and S. Zhong (Eds.): MSN 2017, CCIS 747, pp. 19–31, 2018.
https://doi.org/10.1007/978-981-10-8890-2_2

since the transport layer is the lowest layer to maintain the end-to-end connection and no change needs to be made at the intermediate nodes. Multipath TCP (MPTCP) [7] has become a new standard supported by IETF MPTCP working group. It can utilize multiple network interfaces simultaneously while is also compatible with existing network systems. Thus, it has received much attention from both academia and industries.

MPTCP could aggregate bandwidth resources and improve overall throughput. However, different from TCP which only uses one path to transmit data, using multiple paths will cause new problems, like the out-of-order problem and load imbalance problem. These problems will lead to the degradation of overall network performance. Especially in today's heterogeneous networks, which has many wireless links and different path parameters. Wireless networks lead to more packet loss and different paths lead to asymmetrical scenarios, will make it harder to collaborate different paths, and the impact will be even severer.

Specifically, out-of-order packets will cause buffer bloat in receive buffer, which will block the data transmission and decrease the throughput. This problem can be solved using scheduling algorithm [8]. The main idea is to schedule the packets and make the packets arrive at receiver in-order. However, there are still some limitations in the scheduling algorithms. Scheduling algorithms are suitable for the situation where there are obvious differences among different subflows' round-trip time (RTT). If the difference is within two times, it will be hard for scheduling algorithms to achieve good performance. On the other hand, scheduling algorithms always reserve a block of sending buffer for the subflow with smaller RTT. If the size of the buffer is limited and insufficient for every subflow, less data will be sent on the subflow with larger RTT, which will then cause the load imbalance problem.

The other method to reduce the out-of-order packets is controlling the traffic flow on each subflow independently according to the characteristics of subflow. In the original flow control of MPTCP, subflows share one receive buffer. The subflows compete against each other, which will cause unreasonable distribution of receive buffer among subflows and make the out-of-order problem even worse. MPTCP uses multiple paths for parallel transmission, where each subflow can easily implement separate flow control. Meanwhile, an independent control for each subflow will lead to better use of the different characteristics among subflows and a more reasonable data distribution. The idea of flow control with evenly divided buffer has been mentioned in CMT-SCTP [9]. But this mechanism does not consider the path difference between subflows.

In this paper, we propose a Receive Buffer Pre-division based flow control For MPTCP (RBP). RBP enables flow control on each subflow separately according to buffer pre-division, which can control the data distribution among subflows reasonably and solve the above-mentioned problems effectively. The main contributions of our work can be summarized as follows:

- We propose a new flow control mechanism based on receive buffer pre-division, which can distribute data according to the performance of subflows. This scheme decreases the influence of bufferbloat and improves the performance of MPTCP.

- We propose a scheme estimating the buffer occupancy of each subflow which dynamically adjusts to the actual situation, thus is more adaptable to the real network.
- Simulation results show that the proposed scheme can effectively improve the throughput of MPTCP.

The rest of this paper is organized as follows. In Sect. 2, we will introduce the flow control of TCP and MPTCP. The details of our algorithm will be described in Sect. 3. In Sect. 4, we evaluated the performance of the proposed algorithm. Finally, we will conclude our work in Sect. 5.

2   Related Work

Scheduling algorithm is an approach to enhance the performance of MPTCP. Scheduling algorithm can solve out-of-order problem caused by asymmetry of paths, and try to ensure the packets to reach receiver in order. When a subflow is under scheduling, sender estimates N, the number of packets which can arrive at sender before the first packet at this subflow, and skips these N packets to send. These N packets will be reserved for other subflows.

There are many recearches on scheduling algorithm. Linux-MPTCP scheduling algorithm [10] is a predictive scheduling algorithm supported in Linux-MPTCP kernel code. Linux-MPTCP scheduling algorithm ignores the change of congestion and other factors and just makes $N = \sum_{j,RTT_j<RTT_i}$ $\left(\frac{RTT_i}{RTT_j} \cdot cwnd_j\right)$. Forward Prediction Scheduling (FPS) [11], Fine-grained Forward Prediction based Dynamic Packet Scheduling (F^{2}P-DPS) [12], Offset Compensation based Packet Scheduling (OCPS) [13] are the enhancements of Linux-MPTCP scheduling algorithm, which consider the change of congestion window, wireless packet loss and feedback information respectively, and gradually increase the accuracy of schedule algorithms.

Although the modelling of scheduling algorithm is becoming better designed, there are still some limitations as we mentioned before. The scope of application is limited, and sometimes it needs a large buffer. So we can think about this question from another perspective.

In the original MPTCP, receive buffer is shared, and receiver notifies the overall buffer allowance ($rwnd$), which controls the data flow of the total MPTCP connection. When sender receives an ACK from $subflow_i$, it will change the send window of $subflow_i$ as $Send\_Window_i = min(cwnd_i, rwnd)$, where $cwnd_i$ is the congestion window of $subflow_i$, and $rwnd$ is the total advertisement window carried in ACK. If $Send\_Window_i - Outstanding_i > 0$, $subflow_i$ is able to send new data, where $Outstanding_i$ is the unACKed data of $subflow_i$ on subflow level.

In the original MPTCP protocol, $cwnd_i$ is the congestion window of subflow level, and $rwnd$ is the receive window of connection level. Sender makes use of $cwnd_i$ and $rwnd$ to control the data sent on $subflow_i$, which will lead to a mess in different subflows, and cause a decline in the global throughput. If sender can keep all of the packets arriving at receiver in order or receiver has an infinite buffer, it will be unnecessary to keep flow control on each subflow independently. However, the capacity of different subflows is always different, and it is impossible to make all the packets arriving at receiver in order because of different RTTs and packet loss. In this case, to distinguish each subflow and make an individual flow control will become a better choice.

Concurrent Multipath Transfer using SCTP (CMT-SCTP) [14] is also a multipath protocol on transport layer. Although the discussion of SCTP is gradually weakening, MPTCP could also draw lessons from the thought of flow control scheme. CMT-SCTP came up with a flow control scheme based on buffer allocation [9]. The basic idea is to evenly divide the buffer space into N parts (where N is the number of subflows), and make an independently flow control on each subflow.

However, subflows are always asymmetric in the real station, evenly dividing the buffer space does not consider the inconsistency between parameters of different subflows. Therefore it will not adapt to the actual network well. Sender should consider the capacity of different subflow, and adjust with the actual situation.

3   Receive Buffer Pre-division Based Flow Control Algorithm

To address the problems caused by asymmetric paths of subflows and improve the global throughput of MPTCP in heterogeneous networks, we propose a Receive Buffer Pre-division based flow control algorithm (RBP) for MPTCP. The basic idea of RBP is to distribute the overall $rwnd$ into $rwnd_i$ on each subflow according to the capacity of different subflows. To achieve this goal, we make some modification on the sender. The receiver do not need to make any changes. The receiver still notice the overall receive window to the sender. Then the sender estimates the buffer occupancy of each subflow, and then divides the receive window according to the estimation.

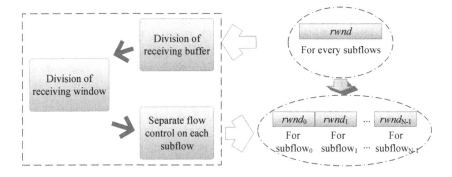

Fig. 1. Receive buffer pre-division based flow control algorithm

Figure 1 shows the basic idea of RBP. The sender first estimates the average maximum buffer occupancy of each subflow in MPTCP, and then divides the receive buffer according to the estimation. After that, the sender counts the unACKed packets on connection level of each subflow, and sets the receive window to the remaining buffer capacity. Finally, the variable *rwnd* will be distributed among all the subflows and the results will be used for flow control on each subflow.

RBP consists of three parts: (1) division of receive buffer; (2) division of receive window; and (3) separate flow control on each subflow. Next, we will describe them in details.

3.1   Division of Receive Buffer

In RBP, the sender first estimates the average maximum buffer occupancy of each subflow, and distributes the buffer based on the estimation results. Buffer occupancy depends on the congestion window and RTT. Notice that congestion window will be changed by congestion control algorithms according to varying path condition, especially in wireless networks with serious packet loss. In order to estimate the congestion window, we assume that the path condition is stable during the estimation.

We use $acwnd_i$ to denote the short-time average size of the congestion window of $subflow_i$. When $cwnd_i$ changes, $acwnd_i$ will be updated as follows:

$$acwnd_i \longleftarrow (1 - \beta) \cdot acwnd_i + \beta \cdot cwnd_i, \tag{1}$$

where β is the weight between 0 and 1. Here, we take $\beta = 1/16$, which refers to the update of congestion degree in [15].

Figure 2 illustrates an example of two subflows. The round-trip times of $subflow_0$ and $subflow_1$ are denoted as RTT_0 and RTT_1, respectively. Here,

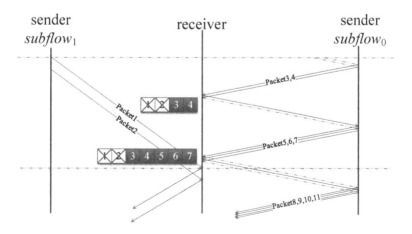

Fig. 2. Estimation of buffer occupy

we assume that $RTT_0 < RTT_1$. The sender estimates the average size of the congestion window for $subflow_0$ as $acwnd_0$.

As shown in Fig. 2, $subflow_1$ will cause out-of-order packets received from $subflow_0$ in the receive buffer. If $subflow_1$ sends its first packet before $subflow_0$, there will be $\left\lceil \frac{RTT_1}{2 \cdot RTT_0} + \frac{1}{2} \right\rceil \cdot acwnd_0$ out-of-order packets in the receive buffer. Otherwise, there will be $\left(\left\lceil \frac{RTT_1}{2 \cdot RTT_0} + \frac{1}{2} \right\rceil - 1 \right) \cdot acwnd_0$ out-of-order packets in the receive buffer. The probabilities of these two cases are both $\frac{1}{2}$. Also, there will be $acwnd_0$ packets that are in transmission from the sender to the receiver, which should also be considered. Therefore, the average buffer occupancy of $subflow_0$ is $acwnd_0 \cdot \left(\left\lceil \frac{RTT_1}{2 \cdot RTT_0} + \frac{1}{2} \right\rceil + \frac{1}{2} \right)$.

When there are more than two subflows in a MPTCP connection, the calculation on the number of out-of-order packets and the average buffer occupancy is similar to that in the above example. For $subflow_i$, every $subflow_j (j \neq i)$ will cause $acwnd\_i \cdot \left(\left\lceil \frac{RTT_j}{2 \cdot RTT_i} + \frac{1}{2} \right\rceil + \frac{1}{2} \right)$ out-of-order packets in the receive buffer. The number of out-of-order packets from $subflow_i$ depends on the maximum value of them, i.e., $\max_{j \neq i} acwnd\_i \cdot \left(\left\lceil \frac{RTT_j}{2 \cdot RTT_i} + \frac{1}{2} \right\rceil + \frac{1}{2} \right)$.

Then, the average maximum buffer occupancy of the $subflow_i$ can be calculated as follows:

$$Buf_i = acwnd\_i \cdot \left(\left\lceil \frac{\max_{j \neq i} RTT_j}{2 \cdot RTT_i} + \frac{1}{2} \right\rceil + \frac{1}{2} \right), \tag{2}$$

where Buf_i is the estimation of the average maximum buffer occupancy of $subflow_i$.

After estimating the average maximum buffer occupancy, the receive buffer will be allocated among all the subflows and the distribution is proportional to the estimated average maximum buffer occupancy, which is shown as follows:

$$B_i = recvBuffer \cdot \frac{Buf_i}{\sum_{i=0}^{N-1} Buf_i}. \tag{3}$$

Suppose there are N subflows in total, B_i is the allocation of available receive buffer to $subflow_i$ and $recvBuffer$ is the variable that contains the size of the receive buffer and will be transmitted to the sender from the receiver at the beginning of the transmission.

3.2   Division of Receive Window

In this part, the sender records the amount of unACKed data on the connection level, and calculates the size of residual available buffer for each subflow. Then, it will allocate $rwnd$ based on the residual available buffer size of each subflow. Each subflow $subflow_i$ obtains $rwnd_i$, which is the receive window on subflow level. Then, the send window of $subflow_i$ will be determined by $rwnd_i$ as follows:

$$rwnd_i = \begin{cases} 0 & B_i \leq unordered_i, \\ \dfrac{rwnd \cdot (B_i - unordered_i)}{\displaystyle\sum_{B_i > unordered_i} (B_i - unordered_i)} & else. \end{cases} \quad (4)$$

Here, $rwnd_i$ is the resudual buffer size distributed to $subflow_i$, $rwnd$ is the size of the total available buffer noticed by the receiver, and $unordered_i$ is the amount of unACKed data on connection level of $subflow_i$. We can observe that the sender allocates $rwnd$ based on the ratio of $(B_i - unordered_i)$. If $(B_i - unordered_i) \leq 0$, which indicates there are too many out-of-order packets from $subflow_i$, the sender will temporarily stop sending data on $subflow_i$.

3.3   Separate Flow Control on Each Subflow

After the above two steps, the shared receive window $rwnd$ will be divided into a set of receive windows $rwnd_i$ for each subflow $subflow_i$. The amount of data transmitted on each subflow will be controlled by the $rwnd_i$. The send window on subflow level slides according to the congestion window and the receive window of each subflow. The send window for a subflow cannot exceed the overall send window for the connection.

When $subflow_i$ is able to send data, the send window of $subflow_i$ will be restricted by the congestion window of the subflow as follows

$$Send\_Window_i = min(cwnd_i, rwnd_i), \quad (5)$$

where $cwnd_i$ is the congestion window of $subflow_i$ and $rwnd_i$ is the receive window of $subflow_i$. The send window of $subflow_i$ cannot exceed the minimum of $cwnd_i$ and $rwnd_i$.

Then, the amount of data that $subflow_i$ can send will be controlled by the send window and the size of unACKed data from $subflow_i$ as follows

$$Send\_data_i = Send\_Window_i - Outstanding_i, \quad (6)$$

where $Outstanding_i$ is the size of unACKed data from $subflow_i$, which is different from $unordered_i$. If $Send\_data_i > 0$, $subflow_i$ is able to send new data.

It can be observed that subflows influence each other when they share the same receive buffer. RBP enables independent flow control on each subflow, and restricts the rate of subflow with too many out-of-order packets. Then, the sender could transmit more data on the subflow with higher throughput, which reduces the number of out-of-order packets and achieves load balancing. RBP does not change the congestion window size. When the number of out-of-order packets on the connection level decreases, it will resume the normal throughput quickly, which can achieve good adaptability to the network. The RBP algorithm is described in Algorithm 1.

Algorithm 1. RBP Algorithm Description

Input:

The receive window: $rwnd$;

The congestion window of $subflow_i$: $cwnd_i$;

The average congestion window of each subflow: $acwnd_1, acwnd_2, ..., acwnd_{N-1}$.

Output:

The amount of new data which is able to send on $subflow_i$: $Send\_data_i$

$acwnd_i \longleftarrow (1 - \beta) \cdot acwnd_i + \beta \cdot cwnd_i$

for $j = 0 \rightarrow N - 1$ **do**

$\quad Buf_j = acwnd\_j \cdot \left(\left\lceil \frac{\max_{k, k \neq j} RTT_k}{2 \cdot RTT_j} + \frac{1}{2} \right\rceil + \frac{1}{2} \right)$

end for

for $j = 0 \rightarrow N - 1$ **do**

$\quad B_j = recvBuffer \cdot \frac{Buf_j}{\sum_{j=0}^{N-1} Buf_j}$

end for

if $B_i \leq unordered_i$ **then**

$\quad rwnd_i = 0$

else

$\quad rwnd_i = rwnd \cdot \dfrac{B_i - unordered_i}{\displaystyle\sum_{B_i > unordered_i} (B_i - unordered_i)}$

end if

$Send\_Window_i = min(cwnd_i, rwnd_i)$

$Send\_data_i = Send\_Window_i - Outstanding_i$

4   Performance Evaluation

In this section, we evaluate the efficiency of the RBP algorithm on NS-3 [16] simulator. The basic MPTCP code is provided by Google MPTCP Group [17]. We use the original MPTCP and TCP on each subflow as comparisons at the same time. We evaluate the performance of the RBP algorithm in terms of the overall throughput, the throughput of subflows, and the number of out-of-order packets in receive buffer.

Table 1. Flow parameters of simulation scenario

Parameters	$subflow_0$	$subflow_1$
Path delay	$10\,\text{ms} - 50\,\text{ms}$	$50\,\text{ms}$
Maximum bandwidth capacity	$5\,\text{Mbps}$	$10\,\text{Mbps}$
Packet loss rate	$0.1\% - 5\%$	0.1%
Maximal Segment Size (MSS)	$1400\,\text{Bytes}$	$1400\,\text{Bytes}$
Congestion control algorithm	TCP-Reno	TCP-Reno

The simulation scenario is shown in Fig. 3. There are two subflows in the MPTCP connection, each of which is routed along a separate path. The middle link on each path is the bottleneck, and therefore the maximum bandwidth capacity of $subflow_0$ and $subflow_1$ is 5 Mbps and 10 Mbps respectively. Each subflow has a wireless link for the last hop to the MPTCP receiver, which suffer from random packet loss. In addition, there is a UDP background flow that is transmitted along each path. The traffic of the UDP flows is uniformly distributed and we set the interval between packets to 5 ms.

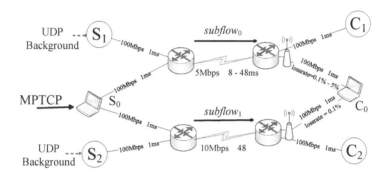

Fig. 3. Simulation scenario

Each subflow has different parameters, such as path delay, packet loss, and so on. Table 1 shows the parameter configuration of $subflow_0$ and $subflow_1$. In addition, the MSS of each subflow is set to 1400 Bytes, and the size of shared receive buffer is 2×65536 Bytes. The receive buffer of single TCP is 65536 Bytes, and the MSS of UDP is set to 1024 Bytes. For each scenario, we take the average values of 50 simulation runs as results.

4.1   Asymmetric Scenario

The different path delay among subflows is an important factor that causes the decrease of overall throughput in asymmetric scenarios. In a network, if two subflows have the same path delay, it will result in the best performance. However, it is difficult to achieve the best performance since different subflows often have different path delay in real network.

In the first scenario, we change the path delay while maintain the other parameters as constants. Specially, the path delay of $subflow_0$ changes from 10 ms to 50 ms, and the delay of $subflow_1$ is always 50 ms. We also set the loss rate of $subflow_0$ to 0.1% in the simulations.

Figure 4 shows the result of overall throughput. It can be observed that the global throughput of these two schemes decrease simultaneously as the path delay of $subflow_0$ increases. Because the throughput of a subflow will be affected by the path delay, and large delay may lead to a decrease in throughput. However,

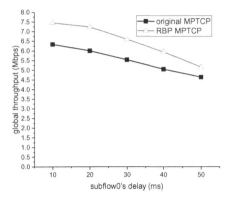
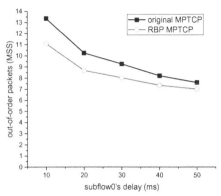

Fig. 4. Comparison of overall through-put with the change of path delay

Fig. 5. Comparison of out-of-order pack-ets with the change of path delay

from Fig. 4 we can see that RBP brings a transmission gain on MPTCP, which will result in a better performance. In the best case, RBP can achieve a gain nearly 20%. However, transmission gain of RBP will be a little lower if the path delay of $subflow_0$ and $subflow_1$ are similar, because the symmetric paths will cause fewer out-of-order packets.

The results on the number of out-of-order packets in the receive buffer is shown in Fig. 5. With the path delay increasing, the difference between the delays of $subflow_0$ and $subflow_1$ becomes smaller, and the number of out-of-order packets will significantly decrease, since the difference of path delay is the most important factor that leads to the out-of-order packets in the receive buffer. In addition, when RBP with independent control on each subflow is used, the number of out-of-order packets will also decrease. At the beginning, when the RTT of $subflow_0$ is much smaller than $subflow_1$, the number of out-of-order packets decreases a lot with RBP algorithm. The gain will become smaller as the difference between two subflows decreasing.

Figure 6 shows the throughput of different subflows with original MPTCP and RBP algorithm. As shown Fig. 4, RBP brings a gain on the total through-put. Figure 6 shows more details of the gain. The throughput of $subflow_0$ does not decrease too much with RBP algorithm, but the throughput of $subflow_1$ increases significantly, which will improve the overall throughput.

4.2   Wireless Scenario

In practice, random packet loss mostly occurs in wireless networks, which may lead to the decrease of throughput. We change the packet loss rate of $subflow_0$ from 0.1% to 5%, and maintain the other parameters as constants. The delay of $subflow_1$ is always 50 ms. We also set the path delay of $subflow_0$ to 20 ms in this scenario.

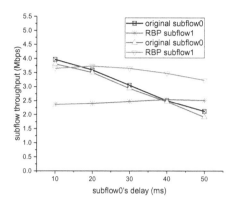

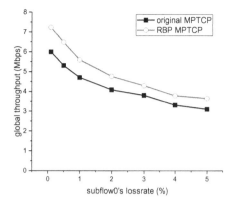

Fig. 6. Comparison of subflow throughput with the change of path delay

Fig. 7. Comparison of overall throughput with the change of loss rate

Figure 7 shows the simulation results of overall throughput. With the random packet loss rate on $subflow_0$ increasing, the throughput of these two schemes decreases. The reason is that a majority of congestion control algorithms are based on packet loss, and large packet loss rate will cause poor throughput. Moreover, large packet loss rate will lead to asymmetric situation of data sending between subflows, which causes more out-of-order packets in connection level, and hence the overall throughput will be further reduced. It can also be observed that RBP still outperforms the original MPTCP.

The results on the number of unordered packets are shown in Fig. 8. Since RBP controls data transmitted on each subflow independently and reasonably distributes data among subflows, it can effectively decrease the number

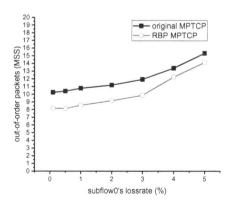

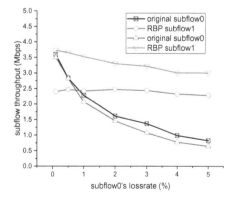

Fig. 8. Comparison of out-of-order packets with the change of loss rate

Fig. 9. Comparison of subflow throughput with the change of loss rate

of out-of-order packets. We can see RBP works better on the scenario with less packet loss, because the packet loss will lead to more out-of-order packets and make it difficult to estimate the transmission state. However, from Fig. 8 we can see RBP still brings a better performance on out-of-order packets in lossy scenarios.

Figure 9 shows the throughput of subflows. When the RBP algorithm is used, the throughput of $subflow_1$ is higher than that with original MPTCP. At the same time, the throughput of $subflow_0$ does not significantly decrease. Thus, RBP still improves the overall throughput. Likewise, we can see that RBP allocates more data on $subflow_1$ than original MPTCP, which indicaets RBP allocates more data on the best subflow, so as to achieve load balance between subflows.

5   Conclusions

MPTCP uses multiple paths for data transmission at the same time, which needs to be more precisely controlled. However, each subflow has its own congestion window, but there is only one receive window on connection level. If there is nothing different between subflows, and each packet can arrive at receiver in order, it will be unnecessary for keeping separate flow control on each subflow. However, the wireless network and asymmetrical paths lead to a degradation of MPTCP, which is caused by misallocation of data among subflows.

RBP scheme makes independent flow control on each subflow and adjusts to the actual situation. Thus it can regulate and control the data sent on each subflow in detail. If there are too many out-of-order packets on one subflow, which is beyond the permitted scope, sender will limit the data on the subflows, so as to reduce the amount of out-of-order packets, and promote throughput of the correct subflows, thus could also reduce bufferbloat and provide a better performance. Therefore RBP can achieve the purposes of improving the overall throughput and balancing traffic load between subflows, which can improve the network performance greatly.

Acknowledgment. This work is supported by the National Natural Science Foundation of China under Grant No. 61379129 and No. 61671420, the Fund of Science and Technology on Communication Networks Laboratory under Grant No. KX162600024, Youth Innovation Promotion Association CAS under Grant No. 2016394, and the Fundamental Research Funds for the Central Universities.

References

1. Habak, K., Harras, K.A., Youssef, M.: Bandwidth aggregation techniques in heterogeneous multi-homed devices: a survey. Comput. Netw. **92**, 168–188 (2015)
2. Lee, W., Koo, J., Park, Y., Choi, S.: Transfer time, energy, and quota-aware multi-RAT operation scheme in smartphone. IEEE Trans. Veh. Technol. **65**(1), 307–317 (2016)

3. Zheng, X., Cai, Z., Li, J., Gao, H.: Scheduling flows with multiple service frequency constraints. IEEE Internet Things J. **4**(2), 496–504 (2017)
4. Amer, P., Becke, M., Dreibholz, T., Ekiz, N., Iyengar, J., Natarajan, P., Stewart, R., Tuexen, M.: Load sharing for the stream control transmission protocol (SCTP). IETF Personal Draft, draft-tuexen-tsvwgsctp-multipath-13 (2016)
5. Li, M., Lukyanenko, A., Ou, Z., Ylä-Jääski, A., Tarkoma, S., Coudron, M., Secci, S.: Multipath transmission for the internet: a survey. IEEE Commun. Surv. Tutor. **18**(4), 2887–2925 (2016)
6. Shailendra, S., Bhattacharjee, R., Bose, S.K.: MPSCTP: a simple and efficient multipath algorithm for SCTP. IEEE Commun. Lett. **15**(10), 1139–1141 (2011)
7. Ford, A., Raiciu, C., Handley, M., Bonaventure, O.: TCP extensions for multipath operation with multiple addresses. IETF RFC, RFC6824 (2013)
8. Xue, K., Han, J., Ni, D., Wei, W., Cai, Y., Xu, Q., Hong, P.: DPSAF: forward prediction based dynamic packet scheduling and adjusting with feedback for multipath TCP in lossy heterogeneous networks. IEEE Trans. Veh. Technol. **67**(2), 1521–1534 (2017)
9. Adhari, H., Dreibholz, T., Becke, M., Rathgeb, E.P., Tüxen, M.: Evaluation of concurrent multipath transfer over dissimilar paths. In: Proceedings of 2011 IEEE Workshops of International Conference on Advanced Information Networking and Applications (WAINA 2011), pp. 708–714. IEEE (2011)
10. Barré, S., et al.: Implementation and assessment of modern host-based multipath solutions. Ph.D. dissertation, UCL (2011)
11. Mirani, F.H., Boukhatem, N., Tran, M.A.: A data-scheduling mechanism for multi-homed mobile terminals with disparate link latencies. In: Proceedings of the 72nd IEEE Vehicular Technology Conference Fall (VTC 2010-Fall), pp. 1–5. IEEE (2010)
12. Ni, D., Xue, K., Hong, P., Shen, S.: Fine-grained forward prediction based dynamic packet scheduling mechanism for multipath TCP in lossy networks. In: Proceedings of the 23rd International Conference on Computer Communication and Networks (ICCCN), pp. 1–7. IEEE (2014)
13. Ni, D., Xue, K., Hong, P., Zhang, H., Lu, H.: OCPS: offset compensation based packet scheduling mechanism for multipath TCP. In: Proceedings of 2015 IEEE International Conference on Communications (ICC 2015), pp. 6187–6192. IEEE (2015)
14. Iyengar, J.R., Amer, P.D., Stewart, R.: Concurrent multipath transfer using SCTP multihoming over independent end-to-end paths. IEEE/ACM Trans. Netw. **14**(5), 951–964 (2006)
15. Kühlewind, M., Wagner, D.P., Espinosa, J.M.R., Briscoe, B.: Using data center TCP (DCTCP) in the internet. In: Proceedings of 2014 IEEE Globecom Workshops (GC Wkshps), pp. 583–588. IEEE (2014)
16. NS3 simulator. www.nsnam.org/
17. MPTCP NS3 code. http://code.google.com/p/mptcp-ns3/

On Complementary Effect of Blended Behavioral Analysis for Identity Theft Detection in Mobile Social Networks

Cheng Wang$^{(\boxtimes)}$, Jing Luo, Bo Yang, and Changjun Jiang

Key Laboratory of Embedded System and Service Computing, Ministry of Education,
Department of Computer Science and Technology, Tongji University, Shanghai, China
{chengwang,jingluo,boyang,cjjiang}@tongji.edu.cn

Abstract. User behavioral analysis is expected to act as a promising technique for identity theft detection in the Internet. The performance of this paradigm extremely depends on a good individual-level user behavioral model. Such a good model for a specific behavior is often hard to obtain due to the insufficiency of data for this behavior. The insufficiency of specific data is mainly led by the prevalent sparsity of users' collectable behavioral footprints. This work aims to address whether it is feasible to effectively detect identify thefts by jointly using multiple unreliable behavioral models from sparse individual-level records. We focus on this issue in mobile social networks (MSNs) with multiple dimensions of collectable but sparse data of user behavior, i.e., making check-ins, posing tips and forming friendships. Based on these sparse data, we build user spatial distribution model, user post interest model and user social preference model, respectively. Here, as the arguments, we validate that there is indeed a complementary effect in multi-dimensional blended behavioral analysis for identity theft detection in MSNs.

Keywords: Mobile social networks · Identity theft detection
Blended behavioral analysis · Complementary effect

1 Introduction

Mobile Internet has been increasingly gaining popularity. To say that a global phenomenon is almost an understatement, as the number of worldwide social network users is expected to grow to around 2.5 billion in 2018, around a third of Earth's entire population. Projections also show that by 2018, over 75% of Facebook users worldwide will access the service through their mobile phone[1].

However, due to the ever increasing number of users and the advent of information boom, people's property is also rapidly digitized (private photos, customer sensitive data, intellectual property, etc.). According to a new survey

---

[1] One of the largest statistics portals, http://www.statista.com/.

© Springer Nature Singapore Pte Ltd. 2018
L. Zhu and S. Zhong (Eds.): MSN 2017, CCIS 747, pp. 32–44, 2018.
https://doi.org/10.1007/978-981-10-8890-2_3

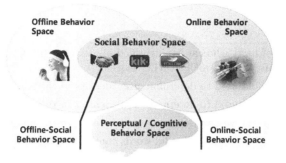

Fig. 1. Modern human behaviors usually take place in multiple spaces, such as the physical space of reality, virtual cyber space and social space.

from security software company Webroot[2], MSNs users are more likely to face security threats such as the loss of financial information, identity theft, and the infringement of the right to privacy. A more common strategy is to hijack a user account, then the hackers send messages to their contacts and deceive them to send money to a "friend in trouble". Because social network is mostly acquaintance network, users can easily relax the vigilance and eventually be deceived. When a user logs in to a social network, he or she will generate a sequence of behaviors. By modeling these behavioral habits, it is possible to derive behavioral characteristics that uniquely discern the user's identity. Studies have shown that private traits and attributes are predictable from digital records of human behavior and computer-based personality judgments are more accurate than those made by humans. Montjoye et al. [1] investigated three months of credit card records for 1.1 million people and showed that four spatiotemporal points are enough to uniquely reidentify 90% of individuals. It strongly proved that the behavior of the track can uniquely identify a person.

The research of user behavior has caused widespread concern in recent years. In a perspective, human beings live in a multiple space, such as the realistic physical space, virtual cyber space and social space. Mobile Internet is essentially to provide users with real-time switching channels. The behavior can be divided into offline behavior in the physical space, online behavior in the cyber space and social behavior in the social space. These form a blended space consisting of offline behavior space, online behavior space and social behavior space, which is illustrated in Fig. 1.

In this work, we grasp the essence of Mobile Internet serving as a portal for users among multiple spaces, e.g. physical and cyber spaces, which makes user behavior blended by multiple dimensional. The main issue to be addressed is if it is feasible to overcome the sparsity of behavioral data by cooperatively using multiple dimensional behavior. More specifically, we focus on behavioral data in three dimensions, i.e., check-ins, tips and friendships. The identity theft detection can be carried out by the comprehensive analysis of the above three behavior

---

[2] The largest privately held cybersecurity organization based in the USA, operating globally across North America, EMEA and APAC, https://www.webroot.com/.

Table 1. Notations

Symbol	Meaning
I_ξ	The set of users who can be identified in each dimension, $\xi \in \{$ DoC, DoT, DoF, DoCT, DoCF, DoTF, DoCTF $\}$
S^{che}_{log}	The threshold used to determine user identity in the method of DoC
D^{tip}_{JS}	The threshold used to determine user identity in the method of DoT
D^{fri}_{JS}	The threshold used to determine user identity in the method of DoF
n^λ_{vow}	The minimum number of valid words contained in corresponding method, $\lambda \in \{$ tip, fri $\}$
θ^λ_{his}	Vector of topic probability distribution, which indicates the behavior characteristic of user historical data, $\lambda \in \{$ tip, fri $\}$
θ^λ_{new}	Vector of topic probability distribution, which indicates the behavior characteristic of user newly generated data, $\lambda \in \{$ tip, fri $\}$

data. We perform the detection on two Location-based Social Networks (LBSNs) data sets [2], i.e., Foursquare and Yelp. We choose several metrics to evaluate the detection performance. One is the *intercept rate* (IR), that is, the proportion of anomalous accounts that are intercepted accurately. The other is the *disturb rate* (DR), which is the proportion of the accounts that are erroneously intercepted to be anomalous in the normal account. In summary, this paper makes the following contributions:

- We propose three detection methods via user behavior for identity theft detection.
- We obtain the performance of user behavior models for identity theft detection on two real-life data sets.
- We validate that there is indeed a complementary effect on multi-dimensional blended behavioral analysis for identity theft detection in MSNs.

2   Problem Description and Settings

Identity theft refers to somebody stealing your personal data and impersonating you to, for example, shop under your name. Statistics showed that six percent of users stated that they suffered from identity theft. In this work, we propose the approach for identity theft detection via user blended behavior in MSNs. We mainly address two issues: For one thing we aim at building the behavior model for each dimension and proposing the corresponding detection method to effectively identify the user authenticity; for another the poor detection performance causing by data sparsity should also be solved due to the complementary effect of the blended behavioral analysis.

Our first object is to build the user's behavior model based on their generated data. User behavior data are the check-in records at the location, online text content, and user-generated social relationship. We build three user behavior models corresponding to each dimension. Corresponding to our work, we call them three dimensions, namely dimension of check-ins (DoC), dimension of tips (DoT) and dimension of friendships (DoF). In Table 1, we give an explanation of the symbols appearing in this paper. Due to various constraints, the behavior data are sparse for a particular user in single dimension. Since the detection is done by the individual-level user behavioral model, we define those who have sufficient data and can be identified by our method of this dimension as *Identifiable Users*. In each model, we need to find the appropriate criteria to distinguish between the user's own and non-users themselves, i.e., S_{log}^{che}, D_{JS}^{tip} and D_{JS}^{fri}. In order to achieve identity theft detection, we chose three metrics to evaluate the detection performance, which are *intercept rate* (IR), *disturb rate* (DR) and *precision rate* (PR), respectively. They are defined as follows:

$$\text{Intercept Rate} = \frac{\#\ \text{users intercepted correctly}}{\#\ \text{all anomalous users}}, \tag{1}$$

$$\text{Disturb Rate} = \frac{\#\ \text{users intercepted wrongly}}{\#\ \text{all normal users}}, \tag{2}$$

$$\text{Precision Rate} = \frac{\#\ \text{users intercepted correctly}}{\#\ \text{all intercepted users}}. \tag{3}$$

3   Detection Method

In this section, we present the user behavior models for each dimension and the methods for identity theft detection via the corresponding models.

3.1   Detection via Check-Ins

Modeling User Spatial Distributions. We model the user spatial distribution (USDM) by using the method based on the kernel density estimation. According to the history data of the users, the probability density function of each user is obtained by using the mixed kernel density estimation (MKDE) method [3]. Let $E = \{e^1, ..., e^n\}$ be a set of historical events where $e^j =<x, y>$ is a two-dimensional spatial location, $1 \leq j \leq n$, and where we have suppressed any dependence on individual i for the moment and dropped dependence on time t. Let E denote the training data set. A simple method for estimating a bivariate density function from such kind of data is to use a single fixed 2×2 bandwidth matrix H and a Gaussian kernel function $K(\cdot)$. More specifically, we assume the bandwidth matrix $H = \begin{pmatrix} h & 0 \\ 0 & h \end{pmatrix}$. This results in a bivariate KDE of the following form:

$$f_{KD}(e|E, h) = \frac{1}{n} \sum_{j=1}^{n} K_h \left(e - e^j\right), \tag{4}$$

$$K_h(x) = \frac{1}{2\pi h} \exp\left(-\frac{1}{2} x^T H^{-1} x\right), H = \begin{pmatrix} h & 0 \\ 0 & h \end{pmatrix}, \tag{5}$$

where e is the location for which we would like to calculate the probability density, and $h > 0$ is a fixed scalar bandwidth parameter for all events in E.

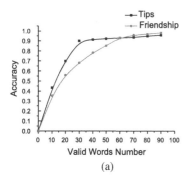 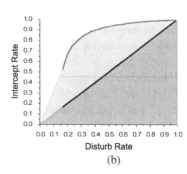

(a)   (b)

Fig. 2. (a) is the number of valid words for identification accuracy about the DoT and DoF, respectively and (b) is the ROC curve of identity theft detection through the social topology. (Color figure online)

To deal with "cold start" problem, we use a mixture model as follows:

$$f_{MKD}\left(e|E,h\right) = \alpha f_{KD}\left(e|E_1\right) + \left(1-\alpha\right)f_{KD}\left(e|E_2\right), \tag{6}$$

where E_1 is a set of an individual's historical events (individual component), E_2 is a set of the friends' historical events (friendship component) and α is the weight for individual component.

Identity Theft Detection. We compute the average log-likelihood of each user i's check-in records in the test set:

$$S_i = -\frac{1}{n_i}\sum_{r=1}^{n_i}\log f_{MKD_i}\left(e^r|E,h_i\right), \tag{7}$$

where n_i is the number of user i's check-in records in the test set. The larger S_i, the more likely the records are conducted by himself. The key is to set the anomalous threshold, and define it as S_{log}^{che}. When the user i's S_i is greater than the baseline, we consider the account to be anomalous.

3.2 Detection via Tips

Modeling User Post Interests. We build the user post interest model (UPIM) by using the user-generated tips in the online behavior space. Each user's historical tips accumulate as a document, and then all the user's tips constitute a large-scale corpus. In LDA [4], each document may be viewed as a mixture of various topics. Through the document generation model, we can get the topic probability distribution of the document. In fact, the topic probability distribution corresponding to each document is the interest probability distribution of the user. We define the vector of topic probability distribution generated by the historical data as θ_{his}^{tip}.

Identity Theft Detection. After the new generated tips are processed, the vector of topic probability distribution can be calculated as θ_{new}^{tip}. We count the number of words assigned to kth topic, and denote it as $n(k)$. α is a hyperparameter, and we set $\alpha = 0.5$. The kth component of the topic proportion vector can be computed as:

$$\theta_{new} = \frac{n(k) + \alpha}{\sum_{i=1}^{K}(n(i) + \alpha)}. \tag{8}$$

In order to ensure that the tips can get a reasonable topic probability distribution, we hope that the accumulation of tips as much as possible. However, considering the efficiency of the model, we need to be able to give the identity judgment in a short time. We solve this problem by experimentally training the number of valid words. Then we define the minimum number of valid words contained in the tips as n_{vow}^{tip}. Through experiments shown in Fig. 2(a), we find that when the number of valid words reaches 30, the accuracy tends to be stable and very impressive, so we set the parameter n_{vow}^{tip} to 30 for the DoT. The interest probability distribution of tips for the user's new post is calculated as θ_{new}^{tip} by using Eq. 8.

For the discrete probability distributions P and Q, the Kullback-Leibler divergence from Q to P is defined as:

$$D_{KL}(p,q) = \sum_{i=1}^{T} p_i \cdot \ln \frac{p_i}{q_i}. \tag{9}$$

An alternative is given via the γ divergence,

$$D_{KL}(p,q) = \gamma D_{KL}(p, \gamma \cdot p + (1-\gamma)q) \tag{10}$$
$$+ (1-\gamma) D_{KL}(q, \gamma \cdot p + (1-\gamma)q),$$

which can be interpreted as the expected information gain about X from discovering which probability distribution X is drawn from, P or Q, if they currently have probabilities γ and $(1-\gamma)$ respectively.

The value $\gamma = 0.5$ gives the Jensen−Shannon divergence by

$$D_{JS}(p,q) = \frac{1}{2}\left[D_{KL}(p,M) + D_{KL}(q,M)\right], \tag{11}$$

where $M = \frac{p+q}{2}$ is the average of the two distributions.

The similarity of two topic probability distributions can be judged by JS divergence. According to its definition, a smaller divergence of JS indicates a higher similarity of the two distributions. In this work, θ_{his}^{tip} is P, and θ_{new}^{tip} is Q. So what we need to calculate is $D_{JS}^{tip}\left(\theta_{his}^{tip}, \theta_{new}^{tip}\right)$. Set the anomalous threshold to D_{JS}^{tip}. When the $D_{JS}^{tip}\left(\theta_{his}^{tip}, \theta_{new}^{tip}\right)$ of two probability distribution is greater than D_{JS}^{tip}, we consider the account to be an anomalous account.

3.3   Detection via Friendships

Modeling User Social Preferences. We use the social relationships and friend-generated tips to build the user social preferences model (USPM). Generally speaking, when the user social relationship is complete, the friendship topological structure can be utilized to model the friendship community. Due to data imperfection, the topology of friendships cannot be utilized to identify users. Figure 2(b) is the ROC (Receiver Operating Characteristic) curve of identity theft detection via the social topology, which shows an extremely poor performance. Especially when the DR is relatively low, the effect of interception is very poor, which can not be used for identity detection.

It is considered that the user's friendship community tends to be stable. If a user follows the new friends who are very different from previous ones, we would like to believe that the account may be anomalous. Therefore, we need to get the characteristics of friendship community for each user according to user's friendship and user-generated content.

Identity Theft Detection. For the new friends of the user, we cluster the preferences of these new friends for each user. Similar to the DoT, we calculate the $D_{JS}^{fri}\left(\theta_{his}^{fri}, \theta_{new}^{fri}\right)$ by using Eq. 11.

The red curve is the process of training the minimum number of valid words which is defined as n_{vow}^{fri} in Fig. 2(a). Therefore, when n_{vow}^{fri} is 60, it can achieve a stable and satisfactory accuracy for the detection method based on USPM. Set the anomalous threshold to D_{JS}^{fri}, which we define it as the baseline of the method for the DoF. When the values of D_{JS}^{fir} of two probability distributions are greater than the baseline, we consider that the preferences between the new and old friends vary in a wide range and the account could be anomalous.

4   Experiments

In this section, we present the experiments to evaluate our models and validate the complementary effect of blended behavioral analysis for identity theft detection in MSNs.

4.1   Data Sets

We present a large-scale study of user behavior for two real-life datasets of Foursquare and Yelp, and conduct experiments of about 70 thousand users that spans a period of more than 100 days. In the location-based mobile social network, we study the check-in record (DoC), online text information (DoT) and social relationship (DoF) for each user, and model the user behavior from three dimensions. Table 2 shows the number of users and the number of identifiable users in each dimension.

Table 2. Number of identifiable users in each dimension.

Dataset	Users	I_{DoC}	I_{DoT}	I_{DoF}
Foursquare	23537	18624	1062	17472
Yelp	43137	29885	1912	18484

4.2 Theft Simulation

The detection of suspicious accounts can be attributed to two types, respectively fake account detection and compromised account detection. For all accounts, we first consider the population-level suspicious behavior detection. Its purpose is to detect the outlier. If the difference is obvious, the account will be blocked as suspicious account. As for compromised account detection, although it passes the population-level suspicious behavior detection successfully, we do not fully trust it. It needs to be further detected, which is individual-level suspicious behavior detection. That is, even if the user's current behavior is not outlier, we have to detect whether the behavior is the same as himself before. If the difference is obvious, we have to doubt his identity. Our work is to solve the last and most critical issue. It means that all the suspicious behavior we have taken into account.

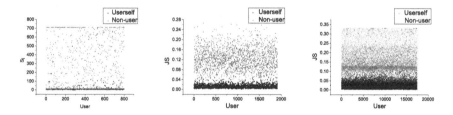

Fig. 3. The experiments of identity theft detection via Check-in, Tips and Friendship. (Color figure online)

It is hard to obtain the real data set marked with identity theft. However, it is not a pain point for our research. For identity theft detection, the main concern is how to simulate identity theft events. Our model presupposes that an attacker who steals an account will immediately start using it as they would have been some other random user of the service. Then the attacker will generate a series of behavioral records with personal characteristics. These behavioral data are those records that we have replaced with others. In fact, it is most difficult to distinguish them in the detection of suspicious behavior. One obvious fact is that if the model can accurately identify these replaced users, that is, simulated thieves, then for those thieves whose behavior is outlier, the detection performance will be more effective.

4.3   Experimental Setup

Firstly, we preprocess the data for each dimension separately according to the above methods. Secondly, we simulate identity theft by randomly replacing part of user's data with others. Thirdly, we determine the threshold of the anomalous account for the methods proposed in Sect. 3. In the DoC, we calculate S_i for each user. In the DoT and DoF, we separately calculate $D_{JS}^{tip}\left(\theta_{his}^{tip}, \theta_{new}^{tip}\right)$ and $D_{JS}^{fri}\left(\theta_{his}^{fri}, \theta_{new}^{fri}\right)$ for each user. Figure 3 is the experimental results on three dimensions. The red scatter is the result of the similarity between the user's new record and the historical data. The black scatter is the result of the similarity between the non-user's new record and the historical data. The results show that these two values are significantly different. Therefore, we can use these differences to carry out identity theft detection.

4.4   Parameter Settings

For identity theft detection, our goal is to improve the IR-DR trade-off, that is, to achieve a high IR via their blended behavior model in the case of a relatively low DR. Figure 4 is the IRs and DRs with the threshold changes in three dimensions, respectively. It can be observed that the DRs will rise sharply when the threshold reaches a certain value. We need to determine the appropriate threshold so that the IRs are as high as possible in the case of tolerable DRs. Therefore, we set the threshold at this critical point for identity anomalies. So, in each dimension, we finally determine the threshold as follows:

(1) In the DoC, we set S_{log}^{Che} to 207.
(2) In the DoT, we set D_{JS}^{tip} to 0.04.
(3) In the DoF, we set D_{JS}^{fri} to 0.08.

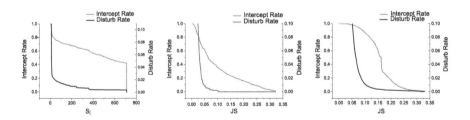

Fig. 4. Trends of different threshold values corresponding to intercept rate and disturb rate.

In the experiment, we randomly selected 1,000 users to replacing their new records with others. Then we use the three methods presented in the Sect. 3 to carry out corresponding identity theft detection. In order to compare the detection performance of our methods, we calculate the experimental results of the IRs, the DRs and the PRs.

4.5   Main Result

We first give the results of the simulation via the three methods we presented in Sect. 3 for two real-life datasets of Foursquare and Yelp. Figure 5 shows the results of three approaches for identity theft detection. The detection method based on check-in has the lowest AUC. The reason is that the data sparsity leads to the low recognition degree of the user spatial distribution. The AUC of DoF detection is the best result, which indicates that social preferences are suitable to reflect user behavior characteristics in MSNs.

As illustrated by the curves in Fig. 5, the effect of identity theft detection is reliable via the above three methods, because the AUC is very large which can reach more than 0.962. However, it is worth emphasizing that the result is obtained on the identifiable users of each dimension. This means that these methods are only feasible for I_{DoC}, I_{DoT}, I_{DoF}, respectively. In fact, behavior data are very sparse for a particular user on each dimension in MSNs. We conduct further experiments to propose an effective method which is detection via their blended behavior.

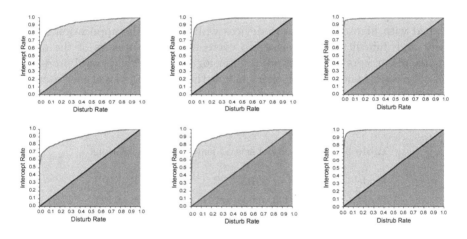

Fig. 5. The ROC curves of three methods on two data set.

We use the blended behavior to perform identity theft detection for all users. We first verify the complementary effect by the fusion between any two dimensions, such as *dimension of check-in and tips* (DoCT). Then, we combine three dimensions together to observe the effect of detection. Table 3 shows the results of seven experiments on two datasets. We get the following conclusions: The first three groups of experiments are the respective results of the above three methods. It is shown that the effect is relatively poor when we consider all users. The *mean intercept rate* (MIR) can only reach 0.518. Secondly, we can observe that when we combine any two dimensions, the performance is significantly improved and the MIR can reach 0.781, while the intercept performance is improved by

50.7%. Thirdly, when we use three dimensions fusion, the IR has reached more than 0.936, which is usually a satisfactory detection performance. At the same time, we also guarantee an acceptable DR at 0.0171. Finally, while the I_{DoT} only accounts for about 4.5%, we can still achieve great detection performance via multi-dimensional fusion due to the complementary effect of blended behavior.

In addition, we also do a similar experiment on the Yelp data, and obtain a similar conclusion. That means the complementary effect of blended behavior can achieve good performance for identity theft detection in MSNs.

5   Literature Review

Identity theft is an ever-present and growing issue in society, where almost all aspects of our lives are digital [5].

Traditional Identification Methods. Studies have shown that the traditional password-based (user-password) authentication technology is still widely used. However the password is easy to leak, easy to forget and easy to copy [6]. Common biometrics usually include fingerprint recognition, face recognition, iris recognition, speech recognition. However, these biometric technology needs to be equipped with high-cost hardware devices which makes the application inconvenient and difficult to popularize. To overcome the drawbacks of the above methods, researchers found that after a user login system, they would produce a series of behaviors and these behaviors include the characteristics of each user. By modeling these behaviors, we can derive behavioral characteristics that uniquely identify the user. Identification based on user behavior came into play [7].

Table 3. Main results of seven identity theft simulations

Model	I_ξ	IR	DR	PR	MIR	MDR	MPR
DoC	18624	0.433	0.008	0.707	0.518	0.006	0.817
DoT	1602	0.336	0.001	0.943			
DoF	17472	0.785	0.008	0.807			
DoCT	18624	0.567	0.009	0.740	0.781	0.012	0.753
DoTF	17681	0.864	0.010	0.806			
DoCF	23525	0.911	0.016	0.713			
DoCTF	23537	0.936	0.017	0.708	0.936	0.017	0.708
DoC	29885	0.226	0.007	0.440	0.396	0.003	0.758
DoT	1912	0.470	0.001	0.977			
DoF	18484	0.492	0.002	0.859			
DoCT	29885	0.648	0.007	0.684	0.681	0.006	0.739
DoTF	19339	0.713	0.002	0.886			
DoCF	42130	0.683	0.009	0.649			
DoCTF	42137	0.872	0.010	0.696	0.872	0.010	0.696

Behavior-Based Identity Analysis. Biometric keystroke recognition technology [9] is through the inherent characteristics of human keystrokes (e.g., keystroke delay and power) for identification, which not only solves the traditional insecurity based on password, but also has the advantages of low cost and high flexibility compared with other biometrics. However, these identification methods usually depend on the specific devices. Once the device is replaced, it takes a long time to retrain. Many researches studied a group or individual behavior features and leverage them to provide a better service [8]. Some of them focused on the spatial-temporal patterns. Cho et al. [2] studied the relation between human geographic movement, its temporal dynamics, and the ties of the social network. Lichman et al. [3] focused on the problem of developing accurate individual-level models of spatial location based on geolocated event data. As one of the most classical probabilistic topic model, LDA is wildly used in modeling text collections (e.g., news articles, research papers and blogs). Yuan et al. [11] propose a novel topic model called SILDA (LDA with Social Interest). Li et al. [10] proposed a new topic model for short texts, named GPU-DMM, which is designed to leverage the general word semantic relatedness knowledge during the topic inference process, to tackle the data sparsity issue. In this paper, we focus on the method for identity theft detection by analyzing user behavior in MSNs.

6   Conclusion

We studied the effectiveness of a promising technique for identity theft detection in mobile social networks, i.e., the method based on user behavioral analysis. To model the user blended behavior in multiple dimensions, we proposed three suitable models in each dimension, such as the user spatial distributions model, user post interests model and user social preferences model. To achieve better detection performance, we proposed a method through multiple dimensions fusion. As a result, we proved the existence of complementary effect of blended behavioral for identity theft detection in MSNs.

Acknowledgments. The research of authors is partially supported by the National Natural Science Foundation of China (NSFC) under Grants 61571331, Shuguang Program from Shanghai Education Development Foundation under Grant 14SG20, Fok Ying-Tong Education Foundation for Young Teachers in the Higher Education Institutions of China under Grant 151066, and the Shanghai Science and Technology Innovation Action Plan Project under Grant 16511100901.

References

1. De Montjoye, Y.A., Radaelli, L., Singh, V.K., et al.: Unique in the shopping mall: On the reidentifiability of credit card metadata. Science 347(6221), 536–539 (2015)
2. Bao, J., Zheng, Y., Mokbel, M.F.: Location-based and preference-aware recommendation using sparse geo-social networking data. In: International Conference on Advances in Geographic Information Systems, pp. 199–208 (2012)

3. Lichman, M., Smyth, P.: Modeling human location data with mixtures of kernel densities. In: Proceedings of the 20th ACM SIGKDD International Conference on Knowledge Discovery and Data Mining, pp. 35–44 (2014)
4. Zhang, J., Chow, C.: CRATS: an lda-based model for jointly mining latent communities, regions, activities, topics, and sentiments from geosocial network data. IEEE Trans. Knowl. Data Eng. **28**(11), 2895–2909 (2016)
5. Zhou, X., Liang, X., Zhang, H., Ma, Y.: Cross-platform identification of anonymous identical users in multiple social media networks. IEEE Trans. Knowl. Data Eng. **28**(2), 411–424 (2016)
6. Daz-Santiago, S., Rodrguez-Henrquez, L.M., Chakraborty, D.: A cryptographic study of tokenization systems. Int. J. Inf. Secur. **15**(4), 413–432 (2016)
7. Naini, F.M., Unnikrishnan, J., Thiran, P., Vetterli, M.: Where you are is who you are: User identification by matching statistics. IEEE Trans. Inf. Forensics Secur. **11**(2), 358–372 (2016)
8. Wang, C., Zhou, J., Yang, B.: From footprint to friendship: modeling user followership in mobile social networks from check-in data. In: SIGIR 2017, pp. 825–828 (2017)
9. Kambourakis, G., Damopoulos, D., Papamartzivanos, D., Pavlidakis, E.: Introducing touchstroke: keystroke based authentication system for smartphones. Secur. Commun. Networks **9**(6), 542–554 (2016)
10. Zuo, Y., Wu, J., Zhang, H., Lin, H., Wang, F., Xu, K., Xiong, H.: Topic modeling of short texts: a pseudo-document view. In: Proceedings of the 22nd ACM SIGKDD International Conference on Knowledge Discovery and Data Mining, San Francisco, CA, USA, 13–17 August, pp. 2105–2114 (2016)
11. He, Y., Wang, C., Jiang, C.: Mining coherent topics with pre-learned interest knowledge in Twitter. IEEE Access **5**, 10515–10525 (2017)

A Hierarchical Framework for Evaluation of Cloud Service Qualities

Qi Wang[⊠], MingWei Liu, KaiQu Chen, Yu Zhang, and Jing Zheng

Shenzhen HuaTech Information Technology Co., Ltd., Shenzhen, China
{wangqi,liumingwei,chenkaiqu,zhangyu,zhengjing}@szhuatechsec.cn

Abstract. The reliability and availability of cloud computing services improved dramatically in recent years. More and more users tend to migrate their business systems to cloud environment. The compliance of SLAs (Service Level Agreement) in cloud services must be efficiently evaluated to ensure the enforcement of SLAs. Traditionally, an Evaluation Center will be established to collecting performance and reliability metrics data of SLAs. However, since the volume of data collected is huge, and the speed of data generation is fast, large bandwidth and computation capacity is needed in the Evaluation Center. This paper proposes a hierarchical architecture for monitoring and evaluating of the compliances of SLAs. In this architecture, a Data Collection Service is deployed in the intranet of each cloud service provider. Metrics data is first collected and analyzed by local Data Collection Service. When SLA violations are detected, related data is packed, signed and sent to the Evaluation Center located on the Internet. Simulations show that the use of local Data Collection Service will effectively reduce the amount of data transferred via Internet and will not cause much overhead in the construction of evaluation infrastructure.

1 Introduction

Cloud Computing is a new computational paradigm with the features of high scalability, availability and extremely inexpensiveness. Nowadays, cloud services have become the best choice for start-up and individual business [1]. However, the centralized, open and shared nature of cloud service makes it vulnerable to various attacks [2–5]. From the user's perspective, losing control of private data makes security and privacy issues more prominent in cloud computing environment. For example, in Sep. 2014, a security issue in the iCloud API caused a serious leak of over 100 celebrities' private photos[1].

Thus, security and quality of cloud service are the most important factors that affect users' choices among different CSPs (Cloud Service Provider). Unlike traditional IT solutions, security and quality of cloud services are difficult to monitor and evaluate since the environment of cloud services is beyond the

---

[1] https://en.wikipedia.org/wiki/ICloud_leaks_of_celebrity_photos.

© Springer Nature Singapore Pte Ltd. 2018
L. Zhu and S. Zhong (Eds.): MSN 2017, CCIS 747, pp. 45–54, 2018.
https://doi.org/10.1007/978-981-10-8890-2_4

reach of common users. Various techniques have been proposed for solving this problem [6–13].

Most of the works proposed so far focused on solving the modeling, monitoring and evaluating aspects of the problem. In these works, a trusted third party, the Evaluation Center, was established to monitor/collect data like service running status, user evaluation, etc. In order to provide reliable and accurate evaluations, these data should be dynamically monitored [14]. However, in traditional centralized and flattened frameworks (Fig. 1), continuously monitoring cloud service quality across different CSPs with thousands of virtual and physical machines will cost a large number of Internet bandwidth and computational resources, making it highly impracticable to build such an Evaluation Center.

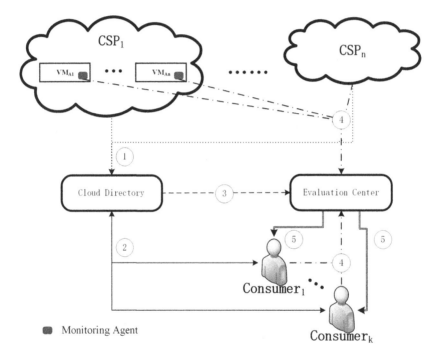

Fig. 1. Architecture for traditional cloud service evaluation framework

In this paper, an Evaluation Framework design with hierarchical architecture is proposed. In order to achieve efficient and cost-effective data collection, a local Data Collection Service will be established in the Intranet of each CSP's cluster. Service quality data will be locally aggregated before sent to the Evaluation Center over the Internet. Moreover, to further reduce the size of data transferred over the network, only data that is useful for assessing the quality of service will be packaged and sent to the Evaluation Center.

The rest of this paper is organized as follows: Sect. 2 briefly introduces related works. In Sect. 3, the architectural design of the hierarchical evaluation framework is described in detail. Section 4 concludes this paper and talks about future improvements.

2   Related Works

As can be seen from Fig. 1, there are four major participants in the interaction of cloud services: (1) a number of Cloud Service Providers (CSPs), (2) the Consumers, (3) the Evaluation Center and (4) the Cloud Directory. Typical working process in this scenario can be described as follows [14]:

1. CSPs publish services at the Cloud Directory. Published service information includes: CSP ID, service ID, service type, service content and SLA, etc.
2. Consumers send request to the Cloud Directory for specific kind of service. Request message contains information like service type, service content, etc.
3. Cloud Directory will find suitable services and send information back to consumers.
4. A negotiation process will be carried out between service provider and consumer. The result will be an SLA. The identities of consumer, CSP, negotiated service, as well as corresponding SLA will be sent to the Evaluation Center.
5. The Evaluation Center will collect objective monitoring data and subjective evaluation data from CSP and Consumer sides respectively. Collected data will be evaluated and combined to produce reports about service quality.
6. Consumers can retrieve service reports from the Evaluation Center.

Current research works focused on several aspects of the above process.

On the modeling aspect of service quality/trustiness. Alhamad et al. [15] pointed out that SLA can be used as the basis for enforcement of service quality since its the agreement signed between service provider and consumer about the level of service. The evaluation result of SLA may help consumers select the most reliable service. Then, in [7], a trust management model for cloud computing based on SLAs is proposed. Essentially, these works are only conceptual descriptions. Gao et al. [16] proposed a trust model based on SLA and consumer evaluations. Evaluation results from SLA and consumers are combined to find the trustworthiest CSP. The evaluation of SLA is statically computed, without continuous monitoring of service at runtime. Zhao et al. [14] proposed a SLA-based dynamic trust evaluation framework for cloud computing. In this framework, monitoring agents are deployed on client-side and cloud-side. SLA related information can be monitored, collected and evaluated to produce a dynamic report on service's trustiness/quality.

On the data collection and evaluation aspects of service quality/trustiness. Various tools, e.g. Netlogger [9], have been devised for effectively monitoring and collecting low level metrics such as available bandwidth, system downtime, etc. However, there is a gap between these low-level metrics and high-level SLA parameters [10]. Vincent et al. proposed a framework named LoM2HiS [10], by which these low level metrics can be combined and mapped to high level

SLA parameters. High level SLA parameters can be used for detecting SLA violations [17].

It can be seen from the above analysis that comprehensive research have been done in modeling and evaluation of service quality in cloud environment. However, since there are a large number of machines (physical and/or virtual) in each cluster of CSPs, the volume of low level metrics data collected for evaluation will be extremely huge. Transferring large amount of data over the internet will pose great burden to underlying ISP networks and computational resources. One of the potential solutions to this problem is aggregating data and detecting violations of SLA inside CSP intranet and send only those data that are related to SLA violations to Evaluation Center over the internet. It is obvious that a hierarchical architecture is required by this solution and will be discussed in detail in the next section.

3   A Hierarchical Service Quality Evaluation Framework

3.1   The Overall Architecture

Figure 2 shows the architecture of the hierarchical cloud service evaluation framework.

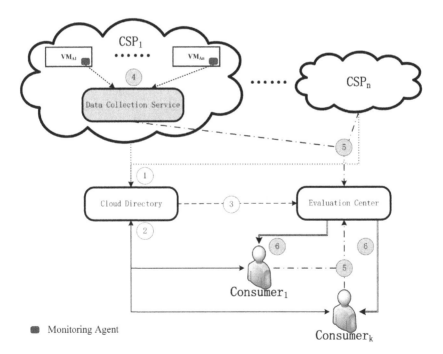

Fig. 2. The hierarchical cloud service evaluation framework

Compared with Fig. 1, an additional local Data Collection Service is established in the intranet of the CSP. Monitoring Agents deployed on every machine (virtual or physical) will continuously monitor low level metrics and send them to the Data Collection Service for local aggregation (Step 4 in Fig. 2). Violations of SLAs can be detected from high level SLA parameters mapped from aggregated low level metrics. If violations of SLAs are detected, only related low level metrics data are extracted, packed, encrypted, signed and sent to the Evaluation Center. If no violation of SLA is detected, a simple service health report will be sent periodically, confirming that all service level requirements are met. Since the possibility of SLA violation is relatively small[2], the amount of data transferred over the network will be reduced drastically.

3.2   The Design of Data Collection Service

The volume of low level metrics data collected by monitoring agents is relatively large. For example, a cluster in the data center of major CSPs may have more than 10,000 physical servers. Each physical server could host approximately 10 to 20 virtual machines, depending on the physical resources and workloads. Monitoring Agents should be deployed on every virtual machines. Various low level service metrics will be measured, packed and sent to Message Queue. The format of data packet sent by monitoring agents is shown in Fig. 3.

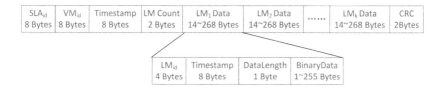

Fig. 3. Data packet structure of monitoring agents

Since different metrics have different data acquisition frequency, monitoring agents will collect, cache data and send data packets in a fixed time interval (for example, one data packet per minute). Figure 3 shows the data packet format, it can be seen that multiple low level metrics data (LM_i Data) are packed into one data packet. Assuming average data packet size is 1 KB, based on the above assumptions, the number of data packets received per hour at the local Data Collection Service will be $10,000 \times 20 \times 60 = 12,000,000$. The size of these data packets will be approximately 11.5 GB.

Obviously, low level metrics data must be processed in a timely manner and can not be saved permanently. In order to achieve high availability and high

---

[2] According to CloudHarmony, the longest downtime (per region) of cloud services by major CSPs in Sep. 2017 is 51.03 min. Data source: https://cloudharmony.com/status-of-compute-group-by-regions.

efficiency, state-of-the-art techniques and frameworks must be applied to build
the Data Collection Service. As shown in Fig. 4, the Data Collection Service
consists of 5 components: Message Queue, Streaming Data Processing, Persistent
Data Storage, SLA Cache and Communication Interface.

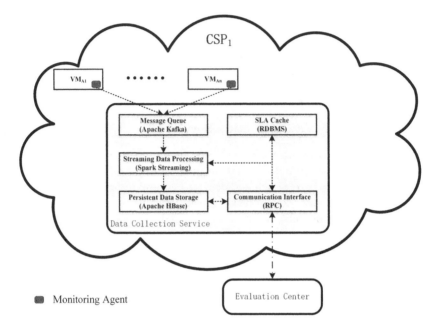

Fig. 4. Architecture overview of the data collection service

SLAs negotiated between CSPs and Consumers are stored in the SLA Cache
which can be built with any mainstream RDBMS. Message Queue can reliably
cache low level metrics data received from monitoring agents. Apache Kafka[3] is
suitable to build such a reliable and high-throughput message queue. Streaming
Data Processing will read and process cached data from message queue in quasi-
real time. Low level metrics data will be mapped to high level SLA parameters
using corresponding rules, then data will be stored into Persistent Data Storage. In case SLA violations are detected, related low level metrics data will be
retrieved from Persistent Data Storage and sent to the Evaluation Center over
the network. In order to reliably store and efficiently access large volume of data,
NoSQL database (e.g. Apache HBase[4]) should be used to build the Persistent
Data Storage.

---

[3] http://kafka.apache.org.
[4] http://hbase.apache.org.

3.3   The Processing of Service Metrics Data

Before discussing details of the low level metrics data processing mechanism, the structure of SLA should be described. The abstract data structure of SLAs used in this paper is given informally as follows:

$$SLA := \langle sp_{id}, c_{id}, sla_{id}, [hp_1, hp_2, \cdots, hp_i] \rangle$$

in which sp_{id}, c_{id} and sla_{id} are identifiers of the CSP, Consumer and SLA, respectively.

$$hp := \langle [lm_1, lm_2, \cdots, lm_k], eval, obj, vio \rangle$$

is the definition of a high level SLA parameter $hp \in H$, consisted of 4 elements:

1. A number of low level metrics $lm_i \in L$,
2. A function $eval(lm_1, lm_2, \cdots, lm_k) : L^* \to H$ that maps values of low level metrics to high level SLA parameter,
3. The negotiated objective $obj \in \mathbb{R}$ for SLA parameter hp, and
4. A function $vio(hp, obj) : H \times \mathbb{R} \to \{TRUE|FALSE\}$ to determine SLA violations.

Using Apache Spark[5] distributed computing platform, low-level metrics data can be processed under the streaming processing paradigm. Data can be ingested from Message Queue, grouped into mini batches (batch interval can be 1 s or 1 min, etc.) and then processed. Algorithm 1 describes the whole process using pseudocode.

Algorithm 1. Low Level Metrics Data Processing

1: **class** LMPROCESS
2:     **method** INITIALIZE(CONTEXT ctx)
3:         Map$\langle sla_{id}, SLA \rangle$ $slas \leftarrow ctx$.readSLAs()
4:     **end method**
5:     **method** PROCESS(TIME $time_s$, TIME $time_e$, RDD$\langle$Packet$\rangle$ lm)
6:         PAIRRDD$\langle$List$\langle\langle sla_{id}, vm_{id}, hp_{id}\rangle, LM\rangle\rangle$ $lmp \leftarrow lm$.FLATMAPTOPAIR($slas$)
7:         PAIRRDD$\langle\langle sla_{id}, vm_{id}, hp_{id}\rangle, List\langle LM\rangle\rangle$ $hp\_g \leftarrow lmp$.GROUPBYKEY()
8:         PAIRRDD$\langle\langle sla_{id}, vm_{id}, hp_{id}\rangle, hp_v\rangle$ $hp\_v \leftarrow hp\_g$.REDUCE($slas$)
9:         PAIRRDD$\langle\langle sla_{id}, vm_{id}, hp_{id}\rangle, hp_v\rangle$ $vio \leftarrow hp_v$.FILTER($slas$)
10:        vio.SAVEASFILE($time_s, time_e$)
11:        hp_g.SAVEINTOHBASE($time_s, time_e$)
12:    **end method**
13: **end class**

Monitored low level metrics data are cached in Message Queue. They are continuously ingested, organized into mini batches and fed to the processing program. The inputs to Algorithm 1 are one batch of low level metrics data

---

[5] http://spark.apache.org.

(lm) as well as the start and end time ($time_s$ and $time_e$) of data in this batch. Each record in lm is a data packet gathered by some monitoring agent. The structure of the data packet was shown in Fig. 3. The output of Algorithm 1 are detected violations (vio, which will be saved into file system) and persisted low level metrics data (hp_g, which will be saved into HBase).

Before computation starts, SLAs are first read into a map named $slas$ (Line 2–4). Then the current batch of low level metrics data (lm) are flat mapped into a sequence of key-value pairs, in which SLA id, virtual machine id and high level parameter id are combined as a compound key, one low level metrics data is used as the value (Line 6). The records in PairRDD lmp are organized into groups according to their keys (Line 7) and further reduced to evaluate the corresponding high level parameter value (Line 8). Evaluated high level parameters are filtered to detect violations to SLAs (Line 9). Detected violations and low level metrics data will be saved into file system and HBase respectively (Line 10–11).

Low level metrics data are persisted into HBase so they can be efficiently retrieved when violations are detected. In HBase, data is organized as tables, which have rows, column families and columns. Data in HBase is uniquely identified by a combination of five dimensional coordinates: Table, Rowkey, Column Family, Column Qualifier, Version. Rows in HBase are sorted lexicographically by rowkey, in other words, rowkey is the only index in HBase. Thus well-designed rowkey can help improve the performance of data access. An HBase table named "lm" is designed for storing low level service metrics data. The schema for this table is shown in Fig. 5:

Fig. 5. Schema for HBase table: "lm"

Rowkey is the most important part of the schema design:

1. A simple hash of the SLA_{id} (Prefix = $SLA_{id}\%256$) is used as the first byte of the rowkey.
2. Data collection time is divided into 5 parts: the year (2 bytes), the month (1 byte), the day (1 byte), the hour (1 byte) and the minute (1 byte). The hour part is used as the second byte of the rowkey. Year, month, day and minute parts occupied the next 5 bytes of the rowkey.

3. The id of SLA (SLA_{id}), Virtual Machine (VM_{id}) and High level Parameter (HP_{id}) are the last three parts of the rowkey.
4. In table "lm", there is currently only one column family (d) and only one column ($data$), in which low level metrics data are serialized and stored.

Using hashed prefix and hour as the first two parts of rowkey, RegionServer hot-spotting in HBase can be effectively avoided. Data collected for different SLAs will be distributed into different portions of the rowkey space. Meanwhile, data collected for the same SLA in one hour will be grouped together. In case violations are detected, related low level metrics data can be efficiently retrieved.

4   Conclusion and Future Work

This paper proposes a prototype cloud service quality evaluation framework. In traditional architectures, large volume of data must be sent over the Internet. In the hierarchical architecture proposed in this paper, data packet is sent to the Evaluation Center only when SLA violations are detected. Thus the volume of data sent over the Internet will be reduced significantly.

Future improvements should be done in the following directions: First, the security and authenticity of the evaluation framework should be considered thoroughly. There are research works on several aspects such as key management scheme [18,19], time synchronization mechanism [20], secure routing protocol [21] and access control [22,23], etc. that should be incorporated into the framework proposed in this paper. Second, data organization and processing should be refined to further reduce the storage and computational resources required to build such a system.

Acknowledgment. The work described in this paper is supported by Shenzhen Science and Technology Project "Research on Key Technologies in Trusted Cloud Architecture" (Project No. JSGG20160229122214337).

References

1. Xiao, Y., Du, X., Zhang, J., Hu, F., Guizani, S.: Internet protocol television (IPTV): the killer application for the next-generation internet. IEEE Commun. Mag. **45**(11), 126–134 (2007)
2. Wu, Z., Xu, Z., Wang, H.: Whispers in the hyper-space: high-bandwidth and reliable covert channel attacks inside the cloud. IEEE/ACM Trans. Netw. **23**(2), 603–615 (2015)
3. Yan, Q., Yu, F.R.: Distributed denial of service attacks in software-defined networking with cloud computing. IEEE Commun. Mag. **53**(4), 52–59 (2015)
4. Green, M.: The Threat in the Cloud. IEEE Educational Activities Department (2013)
5. Hei, X., Du, X., Wu, J., Hu, F.: Defending resource depletion attacks on implantable medical devices. In: IEEE Global Telecommunications Conference (GLOBECOM 2010), pp. 1–5, December 2010

6. Wang, M.C., Wu, X., Zhang, W., Ding, F.Q., Zhou, J., Pei, G.C.: A conceptual platform of SLA in cloud computing. In: IEEE Ninth International Conference on Dependable, Autonomic and Secure Computing, pp. 1131–1135 (2011)

7. Alhamad, M., Dillon, T., Chang, E.: SLA-based trust model for cloud computing. In: 13th International Conference on Network-Based Information Systems (NBiS), pp. 321-324. IEEE (2010)

8. Hogben, G., Dekker, M.: Procure secure: a guide to monitoring of security service levels in cloud contracts. Technical report, European Network and Information Security Agency (ENISA) (2012)

9. Gunter, D., Tierney, B., Crowley, B., Holding, M., Lee, J.: NetLogger: a toolkit for distributed system performance analysis. In: Proceedings of the 8th International Symposium on Modeling, Analysis and Simulation of Computer and Telecommunication Systems (Cat. No. PR00728), pp. 267–273 (2000)

10. Emeakaroha, V.C., Brandic, I., Maurer, M., Dustdar, S.: Low level metrics to high level SLAs - LoM2HiS framework: bridging the gap between monitored metrics and SLA parameters in cloud environments. In: International Conference on High Performance Computing Simulation, pp. 48–54, June 2010

11. Shou-Xu, J., Jian-Zhong, L.: A reputation-based trust mechanism for P2P E-commerce systems. J. Softw. 18(10), 2551–2563 (2007)

12. Du, X., Chen, H.: Security in wireless sensor networks. IEEE Wirel. Commun. 15(4), 60–66 (2008)

13. Xiao, Y., Rayi, V.K., Sun, B., Du, X., Hu, F., Galloway, M.: A survey of key management schemes in wireless sensor networks. Comput. Commun. 30(11), 2314–2341 (2007). Special issue on security on wireless ad hoc and sensor networks

14. Zhao, P., Han, Z., He, Y.: SLA-based dynamic trust evaluation for cloud computing. J. Beijing Jiaotong Univ. 37(5), 80–87 (2013)

15. Alhamad, M., Dillon, T., Chang, E.: Conceptual SLA framework for cloud computing. In: IEEE International Conference on Digital Ecosystems and Technologies, pp. 606–610 (2010)

16. Gao, Y.-L., Shen, B.-J., Kong, H.-F.: Trust model for cloud computing based on SLA and user ratings. Comput. Eng. 38(8), 28–30 (2012)

17. Emeakaroha, V.C., Calheiros, R.N., Netto, M.A.S., Brandic, I., Rose, C.A.F.D.: DeSVi: an architecture for detecting SLA violations in cloud computing infrastructures. In: Proceedings of the 2nd International ICST Conference on Cloud Computing (CloudComp 2010) (2010)

18. Du, X., Xiao, Y., Guizani, M., Chen, H.H.: An effective key management scheme for heterogeneous sensor networks. Ad Hoc Netw. 5(1), 24–34 (2007). Security Issues in Sensor and Ad Hoc Networks

19. Du, X., Guizani, M., Xiao, Y., Chen, H.H.: A routing-driven elliptic curve cryptography based key management scheme for heterogeneous sensor networks. IEEE Trans. Wirel. Commun. 8(3), 1223–1229 (2009)

20. Du, X., Guizani, M., Xiao, Y., Chen, H.H.: Secure and efficient time synchronization in heterogeneous sensor networks. IEEE Trans. Veh. Technol. 57(4), 2387–2394 (2008)

21. Du, X., Xiao, Y., Chen, H.H., Wu, Q.: Secure cell relay routing protocol for sensor networks. Wirel. Commun. Mob. Comput. 6(3), 375–391 (2006)

22. Hei, X., Du, X.: Biometric-based two-level secure access control for implantable medical devices during emergencies. In: 2011 Proceedings of IEEE INFOCOM, 346–350, April 2011

23. Yao, X., Han, X., Du, X., Zhou, X.: A lightweight multicast authentication mechanism for small scale iot applications. IEEE Sens. J. 13(10), 3693–3701 (2013)

Facility Location Selection Using Community-Based Single Swap: A Case Study

Rixin Xu[1], Zijian Zhang[1($\boxtimes$)], Jiamou Liu[2($\boxtimes$)], Nathan Situ[2], and Jun Ho Jin[2]

[1] Beijing Institute of Technology Beijing, Beijing, China
{xurixin,zhangzijian}@bit.edu.cn
[2] University of Auckland, Auckland, New Zealand
jiamou.liu@auckland.ac.nz

Abstract. This paper focuses on the uncapacitated k-median facility location problem, which asks to locate k facilities in a network that minimize the total routing time, taking into account the constraints of nodes that are able to serve as servers and clients, as well as the level of demand in each client node. This problem is important in a wide range of applications from operation research to mobile ad-hoc networks. Existing algorithms for this problem often lead to high computational costs when the underlying network is very large, or when the number k of required facilities is very large. We aim to improve existing algorithms by taking into considerations of the community structures of the underlying network. More specifically, we extend the strategy of *local search with single swap* with a community detection algorithm. As a real-world case study, we analyze in detail Auckland North Shore spatial networks with varying distance threshold and compare the algorithms on these networks. The results show that our algorithm significantly reduces running time while producing equally optimal results.

Keywords: Facility location · k-median problem
Community structures · Spatial networks · Auckland Open Data
Single swap algorithm

1 Introduction

Facility location problem concerns with the deployment of decentralized service across a network of interconnected nodes. The goal is to choose a set of nodes to host facilities which lead to a minimized overall cost. Consider, as an example, a *wireless sensor network* [20], which consists of self-organizing sensors that communicate through wireless transmission without a pre-designated infrastructure. It is often more cost-effective to designate nodes in the networks to host

Z. Zhang—This work is partially supported by China National Key Research and Development Program No. 2016YFB0800301.

L. Zhu and S. Zhong (Eds.): MSN 2017, CCIS 747, pp. 55–69, 2018.
https://doi.org/10.1007/978-981-10-8890-2_5

servers (or "hubs") that collect and aggregate sensory data [14]. The costs associated with this scheme include resources consumed by the servers, as well as the communication costs between sensors to servers. To minimize costs, a challenge lies in the selection of server locations so that every sensor reaches a nearby server while keeping the number of servers reasonable. This would mean an even distribution of workload carried out by the servers and thus reliable network performance. One needs to deal with two central questions: how many servers should there be and on which nodes should servers be placed?

This paper focused on (uncapacitated) *k-median facility location problem.* Abstractly, complex networks such as communication, physical or social networks are characterized by interactions between its nodes; channels of interactions are represented as edges and are typically weighted to reflect distance or strength of the connection. Nodes are classified into ones that are resource-rich and resource-poor, and facilities (or "servers") may be placed on resource-rich nodes. When a facility is opened on a node, the node becomes a *server nodes* and it may provide services to others. A non-server node is also called a *client node,* and it is designated a particular server node to communicate with. As client nodes may have different levels of demand for service from their designated server, the communication cost for a client is captured by (1) the distance between the client and its nearest server; and (2) the demand level of this client. The problem takes a parameter k and seeks for k nodes to act as server nodes that minimize total communication costs among all client nodes.

The facility location problem has many potential applications in wireless communication. Apart from the application in sensor networks discussed above, consider, as a second application, an urban *cellular network.* An important problem of cellular networks is to reduce energy consumption through the use of base stations with low transceiver power budget. The main challenge here is to place such base stations in appropriate locations that meet the QoS requirement of every user while minimizing energy consumption. This challenge can be rephrased in terms of facility location problem, where the facilities correspond to base stations and the costs correspond to energy consumption [16]. A third potential application involves information-centric networking (ICN), which transmits data directly between devices without the need for a pre-existing infrastructure [3]. In particular, *opportunistic networks* present as an efficient, scalable and robust scheme to delivery contents. Here, communications are supported through mobile ad hoc networks (MANETs) and contacts are opportunistically established between devices [18]. To facilitate reliable delivery of contents, one may deploy a number of "hub storage" of user contents. These storages can be selected via a facility location problem: the underlying network in this scenario contains social contact patterns among users, i.e., the frequency of contacts between people implies the potential to deliver message between their devices. The facilities correspond to storage hubs, and the cost is associated with how easy or likely a node may reach a facility via multi-hop paths [28].

This paper's main aim is three-fold. Firstly, due to the high computational complexity of facility location problem, attention has mostly been concentrated on designing heuristics to approximate optimal solutions of the facility location problem. Classical solutions, such as the *reverse greedy algorithm* and the *single-swap algorithm* incur a large computation cost when applied to complex networks or when a lot of facilities are required to be placed on the network [5,10]. Thus the first goal of the paper is to design more efficient heuristic to solve the problem. Secondly, community structure is a prevalent property of complex networks in the real world and has been intensively studied in the context of large and complex networks. Intuition tells us that facilities should be placed to serve local communities. However, to the authors' knowledge, no work has so far emphasized on the potential that community structure may support the selection of facility locations within a network; The goal of the research is to explore this potential. Thirdly, by processing government open-access GIS dataset, we obtain geospatial networks representing Auckland's North Shore, a major urban region in New Zealand. Nodes in the network correspond to land zones and edges represent geodesic proximity. We investigate the facility location problem in the context of this region as a real-world case study. The findings would potentially provide us more insights on the urban topology of the city.

Paper organization. Section 2 discusses background and related works. Section 3 introduces the facility location problem, the reverse greedy and single swap algorithm. Section 4 presents our two community-based methods: the community select and community swap algorithms. Section 5 discusses our case study on North Shore dataset and experimental results obtained on the spatial networks. Section 6 concludes with future works.

2   Background and Related Works

2.1   Main Themes and Background

Selecting facility locations to effectively serve a region has been an important problem in operation research [4,11,17]. There are two main versions of the problem that are closely related: Firstly, the *classical facility location problem* seeks not only to decide on the location but also the number of facilities to be placed. Secondly, the *k-median facility location problem* assumes that the number k of facilities is given as an input, and lifts the restriction on the coverage of each server. The focus of this paper is on the k-median facility location problem.

Real-world networks are seldom uniformly distributed, but rather, exhibit distinguishing patterns such as scale-freeness (i.e., power-law degree distribution) and small-worldness (i.e., short average path length and high clustering coefficient) [6,25,29,30]. A real-world network is typically composed of a collection of densely connected regions, which are sparsely connected between themselves [23,26]. Detecting these dense regions allows us to develop a macro-level topology of the network, where each such dense region is called a *community*. Intuition tells us that it is reasonable to place servers at the center of communities so that they dedicate their services towards their own communities.

Spatial analysis studies geometric and topological properties of physical locations through geographical information systems [22, 24, 31]. The field has been widely applied to urban planning [32], transportation [7], and telecommunication engineering [19]. Auckland North Shore (formerly North Shore City) comprises of the 4th largest urban area in New Zealand and it has become an integrated part of Auckland since 2010. Auckland City Council has published data of North Shore which contains detailed accounts of geographic information. This allows us to extract distance-based networks of land areas in the region and perform analytics over these networks.

2.2   Related Works

Here we briefly survey important algorithms for solving the facility location problem. Chaudhuri et al. in [9] discussed the k-median facility location problem by exploiting the notion of *distance-d dominating sets* [12]. This approach ignores the varying service requirements from nodes, furthermore, the identification of dominating sets is, in general, a computationally hard problem.

Chrobak et al. in [10] focuses on greedy approaches to solve the k-median facility location problem. The naive greedy approach minimizes cost with each addition of server node but only produces solutions with $\Omega(n)$ approximation ratio. The *reverse greedy algorithm*, on the other hand, starts with all nodes being servers and iteratively removes nodes from the solution set. This method results in a much-improved approximation ratio of between $\Omega(\log n/\log\log n)$ and $O(\log n)$ when the distance is metric. In our experiments, we will use this method as a benchmark algorithm.

The local search with swap strategy was introduced in [5]. The algorithm works by choosing an initial set of k facilities. The algorithm then examines possible ways to swap a current server location with another client node for possible improvements over the current cost and executes the best swap. The procedure repeats until when no swap may reduce the cost. In the worst case, the solution produced will create a cost of $(3 + 2/p)$-times the optimal cost, where p is the number swaps that are being done at one time. In this paper, we aim to improve upon this algorithm by extending swap strategy above with community structure of the underlying graph.

Liao et al. in [21] explored clustering-based location-allocation methods. Their method utilizes Euclidean distances between physical locations. The main difference between this algorithm and our proposed algorithm is that we use pre-computed clusters and execute a local search to take place within computed communities, whereas their approach also identifies clusters along with the process. Therefore, our algorithm may utilize a wide range of community detection algorithms to provide community structures of different granularity.

3   Problem Formulation and Existing Solutions

We consider models of wireless networks that consist of undirected links between nodes. Formally, we define the model as follows:

Definition 1. *A* facility location (FL) network *is represented by a weighted graph* $G = (V, E, V_f, \rho, w)$ *where V is the set of* nodes *and E is a set of (undirected)* edges; *no multi-edge nor self-loop is allowed. The subset $V_f \subseteq V$ contains nodes that are candidate locations of servers while $V \setminus V_f$ contains client nodes. The function $\rho \colon V \setminus V_f \to \mathcal{R}$ is the* demand function *that assigns a* demand level *of service to each client node. The weight $w \colon E \to \mathcal{R}$ is a* distance function *measuring how close two neighboring nodes are.*

A *path* in the network is a sequence of edges $\{v_0, v_1\}, \ldots, \{v_{k-1}, v_k\}$ in E; k is the *length* of the path. The *distance* between two nodes u, v is the minimum length of a path connecting u and v and is denoted $\mathrm{dist}(u, v)$. The dist function is a *metric* as for all nodes $u, v, w \in V$, $\mathrm{dist}(u, w) \leq \mathrm{dist}(u, v) + \mathrm{dist}(v, w)$. We also assume that $\mathrm{dist}(u, v) < \infty$ for any pairs of nodes u, v (i.e., G is connected).

We are interested in ways to place servers on nodes in G. Since we are going to focus on uncapacitated version of the facility location problem, each client node will implicitly connect to the server node that has the least distance.

Definition 2. *Given FL network* $G = (V, E, V_f, \rho, w)$, *and $k \in \mathbb{N}$, a k-facility location (FL) instance* on G *is a set $S \subseteq V_f$ containing k server nodes. The* cost *of a k-FL instance S is* $\mathrm{cost}(S) = \sum_{v \in V} \min\{\mathrm{dist}(v, u) \mid u \in S\} \cdot \rho(v)$.

The *k-means facility location problem* seeks a k-FL instance with minimum cost. Hence the problem is formally defined as

INPUT   An FL network $G = (V, E, V_f, \rho, w)$, $k \in \mathbb{N}$.
OUTPUT   A k-FL instance with minimum cost.

The problem has long been known to be NP-hard [10] through a reduction from dominating set problem. Next, we review two important approximation algorithms with known approximation ratios.

Reverse Greedy Algorithm [10]. Reverse greedy algorithm is a simple greedy algorithm that starts with setting the solution set $S = V_f$ and iteratively reduces the set by removing server nodes that leads to the least cost. The procedure repeats until $|S| = k$. More precisely, the algorithm is described in Algorithm 1. The algorithm repeats $n - k$ iterations where each iteration i computes costs for $n - i$ sets S', each taking $O(n(n - i))$ in a naive implementation, where $n = |V|$. Assuming that computing all-pair shortest path distance takes time $O(g(n))$. The total running time of the algorithm is thus $O\left(g(n) + (n - k)\sum_{j=k}^{n} j^2\right) = O(g(n) + (n - k)n^3)$.

Single-Swap Algorithm [5]. The algorithm starts with a set of k randomly selected facility locations. It then loops over pairs of nodes (u, v) where u is a currently selected location and v is not, and compares the costs of the k-FL instances before and after when u is swapped with v. After identifying the pair (u, v) which will result in maximum improvement in the cost, the algorithm performs the swap. This action will guarantee that the cost goes down with each iteration. The algorithm terminates when no pair (u, v) is found that reduces

Algorithm 1. RevGreedy(G, k)

[INPUT] FL network $G = (V, E, V_f, \rho, w)$, integer k
[OUTPUT] FL instance $S \subseteq V_f$
$S \leftarrow V_f$
while $|S| > k$ **do**
$\quad m \leftarrow \infty$
$\quad$ **for** $u \in S$ **do**
$\quad\quad S' \leftarrow S \setminus \{u\}$
$\quad\quad$ **if** cost(S') $< m$ **then**
$\quad\quad\quad v \leftarrow u$
$\quad S \leftarrow S \setminus \{v\}$
return S

the cost any further, at which point we are sure to reach a local optimum. The algorithm is named *single-swap algorithm*. Note that as each facility can only be swapped-in at most once, the algorithm will always terminate. Each iteration of the algorithm runs in time $O(k(n - k)n)$ and there may be at most $O(n)$ iterations. Assuming an $O(g(n))$ algorithm to compute all-pair shortest path, the algorithm runs in time $O(g(n) + kn^3)$.

Algorithm 2. SingleSwap(G, k)

[INPUT] FL network $G = (V, E, V_f, \rho, w)$, integer k
[OUTPUT] FL instance $S \subseteq V_f$
$S \leftarrow$ Initialize(G, k); $c \leftarrow$ cost(S); swap $\leftarrow$ true
while swap **do**
$\quad T \leftarrow S$
$\quad$ **for** every pair $(u, v) \in V_f \times (V \setminus V_f)$ **do**
$\quad\quad S' \leftarrow (S \setminus \{u\}) \cup \{v\}$; swap $\leftarrow$ false
$\quad\quad$ **if** cost(S') $< c$ **then**
$\quad\quad\quad T \leftarrow S'$; swap $\leftarrow$ true; $c \leftarrow$ cost(S')
$\quad S \leftarrow T$
return S

4   Community-Based Algorithms

Community structure refers to a notable property of a network where nodes are typically clustered into several subgraphs, i.e., *communities*, which are densely connected on the inside, and sparsely connected on the outside [15]. The property naturally arises from small-world networks and gives rise to a modular view of the overall network structure that enabled a wide range of applications. Over the last 10–15 years, a vast literature has been devoted to the description and detection of communities in a network [13,27], which has lead to a number of well-established methods. In particular, *modularity maximization* has been a widely-used approach that maximizes the concentration of edges within communities compared with a random null model. In particular, given a partition of nodes into clusters $C_1, C_2, \ldots, C_k$, the *modularity* is defined as

$$Q = \frac{1}{2m} \sum_{i,j \in V} \left[A_{i,j} - \frac{d_i d_j}{2m} \right] \delta(i,j)$$

where m is the sum of edge weights, $A_{i,j}$ is the edge weight between nodes i and j, d_x is the sum of edge weights adjacent to node $x \in \{i,j\}$, and $\delta(i,j)$ is 1 if i, j are in the same cluster and is 0 otherwise. An ideal community structure is a partition that maximizes Q. Finding a partition with maximum modularity is NP-hard in general. In our experiments, we use Louvain method that uses an agglomerative greedy heuristic to approximate communities [8].

Past works which bring network clustering and facility location problem together normally select server nodes in hope to find communities in networks. The logic flow goes as follows: An algorithm picks a set of server nodes in the network and at the same time, decides on which client nodes would be assigned to a server. Thus the process identifies clusters of nodes that are within close proximity to each server node, giving rise to a community structure. In this work, we adopt a different perspective: Assuming an extraneous mechanism truthfully identifies communities in the network. The ideal selection of server nodes in the network would then rely on this identified community structure. Namely, when picking server nodes, it would be sufficient to identify one or a few server nodes within single communities, hence more efficiently identify k-FL instances with low costs. In this line of thoughts, we propose two algorithms: *community select* and *community swap*.

4.1 Community Select Algorithm

The community select algorithm takes the identified community structure and selects a server node in each community that leads to minimum cost within this community. See Algorithm 3. The algorithm is simply implemented with running time $O(f(n) + g(\tilde{n}) + k\tilde{n}^2)$ where $f(n)$ is the running time of the extraneous community detection algorithm, $\tilde{n}$ is the largest size of a community, $g(\tilde{n})$ is the running time to compute all-pair shortest path on a graph with $\tilde{n}$ nodes.

Algorithm 3. CommunitySelect(G, k)

[INPUT] FL network $G = (V, E, V_f, \rho, w)$, integer k
[OUTPUT] FL instance $S \subseteq V_f$
Set $\mathcal{C} = (C_1, C_2, \ldots, C_k) \leftarrow$ CommunityDetect(G, k)
$\qquad\qquad\qquad\qquad\qquad\qquad\quad \triangleright$ Apply a community detection algorithm on G
for $C_i \in \mathcal{C}$ **do**
$\quad V_{f,i} = C_i \cap V_f$
$\quad v_i \leftarrow \arg\min_u \left\{ \sum_{v \in C_i \backslash V_f} \text{dist}(v, u) \cdot \rho(v) \mid u \in V_{f,i} \right\}$
Return $S \leftarrow \{v_1, v_2, \ldots, v_k\}$

4.2   Community Swap Algorithm

The community swap algorithm extends from the single swap algorithm by incorporating the community structure. As opposed to the community select algorithm, it does not just pick the single optimal server node in each community, but rather, it applies local search and swaps to reach optimize costs. The difference between the classical single swap algorithm is that, when identifying possible pairs (u, v) to swap, the algorithm only looks at pairs (u, v) where u and v belong to the same community. In this way, the algorithm drastically reduces the running time. See Algorithm 4 for a detailed description.

Algorithm 4. CommunitySwap(G, k)

[INPUT] FL network $G = (V, E, V_f, \rho, w)$, integer k
[OUTPUT] FL instance $S \subseteq V_f$
Set $\mathcal{C} = (C_1, C_2, \ldots, C_k) \leftarrow$ CommunityDetect(G, k)
                                                    ▷ Apply a community detection algorithm on G
for $1 \leq i \leq k$ **do**
   $v_i \leftarrow$ Select(C_i, V_f) ▷ Initialize a server node in V_f
   $S \leftarrow S \cup \{v\}$
$c \leftarrow \text{cost}(S)$
for $1 \leq i \leq k$ **do**
   swap $\leftarrow$ true
   while swap **do**
      $T \leftarrow S$
      for every $u \in (C_i \setminus V_f)$ **do**
         $S' \leftarrow (S \setminus \{v_i\}) \cup \{u\}$; swap $\leftarrow$ false
         if $\text{cost}(S') < c$ **then**
            $T \leftarrow S'$; swap $\leftarrow$ true; $c \leftarrow \text{cost}(S')$
      $S \leftarrow T$
return S

This algorithm repeats the swapping process for each community $C_1, \ldots, C_k$; every community C_i may run in $O\left(\tilde{n}^2 n\right)$ where $\tilde{n}$ is the size of the largest community. Thus the total running time of the swapping process is $O\left(k\tilde{n}^2 n\right)$. The algorithm runs in time $O\left(f(n) + g(n) + k\tilde{n}^2 n\right)$ where $g(n)$ is the time of computing all-pair distance and $f(n)$ is the time of community detection.

5   Case Study: Auckland North Shore Networks

5.1   Data Set and Network Definition

With an area of $130\,\text{km}^2$ and $141\,\text{km}$ coastline, the former North Shore City was the fourth largest urban area in New Zealand prior to its merge with other local councils to form the current Auckland City Council. We take Auckland Open Data offered by Auckland City Council with geographical information of

North Shore zoning [2]. The data set (Auckland Council District Plan Operative North Shore Section 2002) contains maps and descriptions of all land and sea zones in the region, each labeled by length, area, and zone types. Zone types include residential (7 classes), recreational (4 classes), rural (4 classes), business (12 classes), sea, road, and other. For clarification, zone types specify how the zone can be used and possible developments. For example, only a business can be placed in a business zone, and housing can only be placed in a residential zone. The zone class determines further restrictions on how buildings in that zone can be placed. For example, a Residential 6 zone is classified as an intensive housing zone where high-density housing is placed near specific commercial sites. The dataset can be processed and visualized using GIS applications such as ArcGIS[1], from which we are able to extract location (vectorization) of each zone, and the centroid of each zone. Further details and usage of the data set can be found in [1].

Our goal is to draw up simulated wireless mesh networks of North Shore given the zoning data set. Here, each land zone is going to be a node in our network (e.g., assume a device is placed at the centroid of the zone). The data set contains 3986 land zones. We calculate distances between centroids of each pair of zones, which become the edge weight. Thus the data set would result in a complete graph. To further reveal topological structures, we set a *threshold θ* so that the network only contains edges $\{u, v\}$ when the distance between u and v is no more than θ meters. Such edges represent simulated wireless connections based on proximity. We set all business zones on this network as potential facility locations. From Auckland City Council, we also obtain policies on allowable housing densities on residential zones of different classes. By combining density with zone area, we obtain estimates on the population of each residential zone. This allows us to assign a service demand to each residential zone. Here is the formal definition of the FL network $NS\theta = (V, E_\theta, w, V_f, \rho)$:

- V contains all land zones from North Shore.
- The set E_θ of edges contains pairs of nodes $\{u, v\}$ whose are within θ meters.
- $w(u, v) \in [0, \theta]$ represents the distance between u and v.
- The set V_f consists of all business zones.
- The service demand $\rho(v)$ of a node $v \in V \setminus V_f$ equals to the estimated population of v if v is residential, and 0 if v is of other types.

For our experiment, we set $\theta \in \{200, 300, 400\}$; the corresponding networks are called NS200, NS300, and NS400 networks, respectively. Figure 1 illustrates a map of North Shore with all land zones and illustrates the Fruchterman-Reingold visualization of the three networks. The network structures all exhibit strong community structures. Table 1 lists various properties of the networks including average clustering coefficient (ACC), density and average degree. It is clear that the networks are all sparse networks with very low density, however, with high clustering coefficients, meaning that they exhibit small-world property.

---

[1] www.arcgis.com.

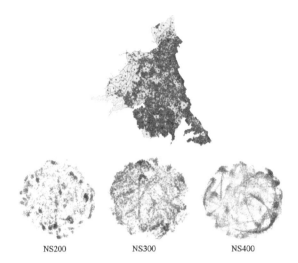

NS200   NS300   NS400

Fig. 1. Above: Auckland North Shore map and land zones. Below: Fruchtermar-Reingold layout of the networks NS200, NS300, and NS400.

Table 1. Properties of the graphs used

Graph	#Node	#Edge	ACC	Density	Avg deg
NS200	3986	12001	0.507	0.00151	6.02
NS300	3986	25544	0.593	0.00322	12.8
NS400	3986	42936	0.625	0.00541	21.5

Applying Louvain method, we identify the following community structure of the NS400 network. The NS400 network exhibits 18 non-trivial communities as shown in Fig. 2(a). The result is remarkably consistent with the real-world administrative divisions. For example, community 0 (in red) aligns very well with the suburb of Northcote, while community 14 (in violet) and 17 (in blue) align closely to the suburbs of Albany and Devonport, resp. Also noticeable is that the communities are clearly divided by State Highway 1 which divides North Shore vertically into eastern and western regions.

It is important to point out that, due to stochastic nature of the Louvain method, different runs of the algorithm will result in different communities. In our experiments, we need to set a parameter k indicating the number of communities identified from the data set. This results in different communities being found. In particular, we choose k largest communities in the process whenever these communities cover an area that is at least 75% of the overall area.

Below we illustrate our facility location algorithms when applied on the NS300 network. Fig. 2(b) shows the result of the community select algorithm with $k = 4$. The four identified communities roughly overlap with the four district boards: Devenport-Takapuna (green), Kaipatiki (brown), Upper Harbour (purple), and Hibiscus And Bays (blue).

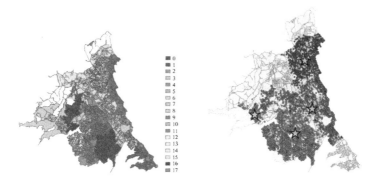

Fig. 2. Left (a): The 18 found communities of North Shore; Right (b): The result of CommunitySelect with $k = 4$ on NS300. Stars indicate the locations of the selected server nodes. (Color figure online)

Fig. 3. The result of CommunitySwap with $k = 4$ on NS300. Left: the selected server nodes before swapping. Right: server nodes after swapping.

Figure 3 shows the result of the community swap algorithm. The algorithm identifies four different communities and initialized a random location in each community, which are visibly not optimal. Through local search and swapping, the algorithm is able to adjust the server nodes so that eventually produce a reasonable 4-FL instance.

5.2 Experiments

Our experiments aim to compare the performance of our community-based algorithm against the reverse greedy and single swap algorithms. The metrics that we use in our comparison include the cost of the resulting FL instance computed by each algorithm as well as the running time. The running time of the algorithms take into account also the time for computing shortest path distance between nodes as well as the time for detecting communities. To measure the performance of algorithms as k changes, we set $k \in \{1, 3, 5, 7, 9, 11\}$. In implementing the community select and community swap algorithms, we used Louvain method to compute k communities. Due to the inherent randomness of the Louvain method, for each network and each value of k, we run each algorithm 5 times and calculate the average outcome.

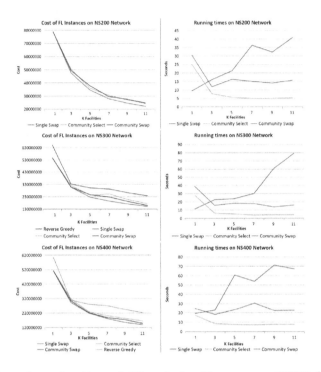

Fig. 4. Costs and running time of different algorithms ran on NS200 (top), NS300 (middle), NS400 (bottom) Network.

As illustrated in Fig. 4, results on all three networks are consistent: all four algorithm result in expected downwards trend in the cost as k increases. Despite its logarithmic theoretical approximation ratio, the reverse greedy produces significantly worse results than the other algorithms in terms of both cost and running speed by several magnitudes. We omit it in the NS200 network. In particular, the running time of the reverse greedy algorithm is about 30–100 times longer than community select algorithm (e.g. choosing 3 server nodes in NS300 network using community swap takes roughly 30 s, while using reverse greedy takes more than 30 min), so including it in the plot will trivialize the running time of all other algorithms. Thus we omit reverse greedy algorithm in all running time plots. On the other hand, the single swap algorithm in general produces FL instances with the lowest cost, however, in all three networks, the costs resulted from the community select and community swap algorithms are very close to single swap. Moreover, single swap algorithm results in much longer running time as compared with the community-based algorithm as $k > 3$.

Another remarkable point of the experimental result is regarding the running time comparisons between single swap with the community-based algorithms. While the single swap algorithm takes longer running time as k increases (this is consistent with the theoretical worst-case running time analysis in this paper), both community-based algorithms exhibit a flat or even downward trend in running time as k increases. This may be due to the fact that with a higher value of k, we divide the region into a larger number of communities, each having a smaller size. As the crucial factor in the running time depends on the largest size $\tilde{n}$ of a community, the running time of the community-based algorithm does not increase, resulting in almost constant-time algorithms.

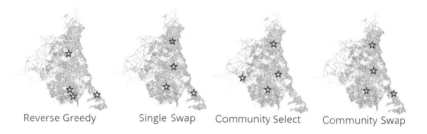

Reverse Greedy   Single Swap   Community Select   Community Swap

Fig. 5. Results from all four algorithms on NS300 Network where $k = 4$

The maps in Fig. 5 contain four server nodes picked from the NS300 network. The maps are to give an indication of why the cost of each algorithm within the network is displayed in that order, i.e. reverse greedy having the highest cost, community select having a somewhat evenly spaced facility locations and community swap and single swap having very similar results. In particular, when comparing with the real-world situation, the results produced by single swap and community swap are the most intuitive as all four facilities fall into well-recognized industrial areas that are also close to dense residential areas.

6   Conclusion and Future Work

This work focuses on the k-median facility location problem and proposes algorithms that incorporate a pre-determined community structure of the network. We analyze the performance of the algorithms on a real-world case study, i.e., spatial networks generated from Auckland North Shore. The experimental results reveal that the community swap algorithm produces outputs that are very close to the single swap algorithm while achieving almost constant time due to small search space. As a result, the community-based algorithms demonstrate a high potential to be used in real-world network data to solve this problem.

Our future work will be focused on adding more parameters to community swap so that it gives results that are useful for real-life networks. For example, it would be interesting to investigate the performance of the algorithm on road networks of land adjacency networks. Another future work concerns with more sophisticated application scenarios of the facility location problem. E.g., introducing competing and existing facilities in the problem domain. When competing facilities are considered we must take into account whether the algorithm is trying to take away as many customers away from the existing facilities or whether we are trying to avoid the existing algorithms so that it is connected to as customers as possible. A third direction to extend this work is to introduce capacity to server nodes. Our work only deals with uncapacitated facility location algorithms and therefore the next goal is to extend all our implemented facility location algorithms so that facilities have capacities in them.

References

1. Auckland council district plan operative north shore section 2002. Accessed 30 Sept 2017. http://temp.aucklandcouncil.govt.nz/EN/planspoliciesprojects/plansstrategies/DistrictRegionalPlans/northshorecitydistrictplan/Pages/home.aspx
2. Auckland open data. Accessed 30 Sept 2017. https://aucklandopendata-aucklandcouncil.opendata.arcgis.com/datasets
3. Ahlgren, B., Dannewitz, C., Imbrenda, C., Kutscher, D., Ohlman, B.: A survey of information-centric networking. IEEE Commun. Mag. **50**(7), 26–36 (2012)
4. Aikens, C.H.: Facility location models for distribution planning. Eur. J. Oper. Res. **22**(3), 263–279 (1985)
5. Arya, V., Garg, N., Khandekar, R., Meyerson, A., Munagala, K., Pandit, V.: Local search heuristics for k-median and facility location problems. SIAM J. Comput. **33**(3), 544–562 (2004)
6. Barabási, A.-L., Albert, R.: Emergence of scaling in random networks. Science **286**(5439), 509–512 (1999)
7. Bell, M.G., Iida, Y., et al.: Transportation Network Analysis. Wiley, New York (1997)
8. Blondel, V.D., Guillaume, J.-L., Lambiotte, R., Lefebvre, E.: Fast unfolding of communities in large networks. J. Stat. Mech. Theor. Exp. **2008**(10), P10008 (2008)
9. Chaudhuri, S., Garg, N., Ravi, R.: The p-neighbor k-center problem. Inf. Process. Lett. **65**(3), 131–134 (1998)
10. Chrobak, M., Kenyon, C., Young, N.E.: The reverse greedy algorithm for the metric K-median problem. In: Wang, L. (ed.) COCOON 2005. LNCS, vol. 3595, pp. 654–660. Springer, Heidelberg (2005). https://doi.org/10.1007/11533719_66
11. Church, R., Velle, C.R.: The maximal covering location problem. Pap. Reg. Sci. **32**(1), 101–118 (1974)
12. Dai, F., Wu, J.: On constructing k-connected k-dominating set in wireless networks. In: Proceedings of the 19th IEEE International Parallel and Distributed Processing Symposium, 10 pp. IEEE (2005)
13. Fortunato, S.: Community detection in graphs. Phys. Rep. **486**(3), 75–174 (2010)
14. Frank, C., Römer, K.: Distributed facility location algorithms for flexible configuration of wireless sensor networks. In: Aspnes, J., Scheideler, C., Arora, A., Madden, S. (eds.) DCOSS 2007. LNCS, vol. 4549, pp. 124–141. Springer, Heidelberg (2007). https://doi.org/10.1007/978-3-540-73090-3_9
15. Girvan, M., Newman, M.E.: Community structure in social and biological networks. Proc. Natl. Acad. Sci. **99**(12), 7821–7826 (2002)

16. González-Brevis, P., Gondzio, J., Fan, Y., Poor, H.V., Thompson, J., Krikidis, I., Chung, P.-J.: Base station location optimization for minimal energy consumption in wireless networks. In: IEEE 73rd Vehicular Technology Conference (VTC Spring), pp. 1–5. IEEE (2011)
17. Guha, S., Khuller, S.: Greedy strikes back: improved facility location algorithms. J. Algorithms **31**(1), 228–248 (1999)
18. Huang, C.-M., Lan, K.-C., Tsai, C.-Z.: A survey of opportunistic networks. In: 22nd International Conference on Advanced Information Networking and Applications-Workshops, AINAW 2008, pp. 1672–1677. IEEE (2008)
19. Lambiotte, R., Blondel, V.D., De Kerchove, C., Huens, E., Prieur, C., Smoreda, Z., Van Dooren, P.: Geographical dispersal of mobile communication networks. Phys. A Stat. Mech. Appl. **387**(21), 5317–5325 (2008)
20. Lewis, F.L., et al.: Wireless sensor networks. In: Smart Environments: Technologies, Protocols, and Applications, pp. 11–46 (2004)
21. Liao, K., Guo, D.: A clustering-based approach to the capacitated facility location problem. Trans. GIS **12**(3), 323–339 (2008)
22. Liu, J., Minnes, M.: Deciding the isomorphism problem in classes of unary automatic structures. Theor. Comput. Sci. **412**(18), 1705–1717 (2011)
23. Liu, J., Wei, Z.: Community detection based on graph dynamical systems with asynchronous runs. In: Second International Symposium on Computing and Networking (CANDAR), pp. 463–469. IEEE (2014)
24. Miller, H.J., Han, J.: Geographic Data Mining and Knowledge Discovery. CRC Press (2009)
25. Moskvina, A., Liu, J.: How to build your network? A structural analysis. In: Proceedings of the Twenty-Fifth International Joint Conference on Artificial Intelligence, pp. 2597–2603. AAAI Press (2016)
26. Moskvina, A., Liu, J.: Togetherness: an algorithmic approach to network integration. In: IEEE/ACM International Conference on Advances in Social Networks Analysis and Mining (ASONAM), pp. 223–230. IEEE (2016)
27. Newman, M.E.: Modularity and community structure in networks. Proc. Natl. Acad. Sci. **103**(23), 8577–8582 (2006)
28. Pantazopoulos, P., Stavrakakis, I., Passarella, A., Conti, M.: Efficient social-aware content placement in opportunistic networks. In: Seventh International Conference on Wireless On-Demand Network Systems and Services (WONS), pp. 17–24. IEEE (2010)
29. Watts, D.J., Strogatz, S.H.: Collective dynamics of 'small-world' networks. Nature **393**(6684), 440 (1998)
30. Yan, B., Chen, Y., Liu, J.: Dynamic relationship building: exploitation versus exploration on a social network. In: Bouguettaya, A., et al. (eds.) WISE 2017. LNCS, vol. 10569, pp. 75–90. Springer, Cham (2017). https://doi.org/10.1007/978-3-319-68783-4_6
31. Yang, K.-Q., Yang, L., Gong, B.-H., Lin, Z.-C., He, H.-S., Huang, L.: Geographical networks: geographical effects on network properties. Front. Phys. China **3**(1), 105–111 (2008)
32. Zhong, C., Arisona, S.M., Huang, X., Batty, M., Schmitt, G.: Detecting the dynamics of urban structure through spatial network analysis. Int. J. Geogr. Inf. Sci. **28**(11), 2178–2199 (2014)

Message Transmission Scheme Based on the Detection of Interest Community in Mobile Social Networks

Ying Cai$^{(\boxtimes)}$, Linqing Hou, Yanfang Fan, and Ruoyu Chen

School of Computer Beijing Information Science and Technology University,
Beijing, China
ycai@bistu.edu.cn

Abstract. The storage-carrying-forwarding of messages of the node is a way of short-distance communication in the mobile social networks, and the transmission performance is the key factor that affects the user interaction experience. If the user can transmit the message according to the interest or the community, the transmission performance can be improved. For the short-distance communication in the mobile social networks, the existing research is mainly either interest-based or community-based transmission. In order to make users to have a better interactive experience, we proposed InComT (Interest Community based Transmission) which combines the user interest with the community. We measure the interest value of a node in the mobile social networks, and the community is divided according to its interest value to determine the whole community interest value. Then the relay community and the relay node are selected by the interest value to realize the transmission of the message. The simulation results show that the scheme can get a higher transmission success rate with low transmission overhead and low average delay.

Keywords: Interest community · Detection · Mobile Social Networks (MSNs)

1 Introduction

With the emergence and rapid development of smart mobile devices, the short distance communication technologies such as Bluetooth, WiFi and etc., provide support to distribute the message for the user to access the Internet anytime and anywhere [1–3]. The intelligent device that people carried is regarded as a node, different nodes are forming a social networks through contacting with each other. Due to the technology of Bluetooth and WiFi's communicate distance are limited, which combine the node mobility to constitute the Mobile Social Networks (that is MSNs) [5], the message transmission of the node is realized through the way in storage-carrying-forwarding.

The end-to-end connection between the mobile nodes (i.e., the device or user) in the mobile social networks may be disconnected due to the rapid movement, and the information cannot be exchanged directly; at the same time, each node has a preference for a particular content. The messages transmission in mobile social networks is managed by the mobile devices, and each node only knows the interest of the node whom they contact with. To facilitate the process of sending messages to the destination node,

© Springer Nature Singapore Pte Ltd. 2018
L. Zhu and S. Zhong (Eds.): MSN 2017, CCIS 747, pp. 70–83, 2018.
https://doi.org/10.1007/978-981-10-8890-2_6

the source node should carry the copies of the message and move. If the source node deliver the message copies to each encounter node, it can reduce the delay, but these copies will be full of the network storage very soon and cannot be directly applied to resource-constrained mobile social networks.

The use of social relationships between users and the social properties of the user (such as interest) can effectively improve the transmission performance. Nodes with social properties follow the fact that a node go to some locations has a greater likelihood of meeting a node with common interest than that does not. The people will be together because of a common interest, such as working in a workplace colleagues, friends gathered in a party, etc. [6].

The research on the message transmission in the mobile social networks are mostly based on the interest of the single node or designed based on the community. Without considering the overall interest of the community as the relay selection condition in the message transmission, the communication reliability of the mobile social networks will be lower, and the purpose of the message transmission is also lack of assurance. At the same time, it consumes consuming a lot of network resources but not achieve the expected transmission performance [7]. In order to reduce the transmission delay more effectively and improve the performance, this paper proposes the InComT (Interest Community based Transmission strategy) based on the interest community, social ties and the contact history information. Through measuring the interest of the nodes, we can further measure the overall communities, and then looking for relay communities and destination communities to transmit the message. Users only receive their own content of interest and relay messages of the same interest node. Not only save the buffer for the resource limited intelligent mobile devices, but also generate the low costs while improving the transmission efficiency.

2 Related Work

2.1 Community Detection Algorithm

There are a lot of research for community detection in mobile social networks, which can be divided into global community detection and local community detection. Global community detection need to offline working, requiring higher resource availability. And all communities in the networks need to centralized management as well as each node should know well the entire network topology. Newman [8] first grouped people together as a "community" and found that the links between people in the intra community were closer than those inter communities. The "modularity" which is introduces as the evaluation standard for community by Newman in [9]. Modularity is defined as the closeness in intra-community and the looseness in inter-community. Then evaluate the community by measuring the module degree of the nodes in the network. Nguyen et al. [10] studied how to detect the overlapping community structures in dynamic networks, with a focus on the adaptive update of community structures for mobile applications. There are also several recent studies on how to evaluate the communities. To detect overlapping communities, the authors of QCA designed AFOCS [11]. With the similar idea of slicing the network into time-dependent snapshots, AFOCS detects the initial overlapping community structure from the first network snapshot and then updates it when taking the next snapshot. First, local communities are located around the edges. Specifically, a local community C around edge (u, v) is formed by u, v and their common neighbors if the internal connections of C is larger than its density function [12]. Subsequently, local communities that have an overlapping score lager than a threshold are merged as one community, or else they remain as separate communities.

Although the above community detection method solves the problem of detecting overlapping community to a certain extent, there are still some limitations to the dynamic mobile social networks. Firstly, it needs to obtain the information of the whole network structure and the prior knowledge relate to the community; Then, global search and calculation will greatly reduce the speed of the algorithm and the utilization of network resources.

To cope with the limitations of above mentioned, researchers have proposed local community detection methods in mobile social networks. It is based on the local topology of the network to depict the local or the entire network of community structure. Compared with the global community, the local community detection method does not need to understand the information of complete network structure and the priori knowledge, so that the calculation cost is greatly reduced for the large and dynamic social networks. This kind of community characteristic is especially obvious in the large-scale social networks, which becomes the hotspot of the research on the community detection in mobile social networks currently.

TopGC method (Top Graph Cluster) [13] uses locality sensitive hashing which means that same community shares the same hash value. It could finds a set of nodes whose neighborhoods are highly overlapping and these nodes should be clustered together to form communities. So it can only search for overlapping users with higher density. Although the resource requirement is less, but only can detect the overlapping communities up to a given percentage. The algorithm can also detect directed, weighted and disjoint communities.

The SLPA method (Speaker-Listener Label Propagation Algorithm) [13] is an agent-based algorithm. Each node sends its unique label value and listens to each of its neighbors. Then each node detects the community by choosing the most common label in its memory after repeating the process multiple times. So, it use more memory as each node stores labels of all its neighbors. A single common label means a single community. A multiple label means an overlapping community. Although it is scalable but need to process more label in large networks. Therefore, the time complexity also scales linearly with the number of edges. It is good for detecting low overlapping density communities.

PEC method (Periodic Encounter Communities) [14] is a decentralized algorithm to detect periodic communities. Each node can detect and share its community periodicity by mining its encounter history and extract globally maximal PEC. It assumes sufficient opportunities for exchanging information among nodes which are not always possible in real-world. But, the current algorithm is not able to maintain an updated view of the knowledge base as it does not prune old encountered nodes. The algorithm performance decreases with increase in the size of the community, so it is not good for large networks.

DOCNET method (Detecting Overlapping Community in NETwork) [16] is based on local optimization of a fitness function and a fuzzy belonging degree of different nodes. It greedily extends from a seed node until a stopping criterion is not met. It builds community in an agglomerative manner as a two steps process: build core and then extend the core. It can find homogeneous communities and community exhibiting antagonistic behaviors which means set of community pairs behaving opposite to each other.

Above local community detection algorithms eliminate some limitations of the global community detection, the shortcomings still exist. It cannot well represent the social properties of the network nodes and the social relations. Therefore, this article is to solve the problems caused by these shortcomings.

2.2 Message Transmission Strategy

The data transmission is delay tolerant in the mobile social networks, and considering the carrier in the network as a node. Each node has its own social properties, the node communicate with each other through the mobile device in the short range to transmit the message. At the same time, the security problem in wireless sensor networks is also one of the hot spots in the field of mobile ad hoc networks [18–22]. In this paper, the security problems in the process of mobile social networks transmission are not considered for the moment.

The classical message transmission strategy include the Epidemic Routing [23], PRoPHET [24] and Spray and Wait [25]. The Epidemic Routing distributes the message to the node in the same connected subnet (called the carrier), and transmit the message to the final destination node through the contact of the carrier with other nodes in the connected subnet. It assumed that the nodes walks randomly, in order to balance the relationship between the number of relay nodes and the probability of transmission, authors in [24] argues that the real nodes are usually moved in a predictability, and inferred the mobility according to a period of repeated behavior. Based on this assumption, a probabilistic routing protocol based on encounter history and transitivity is proposed, to maximize the probability that the message was delivered to the destination node. The Spray and Wait routing is similar to Epidemic, but the replicate is restricted for each forwarding data so as to reducing the forwarding overhead.

Recently, the social-based transmission mechanism [25–27] has proposed to use the network nodes with social properties on designing the transmission strategy. Then proved the transmission performance could be greatly improved. In [28], the protocol ensures that the content given to user as "fresh" as possible by the download link capacity was limited by the service provider. Combined with the interest and behaviors of nodes in mobile social networks, a node with the same or similar interest is more likely to travel to a location in the future. Moghadam et al. [29] proposed an interest-based routing protocol in Social Aware Network (called as SANE), the content will only transmitted to the interested in node. Meanwhile, SANE nodes will only receive the data with the similar interests. In order to transmit the message to the user most interested in timely, PeopleRank [30] arranges the nodes according to the tunable weighted social information. If a node connected to another node with a larger sociability, then it will get a larger weight value. User-centric [33] attempts to select the least number of relay nodes to forward message to users who are interested in as much as possible. PrefCast [34] take the different interests of the users into account so that each forwarder in the network could choose the optimal message forwarding sequences to maximize the total utility of all users. It also described the message transmission in the mobile social networks from different perspectives [35–38]. However, they did not combine the user's interest with the community, resulting in the performance of the message transmission did not optimality.

In the mobile social networks, the node have some social properties (such as interest). In this paper, it will use the user's interest as a factor of community detection, which the users with the same hobbies or similar interests will be divide into the same community. The interest of the community is measured by measuring the interest of the nodes, and the local extension is used to measure the similarity of each node and the matching nodes in the same geographical area. If the similarity of interest exceeds a threshold, then divided them into the same community. Selecting the communities from the same interest nodes to determine the similarity of community and closest to the target community. Learned from the recommended idea in the community to recommend candidate relay nodes for the carrier. Select the candidate node with the largest similarity with the destination node as the optimal relay forwarding node, and realize the hop-to-hop forwarding between the intra-communities and the inter-communities. Finally, simulation and analysis were carried out.

3 The Community Detection Based on Interest

3.1 Network Model

In the mobile social networks, users tend to communicate with each other according to their interests, and they will gather together with the same interest to form a community. Links between nodes in different communities more sparse, and within the same community more closely. Therefore, in the design of the routing algorithm only need to consider the node where the community and frequent contacts between the nodes in the community, without having to consider the every node. In this paper, the network model has the following assumptions:

- Nodes are collaborative each other, there is no misbehavior between the nodes;
- A node can have multiple interests, and each node is allowed to exist in multiple communities;
- Each node has its own interest table for calculate the similar interests with others and then was divided into communities;
- The delivery of messages consists of two phases: inter-community message delivery and intra-community message delivery.

3.2 Community Detection Strategy

Assuming that there have n topics of interests in the networks, whether node i is interested in j topics $Int_{i,j}$ can be expressed as

$$Int_{i,j} = \begin{cases} 0, & node\ i\ is\ not\ interest\ in\ j\_th\ topic \\ 1, & node\ i\ is\ interest\ in\ j\_th\ topic \end{cases} j \in [1, n]$$

The interest weight of node i for topic j is expressed as

$$weg_{i,j} \in [0, 1], \quad j \in [1, n]$$

Therefore, taking the user i as an example, the user's interest table is shown in Table 1.

Table 1. The interest table of user i

Interest number P_i	$P_i^{(1)}$	$P_i^{(2)}$	...	$P_i^{(j)}$	...	$P_i^{(n)}$
Interest	$Int_{i,1}$	$Int_{i,2}$	...	$Int_{i,j}$	...	$Int_{i,n}$
Weight	$weg_{i,1}$	$weg_{i,2}$	...	$weg_{i,j}$	...	$weg_{i,n}$

At the initialization, the interest weight of each user in the interest table for different interests are normalized according to the formula $weg_{i,j} = weg_{i,j} / \left(\sum_{i=1}^{n} weg_{i,j} \right)$. The purpose is to ensure the completeness of the weights so that the sum of the weights of each user is one. Then, in accordance with the weight of interest in descending order, the weight of the greatest interest is considered the user's main interest. When the two users meet, they will exchange the interest table with each other and can know the each other's interest information. Simultaneously, compare the interest number of the two users' main interests, $P_i^{(k)}$ represents the serial number of the k-th topic in the interest table of the user i. For example, $P_i^{(1)}$ said that with i's first topic of interest number, that is, the user i's interest number with main interest. If the main interest are same between the user i and j, i.e. $P_i^{(1)} = P_j^{(1)}$, then calculate the interest similarity of them by the following equation

$$Sim_{i,j} = \frac{\sum_{k=1}^{n} \left[(Int_{i,k} \cdot weg_{i,k}) \times (Int_{j,k} \cdot weg_{j,k}) \right]}{\sqrt{\sum_{k=1}^{n} weg_{i,k}^2} \cdot \sqrt{\sum_{k=1}^{n} weg_{j,k}^2}}$$

Set the threshold $thr_{sim} = 0.5$ for interest similarity based on the experience value. If $Sim_{i,j} \geq thr_{sim}$, it indicates that user i has the similar interests with user j, then divide them into a community. The detail algorithm is shown in Table 2.

Table 2. Interest community detection algorithm

Input: N, thr_{sim}, n

Output: C_1, C_2, $\cdots C_b$;

1. $m = b = 0$, $C_m = \emptyset$

2.   while($P_i^{(1)} == P_j^{(1)}$), then

3.   calculate $Sim_{i,j}$

4.   if $Sim_{i,j} \geq 0.5$, then

5. $C_m = C_m \cup \{i,j\}$, $i = C_m$

6.   update the interest table

7.   end if

8. $b = m + 1$, $m + +$

9.   end while

10. for every community C_a,

11.   if $C_a = \emptyset$, $a \in [1,m]$, then

12.   delete C_a, $b - -$

13.   end if

14. end for

15. return C_1, C_2, $\cdots$, C_b

---

4   The Message Transmission Strategy of InComT

4.1   Inter-community Message Transmission

Before the inter-community message transmission, we first defined the geographical distance between two node i and j as $Geo_{i,j}$. According to the GPS in the smart device to obtain the location of each node (with two-dimensional coordinates). Assume that the position of nodes i and j are expressed as $L_i = (X_i, Y_i)$ and $L_j = (X_j, Y_j)$, then the geographical distance of them can calculate using the equation below

$$Geo_{i,j} = \sqrt{(Y_j - Y_i)^2 + (X_j - X_i)^2}$$

Assuming the message msg is generate by the source node S in the source community C_s, and the destination node d is located in community C_d. The message delivery in intercommunity is based on the main interest of message in selecting the relay community. Due to the message exists in a community, the main interest of the message I_s is consistent with its community. The main interest of the destination community is I_d, since there is an overlap between communities in this paper. So we select the community from the overlapping nodes, whose main interest is same as I_d and the geographical distance is closest to the destination community as a relay community for inter-community message transmission. The algorithm for message delivery in inter-community is shown in Table 3 below.

Table 3. Message transmission algorithm in inter-community

Input: C_1, C_2, $\cdots$, C_b, I_s, I_d

Output: relay community C_{R_1}, $\cdots$, C_{R_m}

1. if $C_s \mathrel{!=} C_d$, then
2.   if $\exists$ overlapping communities $C_{O1} \cdots C_{Oi} \cdots C_{Ok}$, then
3.   for every overlapping node in C_{Oi}
4.   while $(I_{Oi} == I_d)$
5.   calculate the $Geo_{i,d}$
6.   end while
7.   rank the $Geo_{i,d}$ with descending
8.   choose the minimum value of $Geo_{i,d}$
9.   end for
10.   end if
11. end if
12. return C_{R_1}, $\cdots$, C_{R_m}

4.2   Intra-community Message Transmission

Message transmission in intra-community occurs when the message has been delivered to the destination community but has not yet reached the destination node. The strategy of message transmission in the intra-community is that if the neighbor node of the source node is not the destination node, then calculate the interest similarity between the neighbor node j of s and the destination node d. When the similarity of them is greater than the threshold value of 0.5, the node j is recommended to s as the candidate relay node. Finally, the node s select the node from the candidate sets candidate(s), which the largest similarity as the optimal relay forwarding node. The process is looped until the destination node is encountered and the message is delivered successfully. The detailed algorithm is shown in Table 4 below.

Table 4. Message transmission algorithm in intra-community

Input: s, d

Output: R

1. while $(d \notin N(s))$ then
2.   for every node $j \in N(s)$
3.   calculate the $SInt_{j,d}$
4.   if $\left(SInt_{j,d}\right) \geq 0.5$ then
5.   add j to candidate(s)
6.   end if
7.   end for
8.   if $(candidate(s)! = \emptyset)$ then
9.   rank the candidate(s) with descending
10.   Choose the first node I as realy node
            from candidate(s)
11. $R = R \cup \{i\}$
12.   deliver msg from node s to node i, $s \leftarrow i$
13.   end if
14. end while
15. return R

---

5 Performance Evaluation

5.1 Experiment Setup

In this paper, the performance evaluation of InComT is carried out using ONE (Opportunistic Network Evaluation) platform [39], the comparison algorithms are Epidemic Routing, FirstContact Routing and Spray and Wait Routing respectively. With the change of Time-To-Live (TTL), compare the proposed algorithm with the classic algorithms in the average delivery ratio, the average delivery overhead and the average delivery delay. The simulation parameters are summarized in Table 5.

5.2 Simulation Results

Message delivery ratio: The message delivery ratio is the ratio of the number of messages successfully transmitted to the destination to the total number of messages created. As shown in Fig. 1 below, the delivery ratio of the InComT is increasing at

Table 5. The simulation parameters

Parameters	Value
Simulation area/m^2	4500 * 3400
End time/s	43200
Nodes number	76
Transmit speed/kbps	250
Update interval/s	0.1
Transmit range/m	10
Buffer/M	5
Movement model	ShortestPathMapBasedMovement
Message size/K	50
Move speed/(m/s)	0.5–1.0
TTL/(min)	30 60 120 180 240 300 360

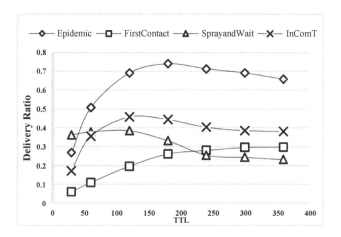

Fig. 1. Message TTL (Minute) and delivery ratio

TTL < 120, then it shows slow down when TTL > 120, which indicates that it can get a better delivery ratio when the time-to-live of the message is set in 120 min. Epidemic routing have the highest success rate, but a large number of copies in the network lead to the network congestion with the increase in TTL, and the delivery ratio began to decline at TTL > 200. When TTL > 240, the delivery ratio of SprayandWait and FirstContact Routing is stable.

Message delivery overhead: The message delivery overhead is the ratio of the number of messages that are relayed but not successfully transmitted to the total number of transmissions. The simulation results in Fig. 2 reveal that InComT is closest to the SprayandWait algorithm on message delivery overhead. This is because the interest of the message is sorted before the message is forwarded in the proposed system, and reduce the number of relay forwarding by selecting the same interest of the

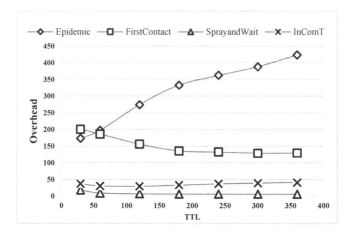

Fig. 2. Message TTL (Minute) and overhead on average

user as a relay. Additionally, Epidemic Routing caused the highest overhead due to it does not have replicate control strategy.

Message delivery delay: Figure 3 below reflects the variety of the average delivery delay by the time-to-live increasing. The delay for each algorithm is increasing with the increase of TTL. The proposed algorithm has the lowest delay and the change is small with the increase of TTL. However, the other three algorithms are higher than InComT. Because the InComT divides the users with the same interest into a community which the other three algorithms are not, the message transmission process is relayed by these users with the same interest, and can effectively reduce the waiting time for relay user to carry and forward the message.

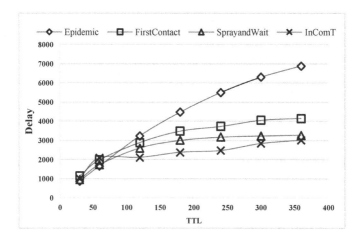

Fig. 3. Message TTL (Minute) and delivery delay

6 Conclusion

We proposed an Interest Community based message transmission in MSNs, namely InComT, to promote the message forwarding efficiency. At first, measure the user's interest and detect the community based on the interest, so that the message can be delivered based on the division community. The purpose is to make the user more purposeful for selective the relay nodes and relay community, thereby improving the transmission performance. The simulation results show that the delivery ratio in InComT is improved compare with the FirstContact and SprayandWait algorithms, the delivery overhead and delay are obviously reduced.

Acknowledgement. This work was supported by the National Natural Science Foundation of China under Grant 61672106 and by Governmental Special Funds to Promote Regional Development of Science and Technology under Grant Z171100004717002.

References

1. Xiao, Y., Rayi, V., Sun, B., Du, X., Hu, F., Galloway, M.: A survey of key management schemes in wireless sensor networks. J. Comput. Commun. **30**(11–12), 2314–2341 (2007)
2. Du, X., Xiao, Y., Guizani, M., Chen, H.H.: An effective key management scheme for heterogeneous sensor networks ad hoc networks. Elsevier **5**(1), 24–34 (2007)
3. Du, X., Guizani, M., Xiao, Y., Chen, H.H.: A routing-driven elliptic curve cryptography based key management scheme for heterogeneous sensor networks. IEEE Trans. Wirel. Commun. **8**(3), 1223–1229 (2009)
4. Index, Cisco Visual Networking. Global Mobile Data Traffic Forecast Update 2015–2020 White Paper, February 2016. www.cisco.com/go/offices
5. Hu, X., Chu, T.H.S., Leung, V.C.M., et al.: A survey on mobile social networks: applications, platforms, system architectures, and future research directions. IEEE Commun. Surv. Tutor. **17**, 1557–1581 (2015)
6. Vastardis, N., Yang, K.: Mobile social networks: architectures, social properties, and key research challenges. IEEE Commun. Surv. Tutor. **15**, 1355–1371 (2013)
7. Zhu, Y., Xu, B., Shi, X., et al.: A survey of social based routing in delay tolerant networks: positive and negative social effects. IEEE Commun. Surv. Tutor. **15**, 387–401 (2013)
8. Newman, M.E.J.: Fast algorithm for detecting community structure in networks. Phys. Rev. E **69**, 066133 (2004)
9. Hui, P., Yoneki, E., Chan, S.Y., Crowcroft, J.: Distributed community detection in delay tolerant networks. In: Workshops -2nd ACM International Workshop on Mobility in the Evolving Internet Architecture, pp. 1–8 (2007)
10. Nguyen, N.P., Dinh, T.N., Tokala, S., et al.: Overlapping communities in dynamic networks: their detection and mobile applications. In: Proceedings of the 17th Annual International Conference on Mobile Computing and Networking, pp. 85–96. ACM (2011)
11. Fortunato, S., Castellano, C.: Community structure in graphs. In: Meyers, R. (ed.) Computational Complexity, pp. 490–512. Springer, New York (2012). https://doi.org/10.1007/978-1-4614-1800-9
12. Macropol, K., Singh, A.: Scalable discovery of best clusters on large graphs. Proc. VLDB Endow. **3**, 693–702 (2010)

13. Xie, J., Szymanski, B.K., Liu, X.; SLPA: uncovering overlapping communities in social networks via a speaker-listener interaction dynamic process. In: IEEE 11th International Conference on Data Mining Workshops (ICDMW), pp. 344–349 (2011)
14. Williams, M.J., Whitaker, R.M., Allen, S.M.: Decentralised detection of periodic encounter communities in opportunistic networks. Ad Hoc Netw. **10**, 1544–1556 (2012)
15. Chen, Q., Wu, T.T., Fang, M.: Detecting local community structures in complex networks based on local degree central nodes. Phys. Stat. Mech. Appl. **392**, 529–537 (2013)
16. Rhouma, D., Ben Romdhane, L.: An efficient algorithm for community mining with overlap in social networks. Expert Syst. **41**, 4309–4321 (2014)
17. Wei, K., Liang, X., Xu, K.: A survey of social-aware routing protocols in delay tolerant networks: applications, taxonomy and design-related issues. IEEE Commun. Surv. Tutor. **16**, 556–578 (2014)
18. Du, X., Chen, H.H.: Security in wireless sensor networks. IEEE Wirel. Commun. Mag. **15**(4), 60–66 (2008)
19. Du, X., Guizani, M., Xiao, Y., Chen, H.H.: Secure and efficient time synchronization in heterogeneous sensor networks. IEEE Trans. Veh. Technol. **57**(4), 2387–2394 (2008)
20. Du, X., Xiao, Y., Chen, H.H., Wu, Q.: Secure cell relay routing protocol for sensor networks. Wirel. Commun. Mob. Comput. **6**(3), 375–391 (2006)
21. Hei, X., Du, X., Wu, J., Hu, F.: Defending resource depletion attacks on implantable medical devices. In: Proceedings of IEEE GLOBECOM 2010, Miami, Florida, USA, December 2010
22. Hei, X., Du, X.: Biometric-based two-level secure access control for implantable medical devices during emergency. In: Proceedings of IEEE INFOCOM 2011, Shanghai, China, April 2011
23. Vahdat, A., Becker, D.: Epidemic routing for partially connected ad hoc networks (2000)
24. Lindgren, A., Doria, A., Schelén, O.: Probabilistic routing in intermittently connected networks. In: Dini, P., Lorenz, P., de Souza, J.N. (eds.) SAPIR 2004. LNCS, vol. 3126, pp. 239–254. Springer, Heidelberg (2004). https://doi.org/10.1007/978-3-540-27767-5_24
25. Spyropoulos, T., Psounis, K., Raghavendra, C.S.: Spray and wait: an efficient routing scheme for inter-mittently connected mobile networks. In: Proceedings of the ACM SIGCOMM Workshop, pp. 252–259 (2005)
26. Daly, E.M., Haahr, M.: Social network analysis for routing in disconnected delay-tolerant manets. In: Proceedings of the 8th ACM International Symposium on Mobile Ad Hoc Networking and Computing, pp. 32–40. ACM (2007)
27. Hui, P., Crowcroft, J., Yoneki, E.: Bubble rap: social-based forwarding in delay tolerant networks. ACM MobiHoc (2008)
28. Gao, W., Li, Q., Zhao, B., et al.: Multicasting in delay tolerant networks: a social network perspective. In: Proceedings of the Tenth ACM International Symposium on Mobile Ad Hoc Networking and Computing, pp. 299–308. ACM (2009)
29. Ioannidis, S., Chaintreau, A., Massoulié, L.: Optimal and scalable distribution of content updates over a mobile social network. In: INFOCOM 2009, pp. 1422–1430 (2009)
30. Moghadam, A., Schulzrinne, H.: Interest-aware content distribution protocol for mobile disruption-tolerant networks. In: IEEE International Symposium, pp. 1–7 (2009)
31. Mtibaa, A., May, M., Diot, C., et al.: Peoplerank: social opportunistic forwarding. In: Infocom Proceedings IEEE, pp. 1–5 (2010)
32. Hui, P., Crowcroft, J., Yoneki, E.: Bubble-rap: social-based forwarding in delay-tolerant networks. IEEE Trans. Mob. Comput. **10**(11), 1576–1589 (2011)
33. Gao, W., Cao, G.: User-centric data dissemination in disruption tolerant networks. In: INFOCOM IEEE, pp. 3119–3127 (2011)

34. Lin, K.C.J., Chen, C.W., Chou, C.F.: Preference aware content dissemination in opportunistic mobile social networks. In: INFOCOM Proceedings IEEE, pp. 1960–1968 (2012)
35. Wu, J., Wang, Y.: Social feature-based multi-path routing in delay tolerant networks. In: INFOCOM, Proceedings IEEE, pp. 1368–1376 (2012)
36. Xu, Y., Chen, X.: Social-similarity-based multicast algorithm in impromptu mobile social networks. In: Global Communications Conference (GLOBECOM), pp. 346–351. IEEE (2014)
37. Didwania, A., Narmawala, Z.: A comparative study of various community detection algorithms in the mobile social network. In: Engineering Nui-CONE 5th Nirma University International Conference, pp. 1–6. IEEE (2015)
38. Mao, Z., Jiang, Y., Min, G., et al.: Mobile social networks: design requirements, architecture, and state-of-the-art technology. Comput. Commun. **100**, 1–19 (2017)
39. Keränen, A., Ott, J., Kärkkäinen, T.: The one simulator for dtn protocol evaluation. In: Proceedings of the 2nd International Conference on Simulation Tools and Techniques, p. 55. ICST (Institute for Computer Sciences, Social-Informatics and Telecommunications Engineering) (2009)

An Improved Lossless Data Hiding Scheme in JPEG Bitstream by VLC Mapping

Yang Du[1], Zhaoxia Yin[1,2(✉)], and Xinpeng Zhang[2]

[1] Key Laboratory of Intelligent Computing and Signal Processing,
Ministry of Education, Anhui University, Hefei 230601, People's Republic of China
yinzhaoxia@ahu.edu.cn
[2] School of Communication and Information Engineering, Shanghai University,
Shanghai 200072, People's Republic of China
xzhang@shu.edu.cn

Abstract. This paper proposed a lossless data hiding scheme by variable length code (VLC) mapping, which focused on embedding additional data into JPEG bitstream. The entropy-coded data in JPEG bitstream consists of a sequence of VLCs and the appended bits. Not all VLCs defined in the JPEG file header are used in the entropy-coded data and the replacement of unused-VLCs do nothing with image decompression. Hence, additional data can be embedded by mapping the unused-VLCs to the used-VLCs. To obtain higher embedding capacity, we improved the mapping rules in this paper. Employing the proposed mapping scheme, larger embedding capacity and no image distortion are both achieved while the filesize of JPEG is preserved after data embedding.

Keywords: Data hiding · JPEG bitstream · VLC · Lossless

1 Introduction

Data hiding is a technique for hiding secret message into digital cover, which developed for the last decades. Data hiding is widely used in military, commercial, medical, financial, etc. People transmit or share multimedia data more and more widely with the rapid development of computer technology. To transmit or share multimedia data quickly in the net, most multimedia data are stored in compressed formats. JPEG is the most popular file format in relation to digital images, which compresses image data effectively. Therefore, the research of data hiding for JPEG images has practical significance.

Traditional data hiding techniques usually change the original data irretrievably, such as modifying the DC components [1], modifying the AC coefficients by histogram shifting [2], etc. However, the distortion due to embedding cannot be accepted in some application areas, like medical, military and law. Hence,

© Springer Nature Singapore Pte Ltd. 2018
L. Zhu and S. Zhong (Eds.): MSN 2017, CCIS 747, pp. 84–98, 2018.
https://doi.org/10.1007/978-981-10-8890-2_7

the lossless data hiding techniques are required. As a branch of data hiding techniques, lossless data hiding techniques can embed additional data into cover signal and leave no signal distortion.

Recently some lossless data hiding methods for JPEG images have been proposed. For instance, Fridrich et al. [3] proposed three lossless data embedding methods for embedding data in the quantized DCT coefficients reversibly. Hence, it is possible to reconstruct from the marked JPEG file. Xuan et al. [4] proposed a lossless data hiding method by histogram shifting. The quantized DCT coefficient histogram is shifted to embed high capacity secret data. However, the filesize will increase after data embedding by using the lossless methods introduced above. Then, some lossless and filesize preservation methods for JPEG images appear. A novel lossless method by code mapping is proposed by Mobasseri et al. [5]. The method performs in JPEG bitstream and preserves the image quality and filesize. To improve the embedding capacity, an improved method was proposed by Qian and Zhang [6]. The method improved the code mapping relationships and achieved higher embedding capacity. Recently, Hu et al. [7] improved the mapping relationships further but not optimally.

Similar to the previous methods, we only replace the unused-VLCs for hiding additional data in this paper. Then both the image visual quality and the JPEG filesize are preserved. But the embedding capacity can be improved because of the proposed optimal VLC mapping rules. The rest of this paper is organized as follows. Section 2 briefly introduces the structure of JPEG images and Hu et al.'s method [7]. Section 3 presents the proposed scheme in detail. The experimental results with analysis and comparisons are given in Sect. 4. Section 5 concludes the paper.

2 Related Works

Since the proposed method works on JPEG bitstream, the knowledge of JPEG image structure is required. Furthermore, inspired by Liu et al. method, we proposed a lossless and reversible data hiding method. Thus, we introduce the structure of JPEG image at first and Liu et al. method. Since we aim to propose the optimal VLC mapping of JPEG bitstream based on Hu et al.'s method [7] in this paper, we introduce the structure of JPEG bitstream at first in Subsect. 2.1. Because Hu et al. [7] improved the payload based on Qian and Zhang's method [6] Subsect. 2.2 will include the method proposed by Qian and Zhang [6]. Finally, we will introduce Hu et al.'s method in Subsect. 2.3.

2.1 The Structure of JPEG Bitstream

In general, JPEG bitstream consists of a sequence of segments, each beginning with a marker. Each marker begins with a 0xFF byte followed by a byte indicating what kind of marker it is. For the decoding phase, there are two key segments, the Define Huffman Table (DHT) segment and the Start of Scan (SOS) segment. Figure 1 shows the detail structure of the two segments.

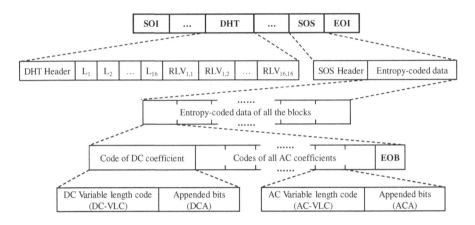

Fig. 1. The structure of the JPEG bitstream.

According to the JPEG guideline, after some preprocessing works, the pixel values of each 8×8 block in the image are transformed into AC/DC coefficients by Discrete Cosine Transformation (DCT). For each block's upper left corner first coefficients, define it as DC coefficients. For the remaining 63 coefficients of each block, define them as AC coefficients. To compress the image filesize, the AC coefficients are encoded in Run-Length encoding format as intermediate symbols, (Run, Length) and (Amplitude). Further, to improve the compress rate, (Run, Length) is encoded in the format of Variable Length Code (VLC), and (Amplitude) is encoded in Variable Length Integer (VLI) format, which calls it as appended bits.

The DHT segment contains the Canonical Huffman table information, which is used for obtaining the VLCs. Figure 1 shows the structure of DHT segment, in which L_i equals the number of the same length VLCs and $RLV_{i,j}$ represents the run/length value (RLV) corresponding to the first j VLC of length i. Each VLC is corresponded to a specific RLV that represents an AC coefficient in entropy-coded data. The VLCs are encoded by Canonical Huffman code, for instance, if the run/length value is '0/4', the corresponding VLC is '1011'. For AC coefficients of luminance component, 162 different VLCs are corresponded to the run/length value from '0/1' to 'F/A' accompanied with '0/0' (End of Block) and 'F/0' (Zero Run Length). The length of VLC is between 2 to 16 bits. The statistical results indicate that not all of the VLCs appear in the entropy-coded data. As discussed in Sect. 1, many researchers make use of this condition to embed data [6,7].

2.2 Qian and Zhang's Method

Qian and Zhang proposed a lossless data hiding method [6] by Huffman code mapping, which can preserve the modified image with no distortion and provide more embedding capacity than [5]. In addition, their method can preserve the filesize with not changed.

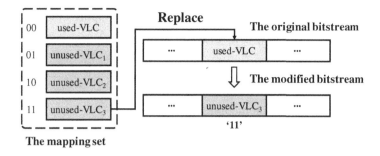

Fig. 2. An embedding instance by VLC mapping.

As mentioned in Sect. 1 and Subsect. 2.1 that not each kind of VLC appears in the entropy-coded data. Qian and Zhang used this condition to establish mapping relationships between used-VLCs and unused-VLCs. Then replace the used-VLC by the any VLC in the mapping sets to embed data. Figure 2 shows an instance about embedding data by VLC mapping. In Fig. 2, the mapping set includes four VLCs, used-VLC, $unused - VLC_1$, $unused - VLC_2$ and $unused - VLC_3$. Therefore, the four VLCs can stands for all the 2^2 situations of two binary bits. Then find the used-VLC in the entropy-coded data and replace it by any of the mapping set. For instance, if we replace the used-VLC by the $unsed - VLC_3$, the data '11' will be embedded.

Their embedding phase can be described as following steps.

Step 1: Parse the JPEG bitstream and extract all the VLCs in the entropy-coded data.

Step 2: Establish the mapping relationships according to the statistical results of the used-VLCs and unused-VLCs.

Step 3: Modify the corresponding run/size value in the DHT segment according to the mapping relationships.

Step 4: Replace the VLCs in the entropy-coded data with the corresponding unused-VLCs to embed data.

To preserve the filesize with not changed, Qian and Zhang only replace the used-VLC by the unused-VLC with same length. Therefore, all the VLCs are classified into 16 categories:

$$\{C_1, C_2, \ldots, C_{16}\}$$

by their code length and category C_i has L_i VLCs of length $i(i = 1, 2, \ldots, 16)$, which can be represented in the following equation:

$$C_i = \{VLC_{i,1}^u, \ldots, VLC_{i,p_i}^u; VLC_{i,1}^n, \ldots, VLC_{i,q_i}^n\} \tag{1}$$

where $VLC_{i,1}^u, \ldots, VLC_{i,p_i}^u$ are used-VLCs, $VLC_{i,1}^n, \ldots, VLC_{i,q_i}^n$ are unused-VLCs, and $p_i + q_i = L_i$.

To obtain more payload, they have proposed two mapping manners:

(1) For the case $p \geq q$ and $q > 0$, VLCs in each category are mapped by one-to-one manner.

$$C_i = \{\{VLC_{i,1}^u \leftrightarrow VLC_{i,1}^n\}, \ldots, \{VLC_{i,q_i}^u \leftrightarrow VLC_{i,q_i}^n\}\} \qquad (2)$$

where "$\leftrightarrow$" represents the mapping relationship.

(2) For the cases $q \geq p$ and $p > 0$, VLCs in each category are mapped in the manner of one-to-k. This One-to-k manner can stand for $log_2(k+1)$ binary bits data, where $log_2(k+1)$ is a positive integer.

Qian and Zhang's method is mapping the same number of the unused-VLCs to each used-VLC in each category. The mapping manner could be described as follows:

$$M_i = \left\{ \begin{array}{l} \{VLC_{i,1}^u \leftrightarrow \{VLC_{i,1}^n, \ldots, VLC_{i,k_i}^n\}\}, \ldots, \\ \{VLC_{i,p_i}^u \leftrightarrow \{VLC_{i,(p_i-1)\times k_i-1}^n, \ldots, VLC_{i,p_i \times k_i}^n\}\} \end{array} \right\} \qquad (3)$$

where $k_i = 2^{\lfloor log_2(q_i/p_i+1) \rfloor - 1}$ and "$\lfloor x \rfloor$" stands for the floor function.

After establishing the mapping relationships, the additional data can be successfully embedded into JPEG bitstream. However, there are still free space to obtain more payload.

2.3 Hu et al. Method

Hu et al. have discovered the potential free space to improve the payload based on Qian and Zhang's method [6]. They have considered the statistical results of used-VLCs and unused-VLCs and explored to increase the payload. The key contribution of Hu et al.'s method is improving the one-to-k mapping manner by considering the frequency of each used-VLC in the entropy-coded data.

For the VLCs, the largest category is C_16 which has 125 VLCs, and the total number of VLCs is 162. Hence use one-to-k manner can represent 6 ($\lfloor log_2(125 + 1) \rfloor$) data in C_16. In each category C_i, Hu et al.'s method assumed the number of one-to-$(2j-1)$ manner mapping sets is $m_{i,j}$ ($1 \leq j \leq 6$). The selection of $m_{i,j}$ should satisfy the following condition:

$$\mathbf{max} \quad \mathbf{Z} = \sum_{j=1}^{6} j \cdot m_{i,j}$$

$$\mathbf{s.t.} \quad \left\{ \begin{array}{l} \sum_{j=1}^{6} m_{i,j} \leq p_i \\ \sum_{j=1}^{6} (2^j - 1) \cdot m_{i,j} \leq q_i \\ m_{i,j} \geq 0, j = 1, 2, \ldots, 6 \\ m_{i,j} \in N^*, j = 1, 2, \ldots, 6 \end{array} \right. \qquad (4)$$

After 4 is solved, all code mapping relationships are established which could be described as:

$$M_i = \begin{cases} \{VLC_{i,1}^u \leftrightarrow \{VLC_{i,1}^n, \ldots, VLC_{i,63}^n\}\}, \ldots, \\ \{VLC_{i,m_{i,6}}^u \leftrightarrow \{VLC_{i,63\cdot(m_{i,6}-1)+1}^n, \ldots, VLC_{i,63\cdot m_{i,6}}^n\}\}, \\ \{VLC_{i,m_{i,6}+1}^{(u} \leftrightarrow \{VLC_{i,63\cdot m_{i,6}+1}^n, \ldots, VLC_{i,63\cdot m_{i,6}+31}^n\}\}, \ldots, \\ \{VLC_{i,\sum_{j=1}^6 m_{i,j}}^u \leftrightarrow VLC_{i,\sum_{j=1}^6[(2^j-1)\cdot m_{i,j}]}^n\} \end{cases} \quad (5)$$

where $VLC_{i,j}^u$ are the used-VLCs after sorted in descend order and $VLC_{i,1}^n, \ldots, VLC^{(n)}{}_{i,j}$ are unused-VLCs.

This means that the first $m_{i,6}$ sorted used VLCs follow the one-to-63 manner, the next $m_{i,5}$ sorted used VLCs follow the one-to-31 manner, ... , and the last $m_{i,1}$ sorted used VLCs follow the one-to-one manner.

Since each used-VLC each time occurs in the entropy-coded segment can be embedded $log_2(k+1)$ bits data, Hu et al.'s method maps more unused-VLCs to the used-VLC which occurs more in the entropy-coded data. By considering each used-VLC's frequency (occurrences number) in the mapping relationships, Hu et al.'s method gained more payload than Qian and Zhang's method. Whereas only consider the first six high frequency VLCs may ignore the potential free space. The statistical results indicate that the frequency of each used-VLC in the same category also vary distinctly. Hence, the payload can be further increased by considering the frequency of each used-VLC. That is the key point of the proposed method that will be described in detail in Sect. 3.

3 Proposed Method

The proposed method can further increase the payload based on Hu et al.'s method [7] by improving the VLCs' mapping relationships. The improved algorithm, the data embedding and data extraction procedures are introduced in the following sections. Figure 3 illustrates the framework of our proposed method. First, parse the JPEG bitstream and extract all the VLCs. Then establish the VLC mapping relationships by our proposed mapping rules. According to the optimal mapping relationships, we can embed more additional data.

3.1 Algorithm of Optimized VLC Mapping

According to the JPEG guideline, there are 162 kinds of VLCs to represent AC coefficients and 12 kinds of VLCs to represent DC coefficients. The statistical results show that the VLCs for DC coefficients are all used in the entropy-coded data, but for AC coefficients, not all of the VLCs are used. Hence, the algorithm is suitable for AC coefficients. The unused-VLCs' corresponding RLVs can be modified to the same value as the used-VLCs' corresponding RLVs, thus the unused-VLCs can be mapped to the used-VLCs. In order to preserve the image filesize, the code length of the used-VLCs and the mapped unused-VLCs must be consistent.

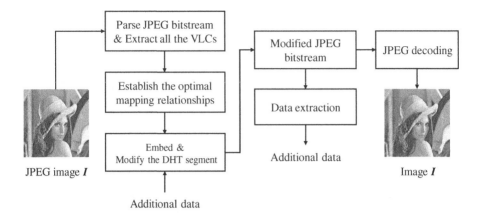

Fig. 3. The framework of proposed method.

The steps of the VLCs' classifying, occurrences recording and VLCs sorting are the same as Hu et al.'s method. After the above steps completed, each category can be represented in the following form:

$$C_i = \{VLC_{i,1}^{(u)'}, \ldots, VLC_{i,p_i}^{(u)'}; VLC_{i,1}^{n}, \ldots, VLC_{i,q_i}^{n}\} \tag{6}$$

where $VLC_{i,1}^{(u)'}, \ldots, VLC_{i,p_i}^{(u)'}$ are the used-VLCs after sorted in descend order and $VLC_{i,1}^{n}, \ldots, VLC_{i,q_i}^{(n)}$ are unused-VLCs.

After the above steps are completed, the mapping relationships will be established. Each category's mapping rule depends on p_i and q_i. For the case $p \geq q$ and $q > 0$, C_i employs the one-to-one mapping rule. For the case $q \geq p$ and $p > 0$, C_i employs the one-to-k mapping rule. If both the two cases are not satisfied, C_i does not employ any mapping rule. A detailed description of the different mapping rules is given in the following subsection.

One-to-One Mapping Rule. For the case $p \geq q$ and $q > 0$, VLCs in each category are mapped by one-to-one rule which the same as Hu et al.'s method:

$$C_i = \{\{VLC_{i,1}^{(u)'} \leftrightarrow VLC_{i,1}^{n}\}, \ldots, \{VLC_{i,q_i}^{(u)'} \leftrightarrow VLC_{i,q_i}^{n}\}\} \tag{7}$$

where "$\leftrightarrow$" represents the mapping relationship. Figure 4 illustrates the one-to-one mapping rule. As shown in Fig. 4, each unused-VLC is mapped to a different used-VLC.

One-to-k Mapping Rule. For the case $q \geq p$ and $p > 0$, the mapping rule will change to one-to-k manner. Hu et al.'s method assign the corresponding unused-VLCs to used-VLCs according to their sorted order. Both of Qian and Zhang' method [6] and Hu et al.'s method [7] are particular cases. Different from Qian and Zhang's method and Hu et al.'s method, the proposed method takes each

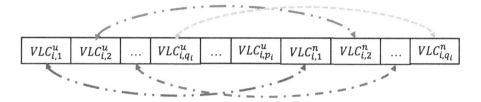

Fig. 4. The diagram of the one-to-one mapping rule.

used-VLC's frequency into consideration. However, how many unused-VLCs to be mapped to each used-VLC is a pure integer nonlinear programming $(PINLP)$ problem. Assuming the number of unused-VLCs which mapped to each used-VLC in the category C_i is $x_{i,j}$ and the frequency of each used-VLC is $f_{i,j}$, the selection of $x_{i,j}$ should satisfy the following condition:

$$\mathbf{max} \quad Z_i = \sum_{j=1}^{p_i} f_{i,j} \cdot log_2(x_{i,j} + 1)$$

$$\mathbf{s.t.} \quad \begin{cases} \sum_{j=1}^{p_i} x_{i,j} \leq q_i \\ x_{i,j} \geq 0 \\ x_{i,j} \leq q_i \\ x_{i,j} \in N^* \\ log_2(x_{i,j} + 1) \in N^* \end{cases} \tag{8}$$

where Z_i represents the embedding capacity of the category C_i and $log_2(x_{i,j}+1)$ means $log_2(x_{i,j} + 1)$ additional data can be represented by each VLC belonging to the corresponding mapping set. For instance, if there are 63 unused-VLCs mapped to a used-VLC, 6 additional data can be represented by each of the same used-VLCs. According to Eq. (8), there is a positive correlation between $x_{i,j}$ and $f_{i,j}$. After Eq. (8) is solved, all code mapping relationships are established which can be described as:

$$M_i = \begin{cases} \{VLC_{i,1}^u \leftrightarrow \{VLC_{i,1}^n, \dots, VLC_{i,x_{i,1}}^n\}\}, \\ \{VLC_{i,2}^{(u} \leftrightarrow \{VLC_{i,x_{i,1}+1}^n, \dots, VLC_{i,x_{i,1}+x_{i,2}}^n\}\}, \dots, \\ \{VLC_{i,p_i}^{(u} \leftrightarrow \{VLC_{i,q_i-x_{i,p_i}}^n, \dots, VLC_{i,q_i}^n\}\}, \end{cases} \tag{9}$$

Figure 5 illustrates the one-to-k mapping rule. In Fig. 5, $VLC_{i,1}^u$ is mapped to k_1 different unused-VLCs. Thus the mapping rule for is one-to-k_1. In the same way, the mapping rule for $VLCVLC_{i,k}^u$ is one-to-k_2.

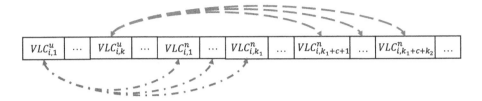

Fig. 5. The diagram of the one-to-k mapping rule.

3.2 Data Embedding and Extraction

The embedding procedure can be summarized as follows:

Input: An original JPEG bitstream and a secret bitstream.

Output: A stego JPEG bitstream.

Step 1: Parse the entropy-coded data, extract all of the used-VLCs and unused-VLCs.

Step 2: Establish the mapping relationships based on the mapping method mentioned in Sect. 3.1.

Step 3: Modify the corresponding RLVs in DHT segment, embed these by replacing the VLCs. Figure 6 shows the process of embedding additional data by replacing VLCs. In Fig. 6, $VLC_{i,m}^u$ is mapped to three different unused-VLCs $VLC_{i,k}^n, VLC_{i,l}^n$, and $VLC_{i,n}^n$. After replacing the three unused-VLCs' corresponding RLVs by $VLC_{i,m}^u$'s corresponding RLV $RLV_{i,m}^u$, these four VLCs can represent the same RLV. We can then embed additional data by replacing the original VLC by the four VLCs. Figure 7 shows one of the groups of additional

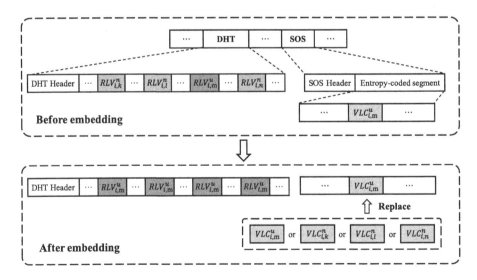

Fig. 6. The diagram of embedding additional data by replacing VLCs.

VLC	RLV		VLC	RLV	Data
$VLC_{i,m}^{u}$	$RLV_{i,m}^{u}$		$VLC_{i,m}^{u}$	$RLV_{i,m}^{u}$	00
$VLC_{i,k}^{n}$	$RLV_{i,k}^{n}$	$\Rightarrow$	$VLC_{i,k}^{n}$	$RLV_{i,m}^{u}$	01
$VLC_{i,l}^{n}$	$RLV_{i,l}^{n}$		$VLC_{i,l}^{n}$	$RLV_{i,m}^{u}$	10
$VLC_{i,n}^{n}$	$RLV_{i,n}^{n}$		$VLC_{i,n}^{n}$	$RLV_{i,m}^{u}$	11

Fig. 7. One of the group of additional data.

data. If we use the group as described in Fig. 7, when we replace the original VLC with $VLC_{i,k}^{n}$, additional data '01' will be embedded in the bitstream.

On the receiver side, the data extraction procedure can be summarized as follows:

Input: A stego JPEG bitstream.
Output: An original JPEG bitstream and a secret bitstream.
Step 1: Read the DHT segment and find the RLVs with same values.
Step 2: Classify the same RLVs into a set and record the RLVs, the corresponding VLCs and each corresponding additional data.
Step 3: Parse the JPEG bitstream and extract the embedded data according to the records from the entropy-coded data.

4   Experimental Results and Analysis

4.1   Experimental Results

To test the performance of our proposed method, firstly we used the images from the USC-SIPI database as mentioned in [8]. Figure 8 shows the ten test

Baboon	Boat	Bridge	Elaine	F-16

Gray21	Lena	Peppers	Splash	Tiffany

Fig. 8. The ten test grey-scale images

Table 1. Embedding capacity comparison with JPEG quality factors from 10 to 90 (bits)

Image	Method	10	20	30	40	50	60	70	80	90
Baboon	Hu et al.	6596	3475	1753	1755	1245	1272	1317	713	585
	Proposed	6596	3475	1754	1789	1271	1305	1358	757	675
Boat	Hu et al.	950	549	681	547	647	738	617	960	1776
	Proposed	950	549	691	571	687	811	679	1000	1929
Bridge	Hu et al.	1802	982	666	829	1007	691	795	569	555
	Proposed	1802	989	713	860	1035	714	817	596	615
Elaine	Hu et al.	341	264	200	414	553	326	407	787	1739
	Proposed	341	264	200	414	553	326	408	788	1745
F16	Hu et al.	791	764	904	863	721	670	527	366	332
	Proposed	791	764	904	961	886	860	741	920	928
Gray21	Hu et al.	235	502	904	982	884	892	1383	1398	2658
	Proposed	235	472	904	982	884	929	1510	1675	3207
Lena	Hu et al.	564	326	262	293	363	195	285	343	562
	Proposed	564	326	262	293	370	197	286	351	583
Peppers	Hu et al.	567	518	679	427	429	550	363	261	1537
	Proposed	567	427	717	492	556	644	450	633	1553
Splash	Hu et al.	496	597	1062	1330	1340	1429	1042	881	456
	Proposed	496	597	1086	1344	1380	1545	1184	1153	719
Tiffany	Hu et al.	4721	1152	656	864	736	786	856	761	625
	Proposed	4721	1152	682	908	782	880	997	956	744

grey-scale images. First, we convert these images to grey-scale images and then compress these to generate the JPEG images with different quality factors.

Since we only replace the used-VLCs by the same length unused-VLCs, the filesize of the modified JPEG bitstream is not changed. Moreover, because the corresponding RSV of the replaced VLC is the same as the original VLC, the decoded results are not changed. Thus, the decoded image has no distortion left. For the reason that our proposed method is lossless with filesize not changed, we only compare the embedding capacity with the other earlier method.

The embedding capacity results of both our proposed method and Hu et al.'s method are shown in Table 1, which the JPEG quality factors are from 10 to 90. From Table 1, we can see the improvement of capacity by our proposed method.

To compare the embedding capacity of these methods further, we has also tested the entire 1338 images from UCID image database [9]. Figure 9 shows the average payload of these 1338 JPEG images with different quality factors by these methods. Table 2 lists the average payload of the three methods. As shown in Fig. 9, the higher the quality factor, the more obvious the improvement of our proposed method. Table 3 shows the specific improvements of our proposed method compared to the other methods. Therefore, to indicate the improvement clearly, we has generated three scatter plots Figs. 10, 11 and 12, which the quality factors are 70, 80, and 90 respectively. From the three scatter plots, we can see that the improvement is steady and clear.

4.2   Analysis

From Table 3 and Fig. 9, we can see the improvement of our proposed method is much obvious for the high-QF JPEG images. However, from Table 2, the average payload of the high-QF JPEG images is less than the low-QF JPEG images, regardless of obtained by using any of the three methods. The reason can be concluded as the following two points.

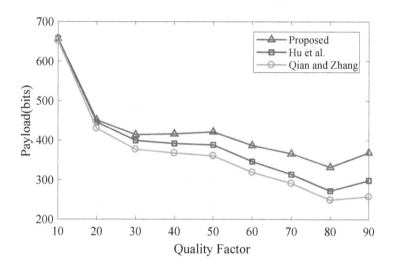

Fig. 9. The comparison of average payload of the JPEG images from UCID.

Table 2. The average payload of the three methods.

Quality factor	Payload(bits)		
	Proposed	Hu et al.	Qian and Zhang
10	1115.667	1114.771	1104.443
20	703.194	692.469	660.613
30	628.033	598.496	554.406
40	632.213	583.499	535.963
50	642.400	576.840	521.901
60	573.980	493.093	438.634
70	532.930	428.234	383.388
80	464.750	345.194	298.259
90	538.026	397.435	315.119

Table 3. The improvements of proposed method compared to the other methods.

Quality factor	Increased than Qian(%)	Increased than Hu(%)
10	1.016	0.080
20	6.446	1.549
30	13.280	4.935
40	17.958	8.349
50	23.088	11.365
60	30.856	16.404
70	39.005	24.448
80	55.821	34.634
90	70.738	35.375

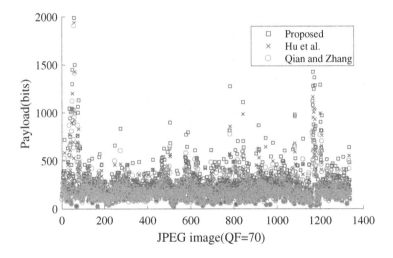

Fig. 10. The payload of each JPEG image with QF = 70 from UCID.

First point: The shorter the length of VLC, the higher the frequency (occurrence number) in the entropy-coded data generally. This is because the VLC is encoded by the format of Canonical Huffman Code.

Second point: The lower the QF, the higher possibility of unused-VLCs with shorter length exists. The QF stands for the compressed degree of a JPEG image. The high-QF means the compressed degree is low. The lower the QF, the more zero-AC coefficients, which means the less kinds of used-VLCs in the entropy-coded data. Correspondingly the possibility of unused-VLCs with shorter length exists is more.

Base the two points we can embed more data into low-QF JPEG images than high-QF JPEG images. Because the payload is determined by both the frequency of used-VLC and the amount of information, which each used-VLC can stands

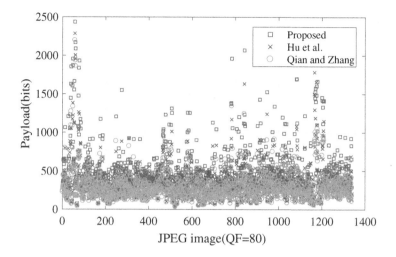

Fig. 11. The payload of each JPEG image with QF = 80 from UCID.

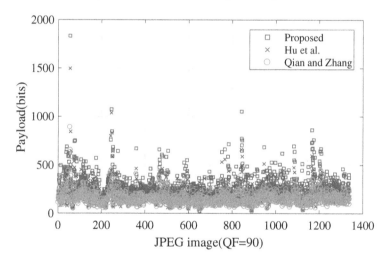

Fig. 12. The payload of each JPEG image with QF = 90 from UCID.

for. However, the frequency of used-VLC affects more. Because the possibility of the unused-VLC with shorter length exists in low-QF JPEG images is higher, the used-VLC with shorter length is more possible to establish mapping relationship. In addition, the frequency of the used-VLC with shorter length is much high, so we can embed more data than high-QF JPEG images.

However, the high-QF JPEG images are used more widely than low-QF JPEG images, which is because the distortion is less than low-QF JPEG images. Therefore, for most JPEG images in daily life, our method can obtain obvious improvement than the other methods.

5   Conclusions

In this paper, a lossless data hiding scheme for JPEG images is proposed. After introducing the established VLC mapping algorithm for JPEG bitstream, we develop the optimal VLC mapping according to the statistical results of VLCs. Thus, the proposed method obtains more free space to embed additional data.

Ackonwledgement. This research work is partly supported by National Natural Science Foundation of China (61502009, 61525203, 61472235, U1636206), Undergraduates Training Foundation of Anhui University, Anhui Provincial Natural Science Foundation (1508085SQF216) and Key Program for Excellent Young Talents in Colleges and Universities of Anhui Province (gxyqZD2016011).

References

1. Wong, P.H.W., Au, O.C.L., Wong, J.W.C.: Data hiding and watermarking in JPEG-compressed domain by DC coefficient modification. In: Proceedings of SPIE-The International Society for Optical Engineering, pp. 237–244 (2000)
2. Huang, F., Qu, X., Kim, H.J., et al.: Reversible data hiding in JPEG images. IEEE Trans. Circuits Syst. Video Technol. **26**(9), 1610–1621 (2016)
3. Fridrich, J., Goljan, M., Du, R.: Lossless data embedding for all image formats. In: International Society for Optics and Photonics, Electronic Imaging, pp. 572–583 (2002)
4. Xuan, G., Shi, Y.Q., Ni, Z., Chai, P., Cui, X., Tong, X.: Reversible data hiding for JPEG images based on histogram pairs. In: Kamel, M., Campilho, A. (eds.) ICIAR 2007. LNCS, vol. 4633, pp. 715–727. Springer, Heidelberg (2007). https://doi.org/10.1007/978-3-540-74260-9_64
5. Mobasseri, B.G., Berger, R.J., Marcinak, M.P., et al.: Data embedding in JPEG bitstream by code mapping. IEEE Trans. Image Process. **19**(4), 958–966 (2010)
6. Qian, Z., Zhang, X.: Lossless data hiding in JPEG bitstream. J. Syst. Softw. **85**(2), 309–313 (2012)
7. Hu, Y., Wang, K., Lu, Z.M.: An improved VLC-based lossless data hiding scheme for JPEG images. J. Syst. Softw. **86**(8), 2166–2173 (2013)
8. The USC-SIPI Image Database. http://sipi.usc.edu/database/
9. The UCID Image Database. http://vision.doc.ntu.ac.uk/

Co-saliency Detection Based on Siamese Network

Zhengchao Lei, Weiyan Chai, Sanyuan Zhao$^{(\boxtimes)}$, Hongmei Song, and Fengxia Li

Beijing Laboratory of Intelligent Information Technology, School of Computer Science, Beijing Institute of Technology, Beijing 100081, People's Republic of China
zhaosanyuan@bit.edu.cn

Abstract. Saliency detection in images attracts much research attention for its usage in numerous multimedia applications. Beside on the detection within the single image, co-saliency has been developed rapidly by detecting the same foreground objects in different images and trying to further promote the performance of object detection. This paper we propose a co-saliency detection method based on Siamese Network. By using Siamese Network, we get the similarity matrix of each image in superpixels. Guided by the single image saliency map, each saliency value, saliency score matrix is obtained to generate the multi image saliency map. Our final saliency map is a linear combination of these two saliency maps. The experiments show that our method performs better than other state-of-arts methods.

Keywords: Co-saliency detection · Siamese network
Feature extraction

1 Introduction

The purpose of saliency detection is to find the regions that humans are most interested in. Following this idea, the images or videos can be compressed more effectively and accurately. In this paper, we mainly focus on the saliency detection area instead of the network problem. In the past decades, saliency prediction models have changed remarkably and applied to many fields, such as image search, redirection and segmentation. There are two main methods for detecting salient area, one is global detecting, the other is local detecting, which are similar to methods in image processing.

Local saliency detection method mainly focuses on the different features that appear in the adjacent local region. Nowadays there exist many mature models for detecting local salient regions, including visual saliency detection based on graph model, saliency based on feature learning, and interpolation method of local region. Local saliency detection initially utilizes image pyramids to generate color and orientation features, which means the images will be sampled by stages. [1] calculated the color difference of each pixel around the center in the fixed adjacent region and extracted local saliency map. The most important part

© Springer Nature Singapore Pte Ltd. 2018
L. Zhu and S. Zhong (Eds.): MSN 2017, CCIS 747, pp. 99–109, 2018.
https://doi.org/10.1007/978-981-10-8890-2_8

of the local sampling method is to determine the size of sampling area. Besides, the edge information with high contrast is not necessarily in foreground. [2] adopted the multilevel saliency detection method which divided image into multi layers from depth, and then integrated the results with graph models. Global saliency detection method starts from the global characteristics of images. Generally, image frequency or spatial domain computing methods are adopted. [3] introduced a method to subtract the mean value in color space through lowpass filter. [4] extended histograms to three dimensional color space. However Both of these methods were mere to find the pixels that stand out in the whole image instead of considering the spatial distribution. [5] tried to describe the spatial distribution of colors, which may be difficult for similar elements both in the foreground and background.

Both local and global saliency detection methods are single image saliency detection, while Co-saliency detection aims at extracting common objects from a set of images. The extraction of same objects in a set of images is one of the most important application in computer vision and has been widely used in image matching, pattern recognition and synergetic recognition. [6] gave a more precise definition to co-saliency detection. Meanwhile a new method was introduced that co-saliency detection contains single image saliency map and multi images saliency maps which were generated by super pixel segmentation and feature extraction. By using mathematical method, the two results are joined together to obtain the final saliency map. And this approach has been continuously improved. In 2015, [7] tried to eliminate the common background except for extracting common foreground in multiple images. The single image and multi image saliency detection now are known as Intrasaliency and Intersaliency.

Co-segmentation is also closely related to co-saliency detection. The purpose of co-segmentation is to segment the same area from a set of images, which was originally used as histogram matching method. At present, there are two types of co-segmentation. One is collaborative segmentation based on graph models and the problem is converted into maximum flow problem. The other is cooperative segmentation method based on clustering problem. The results of saliency detection are often used to conduct the co-segmentation problem. [8] proposed a co-segmentation method based on cosine similarity and guided by salient features. They optimized the clustering step, and made the algorithm perform better with faster speed.

It is easy to see that both single image saliency and co-saliency detection are based on human cognition. Salient object is the region that is quite different from the adjacent area, or the common object repeated in a number of images. Therefore, the artificial intelligence based methods are suitable for saliency detection. This paper we introduce deep learning method assisting us to accomplish co-saliency detection. In 2015, [9] utilized deep convolution neural network(CNN) to learn and express high-level features to detect the saliency region. [7] extended to deep learning framework SDAE. Most of the co-segmentation and co-saliency detection methods are mainly achieved by unsupervised learning, such as clustering and so on. However, both of the deep neural network based method are time and resource consuming because of the training steps. Therefore, we proposed a new siamese network based method to reduce the computing cost in train step and obtained a better performance in co-saliency detection. Our approach is summarized below. 1. A traditional method is used to generate the single image saliency map. 2. By utilizing the deep learning network-Siamese Network to train the feature difference model, we obtain the similarity parameter matrix of each superpixel between interimages. 3. The multi-image saliency map can be achieved by based on the vote of similarity matrix and the score of single image saliency map. 4. In the final step, we linearly combine the single image saliency map with multi image saliency map to obtain the final saliency map. Note that the siamese network in our work is to generate the feature differences between the input images instead of extracting features.

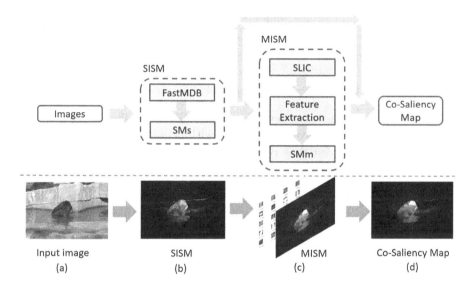

Fig. 1. Illustration of our algorithm

2 Related Work

2.1 Single Image Saliency Detection

There exist lots of saliency detection method for single image [4,5,10,11]. Taking into account time consuming and performance, we choose Fast-MDB [11] as our single image detection approach. Minimum Barrier Distance(MDB) [10] is a fast algorithm designed to generate the saliency map of an image. Barrier connectivity information has always been one of the effective methods for saliency generation. However, this step is also the bottleneck of methods. The MBD algorithm omitted the regional extraction process and improved the original method. At the same time, Fast-MBD algorithm provided an approximate approach based on MBD algorithm, which generated saliency map in milliseconds.

2.2   Siamese Network

The image similarity plays an important role in computer vision and has been applied in the field of image super resolution, dynamic structure, object recognition, image classification. Variety of methods have been explored to determine whether two images are the same. In mathematical, Hu invariant moments are widely used to extract features that insensitive to translation, rotation and scaling in images, and already available in fingerprint matching. Another important method to match images is SIFT.

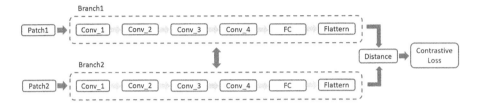

Fig. 2. Siamese network used in our method

Recent years, with the rapid development of artificial intelligence techniques, many researchers tried to solve this problem with neural network. [12] explored to describe the feature through AlexNet network, and they found that deep learning exceed the performance of SIFT algorithm in many cases. [13] verified deep learning method on some data sets. The method achieved good performance only in particular cases. [14] constructed a model to compare images through CNN. In this paper, we introduced siamese network for matching image patches in feature extraction.

Figure 2 demonstrates the siamese network structure used in our method. The network contains two branches and the input is image pair with same height, width and channel. Each branch consists of 4 convolution layers, 1 fully convolution layer and flattern layer. The kernel size for each convolution layer is 7×7, 5×5, 3×3, 1×1. The contrastive loss function is defined as the euclidean distance of two branch output. Branches and last output in our network can be considered as the descriptor and similarity function respectively. In traditional methods, each image was represented with the same feature, that is why branches in our network share the same weight. At the same time this will reduce the training cost significantly. We utilize the network to obtain an image comparison model to distinguish the same patches among images.

In addition to the siamese network, there are some similar networks can be used for comparison of images in experiments. The pseudo siamese network is the same as the siamese network in structure. The only difference between them is that the pseudo network does not share weight. In this way, the computation time of pseudo siamese and siamese is the same in the forward process. However in learning process, pseudo siamese should learn much more weight and need more time. This is another reason why we set the same weight of branches in our network.

3   Proposed Method

The procedure of the proposed framework is summarized in Fig. 1. The input of our network is the superpixels of images divided by [3]. Firstly, We obtain the single image saliency map through Fast-MDB algorithm in SISM step. At the beginning of MISM step, an image comparison model based on siamese network is trained. By utilizing this model, we obtain the similarity parameter matrix of each superpixel between interimage and intraimage. The multi image saliency map is generated combining the similarity matrix with scores of single image saliency map. The final saliency map is the linear combination of single and multi image saliency map.

Fig. 3. Cifar-10 dataset for training

3.1   Multi Images Saliency Detection

Network Training. Because of the particularity of siamese network structure, the loss function and training step of siamese network are different from those of the ordinary single branch deep learning network. The training of siamese network generally uses contrast loss as the loss function. Similar to classification, Siamese network mainly focuses on the difference of image features instead of the classification score. As shown in Fig. 2, the distance function in our network is defined as:

$$D_W(\overrightarrow{X_1}, \overrightarrow{X_2}) = \left\| G_W(\overrightarrow{X_1}) - G_W(\overrightarrow{X_2}) \right\|_2 \tag{1}$$

$\overrightarrow{X_1}$ and $\overrightarrow{X_2}$ is the input pair of our network, and G_W means the operation done in each branch. In fact, the distance function is the Euclidean distance of two network outputs. The loss function is defined as follows.

$$L = (1 - Y)L_S(D_w) + Y L_D(D_w) \tag{2}$$

Where Y represents the label of the input pair. For example, $Y = 1$ indicates that two inputs are the same, otherwise $Y = 0$. Obviously, L_S means the partial loss for the same inputs and L_D represents for the different. For L_S and L_D, it is necessary to ensure that L is smaller when the inputs are the same and larger when different after training. After experiments, we obtain our loss function:

$$L = \frac{1}{2}(1 - Y)(D_W)^2 + \frac{1}{2}Y[\max(0, m - D_W)]^2 \tag{3}$$

We adopt Cifar-10 as our training dataset as shown in Fig. 3. Cifar-10 has a number of advantages: the regular images and label format; easy to read; large number of images in each class for training. Compared to MNIST, image in Cifar-10 is smaller enough with 32 height and 32 width, and this will reduce the complexity of training. In the training step, we first select an image from each class as one input, and select another image from the same class while setting the label $Y = 1$. At the same time, we select another image from the different class and set the $Y = 0$. After numbers of iterations, the image comparison model will be obtained.

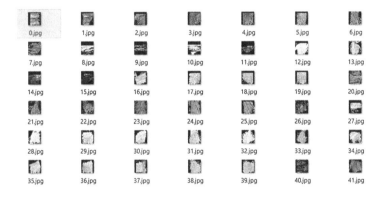

Fig. 4. Result of image preprocessing

Preprocessing. For multi image saliency detection, each image should be divided into a number of superpixels firstly. Each superpixel will be filled to an image patch with black background. Center of the superpixel locates at the center of image patch. Other pixels will be put in the patch according to the original location. Since the generated superpixels vary greatly in sizes, the image patch should be adaptive to cover all the pixels in each superpixel without being too small. In our experiments, we assume that S_k is the quantity of superpixels, and the size of the patch is $A/(\sqrt{S_k} - n)$. While A means the length of original image, and n is an adjustable parameter. This doesn't always get the best result. However it ensures that the computation complexity is still about the linear time of the image size, which is independent of the number of superpixels. According to the size of Cifar-10, each image patch will be reshaped to 32×32 finally and stored in hard drive shown in Fig. 4.

Fig. 5. Result of image preprocessing

Feature Extraction and Comparison. Our proposed method is to use the forward transmission of siamese network to directly replace the feature extraction and matching. For forward transmission, the input is the image patch pairs of the same image generated by preprocessing. By computing the feature differences between one image patch with all other patches in the same image, we can get the similarity of this patch. The other similarities can be computed in the same way. Finally, similarity matrix is obtained for each image. Based on this matrix, We define our score function as

$$Score_c = 0.5 + m - Sigmoid(2/d) \tag{4}$$

d represents the contrastive loss of two input patches. When d is large, which means there is big differences between two image patches, the score is close to 0. Otherwise, the score is close to 1. The score function reflect the negative feedback relationship between distance and score. However, there are some problems in our approach. As shown in Fig. 5, the grassland should be labeled as background. However the similarity matrix treats this area as the most frequently parts and labels foreground. Therefore, we make use of the single image saliency map to guide the generation of multi image saliency map. In our method, we construct a saliency score matrix S_s based on single image saliency map in superpixels. The saliency score matrix is

$$Score_{si} = \frac{\sum_{p_j \in SP_i} SISM(p_j)}{NUM} \tag{5}$$

SISM stands for the saliency value of single image saliency map. p_j is a pixel of image. NUM means the count of pixels for the i-th superpixel SP_i. As a consequence, $Score_{si}$ is the saliency score for the i-th superpixel. The final saliency value R for multi image is summarized

$$R = (Score_c + c_1) \times (Score_{si} + c_2) \tag{6}$$

While c_1 and c_2 are the gaussian noise avoiding too many zeros. Afterward, R is normalized to R_f, where R_f is the final saliency value for multi image.

3.2 Final Saliency Map

We obtain our final saliency map by linear combination with the single image saliency map and multi image saliency map. The equation is as follows.

$$SS(I_i) = \alpha_1 \cdot S_s(I_i) + \alpha_2 \cdot S_m(I_i) \tag{7}$$

S_s and S_m are the saliency map for single and multi image respectively. α_1 and α_2 stand for the weight. In our experiments, we set $\alpha_1 = 0.2$ and $\alpha_1 = 0.8$ to increase the weight of our multi image saliency map.

4 Experiments and Results

In this section, we describe our evaluation protocol and implementation details, provide exhaustive comparison results over two datasets, analysis the performance our methods.

4.1 Dataset and Metrics Method

We evaluate our method on two public datasets, including iCoseg [15] and MSRC [16]. The iCoseg dataset consists of 38 classes with 643 images. MSRC-v1 contains 9 object classed and 240 images. The results are compared with several state-of-art method, including Kim [17], Jou [18] and Fast-MDB [11]. Each image is segmented into 400 superpixels. We leverage the Precision(P) and Jaccard similarity coefficient(J) as evaluation indicators. P represents the proportion of the correct pixels in the final saliency map. J refers to the similarity between the detection result R and the ground true G, and it can be defined as

$$J = \frac{R \cap G}{R \cup G} \tag{8}$$

4.2 Results

Quantitative Results. Table 1 is the results of iCoseg dataset. As shown our method performs better than Kim and Jou in precision. However, our method does not have the advantage in J. It is worth noting that all the other methods, such as Kim, is actually a method for image cosegmentation. Although it is similar to saliency detection, the segmentation results generally guarantee the edge smoothing, and the final result is strong connectivity. Therefore, J can be higher than saliency method. For our method, loss of some low saliency values and wrong annotations lead to the lower J.

Compared to Fast-MDB, our method works little better in P and J. Nonetheless, our method labels some images that are not detected by Fast-MDB shown in Fig. 6. The two warriors belong to the foreground. However, Fast-MDB only labels some parts of edge while our method annotates the right warrior.

Table 1. Comparison with other methods

	Kim	Jou	Fast-MDB	Ours
P	70.2	70.4	82.8	83.2
J	42.6	39.7	38.7	41.4

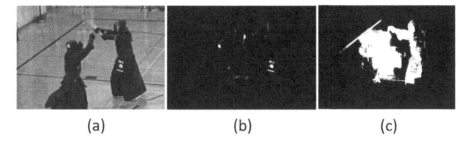

(a) (b) (c)

Fig. 6. Results of our method

Visualization. Combined with single and multi image saliency map, our method can correctly locate the approximate salient objects in the image. Figure 7 is an image chosen from iCoseg. (a) is the source image and (b) is the result segmented by [19]. (c) represents the saliency map generated by Fast-MDB. As we can see that some sharp edges, such as the stone crevice, make the map noisy. When the co-saliency method is added, it can better filter the noise below. The multi image saliency map plays an important role in co-saliency detection. The graph neutralizing the bear's own color close to the tree trunk and the obvious shadow can not be removed, which is also related to the limitations of the fast MDB algorithm itself focusing on the center of image.

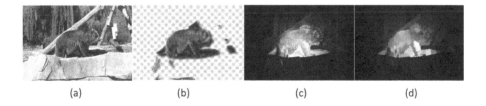

(a) (b) (c) (d)

Fig. 7. Visualization of result

5 Conclusion

We proposed a new co-saliency detection method based on siamese network. The proposed method consists of two parts. One is to detect the single image saliency region with traditional method. Another is to generate the multi image saliency map through siamese network. The network is trained to evaluate the difference between two input image features. Therefore, similarity matrix is generated for each image in superpixels. Combing with saliency score matrix Guided by the exist single image saliency map, we can get the multi image saliency map. Afterward, the co-saliency map is the linear combination of single and multi image saliency maps. Finally, we conduct experiments on two public datasets, and the experiments show that our method performs better in metrics P and J. Our method provide an idea of network transmission. We can improve the compression algorithm to keep the saliency area as much as possible while reduce the size of images and videos.

References

1. Ma, Y., Zhang, H.: Contrast-based image attention analysis by using fuzzy growing. In: ACM International Conference on Multimedia, pp. 374–381 (2003)
2. Yan, Q., Xu, L., Shi, J., Jia, J.: Hierarchical saliency detection. In: 2013 IEEE Conference on Computer Vision and Pattern Recognition(CVPR), pp. 1155–1162 (2013)
3. Achanta, R., Shaji, A., Smith, K., Lucchi, A., Fua, P., Süsstrunk, S.: SLIC superpixels compared to state-of-the-art superpixel methods. IEEE Trans. Pattern Anal. Mach. Intell. **34**(11), 2274–2282 (2012)
4. Cheng, M., Zhang, G., Mitra, N., Huang, X., Hu, S.: Global contrast based salient region detection. In: 2011 IEEE Conference on Computer Vision and Pattern Recognition (CVPR), vol. 37(3), pp. 409–416 (2011)
5. Perazzi, F., Krahenbuhl, P., Pritch, Y., Hornung, A.: Saliency filters: contrast based filtering for salient region detection. In: 2012 IEEE Conference on Computer Vision and Pattern Recognition (CVPR), pp. 733–740 (2012)
6. Li, H., Ngan, K.: A co-saliency model of image pairs. IEEE Trans. Image Process. **20**(12), 3365–3375 (2011)
7. Zhang, D., Han, J., Han, J., Shao, L.: Cosaliency detection based on intrasaliency prior transfer and deep intersaliency mining. IEEE Trans. Neural Netw. Learn. Syst. **27**(6), 1163–1176 (2016)
8. Tao, Z., Liu, H., Fu, H., Fu, Y.: Image cosegmentation via saliency-guided constrained clustering with cosine similarity. In: 13th AAAI Conference on Artificial Intelligence (2017)
9. Zhang, D., Han, J., Li, C., Wang, J.: Co-saliency detection via looking deep and wide. In: 2015 IEEE Conference on Computer Vision and Pattern Recognition (CVPR), pp. 2994–3002 (2015)
10. Strand, R., Ciesielski, K.C., Malmberg, F., Saha, K.: The minimum barrier distance. Comput. Vis. Image Underst. **117**(4), 429–437 (2013)
11. Zhang, J., Sclaroff, S., Lin, Z., Shen, X., Price, B., Mech, R.: Minimum barrier salient object detection at 80 FPS. In: 2015 IEEE International Conference on Image Processing, pp. 1404–1412 (2015)
12. Philipp, F., Alexey, D., Thomas, D.: Descriptor Matching with Convolutional Neural Networks: a Comparison to Sift. Computer Science (2014)
13. Žbontar, J., LeCun, Y.: Computing the stereo matching cost with a convolutional neural network. In: 2015 IEEE Conference on Computer Vision and Pattern Recognition (CVPR), pp. 1592–1599 (2015)

14. Zagoruyko, S., Komodakis, N.: Learning to compare image patches via convolutional neural networks. In: 2015 IEEE Conference on Computer Vision and Pattern Recognition (CVPR), pp. 4353–4361 (2015)
15. Dhruv, B., Adarsh, K., Devi, P., Luo, J., Chen, T.: iCoseg: interactive cosegmentation with intelligent scribble guidance. In: 2015 IEEE conference on Computer Vision and Pattern Recognition (CVPR), pp. 3169–3176 (2010)
16. Microsoft Research. http://research.microsoft.com/en-us/projects/objectclassrecognition/
17. Kim, G., Xing, E., Li, F., Kanade, T.: Distributed cosegmentation via submodular optimization on anisotropic diffusion. In: 2011 International Conference on Computer Vision, pp. 169–176 (2011)
18. Joulin, A., Bach, F., Ponce, J.: Multi-class cosegmentation. In: 2012 IEEE Conference on Computer Vision and Pattern Recognition (CVPR), pp. 542–549 (2012)
19. Rubinstein, M., Joulin, A., Kopf, J., Liu, C.: Unsupervised joint object discovery and segmentation in internet images. In: 2013 IEEE Conference on Computer Vision and Pattern Recognition (CVPR), pp. 1939–1946 (2013)

An Efficient Privacy-Preserving Fingerprint-Based Localization Scheme Employing Oblivious Transfer

Mengxuan Sun[✉], Xiaoju Dong, Fan Wu, and Guihai Chen

Shanghai Key Laboratory of Scalable Computing and Systems,
Shanghai Jiao Tong University, Shanghai, China
sunmengxuan@sjtu.edu.cn, {dong-xj,fwu,gchen}@cs.sjtu.edu.cn

Abstract. The tremendous growth of WiFi fingerprint-based localization techniques has significantly facilitated localization services. The traditional techniques pose a threat to both client's and server's privacies,
because it is likely to reveal sensitive information about the client and the
server during providing localization services. Many existing works have
proposed privacy preserving localization schemes based on homomorphic cryptographic systems. However, the state of the art homomorphic
cryptographic systems turn out to bear a time-consuming process for
recourse-constrained devices. Hence, preserving location privacy while
guaranteeing efficiency and usability is still a challenging problem. In
this paper, we propose a privacy preserving indoor localization scheme
employing oblivious transfer, called OTPri, to preserve the privacy of
both clients and server in the process of localization in an efficient way.
Our method enables a client to efficiently compute her location locally at
client side with a small amount of additional overhead compared with the
non-privacy-preserving scheme. Meanwhile, we conduct comprehensive
experiments, including single-floor and multi-floor scenarios in our office
building. The evaluation results demonstrate the efficiency improvement
and overhead reduction of our proposed scheme compared with a classical
privacy-preserving indoor localization scheme.

1   Introduction

The explosive popularity of portable mobile devices such as smartphones and
tablets are fostering the emergence of location-aware applications and services
for mobile users. Exemplary applications [19] include sounding the security alert
when entering dangerous areas, posting location-based advertisements, locating
a friend, etc. Due to the lack of GPS signals for indoor localization, a large body
of research has come up with numerous techniques. A prevalent method is to
measure received signal strength as a fingerprint, and match it with the sampled
fingerprints in the database, including radio frequency [2,5,33], acoustic signals
[12,23,24], infrared ray [28], GSM [21], the combination of ambience features
[1,30], etc. A common idea among all these techniques is to reduce the site survey

© Springer Nature Singapore Pte Ltd. 2018
L. Zhu and S. Zhong (Eds.): MSN 2017, CCIS 747, pp. 110–132, 2018.
https://doi.org/10.1007/978-981-10-8890-2_9

effort and distance error to realize indoor localization. Nevertheless, the majority of clients are reluctant to disclose their privacy while asking for an accurate service. Meanwhile, the server has to protect its database from unauthorized acquisition. Therefore, protecting privacy while guaranteeing the usability of the WiFi fingerprint-based localization system is an important foundation to ensure practicability.

Typically, the WiFi fingerprint-based localization system consists of two phases [29], including offline training and online operating phase. In the offline training phase, the server acquires the received signal strengths and the corresponding coordinate information of sampled locations and stores them in the database for future reference. During the online operating phase, a client who needs a localization service first measures the signal strength at current location and then submits it to the server for matching. Finally, the server employs an algorithm to determine client's location.

Although regarded as a promising approach for indoor localization, there are still considerable potential privacy leakages in such a paradigm of localization service. From client's perspective, the client has to expose its fingerprint and location directly to the server when requesting services, which will enable the server to trace client's location, and give third-party an opportunity to breach the client's privacy. Existing works indicate that the adversary can steal the individuals habits, activities, and relationships by location traces [18,25]. Therefore, the loss of privacy can lead to bad consequences [8], including location-based spams, damage of reputation or economic and physical violences. From server's perspective, although the transmission of complete database to the client may protect client's privacy [15], the database may be disclosed and utilized for commercial profit. Meanwhile, the continuous transmission of massive amounts of data will consume the device's resource, extend query process and compromise the network health. Moreover, the service provider has a strong demand for the protection for its WiFi fingerprint database from the unauthorized reveal. Hence, a privacy preserving scheme should be carefully designed to ensure confidentiality and usability.

According to the potential privacy leakage and the corresponding requirements, there are several challenges in designing a privacy-preserving localization scheme [7]. First, the scheme should meet both client's and server's requirements for data privacy, which means keeping their data safe from each other and malicious third party while acquiring all necessary information to achieve accurate localization, thus it makes the design much more complicated than the localization itself. Second, considering the resource-constrained characteristic of portable devices, the scheme should avoid complicated computation and large amount of communication overhead to ensure quick response and low cost, however, existing privacy-preserving localization schemes employing homomorphic cryptographic turn out to be a time-consuming process for portable devices and the performance degrades in larger scenarios. Third, since precision is a core objective of localization system, it directly influences the usability and user experience of the system. Nevertheless, the introduction of privacy-preserving function certainly will influence the accuracy of the localization scheme, thus we should improve the accuracy to the greatest extent. Therefore, it is a challenging problem to achieve an overhead-performance balanced system while guaranteeing the data privacy of both sides.

To protect clients' location privacy in location-based services, some approaches including k-anonymity [17,31] and mix zones [4]) have been proposed. However, WiFi fingerprint-based localization lacks trusted third parties to apply them. Furthermore, these works submit the users' location information with the requests to protect the location privacy of the users requesting location-based services, which assumes that each client has obtained service without any privacy concern.

Considering the challenges as stated, toward this end, we are motivated to design a privacy-preserving localization system based on oblivious transfer [6] named OTPri.

To avoid the exposure of client's fingerprint, the localization scheme should protect any side information that may lead to a coarse estimate of the location in addition to the protection of the exact location of the client, meanwhile, the client has to provide as few information as possible to acquire the information that meets the requirement of accurate localization. Therefore, whenever a client needs to be localized, she sends an AP id from her vicinity to the server, then the server will choose the corresponding data entries which are stored at its side. Even though the id of the vicinity AP is exposed, the server can only confirm a wider area of the client's location, which meets the demand for client privacy. Moreover, due to the characteristic of oblivious transfer, the server cannot figure out which data entries the client has chosen, and the client cannot get any other information except her choices, besides, the server can put constraint on the number of data entries that the client can obtain during one localization process and the total number of requests a single client can achieve, thus preserving the server's data security to the greatest extent (Fig. 1).

The major contributions of this paper are summarized as two-fold:

- We present and formulate a privacy-preserving indoor localization scheme employing oblivious transfer to achieve a privacy-overhead-balanced construction to solve the privacy issues during the localization process. Meanwhile, we reduce the computation and communication overhead to the utmost extent, which has a decrease of nearly 40% considering the computation and communication overhead. And the localization process is conducted locally at the client side.
- We elaborate the privacy property for the proposed scheme and evaluate its performance by comprehensive experiments in both single-floor and multiple-floor scenarios in our office buildings. By comparing with existing privacy-preserving localization solutions, we verify the efficiency improvement and overhead reduction of the proposed scheme compared with PriWFL algorithm [6].

The remainder of this paper is organized as follows. In Sect. 2, we define the system model and present the threat model and technical preliminaries. In Sect. 3, we present the design motivation of the proposed privacy-preserving localization

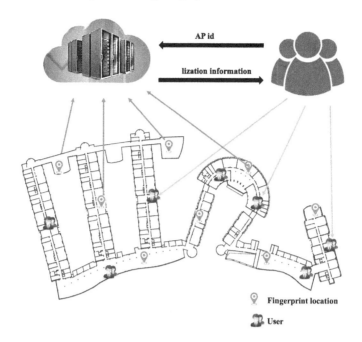

Fig. 1. OTPri system design

scheme, its details and privacy analysis. Section 4 reports our extensive experiments on this scheme. Section 5 briefly discusses the related work. Finally, in Sect. 6, we conclude our work.

2   Background and Attack Model

2.1   Overview of WiFi Fingerprint-Based Localization

WiFi fingerprint-based localization uses the WiFi signal strength to infer the location of a user. WiFi fingerprint-based localization is mainly composed of two phases [2], including offline phase and online phase. In the offline phase, the server selects N WiFi access points to represent fingerprints, then the service provider measures the average WiFi signal strength of the WiFi access points at M locations in the interested area, denoted as $V_i = \{v_1, v_2, ..., v_j, ..., v_N\}$, $i \in [1, M]$, where v_j is the average WiFi signal strength at (x_i, y_i) from the jth access point AP_j, and N is the totality of access points. Then the service provider stores the sampled fingerprints and their corresponding coordinates $(i, (x_i, y_i), V_i)$ in the WiFi fingerprint database D.

In the online phase, a client who intends to locate herself first measures the signal strengths from N access points, indicated as $V' = (v'_1, v'_2, ..., v'_j, ..., v'_N)$, and sends its fingerprint to the server. Then, the server computes the Euclidean distances between V' and all the M sampled fingerprints as $d_i = ||V' - V_i||^2, i \in [1, M]$.

$$d_i = \| V' - V_i \|^2 = \sum_{j=1}^{N} (v_{i,j} - v'_j)^2$$

$$= \sum_{j=1}^{N} v_{i,j}^2 + \sum_{j=1}^{N} (-2v_{i,j} * v'_j) + \sum_{j=1}^{N} v'^2_j \qquad (1)$$

In the last step, the server selects k smallest values of d_i and finds out the corresponding coordinates of these d_is, then estimates the client's location by computing the centroid of these locations.

2.2 Threat Model

The clients and service providers act in a semi-honest manner [10], in which they independently follow the protocol during localization process, but will try to extract useful information from the communication. Besides, we also assume that the third-party cannot steal privacy through eavesdropping the communication because of the encryption of the message sent between the client and server. Thus, in this paper, the prevention of privacy leakage in a normal localization operation is considered.

Our study considers both the client's location privacy and the service provider's data privacy. From the client's perspective, the client intends to acquire the localization service without compromising its location privacy. The location information can be theft by a curious service provider who collects the locations of the customers to make marketing and sales strategies or sells them for profit, namely *client privacy attack*. Therefore, the proposed scheme should prevent the attackers from stealing client's information, including the client's location and her sampled WiFi RSS signals, while providing accurate localization service.

From the service provider's perspective, the fingerprint database should be protected from unauthorized reveal. The database of the server may be downloaded or simulated by a malicious client to make profit, namely *database privacy attack*. Consequently, the server needs to protect its collected fingerprint database from learning or simulating by others in the process of localization.

2.3 Security Model

In privacy-preserving indoor localization scheme, we use the standard security model [9,11] in presence of semi-honest participants, in which the client and the server will follow the scheduled protocol, but might try to compute additional information by received messages. We use simulation argument to define security in this setting: if no additional information is revealed to the participants during protocol execution, which means no party can compute the view of protocol execution using that party's input and output only, the protocol is unconditionally secure. The notion of privacy-preserving for semi-honest participants is formalized using the definition below:

Definition 1. The client and the server engage in a protocol t, in which they cooperatively compute function $f(in_1, in_2) = (out_1, out_2)$, where in_i and out_i respectively represent input and output of client and server. During the execution of protocol t, we use $VIEW_t(P_i)$ to denote the view of a participant. More precisely, the participants' input, random coin tosses r_i and messages $m_1, ..., m_t$ passed between the parties during protocol execution form $P_i's$ view: $VIEW_t(P_i) = (in_i, r_i, m_1, ..., m_t)$. We define time simulator S_i such that:

$$S_i(in_i, f(in_1, in_2)) \equiv VIEW_p(P_i), out_i \tag{2}$$

where "$\equiv$" denotes computational indistinguishability. If for each party P_i, such a probabilistic polynomial time simulator exists, the protocol t is unconditionally secure.

Indistinguishability. Two probability ensembles X_i and Y_i, indexed by i, are (computationally) indistinguishable if for any PPTM D, polynomial $p(n)$ and sufficiently large i, it holds that

$$|P_r[D(X_i) = 1] - Pr[D(Y_i) = 1]| \leq 1/p(i) \tag{3}$$

2.4 Security Assumptions

For our privacy-preserving scheme against semi-honest client, we assume the hardness of Decisional Diffie-Hellman (DDH) problem [6].

Decisional Diffie-Hellman (DDH). Let $p = 2q + 1$ where p, q are two primes, and G_q be the subgroup of Z_p^* with order q. The following two distribution ensembles are computationally indistinguishable:

- $Y_1 = (g, g^a, g^b, g^{ab})_{G_q}$, where g is a generator of G_q, and $a, b \in {}_R Z_q$.
- $Y_2 = (g, g^a, g^b, g^c)_{G_q}$, where g is a generator of G_q, and $a, b, c \in {}_R Z_q$.

2.5 k-out-of-n Oblivious Transfer

In this paper, we adopt k-out-of-n Oblivious Transfer [6] to protect both the client's privacy and the server's fingerprint database. Therefore, we briefly review the fundamental of k-out-of-n oblivious transfer.

Oblivious transfer (OT) is an important primitive used in many cryptographic protocols. An oblivious transfer protocol involves two parties, the sender S and the receiver R. S has some messages and R wants to obtain some of them via interaction with S. The security requirement is that S wants R to obtain the message of her choice only and R does not want S to know what she chooses. A k-out-of-n OT (OT_n^k) scheme is an OT scheme in which R chooses k messages at the same time, where $k < n$.

The sender S has n secret messages $m_1, m_2, ..., m_n$ from message space G_q, and the semi-honest receiver R wants to get k of them.

In our scheme, there is no need for trapdoor specification or initialization, which means the system parameters can be repeatedly used by all senders and receivers, and each pair of sender and receiver does not need to hold any secret key.

3   Design of OTPri

In this section, we propose the construction of our privacy preserving indoor localization scheme employing oblivious transfer (OTPri), a WiFi fingerprint-based indoor localization employing oblivious transfer to preserve privacy.

3.1   Preliminary Design

Our proposed scheme protects both client's and server's information, and achieves high efficiency in the process of indoor localization. The key idea of our scheme is to mask the query by oblivious transfer [6], thus the server cannot know the client's choice. Meanwhile, the client only obtains the information of her choice. We demonstrate the challenges and our corresponding solutions in this subsection.

Privacy Preservation in Indoor Localization. To avoid the exposure of client's fingerprint, the localization scheme should protect any side information that may lead to a coarse estimate of the location in addition to the protection of the exact location of the client. In the query process of other fingerprint-based localization methods, the server has access to client's fingerprint and estimated location. Therefore, the privacy of client's location is leaked to the server. To avoid this kind of threats, we integrate oblivious transfer with traditional fingerprint-based localization scheme, which allows the client to choose the necessary information for localization on her own and keep her choices from the others. Meanwhile, due to the characteristic of oblivious transfer, the client cannot learn anything other than her choices. And the server can put constraint on the number of data entries that the client can obtain during one localization process and the total number of requests a single client can achieve, thus preserving the server's data security to the greatest extent.

Time Efficiency. Privacy-preserving indoor localization has been researched very extensively in the last few years. Many schemes use homomorphic encryption. However, it requires computationally expensive public-key operations that scale very inefficiently for larger security parameters, which is a time-consuming process for resource-constrained devices such as smartphones. Moreover, the user has to generate a pair of keys each time when it needs to be localized. To shorten the process of query, our scheme employs oblivious transfer in which the parameters can be used repeatedly by all possible clients and servers without any initialization.

3.2   Scheme Details

Our scheme involves three phases, including Pre-Process Phase, Oblivious Transfer Phase and Location Determination Phase.

Pre-process Phase. After collecting the fingerprints from a building $(i, (x_i, y_i), V_i = ((v_{ij})|_{j=1}^N)_{i=1}^M)$, where i is an index, M is the total number of sampled locations, N is the totality of APs, (x_i, y_i) is the coordinate of the specific location, V_i represents the WiFi fingerprint at the specific location (x_i, y_i), the server stores the results in a 2-D matrix $MATRIX[N][M]$, which records the RSS value of N APs at M geo-locations. Moreover, the server stores the table $T = (i, (x_i, y_i))_{i=1}^M$ which records the indices and their corresponding coordinates of sampled locations. The Radiomap MATRIX can be of the following format:

$$\text{Radiomap(MATRIX)}$$
$$AP_{1,1}, AP_{1,2}, ..., AP_{1,M} \Rightarrow x_1, y_1$$
$$AP_{2,1}, AP_{2,2}, ..., AP_{2,M} \Rightarrow x_2, y_2$$
$$AP_{3,1}, AP_{3,2}, ..., AP_{3,M} \Rightarrow x_3, y_3$$
$$...$$
$$AP_{N,1}, AP_{N,2}, ..., AP_{N,M} \Rightarrow x_N, y_N$$

Each row in this radiomap represents a data entry. This process can be executed before a client uses the localization service, and only needs to be performed once. Whenever a client needs a localization service, she first measures its WiFi RSS value of each AP at current location, denoted as $V' = (v'_1, v'_2, ..., v'_N)$. Then she chooses one AP-id, named j, from her vicinity and sends this AP-id (j) to the server. After receiving the port number of the AP, the server searches its MATRIX and finds out all the data entries that have nonzero signal value at this AP, where $AP_{i,j} \neq 0$, $i \in (\alpha_1, \alpha_2, ..., \alpha_l)$, then the server renumbers the indices of those data entries and forms a map $(i, signal)_{i=1}^l$ between the renumbered indices and their corresponding signal values at this AP, after that the server sends the map to the client. Meanwhile, the server finds out the union set of APs that have nonzero signal value at these data entries, $C = \{\beta_1, \beta_2, ..., \beta_n\}$ where $AP_{\alpha_1, \beta_1}, AP\alpha_2, \beta_2, ..., AP\alpha_l, \beta_n \neq 0$, and sends the set of port numbers of these APs $(C = \{\beta_1, \beta_2, ..., \beta_n\})$ to the client, which indicates the delivery order of signal values at Oblivious Transfer Phase. The sever will send these signal values and their corresponding coordinates by column. For example, if 2 is included in $\{\beta_1, \beta_2, ..., \beta_n\}$, then the server will send the signal value at AP_2 of these chosen data entries in a transfer process in Oblivious Transfer Phase.

Oblivious Transfer Phase. Considering the map $(i, signal)_{i=1}^l$ received by the client, first, the client finds out the k nearest data entries based on their RSS values, then masks her choices $C = \{\sigma_1, \sigma_2, ..., \sigma_k\}$ by oblivious transfer. Eventually, the server sends other APs' signal values in accordance with the order in $C = \{\beta_1, \beta_2, ..., \beta_n\}$ and their corresponding coordinates one by one.

For system parameters, g, h is two generators of G_q, and $\log_g h$ is not revealed to any party. (g, h, G_q) are universal parameters, which means they can be used repeatedly by all possible clients and the server if $\log_g h$ is not revealed.

During each transfer, the server sends the signal value of l data entries at AP_j, $j \in \{\beta_1, \beta_2, ..., \beta_n\}$, denoted as $m_1, m_2, ..., m_l$. The procedure of each transfer of signal value is as follows:

– System parameters: (g, h, G_q);
– Server has messages: $m_1, m_2, ..., m_l$;
– Client's choices: $\sigma_1, \sigma_2, ..., \sigma_k$;
  1. Client chooses two polynomials:

$$f(x) = a_0 + a_1 x + ... + a_{k-1} x^{k-1} + x^k \tag{4}$$

$$f'(x) = b_0 + b_1 x + ... + b_{k-1} x^{k-1} + x^k \tag{5}$$

  where $a_0, a_1, ..., a_{k-1} \in Z_q$ and $b_0 + b_1 x + ... + b_{k-1} x^{k-1} + x^k = (x - \sigma_1)(x - \sigma_2)...(x - \sigma_k) \bmod q$.
  2. Client to Server:

$$A_0 = g^{a_0} h^{b_0}$$
$$A_1 = g^{a_1} h^{b_1}$$
$$...$$
$$A_{k-1} = g^{a_{k-1}} h^{b_{k-1}} \tag{6}$$

  3. Server computes

$$d_i = (g^{k_i}, m_i B_i^{k_i}) \tag{7}$$

  where $k_i \in Z_q^*$ and

$$B_i = g^{f(i)} h^{f'(i)}$$
$$= A_0 A_1^i ... A_{k-1}^{i^{k-1}} (gh)^{i^k} \bmod p \tag{8}$$

  for $i = 1, 2, ..., l$.
  4. Server to Client: $d_1, d_2, ..., d_l$.
  5. Let $d_i = (U_i, V_i)$, the client computes $m_{\sigma_i} = V_{\sigma_i} / U_{\sigma_i}^{f(\sigma_i)} \bmod p$ for each σ_i.

First, the client constructs a k-degree polynomial $f'(x)$, which satisfies $f'(i) = 0$ if and only if $i \in \{\sigma_1, \sigma_2, ..., \sigma_k\}$. Next, another random k-degree polynomial $f(x)$ is selected to mask the chosen polynomial $f'(x)$. Then, the client sends the masked choices $A_0, A_1, ..., A_{k-1}$ to the server.

After the server receives these requests, he first computes $B_i = g^{f(i)} h^{f'(i)}$ by computing $A_0 A_1^i ... A_{k-1}^{i^{k-1}} (gh)^{i^k} \bmod p$. The server has no idea of which $f'(i)$ is equal to zero, for $i = 1, 2, ..., n$ because of the random polynomial $f(x)$. Next, the server encrypts each message m_i by public key B_i. Then, the server sends the encrypted messages $d_1, d_2, ..., d_k$ to the client.

For each d_i, $i \in \{\sigma_1, \sigma_2, ..., \sigma_k\}$, since $B_i = g^{f(i)}h^{f'(i)} = g^{f(i)}h^0 = g^{f(i)}$, the client can get these messages with secret key $f(i)$. If $i \notin \{\sigma_1, \sigma_2, ..., \sigma_k\}$, since the client cannot compute $(g^{f(i)}h^{f'(i)})^{k_i}$ with the knowledge of g^{k_i} and $f(i), f'(i)$ only, the client gets no access to the message m_i.

Correctness. For each message received by the client $d_i = (U_i, V_i)$, the chosen messages m_{σ_i}, $i = 1, 2, ..., k$, are computed as

$$
\begin{aligned}
V_{\sigma_i}/U_{\sigma_i}^{f(\sigma_i)} &= m_{\sigma_i} * (g^{f(\sigma_i)}h^{f'(\sigma_i)})^{k_{\sigma_i}}/g^{k_{\sigma_i}f(\sigma_i)} \\
&= m_{\sigma_i} * (g^{f(\sigma_i)} * 1)^{k_{\sigma_i}}/g^{k_{\sigma_i}f(\sigma_i)} \quad (9) \\
&= m_{\sigma_i}
\end{aligned}
$$

Location Determination Phase. In this phase, the user computes the squared Euclidean distance d_i between V' and V_i, $i = 1, 2, ..., k$. Then, it sorts the distances and determines the q smallest distances $d_{I_1}, d_{I_2}, ..., d_{I_q}$. These q nearest neighbors form C. Finally, the client estimates her location by computing the centroid of the q neighbors.

$$
\begin{cases}
\| V'_h - V_1 \| = \sum_{j=1}^{N}(v'_{h,j} - v_{1,j})^2 = d_{h,1} \\
\| V'_h - V_2 \| = \sum_{j=1}^{N}(v'_{h,j} - v_{2,j})^2 = d_{h,2} \\
... \\
\| V'_h - V_k \| = \sum_{j=1}^{N}(v'_{h,j} - v_{k,j})^2 = d_{h,k}
\end{cases} \quad (10)
$$

$$
\begin{cases}
x = \frac{\sum_{j \in C} x_j}{q} \\
y = \frac{\sum_{j \in C} y_j}{q}
\end{cases} \quad (11)
$$

3.3   Parameter Set

Considering the accuracy-overhead balanced construction and the restriction of oblivious transfer protocol, we must carefully choose parameters which are involved in the localization process.

Locations and Access Points. As the previous descriptions have stated, N access points are selected to measure WiFi signal strengths to represent a specific indoor location, and these access points should be chosen to efficiently differentiate each location. For example, an AP that has very low RSS values on all locations should be eliminated due to its neglectable effect on localization process. Moreover, the M sampled locations should be distinct from each other and evenly distributed to represent the building's floor plan as detailed as possible.

Number of Data Entries in the Map. After receiving the port number of the AP from the client, the server searches its MATRIX and finds out all the data entries that have nonzero signal value at this AP, then the server forms a map $(i, signal)$, $i \in [1, l]$ and sends it to the client. Note that the number of data entries in the map is the totality of choices in Oblivious Transfer Phase, which remains as a constant during localization process, denoted as l. Different queries may have different l because the AP id chosen by the client may vary when her current location varies, and the number of data entries that have nonzero signal value at this chosen AP varies as the AP id changes. According to the system process displayed before, l has a deep influence on system performance.

Size of k. In Oblivious Transfer Phase, the client finds out the k nearest data entries based on their RSS values, then masks her choices by oblivious transfer. An oversize k will lead to the unnecessary exposure of server's database and extend the process of query. However, if the size of k is too small, the alternative set will be too small that the client will be unable to compute her location accurately. Thus, an appropriate k is needed to balance precision, privacy and overhead.

3.4   Communication Cost

The communication cost in localization scheme mainly centers on Oblivious Transfer Phase which uses two rounds, $O(k)$ messages are sent in the first round, where the client asks for k data entries from the server, then $O(l)$ messages are sent in the second round, where the server responds for the request. As for computation, the client computes $3k + 2$ and the server computes $(k + 2)l$ modular exponentiations. The complexity analysis results are summarized in Table 1.

Table 1. Complexity analysis results

Phases	Communication	Computation (Exp)
Client to Server	$O(k)$	$3k + 2$
Server to Client	$O(l)$	$(k + 2)l$

3.5   Security Analysis

In Sect. 2, we presented two attack models related to the privacy of user and database. The security analysis of these models is represented in this section.

Theorem 1. OTPri is resistent to user privacy attack.

Proof. Pre-process Phase: From the client's perspective, the client only provides the server with the id of AP from her vicinity. Therefore, the server can only confirm a wider area of the client's location.

Oblivious Transfer Phase: Client's privacy-indistinguishability-If there is x in C, but not in C', or vice versa, we say two sets C and C' are diverse. In oblivious transfer phase, the transcript of the choice $C = \{\sigma_1, \sigma_2, ..., \sigma_k\}$ received by the server is indistinguishable from the transcript of $C' = \{\sigma'_1, \sigma'_2, ..., \sigma'_k\}$. Which means if the received messages of the server for C and C' are identically distributed, the choices of the client are unconditionally secure.

For choices $C = \{\sigma'_1, \sigma'_2, ..., \sigma'_k\}$, every tuple $(b'_0, b'_1, ..., b'_{k-1})$ that represents the choices corresponds to a tuple $(a'_0, a'_1, ..., a'_{k-1})$ that satisfies $A_i = g^{a'_i} h^{b'_i}$ for $i = 0, 1, ..., k - 1$. Therefore, the client's choices are unconditionally secure.

Location Determination Phase: Since Location Determination Phase is conducted locally at the client's side, neither server nor any other third party can acquire the client's location or her sampled WiFi RSS signals, thus the client's location privacy is naturally preserved.

Theorem 2. OTPri is resistent to database privacy attack.

Proof. Pre-Process Phase: Since the index of map $(i, signal)$, $i \in [1, l]$ sent from the server to the client is renumbered before sending it to the client, the client is unable to realize the original mapping between index and RSS signal value of the MATRIX.

Oblivious Transfer Phase: Server's security-indistinguishability-For any choices that don't belong to set $C = \{\sigma_1, \sigma_2, ..., \sigma_k\}$, they should be indistinguishable from the random ones. Which means the client gets no information about messages m_i if she is semi-honest, $i \notin \{\sigma_1, \sigma_2, ..., \sigma_k\}$.

We prove that m_is look random if the DDH assumption holds, $i \notin \{\sigma_1, \sigma_2, ..., \sigma_k\}$. First, the random variable for the unchosen messages is defined below:

$$C = (g, h, (g^{k_{i_1}}, m_{i_1}(g^{f(i_1)}h^{f'(i_1)})^{k_{i_1}}), ...,$$
$$(g^{k_{i_{i-k}}}, m_{i_{n-k}}(g^{f(i_{n-k})}h^{f'(i_{n-k})})^{k_{i_{n-k}}}))$$

where $k_{i_1}, k_{i_2}, ..., k_{i_{n-k}} \in {}_R Z_q^*$. Since the polynomial $f(x)$ and $f'(x)$ are selected by the client, besides, $f'(i_1), ..., f'(i_{n-k}) \neq 0$, C can be simplified as below:

$$C' = (g, h, (g^{k_{i_1}}, h^{k_{i_1}}), ..., (g^{k_{i_{n-k}}}, h^{k_{i_{n-k}}}))$$

In multiple samples, the indistinguishability is preserved. Therefore, the prove of the following two distributions

- $C = (g, h, g^r, h^r)$, where $h \neq 1$, $r \in {}_R Z_q^*$
- $X = (g, h, x_1, x_2)$, where $h \neq 1$, $x_1, x_2 \in {}_R G_q$

are distinguishable by a polynomial-time distinguisher D is necessary. To solve the DDH problem, we can construct another polynomial-time machine D', whose sub-routine is D.

Machine D'

Input : (g, u, v, w) (eitherfrom Y_1 or Y_2 in DDH)

Output : $D(g, u, v, w)$

If D distinguishes C and X with non-negligible advantage ε, D' distinguishes Y_1, Y_2 in the DDH problem with at least non-negligible advantage $\varepsilon - 2/q$, where $dist(C, Y_1) = 1/q$ and $dist(X, Y_2) = 1/q$.

Therefore, the indistinguishability is naturally proved.

Even if the communication between the server and client is intercepted by a third-party, due to the characteristic of oblivious transfer, the third-party cannot obtain the data because the message between the server and client is encrypted in Oblivious Transfer Phase, and the decryption requires the knowledge of client's choices, which are only grasped by the client.

4 Experiment Results

In this section, several experiments are conducted to demonstrate the performance of OTPri scheme. And We compare the performance of OTPri system with another privacy-preserving fingerprint-based localization system PriWFL [15].

4.1 Experiment Setup

To simulate the real circumstances to the greatest extent and thoroughly evaluate the performance of OTPri, we employ two scenarios in our experiment. One is a single-floor scenario, and the other one is a two-floor scenario. The experiment is carried out in our department's compound buildings, consisting of five buildings connected by two corridors, including laboratory rooms with different sizes, long narrow corridors and arc spaces. Its purpose is to evaluate the performance of our scheme in the context of a large and complicated scenario.

In the data collection process of our experiment, at each sampled location, we measure the values of received signal strength of 425 WiFi APs and sustain the measurement for 30 s to record the change of the RSS values during this period, then take the average as the averaged RSS values. We use DELL Vostro 2420 Laptop with Linux system and an IEEE 802.11 Atheros Communications AR9485 Wireless Network Adapter to receive signals from each access point. Here we regard the various APs as the same because the type of them cannot be controlled.

4.2 Performance in a Single Floor

First, our experiment is conducted in the first floor of our office building. We choose 111 points to build the database and 40 points as queries. The queries are selected to represent as many typical places as possible. This data set contains 353 APs. Our experiments in this section mainly discuss how variables influence the precision and time performance of our proposed scheme. We use localization precision and time cost for a query as two metrics to evaluate the performance of our scheme.

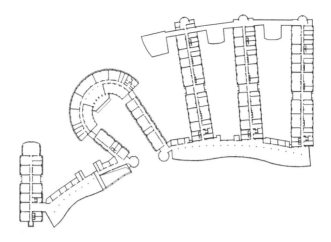

Fig. 2. Floor plan of department building

Precision vs. k. In this section, we vary k to explore the relationship between the precision of our scheme and the variable k. As analyzed before, an appropriate k is needed to balance precision, privacy and overhead. Figure 3 shows the cumulative distribution function (CDF) of localization errors both in the baseline algorithm PriWFL and the proposed scheme OTPri in this paper. As depicted in the figure, OTPri provides a 40% error of 3.6 m and a 80% error of 6.6 m when $k = 5$, then the precision remains almost the same when k continues to grow, which achieves a similar accuracy with PriWFL. In order to obtain the best performance, at least 5 candidates are needed to determine the client's location (Fig. 2).

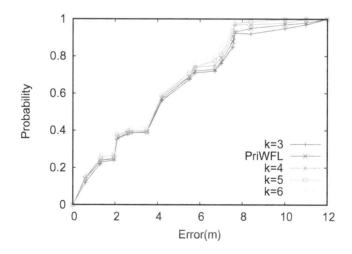

Fig. 3. Precision in a single floor when k varies

Time vs. l. As analyzed in Sect. 3, the major time cost is from Oblivious Transfer Phase. Since it is k-out-of-l oblivious transfer, the scheme performance will be influenced as l varies. As experiment setup, we set k as 3 and configure l as 6, 8, 10, 12 and 14 to evaluate the average run time of the scheme. Figure 4 depicts the relationship between the time cost and l. From this figure we can observe that the time cost increases from 3.003 s to 7.018 s as l increases. Compared with other privacy-preserving scheme that costs at least 12 s each query when 15 access points are considered [15], our scheme is more practical and efficient, thus showing enormous potential in practical utility.

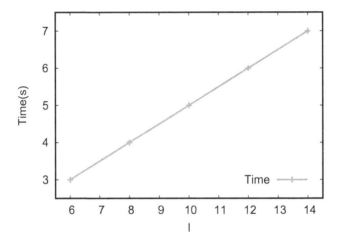

Fig. 4. Time for query in a single floor when l varies

Time vs. k. In this section, we evaluate the time performance of the scheme when k varies, we set l as 8 by default and configure k as 2, 3, 4, 5 and 6, then measure the time cost under different k settings. As depicted in Fig. 5, the time cost increases from 3.153 s to 7.250 s as k increases.

4.3   Performance in Multiple Floors

We test the performance of our scheme in a multi-floor scenario. In this scenario, there are as many as 425 APs. The fingerprint database consists of 222 locations and 84 queries, separately 40 and 44 for the first and second floor. The arrangement of fingerprint database locations and queries are mostly symmetric in the two floors. Apart from (x, y) coordinates to locate the points, we add the third dimension z to form a 3D scenario. Separately we assume the points in the first and second floor have $z = 8$ and 12. When the estimated z for each query is less than 10, we believe it is in the first floor and when z is larger than 10, it is in the second floor. We analyze the precision achieve and time cost reduction by our scheme in this section.

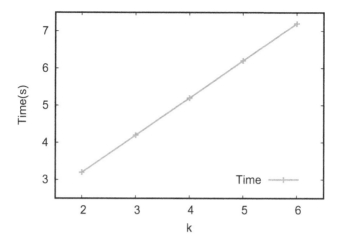

Fig. 5. Time for query in a single floor when k varies

Precision in Multiple Floors. First we calculate the cumulative distribution function (CDF) of the error. The default configuration is $k = 5$. As shown in Fig. 6, our OTPri scheme performs with a 25% error of 1.9 m and 60% error of 4.7 m, while PriWFL has a 25% error of 2.3 m and 60% error of 5.0m. It is obvious that our scheme works better in this case. We can see from this result that turning the 2D floor plan into 3D does not influence much of the precision. In fact, of all queries, 100% of them are located correctly to their own floors. The maximum estimated height of the first-floor points is 8.8 m and the minimum estimated height of the second-floor points is 10.7 m.

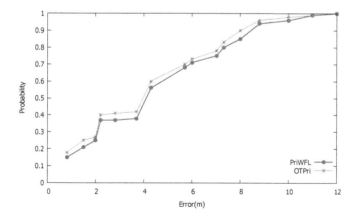

Fig. 6. Precision in multi-floor scenario

To further look into how floors are identified for the queries, we record the top 5, 10, 20, 50 and 100 candidates with the nearest signal values at a specific AP and count their occurrences. The histogram is shown in Fig. 7. Averagely 92.5% of the top 5 candidates for queries in floor 1 are in the same floor. For queries in floor 2, the number is 90.9%. This is enough to identify a query's floor since most choices of the client are within 5. Naturally, as c grows, there's a tendency that this percentage decreases because more candidates that have a near distance in other floors are added. As c increases, the percentage of candidates being in the same floor with queries approximates 0.5.

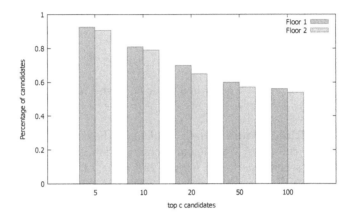

Fig. 7. Percent of candidates

Time Cost in Multiple Floors

Time vs. l. As experiment setup, we set k as 5 and configure l as 6, 8, 10, 12 and 14 to evaluate the average run time of the scheme. Figure 8 depicts the relationship between the time cost and l. From this figure we can observe that the time cost increases from 3.013 s to 6.961 s as l increases. Comparatively, our scheme shows a great advantage in practical uses even in larger scenario. Moreover, the query time grows linearly with l, showing a predictable upper bound for any l.

Time vs. k. We evaluate the time performance of the scheme in multi-floor scenario when k varies, we set l as 8 by default and configure k as 2, 3, 4, 5 and 6, then measure the time cost under different k settings. As depicted in Fig. 9, the time cost increases from 3.253 s to 7.321 s as k increases.

Analysis on Wi-Fi Access Point Number and Database Size. So far in all of our experiments, the full database is used, consisting of 425 Wi-Fi access points and 222 database locations in the two floors. However, in this section, we perform a sensitivity analysis to see how many APs and locations in the database

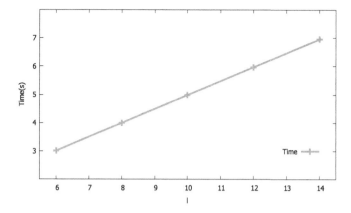

Fig. 8. Time for query in multi floors when l varies

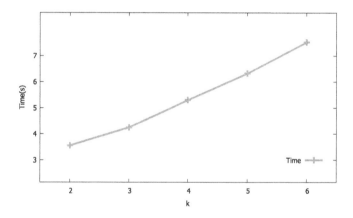

Fig. 9. Time for query in multi floors when k varies

are actually needed to calculate an accurate coordinate of a query. We keep certain portion of APs and database points, and run our OTPri scheme to see the median value of errors. Specifically, the APs and points are chosen evenly with a certain stride. For instance, we select APs with order number 1, 4, 7, 10, ...

Figures 10 and 11 shows the median error when different number of Wi-Fi access points n and location points m are used. It is obvious that larger m and n both lead to smaller errors. In order to obtain the best performance, at least 50 Wi-Fi APs and 80% of the fingerprint database are needed. In the case of Wi-Fi APs, the median error decreases sharply from around 20 m to 3 m until AP number reaches 50, then it remains almost the same when AP number continues to grow. So we can safely use an AP number of 50 in this scenario. As for the points in the fingerprint database, though the median error also declines very fast till 60% of the database is used, it continues to decline at a much lower rate when more than 60% is used, indicating that a larger data set still leads to a better performance.

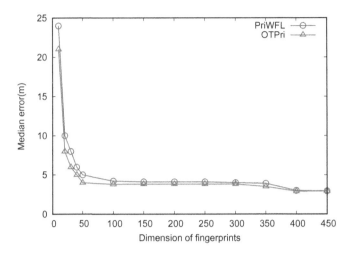

Fig. 10. Median error with different AP numbers

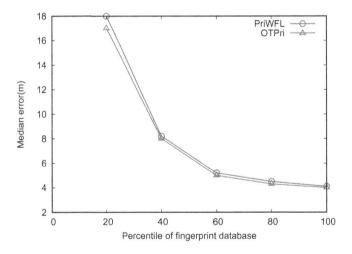

Fig. 11. Median error with different database size

Bandwidth Cost in Oblivious Transfer Phase. In this section, we configure k as 5 and the number of WiFi access points as 425, then investigate the impact of database size M on the bandwidth cost of Oblivious Transfer Phase and compare the results with PriWFL [15]. We observe from Fig. 12 that as M increases from 50 to 400, the bandwidth cost increases from 6.018 KB to 50.009 KB, which is much less than PriWFL [15].

Discussion. The experimental results show that our scheme achieves a similar performance approach in terms of precision but significantly lower online computation overhead and thus total protocol execution latency and energy

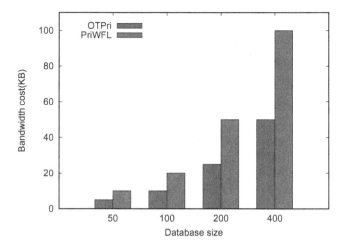

Fig. 12. Bandwidth cost

consumption compared with PriWFL, making it more practical than PriWFL to realize privacy-preserving indoor localization.

Two directions need to be investigated to further reduce the execution time delay of our scheme. First, we can employ advanced network with higher transmission speed to reduce the transmission time [32]. Since a growing number of existing mobile devices support advanced network, the transmission time will be substantially reduced. Second, we can further optimize the Java implementation of Oblivious Transfer [13] to reduce the online operation time.

5   Related Work

In this section, we discuss two related research works, including indoor localization based on signal-fingerprint and privacy-preserving indoor localization.

5.1   Fingerprint-Based Indoor Localization

Among all of the fingerprint-based localization schemes, there are other methods apart from harnessing WiFi signal strengths as fingerprints for locating. Classical works including the famous RADAR [2,3], Horus [33], OIL [22], PlaceLab [14], LANDMARC [20] employ RF signals as identification for each location. And other sources of signatures have also been explored, including geo-magnetism, FM radio [5], background acoustic noise, etc. SurroundSense [1] uses ambience features like sound, light, color as fingerprints, thus the options for fingerprinting techniques are largely diversified. Through abstracting these signatures into fingerprints, a location in indoor area can be represented by these fingerprints, and a nearer fingerprint usually indicates a nearer location, thus we can utilize these fingerprints to estimate user's location. However, these approaches demand a thorough site survey to build up the fingerprint database. If these fingerprints can be abstracted into numbers, our proposed scheme can be applied.

5.2 Privacy-Preserving Indoor Localization

To protect the client's location privacy and the server's data security during localization process, several techniques have been proposed to achieve privacy-preserving indoor localization. A common approach is to encrypt the communication between users and servers with cryptosystems. Li et al. proposed Pri-WFL scheme [15] to encrypt the localization process with Paillier cryptosystem. Though secure enough, the performance decreases in larger scenarios. Li and Jung [16] designed a suite of privacy-preserving location query protocols to balance the required privacy guarantee and computation overhead. In another similar work, Shu et al. [26] employed information hiding and homomorphic encryption techniques to design multi-lateral privacy-preserving localization protocols for three privacy levels. Other schemes, including k-anonymity [11,17,31] and mix zones [4], employ pseudonyms to prevent server from tracking of user's real location or its long-term movements. Vu et al. [27] used locality-sensitive hashing to partition the users into k-anonymous groups. There are four categories in protection strategy of location privacy: (1) regulatory approaches, (2) privacy policy based approaches, (3) anonymity based approaches, and (4) obfuscation based approaches.

Most of these techniques require communication through a trusted third intermediary, which may not be not practical in some real-life settings.

6 Conclusion and Future Work

In this work, we have proposed a privacy-preserving WiFi fingerprint-based localization scheme employing oblivious transfer called OTPri. By employing oblivious transfer in this scheme, the client can locally compute her location with no need for transmission of the whole database. Meanwhile, the client only has to expose a single AP id from its vicinity, moreover, the client cannot learn anything other than her choices, thus preserving the client's and server's data privacy. Through analysis, we have proved that this scheme guarantees fast localization and small overhead while preserving both the privacy of server and clients via oblivious transfer. Finally, experiments based on comprehensive dataset are conducted to prove the effectiveness of the scheme, and the results show that OTPri achieves a much better time performance and much less overhead compared with PriWFL approach. Meanwhile, the experimental studies have shown that OTPri achieves a similar performance compared with the PriWFL approach in terms of precision.

We can investigate a few directions for our future work. First, there are other efficient schemes for privacy-preserving indoor localization. Second, it would be interesting if we expand the experiments to additional public facilities with WiFi coverage, such as coffee shops, libraries, or grocery stores, to characterize and measure the performance of the proposed scheme, and use different measurements for location privacy, such as the one in [25].

References

1. Azizyan, M., Constandache, I., Choudhury, R.R.: Surroundsense: mobile phone localization via ambience fingerprinting. In: Proceedings of the 15th Annual International Conference on Mobile Computing and Networking, pp. 261–272. ACM (2009)
2. Bahl, P., Padmanabhan, V.N.: RADAR: an in-building RF-based user location and tracking system. In: Proceedings of the Nineteenth Annual Joint Conference of the IEEE Computer and Communications Societies (INFOCOM 2000), vol. 2, pp. 775–784. IEEE (2000)
3. Bahl, P., Padmanabhan, V.N., Balachandran, A.: Enhancements to the radar user location and tracking system. Microsoft Research, 2(MSR-TR-2000-12), pp. 775–784 (2000)
4. Beresford, A.R., Stajano, F.: Mix zones: user privacy in location-aware services. In: Proceedings of the Second IEEE Annual Conference on Pervasive Computing and Communications Workshops, pp. 127–131. IEEE (2004)
5. Chen, Y., Lymberopoulos, D., Liu, J., Priyantha, B.: FM-based indoor localization. In: Proceedings of the 10th International Conference on Mobile Systems, Applications, and Services, pp. 169–182. ACM (2012)
6. Chu, C.-K., Tzeng, W.-G.: Efficient k-out-of-n oblivious transfer schemes with adaptive and non-adaptive queries. In: Vaudenay, S. (ed.) PKC 2005. LNCS, vol. 3386, pp. 172–183. Springer, Heidelberg (2005). https://doi.org/10.1007/978-3-540-30580-4_12
7. Du, X., Chen, H.H.: Security in wireless sensor networks. IEEE Wireless Commun. **15**(4), 60–66 (2008)
8. Du, X., Guizani, M., Xiao, Y., Chen, H.-H.: Secure and efficient time synchronization in heterogeneous sensor networks. IEEE Trans. Veh. Technol. **57**(4), 2387–2394 (2008)
9. Du, X., Xiao, Y., Chen, H.-H., Wu, Q.: Secure cell relay routing protocol for sensor networks. Wirel. Commun. Mob. Comput. **6**(3), 375–391 (2006)
10. Du, X., Xiao, Y., Guizani, M., Chen, H.-H.: An effective key management scheme for heterogeneous sensor networks. Ad Hoc Netw. **5**(1), 24–34 (2007)
11. Hei, X., Du, X., Wu, J., Hu, F.: Defending resource depletion attacks on implantable medical devices. In: Global Telecommunications Conference (GLOBECOM 2010), pp. 1–5. IEEE (2010)
12. Huang, W., Xiong, Y., Li, X.-Y., Lin, H., Mao, X., Yang, P., Liu, Y.: Shake and walk: acoustic direction finding and fine-grained indoor localization using smartphones. In: Proceedings of IEEE INFOCOM, pp. 370–378. IEEE (2014)
13. Ishai, Y., Kilian, J., Nissim, K., Petrank, E.: Extending oblivious transfers efficiently. In: Boneh, D. (ed.) CRYPTO 2003. LNCS, vol. 2729, pp. 145–161. Springer, Heidelberg (2003). https://doi.org/10.1007/978-3-540-45146-4_9
14. LaMarca, A., et al.: Place lab: device positioning using radio beacons in the wild. In: Gellersen, H.-W., Want, R., Schmidt, A. (eds.) Pervasive 2005. LNCS, vol. 3468, pp. 116–133. Springer, Heidelberg (2005). https://doi.org/10.1007/11428572_8
15. Li, H., Sun, L., Zhu, H., Lu, X., Cheng, X.: Achieving privacy preservation in wifi fingerprint-based localization. In: Proceedings of IEEE INFOCOM, pp. 2337–2345. IEEE (2014)
16. Li, X.-Y., Jung, T.: Search me if you can: privacy-preserving location query service. In: Proceedings of IEEE INFOCOM, pp. 2760–2768. IEEE (2013)

17. Liu, X., Liu, K., Guo, L., Li, X., Fang, Y.: A game-theoretic approach for achieving k-anonymity in location based services. In: Proceedings of IEEE INFOCOM, pp. 2985–2993. IEEE (2013)

18. Ma, L., Teymorian, A.Y., Cheng, X.: A hybrid rogue access point protection framework for commodity wi-fi networks. In: The 27th Conference on Computer Communications (INFOCOM 2008), pp. 1220–1228. IEEE (2008)

19. Mohapatra, D., Suma, S.: Survey of location based wireless services. In: IEEE International Conference on Personal Wireless Communications (ICPWC 2005), pp. 358–362. IEEE (2005)

20. Ni, L.M., Liu, Y., Lau, Y.C., Patil, A.P.: LANDMARC: indoor location sensing using active RFID. Wirel. Netw. **10**(6), 701–710 (2004)

21. Otsason, V., Varshavsky, A., LaMarca, A., de Lara, E.: Accurate GSM indoor localization. In: Beigl, M., Intille, S., Rekimoto, J., Tokuda, H. (eds.) UbiComp 2005. LNCS, vol. 3660, pp. 141–158. Springer, Heidelberg (2005). https://doi.org/10.1007/11551201_9

22. Park, J.-G., Charrow, B., Curtis, D., Battat, J., Minkov, E., Hicks, J., Teller, S., Ledlie, J.: Growing an organic indoor location system. In: Proceedings of the 8th International Conference on Mobile Systems, Applications, and Services, pp. 271–284. ACM (2010)

23. Priyantha, N.B., Chakraborty, A., Balakrishnan, H.: The cricket location-support system. In: Proceedings of the 6th Annual International Conference on Mobile Computing and Networking, pp. 32–43. ACM (2000)

24. Priyantha, N.B., Miu, A.K., Balakrishnan, H., Teller, S.: The cricket compass for context-aware mobile applications. In: Proceedings of the 7th Annual International Conference on Mobile Computing and Networking, pp. 1–14. ACM (2001)

25. Shokri, R., Theodorakopoulos, G., Le Boudec, J.-Y., Hubaux, J.-P.: Quantifying location privacy. In: IEEE Symposium on Security and Privacy (SP), pp. 247–262. IEEE (2011)

26. Shu, T., Chen, Y., Yang, J., Williams, A.: Multi-lateral privacy-preserving localization in pervasive environments. In: Proceedings of IEEE INFOCOM, pp. 2319–2327. IEEE (2014)

27. Vu, K., Zheng, R., Gao, J.: Efficient algorithms for k-anonymous location privacy in participatory sensing. In: Proceedings of IEEE INFOCOM, pp. 2399–2407. IEEE (2012)

28. Want, R., Hopper, A., Falcao, V., Gibbons, J.: The active badge location system. ACM Trans. Inf. Syst. (TOIS) **10**(1), 91–102 (1992)

29. Xiao, Y., Du, X., Zhang, J., et al.: Internet Protocol Television (IPTV): the killer application for the next-generation Internet. IEEE Commun. Mag. **45**(11), 126–134 (2007)

30. Xiao, Y., Rayi, V.K., Sun, B., Du, X., Hu, F., Galloway, M.: A survey of key management schemes in wireless sensor networks. Comput. Commun. **30**(11), 2314–2341 (2007)

31. Yang, D., Fang, X., Xue, G.: Truthful incentive mechanisms for k-anonymity location privacy. In: Proceedings of IEEE INFOCOM, pp. 2994–3002. IEEE (2013)

32. Yao, X., Han, X., Du, X., Zhou, X.: A lightweight multicast authentication mechanism for small scale IoT applications. IEEE Sens. J. **13**(10), 3693–3701 (2013)

33. Youssef, M., Agrawala, A.: The Horus WLAN location determination system. In: Proceedings of the 3rd International Conference on Mobile Systems, Applications, and Services, pp. 205–218. ACM (2005)

An Efficient Sparse Coding-Based Data-Mining Scheme in Smart Grid

Dongshu Wang, Jialing He, Mussadiq Abdul Rahim,
Zijian Zhang$^{(\boxtimes)}$, and Liehuang Zhu

Beijing Institute of Technology, Beijing, China
zhangzijian@bit.edu.cn

Abstract. With the availability of Smart Grid, disaggregation, i.e. decomposing a whole electricity signal into its component appliances has gotten more and more attentions. Now the solutions based on the sparse coding, i.e. the supervised learning algorithm that belongs to Non-Intrusive Load Monitoring (NILM) have developed a lot. But the accuracy and efficiency of these solutions are not very high, we propose a new efficient sparse coding-based data-mining (ESCD) scheme in this paper to achieve higher accuracy and efficiency. First, we propose a new clustering algorithm – Probability Based Double Clustering (PDBC) based on Fast Search and Find of Density Peaks Clustering (FSFDP) algorithm, which can cluster the device consumption features fast and efficiently. Second, we propose a feature matching optimization algorithm – Max-Min Pruning Matching (MMPM) algorithm which can make the feature matching process to be real-time. Third, real experiments on a publicly available energy data set REDD [1] demonstrate that our proposed scheme achieves a for energy disaggregation. The average disaggregation accuracy reaches 77% and the disaggregation time for every 20 data is about 10 s.

Keywords: Smart Grid · Energy disaggregation · Sparse coding
Data mining

1 Introduction

Data mining is an efficient technique that shows the interesting patterns or knowledge from huge amount of data. These patterns play an important role in marketing, business, medical analysis, intrusion detection, and other applications where these patterns are of paramount importance for strategic decision making [21].

In Smart Grid, Energy disaggregation, the task of separating the whole energy signal of a residential, commercial, or industrial building into the energy signals of individual appliances, is a kind of important data mining method for energy-saving and by Energy disaggregation, we can disaggregate electricity consumptions to infer what device is used, how often this device is used. If this data

L. Zhu and S. Zhong (Eds.): MSN 2017, CCIS 747, pp. 133–145, 2018.
https://doi.org/10.1007/978-981-10-8890-2_10

is used by the supplier, amount of advertising fees may be saved and they can make a precise advertising for each family. They can even know which device needs to be fixed [24,25].

Studies on energy disaggregation date back to about thirty years ago. The early approaches look for sharp edges (corresponding to device on/off events) in both the real and reactive power signals, and cluster devices according to these changes in consumption [2–6]. A number of different directions has been explored, [22,23] computing harmonics of steady-state power to determine more complex device signatures, [24] analyzed the transient noise of a device circuit when the device changes state. But now for costs and convenience more and more researches focus on disaggregate electricity using low-frequency-resolution [7–9]. In this paper, we use a novel clustering algorithm based on sparse coding to disaggregate electricity in low frequency data set.

In this paper, we propose a new scheme–ESCD to make Energy disaggregation. The main contributions are as follows:

1. In the scheme we first proposes a new clustering algorithm–Probability Based Double Clustering (PBDC) based on Fast Search and Find of Density Peaks Clustering (FSFDP) algorithm in energy disaggregation, which can cluster the device consumption features fast and efficiently.
2. Our scheme proposes a feature matching optimization algorithm – Max-Min Pruning Matching (MMPM) algorithm, without any constraint condition, our algorithm can make the feature matching process to be real-time.
3. Experiments show that our scheme (ESCD) has a better Energy disaggregation accuracy and real-time performance than the sparse-coding based schemes before.

2   Related Work

The basic problem in this paper is energy disaggregation (the task of determining the component appliance contributions from an aggregated electricity signal) [1]. The user's behavior of electricity consumption can be obtained by energy disaggregation, the solutions of which are varied. According to different types of basic data sets, the solutions can be divided into two categories. The first is the scheme based on the high frequency data [10–12], and the second is based on the low frequency data [7–9,13–18]. The schemes based on the high frequency data can obtain more accurate analysis results. But the hardware for data sampling is very expensive. It requires one or more than one sensor per appliance to perform Appliance Load Monitoring (ALM). Namely Intrusive Load Monitoring (ILM) that is contrary to the issue studied in this paper. The scheme based on the low frequency data just requires only a single meter for per house or a building, the scheme is called Non-Intrusive Load Monitoring (NILM). The NILM schemes are divided into supervised [15–17] and unsupervised [7–9,18] disaggregation algorithms. Most unsupervised disaggregation algorithms are developed based on the HMM. They can have good results in estimating the total electricity consumption per device, while the analysis for the time-sharing of each device is not good compared to the supervised ones [26]. Most supervised disaggregation algorithms are based on the sparse coding. For example, [16] uses a data set provided by Plugwise which contains ten broad categories of electrical devices from several houses. It models the entire signal of each device over a long period of time, such as a week, as a sparse linear combination of the atoms of an unknown dictionary [27]. However, the drawbacks of the algorithm are that it requires a large training dataset to capture all possible times that the same device may operate and the classification times cost too long. [15] uses the data set REDD, it proposes a concept: powerlets – a small period time, the electricity consumption of device measured by 'powerlets' and decoded by Dissimilarity-based Sparse subset Selection (DS3) [19] algorithm. The scheme can achieve the energy disaggregation accuracy of 72%, and the energy disaggregation speed is about 15 s. It is an efficient and accurate scheme, but it requires a lot of constraints, which causes the bad effect on the actual effect of this scheme. We propose a scheme in this paper, which improves the algorithm in [20]. We first use FSFDP algorithm and propose a feature matching optimization algorithm – max-min Pruning algorithm.

3   Preliminaries

We make a brief introduction to fast search and find of density peaks clustering and sparse coding.

3.1   Fast Search and Find of Density Peaks Clustering (FSFDP)

Clustering algorithm is an effective tool for data mining. Specifically, clustering analysis automatically groups things in the absence of category tag information. Each packet is self-identifying and differentiated from other groups [28].

Fast search and find of density peaks Clustering is a clustering algorithm, it is based on the idea that cluster centers are characterized by a higher density than their neighbors, and by a relatively large distance from points with higher densities. In FSFDP, the number of clusters arises intuitively, outliers are automatically spotted and excluded from the analysis, and clusters are recognized regardless of their shape and the dimensionality of the space in which they are embedded [21].

Assume that the data set $S = \{x_i\}_{i=1}^{N}$, $I_S = \{1, 2, \ldots, N\}$ to be clustered is the corresponding set of indices, and d_{ij} represents the defined distance between the data points x_i and x_j. For any data point x_i in S, we can define two quantities of ρ_i and δ_i, which are the two characteristics of the clustering center mentioned above: local density and distance, respectively.

Local density ρ_i is calculated by two ways: Cut-off kernel or Gaussian kernel. Cut-off kernel and Gaussian kernel are calculated by Eqs. 1 and 2:

$$\rho_i = \sum_{j \in I_s \backslash \{i\}} \chi(d_{ij} - d_c)\chi(x) = \begin{cases} 1, x < 0; \\ 0, x \geq 0. \end{cases} \tag{1}$$

$$\rho_i = \sum_{j \in I_s \setminus \{i\}} e^{-\left(\frac{d_{ij}}{d_c}\right)^2} \tag{2}$$

The parameter $d_c > 0$ is the cutoff distance and must be specified in advance. ρ_i represents the number of data points in the S where the distance is less than d_c (regardless of the itself). In Gaussian kernel, the distance between the data point j and i$(d_{ij} < d_c)$ is greater, the value of ρ_i is greater. The only difference is that the cut-off kernel is a discrete value and the Gaussian kernel is a continuous value, the probability of the latter is conflicting (i.e., the local density values of the same data points with the same distance) are smaller.

We calculate the distance δ_i as follows:

Let $\{q_i\}_{i=1}^N$ be a descending order of $\{\rho_i\}_{i=1}^N$, $\rho_{q_1} \geq \rho_{q_2} \geq \cdots \geq \rho_{q_N}$.

$$\delta_{q_i} = \begin{cases} \min_{q_j, j} \{d_{q_i q_j}\}, i \geq 2; \\ \max_{j \geq 2} \{d_{q_i q_j}\}, i = 1. \end{cases} \tag{3}$$

$$\delta_i = \begin{cases} \min_{j \in I_s^i} \{d_{ij}\}, I_s^i \neq \Phi; \\ \max_{j \in I_s} \{d_{ij}\}, I_s^i = \Phi. \end{cases} \tag{4}$$

The set $I_s^i = \{k \in I_s : \rho_k > \rho_i\}$, when x_i has the maximum local density, δ_i represents the distance between the data point and x_i with the largest distance from x_i in S, otherwise δ_i represents the shortest distance that in all data points with local density greater than x_i. We can choose some appropriate value of ρ_i and δ_i as critical value to cluster.

3.2 Sparse Coding

Sparse coding is a class of unsupervised methods for learning sets of over-complete bases to represent data efficiently. The aim of sparse coding is to find a set of basis vectors ϕ_i such that we can represent an input vector X as a linear combination of these basis vectors [21]:

$$X = \sum_{i=1}^k a_i \phi_i \tag{5}$$

We define sparsity as having few non-zero components or having few components not close to zero. The requirement that our coefficients a_i be sparse means that given a input vector, we would like as few of our coefficients to be far from zero as possible. The choice of sparsity as a desired characteristic of our representation of the input data can be motivated by the observation that most sensory data such as natural images may be described as the superposition of a small number of atomic elements such as surfaces or edges. Other justifications such as comparisons to the properties of the primary visual cortex have also been advanced [22].

We define the sparse coding cost function on a set of m input vectors as [23]:

$$\min_{a_i^{(j)}} \phi_i \sum_{j=1}^{m} \left\| X^{(j)} - \sum_{i=1}^{k} a_i^{(j)} \phi_i \right\|^2 + \lambda \sum_{i=1}^{k} S(a_i^{(j)}) \tag{6}$$

where S(.) is a sparsity cost function which penalizes a_i for being far from zero. We can interpret the first term of the sparse coding objective as a reconstruction term which tries to force the algorithm to provide a good representation of X and the second term as a sparsity penalty which forces our representation of X to be sparse. The constant λ is a scaling constant to determine the relative importance of these two contributions [29].

Although the most direct measure of sparsity is the 'L0' norm ($S(a_i) = 1(|a_i| > 0)$), it is non-differentiable and difficult to optimize in general. In practice, common choices for the sparsity cost S(.) are the L_1 penalty $S(a_i) = |a_i|_1$ and the log penalty $S(a_i) = \log(1 + a_i^2)$.

In addition, it is also possible to make the sparsity penalty arbitrarily small by scaling down a_i and scaling ϕ_i up by some large constant. To prevent this from happening, we will constrain $\|\phi^2\|$ to be less than some constant C. The full sparse coding cost function including our constraint on ϕ is

$$\min_{a_i^{(j)}} \phi_i \sum_{j=1}^{m} \left\| X^{(j)} - \sum_{i=1}^{k} a_i^{(j)} \phi_i \right\|^2 + \lambda \sum_{i=1}^{k} S(a_i^{(j)}) \tag{7}$$
$$\text{subject to } \|\phi\|^2 \le C, \forall i = 1, \dots, k$$

4   Efficient Sparse Coding-Based Data-Mining (ESCD) Scheme

In this section we propose a novel energy disaggregation scheme, ESCD Scheme. Based on sparse coding, this is an efficient and fast scheme for energy disaggregation. First, we carry out a detailed description of the problem. We assume that there are n electrical devices in a building, where $x_i(t)$ denotes the energy signal of device i at time t. $y(t)$ denotes the aggregate energy signal, recorded by a smart meter, at time t. We can write

$$y(t) = \sum_{i=1}^{n} x_i(t) \tag{8}$$

Given only the whole power consumption $y(t)$, the goal of energy disaggregation is to recover the power signal of each of the appliances, i.e., to estimate $x_i(t)$ for i $\in \{1, 2, 3, \dots, n\}$. It is very difficult to solve the formula (8) because $x_i(t)$ represents the $i - th$ electricity consumption of the device at the time t, and the electrical device is operated by the person. We can not judge the human behaviour at time t that we can't get $x_i(t)$.

In this paper, we model each electrical device with sparse coding. For every $i = 1, 2, 3, \dots, n$, n, we learn a feature matrix from training set whose frequency is q Hz, $X_i \in R^{m_i \times T_w}$, T_w we call sliding window time represents a continuous period of time from training time T_{tr} and $T_w \ll T_{tr}$. m_i represents the number of features in the $i - th$ electrical device. If we have got enough features from the $i - th$ electrical device, we can use the approximation

$$T_w \left(x_i \left(t \right) \right) \approx X_i a_i \left(t \right), T_w \left(x_i \left(t \right) \right)$$
$$= \left(x_i \left(t \right), x_i \left(t + \tfrac{1}{q} \right), x_i \left(t + 2 \times \tfrac{1}{q} \right), \ldots, x_i \left(t + T_w \right) \right) \tag{9}$$

We call the vector $T_w \left(x_i \left(t \right) \right)$ sliding window, $a_i \left(t \right)$ is the activations of feature matrix X_i, $a_i \left(t \right)$ is sparse that contain mostly zero elements and only a 1 elements. We propose a matching algorithm to get the $a_i \left(t \right)$ so that we can calculate $X_i a_i \left(t \right)$ to get an approximate solution for each device. Our scheme based on sparse coding is consist of two stages, learning feature matrix and energy matching.

4.1   Learning Feature Matrix

We propose a Probability Based Double Clustering (PBDC) algorithm to learning each of the electrical devices feature matrix. As described above, the time length of training data is T_{tr}, frequency is q Hz, there are $(T_{tr} - T_w + 1) \times q$ sliding windows, for each sliding window, we have $T_w \times q$ elements. Assume that every sliding window is a data point $P_i \in (1, (T_{tr} - T_w + 1) \times q)$, after removing the repeated points we get k unique points set P_{uniq} and a vector representing the repeat times of data points $R = (r_1, r_2, r_3, \ldots, r_k)$, we define the distance between two point $d_{ij} = \|P_i - P_j\|_2$, the distance matrix D is a k × k scale symmetric matrix with a diagonal of 0, $D = \{d_{ij}, i, j \in \{1, 2, 3, \ldots, k\}\}$, PBDC algorithm is based on FSFDP, the FSFDP algorithm needs to manually specify the minimum value of ρ and δ to determine the boundary of the cluster that to determine the number of clustering centres, this operation will lead to the instability of the number of clustering centres and can not get the scheme to be automated.

In this paper, the algorithm is improved by setting a upper limit of the number m, when clustering we will compare the difference of m and the number of clusters, and make a automatically correct until the number of clusters is similar to m. In this improved algorithm, it is only necessary to specify the upper limit of the number m of clustering centres before clustering instead of manually specify the minimum value of ρ and δ during clustering. Therefore, we can have an efficient clustering and the number of clustering centres can be stabilized at a certain controllable value. Every clustering centre is an electrical device feature, a controllable number of electrical device feature is necessary for reduce the algorithm complexity of energy matching.

After first clustering, we find some problem, the clustering result is not what we really want. According to the power consumption of electrical equipment and the relationship between time, as shown in Fig. 1.

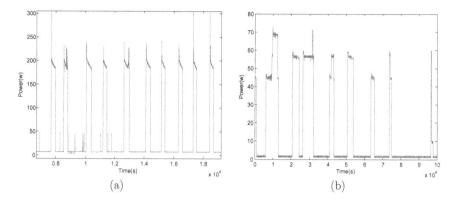

Fig. 1. (a) and (b) are the electricity consumption of refrigerator and lighting.

Algorithm 1. Learning Feature Matrix

Input: Device training data set D_{tr},
       Sliding window size w,
       The number of feature vector m.
Output: Device feature matrix X.
1. Compute P_{uniq} and R from D_{tr}
2. Compute distance matrix D:
3. **for** $i = 1, ..., size(R)$ **do**
4.   **for** $j = i, ..., size(R)$ **do**
5. $d_{ij} = \|P_i - P_j\|_2$
6.   **end for**
7. **end for**
8. First Clustering: improved FSFDP(D,m/10)
9. Second Clustering:
10. **for** $k = 1, ..., size(clusters)$ **do**
11. $C_i = num(cluster_i)/\|R\|_1$
12.   improved FSFDP(D_i,$m * C_i$)
13.   clustering result is collected to X
14.**end for**
15.**retrun** X

It is clear that after the first clustering, the centre point represents the larger distance from the data points, and the result is just judged by the data value difference, this will lead a result that some data points with small value is buried in large. In fact, we need a more comprehensive clustering to make a second clustering for improving this result.

In the second clustering, we need to do cluster for every clusters calculated in the first clustering. And we set the number of cluster by the probability set C that includes the probability C_i of each cluster. Considering the repeated points, the probability C_i of each cluster can be calculated by formula 10 and 11.

$$C_i = \frac{num\,(Cluster_i)}{\sum_{i=1}^{k} r_i} \tag{10}$$

$$num\,(Cluster_i) = \sum r_i, r_i \in \{Cluster_i\} \tag{11}$$

Assume that we need about m features in each electrical device, we can set the upper limit m × C_i for each cluster and clustering again. The algorithm details describe in Algorithm 1.

4.2   Energy Matching

According to the first stage, we obtain the feature matrix of each device X_i, as seen in formula (9), in this stage, we need to calculate $a_i\,(t)$. Considering the constraint of $a_i\,(t)$ that $a_i\,(t)$ has only one element is 1 and other is 0.

Algorithm 2. MMPM algorithm

Input: Device feature matrix $X_1 X_2 \ldots X_n$
      Test data Y.
      Pruning threshold u
Output: Disaggregation result $\tilde{Y}_1 \tilde{Y}_2 \ldots \tilde{Y}_n$
1. get the windows size w and each device feature numbers m_i
2. **while** $X_1 \neq NULL$
3.   get one feature vector form X_1
4.   compute the remainder energy $T_w\,(\mathrm{y}\,(t))$ and arg_{max}
5.   **if**$(arg_{max} > \mu || min(T_w\,(\mathrm{y}\,(t))) + \mu < 0)$
6.   break;
7.   **end if**
8.   overlay record the feature vector into $\tilde{Y}_1$
9.   ...
10.   **while** $X_n \neq NULL$
11.   get one feature vector form X_n
12.   compute the remainder energy $T_w\,(\mathrm{y}\,(t))$ and arg_{max}
13.   **if**$(arg_{max} > \mu || min(T_w\,(\mathrm{y}\,(t))) + \mu < 0)$
14.   break;
15.   **end if**
16.   overlay record the feature vector into $\tilde{Y}_n$
17.   **end while**
18.   ...
19.**end while**

In general, in order to get a globally optimal solution with n electrical devices, if the number of feature matrix in each electrical device X_i is m_i, the algorithm complexity is $O\left(\prod_{i=1}^{n} m_i\right)$. We can find that the complexity of the algorithm increases exponentially with each additional device, and the complexity of this algorithm is unacceptable. We need to do some algorithm optimization, consider that n is a constant determined by the number of equipment and m_i is the number of electrical device feature, it will lead to a poor accuracy if we reduce the m_i. We propose a Max-Min Pruning Matching (MMPM) algorithm.

The purpose of the algorithm is to perform the pruning optimization of the matching algorithm under the condition of guaranteeing the global optimum. This optimization can be divided into two operations: minimum pruning and maximum pruning, set the maximum pruning parameters for arg_{max}, the pruning threshold for μ. We first discuss the minimum pruning.

The goal of maximum pruning can make sure that we can get the global optimal solution and end the loop as soon as possible when we get the global optimal solution. To do this option, we should get the order j of the maximum element in $T_w\left(y\left(t\right)\right)$. And then sort in each feature matrix $X_i, i \in \{1, 2, 3 \ldots, n\}$ by the j-th element in descending order, we set the maximum element of feature matrix X_i in j-th column max_i. We calculate the maximum pruning parameters as below

$$arg_{max} = y\left(t + \left(j - 1\right)q\right) - \sum_{i=n-i}^{n} max_i \tag{12}$$

When $arg_{max} > \mu$, it means that the arg_{max} in remaining loop will large than the pruning threshold, the remaining loop should be cutoff.

The goal of minimum pruning aids to cut the invalid loop when the sliding windows vector is to small. In each loop, we get a remainder energy $T_w\left(r\left(t\right)\right)$ which is the difference between total energy $T_w\left(y\left(t\right)\right)$ and the upper loop, we make a minimum pruning judgement condition

$$\min\left(T_w\left(r\left(t\right)\right)\right) + \mu < 0 \tag{13}$$

If this judgement condition is set up, that proves it the remaining loop will make the $\min\left(T_w\left(r\left(t\right)\right)\right)$ more and more small, we should cut off the remaining invalid loop. The algorithm details describe in Algorithm 2.

5   Experiment Analysis

In this section, we evaluate our propose scheme on the real-world REDD data set [1], a publicly available data set for electricity disaggregation. The data set consists of power consumption signals from six different houses, where for each house, the whole electricity consumption as well as electricity consumptions of about twenty different devices are recorded. The signals from each house are collected over a period of two weeks with a low frequency sampling rate of $1/3\,\mathrm{Hz}$. The House 5 data set is excluded because of its data contains very few fluctuation that we could not extract enough features to do energy disaggregation.

In the experiment, in every house we use a month of recorded electricity signals that include 5 important household appliances, one week for learning feature matrix and the rest for energy matching. We set the size of feature matrix as $20 \times m$ that means the size of a feature vector is set to 20 and the numbers

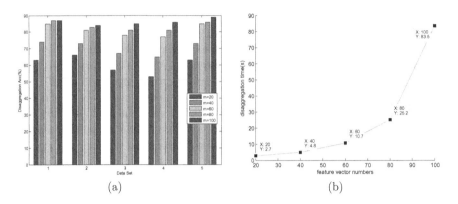

Fig. 2. (a) and (b) are the relationship of disaggregation accuracy and time with feature vector numbers.

of feature vector is set to m. The size of feature vector too small or to large may lead to a low performance because that a small size could cause excessive training and a large size could confusion the features. In order to make a real-time energy matching the numbers of feature vector m must be less than 100. With these settings, we can get five feature matrix for five household appliances, it takes about 10 s to perform energy matching on a temporal window. We compute the disaggregation accuracy, similar to [1]:

$$acc_{\text{energy matching}} = 1 - \frac{\sum\limits_{t \in \psi} \sum\limits_{i=1}^{M} \left\| T_w(x_i(t)) - \tilde{T}_w(x_i(t)) \right\|_1}{2 \sum\limits_{t \in \psi} \| T_w(x_i(t)) \|_1} \tag{14}$$

where $\psi = \{1, T_w + 1, 2T_w + 1, \dots\}$ and the 2 factor in the denominator comes from the that the absolute value results in double counting errors. We compare our method with the PED algorithm [15], FHMM algorithm (in its supervised setting) [1] and a Simple Mean prediction algorithm, which estimates the total consumption percentage of each device and predicts that the whole electricity signal breaks down according to this percentage at all time.

Figure 2 shows the disaggregation accuracy and time of our algorithm for different houses as a function of feature vector numbers m when size of a feature vector is set to 20. Table 1 shows the disaggregation results for all the six houses (exclude the House 5) in the REDD data set. Our algorithm performs better than PED, FHMM and the naive Simple Mean on the data set, achieving about 5.4% higher accuracy overall. Figure 3 shows the actual and estimated energy consumption obtained by our method for refrigerator and lighting in the House 1. Our scheme captures transients and different steady states in each device.

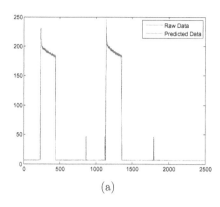
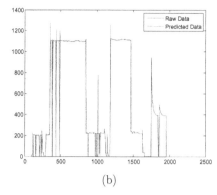

(a)   (b)

Fig. 3. (a) and (b) the actual and estimated energy consumption obtained by ESCD scheme for refrigerator and lighting in the House 1

Table 1. Energy disaggregation accuracies (%)

	House 1	House 2	House 3	House 4	House 6	Average
Simple	41.4%	39.0%	46.7%	52.7%	33.7%	42.7%
FHMM	71.5%	59.6%	59.6%	69.0%	62.9%	64.5%
PED	81.6%	79.0%	61.8%	58.5%	79.1%	72.0%
ESCD	84.3%	82.7%	70.2%	71.0%	78.9%	77.4%

6   Conclusion

In this paper, we propose a new algorithm for energy disaggregation which consists of the two steps of learning feature matrix of power consumption signatures and a energy matching for disaggregation. To learn feature matrix, based on FSFDP algorithm we propose the Probability Based Double Clustering (PBDC) algorithm to learning each of the electrical devices feature matrix, the PBDC algorithm can make a second clustering according to the first clustering points distribution probability and ensure that the clustering can extract sufficient feature vector and avoid excessive training. After we calculate feature matrix of each devices, we propose a Max-Min Pruning Matching (MMPM) energy matching algorithm for disaggregation. The MMPM algorithm can minimize computational complexity make the disaggregation be a real-time calculation. Our experiments are based on a real energy data set, we show that our scheme provides promising results for energy disaggregation.

Acknowledgment. This work is partially supported by China National Key Research and Development Program No. 2016YFB0800301.

References

1. Kolter, J.Z., Johnson, M.J.: REDD: a public data set for energy disaggregation research. In: Workshop on Data Mining Applications in Sustainability (SIGKDD), San Diego, CA, vol. 25, pp. 59–62 (2011)
2. Pinkas, B.: Cryptographic techniques for privacy-preserving data mining. SIGKDD Explor. Newsl. **4**(2), 12–19 (2002)
3. Hart, G.W.: Nonintrusive appliance load monitoring. Proc. IEEE **80**(12), 1870–1891 (1992)
4. Berges, M., Goldman, E., Matthews, H.S., Soibelman, L.: Learning systems for electric comsumption of buildings. In: ASCI International Workshop on Computing in Civil Engineering (2009)
5. Shaw, S.R., Abler, C.B., Lepard, R.F., et al.: Instrumentation for high performance nonintrusive electrical load monitoring. J. Sol. Energy Eng. **120**(3), 224–230 (1998)
6. Patel, S.N., Robertson, T., Kientz, J.A., Reynolds, M.S., Abowd, G.D.: At the flick of a switch: detecting and classifying unique electrical events on the residential power line. In: 9th International Conference on Ubiquitous Computing (UbiComp 2007) (2007)
7. Shao, H., Marwah, M., Ramakrishnan, N.: A temporal motif mining approach to unsupervised energy disaggregation. In: Proceedings of the 1st International Workshop on Non-Intrusive Load Monitoring, Pittsburgh, PA, USA, 7 May 2012
8. Zhong, M., Goddard, N., Sutton, C.: Interleaved factorial non-homogeneous hidden Markov models for energy disaggregation (2014). arXiv preprint: arXiv:1406.7665
9. Lange, H., Bergs, M.: Efficient inference in dual-emission FHMM for energy disaggregation. In: AAAI Workshop: AI for Smart Grids and Smart Buildings (2016)
10. Norford, L.K., Leeb, S.B.: Non-intrusive electrical load monitoring in commercial buildings based on steady-state and transient load-detection algorithms. Energ. Build. **24**, 51–64 (1996)
11. Shaw, S.R., Leeb, S.B., Norford, L.K., Cox, R.W.: Nonintrusive load monitoring and diagnostics in power systems. IEEE Trans. Instrum. Meas. **57**, 1445–1454 (2008)
12. Gupta, S., Reynolds, M.S., Patel, S.N.: ElectriSense: single-point sensing using EMI for electrical event detection and classification in the home. In: Proceedings of the 12th ACM International Conference on Ubiquitous Computing, Copenhagen, Denmark, pp. 139–148, 26–29 September 2010
13. Srinivasan, D., Ng, W., Liew, A.: Neural-network-based signature recognition for harmonic source identification. IEEE Trans. Power Del. **21**, 398–405 (2006)
14. Kim, H., Marwah, M., Arlitt, M., Lyon, G., Han, J.: Unsupervised disaggregation of low frequency power measurements. In: Proceedings of the 11th SIAM International Conference on Data Mining, Mesa, AZ, USA, 28–30 April 2011
15. Elhamifar, E., Sastry, S.: Energy disaggregation via learning powerlets and sparse coding. In: AAAI, pp. 629–635 (2015)
16. Kolter, J.Z., Batra, S., Ng, A.Y.: Energy disaggregation via discriminative sparse coding. In: Advances in Neural Information Processing Systems, pp. 1153–1161 (2010)
17. Gupta, M., Majumdar, A.: Nuclear norm regularized robust dictionary learning for energy disaggregation. In: 2016 24th European Signal Processing Conference (EUSIPCO), pp. 677–681. IEEE (2016)
18. Kolter, J.Z., Jaakkola, T.: Approximate inference in additive factorial HMMs with application to energy disaggregation. J. Mach. Learn. Res. **22**, 1472–1482 (2012)

19. Elhamifar, E., Sapiro, G., Sastry, S.S.: Dissimilarity-based sparse subset selection. IEEE Trans. Pattern Anal. Mach. Intell. **38**(11), 2182–2197 (2016)
20. Rodriguez, A., Laio, A.: Clustering by fast search and find of density peaks. Science **344**(6191), 1492–1496 (2014)
21. Lee, H., Battle, A., Raina, R., et al.: Efficient sparse coding algorithms. In: Advances in Neural Information Processing Systems, pp. 801–808 (2007)
22. Hoyer, P.O.: Non-negative sparse coding. In: Proceedings of the 2002 12th IEEE Workshop on Neural Networks for Signal Processing, pp. 557–565. IEEE (2002)
23. Bao, C., Ji, H., Quan, Y., et al.: Dictionary learning for sparse coding: algorithms and convergence analysis. IEEE Trans. Pattern Anal. Mach. Intell. **38**(7), 1356–1369 (2016)
24. Du, X., Guizani, M., Xiao, Y., Chen, H.H.: Secure and efficient time synchronization in heterogeneous sensor networks. IEEE Trans. Veh. Technol. **57**(4), 2387–2394 (2008)
25. Hei, X., Du, X., Wu, J., Hu, F.: Defending resource depletion attacks on implantable medical devices. In: Proceedings of IEEE GLOBECOM 2010, Miami, Florida, USA, December 2010
26. Yao, X., Han, X., Du, X., Zhou, X.: A lightweight multicast authentication mechanism for small scale IoT applications. IEEE Sens. J. **13**(10), 3693–3701 (2013)
27. Xiao, Y., Rayi, V., Sun, B., Du, X., Hu, F., Galloway, M.: A survey of key management schemes in wireless sensor networks. J. Comput. Commun. **30**(11–12), 2314–2341 (2007)
28. Du, X., Xiao, Y., Chen, H.H., Wu, Q.: Secure cell relay routing protocol for sensor networks. Wirel. Commun. Mob. Comput. **6**(3), 375–391 (2006)
29. Du, X., Guizani, M., Xiao, Y., Chen, H.H.: A routing-driven elliptic curve cryptography based key management scheme for heterogeneous sensor networks. IEEE Trans. Wirel. Commun. **8**(3), 1223–1229 (2009)

Achieving Communication Effectiveness of Web Authentication Protocol with Key Update

Zijian Zhang, Chongxi Shen, Liehuang Zhu[✉], Chen Xu,
Salabat Khan Wazir, and Chuyi Chen

Beijing Institute of Technology, Beijing, China
liehuangz@bit.edu.cn

Abstract. Today, with the presence of a large number of Man-In-The-Middle (MITM) attacks, identity authentication plays an important role in computer communication network. Series of authentication protocols have been proposed to resist against MITM attacks. Due to the lack of two-way certification between the client and the server, an attack named Man-In-The-Middle-Script-In-The-Browser (MITM-SITB) still works in most protocols. In order to protect against this kind of attack, a Channel-ID based authentication protocol named Server-Invariance-with-Strong-Client-Authentication (SISCA) is put forward. This protocol can not support key update and execute inefficiently. To solve this problem, we propose a Communication-Effectiveness-of-Web-Authentication (CEWA) protocol. We design a new certification process to make the protocol support key update, thus avoiding the risk of key leaks. Simultaneously, We designed the key storage method to manage the keys. We improve the efficiency of implementation. We also analyze its security and the experimental analysis shows the better performance of the efficiency than that in SISCA protocol.

Keywords: Man-In-The-Middle (MITM) Attack · TLS · Channel ID
Web authentication · Key update

1 Introduction

Web authentication becomes critical in computer communication network. Currently, attacks such as TLS Man-In-The-Middle (MITM) attack post a serious threat to network communication security [1,18,21,24]. Therefore, it is necessary to enable legitimate users to access authenticated server within the legal status of the user.

Several research on web authentication has been proposed. Some protocols strengthen client or server authentication to prevent attacks.

© Springer Nature Singapore Pte Ltd. 2018
L. Zhu and S. Zhong (Eds.): MSN 2017, CCIS 747, pp. 146–162, 2018.
https://doi.org/10.1007/978-981-10-8890-2_11

Origin-Bound Certificates protocol is a fresh approach to strong client authentication for the web and now people used to call it TLS Channel ID. The strengthening of client authentication enhances the entire web authentication [6].

Server Invariance with Strong Client Authentication (SISCA) is another protocol of web authentication. It enhanced the server authentication on the basis of TLS Channel ID to against the TLS MITM attacks. SISCA can effectively protect the protocol from attack, even if the attacker is able to successfully impersonate the server [7].

However, the above protocols do not have a complete and effective defense for web attacks. Some protocols have some imperfections that can be exploited by attackers. Some protocols are difficult to implement because of complex designs. Due to the realization of the method, some protocols will take up a lot of memory space and have low efficiency. None of the protocols take into account the key update problem.

In this paper, we present our scheme to solve the problems above. We summarize our contributions as described below:

(1) We propose a Communication Effectiveness of Web Authentication (CEWA) scheme, introduce its interaction process under basic model and cross-origin communication model in detail. We show that how it prevents attacks by a attack model and elaborate that how it supports key update.
(2) We formally give the security proof of the CEWA scheme through the security analysis.
(3) We show the performance of CEWA scheme comparing with SISCA through some experiments.

The rest of this paper is organized as follows. Section 2 introduces TLS channel ID, attack model and the process of SISCA. In Sect. 3, we propose the CEWA scheme under basic model and cross origin communication model. In Sect. 4, CEWA scheme is proved to be security by the security analysis. Section 5 gives an exhibition of performances between CEWA and SISCA by some experiments. Section 6 reviews the related work. Section 7 draws the conclusion.

2 Preliminaries

2.1 TLS Channel ID

With the extensive application of TLS protocol, network communication security is guaranteed. However, attacks against the TLS protocol are still endless. The presence of a man-in-the-middle attack poses a great challenge to the security of the TLS protocol [2–5].

In the TLS Handshake phase, it is assumed that an attacker can hijack a TLS session. When the client sends a ClientHello message to the server, the attacker hijacks the message and fakes the server to send a ServerHello message to the client and a forged certificate. Then the client passes the follow-up handshake protocol to achieve the communication with the attacker. While the attacker fakes the client and establishes a TLS session with the legitimate server. In the subsequent communication, the attacker can use the identity of its middleman to steal, tamper and monitor the communication between the client and the server.

In order to solve the problem of such attacks, the Origin-Bound Certificates (OBCs) protocol was proposed. The Origin-Bound Certificates protocol is a new way to enhance web authentication, which is now known as the TLS Channel ID(cid_b) [7]. It enhances the Web authentication by enhancing client authentication.

Now we briefly introduce the TLS Channel ID handshake protocol. When the client decides to establish a TLS session with the server using the cid_b, the client informs the server in the initial ClientHello message that the TLS-OBC extension is used. If the server chooses to accept using cid_b, it will respond in the SeverHello message. Then the server sends a CertificateRequest message to the client to indicate the type of certificate it supports (ECDSA, RSA, or both) [22]. The cid_b is a self-signed client certificate. When the client receives a CertificateRequest message, the client checks that whether it has generated cid_b for this server. If this cid_b already exist, the client sends this certificate to the server through the client's Certificate message. If the client links to the server for the first time or there is no acceptable cid_b, the client will generate the corresponding cid_b and send the certificate to the server through the Certificate message.

After the TLS Channel ID handshake protocol is complete, the server associates the client's cid_b with the client. When the subsequent TLS connections are initiated for communication, the server will use the cid_b to authenticate the client. When an attacker fakes the client to create TLS sessions to the server, the cid_b for the attacker will tells the server that this client is not the same client as it linked with before. Unless the attacker can still steal the private key associated with the client cid_b. Of course, this is difficult to achieve.

The TLS Channel ID is effective against some middleman attacks. However, due to the lack of the client's authentication for the server, TLS Channel ID will not be able to resist its attack when the attacker can successfully simulate the legitimate server for the client.

2.2   MITM Attack on Channel ID-Based Authentication

There are several MITM attacks exist in network communication, now we show one of them. The attacker intercepts the information among the client and server via the malicious script in the client's browser. This attack is called Man-In-The-Middle-Script-In-The-Browser (MITM-SITB) [8,9].

We assume that an attacker can successfully impersonate the legitimate server that the client will access. There are two ways to achieve this effect. One way is that the attacker has a legitimate certificate for the target server. It binds the legal public key to its own server, and has the corresponding private key. We ignore how the attacker gets the legitimate certificate. Due to the existence of the key steal attack, or the server in the key management loopholes, such assumptions exist. The second method is based on the client's awareness. The attacker did not get the legitimate server certificate or only get an invalid certificate. But because the client ignores the browser's security warning, the attacker can still successfully imitate the server to the client. We know that in order to enrich the Web application and improve the user experience, the Web server will send the scripting code to the browser and JavaScript is more used. In addition, a browser connects with a server, it can set up multiple TLS connections. Alternatively, when the browser loads a web page, it need to set up TLS connections with multiple servers. When a JavaScript loaded in the browser's TLS connections is allowed to execute, the malicious code will threaten the security of this browser if this JavaScript is malicious.

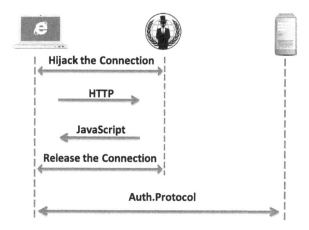

Fig. 1. MITM attack on channel ID-based authentication

Figure 1 shows the detail steps how the attacker monitors information from the communication between the client and the server. When the browser establishes a TLS session to the server, the attacker hijacks the connection so that the browser is connected to the attacker's server. After the connection is established, the browser sends an HTTP request to the attacker's server. Then the attacker's server sends a response message to the browser which contains a malicious JavaScript. Because the browser recognizes the connected server is a legitimate server, the malicious JavaScript will be executed by the browser. Then the attacker releases the connection. When the browser finds that the connection is broken, it will reestablish a new connection to the server for subsequent requests. The attacker will not hijack the connection at this time. Then the browser connects to the legitimate server and makes subsequent communications. Due to the operation of malicious code in the browser, the communication between the browser and the legitimate server will be attacked [1,7].

2.3   Server Invariance with Strong Client Authentication

Server Invariance with Strong Client Authentication (SISCA) protocol is a Channel ID-based protocol [7]. When the browser establishes a TLS connection with the server, the browser's Channel ID is called cid_b.

We now describe the server invariance protocol of SISCA in detail. This protocol includes two phases, initialization and verification.

Figure 2 illustrates the protocol. Before the connection, the server does a preparation work for the keys. It generates two keys ks_1 and ks_2. The keys are called SISCA keys. The use of the keys will run through the entire protocol process and will not leak. Accompanied by TLS connection, the client's browser will create a Channel ID cid_b.

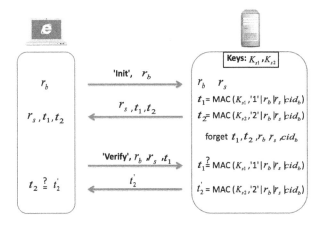

Fig. 2. Server invariance with strong client authentication

INITIALIZATION. In a browsing session, For the first time the client's browser establishes a TLS connection to the server, the initialization phase occurs. Firstly, the browser creates a random number r_b. Then it sends a request message to the server. This message includes two members, $<'Init', r_b>$ ('Init' is a string constant). Secondly, when the server receives this message, it creates a random number r_s and computes these data which are called message authentication tags as follows:

$$t_1 = MAC(ks_1,'1'|r_b|r_s|cid_b) \tag{1}$$

$$t_2 = MAC(ks_2,'2'|r_b|r_s|cid_b) \tag{2}$$

The numbers '1' and '2' in the MAC are strings constants. cid_b is the Channel ID created by the browser. Finally, the server sends a response message to the browser. This message includes three members, $<r_s, t_1, t_2>$. When the client's browser receives this message, it stores $<r_b, r_s, t_1, t_2>$. However, the server forgets $<r_b, r_s, t_1, t_2, cid_b>$. It only stores the tow SISCA keys. After these processes, the initialization phase is done.

VERIFICATION. In the same browsing session, browser's every subsequent TLS connection to the server, the initialization phase occurs. Firstly, the browser sends a request message to the server. It includes $<'Verify', r_b, r_s, t_1>$ ('Verify' is a string constant). Secondly, When the server receives the request message, it extracts the data from this message and checks if

$$t_1 \overset{?}{=} MAC(ks_1, '1'|r_b|r_s|cid_b) \qquad (3)$$

Because these two requests occur in one TLS session, cid_b from two requests are the same. If one attacker impersonates the client and intercepts the TLS connection, the cid_b is changed. The verification t_1 must be not passed. Then the server will close this session. This attack is failed. The verification will be passed with no attack. Then the server computes

$$t_2' = MAC(ks_2, '2'|r_b|r_s|cid_b) \qquad (4)$$

and sends a response message $<t_2'>$ to the browser. Finally, when the browser receives the response message, it checks if $t_2' \overset{?}{=} t_2$. If the verification is passed, the browser thinks that server invariance holds for this TLS connection.

2.4 SISCA Cross-Origin Communication

In today's web applications, many websites perform cross-origin requests. In order to solve the safety of SISCA in the cross-origin situation, the processes are changed. This leads to a SISCA protocol for cross-origin as shown in Fig. 3.

This protocol also includes two phases, initialization and verification. As we know, one client connects to different servers using different TLS Channel IDs. Therefore, how to make the verification being passed across different servers is the key to solve this problem.

The initialization phase is the same as it in SISCA. The client's browser creates a TLS connection with $server_1$ using cid_b. The cid_b is different from it in SISCA. It contains two keys, the public key pk_b and the private key sk_b.

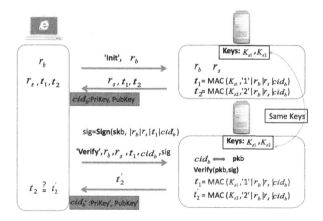

Fig. 3. SISCA cross-origin communication

Now we tell the verification phase directly. When the connection is cross to $server_2$, $server_1$ will share the SISCA keys to $server_2$. A new TLS connection is created between the client's browser and $server_2$, the browser uses a new TLS Channel ID cid_b' which contains the public key pk_b' and the private key sk_b'. Before the browser sends the request message, it signs cid_b' using the private key sk_b from cid_b. The signed data is called sig. Then the browser sends $<'Verify', r_b, r_s, t_1, sig, cid_b>$ to $server_2$. This means that the browser tells $server_2$ to verify using cid_b. Before $server_2$ makes the verification, it will make sure the request message's legality. $server_2$ decrypts sig using pk_b and compares cid_b' from sig with cid_b' from the connection. If they are matched, it means the browser owns both cid_b and cid_b' and it is legitimate. Then $server_2$ verifies t_1 and computes t_2' using cid_b. After receiving the request message with t_2' from $server_2$, the browser checks if $t_2' \overset{?}{=} t_2$.

Although SISCA can prevent MITM attack effectively, there are some security problems in caching of static resources. As we know, in order to reduce web page loading times, browser will cache static resources, such as scripts and images [13]. This will bring SISCA security risks. MITM attacker will use these static resources to do some of the attacks.

For example, when a browser plans to connect to a server, the attacker impersonates the server and intercepts the TLS connection. During the execution of the protocol, the attacker injects some static resources with malicious script into the browser. After the browser disconnects from the attacker, the static resources with malicious script in the browser will work in later processes. When the browser connects to the server, it will invoke the static resources and the malicious script in them will let the attacker monitor this communication.

To prevent this attack, SISICA let the browser make some changes in caching static resources. The browser will use Entity Tags (ETags) [23] which contain a cryptographic hash of the file when it caches static resources. Before uses the static resources, the browser will check that whether the static resources are the most recent version. The browser sends the ETags of the static resources to the server and the server checks the version. If the version does not meet the requirements, the browser will delete the static resources and the server will returns a new version.

With the increase in the number of browser usage, the caching of static resources will increase. Every time the browser uses the caching of static resources, it will verify first. This will reduce the efficiency. Also SISCA don't support key update. The two keys ks_1 and ks_2 generated by the server during the authentication phase remain unchanged. As the use of time increases, the risk of key leakage increases [14–16]. This will undoubtedly increase the insecurity. Every time before the browser uses the cached version of the file, it first verifies that the local version matches the version of the server. We know that one web page can caches lots of static resources. Browser frequent verification will reduce efficiency.

3   Communication Effectiveness of Web Authentication

3.1   The Vulnerability in SISCA

Due to the nonsupport key update, SISCA is flawed easily attacked by the attackers described in MITM attack model. The attacker can successfully pass the authentication when he gets the SISCA keys from the server. We introduce this situation as follows. When the client plans to connect the server for the first time. The attacker impersonates the server and lets the client connect with him. The client generates a random number sends r_b and sends initialization message r_b to the attacker. The attacker generates a random number r_s and computes the message authentication tags t_1, t_2 using the SISCA keys get from the server and the cid_b between attacker and client. Then he sends r_s, t_1, t_2 and the malicious script back to the client. Then the attacker lets the client connect to the server using cross-origin communication and releases the connection. The client considers the initialization phase to be completed. When starting the validation phase, it uses the SISCA cross-origin communication process to communicate with the server for the next validation communication. The client passes the authentication on the server because that the attacker has the same SISCA keys with the server. After the authentication phase, the client begins to communicate with the server. The malicious script injected into the client starts working. The attack is complete.

3.2   Communication Effectiveness of Web Authentication

We now describe the protocol of CEWA in detail. It is like a enhanced version of SISCA. We present that how CEWA support key update at first. Then we explain the problem of the storage of updated keys. Finally, we show the solution to the problem of the efficiency of the resource cache.

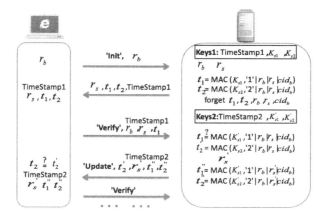

Fig. 4. Communication effectiveness of web authentication (CEWA)

Figure 4 illustrates the protocol. The same as SISCA, this server generates two keys ks_1 and ks_2, and generates a time stamp TimeStamp1 to mark these two keys. Now we call them CEWA keys.

INITIALIZATION. When the initialization phase begins, firstly, the browser creates a random number r_b. Then it sends a request message to the server. This message includes two members, $<'Init', r_b>$ ('Init' is a string constant). Secondly, when the server receives this message, it creates a random number r_s and computes these data which are called message authentication tags as follows:

$$t_1 = MAC(ks_1, '1'|r_b|r_s|cid_b) \tag{1}$$

$$t_2 = MAC(ks_2, '2'|r_b|r_s|cid_b) \tag{2}$$

The numbers '1' and '2' in the MAC are strings constants. cid_b is the Channel ID created by the browser. Finally, the server sends a response message to the browser. Different from SISCA, This message includes four members, $<r_s, t_1, t_2, TimeStamp1>$. When the client's browser receives this message, it stores $<r_b, r_s, t_1, t_2, TimeStamp1>$. The same way, the server forgets $<r_b, r_s, t_1, t_2, cid_b>$. It only stores the two CEWA keys as SISCA protocol. After these processes, the initialization phase is done.

In one keys period, the CEWA keys don't be changed. While when the keys expired, the keys will be updated. The server generates two new keys ks_1' and ks_2', and generates a new time stamp TimeStamp2 to mark these two keys. However, the server don't forget the old keys. It sets up a key list to store these keys in turn. It will store some newest key groups and forget the oldest one. We will introduce the way of key storage in later section.

VERIFICATION. When the verification phase takes place, the validation process consists of two cases whether the CEWA keys are matched.

At first, the browser sends the verification message $<'Verify', r_b, r_s, t_1, TimeStamp1>$ to the server ('Verify' is a string constant). When the server receives the verification message, he first checks whether the parameter TimeStamp1 is matched to the time stamps in its time stamp list.

In the first case, if there is a time stamp in the list that is matched to TimeStamp1 and TimeStamp1 is the newest one. Then, the verification process is the same with that in SISCA. If TimeStamp1 is not the newest one, that means the keys are updated, the server computes the following message authentication tags:

$$t_1{}' = MAC(ks_1, '1'|r_b|r_s|cid_b) \tag{3}$$

$$t_2{}' = MAC(ks_2, '2'|r_b|r_s|cid_b) \tag{4}$$

The server checks if $t_1{}' \overset{?}{=} t_1$. If they don't match, the server will send a alert message to the browser and closes the session because it considers the client is not legitimate. If they match, the server picks a new random number r_s', and computes the following message authentication tags:

$$t_1{}'' = MAC(ks_1', '1'|r_b|r_s'|cid_b) \tag{5}$$

$$t_2{}'' = MAC(ks_2', '2'|r_b|r_s'|cid_b) \tag{6}$$

After the completion of the above work, the server sends a message to the browser and forgets all of the parameters generated in the above process except CEWA keys, this message includes these parameters: 'Update', t_2', r_s', t_1'', t_2'' ('Update' is a string constant). We express this message as $<Update, t_2', r_s', t_1'', t_2'', TimeStamp2>$. When receiving the update message, the browser checks if $t_2' \overset{?}{=} t_2$ at first. If they don't match, the browser closes the session and wipes the caches because it considers the server is not legitimate. If they match, it means that the server invariance holds for this TLS connection, The browser forgets $<r_s, t_1, t_2, TimeStamp1>$ and stores $<r_b, r_s', t_1'', t_2'', TimeStamp2>$.

In the second case, If the time stamp matching is not successful, the server will send a alert message to the browser and closes the session because it considers the client is not legitimate or the time stamp of the browser is out of date.

3.3   Cross-Origin Communication

The same with SISICA, CEWA has a Cross-Origin communication model, too. This protocol also includes two phases, initialization and verification, as shown in Fig. 5. The initialization phase is the same as it in CEWA. The client's browser creates a TLS connection with $server_1$ using cid_b which contains the public key pk_b and the private key sk_b.

Now we tell the verification phase. After $server_1$ is cross to $server_2$, $server_1$ shares the key list of the browser with $server_2$. A new TLS channel ID cid_b' is produced when a new TLS connection between the client's

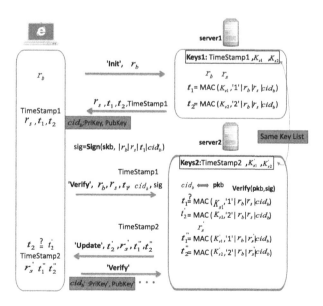

Fig. 5. CEWA cross-origin communication

browser and $server_2$ occurs. The browser signs cid'_b using sk_b at the first time, too. The signed data is called sig. Then it sends the request message $<'Verify', r_b, r_s, t_1, TimeStamp1, sig, cid_b>$ to $server_2$.

After $server_2$ makes sure that the message's legality sig and comparing cid'_b from sig with cid'_b from the connection. If they are matched, they do the subsequent verification processes as CEWA.

We let the browser only do one initialization to the same server. After the first time the browser initializes the server, the browser only verifies when the browser initiates a session on the same server again. If the authentication passes, the browser communicates directly with the server. If the server puts the browser update, the browser will update the data, clear the cache, and re-authenticate with the server. Else if the authentication does not pass, the browser will interrupt the session, clear the cache and re-initialization with the server. This solves the security damage caused by malicious caching.

3.4 Key Storage

With the constant update of the server's CEWA keys, it is bound to generate a series of keys. Some old keys will be used to authenticate the verification messages so that they must be properly stored. With the increasing of the old keys, the storage space will be filled if all of them are stored. So we design a scheme for efficient keys storage.

As we know, the CEWA keys are the existence of groups. One group contains three members: TimeStamp, ks_1, ks_2. So we set up a key list to store the keys in groups. Taking into account the storage space problem, we set up a suitable capacity for the key list. Working likes a queue, the key list stores the new keys groups when the keys are updated and deletes the keys groups earliest when the capacity is full. The keys renewal period will be based on the maximum lifetime of js-cookie and the capacity will be set according to the size of memory (Table 1).

Table 1. Key storage

Key List	
TimeStamp1	K_{s1}, K_{s2}
TimeStamp2	K'_{s1}, K'_{s2}
TimeStamp3	K''_{s1}, K''_{s2}
...	...

4   Security Analysis

Theorem 1. If MAC is existentially unforgeable under an adapture chosen-attack, the CEWA protocol with key update in single domain is secure to authenticate client.

Proof. Assure CEWA protocol with key update in single domain is not secure to authenticate client. Assure the $q(n)s$ CEWA sessions adversary run. There exists adversary $\mathcal{A}$ that can impersonate server to communicate with client. If so, we construct a simulation experiment to attack the MAC algorithm.

In message authentication experiment,

1. Generate a random key k.
2. We choose a random number Sr from 1 to $q(n)$.
3. When $\mathcal{A}$ asks client and server to create a CEWA cession, we imitate client and server execute the protocol as in Fig. 4, except that when $s = Sr$.
   a. When $\mathcal{A}$ asks a client to generate the initial message, we generate a random number r_b^s and send $'Init'$, r_b to $\mathcal{A}$.
   b. When $\mathcal{A}$ sends $'Init'$, r_b^A to the server, we first generate two random numbers r_b^s, r_s^s and call the MAC oracle to compute the MAC for $('1'|r_b^s|r_s|cid_b)$, and $('2'|r_b|r_s|cid_b)$. After the MAC oracle responds two MAC t_1^s and t_2^s, send $r_s^s, t_1^s, t_2^s, TimeStamp1$ to $\mathcal{A}$.
   c. When $\mathcal{A}$ sends $r_s^A, t_1^A, t_2^A, TimeStamp1^A$ to client and pass the verification. We verify $t_1^A \overset{?}{=} t_1^S, t_2^A \overset{?}{=} t_2^S$. If they are the same, forward them to client. Else if $t_1^A \neq t_1^S$, output $('1'|r_b^s|r_s^A|cid_b, t_1)$. Else, output $('2'|r_b^s|r_s^B|cid_b, t_2)$.
   d. When $\mathcal{A}$ asks client to generate 'Verify' message, we send $'Verify'$, r_b^s, r_s^A, t_1^A to $\mathcal{A}$.
   e. When $\mathcal{A}$ sends $'Verify'$, $r_b^{A'}$, $r_s^{A'}$, $t_1^{A'}$ to server, we check $r_b^{A'} \overset{?}{=} r_b^A$, $r_s^{A'} \overset{?}{=} r_s$ and $t_1^{A'} \overset{?}{=} t_1$. If not, abort. Else, we generate a random number $r_s', t_1^{s''}, t_2^{s''}$. Then we rum two MAC oracles to compute MAC for messages $('1'|r_b^A|r_s'|cid_b)$ and $('2'|r_b^A|r_s'|cid_b)$ respectively. Finally, we send $'Update', t_2^s, r_s', t_1^{s''}, t_2^{s''}$ to $\mathcal{A}$.
   f. When $\mathcal{A}$ sends $'Update', t_2^{A'}, r_s^A, t_1^{A''}, t_2^{A''}$ to client, we verify the MAC $t_1^{A''}$, and $t_2^{A''}$. If they pass, we check whether $t_1^{A''} \overset{?}{=} t_1^{S''}, t_2^{A''} \overset{?}{=} t_2^{S''}$. If $t_1^{A''} = t_1^{S''}$ and $t_2^{A''} = t_2^{S''}$, we abort. Else if $t_1^{A''} \neq t_1^{S''}$, we output $('1'|r_b^A|r_s^{A'}/|cid_b, t_1^{A''})$. Else, we output $('2'|r_b^A|r_s^{A'}|cid_b, t_2^{A''})$.

The successful probability for us is $Pr[we\ win] = \frac{1}{q(n)} * Pr[\mathcal{A}\ wins]$. Because if $\mathcal{A}$ wins, there must exists a session such that $t_1^A \neq t_1^S$ or $t_2^{A}! = t_2^S$ or $t_1'' \neq t_1^{S''}$ or $t_2^{A''} \neq t_2^{S''}$. When either of that occurs, we output a corresponding message m and MAC t such that t is a valid tag of m, and m has not been asked in the MAC oracle. Assure $Pr[\mathcal{A}\ wins]$ is $e(k)$ which is a nonnegotiable function of k since $q(k)$ is a polynomial function of k, $Pr[we\ win]$ is also nonnegotiable.

Theorem 2. If MAC is existentially unforgeable under an adapture chosen-attack, the CEWA protocol with key update in cross domain is secure to authenticate client.

Proof. The proof is similar with that in Theorem 1 except the steps in Fig. 5. We omit the details for space reason.

5 Performance

We give an evaluation of CEWA protocol and measure the performance improvement compared to SISCA. We use python standard library httplib and Base-HTTPServer to implement CEWA and SISCA protocol. And we use 128-bit random values (rb and rs), 256-bit keys(ks1 and ks2), HMAC-SHA256 for message authentication code, 1024-bit RSA for signature. The key is rotated every 2 h. The server runs on a Dell personal computer which has a 3.30 GHz Intel Core i5-4590 CPU, 8 GB of RAM running Win10 64bit. The client runs on a Dell N430 notebook which has a 2.50 GHz Intel Core i5-2450M CPU, 6 GB of RAM running Win8 64bit. The server and the client are connected through the campus network. First we evaluate the performance improvement of CEWA when accessing a website which has many static resources that can be cached. In order to prevent resource poison attack, SISCA ignore the max-age parameter of the static resources which can be cached and only use ETag to confirm that the static resource is not modified or poisoned by attackers. On the contrary, CEWA will take full advantage of max-age and ETag. Therefore, SISCA will perform an addition communication with the server when requesting a static resource which is already cached.

We set different numbers N of the static resources in an interval 10 and analysis the time-consuming in single domain case and cross domain case. From Fig. 6, we can see that SISCA cost more time than CEWA due to the additional communications with the server, and in cross domain case, SISCA will perform an addition signature-verify operation. CEWA use max-age parameter to learn that there is no need to re-request the resource without communicating with server. So no matter single domain or cross domain, CEWA use very short time.

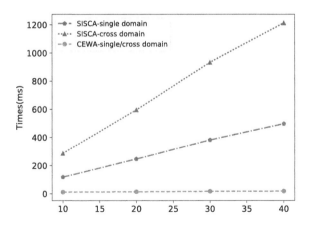

Fig. 6. Time-consuming of requesting N static resources

Next we evaluate the performance overhead when CEWA perform key update operation. We compare the total time-consuming cost by N "Verify" operation performed by SISCA and N "Verify Update" operation performed by CEWA. For every 'Verify Update' operation, CEWA perform two more MAC calculation than normal "Verify" operation. From Fig. 7, we can learn that both in single domain case and cross domain case, CEWA just cost slightly more time that SISCA.

Recall that "Verify Update" operation is performed only once at most per TLS connection and not on every HTTP request/response. So the time overhead of CEWA compared to SISCA is negligible.

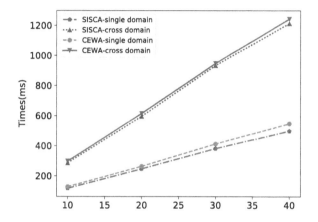

Fig. 7. Time-consuming of N times verify and update operations

Finally, we evaluate the storage overhead of CEWA. In CEWA protocol, key pairs in a recent period must be stored. The key pair contains two 256-bit keys Ks1, Ks2 and a 32-bit timestamp. So every key pair occupy 132 Bytes memory space. Considering we are using a 2-h key rotation frequency, key pairs stored every day will occupy 816 Bytes memory space. In CEWA, we store key pairs of at most 10 days, so the total storage overhead is about 8MB which is negligible for a https server.

6   Related Work

A research on hardening web browsers to keep web authentication's security is context-sensitive certificate verification (CSCV). Due to the bad habits of the user, the browser allows the user connect to the server despite the verification failure. CSCV orders the browser to interrogate the user about the context in which a certificate verification error occurs and give specific password warnings when user is going to send password in an insecure way [10]. Obviously, it's not enough to just do some restrictions on the browser. We can't make sure that every browser can be set up as required, and we need find a way to prevent by study authentication process.

AUTHSCAN protocol tells another way for web authentication. It automatically extracts the formal specifications of authentication protocols from their implementations. Then, these specifications are directly checked for authentication and secrecy properties using off-the-shelf verification tools. It can automatically confirm the candidate attacks generated by the verification tools and report the true positives [11]. According to the analysis, the protocol is susceptible to several MITM attacks by a web attacker. However, too many specifications of the extraction will take up lots of cache, and checking for authentication every time is bound to Influence efficiency.

In order to ensure the security of network communication, Netscape put forward the SSL (Secure Sockets Layer) protocol to ensure that the data in network communication process is not intercepted or steal in the mid-90s of last century [1]. After continuous development, SSL protocol is updated to version 3.0. SSL protocol is widely used in the authentication and data security transmission between Web browser and server. Then it has become a de facto standard in the Internet. In 1999, the Internet Engineering Task Force (IETF) standardized the SSL protocol and renamed the Transport Layer Security (TLS). So the TLS protocol is actually a new version of the SSL protocol [17,19]. TLS consists of TLS Record (TLS Record) and TLS Handshake protocol (TLS Handshake) two-tier protocols [20]. The TLS handshake protocol handles the authentication of peer users, using the public key and certificate at this level, negotiating the algorithm and encrypting the actual data transmission key, which is performed on the TLS record protocol. The TLS record protocol uses encryption keys negotiated in the TLS handshake protocol in the encryption algorithm to provide data privacy and consistency protection. With the emergence of a large number of man-in-the-middle attacks, TLS has a lot of security risks.

Another study focuses on the client authentication is Origin-Bound Certificates protocol (TLS Channel ID). TLS Channel ID is a protocol of TLS extension. It bounds certificates on both sides of TLS connects. To enhance the security of the TLS protocol, Michael Dietz et al. designed a TLS extension to protect against a large number of attacks by strengthening client authentication. They modified the version of the TLS client certificate, called Origin-Bound Certificates (OBCs) [6] or TLS Channel IDs(cid_b) [7]. When the browser and the server establish the first TLS connection, it creates the cid_b for the server. cid_b contain a private key and a public key. The server will authenticate the browser by using the public key. When the browser again establishes a TLS connection with the same server, it will use the same cid_b. The server can identify that the browser he connects again is the same one by cid_b. The protocol allows much of the existing infrastructure of the web to remain unchanged, while at the same time strengthening client authentication considerably against a wide range of attacks [6]. But without server authentication, TLS Channel ID cannot resists the attacks, where the attacker is able to successfully impersonate the legitimate server to the user.

To resolve the problem, Nikolaos Karapanos et al. present a scheme called Server Invariance with Strong Client Authentication (SISCA) which support both client authentication and server authentication. In this scheme, when the user intends to access target server, he must send init message to the server at first. Then the server generate parameters due to the init message and send the parameters to the user. When the user wants to access the same server, he send verify message with the parameters to the server. Then the server generates new parameters and check whether the parameters generated in two times are the same and send the new parameters to the user. The user does the same verification. After such a process, both user and server are verified [7]. But the keys in parameters generation are not update. Initialization is too frequent, and efficiency will be reduced.

7 Conclusion

In this paper, we introduced some web authentication protocol which are used to resist TLS MITM attacks. We show how Channel ID-based authentication still allows a MITM attacker to successfully impersonate the user. In order to illustrate the solution to this problem, we describe a Channel ID-based authentication with server invariance which is called SISCA. In the light of some problems of key update and efficiency in SISCA, we propose our solution, CEWA. We detail the session process of this protocol to show that how it support key update in a security way. The security analysis in this paper fully proves the security of the protocol. At last, We show the better performance of this protocol than that in SISCA through several experiments.

Acknowledgment. This work is partially supported by China National Key Research and Development Program No. 2016YFB0800301.

References

1. Oppliger, R., Hauser, R., Basin, D.: SSL/TLS session-aware user authentication - or how to effectively thwart the man-in-the-middle. Comput. Commun. **29**(12), 2238–2246 (2006)
2. Callegati, F., Cerroni, W., Ramilli, M.: Man-in-the-middle attack to the HTTPS protocol. IEEE Secur. Priv. **7**(1), 78–81 (2009)
3. Stricot-Tarboton, S., Chaisiri, S., Ko, R.K.L.: Taxonomy of man-in-the-middle attacks on HTTPS. In: TrustCom/BigDataSE/ISPA (2017)
4. Huang, L.S., Rice, A., Ellingsen, E., et al.: Analyzing forged SSL certificates in the wild. In: IEEE Symposium on Security and Privacy, pp. 83–97 (2014)
5. Mayer, W., Zauner, A., Schmiedecker, M., et al.: No need for black chambers: testing TLS in the e-mail ecosystem at large, pp. 10–20 (2015)
6. Dietz, M., Czeskis, A., Balfanz, D., et al.: Origin-bound certificates: a fresh approach to strong client authentication for the web. In: USENIX Conference on Security Symposium, p. 16 (2012)

7. Karapanos, N., Capkun, S.: On the effective prevention of TLS man-in-the-middle attacks in web applications. In: 23rd USENIX Security Symposium, pp. 671–686 (2014)
8. Karlof, C., Shankar, U., Tygar, J.D., et al.: Dynamic pharming attacks and locked same-origin policies for web browsers. In: ACM Conference on Computer and Communications Security, CCS 2007, Alexandria, Virginia, USA, pp. 58–71, October 2007
9. Chen, K., Lin, D., Yan, L., Sun, X.: Environment-bound SAML assertions: a fresh approach to enhance the security of SAML assertions. In: Lin, D., Xu, S., Yung, M. (eds.) Inscrypt 2013. LNCS, vol. 8567, pp. 361–376. Springer, Cham (2014). https://doi.org/10.1007/978-3-319-12087-4_23
10. Xia, H.: Hardening web browsers against man-in-the-middle and eavesdropping attacks. In: International Conference on World Wide Web, WWW 2005, Chiba, Japan, pp. 489–498, May 2005
11. Bansal, C., Bhargavan, K., Maffeis, S.: Discovering concrete attacks on website authorization by formal analysis. In: IEEE Computer Security Foundations Symposium, pp. 247–262 (2012)
12. Zhou, Y., Evans, D.: SSOScan: automated testing of web applications for single sign-on vulnerabilities. In: USENIX Security Symposium (2014)
13. Chang, P.H., Kim, W., Agha, G.: An adaptive programming framework for web applications. In: Proceedings of the International Symposium on Applications and the Internet, pp. 152–159 (2004)
14. Xiao, Y., Rayi, V., Sun, B., Du, X., Hu, F., Galloway, M.: A survey of key management schemes in wireless sensor networks. J. Comput. Commun. 30(11–12), 2314–2341 (2007)
15. Du, X., Xiao, Y., Guizani, M., Chen, H.H.: An effective key management scheme for heterogeneous sensor networks. Ad Hoc Netw. 5(1), 24–34 (2007)
16. Du, X., Guizani, M., Xiao, Y., Chen, H.H.: A routing-driven elliptic curve cryptography based key management scheme for heterogeneous sensor networks. IEEE Trans. Wirel. Commun. 8(3), 1223–1229 (2009)
17. Dierks, T., Rescorla, E.: RFC 5246 - The transport layer security (TLS) protocol - Version 1.2 (2008)
18. Xiao, Y., Du, X., Zhang, J., Guizani, S.: Internet protocol television (IPTV): the killer application for the next generation internet. IEEE Commun. Mag. 45(11), 126–134 (2007)
19. Lennox, I.D.J., Rosenberg, J., Schulzrinne, H.: Internet Engineering Task Force. RFC, pp. 82–89, 11 August 2001
20. Tschofenig, H., Fossati, T.: Transport layer security (TLS)/datagram transport layer security (DTLS) profiles for the internet of things. Physiol. Rev. 66(4), 1121–1188 (2016)
21. Du, X., Chen, H.H.: Security in wireless sensor networks. IEEE Wirel. Commun. Mag. 15(4), 60–66 (2008)
22. Yee, P.: Updates to the internet X.509 public key infrastructure certificate and certificate revocation list (CRL) profile. Harefuah 131(5–6), 184 (2013)
23. Fielding, R., Gettys, J., Mogul, J., et al.: RFC 2616: Hypertext Transfer Protocol - HTTP/1.1. Comput. Sci. Commun. Dict. 7(9), 3969–3973 (1999)
24. Du, X., Guizani, M., Xiao, Y., Chen, H.H.: Secure and efficient time synchronization in heterogeneous sensor networks. IEEE Trans. Veh. Technol. 57(4), 2387–2394 (2008)

Placement Fraud Detection on Smart Phones: A Joint Crowdsourcing and Data Analyzing Based Approach

Bo Wang, Fan Wu$^{(\boxtimes)}$, and Guihai Chen

Department of Computer Science and Engineering, Shanghai Jiao Tong University, 800 Dongchuan Road, Minhang District, Shanghai, China
wangbo727@outlook.com, {fwu,gchen}@cs.sjtu.edu.com

Abstract. With the widespread use of mobile devices, mobile online advertising is taking more and more market share. Cost per click and cost per view are the most popular pricing modes in mobile internet advertising, which take effective clicks or displaying duration as the charging basis. However, at the same time, ad fraud, which uses illegal and invalid clicks to fraud advertisers in order to obtain unreasonable income, become a serious problem. Most of the previous studies on click fraud in website focused on network traffic data analysis. This makes them cannot solve the placement fraud problem, which use invalid placement to mislead user to click on it in mobile apps. In this paper, we propose a joint crowdsourcing and data analyzing based placement click fraud detection system. For the characteristic of placement fraud in mobile apps, automatic processing cannot cover every possible fraud. To overcome this, our report system provides a platform to find all possible placement fraud through crowdsourcing. Report system has three main services: a monitor service for monitoring user's call; a layout service for recording the screen; a data service for recording the backend data. Because the placement fraud only appears when users use the apps, the report system based on crowdsourcing can cover every possible placement fraud. We implement our system in 10 tablets with 500 apps to evaluate its effectiveness. Experiment result shows that our approach can record enough data to analysis which app has placement fraud. What's more, our system can figure out some special placement fraud which pop ads when user is using other apps. This placement fraud cannot be solved through automatic method in previous studies.

Keywords: Placement fraud · Crowdsourcing · Data analyzing

1 Introduction

As a major economic driver in the Internet economy, online advertising has become an indispensable part of all kind of internet content, such as website, search engine and mobile apps. It uses the internet as intermediary to deliver

© Springer Nature Singapore Pte Ltd. 2018
L. Zhu and S. Zhong (Eds.): MSN 2017, CCIS 747, pp. 163–179, 2018.
https://doi.org/10.1007/978-981-10-8890-2_12

ad to consumers. After the first online advertising originated in United States in 1994, online advertising revenues has exceeded cable television advertising revenues in 2011 [1], and reach 72.5$ billion which is twice as much as the number in 2011 [2].

Mobile advertising is ad copy delivered through mobile devices such as smart-phones, or tablets. For more mobile devices spread more widely with higher screen resolutions and better performance, mobile advertising is growing rapidly in recent years. Facebook reported that mobile advertising accounted for 84% of its 2016 fourth-quarter revenue.

In mobile ad, the major charging model is cost per click (CPC). Publisher charge the ad exchange platform for every click. However, studies found that up to 43% of user clicks are fraudulent or accidental [3], meaning advertisers are frequently wasting their budgets on clicks with low or non-existant conversion rates.

Click fraud has been studied in the context of web advertising for a long time. Metwally et al. [4,5] studied the advertisers duplicate clicks detection method, and proposed a detection method corresponding correlation analysis in data min-ing; Blundo [6] developed a web measuring system which is specifically for the advertising on search engine site. It can make a judgement result of the adver-tising enterprises which suffered click frauds. Immorlica et al. [7] used machine learning algorithm which is based on user's ad click activity to detect whether the click is from real human or a botnet. Tuzhilin [8] mentioned that Google used online filtering technology to filter click fraud, and gave a detailed explanation on the short coming of this technology and difficulty when face to complicated problem. Kantardzic et al. [9] developed a system CCFDP to do real-time detec-tion of click fraud, namely in real-time click stream to detect. Costa et al. [10] used clickable system called CAPTCHA proposed differentiation test to detect human-computer click fraud, which belongs to authenticated Code mecha-nism category, and the detection performance of using this method alone has limitation.

Several recent studies have pointed out that internet advertising in apps on mobile devices (such as smart-phones and tablets) is also plague by different types of frauds. In 2013, it is considered that mobile apps advertisers lose nearly 1 billion dollars which is 12% of the mobile ad budget due to click fraud [11]. Mobile apps publishers are also incented to commit advertising frauds since ad exchange platform pay them based on cost per thousand impression pricing mode [4], cost per click pricing mode, or more commonly, based on the combinations of both pricing mode. Bot-driven ad frauds have been studied recently [12,13], but placement frauds in mobile apps have not received much attention.

Liu et al. [14] proposed a system named DECAF to detect placement fraud in mobile apps before the click fraud occurs. DECAF is based on a software named *Monkey* which is used to get the frame of the app. It can be viewed as traversal on a state-transition graph which from one state to the next state based on UI inputs such as clicking, swiping and scrolling. Then it analysis the frame UI structure to find if it has potential to cause placement fraud. This work can intensively process many apps in the server before the app come to customers. However, it does not have high accuracy. For some FPS game in mobile devices, *Monkey* cannot get every UI frame of it. Therefore, it is hard to detect if there is a placement fraud in the game.

Crussell et al. [15] proposed a system to detect click fraud in mobile apps. It analyses every app's UI and build a request tree to analysis whether the request tree is normal or have some illegal content which can trigger click fraud. Besides it also analysis the web package to find if there is click fraud. So, similar to the Liu's work, this method is also intensively processing app in one place automatically, which cannot catch every UI frame for some large apps. Dave's work [16] suits for both mobile and non-mobile which have not concerned the characteristic of mobile devices.

In this paper, we propose a report system to detect and report placement fraud through crowd sourcing. Based on the characteristics of the mobile apps placement fraud, the report system can take screen capture of the current app, and figure out where is the placement fraud by user's drawing on the screen capture. At the same time, the system can collect the data package, and analysis it to get the information of the app which has the placement fraud. We implement our report system on 10 tablets with more than 500 mobile apps to test our report system, and analysis the data we collected. The result shows that our system is effective, and can figure out some special placement fraud that never be mentioned in previous studies.

Our contributions are summarized as follows:

- Compare to the previous studies on automatically detecting click fraud in mobile apps, our system can recall almost every placement fraud based on crowdsourcing.
- We implement the report system and evaluate its performance which perfectly demonstrates its effectiveness in real-world environment.
- We analysis the data collected from real-world experiment, result shows the effect of our system and some feature of apps and placement fraud.

The remainder of this paper is organized as follows: In Sect. 2, some background, motivation and challenge will be provided. In Sect. 3, we will present the design and implement detail of the report system. In Sect. 4, we will evaluation the performance of our report system. In Sect. 5, a conclusion about our work is given.

2   Background, Motivation and Challenge

2.1   Background

Similar with the traditional media, a typical mobile advertising model is composed by three roles involved advertiser, ad exchange and publisher. Publisher is the owner of the apps on mobile phone. Advertisers are those who want to post their ad online, and willing pay for it. Ad exchange provides a platform for bringing the publisher and advertiser together to negotiate and transact ad. When users use the apps on the mobile phone with an empty ad slot, the publisher will send an ad request to the ad exchange which it previously embedded the apps. When the ad exchange receiving the ad request, it will choose a set of ad which may be chosen according to some user's profile. Then the ad exchange will ask the advertisers of selected ad for a bid. In response, advertisers will send their bids back to the ad exchange, which is the amount of money they will pay for displaying their ads on that empty slot on app. Once receive the bids, ad exchange will conduct an auction to choose the winner to deliver to the publisher. Then, the publisher will display the ads on the ad plot. When the ad is displayed to user, the publisher will charge the ad exchange or advertiser according to some evaluation method, such as cost per click (CPC) or cost per view (CPV). For CPC model, the number of clicking is regarded as the measurement of charging. When click on ad, ad exchange platform will think this click is attracted by ad showed to user, and give a reward to publisher. For CPV model, which is similar to CPC model, the duration of displaying the ad is regarded as the measurement. Therefore, the more ads publishers show in the apps, the more revenue they get (Fig. 1).

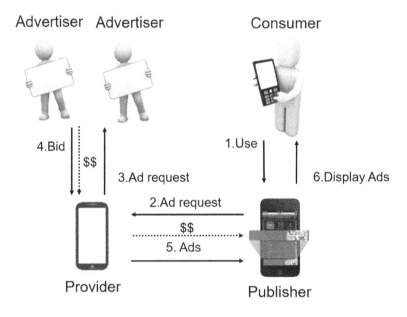

Fig. 1. Mobile advertising model.

To be fair to advertisers, ad exchange platform usually imposes strict guidelines on how should publisher place ad slot in their apps. Google AdMobs terms dictate that "Ads should not be placed very close to or underneath buttons or any other object which users may accidentally click while interacting with your app and Ads should not be placed in areas where users will randomly click or place their fingers on the screen" [17]. Similarly, Microsoft Mobile Advertising stipulates that a publisher must not edit, resize, modify, filter, obscure, hide, make transparent, or reorder any advertising and must not "include any Ad Inventory or display any ads ... that includes materials or links to materials that are unlawful (including the sale of counterfeit goods or copyright piracy), obscene, ..." [18]. However, for getting more reward, some publishers still place the ad slot at a special location which can mislead user to click on it to send a meaningless clicking to ad exchange platform, or place the ad slot at obscure position to make it display all the time without user's attention. To avoid the inspection of ad exchange platform, they can make the ad appears at anytime and anywhere.

2.2 Motivation and Challenge

The ad exchange is an important carrier of internet adverting, and the number of them is growing at an alarming rate. Therefore, in the internet advertising, integrity is very important to every ad exchange platform. The proliferation of fraudulent clicks makes the ad exchange platform of confidence level declined which lead to advertiser declining, and decreasing the revenue of the platform. Reliability declining will push advertiser switch to other ad exchange platforms. For all ad exchange platforms, reliability declining will reduce the number of network advertising. Furthermore, it will damage the online marketing and threat internet advertising industry. Such fraudulent clicks need an effective strategy to prevent to guarantee the benefit of all parties. What's more, these fraud with uncomfortable location not only cause an unintentional click, but also always interrupt the browsing or gaming which will do great harm user experience. Correcting this phenomenon will bring more comfortable use experience, reduce the hazard caused by an unintentional and unexpected click.

Placement fraud in mobile apps is not bot-driven, the clicking behavior is done by real users which do not act like a botnet. Main method of previous studies on placement fraud in mobile app is analysis layout structure or UI structure in a centralized way. They can just detect those placement frauds which violate the guidelines of ad exchange platform with a static location. For the types of placement fraud which may appear at anytime and anywhere, these methods can not cover every situation.

Therefore, to solve the placement fraud, there are two challenges need to be considered:

- Different with the bot-driven fraud, it manipulates visual layouts of ad to trigger ad impressions and unintentional clicks when a real user is using the app. Because clicking behavior is done by real users, it is hard to figure it out with feature analysis.
- The ad slot may appear at any time during user use the apps. Therefore, it is hard to catch every fraud when it appears to user by centralized automated processing.

3   System Design and Implementation

To solve these challenges, we propose a report system based on crowdsourcing. In this section, we will first present the goal of our system. Then we will introduce the system design of the report system. Finally, some details of implementation are introduced.

3.1   Goals

The place where fraud happened should be recorded firstly, when the fraud happened. Then, we need to record the fraud in detail for reporting the fraud to advertiser and ad exchange platform. What's more, responding the user's call should be considered in the system. To achieve the above goals we need to accomplish the following functions to record fraud information:

- Capture screen capture.
- Figure out the placement fraud.
- Record the fraud information.
- Be called in anytime.
- Be called whatever the foreground apps are.

3.2   System Design

Our report system is divided into two parts to achieve our designed goals. One part is used to store the data when fraud happened which include screen capture and data recording service; the other part is monitoring user's call to make the report system can response the user in anytime. To store the data, the system consists of two services. One is an interactive part named layout service which need user do some operation to catch screenshot and figure out the where is the placement fraud. Almost all operation of this service is about frame layout. Another part is a backstage part named data service which do not need any user operation. It is used to record the real-time apps information and store it when the layout part is called. These two parts will save data in a same name with different types. The layout service starts when user calls, and the data service starts together with monitor service when the report system starts.

The Fig. 2 shows the system structure. The Fig. 3 shows our system work flow. When the report system starts, data service and layout service will start together to wait a user call. When user calls the report system, Layout service will take the screen capture, and display it to user. At the same time, the data service will store the recorded information. Then, user can figure out where is the placement fraud, and store the screen capture and data together. Report system will package these data to send it to server. The following part will introduce the detail of two service.

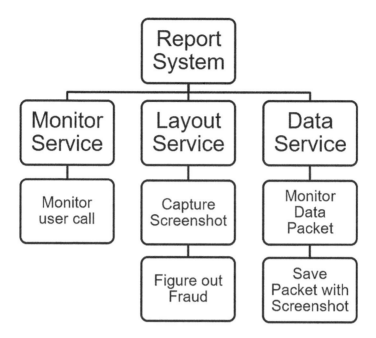

Fig. 2. Structure of report system.

Monitor Service. The Monitor service need to answer user call at anytime, anywhere. When the user wants to activate the report system to record the placement fraud, the monitor service should respond it immediately. It means that the service must be in long-term active. Apparently, a long-term complicated service will take many system resources. To save the system resource, we just need a small long-term service for monitoring and waiting for the user call. This small service is not complicated. It just need to invoke the layout service when the user calls the report system without any other operation. According to the android system, a service class suits for the small service. There is another reason to choose a service as monitor instead of starting up a new app when user calls report system. Starting a new app is slow than invoke function from service. If we want to reduce the complexity of the interaction operation of report system, a rapid reaction speed is essential. What's more, start a new app need a third-party entrance for convenient and fast start it. It may complicate the report system.

Beside the long-term monitoring, we should provide a interface to call the service. As we said before, we do not want a third-part app to support a convenient and fast entrance, but we need to find a way to call the service in anytime, in any apps. There are two potential choice to active the service: gesture and notification. For the gesture way, the gesture we chosen to active the service may be similar to some gestures of other apps, the conflict problem is hard to be solved. Therefore, we use notification bar. The notification bar can be pulled out

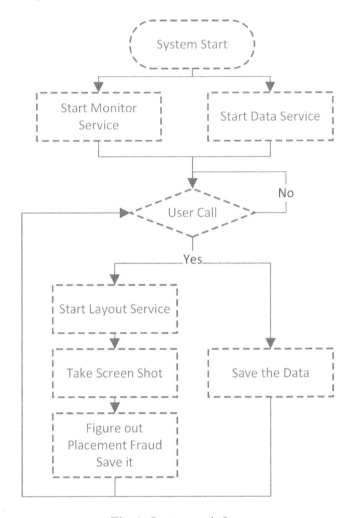

Fig. 3. System work flow.

in anytime in any apps after android 4.X system. We can make a notification in the bar. Then it will appear after the notification bar is pulled out. Same as the monitor service, this notification bar also takes very small system resource.

Layout Service. The major part of layout service is screen capture. Android system support the screen capture function. Pressing power key and volume down key at the same time will take a current screen capture. Android as a open source system should provide the screen shot API. We just need to put the take screen capture method into the monitor service as invoke key. When we invoke the screen capture method, it will take a screen capture and save it into memory. The screen capture named after timestamp. Then we need to load the screen capture and let user to figure out the placement fraud. The figure out function can be supported by drawing service.

When the placement fraud place is figured, the new picture with placement fraud information will cover old screen shot file, save in storage named with timestamp. When this layout service finished, the monitor service starts is waiting for the next call.

Information Service. The information service does not need user's operation. All its functions are linked with layout service. Once layout service starts to save original screen capture, the information service records the current system information at the same time.

Our purpose is reporting apps with placement fraud to ad exchange platform. Therefore, the apps name and package name of the app which has placement fraud are essential, the ad plot embedded in the system is belong to which ad exchange platform, and the ad displayed is from which advertiser. Therefore, the information we need to know is clear:current app, ad provider, and advertiser.

Compare to the ad exchanger and advertiser, the app statues are easy to get. The app is running in the android system, which uses linux core. The worst case is getting apps information in a linux-like way. But consider many other android process manager app. The process information is not so hard to get. What we need is a root authority. Actually, android system provide method to get the foreground app information about process ID, app name and so on. But there is another problem. We need to save the system information at the same time with the layout service is called. At that time, the foreground app is screen capture and drawing part which is all the report system but not the app which is user used before. What we can get is just the running app, it is not easy to get which app is in foreground just second ago. Moreover, we cannot let the information services wait for the layout service finished. That cannot guarantee the correlation between the two records and the two services. So far, we can just get the running apps list, and need more experiment to get the foreground app.

Ad exchange platform and advertiser information are more difficult to get, we cannot operate apps inside like android system. There is no any port to some specific information of all apps. But we can get another thing from system but generated by the app which is TCP package. Since the publisher need send an ad request to ad exchange platform, the IP information is store in the TCP package. We want to use this internet information corresponding with process information to infer the ad exchange platform information.

3.3   Implementation Details

Our System is implement on the Android system. All the test and development are focus on android apps. In report system, three services need to be implement in Android system.

Monitor Service. As we mentioned above, monitor service need is implemented as a notification bar (Fig. 4).

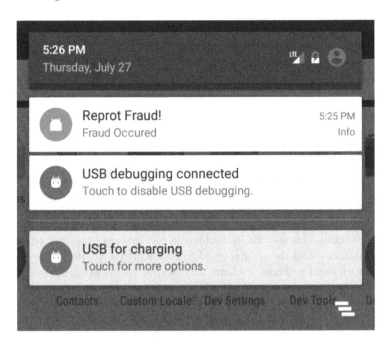

Fig. 4. Report in notification bar.

Layout Service. Android is a core based on Linux and open source. But Android system also have some hidden or set the permissions of the framework APIs which brings me a big problem in the system implementation.

To implement report system, we should solve the two import function: screen shot and drawing. Unfortunately, the screen shot API "ScreenShot" is hidden. Developer cannot use the API in the regular Android SDK because the SDK didn't compile the API. To solve the problem, we found three feasible method at first:

- Build a SDK by ourselves.
- Build our system in the source code.
- Because android is linux core, linux shell command "screencap" is also work.

The first two methods need AOSP (Android open source project) source code to achieve full compile. The last two methods need an extra system authority which make them as a system app. There are two methods to get the authority: compile it in source code, or sign the app with key while both key and sign app are from source code. As a result, first two methods need android source code. What's more, these two methods are highly depends on the android system version that we used to develop the report system. When we change it to another android system, the ScreenCap API is totally changed. Even if we compile our project in the source code, the screen cap is still invalid. Only one way to make it valid is to change the source code of Screen Cap API and rebuild the system.

We tried several times but failed. It is a little bit difficult to debug the whole android source code by myself in a short time. Finally, we chose the third method, run linux command with root authority by android function. Drawing part is just use Bitmap method to load screen capture, put the bitmap to a canvas, drawing on canvas, and save canvas to a bitmap.

Data Service. In Data Service, we need to store the app information which include fore ground app's name, package name, tcp package. For the app name, android system provides api to get the running processes' name and ID. The running processes list in time order which can apparently show the last used apps. For TCP package, we use tcpdump to monitor the TCP package and store the data recurrently.

4   Evaluation

In this section, we implement our system and evaluate the performance of our report system.

4.1   Methodology

We implement the report system in Android 6.0 system on 10 devices. 5 of them are Nexus 7-I, and another 5 of them are Nexus 7-II. To evaluate our report system generally, we collect more than 500 apps, and install all of them on the devices in 10 or 11 batches. Because of the different performance of these two types of devices, the number of apps installed on it are different. Table 1 shows all types apps we install on the 10 devices.

4.2   Experiment Result

We employed 10 users to use these apps with our report system in three months, and collected 520 reports which include 509 valid reports and 11 invalid reports.

Table 2 show the reports data of different apps on different devices. The report rate here is defined as $total \div (Nexus7I * 5 + Nexus7II * 5)$. It is clear that placement frauds are happened more frequently in game than the other apps. 37.2% game apps have 60.1% reports, and the total report rate is three times of the other apps report rate. The travel apps have least report rate. The apps of this type are all about booking, ticketing, map service and some other service like this, which are only provided by large enterprise whose reputation are higher. Therefore, their apps have less illegal behaviors. The other two types with less report rate are Office and System which need more complicated technology to develop. It induces to higher violation cost to use placement fraud to get revenue. In games, the racing game has the least report rate, where business, simulator and chess games have relatively higher report rate. It is because these games have less cost of development which induces less violation cost. In summary, the higher the cost of development, the less the probability of violating the rules.

Table 1. Applications installed on devices

Type		Total	Nexus7-I	Nexus7-II
Office		55	55	55
Theme		42	42	42
Travel		44	43	43
Shooting		56	51	53
Life		50	48	49
System		44	42	43
Audio		40	39	40
Information		39	37	39
Total		370	357	364
Game	Action	25	19	25
	Acting	25	21	25
	Business	27	22	27
	Simulator	29	16	29
	Chess	28	20	27
	Racing	33	21	32
	Sports	26	23	25
	Leisure	26	19	26
	Total	219	161	216
Total		589	518	580

Figure 5 shows the number of report collected from 10 users. The light-blue denote Nexus 7-I, where the darkblue denotes Nexus7-II. According to the result, different device influences is little. Since the apps for the 10 users are same, Fig. 5 shows that for different people, the tolerances of placement fraud are different. For those people who dislike ad, they may report the apps when ad appears in apps. For those who do not care the ad, they may report the app when the placement fraud really disturbs their normal usage of the app. Therefore, in these 509 available reports, 185 apps are reported as placement fraud. Figure 6 shows the times of applications are reported. 81 apps are reported only once, 32 apps are reported twice. However, due to the difference of the two kinds of devices, some apps cannot be install on Nexus7-I. According the report result, 27 reported apps cannot be install on Nexus7-I. Because, the users with different type of devices behave similarly, we can simply assume the report times of Nexus7-I is same as Nexus7-II. Then, the report data is updated as follow:

Figure 7 and Table 3 show the result after adding the Nexus7-I's report. The trend of the result is similar to the before with a little increase.

In the experiment, every app is installed once for every user. However, in the report result, 3 apps which are reported more than 10 times, 2 of them are reported more than 20 times. To find the reason that induces these three

Table 2. Reports of different apps on different devices

Type		Total	Nexus7-I	Nexus7-II	Report rate
Office		26	18	8	4.73%
Theme		27	10	17	6.43%
Travel		7	3	4	1.63%
Shooting		42	20	22	8.08%
Life		37	27	10	7.63%
System		9	1	8	2.12%
Audio		29	12	17	7.34%
Information		26	12	14	6.84%
Total		203	103	100	5.63%
Game	Action	42	24	18	19.09%
	Acting	18	10	8	7.83%
	Business	62	35	27	26.12%
	Simulator	60	34	26	26.67%
	Chess	56	34	22	23.83%
	Racing	11	6	5	4.15%
	Sports	25	14	11	10.42%
	Leisure	32	21	11	14.22%
	Total	306	178	128	16.34%
Total		509	281	228	9.31%

anomalies, we analysis the original report of these three apps. The screen capture structure of all these three apps are similar: an advertisement on the top of screen with an app under it. The difference is the apps which are under the ad are totally different. The name we recorded in report is not same as the one beneath the ad. After we installed these apps, we found the reason. The ad is not embedded in the app when the ad appears. It belongs to some other app which is installed before. The ad does not appear during that app is running foreground, just appears when the other app starts. This is a new placement fraud which are really disturb user experience, and cannot be found by some automatic detection mechanism.

Besides these, we also record the internet information when placement fraud happened. But when we analyze the collected reports, we cannot match the internet information with fraud app appropriately. We do not have enough information to determine which ad exchange platform is used when fraud occurred. The privacy protection of mobile advertising is good.

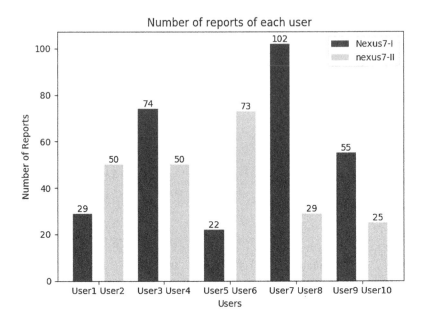

Fig. 5. Reports from different user. (Color figure online)

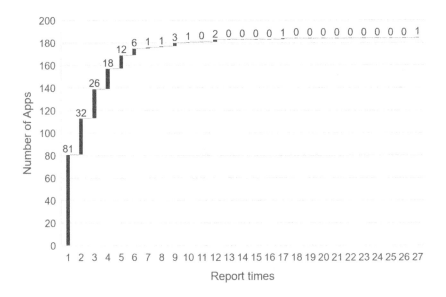

Fig. 6. Report times of apps.

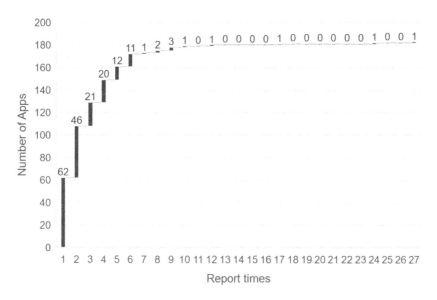

Fig. 7. Report times after emendation.

Table 3. Reports of different apps on different devices

Type		Total	Nexus7-I	Nexus7-II	Report rate
Office		26	18	8	4.73%
Theme		27	10	17	6.73%
Travel		7	3	4	1.63%
Shooting		42	22	22	8.27%
Life		39	29	10	7.84%
System		9	1	8	2.12%
Audio		30	13	17	7.59%
Information		28	14	14	7.37%
Total		210	110	100	5.77%
Game	Action	49	31	18	22.27%
	Acting	18	10	8	7.83%
	Business	82	55	27	33.47%
	Simulator	69	43	26	30.67%
	Chess	63	41	22	26.81%
	Racing	15	10	5	5.66%
	Sports	26	15	11	10.83%
	Leisure	36	25	11	16.00%
	Total	358	230	128	18.94%
Total		568	340	228	10.29%

5   Conclusion

In this paper, we propose a report system can record and report the placement fraud in mobile app. Compared with previous studies, our system based on crowdsourcing instead of intensively operation with automatic program. The report system can record the screen capture and the apps information when placement fraud occurred. Our evaluation results have shown that the report system can detect some special placement fraud that cannot be find in automatic detection.

References

1. IAB Internet Advertising Revenue Report, 2012 Full Year Results. https://www.iab.com/wp-content/uploads/2015/05
2. IAB Internet Advertising Revenue Report, 2016 Full Year Results. https://www.iab.com/wp-content/uploads/2016/04
3. The Truth About Mobile Click Fraud. http://www.imgrind.com/the-truth-aboutmobile-click-fraud
4. Metwally, A., Agrawal, D., El Abbadi, A.: Duplicate detection in click streams. In: 14th International Conference on World Wide Web, pp. 12–21. ACM (2005)
5. Metwally, A., Agrawal, D., Abbadi, A.E.: Using association rules for fraud detection in web advertising networks. In: 31st International Conference on Very Large Data Bases, pp. 169–180. VLDB Endowment (2005)
6. Blundo, C., Cimato, S.: SAWM: a tool for secure and authenticated web metering. In: 14th International Conference on Software Engineering and Knowledge Engineering, pp. 641–648. ACM (2002)
7. Immorlica, N., Jain, K., Mahdian, M., Talwar, K.: Click fraud resistant methods for learning click-through rates. In: Deng, X., Ye, Y. (eds.) WINE 2005. LNCS, vol. 3828, pp. 34–45. Springer, Heidelberg (2005). https://doi.org/10.1007/11600930_5
8. The Lan's Gifts v. Google Report. http://googleblog.blogspot.com/pdf/Tuzhilin_Report.pdf
9. Kantardzic, M., Walgampaya, C., Wenerstrom, B., Lozitskiy, O., Higgins, S., King, D.: Improving click fraud detection by real time data fusion. In: IEEE International Symposium on Signal Processing and Information Technology, ISSPIT 2008, pp. 69–74 (2008)
10. Costa, R.A., de Queiroz, R.J., Cavalcanti, E.R.: A proposal to prevent click-fraud using clickable CAPTCHAs. In: 2012 IEEE Sixth International Conference Software Security and Reliability Companion (SERE-C), pp. 62–67. IEEE (2012)
11. Bots Mobilize. http://www.dmnews.com/bots-mobilize/article/291566/
12. Blizard, T., Livic, N.: Click-fraud monetizing malware: a survey and case study. In: 2012 7th International Conference Malicious and Unwanted Software (MALWARE), pp. 67–72. IEEE (2012)
13. Miller, B., Pearce, P., Grier, C., Kreibich, C., Paxson, V.: What's clicking what? Techniques and innovations of today's clickbots. In: Holz, T., Bos, H. (eds.) DIMVA 2011. LNCS, vol. 6739, pp. 164–183. Springer, Heidelberg (2011). https://doi.org/10.1007/978-3-642-22424-9_10
14. Liu, B., Nath, S., Govindan, R., Liu, J.: DECAF: detecting and characterizing ad fraud in mobile apps. In: NSDI, pp. 57–70 (2014)

15. Crussell, J., Stevens, R., Chen, H.: Madfraud: investigating ad fraud in android applications. In: 12th Annual International Conference on Mobile Systems, Applications, and Services, pp. 123–134. ACM (2014)
16. Dave, V., Guha, S., Zhang, Y.: Measuring and fingerprinting click-spam in ad networks. ACM SIGCOMM Comput. Commun. Rev. **42**(4), 175–186 (2012)
17. AdMob Publisher Guidelines and Policies. http://support.google.com/admob/answer/1307237?hl=en&topic=1307235
18. Microsoft pubCenter Publisher Terms and Conditions. http://pubcenter.microsoft.com/StaticHTML/TC/TCen.html

A Reinforcement Learning Approach
of Data Forwarding in Vehicular Networks

Pengfei Zhu$^{(\boxtimes)}$, Lejian Liao, and Xin Li

School of Computer Science, Beijing Institute of Technology, Beijing, China
zhu_pengfei0408@163.com, {liaolj,xinli}@bit.edu.cn

Abstract. As the basis of vehicle ad hoc networks, the method of forwarding data is one of the most important parts which ensures the stability and efficiency of network communication. However, the high-speed mobile vehicle nodes cause frequent changes of network topology and disconnections of network links, casting a big challenge to the performance of network data delivery. Data forwarding methods based on the prior knowledge of vehicle's trajectory are difficult to adapt to the changing vehicle trajectory in real world applications, while getting destination vehicles' positions in broadcast way are extremely costly. To solve the above problems, we have proposed an association state based optimized data forwarding method (ASODF) with the assistance of low loaded road side units (RSU). The proposed method maps the urban road network into a directed graph, utilizes the carry-forward mechanism and decomposes the data transmission into decision-making data forwarding at intersections and data delivery on roads. The vehicles carried data combine the destination nodes locations obtained by low loaded road side units and their locations into association states, and the association state optimization problem is formalized as a Reinforcement Learning problem with Markov Decision Process (MDP). We utilized the value iteration scheme to figure out the delay-optimal policy, which is further used to forward data packets to obtain the best delay of data transmission. Experiments based on a real vehicle trajectory data set demonstrate the effectiveness of our model ASODF.

1 Introduction

With the improvement of the vehicle information technology and the development of the wireless communications technology, Vehicular Ad-hoc Network (VANET) has developed rapidly. VANET is a self-organizing network which is specially designed for inter-vehicle communication based on Mobile Ad-hoc Network (MANET). The communication in VANET can be divided into three types, including vehicle to vehicle (V2V), vehicle to infrastructure (V2I) and infrastructure to vehicle (I2V). The core of Vehicular Network is the speed and efficiency and the security of data transmission in the network which consist of vehicles and road side units. However, the characteristics of large amount of nodes and quickly movement of nodes make it difficult to use the effective routing

© Springer Nature Singapore Pte Ltd. 2018
L. Zhu and S. Zhong (Eds.): MSN 2017, CCIS 747, pp. 180–194, 2018.
https://doi.org/10.1007/978-981-10-8890-2_13

protocol algorithms in Internet and wireless sensor networks, e.g., literature [1] proposed secure cell relay routing protocol, and also including some exists key management schemes in wireless sensor network [2], e.g, Du et al. proposed some key management schemes [3,4]. And some other exists work for the problems of wireless sensor network elaborated in literature [5] and the time synchronization scheme proposed in literature [6] also can't be applied in VANETs. Additionally, network performance is critical to the data transmission mechanism, due to that the performance of network are influenced by many factors, including instability and uncertainty of the channel quality. Therefore, some particular methods have been proposed to solve these problems.

The exists work of data transmission in Vehicular Network can be divided into three types. First is methods based on topology. This type of methods can also be divided into two subtype: Proactive and Reactive. **Destination Sequenced Distance Vector** (DSDV) [7] and **Optimized Link State Routing protocol** (OLSR) [8] are two classical Proactive methods. These type of methods have a obvious disadvantages is that the node needs to update the routing information at any time, which consumes a lot of bandwidth. **Dynamic Source Routing** (DSR) [9] and **Ad hoc on Demand Distance Vector routing** (AODV) are two reactive methods. But due to the use of broadcast mode, DSR has a poor scalability which is not suitable for such a large-scale mobile network ad hoc networks. AODV can suitable for large-scale network, but it still has some problem, e.g., larger network overhead and expired routing problem.

Second, since VANET has the characteristic of frequent changes in its topology, it is very difficult for network nodes to set up and maintain a stable routing table. Therefore, topology-based data transmission schemes are not suitable for vehicular networking. With the popularization of GPS equipment, the data transmission method based on geographic location has been proposed. **Greedy Perimeter Stateless Routing** (GPSR) [10] and **Geographic source routing** (GSR) [11] are two methods based on geographic location. GPSR uses a greedy model to transmission data which has a locally optimal problem. GSR is different to these model whose nodes are able to randomly move, it utilizes the fact that vehicle can only drive on road. So data transmission can only occurs at a intersection. The GSR does not take into account the real-time traffic conditions in the road network and may result in a lack of connectivity due to too few vehicles on the road sections selected at the intersection.

Third, due to the frequent disconnection of network links in vehicular ad hoc networks and the inability to establish end-to-end routing of source nodes to destination nodes, researchers creatively introduced the mechanism of tolerates time-delay networks and opportunistic networks into vehicular network, proposed a data transmission scheme based on store-and-forward and carry-forward mechanism. **Static Node Assisted Adaptive Routing** (SADV) [12] and **Vehicle Assisted Data Delivery** (VADD) [13] are two methods based on Store and Forward mechanism. SADV deploys static nodes at intersections, i.e., roadside units (RSU), to aid in the transmission of data. SADV draws on the VADD's section delay model and the optimal path selection. SADV utilizes the store-and-forward and carry-forward mechanism, which make it be a efficient data routing solution. However, The need to deploy infrastructure at each intersection makes SADV unsuitable for large-scale network environments. VADD is a method that proposed for sparse environment. First, VADD extracts a delay model from real vehicle trajectory data. Then VADD calculates the total delay of packets from the current intersection to the destination node through the adjacent crossroads according to the delay model. Finally VADD ranks the total delay to select the optimal routing.

Fourth, the model based on store-and-forward and carry-forward mechanism is a good solution to the problem of link disconnection caused by sparse vehicles. But they are still do not take the road restrictions and human behavior patterns caused by a certain trajectory of the vehicle into consideration. Therefore, the models based on vehicle trajectory are proposed. These models can be divided into two types. One is the models in which the vehicles' trajectory is fixed in advance. Another is models based on trajectory prediction. **Anchor based Street and Traffic Aware Routing** (A-STAR) [14], **Geographical Opportunistic Routing** (GeOpps) [15] and **Mobile Gateway based Forwarding** (MGF) [16] are several models with fixed trajectory. The vehicle nodes in A-STAR model will choose the route with high connectivity, which will cause too heavy or even congestion. GeOpps can obtain the fixed trajectory of the vehicle node through the navigation system, and utilize the trajectory information to send packets to vehicles close to the destination node selectively. But due to too much dependency of trajectory, it is limited to the navigation system and driver's driving habits. MGF only use bus to transmission data which makes it only available on buses. Different to the above model, **Trajectory-Based Data Forwarding** (TBD) [17], **Trajectory-based Statistical Forwarding** (TSF) [18], **Shared-Trajectory-based Data Forwarding Scheme** (STDFS) [19], **Trajectory Improves Data Delivery in Vehicular Networks** (Trajectory) [20] and **Delay-Optimal Data Forwarding** (OVDF) [21] are several models with trajectory prediction. However, TBD and TSF only suitable for some certain situations. STDFS is not very reliable due to overdependence on the trajectory. OVDF also assists data transmission with the aid of bus fixed tracks. The Trajectory model adopt Markov Chain to do trajectory prediction, it is a efficient model.

Last, the models based on road side units (RSU) are another type of scheme of data transmission in vehicular network, including the above models of TBD, TSF, MGF, SADV, STDFS, OVDF. ROAMER [22] further used RSU to transmit data with the dependence of wired backbone network which is contrary to the concept of VANET transmit data from vehicle node, and this model has high requirements to RSU.

In summary, there are two problems: (1) data forwarding models based on the prior knowledge of vehicle trajectory assumptions are difficult to adapt to changing vehicle trajectories in real-world applications, (2) whereas broadcast network based approaches has a large network overhead when obtaining destination vehicle's positions. Inspired by the exists work, we proposed an association state based optimal data forwarding model (ASODF) to solve the above problem. Our model is a mixed model which include V2I and V2V data transmission.

2   Background

In this section, we give a brief review of Markov Decision Process and it's value based methods.

2.1   Markov Decision Process

Markov Decision Process (MDP) is an optimal decision process based on the Markov process theory for stochastic dynamical systems. It is widely used to solve the sequential problems that need to make the best decisions at all stages [23]. A sequential decision problem with known environment dynamics is usually formalized as a MDP, which is characterized by a 5-tuple $\langle S, A, T, R, \gamma \rangle$, where S is the set of states and is non-empty, A is the set of actions and is also non-empty, $T : S \times A \to \Pi(S)$ is the transition function, it gives the probability of the next state when an agent execute a action $a \in A$ at state $s \in S$, where $\Pi(S)$ represent the set of probability distribution on S, R represent the Reward function, it give the immediate reward when an agent execute a action $a_t \in A$ at state $s_t \in S$ and the state transit to state $s_{t+1} \in S$, then the reward is $R_t = R(s_t, a_t, s_{t+1})$, γ is the discount factor to calculate the expected reward. MDP based on Markov Property, i.e., no post-efficiency. That means that the transition function $T(s_t, a_t, s_{t+1})$ is depends only upon the present state, whereas has no relate with past other state, i.e., $T(s_t, a_t, s_{t+1}) = P(s_{t+1}|s_t, a_t)$. The goal to solve a MDP question is obtain a optimal policy π, which gives the best decision of all state when an agent is making a decision, so that the agent can get most rewards finally.

When the original state is s_0 of an agent[1], agent will select and execute an action a_0, then the environment will transit to next state s_1, and agent will select and execute an action again, until it arrive terminal state. And the model will gives a optimal policy π when it converged through iteration. The policy give the optimal action of a state, i.e., $a = \pi(s)$.

Value function is always used to evaluate a policy. Value function also been called cumulative discount rewards, it gives a estimation of an agent will get finally from current state s_t, i.e.,

$$V^\pi(s_t) = E^\pi[R(s_t) + \gamma R(s_{t+1}) + \gamma^2 R(s_t + 2) + \cdots] \tag{1}$$

We can easily transform it to a simple form according to Bellman Equation,

$$V^\pi(s_t) = R(s_t, a_t, s_{t+1}) + \gamma \sum p(s_{t+1}|s_t, a_t)V^\pi(s_{t+1}) \tag{2}$$

The optimal policy should be the policy which can gives the decisions to get most cumulative reward from each state. So, the most reward of each state s_i is:

$$V^*(s_i) = R(s_i, a_i, s_j) + \max_\pi \sum_{j \in S} p(s_j|s_i, a_i)V^*(s_j) \tag{3}$$

---

[1] MDP assume that agent can get true state of environment, i.e., $s^{agent} = s^{env}$.

So the optimal policy from state s_i to terminal state is:

$$\pi^*(s_i) = \arg\max_{a_i} \sum p(s_j|s_i, a_i)V(s_j) \tag{4}$$

The methods of solve MDP to get a optimal solution including value iteration and policy iteration and other linear programming methods. In this paper, we will use value iteration methods to solve MDP problem. The process of Value Iteration shows in literature [24].

2.2   Data Delivery on Road

Carry-forward mechanism over is a good way to overcome the shortcomings of frequent disconnection of VANET links, which are widely used in data transmission research of vehicular network. The carry-forward mechanism of data delivery model on road is shown in Fig. 1. When there are vehicles in the communication of the vehicle carried data and the vehicle is closer to next intersection than current vehicle, then select and delivery these data to the vehicle closest to next intersection. If no vehicle, then the vehicle will continue carry the data. This is a greedy model, i.e., select the best vehicle of current situation, so that data package can be delivery to next intersection with fastest speed and the minimum number of forward. Since the transmission process is composed with vehicle store and wireless forward, the delay of data transmission is affected by two factors, one is the vehicle density, and another is vehicle wireless device communication range. Learn from literature [13], we use ρ_{ij} represent the density of road e_{ij}, R represent the radius of wireless communication range. VADD assume that the distribution of distance of two vehicle meet the exponential distribution with parameter $1/\rho_{ij}$. So, the delay d_{ij} on the road e_{ij} is:

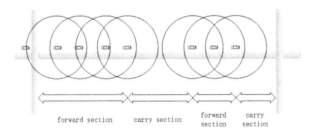

Fig. 1. Data delivery on road

$$d_{ij} = (1 - e^{-R\cdot\rho_{ij}})\frac{l_{ij}c}{R} + e^{-R\cdot\rho_{ij}}\frac{l_{ij}}{v_{ij}} \tag{5}$$

Where l_{ij} represent the distance of road e_{ij}, c indicate the time needed to delivery data to next hop, v_{ij} represent the average speed on the road e_{ij}. These parameters can be obtained through the use of GPS devices by road traffic statistics or analysis of historical trajectory data.

2.3   Association State of Tag Game

Different to the exists application of MDP in data transmission, the state in MDP used in our paper is association state learn from Tag Game [25]. There are two roles in Tag Game, robot and opponent, The process is that the robot keeps chasing opponent until the robot catches up with opponent, which is shown in Fig. 2.

a. Robots playing Tag   b. Tag configuration

Fig. 2. Tag Game

Tag Game can be see as a Partially Observable MDP task, in which state are composed of the positions of robot and opponent, i.e., association state. The set of state of robot is $\{s_0, \cdots, s_{29}\}$, the set of state of opponent is $\{s_0, \cdots, s_{29}, s_{tagged}\}$, the association state is $s = \{Robot, Opponent\}$. The robot will execute one action of the set $North, South, West, East, Tag$, and then robot will get a immediate reward. When robot and opponent are in the same box, i.e., $Opponent = s_{tagged}$, then robot will catch up opponent and get the highest reward and game over.

3   Association State Based Data Forwarding Model

MDP has widely used to solve sequential decision-making tasks. Since the vehicle carrying data will meet other vehicles with different probabilities, the data forward in VANET can be formed to a Sequential decision making problem. We can consider the process of transmitting a data from source node to destination vehicle as the robot chasing the opponent in Tag Game, i.e., the data package chasing the destination vehicle and the vehicle carrying data are keep changing. In this section, we will form this problem to a MDP task.

3.1   Association State

Association State is the core of getting the position of destination vehicle dynamically and forwarding data optimally. With the use of association state, we can add the position information of destination vehicle to the MDP model and optimize the network delay of data transmission dynamically.

In our model, we use the current intersection as the current vehicle's state. So the association state consists of the intersection of source vehicle and the intersection of destination vehicle. When the source vehicle node obtains the intersection information of the destination vehicle node, the low-load roadside unit and its wired backbone-assisted communication are utilized. We assume that each vehicle will register information on the roadside unit when it enter the coverage area of roadside unit of a intersection. Once the roadside unit detects the destination vehicle node, the intersection information will be transmitted to the roadside unit closest to the source vehicle node through the roadside unit backbone network. Then, the position information of destination vehicle node will be transmitted to the source vehicle node so that it can get the current association state. Due to the use of the roadside unit backbone network, the time delay can be ignored. The next state is also a necessary condition for solving a MDP problem.

In our model, the information of destination vehicle including speed, position, direction and etc. We can also obtain the next intersection of the current vehicle when it has not enter the coverage of the next intersection yet through the this information. Therefore, we can get the next association state.

3.2   Decision-Making of Association State

As we has described the transmission on road section, we will show the process of data transmission at a intersection. We will give priorities on the directions which is shown in Fig. 3 according to a fixed policy like VADD [13], where 1 represent the best direction to transmit data, 2 represent the second optimal direction, etc. We will select the optimal direction, i.e., priority is 1. It will transmission data when there is a vehicle in that direction, or will check if it is driving in this direction, if so then don't forward to another vehicle, if not then will select vehicle in the second optimal direction, and etc.

At intersection i, decisions (actions) can be formed as a vector set $U(i)$, where $\pi_i^1 \pi_i^2 \pi_i^3 \cdots \pi_i^{m_i} \in E$ is all m_i road sections connected with intersection i and the order indicates the priority. Our goals is to select the best decision (action) from set $U(i)$ to transmit data at current intersection.

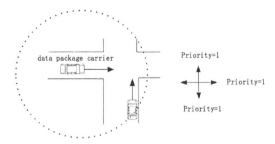

Fig. 3. The decision making of a intersection

3.3   Transition Probability

We use $P(s, \pi_i, s')$ represent the transition probability, where state s consist of the intersections of source vehicle and destination vehicle. So $P(s, \pi_i, s')$ is consist of two parts, the transition probability of source vehicle $P(src_t, \pi_i, src_{t+1})$ and the transition probability of destination vehicle turn to the next intersection $P(des_t, des_{t+1})$.

Assume that the current intersection is i and the policy is π_i, $P_{ij}(\pi_i) = P(src_t, \pi_i, src_{t+1})$ represent the probability that the data be transmitted to next intersection j along the road e_{ij} where $src_t = i, src_{t+1} = j$.

(1) Computation of $P(src_t, \pi_i, src_{t+1})$. We define three probability events:

- **A** represent the event that a vehicle has not met a vehicle which is heading to a road section with a higher priority than road segment e_{ij}.
- **B** represent the event that a vehicle met a vehicle which is drive to the road e_{ij} at intersection i and the vehicle itself doesn't drive to a road whose direction has a higher priority that e_{ij}.
- **C** represent the event that a vehicle drive to the road e_{ij}.

With the above definition, we can derive the probability of $P_{ij}(\pi_i)$:

$$
\begin{aligned}
p(src_t, \pi_i, src_{t+1}) &= P_{ij}(\pi_i) \\
&= P[A \cap (B \cup C)] \\
&= P(A) \times P(B \cup C) \\
&= P(A) \times [P(B) + P(C) - P(B|C)P(C)] \\
&= [\prod_{e_{ik} \in HPe_{ij}(\pi_i)} (1 - p_{ik})] \\
&\quad \times [p_{ij} \times (1 - \sum_{e_{ik} \in HPe_{ij}(\pi_i)} p'_{ik}) + p'_{ij} - p_{ij} \times p'_{ij}]
\end{aligned}
\tag{6}
$$

where $P(A)$ indicate the probability that event **A** occurred, $HPe_{ij}(\pi_i)$ represent the set of roads that have a higher priority that road e_{ij}. p_{ij} represent the probability that a vehicle drive from intersection i to intersection j, p'_{ij} represent the probability that a vehicle meet other vehicles which drive from intersection i to road e_{ij}. In our model, we set $p_{ij} = \frac{\#num(i \to j)}{\#num(i)}$, where $\#num(i \to j)$ is the number of vehicles drive to intersection j when it is at intersection i, $\#num(i)$ is the number of all vehicles reach intersection i. And we set $p'_{ij} = \frac{\#num^{met}(i \to j)}{\#num^{met}(i)}$, where $\#num^{met}(i \to j)$ is the number of vehicles that the vehicle met at intersection i and drive to intersection j, $\#num^{met}(i)$ is the number of all vehicles that the vehicle met at intersection i.

(2) Computation of $P(des_t, des_{t+1})$. In our model, we set $P(des_t, des_{t+1}) = \frac{\#num(des_t \to des_{t+1})}{\#num(des_t)}$, where $\#num(des_t \to des_{t+1})$ is the number of vehicles that reach intersection i at time t and reach intersection j at time $t + 1$, and $\#num(des_t)$ is the number of all vehicles reach intersection i at time t.

So the complete association state transition probability $P(s, \pi_i, s')$ of a carrier vehicle reached intersection i at time t is:

$$
\begin{aligned}
P(s, \pi_i, s') &= P(s_{t+1} = s | a_t = \pi, s_t = s') \\
&= P((src, des)_{t+1} | \pi_i, (src, des)_t) \\
&= P(src_t, \pi_i, src_{t+1}) * P(des_t, des_{t+1}) \\
&= P_{ij}(\pi_i) * P(des_t, des_t + 1)
\end{aligned}
\tag{7}
$$

3.4 Model Derivation

Network time delay is an important indicator of VANET performance. Its value is the accumulation of time delays on the roads that the data package passed, which is corresponds to the composition of the value function in MDP. So we use the time delay as MDP reward.

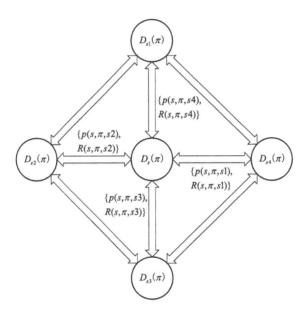

Fig. 4. The Markov Decision Process at state s

Assume that there are four adjacent state at state s, then the transition model from state s is shown in Fig. 4. The $D_s(\pi)$ represent the value function from state s, i.e., the estimated total time delay from the source vehicle which is at state s. So $D_s(\pi)$ can be formed as:

$$
D_s(\pi_s) = \sum_{s' \in N(s)} P(s, \pi_s, s') \times [R(s, \pi_s, s') + D_s'(\pi)]
\tag{8}
$$

$$\begin{aligned}
&= P_{s,s_1} \times (R(s, \pi_s, s_1) + D_{s1}(\pi_s)) \\
&+ P_{s,s_2} \times (R(s, \pi_s, s_2) + D_{s_2}(\pi_s)) \\
&+ P_{s,s_3} \times (R(s, \pi_s, s_3) + D_{s_3}(\pi_s)) \\
&+ P_{s,s_4} \times (R(s, \pi_s, s_4) + D_{s_4}(\pi_s))
\end{aligned} \tag{9}$$

The our goal is to minimize the total time delay, i.e.,

$$\min_{\pi} D_s(\pi), \forall s \tag{10}$$

And the optimal policy we will get is:

$$\pi^* = \langle \pi_s^*, \forall s \in S \rangle \tag{11}$$

The reward $R(s, \pi_i, s')$ we will get is derived as:

$$R(s, \pi_i, s') = R((src_t, des_t), \pi_i, (src_{t+1}, des_{t+1})) \tag{12}$$

$$= \frac{1}{2}(d_{src_{t+1}, src_t} + d_{des_{t+1}, des_t}) \tag{13}$$

3.5 Algorithm

Since our model is still a standard MDP model, we can use the standard Value Iteration to solve this question. The Algorithm is shown in Algorithm 1.

Algorithm 1. ASODF:Association State based Optimal Data Forwarding model

---

Input: Initial the Values of all state to D_0, max iteration τ and threshold θ.
Output: The optimal policy $\pi^* = \langle \pi_s^*, \forall s \in S \rangle$ and the corresponding expected time delay $D_s^*(\pi^*)$
1: initial $g_0 = 0$ and $d_0 = 0$; **Local:** $k = 0$
2: **repeat**
3:    $D_s^{k+1} = \sum_{s' \in N(s)} T(s, \pi_s, s') \times (d_{s,s'} + D_{s'}^{k+1})$
4:    $\pi_s^{k+1} = \arg\min_{\pi_s \in \cap(s)} \sum_{s' \in N(s)} T(s, \pi_s, s') \times (d_{s,s'} + D_{s'}^k)$
5:    $k = k + 1$
6: **until** $\max_{s \in S} \|D_s^k - D_s^{k-1}\| < \theta or k > \tau$
7: $\pi_s^* = \pi_s^*, \pi^* = \langle \pi_s^*, \forall s \in S \rangle$
8: **return** $\pi^*, D_s^*(\pi^*)$

---

4   Experiments

In this section, we will describe our experiments in detail.

4.1 DataSet

In order to make the experimental results more real and convincing, we run experiments on a real vehicle data set of SUVnet of Shanghai [26]. It include 5000 taxis and buses' trajectories data, and we only use the part of taxis' data.

We preprocessed the data set, including:

- Clean the data, including remove duplicate data and error data.
- Repair drift data based on road structure.
- Since the taxi data recorded an average of every 30 s, we interpolated the discontinuous trajectory data and error trajectory data.

4.2 Experiment Settings

We select about 2700 taxis as our object vehicles. In our experiments, we randomly select 200 vehicles as our the source vehicle and the destination vehicles to transmit data. We assume that each data package is the same size. And some hyper parameters are shown in Table 1.

Table 1. Parameter setting of experiments

Parameters	Values (range)
Wireless transmission range	200 m
The number of experimental vehicles	300 to 2700
θ	0.001
τ	1000
The number of vehicles carried data	200
Time difference to the next intersection	10 s
Time to live (TTL)	1 h, 2 h, 3 h

4.3 Experiment Result Analysis

We compared our model ASODF with OVDF-P, which is one of models of OVDF. In OVDF, a data package is successfully be transmitted when it is be transmit to a road side unit and we changed this setting. In our experiments, a data is transmitted successfully when it is transmitted to a moving vehicles.

The results is of average delivery ratio and average delay is shown in Fig. 5(a) and (b) respectively.

The results shown in Fig. 5(a) demonstrate that our model has a high delivery ratio when the number of vehicles are the same, i.e., the density of vehicles is same. And a obvious conclusion is that both model's average delivery ratio will increase with the increase of the number of vehicles. Fig. 5(b) shows that our model has a low delay when the number of vehicles is small, i.e, our model are better when the vehicles in network is sparse. and both the model will have a similar results with the increase of the vehicles.

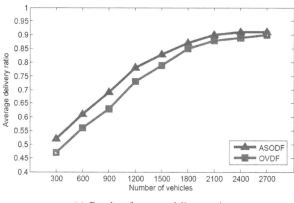

(a) Results of average delivery ratio

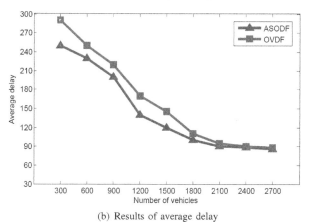

(b) Results of average delay

Fig. 5. POMDP to MDP generalization performance

Table 2. Comparison of average delivery ratio

Vehicle number	ASODF (s)	OVDF (s)	Improvement
300	0.52	0.47	10.64%
600	0.61	0.56	8.93%
900	0.69	0.63	9.52%
1200	0.78	0.73	6.85%
1500	0.83	0.79	5.06%
1800	0.87	0.85	2.35%
2100	0.90	0.88	2.27%
2400	0.91	0.89	2.25%
2700	0.92	0.90	2.22%

Table 3. Comparison of average delay

Vehicle number	ASODF	OVDF	Improvement
300	250	290	13.79%
600	230	250	8.71%
900	200	220	9.09%
1200	140	170	17.65%
1500	120	145	17.24%
1800	100	110	9.10%
2100	90	95	5.26%
2400	88	90	2.52%
2700	86	89	3.37%

The result of comparing two models is shown in Tables 2 and 3. Table 2 shows that with the increase of vehicles, the improvement of our model compare to OVDF tend to a small value of 2.22%. The reason is that with the increase of vehicle density, fewer and fewer vehicle communication links are disconnected, and more and more data packets are transmitted by wireless, the improvement is gradually reduced. And Table 3 shows that the average delay improvement is 13.79% at a low vehicle density. In summary, that our model are better that OVDF, particularly at a low vehicle density.

5   Conclusion

In this paper, we proposed an association state based optimal data forwarding model (ASODF) to improve the data delivery ratio and decrease the delivery delay in VANET. Our model formed the data forwarding to a reinforcement learning tasks and use standard value iteration method to solve it. And Experiments show that our model can get a high delivery ratio and a lower delay, particularly, our model can do better in deal with sparse environment in VANET.

References

1. Du, X., Xiao, Y., Chen, H.-H., Wu, Q.: Secure cell relay routing protocol for sensor networks. Wirel. Commun. Mob. Comput. **6**(3), 375–391 (2006)
2. Xiao, Y., Rayi, V.K., Sun, B., Du, X., Hu, F., Galloway, M.: A survey of key management schemes in wireless sensor networks. Comput. Commun. **30**(11), 2314–2341 (2007)
3. Du, X., Xiao, Y., Guizani, M., Chen, H.-H.: An effective key management scheme for heterogeneous sensor networks. Ad Hoc Netw. **5**(1), 24–34 (2007)
4. Du, X., Guizani, M., Xiao, Y., Chen, H.: Transactions papers a routing-driven elliptic curve cryptography based key management scheme for heterogeneous sensor networks. IEEE Trans. Wirel. Commun. **8**(3), 1223–1229 (2009). https://doi.org/10.1109/TWC.2009.060598

5. Du, X., Chen, H.-H.: Security in wireless sensor networks. IEEE Wirel. Commun. **15**(4) (2008)
6. Du, X., Guizani, M., Xiao, Y., Chen, H.-H.: Secure and efficient time synchronization in heterogeneous sensor networks. IEEE Trans. Veh. Technol. **57**(4), 2387–2394 (2008)
7. Perkins, C.E., Bhagwat, P.: Highly dynamic destination-sequenced distance-vector routing (DSDV) for mobile computers. ACM SIGCOMM Comput. Commun. Rev. **24**(4), 234–244 (1994)
8. Clausen, T., Jacquet, P.: Optimized link state routing protocol (OLSR). Technical report (2003)
9. Lee, S.-J., Gerla, M., Chiang, C.-C.: The dynamic source routing protocol for multi-hop wireless adhoc networks
10. Karp, B., Kung, H.-T.: GPSR: greedy perimeter stateless routing for wireless networks. In: Proceedings of the 6th Annual International Conference on Mobile Computing and Networking, pp. 243–254. ACM (2000)
11. Lochert, C., Hartenstein, H., Tian, J., Fussler, H., Hermann, D., Mauve, M.: A routing strategy for vehicular ad hoc networks in city environments. In: Proceedings of the Intelligent Vehicles Symposium, pp. 156–161. IEEE (2003)
12. Ding, Y., Xiao, L.: SADV: static-node-assisted adaptive data dissemination in vehicular networks. IEEE Trans. Veh. Technol. **59**(5), 2445–2455 (2010)
13. Zhao, J., Cao, G.: VADD: vehicle-assisted data delivery in vehicular ad hoc networks. IEEE Trans. Veh. Technol. **57**(3), 1910–1922 (2008)
14. Costa, P., Frey, D., Migliavacca, M., Mottola, L.: Towards lightweight information dissemination in inter-vehicular networks. In: Proceedings of the 3rd International Workshop on Vehicular Ad Hoc Networks, pp. 20–29. ACM (2006)
15. Leontiadis, I., Mascolo, C.: GEOPPS: geographical opportunistic routing for vehicular networks. In: IEEE International Symposium on World of Wireless, Mobile and Multimedia Networks: WoWMoM 2007, pp. 1–6. IEEE (2007)
16. Chen, L., Li, Z.-J., Jiang, S.-X., Feng, C.: MGF: mobile gateway based forwarding for infrastructure-to-vehicle data delivery in vehicular ad hoc networks. Jisuanji Xuebao (Chin. J. Comput.) **35**(3), 454–463 (2012)
17. Jeong, J., Guo, S., Gu, Y., He, T., Du, D. TBD: trajectory-based data forwarding for light-traffic vehicular networks. In: 29th IEEE International Conference on Distributed Computing Systems, ICDCS 2009, pp. 231–238. IEEE (2009)
18. Jeong, J., Guo, S., Gu, Y., He, T., Du, D.H.: TSF: trajectory-based statistical forwarding for infrastructure-to-vehicle data delivery in vehicular networks. In: 2010 IEEE 30th International Conference on Distributed Computing Systems (ICDCS), pp. 557–566. IEEE (2010)
19. Xu, F., Guo, S., Jeong, J., Gu, Y., Cao, Q., Liu, M., He, T.: Utilizing shared vehicle trajectories for data forwarding in vehicular networks. In: 2011 Proceedings of IEEE INFOCOM, pp. 441–445. IEEE (2011)
20. Wu, Y., Zhu, Y., Li, B.: Trajectory improves data delivery in vehicular networks. In: 2011 Proceedings of IEEE INFOCOM, pp. 2183–2191. IEEE (2011)
21. Choi, O., Kim, S., Jeong, J., Lee, H.-W., Chong, S.: Delay-optimal data forwarding in vehicular sensor networks. IEEE Trans. Veh. Technol. **65**(8), 6389–6402 (2016)
22. Mershad, K., Artail, H.: Performance analysis of routing in VANETs using the RSU network. In: 2011 IEEE 7th International Conference on Wireless and Mobile Computing, Networking and Communications (WiMob), pp. 89–96. IEEE (2011)
23. Bellman, R.: A Markovian decision process. J. Math. Mech. **6**, 679–684 (1957)
24. Sutton, R.S., Barto, A.G., Reinforcement Learning: An Introduction, vol. 1, no. 1. MIT Press, Cambridge (1998)

25. Pineau, J., Gordon, G., Thrun, S., et al.: Point-based value iteration: an anytime algorithm for POMDPs. In: IJCAI, vol. 3, pp. 1025–1032 (2003)
26. Huang, H.-Y., Luo, P.-E., Li, M., Li, D., Li, X., Shu, W., Wu, M.-Y.: Performance evaluation of SUVnet with real-time traffic data. IEEE Trans. Veh. Technol. **56**(6), 3381–3396 (2007)

Privacy-Assured Large-Scale Navigation from Encrypted Approximate Shortest Path Recommendation

Zhenkui Shi[1,2]([envelope]) [ORCID]

[1] Department of Computer Science, City University of Hong Kong,
Hong Kong, S.A.R., China
zhenkshi-c@my.cityu.edu.hk
[2] City University of Hong Kong, Shenzhen Research Institute,
Shenzhen 518057, China

Abstract. As the fast-paced market of smart phones, navigation application is becoming more popular especially when traveling to a new place. As a key function, shortest path recommendation enables a user routing efficiently in an unfamiliar place. However, the source and destination are always critical private information. They can be used to infer a user's personal life. Sharing such information with an app may raise severe privacy concerns.

In this paper, we propose a practical navigation system that preserves user's privacy while achieving practical shortest path recommendation. The proposed system is based on graph encryption schemes that enable privacy assured approximate shortest path queries on large-scale encrypted graphs. We first leverage a data structure called a distance oracle to create sketch information, and we further add path information to the data structure and design three structured encryption schemes. The first scheme is based on oblivious storage. The second scheme takes advantage of the latest cryptographic techniques to find the minimal distance and achieves optimal communication complexity. The third scheme adopts homomorphic encryption scheme and achieves efficient communication overhead and computation overhead on the client side. We also evaluated our construction. The results show that the computation overhead and communication overhead are reasonable and practical.

Keywords: Private navigation · Distance oracle · Oblivious storage
PIR · Homomorphic computation

1 Introduction

As the prosperity of smart phone, location based services (LBS) are becoming very common and useful. It makes our life very convenient especially when traveling to a new place. The most obvious reason is that there is always a built-in

© Springer Nature Singapore Pte Ltd. 2018
L. Zhu and S. Zhong (Eds.): MSN 2017, CCIS 747, pp. 195–211, 2018.
https://doi.org/10.1007/978-981-10-8890-2_14

GPS in a smart phone. At the same time, the current smart phone is very powerful in displaying, computation and communication with a powerful processor, large memory, and storage.

However, LBS application also introduces severe privacy concerns [10,14]. Location information can be used to infer users' context and analyze users' movement patterns [8].

Navigation is one of the most popular LBS applications. The client sends the origin and the destination to the LBS server. The server responds with the shortest path or the fastest route. The user follows the route and the location information provided by the GPS to the destination. The origin and the destination here are more critical. For they introduce same privacy concerns above, may be associated with the user's personal plan [19], and more and more users concern their location privacy, privacy preserving navigation services have attracted much attention. However, there may be many challenges to build up a privacy preserving navigation system. Firstly, any path query which includes the origin and destination may disclose users' privacy. The pair of origin and destination may be personally identifiable [19]. For example, when the destination is a hospital, it may be very severe private information for the user. The second challenge is about how to compute the shortest path privately and efficiently. It is very computation intensive for computing shortest path on large graphs using breadth first search or Dijkstra's algorithm directly. Especially when considering both privacy and users' experience, the efficiency is very critical. The third challenge is how to respond privately to the users. Any plaintext information about the path will disclose the users' location privacy.

Anonymity and obfuscation techniques are common strategies. And there are some previous schemes based on anonymity and obfuscation have been proposed to preserve users' privacy [14,19]. However they always need a trusted third party between the user and the server.

In this paper, we propose a new privacy preserving path recommendation system for navigation based on private approximate queries. Our work is inspired by the latest work about graph encryption scheme based on searchable symmetric encryption (SSE) [9]. Their work is based on distance oracle [4] and SSE. However, their work may be not suitable for privacy preserving navigation. Firstly, the scheme only responds the shortest distance and the corresponding path is not known. In addition, simply adding path information in their structure, their computation may be not work. Secondly, their schemes don't protect access pattern. Whereas in privacy preserving navigation, the access pattern may be used to infer users' the source, destination, and other personal information and will cause severe information leakage.

The contributions are summarized as follows:

1. We propose three privacy preserving shortest path query schemes based on approximate distance/path oracle. To the best of our knowledge, this is the first navigation system based on approximate shortest path query.
2. The proposed schemes leverage the sketch structure. One is based on oblivious storage (OS) and the other is based on computational PIR. The third is based

on PIR and homomorphic encryption which enables computing the shortest path on the server side and achieving minimum computation cost on the client side and communication overhead. We leverage these latest crypto techniques to retrieve the sketches privately.

3. Our schemes can support large scale datasets. We evaluate our system by using real road dataset. The results show that our system provides reasonable latency, computation over head and communication overhead.

The rest of the paper is organized as follows. Section 2 describes the related work. Section 3 presents the problem statement, the adversary model and some preliminaries. Section 4 introduces the path oracle, the scheme based on oblivious storage, the scheme based on computational PIR, the scheme based on PIR and homomorphic computation on the server side, and security analysis. Section 5 presents our concrete experiments, evaluation, further consideration, and optimization. Section 6 concludes the whole work.

2   Related Work

Privacy Preserving Shortest Path Computation. Some general work is about privacy preserving shortest path computation which is based on graph theory [11,18,20]. For example, Wu et al. [18] proposed to compress the next-hop routing matrices in networks such as city street maps, use symmetric PIR for indexes retrieval, and leverage garbled circuits and affine encodings for inner product evaluation. However, the scheme needs to construct a database with N^2 records which will consume large space when n is too large. Xie et al. [20] introduced a scheme based on oblivious storage and KD-tree partition. Mouratidis et al. [11] leveraged the hardware-aided PIR protocol and proposed two schemes. However, both of the preprocessing overhead and auxiliary space are unacceptable.

Privacy Preserving Shortest Distance/Path Query. Besides, there are also some schemes based on privacy preserving shortest distance/path query [9,16]. Meng et al. [9] presented three schemes based on distance oracle and structured encryption which are adaptively semantically-secure with reasonable leakage functions. Although we leverage the notion of distance oracle to build our system, our scheme can return approximate shortest path. And their constructions return only distance without path information and their constructions can't be applied in our construction directly. Simply adding path information may destroy the computation structure. And the most important is that their scheme can't protect the access pattern of the sketches which may reveal the source or the destination information. And the information is very critical for privacy preserving shortest path query and navigation. Wang et al. [16] proposed SecGDB, a secure Graph DataBase encryption scheme. SecGDB supports exact shortest distance/path query. However, the amortized time complexity is based on query history which is stored on the remote server to act as a caching resource. It may take several tens of minutes for a query without history. This is due to the auxiliary computation overhead introduced by implementing a secure Dijkstra's algorithm which is based on additively homomorphic encryption and garbled circuits. In addition, the scheme introduces a third party which doesn't collude with the server.

3   Problem Statement and Preliminaries

3.1   Problem Statement

Here, we formulate the main component of the navigation as the shortest path recommendation problem. Namely, the client holds the origin/source and the destination. It sends the request to the service provider. The service provider holds the map information including the topology.

Formally, the client holds the nodes pair (s, d) as the origin/source and destination. The service provider holds the graph information corresponding to the map $G = (V, E)$. Here, V is the node set of the graph, E is the edge set of the graph, $s \in V$ and $d \in V$. The client sends a shortest path query $q = (s, d)$ to the service provider and asks for the shortest path between s and d.

3.2   Adversary Model

In this paper, we just need to consider two parties without introducing any third party, namely, the server and a client. The server holds the data. When a client has a query for shortest path, it sends the query to the server. The server responds relevant information such as sketches to the client in our case. The server honestly follows the protocols we defined. In addition, the server is curious in learning the source, the destination, the shortest distance, the corresponding path about the client. Specifically, the client wishes to keep the information and the access pattern of retrieved sketches private. Because the access pattern may also leak critical information such as the source and the destination. In addition, we don't consider the information leakage through side channel or timing channel.

3.3   Preliminaries and Notations

$G = (V, E)$ presents a graph where V is the node set and E is the edge set. We denote $q = (u, v)$ as a shortest distance query and $pq = (u, v)$ as a shortest path query. p_{vw} is the shortest path from v to w.

Distance Oracles. Typically, a distance oracle is a type of data structure. It supports approximate shortest distance queries. An obvious construction is that one can pre-compute and store all the shortest distances of different pairs of nodes in the graph. In such a solution, the query complexity is $O(1)$. However, the storage complexity is $O(n^2)$. This is not practical for large graphs. Here, we introduce the sketch-based distance oracle. Das Sarma et al. proposed the first construction of sketch-based distance oracle in 2010 [4]. And we take the

Das Sarma's construction [4] as our study case here. Formally, the sketch-based distance oracle consists of a pair of algorithms, namely, $DO = (Setup, Query)$. The *Setup* algorithm takes three parameters, a graph G, an approximation factor α and an error bound ϵ. Finally, it outputs an oracle $\Omega_G = \{Sk_v\}_{v \in V}$ where Sk_v is the sketch which includes pairs (w, δ), where $w \in V$ and $\delta = dist(v, w)$. The *Query* algorithm takes two parameters, the oracle Ω_G and a shortest distance query $q = (u, v)$ and $d := Query(\Omega_G, u, v)$. DO is (α, ϵ)-correct if for all graphs G and all queries q, $Pr[dist(u, v) < d < \alpha dist(u, v)]$. For the $Query(u, v)$, the query algorithm firstly finds the common nodes set I between Sk_u and Sk_v, and returns $s \in I$ such that $dist(u, s) + dist(s, v)$ is the minimum. If there is no common node, then it returns $\perp$.

4   Our Constructions

In this section, we illustrate our construction for privacy preserving navigation.

4.1   Path Oracle Setup

The sketches created by distance oracles provide our effective data structure for shortest distance queries. It greatly saves the storage. For it is pre-computed and can save computation during runtime. However, only providing the shortest distance is not enough in some cases. In many applications, providing the shortest path is essential. And navigation is one of the cases.

Definition 1 (*Path Oracle*). *A sketch-based path oracle $PO = (Setup, Query)$. The Setup algorithm takes three parameters, a graph G, an approximation factor α and an error bound ϵ. Finally, it outputs an oracle $\Omega_G = \{Sk_v\}_{v \in V}$ where Sk_v is the sketch which includes triples (w, δ, p_{vw}), where $w \in V$, $\delta = dist(v, w)$ and p_{vw} is the shortest path from v to w. The Query algorithm takes two parameters, the oracle Ω_G and a shortest path query $q = (u, v)$ and $(d, p) := Query(\Omega_G, u, v)$ where the pair (d, p) is the shortest distance and path returned by the Query. PO is (α, ϵ)-correct if for all graphs G and all queries q, $Pr[dist(u, v) < d < \alpha dist(u, v)] \geq 1 - \epsilon$.*

We can take advantage of the data structure and construct our path oracles. Similarly, we define a path oracle is a type of data structure which supports approximate shortest path queries. Here, we can construct the path oracle by adding path information to the sketches created by the distance oracle. Suppose that $\Omega_G = (Sk_{v_1}, Sk_{v_2}, ..., Sk_{v_n})$ is the collection of sketches created by a distance oracle. Each sketch Sk_{v_i} consist of λ pairs of $\{(w_z, \delta_z)\}_{0 \leq z \leq \lambda - 1}$, where w_z is a node and $\delta_z = dist(v_i, w_z)$.

Based on the structure, we add path information for each sketch. Without loss of generality, $DO = (Setup, Query)$ is a sketch-based distance oracle. It creates a collection of sketches $\Omega_G = (Sk_{v_1}, Sk_{v_2}, ..., Sk_{v_n})$. We define a path oracle as $PO = (Setup, Query)$. It inherits the sketch-based data structure created by DO. For each sketch Sk_{v_i}, it consists of triple $\{(w_z, \delta_z), p_{v_i w_z}\}_{0 \leq z \leq \lambda - 1}$, where w_z is a node, $\delta_z = dist(v_i, w_z)$, and $p_{v_i w_z}$ is the information about the shortest path from v_i to w_z. $p_{v_i w_z}$ can be pre-computed through classical shortest path algorithm such as Dijkstra's algorithm.

Given a query $q = (u, v)$, it finds the collection common nodes I between Sk_u and Sk_v. Then it find the node $s \in I$ such that $mind = dist(u, s) + dist(s, v)$ is the minimum and return $(mind, pi)$ where $p = p_{us} + p_{sv}$. From the construction, we can get the following lemma.

Lemma 1 (*Path Oracle Construction*). *The construction of path oracle above is (α, ϵ)-correct. For all graphs G and all queries q, $Pr[dist(u, v) < d < \alpha dist(u, v)] \geq 1 - \epsilon$.*

For the path oracle construction, we setup the construction based on the Das Sarma et al. oracle [4] as our study case. There is sub routine *Sketch* used to generate a collection of sketches $(Sk_{v_1}^i, ..., Sk_{v_n}^i)$ where i is the ith call to the sub routine. To create the sketch $Sk_{v_j}^i$, the sub routine samples $r + 1$ sets of nodes $S_0, S_1, ..., S_r$ where the size of S_i is 2^i where $r = \lfloor logn \rfloor$. For each node vj, for all these sets S_i, it computes $w_k, \delta i, p_{w_k, v_j}$ where w_k is the closest node to v_j, $\delta i = dis(v_j, w_k) = dis(v_j, S_i)$ and p_{w_k, v_j} is the corresponding shortest path. After calling the sub routine σ times, it collects σ collections of $(Sk_{v_1}^i, ..., Sk_{v_n}^i)_{i \in [\sigma]}$ where $\sigma = \tilde{\theta}(n^{2/(\alpha+1)})$. The final sketch $Sk_{v_j} = \bigcup_{i=1}^{\sigma} Sk_{v_j}^i$. And finally, it outputs the path oracle as $\Omega_G = (Sk_{v_1}, ..., Sk_{v_n})$.

4.2   A Scheme Based on Oblivious Storage

In this section, we illustrate one of our proposed scheme with strong privacy grantees. The scheme adopts the latest practical techniques, oblivious storage for privacy preserving sketch retrieval.

The proposed architecture is illustrated in Fig. 1. It consists of a client and a server. The server provides oblivious storage service.

Oblivious Storage. Oblivious storage (OS) is defined as a related notion to Oblivious RAM (ORAM). Bonel et al. proposed the notion as a practical implementation of ORAM in [3]. ORAM can provably hide all access patterns. In OS model, clients can outsource the data to the cloud or third parties. when running applications, OS can keep the data from disclose. In our case, we can private retrieval the sketch privately via OS. OS provides strong access pattern protection. The origin and the destination can be well protected.

Typically, there are two kinds of solutions for OS: the Square-Root and the Hierarchical solutions. We adopt the OS scheme based on Path-ORAM [15]. It has non-trivial online latencies on moderate size datasets and doesn't involve any system unavailable time which provides excellent worst-case performance guarantee on large datasets [20].

As illustrated in Fig. 1, the data is stored as a binary tree in the server. In our circumstance, there are N sketches and we pad each sketch to the same length as a block and we call it sketch block. And the hight of the binary tree is $L = \lceil logN \rceil$. Each node of the tree is called a bucket and each bucket contains Z blocks where Z is a small constant (e.g., 3–5). These Z blocks are either real

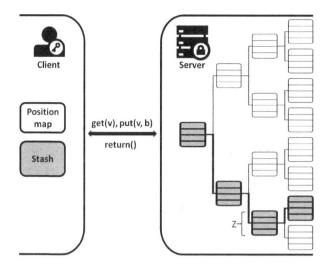

Fig. 1. The architecture based on oblivious storage.

data blocks or dummy blocks. There are two data structures stored on the client, a position map and a stash as illustrated in Fig. 2. The position map maps each of the N sketch blocks to one of the 2^L leaves independently and uniformly, e.g., $i := PosMap[x]$ means that sketch block x is associated leaf i and block x resides in some bucket in the path from the root node to the leaf x, or in the stash. The position map is refreshed as blocks are accessed and remapped.

Oblivious Storage Initialization. The client initializes each sketch as an encrypted block with the same length and sends all the encrypted blocks to the server. The blocks are stored in a binary tree on the server.

On the client side, there is a position map and a stash. The functionality of position map is like an index. Suppose there are N sketches. Each sketch is assigned with an ID. The position map can be used to map each of the N sketches to one of the 2^L leaves which are independently and uniformly at random. The stash is used to store sketch blocks during accessing and overflowed sketch blocks from the binary tree.

On the server side, all the sketch blocks are stored in the binary tree. The height of the tree is $L = \lceil logN \rceil$. Each node of the tree is considered as a bucket which contains Z blocks. Z is independent of N. There are many dummy blocks to make sure that all the buckets appear full.

Private Sketch Retrieval. When the client needs to query a shortest path $pq = (Src, Dst)$ where Src is the source node and Dst is the destination node, the client creates two retrieval requests for the source and the destination respectively. The two requests are in the same form. We take the Src sketch Sk_{Src} retrieval request as an example.

To retrieval sketch block Sk_{Src}, the client and server should take the following steps.

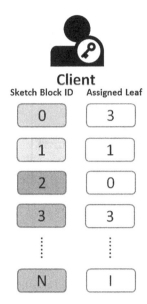

Fig. 2. The data structure on the client side.

1. The client checks the position map and finds the leaf $i := PosMap[Src]$, remaps the sketch block Sk_{Src} to a new random position. Then, it sends a read request to the server. The form of the request is like $(read, PosMap[Src], None)$.
2. The server reads all the buckets along the path from the root node to the leaf node $PosMap[Src]$ and sends all the buckets including $(L + 1) * Z$ blocks to the client.
3. The client decrypts all the $(L + 1) * Z$ blocks, recovers the real sketch blocks, stores in the stash, identifies the sketch block Sk_{Src} and initializes to the sketch format. The dummy blocks are discarded.
4. The client re-encrypts the sketch blocks in the stash with fresh randomness and sends a writing request to the server. The writing path is the same as the read path. The form of the writing request is like $(writing, PosMap[Src], data*)$. The sketch blocks in $data*$ are put as close to the leaves as possible while the buckets where they are must be in the same path as their assigned leaves. If buckets including the root bucket are full of sketch blocks, the remaining sketch blocks will stay in the stash.
5. The server writes the data along the path from the root node to the leaf node $PosMap[Src]$.

In the phase of private sketch retrieval, the client should send two pairs of reading/writing requests to the server and the server completes 2 pairs of reading access and writing access operations, one for the source's sketch and one for the destination's sketch.

Algorithm 1. *ComputeShortestPath*: compute shortest path

Require: Private key SK; source sketch block ssb; destination sketch block dsb.
Ensure: shortest distance and path $\{sdis, spath\}$.
 1: $ssk \leftarrow InitializeSketch(SK, ssb)$;
 2: $dsk \leftarrow InitializeSketch(SK, dsb)$;
 3: $std \leftarrow ssk + dsk$;
 4: $sdis = \perp$;
 5: **for** $v_j \in \{v_1, \cdots, v_m\}$ **do**
 6:    **if** $std[v_j].dis < sdis$ **then**
 7:       $sdis \leftarrow std[v_j].dis$;
 8:       $spath \leftarrow std[v_j].path$;
 9:    **end if**
10: **end for**
11: return $sdis, spath$;

Shortest Path Computation. After retrieving both the origin's sketch and destination's sketch, the client can compute the shortest path locally. The algorithm is illustrated as Algorithm 1. The client firstly initializes the source sketch and the destination sketch as step 1–2. Then the step 3 will add the distances if the nodes are both in the source sketch and the destination sketch. We say these nodes are common nodes and form a set $v_1, v_2, ..., v_m$. Then the step 4–10 of the algorithm find the minimal distance the corresponding common node where $std[v_j].dis$ is the joint distance of the distance from the source to v_j and the distance from v_j to the destination. And the shortest path $std[v_j].path$ is joint of the two paths. If there is no common node, then the algorithm return $\perp$.

4.3   A Scheme Based on PIR

In this section, we illustrate the privacy preserving scheme based on computational PIR. And PIR can provide robust privacy preserving which is equivalent to oblivious RAM storage. The scheme is inspired by the latest privacy preserving techniques XPIR [2] and its application about private media consumption [6]. Although previous work argued that traditional PIR protocols involve considerable computation and/or communication overheads on sizable datasets. Also, some practical PIR scheme may introduce an off-the-shelf hardware secured coprocessor and raise a hardware-aided PIR protocol [17]. By leveraging the usable PIR, [11] proposed two schemes for shortest path queries. But they need unacceptable preprocessing and auxiliary space.

PIR for Private Sketch Retrieval. There are two typical PIR protocols, namely, computational PIR [2] and information theoretic PIR [6]. Due to the fact that the information theoretic PIR protocol needs at least k servers where $k \geq 1$. And any of the servers should not collude. This is a strict setting. Whereas the model for computation PIR is simple and there is only one computationally bound server in computational PIR protocol. And the current crypto scheme for computational PIR is efficient enough [2]. We can realize the privacy preserving

---

Query Construction to retrieve sketch Sk_{v_j} (the client):

1. For i from 1 to n,
   -if $i \neq j$, create a random encryption of zero
   -if $i = j$, create a random encryption of one
2. Send the $q = (pk, q_1, ..., q_n)$ to the server;

Reply Construction (the server): The server performs following computations

1. For i from 1 to n,
   -    $R = Sum_{i=1}^{n} q_i * Sk_{v_i}$
2. Return R

Sketch Extraction (the client):

1. Client decrypts the reply R and recover the sketch Sk_{v_j}.

Fig. 3. The workflow for computational PIR based sketch retrieval.

sketches retrieval through the computational PIR. In our design based on computational PIR, all the sketches form a library as a database. Then the library is $L = \{Sk_{v_1}, Sk_{v_2}, ..., Sk_{v_N}\}$ where N is the number of all nodes in the road network. Suppose that l is the bit length of sketch Sk_{v_i} and l_0 is the bit length that can be used for homomorphic operations. If $l > l_0$, then the sketch should be split into chunks of l_0 bits as $Sk_{v_i} = \{Sk_{v_i,0}, Sk_{v_i,1}, ..., Sk_{v_i,l/l_0}\}$. If $l \leq l_0$, each sketch can be padded as one element entry in the database. The padding scheme just makes sure that one sketch should be contained in only one element entry in the database. This rule guarantees that the client can get the right sketch through one query. And the client should know the mapping of the sketches and the corresponding entries. There are three steps in the traditional computational PIR protocol. For simplicity, we consider each sketch as one element entry. And the workflow can be illustrated in Fig. 3.

Shortest Path Computation. In our scheme, the shortest path computation is on the local side of the client. It shares the same process with the scheme based on oblivious storage as Algorithm 1.

4.4   A Communication Efficient Scheme Based on PIR

In this sub section, we describe a communication efficient scheme. In this scheme, we leverage the PIR to retrieve the source sketch and the destination sketch. However, the server doesn't send the sketch to the client directly. The server computes the shortest path locally and return the result to the client. The scheme includes the following steps.

Setup. Compared with the previous schemes, we need a more structured data structure. We set up a data structure illustrated in Fig. 4. To make the later

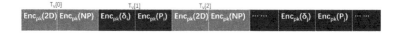

Fig. 4. The sketch hash table for a sketch.

computation effective, we adopt the same homomorphic encryption scheme $HE = (Gen, Enc, Dec, Eval)$ with the following PIR protocol and (pk, sk) is the public/secret key pair. In addition, it makes use of a family of universal hash function H. Given Ω_G, ε, let D be the maximum distance over all the sketches and S be the maximum sketch size. It samples a hash function $h \xleftarrow{\$} H$ with domain V and co-domain $[t]$, where $t = 2 \cdot S^2 \cdot \varepsilon^{-1}$.

For each node $v \in V$, it creates a sketch hash table T_v as Fig. 4. Each table has t cells. Each cell stores two parts, one for the shortest distance and the other for the shortest path. For example, $\{(w_z, \delta_z), p_{v_i w_z}\} \in SK_v$, $T_v[h(w_z)].dis \leftarrow Enc_{pk}(\delta_z)$, and $T_v[h(w_z)].path \leftarrow Enc_{pk}(p_{v_i w_z})$. For all the remaining locations, $T_v[h(w_z)].dis \leftarrow Enc_{pk}(2D)$ and $T_v[h(w_z)].path \leftarrow Enc_{pk}(NP)$ where NP is randomized path information.

Private Sketch Hash Table Identification. This phase is very similar with the scheme based on PIR. We leverage the idea of PIR to identify the source sketch hash table and the destination sketch hash table obliviously. First, the client construct two queries for the source and the destination respectively. The process is same with the PIR protocol. After receiving the queries, the server does the similar computation as PIR protocol. However, it just does the computation and doesn't return the result. After the computation, the server gets the encrypted versions of the source sketch hash table T_s and the destination sketch hash table T_d.

Private Shortest Path Computation. Now the server get the encrypted sketch hash tables T_s and T_d. Then, the server computes the homomorphic additions over each cell and creates the new hash table T_r, where $T_r[i].dis = T_s[i].dis + T_d[i].dis$ and $T_r[i].path$ is the concatenation of $T_s[i].path$ and $T_d[i].path$. Then, the server needs to find the minimum distance and the corresponding path from the new encrypted hash table T_r.

Without loss of generality, we assume that $0 \leq T_r[i].dis, T_r[j].dis < 2^l$ where $i, j \in \{0, ..., t-1\}$. Then, let $T_{i,j} = 2^l + T_r[i].dis - T_r[j].dis$. Let $\widetilde{T_{i,j}}$ be the most significant bit of $T_{i,j}$. And $\widetilde{T_{i,j}}$ can be computed through the following equation

$$\widetilde{T_{i,j}} = 2^{-l} \cdot [T_{i,j} - (T_{i,j} \bmod 2^l)]. \tag{1}$$

In the equation, the subtraction sets the least significant bits to zero, and the multiplication shifts the most significant bit down. Through $\widetilde{T_{i,j}}$, we can compute the minimum distance $T_{i,j}.dis$ and the corresponding path $T_{i,j}.path$ as follows:

$$T_{i,j}.dis = \widetilde{T_{i,j}} \cdot [T_r[i].dis - T_r[j].dis] + T_r[j].dis. \tag{2}$$

$$T_{i,j}.path = \widetilde{T_{i,j}} \cdot [T_r[i].path - T_r[j].path] + T_r[j].path. \tag{3}$$

Algorithm 2. *ComputeShortestPath*: compute shortest path on the server side

---

Require: Private key SK; the hash table T_r.
Ensure: shortest distance and path $\{sdis, spath\}$.
 1: $sdis \leftarrow T_r[0].dis$;
 2: $spath \leftarrow T_r[0].path$;
 3: **for** $n = \{1 : t - 1\}$ **do**
 4:     $sdis_i \leftarrow sdis$;
 5:     $spath_i \leftarrow spath$;
 6:     $sdis_j \leftarrow T_r[n].dis$;
 7:     $spath_j \leftarrow T_r[n].path$;
 8:     follow the secure two-party computation protocol and compute $\widetilde{T_{i,j}}$ using equation1;
 9:     compute $sdis$ using equation 2;
10:     compute $spath$ using equation 3;
11: **end for**
12: return $(sdis, spath)$;

However, there is only one challenge to compute these values over encrypted domain. There is no effective homomorphic operation to compute $(T_{i,j} \mod 2^l)$ over encrypted domain. Here, we try to minimize the computation overhead of the client and introduce a third party, cryptographic service provider (CSP). This similar architecture is widely applied in many scenario [7,12]. Our adversary model follows the similar setting, namely, the server doesn't collude with the CSP. Then, the server and the CSP follow an secure interactive two-party computation protocol to compute $(T_{i,j} \mod 2^l)$ [5,13].

In this architecture, the client and the server uses the homomorphic scheme provided by the CSP. The queries is created by the client through the public key of the CSP. The server runs the PIR protocol under the same homomorphic scheme. Then, the server and the CSP follow the same secure two-party computation protocol as [5].

After that, we can apply a recursive algorithm to compute the shortest distance and the corresponding path. The algorithm is illustrated as Algorithm 2.

After the server computing $sdis$ and $spath$, the server generates two random masks $smask$ and $pmask$, computes $(sdis + smask)$ and $(spath + pmask)$, encrypts $smask$ and $pmask$ using the public key of the client and sends $(sdis + smask)$ and $(spath + pmask)$ to the CSP. The CSP decrypts $(sdis + smask)$ and $(spath + pmask)$, encrypts using the public key of the client, and sends the new encrypted $(sdis + smask)$ and $(spath + pmask)$ to the server. The server sends encrypted $(sdis + smask)$, $(spath + pmask)$, $smask$ and $pmask$ to the client. The client decrypts them and gets the final results through the path information.

5   Evaluation

In this section, we present our experiment and evaluation of our schemes on several real road networks. We implemented the path oracle based on the Das

Sarma et al. distance oracle algorithm [4] and leverage existing building block such oblivious storage scheme based on path ORAM and XPIR [2]. We evaluate the schemes on Microsoft Azure. For simplicity and efficiency, we use the Microsoft Azure virtual machines to simulate the server and the client. We select the standard D4s V3 with 4 cores 16 GB RAM and 30 GB SSD as the server and select the standard D4s V2 with 4 cores 14 GB RAM and 30 GB SSD as the client.

5.1 Evaluation of Path Oracle

We leverage the boost graph library and implement the path oracle in C++11. We also take the real road datasets from [1] as our study case. To evaluate our scheme, we consider the real road network as Table 1. The sketch size is very critical in path oracle. It will affect the communication overhead in both of our schemes and computation overhead in the scheme based on computation PIR. The parameter σ defines the times to call the sub routine to create sketches. We set $\sigma = 3$ as the base [9]. For each node, the oracle program will create a sketch file named with the node ID in a local directory. In the sketch file, a line is an element in the sketch. The format of the file is illustrated as Fig. 5. Suppose that the file is the sketch file of node v_s. Fields like $(v_i, dist(v_s, v_i), Path(v_s, v_i))$ are separated by a comma.

And we run our program to create all the sketch files for different road network. Besides, we also change the times to call the sub routine and check the sizes changing over the times. For the max size of sketch files will affect later processing such as the block size of oblivious storage. We present the max size of sketch files as Fig. 6. In the figure, CA(21048, 21693) means California Road Network which has 21048 nodes and 21693 edges. Through the figure, we can see that the max size is about 6 KB when calling the subroutine 3 times. Even calling the subroutine 18 times, the max size is about 24 KB. In the scheme based on oblivious storage, the size will affect the stash size on the client side and communication overhead. The result shows that the growth rate of max size is all linear or sub linear over times to call the sub routine and the scale of the graph such as the number of nodes and the number of edges.

Table 1. Real road dataset

Name of road network	Number of nodes	Number of edges
California Road Network (CA)	21048	21693
City of San Joaquin County Road Network (TG)	18263	23873
City of Oldenburg Road Network (OL)	6105	7035

5.2   Evaluation of the Scheme Based on OS

To evaluate the scheme based on OS, we focus on the metrics about the query time and communication overhead. It depends mainly on the blocks to transfer and levels to process. We should consider the level of the binary tree $L = \lceil logN \rceil$ and the parameter of OS Z. The level is associated with the number of nodes N. For security reason, we consider the cases when $Z = 4$ [15]. On the client side, we set the security parameter $\lambda = 128$ which means that the failure probability less than $2^{-\lambda}$. And the persistent local storage sizes for the max stash are 147 when $Z = 4$. In addition, the client also requires transient storage used to cache the fetched data from a path on the server. The storage size is $Z * log_2 N$ blocks.

Fig. 5. The file format of sketch file.

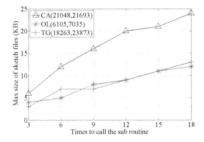

Fig. 6. The max size of sketch files changes over times to call the subroutine.

The time cost is illustrated in Fig. 7. Through the figure, we can see that there is little computation overhead on the server side. The query time is almost for the communication overhead. This is consistent with the oblivious storage protocol. Through the Fig. 7(a), the growth rate of the query time and the time of the server processing is almost linear with the growth rate of the block size. Through the Fig. 7(b), the fluctuation including the server processing time and the whole query time is sub linear over the number of nodes. It can be presented as $f(x) = \alpha \lceil logN \rceil$ where N is the number of nodes and α is a coefficient. This makes the scheme more scalable. And the total time cost is reasonable.

The communication overhead is about $Z * \lceil logN \rceil$. Both the computation overhead and latency are practical.

5.3   Evaluation of the Scheme Based on Computational PIR

To evaluate the scheme based on computational PIR, we focus on the metrics about the query time, computation overhead including the time cost to decrypt results, etc. We pad all the sketches and evaluate different scales of databases. We set the security parameter as 120 for the Ring-LWE encryption. We evaluate the datasets when the number of Nodes $N = 6105, 18263, 21048, 42096$, and the file size $f = 4\,KB$, $8\,KB$, $12\,KB$, $24\,KB$ respectively. The evaluation result is presented in Table 2. Our result focuses on the decrypting time and the query round-trip time (RTT). The RTT grows to 18.6123 s as the number of files increased to 42096 and the file size increased to 24 KB. The client side also should take more time to decrypt the result file.

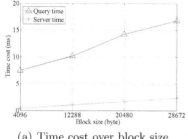   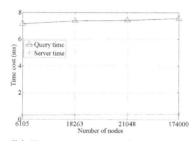

(a) Time cost over block size   (b) Time cost over node number

Fig. 7. Time cost for server and query respectively

Table 2. Evaluation of private sketch retrieval based on computational PIR

Number of files	Max file size of sketch files	Decrypting time (S)	Query RTT (S)
6105	4 KB	0.337939	0.400975
18263	8 KB	1.47355	1.60825
21048	12 KB	2.70837	2.813172
42096	24 KB	18.4685	18.6123

To further investigate the relation ship between the max file size, the query RTT, and computation cost, we fix the number of files, increase the max file sizes and evaluate the metrics. This is due to that the times to call the sub routine also affect the max file size and query correctness. We fix the file number as $N = 21048$. The evaluation result is shown as Fig. 8. Through the results, we can see that both the decrypting time and query RTT grow over the max file size increasing. The query RTT is from 1.8 s to 8.8 s when the max file is from 8 KB to 28 KB respectively.

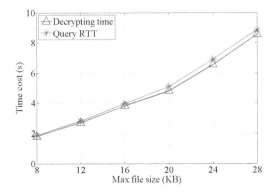

Fig. 8. The time cost of PIR changes over the max file sizes when the number of files is 21048.

6   Conclusion

In this paper, we propose three schemes for approximate shortest path query which aims to protect users' privacy and achieve shortest path query. Our designs provide robust privacy guarantees by leveraging the latest cryptographic progress on oblivious storage and PIR respectively. The first two schemes don't need any third party. In the third scheme, most of the computation is on the server side and can achieve efficient communication overhead. Security and evaluation are conducted to show our design can achieve strong security guarantees with practical performance.

Acknowledgement. This work was supported by the Natural Science Foundation of China (Project No. 61572412) and the Microsoft Azure Research Grant.

References

1. Real datasets for spatial databases: Road networks and points of interest. https://www.cs.utah.edu/~lifeifei/SpatialDataset.htm
2. Aguilar-Melchor, C., Barrier, J., Fousse, L., Killijian, M.-O.: XPIR: private information retrieval for everyone. In: Proceedings of PETS (2015)
3. Boneh, D., Mazieres, D., Popa, R.A.: Remote oblivious storage: making oblivious ram practical (2011)
4. Das Sarma, A., Gollapudi, S., Najork, M., Panigrahy, R.: A sketch-based distance oracle for web-scale graphs. In: Proceedings of ACM WSDM, pp. 401–410 (2010)
5. Erkin, Z., Franz, M., Guajardo, J., Katzenbeisser, S., Lagendijk, I., Toft, T.: Privacy-preserving face recognition. In: Goldberg, I., Atallah, M.J. (eds.) PETS 2009. LNCS, vol. 5672, pp. 235–253. Springer, Heidelberg (2009). https://doi.org/10.1007/978-3-642-03168-7_14
6. Gupta, T., Crooks, N., Mulhern, W., Setty, S.T., Alvisi, L., Walfish, M.: Scalable and private media consumption with popcorn. In: Proceedings of NSDI (2016)

7. Kim, S., Kim, J., Koo, D., Kim, Y., Yoon, H., Shin, J.: Efficient privacy-preserving matrix factorization via fully homomorphic encryption. In Proceedings of ACM ASIACCS (2016)
8. Krumm, J.: A survey of computational location privacy. Pers. Ubiquit. Comput. **13**(6), 391–399 (2009)
9. Meng, X., Kamara, S., Nissim, K., Kollios, G.: Grecs: graph encryption for approximate shortest distance queries. In: Proceedings of ACM CCS (2015)
10. Microsoft Trustworthy Computing. Location based services and privacy (2011). http://www.microsoft.com/en-us/download/confirmation.aspx?id=3250
11. Mouratidis, K., Yiu, M.L.: Shortest path computation with no information leakage (2012)
12. Nikolaenko, V., Ioannidis, S., Weinsberg, U., Joye, M., Taft, N., Boneh, D.: Privacy-preserving matrix factorization. In: Proceedings of ACM CCS (2013)
13. Rahulamathavan, Y., Phan, R.C.-W., Chambers, J.A., Parish, D.J.: Facial expression recognition in the encrypted domain based on local fisher discriminant analysis. IEEE Trans. Affect. Comput. **4**(1), 83–92 (2013)
14. Shin, K.G., Ju, X., Chen, Z., Hu, X.: Privacy protection for users of location-based services. IEEE Wirel. Commun. **19**(1), 1536–1284 (2012)
15. Stefanov, E., Van Dijk, M., Shi, E., Fletcher, C., Ren, L., Yu, X., Devadas, S.: Path ORAM: an extremely simple oblivious RAM protocol. In: Proceedings of ACM CCS, pp. 299–310 (2013)
16. Wang, Q., Ren, K., Du, M., Li, Q., Mohaisen, A.: SecGDB: Graph Encryption for Exact Shortest Distance Queries with Efficient Updates. In: Kiayias, A. (ed.) FC 2017. LNCS, vol. 10322, pp. 79–97. Springer, Cham (2017). https://doi.org/10.1007/978-3-319-70972-7_5
17. Williams, P., Sion, R.: Usable pir. In: Proceedings of NDSS (2008)
18. Wu, D.J., Zimmerman, J., Planul, J., Mitchell, J.C.: Privacy-preserving shortest path computation. arXiv preprint arXiv:1601.02281 (2016)
19. Xi, Y., Schwiebert, L., Shi, W.: Privacy preserving shortest path routing with an application to navigation. Pervasive Mob. Comput. **13**, 142–149 (2014)
20. Xie, D., Li, G., Yao, B., Wei, X., Xiao, X., Gao, Y., Guo, M.: Practical private shortest path computation based on oblivious storage. In: Proceedings of IEEE ICDE, pp. 361–372 (2016)

An Efficient and Secure Authentication Scheme for In-vehicle Networks in Connected Vehicle

Mengjie Duan$^{(\boxtimes)}$, Shunrong Jiang, and Liangmin Wang$^{(\boxtimes)}$

School of Computer Science and Communication Engineering, Jiangsu University,
Zhenjiang, China
duan_ujs@qq.com, jsywow@gmail.com, wanglm@ujs.edu.cn

Abstract. In-vehicle networks which were originally designed to operate in a closed environment without secure concerns are now being connected to external nodes/networks and providing useful services. However, communications with the external world introduce severe security threats to the vehicle. For connected vehicle, many attacks, which were only feasible with physical access to a vehicle, can now be carried out remotely over wireless networks. To overcome this problem, we propose a security protocol to protect in-vehicle networks based on current Controller Area Network specifications. First, we generate the secure in-vehicle networks by using a group key. Then, we make the gateway join the secure in-vehicle networks after authenticating it. Finally, we generate the pairware key to ensure the secure communication between the external node and the gateway. The security analysis and performance evaluation show that the proposed scheme is secure and practical.

Keywords: Connected vehicle · In-vehicle networks
Controller Area Network · Security

1 Introduction

To meet the increasing demand for Intelligent Transportation (IoT), in-vehicle entertainment, and vehicle intelligence, connected vehicle (CV) is proposed to provide Internet connectivity [17], interactivity with mobile devices [1], remote diagnostics [13], firmware updates over the air [16], automatic collision avoidance [5], and so on. With the commercialization of the connected vehicle, in-vehicle networks, which were regarded as a closed network in the past, are now being connected to external nodes/networks and providing useful services.

Traditional in-vehicle networks consist of 70 Electronic Control Units (ECUs) and Controller Area Network (CAN) buses on average [2], where each ECU controls one or more of the electrical systems in a vehicle and CAN buses connect these ECUs via a standard communication protocol. Unfortunately, information security has not been considered in the design of CAN. For example, when data frames are broadcast, CAN does not ensure the confidentiality and the

© Springer Nature Singapore Pte Ltd. 2018
L. Zhu and S. Zhong (Eds.): MSN 2017, CCIS 747, pp. 212–226, 2018.
https://doi.org/10.1007/978-981-10-8890-2_15

authentication of them [11]. Thus, a malicious adversary can easily eavesdrop on data frames or launch a replay attack.

Connected vehicle will be insecure if the nodes in it are not well protected. On the other hand, connecting to external nodes makes attacks more easier than before even without physical contact [4,6,14,20,21]. Thus, before widely adopting connected vehicle, cloud services for vehicles and other sophisticated approaches to the connected vehicle, it is essential to reconsider the security of each node itself.

To achieve secure communication in in-vehicle networks, [8,12] were proposed considering the limited data payload of the CAN data frame. However, these protocols can not be applied to in-vehicle networks since they do not support real-time data processing. To deal with this drawback, [20] proposed their scheme to achieve secure communication in-vehicle networks. They also considered secure connection with external devices such as an automotive diagnostic tool in their work. However, direct communication between the external node and in-vehicle networks introduces two major restrictions for connected vehicle: First, to directly communicate with in-vehicle networks, external nodes should analyze the CAN data frames of car manufacturers while each car manufacture may be different. Second, integration of external devices with in-vehicle networks will have acute security/safety implications [6,18].

To address these concerns, OpenXC [1] may be a better solution which works as a gateway and translation module between external nodes and in-vehicle networks. In addition, Han et al. [9] proposed their authentication mechanism to guarantee the security of the architecture which is composed of external nodes, a gateway, and in-vehicle networks. However, their authentication mechanism is not efficient and does not consider the secure in-vehicle network communication. This motivates us to propose a practical and efficient secure communication scheme in connected vehicle, the contributions of our work are listed as follows:

– In this paper, we propose an efficient and secure scheme based on low-performance ECUs and the limited data payload of a CAN data frame for in-vehicle networks.
– We design the CAN data frames according to our proposed scheme to guarantee the confidentiality, authentication, and practicality while preventing the replay attack.
– The security and performance analysis are carried out to show that the proposed scheme is secure and efficient.

The rest of this paper is organized as follows: Sect. 2 presents the system model and preliminaries. We describe the construction of our scheme in Sect. 3 and give the security analysis in Sect. 4 and provide performance evaluation in Sect. 5. The related work is given in Sect. 6. Finally, Sect. 7 concludes the paper.

2   Related Work

Hoppe et al. [10] and Nilsson et al. [13] pointed out that vulnerabilities of the in-vehicle CAN is the primary reason for cyber attack. Koscher et al. [11] mentioned that the lack of authentication and encryption of data frames is the most severe vulnerabilities of CAN. Schweppe et al. [15] proposed a secure communication architecture for vehicles by EVITA-HSM [3]. They suggested a truncated 32-bit MAC considering the limited data payload of CAN data frames to achieve authentication of in-vehicle networks. However, they did not describe how to generate and transmit a 32-bit MAC. In addition, they did not consider data confidentiality and connectivity to external node. Checkoway et al. [6] discovered that the remote attack is feasible in modern automobiles through wireless communication. They also experimented with short-range and long-range wireless attacks. However, this kind of attack is not practical since it required complex and advanced technologies [6].

To prevent a replay attack in in-vehicle CAN communication environment, Lin et al. [12] and Groza et al. [8] proposed data authentication techniques considering the limited data payload of a CAN data frame. Lin et al. [12] proposed a MAC generation technique by an ID table, message counter, and pairwise symmetric key (PWSK) to address the replay attack. However, the protocol used a PWSK to generate MACs which makes the number of MACs linearly increase with the number of receivers. This will rapidly increase the CAN bus load and is impractical. Groza et al. [8] suggested a CAN data authentication protocol using a TESLA-like protocol. In TESLA, a sender attaches to each data a MAC computed with a key k only known to the sender. A short time later, the sender sends k to the receiver, who can then authenticate the data. We note that key disclosure delay in the TESLA-like protocol should be minimized to ensure real-time processing in CAN. However, the shorter the delay is, the larger the bus load is. In addition, both [12] and [8] did not consider data confidentiality and connectivity with external node.

To achieve confidentiality, authentication, and to prevent the replay attack, Woo et al. [20] proposed their scheme based on the low-performance of ECUs and the limited data payload of a CAN data frame. Their scheme efficiently achieved secure communication of in-vehicle networks and considered communication with external nodes, such as an automotive diagnostic tool. However, in their architecture, the external node directly communicated with in-vehicle networks which makes their scheme may be not practical and convenient.

Han et al. [9] proposed an authentication scheme for a connected vehicle based on the architecture we constructed in this paper. However, their scheme focused on authenticating the entities of the architecture without considering the confidentiality and preventing the replay attack of in-vehicle networks.

3   System Model and Design Objective

3.1   System Model

We consider external nodes connected with in-vehicle networks through a gateway as shown in Fig. 1. The network consists of three entities:

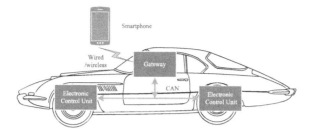

Fig. 1. The system model.

- External node (EN): EN, such as smartphones and tablets, interacts with in-vehicle networks through the gateway. It is capable of handling heavy computation tasks and has a standard communication network architecture.
- Gateway (GW): GW interacts with both the $ECUs$ and EN. GW is usually directly inserted into OBD-II port and communicates with $ECUs$ over in-vehicle networks through CAN buses. It is able to communicate with EN over either a wired connection (e.g., USB) or a wireless connection (e.g., WiFi, Bluetooth). GW has the manufacture-independent interfaces such as Ford's OpenXC [1] which works as a translator between EN and in-vehicle networks.
- ECUs interact with the gateway through CAN buses, and their communication capabilities are limited because of CAN buses.

We assume that the ECUs are not compromised in this paper since this attack model usually needs physical contraction. Both EN and GM are semi-trusted, meaning that they may be compromised or forged by adversaries. Thus, the remote attack model in our paper is that: adversaries can compromise EN or/and GM to attack our in-vehicle networks in order to get the private information of our vehicles (e.g., speed, location, track and so on) or control the car to cause accidents.

3.2   Design Objective

There are three major issues of in-vehicle networks when connecting with external nodes: (1) weak access control; (2) no encryption; and (3) no authentication. In connected vehicle, in order to achieve secure in-vehicle networks, the proposed scheme should satisfy following requirements:

1. Secure in-vehicle networks should guarantee the confidentiality and authentication of CAN data frames.
2. Each software should be checked to protect vehicles against malware attacks [21].
3. The gateway GW connected to in-vehicle networks should be authenticated by in-vehicle networks to enure the valid connection and join the secure in-vehicle networks.

4. Count the number of messages according to different IDs to prevent the replay attack from in-vehicle networks.
5. Each external node EN should be authenticated by GW and a secure communication channel should be set up between EN and GW.

4   The Proposed Scheme

In this section, we define and construct our secure in-vehicle networks. Before describing the detail of our scheme, an overview will be presented.

4.1   Overview

To achieve secure communication of in-vehicle networks, we should authenticate access devices to prevent any malicious device from extracting confidential information from CAN while ensuring the secure communication between EN and in-vehicle networks. The details are described as follows: Before connecting with external nodes, we should build up a secure communication channel for in-vehicle networks by using a generated group key. After that, a gateway GW should be authenticated by in-vehicle networks before it is inserted into the OBD-II port and joining the secure in-vehicle network. Moreover, the software installed in the external node EN should be checked to prevent malware before connecting with the car. After installing the valid software, when the external node connected to the GW, EN should pass the authentication of GW and a secure communication channel should be set up between GW and EN.

4.2   The Proposed Scheme

Our scheme consists of four steps: system initialization, secure in-vehicle networks, connecting with external node, and update.

System Initialization. In order to design our secure in-vehicle networks, we assume that there is a key ECU (KECU) which works as a key management for in-vehicle networks and has higher computing power than general ECUs [20]. Vehicle manufacturers (VMs) initialize the system as follows:

– VM issues a long term key K_{ECU_i} and a forward hash key chain seed K_1^F as shown in Fig. 2 for each ECU_i;
– VM sends a long term key K_{KECU} and a backward hash key chain seed K_1^B as shown in Fig. 2 to $KECU$. $KECU$ also preloads all K_{ECU_i} and K_1^F.

We assume each ECU_i has a identity such as ID_{ECU_i}. Since the resource-constrained property and real-time process of in-vehicle networks, we intend to use the Advanced Encryption Standard-128 (AES-128) and the Keyed-Hash MAC to encrypt the data frame and compute MAC.

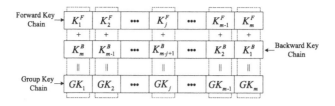

Fig. 2. The hash key chain used to generate the group key.

Secure In-vehicle Networks. A group key should be generated before in-vehicle communication. To generate the group key GK_1, each ECU_i should send a request message to $KECU$ as follows:

$$ECU_i \rightarrow KECU : R_i, ID_{ECU_i}, MAC_1. \tag{1}$$

where $MAC_1 = MAC_{K_{ECU_i}}(R_i, ID_{ECU_i})$ and R_i is a random number chosen by ECU_i.

Upon receiving the message from ECU_i, $KECU$ computes

$$MAC_1^* = MAC_{K_{ECU_i}}(R_i, ID_{ECU_i})$$

and checks $MAC_1^* \stackrel{?}{=} MAC_1$. If the equation holds, $KECU$ will respond the message (2):

$$KECU \rightarrow ECU_i : e_1, MAC_2. \tag{2}$$

where $e_1 = E_{K_{ECU_i}}(R_i, ID_{ECU_i}) \oplus K_m^B$ and $MAC_2 = MAC_{K_{ECU_i}}(R_i, e_1)$. Notice that since we use the AES-128 algorithm to encrypt R_i, ID_{ECU_i}, the result of $E_{K_{ECU_i}}(R_i, ID_{ECU_i})$ is 128 bit. While the maximum size of the CAN data frame payload is 64 bit, we only use the first 64 bits of the ciphertext. The following steps which use AES-128 to encrypt messages also only adopt the first 64 bits.

On receiving the message from $KECU$, ECU_i calculates

$$MAC_2^* = MAC_{K_{ECU_i}}(R_i, e_1)$$

and checks $MAC_2^* \stackrel{?}{=} MAC_2$. If the equation holds, ECU_i will compute

$$e_1' = E_{K_{ECU_i}}(R_i, ID_{ECU_i})$$

and adopt the first 64 bits to compute $K_m^B = e_1' \oplus e_1$. At last, ECU_i computes the current group key GK_1 and MAC key K_{MAC_1} by formula (3).

$$GK_1 || K_{MAC_1} = H(K_1^F || K_m^B). \tag{3}$$

After generating the secure key, each ECU performs encryption and authentication during the in-vehicle network communication.

As mentioned above, we should prevent the replay attack. To overcome this drawbacks, we use a frame ID-based counter [12] to prevent this attack. We assume each ECU_i maintains a set of counters, and each counter corresponds to a data frame ID. Therefore, if a malicious node replays a data frame, receivers can check the corresponding ID counter to see whether this data frame is fresh or not. We assume ECU_1 intends to send a ID_i messages m. Thus, ECU_1 should encrypt the message as $e_m = E_{GK_1}(C_i) \oplus m$, and compute the MAC as $MAC_m = MAC_{K_{MAC_1}}(e_m)$.

Connecting with External Node. We introduce the communication between external nodes and in-vehicle networks as follows steps:

GW$\longleftrightarrow$KECU: When a GW is tested to have been inserted into the OBD-II port, an authentication request message should be send to in-vehicle networks:

$$GW \rightarrow KECU : R_{GW}, ID_{GW}, Cert_{GW}. \tag{4}$$

where R_{GW} is the random number chosen by GW and ID_{GW} is the identity of GW. $Cert_{GW}$ is the certificate issued by the $KECU$ or vehicle owner, which is computed as $Cert_{GW} = MAC_{K_{KECU}}(R_{GW}, ID_{GW})$.

On receiving the broadcast message at time TS_2, $KECU$ executes the authentication process: $KECU$ first checks the certificate revocation lists (CRLs). If $Cert_{GW}$ is in CRLs, it will drop the message and send a warning message to the user. Otherwise, it will compute $Cert^*_{GW} = MAC_{K_{KECU}}(R_{GW}, ID_{GW})$ and check whether $Cert^*_{GW} \stackrel{?}{=} Cert_{GW}$ or not. If equation holds, $KECU$ accepts GW as a valid node.

After that, GW should join the secure communication group of in-vehicle networks. To achieve this, $KECU$ should securely send K^B_{m-j+1} (we assume T_2 is in the $(j-1)$th time slot of group key) to GW as follows:

$$KECU \rightarrow GM : e_2, MAC_3. \tag{5}$$

where $e_2 = E_{K_{GW}}(R_{GW}, ID_{GW}) \oplus K^B_{m-j+1}$ and K^B_{m-j+1} is the group key seed used to calculate the jth group key GK_j as shown in Fig. 2, $MAC_3 = MAC_{K_{GW}}(R_{GW}, e_1)$. $KECU$ also sends K^F_{j-1} to GW as K^B_{m-j+1}.

After receiving the respond message from $KECU$, GW first verifies MAC_3. If the MAC is valid, it will compute $E_{K_{GW}}(R_{GW}, ID_{GW})$ to get the K^B_{m-j+1}. At last, GW computes GK_j and MAC_j as follows:

$$GK_j || K_{MAC_j} = H(K^F_j || K^B_{m-j+1}). \tag{6}$$

$KECU$ also updates the group key of other ECU_i and renews the messages-based counter of each ECU_i.

Malware checking: Before communicating with GW, we should install a special software on EN. Since the malware poses great threat to the security of in-vehicle networks, we should execute the malware check process to protect the vehicle against malware attack. The details can be found in [21].

EN$\longleftrightarrow$ GW: Before connecting with in-vehicle networks through GW, a special software should install in EN. Before that, EN should pass the valid authentication of GW and a pairwise key should be generated to ensure the secure communication. This phase can be realized by using Public Key Infrastructure (PKI) algorithms such as [20].

Notice that the message content between GW and EN is different from in-vehicle networks data format based on OpenXC [1]. Hence, GW should firstly extract the data format of in-vehicle networks, then translate the data format to the message between GW and EN. Thus, we do not consider the authentication process between external nodes and in-vehicle networks.

Update. Since a 32-bit MAC is not enough for secure CAN. In addition, the adversary may compromise GW. Thus we should update the group key. The group update can be divided into two categories: the periodic update and GW changes or gets compromised.

The periodic update: The message of the $(j+1)$th regular periodic update round is

$$KECU \longrightarrow * : e_4, MAC_{UPD_1}. \tag{7}$$

where $e_4 = E_{GK_j}(K^B_{m-j+1}) \oplus K^B_{m-j}$ and $MAC_{UPD_1} = MAC_{K_{MAC_j}}(e_4)$.

When receiving the periodic update message, ECU_i or GW first verifies the validity of MAC_{UPD_1}. If the MAC is valid, GW computes the message to get K^B_{m-j} and checks whether $H(K^B_{m-j}) \overset{?}{=} K^B_{m-j+1}$ holds. Only when the equation holds, ECU_i or GW updates the group key by using K^B_{m-j} and K^F_{j+1}.

Since we use a backward hash chain to generate the group key, during the regular periodic update, the seed of the $(j+1)$th group key is encrypted by using the jth group key which is known by all members of group. Without authenticatin, we can not ensure the update process launched by $KECU$.

GW changes or gets compromised: If an authenticated GW which connected with in-vehicle networks changes or get compromised by the adversary, $KECU$ will launch a session key update process. We plan to use the self-healing group key [7] to revoke GW and update the new group key. However, the limited data payload of the CAN data frame needs many data frames to send the bivariate polynomial $f(x,y)$ used in [7]. Thus, we reconstruct the secure in-vehicle networks one by one as follows:

$KECU$ launches the reconstruction process of secure in-vehicle networks by message (8):

$$KECU \to ECU_i : e_5, MAC_{UPD_2}. \tag{8}$$

where $e_5 = E_{K_{ECU_i}}(K^B_{m-j+1}) \oplus K^B_{m-j}$ and $MAC_{UPD_2} = MAC_{K_{ECU_i}}(e_5) \oplus K^B_{m-j})$.

Upon receiving the message from $KECU$, ECU_i calculates $MAC_{UPD_2} = MAC_{K_{ECU_i}}(e_5)$ and checks whether $MAC^*_{UPD_2} \overset{?}{=} MAC_{UPD_2}$. If the equation holds, ECU_i will computes the encryption message and obtain K^B_{m-j}. Before calculating the new group key, ECU_i should check whether $H(K^B_{m-j}) \stackrel{?}{=} K^B_{m-j+1}$ holds or not. Only when the equation holds, ECU_i computes the current group key and MAC key as in (6).

5   Security Analysis

In this section, we present the security analysis of our scheme.

5.1   Access Control

To achieve access control in connected vehicle, GW should be authenticated by $KECU$ first. When GW is inserted into OBD-II port, the message R_{GW}, ID_{GW}, $Cert_{GW}$ is sent to $KECU$. After authenticating GW, GW can join the secure in-vehicle networks. To each external node, it should be authenticated by GW before connecting with in-vehicle networks. By using access control, we guarantee that only valid node can communicate with in-vehicle networks and achieve the secure communication.

5.2   Confidentiality

Due to the nature of CAN, all data frames of in-vehicle networks are broadcast and it is easy for an attacker to eavesdrop. We use encryption to provide confidentiality for in-vehicle communication. A secure group key is generated among ECU_i. Hence, only valid ECU_i can generate and decrypt the ciphertext data frames, which avoids eavesdropping. After authenticated by $KECU$, GW joins into the secure group. Thus, every data frame of in-vehicle networks can be encrypted to provide confidentiality and the secure communication of connected vehicle can be realized. In addition, to ensure the secure communication between EN and GW (such as wireless), a pair-wise key is generated to encrypt messages. Besides, for the periodic update of group key, upon receiving the update message, we can authenticate the validity of K^B_{m-j} by computing $H(K^B_{m-j}) = K^B_{m-j+1}$ which avoids false update messages from the compromised GW.

5.3   Authentication

We use a 32-bit truncated MAC to authenticate the integrity of frames. A 32-bit MAC can be broken after $O(2^{16})$ queries if an adversary can access the 32-bit MAC generation oracle. This means it is possible for an adversary, who can access the firmware of an ECU, to compromise it. However, we do not consider this type of adversary. It is also possible for the attacker to use the known structure of the input of a MAC to generate meaningful messages. However, the attacker still cannot generate the MAC corresponding to the meaningful message without knowing the MAC key. The key used to generate a MAC is securely shared in the proposed protocol. In addition, we periodically update the MAC key for security of the 32-bit MAC.

5.4 Preventing the Replay Attack

The data frame of in-vehicle networks is identified only by the CAN ID without a sender/receiver ID, which makes the modification and the replay attack of a data frame possible. That is, an adversary with a compromised GW or EN can replay messages. To thwart this type of attack, both the authentication and integrity of the transmitted data should be provided. However, the current CAN specification only offers a CRC code for error detection, not for authentication. We use MAC to guarantee the integrity of messages and update the group key, which ensures the validity of the sender. Moreover, to avoid the replay attack, we use a frame ID-based counter to count the number of each type frame.

5.5 Forward and Backward Security

In-vehicle networks, to ensure the authentication and confidentiality of CAN data frames, GK_j is used to encrypt the message while K_{MAC_j} is used to compute MAC. To guarantee the forward and backward security of the GK_j and K_{MAC_j}, a forward hash key chain K_1^F and a backward hash key chain K_1^B are adopted to generate these two keys. When GW joins in-vehicle networks in the $(j -$ 1)th time slot, $KECU$ sends K_j^F and K_{m-j+1}^B to GW to compute GK_j and K_{MAC_j}. According to the nature of forward hash key chain, it is difficult for GW to compute K_F^{j+1} using K_F^j. Thus, the forward security of the group can be guaranteed. When GW is changed or compromised in the jth time slot, $KECU$ notifies other ECU_i to update the group key. It is also difficult for GW to compute K_{m-j}^B based on K_{m-j+1}^B. Thus, the backward security of the group key can be guaranteed.

6 Performance Evaluation

In this section we analyze the performance of our scheme in terms of secure in-vehicle networks, connection with external node, and update. We first give the asymptotic complexity and then the implement of our scheme. The asymptotic complexity analysis is in terms of different kinds of operations.

6.1 Asymptotic Complexity Analysis

Secure in-vehicle networks: To generate secure in-vehicle networks, a group key should be generated. Each ECU_i should send a request message as R_i, ID_i, MAC_1 to $KECU$. Each message needs a data frame. On receiving the request message, $KECU$ should verify the MAC, then compute e_1 with AES-128 and compute the MAC_2. Then $KECU$ sends the messages to ECU_i, which also consumes one data frame. After ECU_i receives the message, it needs an encryption and MAC verification operation to get K_m^B. Thus, the communication and computation overhead of this phase are $2DF$ and $1ENC + 2MAC$, respectively. DF means a data frame of CAN, ENC means AES-128, and MAC is the MAC.

Thus, for n ECUs, it needs $(2n-1)*(T_{DF}+T_{ENC}+2T_{MAC})$ to achieve secure in-vehicle networks where T_{DF} is communication delay of one data frame, T_{ENC} is the computation delay of a AES-128 operation, and T_{MAC} is the computation delay of a MAC operation.

Connect with external nodes: When a gateway GW connects in-vehicle networks, $KECU$ should firstly authenticate GW by messages R_{GW}, ID_{GW}, $Cert_{GW}$. After authenticated the validity of GW, $KECU$ should send the two seeds K_{j-1}^F and K_{m-j+1}^B of group keys to GW. Thus, the total communication and computation overhead is $3DF$ and $2AES+2MAC$ for GW, respectively. While for GW, it consumes $3DF$ and $2AES+3MAC$. Then, a external node EN can communicate with in-vehicle networks through GW. Since this phase happens outside in-vehicle networks, we omit the detailed description.

Update: There are two kinds of update process: regular update and changed update. When $KECU$ launches the periodic update, it only needs to broadcast $E_{GK_j}(K_{m-j+1}^B) \oplus K_{m-j}^B, MAC_{UPD_1}$ which consumes $1ENC+1MAC$ computation overhead and $1DF$ communication overhead, respectively. When receiving the update message, ECU_i should verify MAC_{UP_1} and encrypt K_{m-j+1}^B to get K_{m-j}^B. In addition, ECU_i checks $H(K_{m-j}^B) \overset{?}{=} K_{m-j+1}^B$. Thus, the computation overhead is $1ENC+1MAC+1HAH$ where HAH means the computation overhead of hash operation. As for changed update, $KECU$ sends the update message to every ECU_i. Thus, $KECU$ consumes $nECU+nMAC$ computation overhead and nDF communication overhead, respectively. Each ECU_i only consumes $1ENC+1MAC+1HAH$ computation overhead.

Finally, we compare our scheme with Woo et al. [20] in Table 1, where C_{comm} and C_{comp} denotes the communication overhead and the computation overhead, respectively. And we assume there are n ECUs in in-vehicle networks.

Table 1. The comparison of communication and computation overhead of update process

		Secure in-vehicle		Regular update		Changed update	
		C_{comm}	C_{comp}	C_{comm}	C_{comp}	C_{comm}	C_{comp}
Our	$KECU$	$2nDF$	$n(1ENC+2MAC)$	$1DF$	$1ENC+1MAC$	nDF	$n(1ENC+1MAC)$
	ECU_i	$2DF$	$1ENC+2MAC$	$1DF$	$1ENC+1MAC+1HAH$	$1DF$	$1ENC+1MAC+1HAH$
[20]	$KECU$	$3nDF$	$3nMAC+1HAH$	$(n+1)DF$	$1ENC+nMAC+2HAH$	$1DF$	$1ENC+1MAC$
	ECU_i	$3DF$	$3MAC+1HAH$	$2DF$	$1ENC+1MAC+1HAH$	$1DF$	$1ENC+1MAC$

Table 2. The execute time for each cryptography algorithm under different CPU clock of DSP-F28335.

	30 MHz	60 MHz	90 MHz	120 MHz
AES/En	856 μs	419 μs	296 μs	214 μs
AES/De	1363 μs	668 μs	471 μs	340 μs
SHA-1	1344 μs	658 μs	465 μs	336 μs
MAC	2669 μs	1308 μs	923 μs	667 μs

6.2   Implementation

In this section, we show the impact of security mechanism on the CAN bus load and messages delay. We first evaluate the execution time for cryptography algorithms (AES-128, SHA-1, MAC) of a CAN data frame running on the 32-bit DSP-F28335 with CPU clock speed 30 MHz to 150 MHz. During the execution, we change the CPU clock rates to 120, 90, 60, and 30 MHz, respectively. We repeat each cryptography algorithm 1,000 times and obtain the average execution time as shown in Table 2 [19] where AES/En is the encryption operation of AES-128 and AES/De is the decryption operation of AES-128. SHA-1 is the hash operation.

We present the computation overhead of ECUs for different schemes under different CPU clock rates as shown in Fig. 3. For our scheme, in different situations (such as secure in-vehicle, regular update, and changed update), the computation overhead is 6.4 ms, 5.1 ms, and 5.1 ms, respectively, when the CPU clock rate is 30 MHz. While for Woo et al.'s scheme, the corresponding computation overhead is 9.3 ms, 5.1 ms, and 3.8 ms, respectively. The computation overhead is acceptable for both schemes. Notice that, the frequency of changed update operation happens lowest. Thus, our scheme is more efficient. It is obvious that as the CPU clock rate increases, the computation overhead will reduce. When the CPU clock rate is 120 MHz, the corresponding computation overhead of our

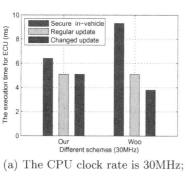

(a) The CPU clock rate is 30MHz;

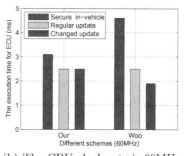

(b) The CPU clock rate is 60MHz;

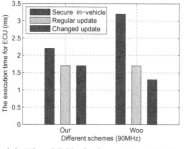

(c) The CPU clock rate is 90MHz;

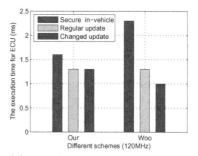

(d) The CPU clock rate is 120MHz;

Fig. 3. The computation overhead of ECUs for different schemes.

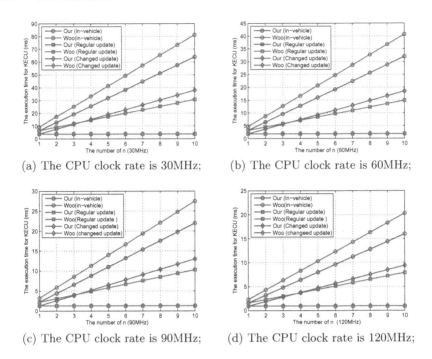

(a) The CPU clock rate is 30MHz;   (b) The CPU clock rate is 60MHz;

(c) The CPU clock rate is 90MHz;   (d) The CPU clock rate is 120MHz;

Fig. 4. The computation overhead of KECU for different schemes.

scheme is 1.6 ms, 1.3 ms, and 1.3 ms, respectively. While for Woo et al.'s scheme, the computation overhead reduces to 2.3 ms, 1.3 ms, and 1 ms, respectively.

In addition, we present the computation overhead of the KECU for different schemes under different CPU clock rates as shown in Fig. 4. Here n is increased from 1 to 10. From Fig. 4(a) to (d), the computation overhead of KECU almost increases linearly with the increasing number of n. And the efficiency of our scheme is obvious, since the frequency of changed update operation is the lowest.

As shown in [19], the basic message transmission delay for each CAN data frame is less than 1 ms even when the bit ratio of the CAN bus is 0.5 Mbit/s. According to the simulation result in Figs. 3 and 4, the secure scheme will greatly influence the response delay of ECUs, especially the KECU. Thus, we should use the high-performance CPU for KECU.

7   Conclusion

Connecting in-vehicle networks to external nodes introduces serious security risks due to their inherent design for operation in an isolated environment. Moreover, it is difficult to directly apply the security mechanisms intended for generic computer networks to in-vehicle networks due to the limited computer resource and payload of CAN bus. Thus, in this paper, we studied the problem of secure in-vehicle networks of connected vehicle. Based on the current CAN bus, we propose an efficient and secure communication scheme to achieve the confidentiality, authentication while preventing the replay attack of in-vehicle networks. The security and performance analysis showed that our scheme is secure and practical.

Acknowledgements. This research is supported by the National Natural Science Foundation of China Grants (No. 61702231), Natural Science Foundation of Jiangsu Province (BK2017 0556), Jiangsu Provincial Research Scheme of Natural Science for Higher Education institutions (No. 17KJB520005), and Key Laboratory for New Technology Application of Road Conveyance of Jiangsu Province (No. BM20082061707).

References

1. http://openxcplatform.com/
2. http://cache.freescale.com/files/microcontrollers/doc/brochure/BRINVEHI CLENET.pdf
3. http://www.evita-project.org/
4. Bariah, L., Shehada, D., Salahat, E., Yeun, C.Y.: Recent advances in vanet security: a survey. In: Vehicular Technology Conference, pp. 1–7 (2016)
5. Biswas, S., Tatchikou, R., Dion, F.: Vehicle-to-vehicle wireless communication protocols for enhancing highway traffic safety. IEEE Commun. Mag. **44**(1), 74–82 (2006)
6. Checkoway, S., McCoy, D., Kantor, B., Anderson, D., Shacham, H., Savage, S., Koscher, K., Czeskis, A., Roesner, F., Kohno, T.: Comprehensive experimental analyses of automotive attack surfaces. In: USENIX Security Symposium, San Francisco (2011)
7. Dutta, R., Mukhopadhyay, S., Collier, M.: Computationally secure self-healing key distribution with revocation in wireless ad hoc networks. Ad Hoc Netw. **8**(6), 597–613 (2010)
8. Groza, B., Murvay, S.: Efficient protocols for secure broadcast in controller area networks. IEEE Trans. Industr. Inf. **9**(4), 2034–2042 (2013)
9. Han, K., Potluri, S.D., Shin, K.G.: On authentication in a connected vehicle: secure integration of mobile devices with vehicular networks. In: ACM/IEEE International Conference on Cyber-Physical Systems (ICCPS), pp. 160–169. IEEE (2013)
10. Hoppe, T., Kiltz, S., Dittmann, J.: Security threats to automotive CAN networks – practical examples and selected short-term countermeasures. In: Harrison, M.D., Sujan, M.-A. (eds.) SAFECOMP 2008. LNCS, vol. 5219, pp. 235–248. Springer, Heidelberg (2008). https://doi.org/10.1007/978-3-540-87698-4_21
11. Koscher, K., Czeskis, A., Roesner, F., Patel, S., Kohno, T., Checkoway, S., McCoy, D., Kantor, B., Anderson, D., Shacham, H.: Experimental security analysis of a modern automobile. In: IEEE Symposium on Security and Privacy, pp. 447–462. IEEE (2010)
12. Lin, C., Sangiovanni-Vincentelli, A.: Cyber-security for the controller area network (CAN) communication protocol. In: 2012 International Conference on Cyber Security (CyberSecurity), pp. 1–7. IEEE (2012)
13. Nilsson, D.K., Larson, U.E., Jonsson, E.: Creating a secure infrastructure for wireless diagnostics and software updates in vehicles. In: Harrison, M.D., Sujan, M.-A. (eds.) SAFECOMP 2008. LNCS, vol. 5219, pp. 207–220. Springer, Heidelberg (2008). https://doi.org/10.1007/978-3-540-87698-4_19

14. Woo, S., Jin, J.H., Choi, W., Chun, J.Y., Park, J., Lee, D.H.: Identifying ecus using inimitable characteristics of signals in controller area networks. arXiv preprint arXiv:1607.00497 (2016)
15. Schweppe, H., Roudier, Y., Weyl, B., Apvrille, L., Scheuermann, D.: Car2x communication: securing the last meter-a cost-effective approach for ensuring trust in car2x applications using in-vehicle symmetric cryptography. In: IEEE Vehicular Technology Conference, pp. 1–5. IEEE (2011)
16. Shavit, M., Gryc, A., Miucic, R.: Firmware update over the air (fota) for automotive industry. Technical report, SAE Technical Paper (2007)
17. Toor, Y., Muhlethaler, P., Laouiti, A.: Vehicle ad hoc networks: applications and related technical issues. IEEE Commun. Surv. Tutorials **10**(3), 74–88 (2008)
18. Vandenbrink, R.: Dude, your car is pwned. SANSFIRE 2012, Washington, DC (2012)
19. Woo, S., Jin, J.H., Kim, I.S., Lee, D.H.: A practical security architecture for in-vehicle CAN-FD. IEEE Trans. Intell. Transp. Syst. **16**, 2248–2261 (2016)
20. Woo, S., Jin, J.H., Lee, D.H.: A practical wireless attack on the connected car and security protocol for in-vehicle can. IEEE Trans. Intell. Transp. Syst. **16**, 993–1006 (2014)
21. Zhang, T., Antunes, H., Aggarwal, S.: Defending connected vehicles against malware: challenges and a solution framework. IEEE Internet Things J. **1**(1), 10–21 (2014)

Research of Task Scheduling Mechanism
Based on Prediction of Memory Utilization

Juan Fang$^{(\boxtimes)}$, Mengxuan Wang, and Hao Sun

Beijing University of Technology, 100 Ping Le Yuan,
Chaoyang District, Beijing, China
fangjuan@bjut.edu.cn, mengxuanw13@emails.bjut.edu.cn

Abstract. With the arrival of big data era, distributed computing framework Hadoop has become the main solution to deal with big data now. People usually promote the performance of distributed computing by adding new computing nodes to cluster. With the expansion of the scale of the cluster, it produces a large amount of power consumption because of lack of reasonable management strategy. So how to make full use of computing resources in the cluster to improve the performance of the whole system and reduce the power consumption has become the main research direction of scholars and industrial circles. For the above, in order to make best use of computing resources and reduce the power consumption, this paper firstly proposes to optimize a reasonable configuration of the parameters provided by Hadoop. Comparing with the default configuration of Hadoop. It shows we can get better performance by parameter tuning. This paper proposes a task scheduling mechanism based on memory usage prediction. In this task schedule, it predicts the future use status of memory in the computing nodes by analyzing the use status before. The task scheduling mechanism can reduce the memory pressure by reducing the allocation of tasks when the computing node is under memory pressure. The task scheduling mechanism can be more flexible by setting the threshold of memory usage. This mechanism based on predicting memory usage can improve the performance of the system by making full use of the computing resources.

Keywords: Big data · High performance · Prediction · Task scheduling

1 Introduction

As people's demand for big data services grows, Hadoop is widely used due to its performance in handling big data. Hadoop is a relatively new technology, the lack of experienced administrators to properly maintain and configure the system. When running the program Hadoop provides users with a lot of parameters for the user configuration, the user does not know whether to configure the corresponding parameters or parameters of the wrong settings will result in system performance degradation or program error.

In order to improve the system performance of Hadoop and provide efficient data application services, it is necessary to experiment with the relevant parameters provided by Hadoop to obtain a reasonable configuration value. With the continuous expansion

© Springer Nature Singapore Pte Ltd. 2018
L. Zhu and S. Zhong (Eds.): MSN 2017, CCIS 747, pp. 227–236, 2018.
https://doi.org/10.1007/978-981-10-8890-2_16

of the cluster size, it is bound to cause the computing node in memory, data processing capacity, storage capacity differences [1]. Based on the parameter configuration in homogeneous mode, the resources of computing nodes cannot be fully utilized, resulting in a decrease of the system Performance. According to the dynamic change of load of each task node and the difference of node performance of different tasks in the heterogeneous Hadoop cluster, [2] presented a novel adaptive task scheduling strategy based on dynamic workload adjustment (ATSDWA). Cheng [3] proposed a self-adaptive task tuning approach, Ant, that automatically searches the optimal configurations for individual tasks running on different nodes. However, these papers did not consider the impact of memory utilization. In order to maximize the performance of Hadoop [4, 5] system and reduce the overall energy consumption during system operation, this paper makes comparative experiments on the related parameters provided by Hadoop and obtains the reasonable value of parameter configuration in heterogeneous mode [6] to improve the performance and reduce energy consumption.

2 Hadoop Parameter Configuration Optimization

2.1 Task Block Parameters

When the client submits the task, Hadoop's runtime environment will generate a configuration object based on the user's configuration of the relevant parameters [9]. When the task is executed, Hadoop will set the conditions for running the task according to the configuration object. After obtaining the task data, JobTracker reads the value of the block size in the generated configuration object and divides the data block provided by the user into multiple data blocks and distributes them to the storage nodes in the cluster. When processing the task block data, obtain the storage location of the relevant data block in the cluster, and then the task allocation is performed according to the migration operation principle to reduce the data migration and complete the task assignment.

Appropriate number of maps can take full advantage of the computing resources in the cluster and play the advantages of distributed computing.

When this parameter is too large, the number of Map running in the system is less, it may not be able to play the advantages of distributed computing. Since the Name-Node data block is stored in memory as an object, if this parameter is too small, the memory of the NameNode is large, causing the performance of the NameNode to deteriorate, scheduling tasks are affected, and cluster expansion is limited.

2.2 Degree of Parallelism Parameters

When scheduling tasks in Hadoop, JobTracker does not take the initiative to assign computing tasks to computing nodes. Instead, it uses the previous heartbeat message to determine whether to schedule tasks. The heartbeat message contains the running status of the node, whether there is a free Map or Reduce task slot (allowing multiple Map or Reduce tasks to run simultaneously on the same compute node). JobTracker according to the heartbeat message related to data for the task of scheduling, the degree of parallelism parameters determines the number of Map tasks that can run at the same time on a compute node [10]. When there are free Map task slots in the compute node, JobTracker will schedule tasks according to the heartbeat message [13].

Through the reasonable setting of this parameter can effectively improve the parallelism of tasks and the overall performance of the system. When this parameter is set too large, it will lead to overuse of the compute node so that the compute node cannot process the assigned task efficiently, resulting in a backlog of tasks. When this parameter is set too small, it will not be able to fully play the computing performance of the computing node, thus affecting the overall performance of the system.

2.3   Experimental Design and Result Analysis

Evaluate Method
The performance of running tasks in Hadoop is a result of many factors, mainly in the following three aspects:

- Configuration of relevant runtime parameters.
- The amount of data allocated to the system to run.
- The complexity of the operation of the data at runtime.

In order to test the configuration of the relevant parameters, by assigning the same number of tasks and computational tasks of the same complexity to machines of different configurations. Run ten runs per experiment and calculate the average to reflect the effect of the relevant parameters. Through the execution time to determine the parameter configuration is reasonable, less time means that the parameters are reasonable and more time represents the parameters are not reasonable.

Experimental Configuration

Task Block Parameters Experiment Settings
Experiment using a master and a slave experimental configuration. This scheme is adopted because in the cluster environment, the data for each experiment needs to be generated by the Hadoop test program and stored in the corresponding compute node. The cluster environment does not guarantee that the state of each data distribution consistent, resulting in task execution time cannot be a single variable dfs.block.size decision, so using a master and a slave experimental configuration.

Tables 1 and 2 are the relevant parameters of master and slave.

Table 1. Configuration of master node.

Parameter	Configuration
Processor	i5-3470CPU@3.20 GHz*4
OS	Ubuntu 12.04
Memory capacity	8 GB

Table 2. Configuration of slave node.

Parameter	Configuration
Processor	i5-3470CPU@3.20 GHz*4
OS	Ubuntu 12.04
Memory capacity	4 GB

Degree of Map Parallelism Experiment Settings

This part mainly carried out two experiments comparing the parameters of running Map tasks in parallel. The first experiment is in a master and a slave by configuring different parameters to compare the parameters of the overall execution time. The second experiment compares the impact of this parameter on the overall execution time by configuring different parameters on the better performing compute nodes in the case of a host and two subordinate heterogeneous clusters.

Result Analysis

Task Block Parameter Experiment Result Analysis

Based on the above experimental setup, two sets of comparative experiments were conducted. One group is in 1 GB data volume, the system execution time changes with this parameter. The other is under 4 GB data volume.

Tables 3 and 4 are the experimental results of two groups of comparative experiments.

Table 3. The experiment results of 1 GB data

Data block (MB)	Average execution time (s)	Variance
64	97.6	2.966479
128	90.2	5.118594
256	90	4.636809
512	89.8	3.962323
1024	88.8	1.788854

Table 4. The experiment results of 4 GB data

Data block (MB)	Average execution time (s)	Variance
64	283	17.67767
128	267.4	4.219005
256	265.2	6.418723
512	271.6	9.2358
1024	283.2	17.72569

In the experiment of running 1 GB data volume, the average execution time of this parameter under 256 MB and 512 MB configuration is short and the performance of the system is stable when the interval changes. In experiments running 4 GB of data, this parameter had the lowest system average execution time under a 256 MB configuration. As the parameter becomes larger, the overall performance of the system shows a downward trend.

Through the analysis of the variance of running results of running 4 GB data, the variance of execution time under the configuration of 1 GB and 2 GB shows that the performance of the system shows an unstable trend with the increase of data blocks. Therefore, the recommended value for parameter setting is 128 MB or 256 MB.

Degree of Map Parallelism Parameter Experiment Result Analysis

Two sets of experiments were conducted in the experimental setup above. One group is running 1 GB data volume, calculate the impact of changes in degree of Map parallelism on system execution time. The other is running 2 GB.

Tables 5 and 6 are the results of two groups of experiments.

Table 5. The experiment results of 1 GB data

Data block (MB)	Average execution time (s)	Variance
2	100.4	9.396808
4	84.8	3.701351
8	80.4	4.393177
12	108.4	20.41568
16	134.4	8.876936

Table 6. The experiment results of 1 GB data

Data block (MB)	Average execution time (s)	Variance
2	237.4	36.0458
4	226.2	19.65197
8	227.4	18.94202
12	252	8.031189
16	270.6	8.502941

According to the experimental results, it is found that in the case of a single compute node, as the parameter becomes larger, the system performance is improved because the computational resources of the compute node are more effectively utilized as the parameter grows. When this parameter exceeds a certain range, the performance of the system as a whole tends to decrease. TaskTalker running multiple tasks in parallel causes the memory node of the compute node to be tense, resulting in a decrease of its computational performance. It is necessary to dynamically configure this parameter on a computable TaskTracker instead of using Hadoop's default parameter configuration values.

It can be seen from the second part of the experiment that in a heterogeneous cluster environment, a reasonable configuration of the parameter is given to the computing node with better computing performance to improve the overall performance.

3 Task Scheduling Mechanism Based on Prediction of Memory Utilization

3.1 Task Allocation Mechanism Design

In the second part, when optimizing the parameters provided by Hadoop, the overall performance of the system is showing a downward trend when the degree of Map parallelism parameters too large. Compute nodes running too many Map tasks in parallel will overload the node's memory and reduce the computational performance of the nodes. Therefore, the compute node's memory usage status is one of the factors to consider when scheduling tasks. If a compute node with higher memory usage is allocated more computational tasks, the computing power of the compute node will decrease, which will eventually affect system performance.

3.2 Predictive Model

In statistics, the concept of least squares is similar to the one used to solve regression problems 错误!未找到引用源。

In the process of solving the objective function, if the data points are in a straight line, we can think of the existence of a one-way function between variables. In order to minimize the deviation between the simulated points on the line and the actual data points, ensure that the user-supplied data points and points on the straight line and the minimum square deviation. for a given N data points (X_i, Y_i), i = 1,..., N, if the objective function to be fitted is $y = a + bx$, it can be transformed into the following system of equations for solving.

The objective function can be transformed into the following binary linear Eqs. (1).

$$\left\{ \begin{array}{l} \varphi_{11}a + \varphi_{12}b = f1 \\ \varphi_{21}a + \varphi_{22}b = f2 \end{array} \right\} \tag{1}$$

The relevant parameters in the (1) can be solved by the following (2) to (7), respectively, where Wi represents the weight of the data point, that is, the number of occurrences of this value.

$$\varphi_{11} = \sum_{i=1}^{n} w_i \tag{2}$$

$$\varphi_{12} = \sum_{i=1}^{n} w_i x_i \tag{3}$$

$$\varphi_{21} = \varphi_{12} \tag{4}$$

$$\varphi_{22} = \sum_{i=1}^{n} w_i x_i^2 \tag{5}$$

$$f1 = \sum_{i=1}^{n} w_i y_i \tag{6}$$

$$f2 = \sum_{i=1}^{n} w_i y_i x_i \tag{7}$$

3.3 Work Process

This section proposes a task allocation scheduling mechanism based on state prediction of compute node memory usage. When the task allocation scheduling is performed, the usage state of the memory of the calculation node is sent as a reference factor to the node responsible for allocating the schedule. The compute node periodically writes its own memory usage to the local file after it starts up. When sending the heartbeat message to the node in charge of scheduling, the historical data of the memory usage of the node is read, and the possible use of the memory in the next phase is predicted through the least squares simulation curve.

When the predicted memory usage is higher than the set value, the node is set to not accept the task in the heartbeat message. In this way, the compute node can make better use of the memory space to calculate the previously assigned tasks, so as to avoid the memory pressure of the node becoming larger due to the excessive assigned tasks, thereby reducing the computing power of the node. When the predicted memory usage is lower than the set value, the node is set to accept the task, so the compute node can maximize the use of memory space to improve overall system uptime.

4 Experimental Design and Result Analysis

4.1 Evaluate Method

On heterogeneous clusters that have been assigned quantitative data processing tasks, the system execution time under three task scheduling mechanisms is compared respectively, including the default task scheduling mechanism, the task allocation mechanism with a higher prediction threshold, and the task allocation mechanism with a lower prediction threshold.

Repeat the experiment several times to calculate the average execution time.

4.2 Experimental Configuration

Experiments on the system architecture of a master and two slaves.

In order to simulate the memory usage under high pressure, the impact of the allocation mechanism on system performance. By setting different numbers of parallel running Map tasks for the smaller compute nodes, verify the proposed design scheme under different prediction thresholds. The compute node with a smaller memory configuration is node1 and the compute node with a larger memory configuration is node2.

Tables 7 and 8 are the related configuration parameters of two slave nodes.

Table 7. Configuration of slave node1.

Parameter	Configuration
Processor	i5-3470CPU@3.20 GHz*4
OS	Ubuntu 12.04
Memory capacity	2 GB

Table 8. Configuration of slave node2.

Parameter	Configuration
Processor	i5-3470CPU@3.20 GHz*4
OS	Ubuntu 12.04
Memory capacity	4 GB

4.3 Results Analysis

Six comparative experiments were conducted in experiments on task allocation mechanism for predicting memory utilization.

In the heterogeneous cluster environment, two groups are configured under different memory pressure conditions by configuring degree of Map parallelism for computing nodes with smaller memory. Use Hadoop's default task scheduling mechanism to experiment with performing fixed task data volumes. Based on the task allocation mechanism predicted by memory utilization, two sets of experiments are used to configure different numbers of parallel running Map tasks on the compute nodes with relatively small memory, and the prediction threshold is low. The remaining two sets of experiments are the same as the previous two sets, and the prediction threshold is set higher.

Table 9 is the experimental results.

Table 9. Configuration of slave node1

Scheduling strategy	Memory pressure value	Average execution time (s)	Variance
Default	8	137.125	18.70399
Threshold 0.9	8	135.625	7.781618
Threshold 0.95	8	129.75	7.106335
Default	12	183.375	13.6898
Threshold 0.9	12	177.5	4.810702
Threshold 0.95	12	183.625	7.170127
Threshold 0.8	8/12	Unable to assign tasks	Unable to assign tasks

The experimental results show that the performance of the system tends to decrease with the increase of the memory usage pressure under the default task scheduling mechanism of Hadoop.

When the memory usage pressure is 8, compared with the default task scheduling mechanism of Hadoop, the task allocation mechanism based on memory usage prediction improves the performance of the whole system when the memory usage threshold is 0.9. Performance has been greatly improved when the threshold is 0.95. When the memory usage pressure is 12, predictive-based mechanisms have limited tuning of overall system performance at a memory usage threshold of 0.95. Experiments show that the improved task allocation mechanism based on memory usage prediction can adjust the allocation of tasks according to the memory state of nodes to improve system performance.

5 Conclusion

Experiments show that the memory factors will affect the computing performance of computing nodes to a certain extent.

This paper proposes a task scheduling mechanism based on prediction of memory utilization. This task allocation mechanism will mathematically calculate the predicted value based on historical values of memory usage. This task allocation mechanism uses mathematical models to calculate predictions based on historical values of memory utilization. When the task is assigned, the task allocation schedule is decided according to the predicted value and the set threshold.

Experiments show that the task allocation mechanism based on memory utilization prediction reduces the average execution time by 6.625 s and improves the performance by 4.25% compared with Hadoop's default task allocation mechanism.

References

1. Bryant, R.E., Katz, R.H., Lazowska, E.D.: Big-data computing: creating revolutionary breakthroughs in commerce, science, and society. Computing Community Consortium, pp. 1–15 (2008)
2. Xu, X., Cao, L., Wang, X.: Adaptive task scheduling strategy based on dynamic workload adjustment for heterogeneous Hadoop clusters. IEEE Syst. J. 10(2), 471–482 (2016)
3. Cheng, D., Rao, J., Guo, Y., et al.: Improving performance of heterogeneous mapreduce clusters with adaptive task tuning. IEEE Trans. Parallel Distrib. Syst. 28(3), 774–786 (2017)
4. Dean, J., Ghemawat, S.: MapReduce: simplified data processing on large clusters. In: Proceedings of Operating Systems Design and Implementation (OSDI), pp. 137–150 (2004)
5. Xiong, S.,Yu, L.,Shen, H., et al.: Efficient algorithms for sensor deployment and routing in sensor networks for network-strucured environment monitoring. In: 2012 IEEE Proceedings of INFOCOM, pp. 1008–1016. IEEE (2012)
6. Bai, X., Xuan, D., Yun, Z., et al.: Complete optimal deployment patterns for full-coverage and k-connectivity wireless sensor networks. In: Proceedings of the 9th ACM International Symposium on Mobile Ad hoc Networking and Computing, pp. 401–410. ACM (2008)

7. Zaharia, M., Konwinski, A., Joseph, A., Katz, R., Stoica, I.: Improving mapreduce performance in heterogeneous environments. In: OSDI, pp. 29–42 (2009)
8. Babu, S.: Towards automatic optimization of mapreduce programs. In: SoCC, pp. 137–142. ACM (2010)
9. Jiang, D., et al.: The performance of mapreduce: an in-depth study. Proc. VLDB Endow. **3**, 472–483 (2010)
10. Dean, J., Ghemawat, S.: Mapreduce: a flexible data processing tool. Commun. ACM **53**(1), 72–77 (2010)
11. Xie, J., Yin, S., Ruan, X.-J., Ding, Z.-Y., Tian, Y., Majors, J., Qin, X.: Improving mapreduce performance via data placement in heterogeneous hadoop clusters. In: Proceedings of 19th International Heterogeneity in Computing Workshop (2010)
12. Jiang, D., et al.: The performance of mapreduce: An in-depth study. Proc. VLDB Endow. **3**, 472–483 (2010)
13. Strutz, T.: Data fitting and uncertainty (A practical introduction to weighted least squares and beyond), Chapter 3. Springer Vieweg

An Effective Method for Community Search in Large Directed Attributed Graphs

Zezhong Wang, Ye Yuan$^{(\boxtimes)}$, Guoren Wang, Hongchao Qin, and Yuliang Ma

School of Computer Science and Engineering, Northeastern University,
Shenyang, China
yuanye@ise.neu.edu.cn

Abstract. Recently there is an increasing need for online community analysis on large scale graphs. Community search (CS), which can retrieve communities efficiently on a query request, has received significant research attention. However, existing CS methods leave edge direction and vertex attributes out of consideration, which results in poor performance of community accuracy and cohesiveness. In this paper, we propose DACQ (directed attribute community query), a novel framework of retrieving effective communities in directed attributed graphs. DACQ first supplements attributes according to the topological structure and generate attribute combinations, after which DACQ finds the strongly connected k-cores ($k\text{-}SCS$) with attributes in the directed graph. Finally, DACQ retrieves effective communities, which are cohesive in terms of the structure and attributes. Extensive experiments demonstrate the efficiency and effectiveness of our proposed algorithms in large scale directed attributed graphs.

Keywords: Community search · Directed graph
Attributed graph · Effective community

1 Introduction

Various real-life complex networks, such as the Internet, social networks, and citation networks, contain communities, which are often defined as relatively compact subgraphs that guarantee structure cohesiveness. Finding communities in real networks is an important analytical task, since communities are imbued with meaning that they are highly correlated with the functionality of the network. The community division are often used to construct indexes in recent researches [21,22]. Community search (CS) is proposed to retrieve more meaningful communities, which are customized for a query request and suitable for quick or online retrieval of communities [2,3,5,13]. However, existing algorithms of retrieving communities remain far away from perfect, as they only use the structure information of the non-attributed and structure-simplified graphs.

© Springer Nature Singapore Pte Ltd. 2018
L. Zhu and S. Zhong (Eds.): MSN 2017, CCIS 747, pp. 237–251, 2018.
https://doi.org/10.1007/978-981-10-8890-2_17

That is, they pay little attention to the *directionality of relationships* and the *attribute of vertices*, which are both significantly important.

The algorithms to retrieve communities [2,3,5,13,18,24] are nearly designed based on the undirected graphs by simplifying real-world networks, in which bidirectional and unidirectional relationships are represented by undirected edges. In a social network, millions of fans $H_1, H_2...H_n$ unidirectionally follow a celebrity A, but A does not follow them. A is not interested in them, so they could not compose a community. However, each community retrieved from the fans in the simplified undirected graph, could contain the celebrity, even with a high structure cohesiveness. Detailed discussion is demonstrated in Example 1. Therefore, simplified graphs cannot completely express relationships, even destroy the structure, and it could reduce accuracy of retrieved communities.

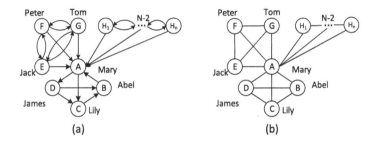

Fig. 1. A social network is simplified by using undirected edges to represent

Example 1. Figure 1(a) is a social network. Jack, Peter and Tom(E, F, G) are good friends and bidirectionally follow all the others. Mary(A) is a singer star, followed by E, F and G, but A is not interested in them. Hence, A is excluded from the community. James, Lily, Abel and Mary(B, C, D, A) exist in a music group and unidirectionally follow some others. Obviously, they are not as closely connected as E, F, and G. In Fig. 1(b), ACQ [5] simplifies the network to a undirected graph. However, it find E, F, G, A as a closely linked 3-core community in the simplified graph, and B, C, D, A has same structure cohesiveness.

In addition, existing community search algorithms also do not consider attributes of vertices. The community retrieved from the algorithms is the mixture of communities with different attribute sets. In Fig. 2, Peter is the query vertex and we could retrieve the community A with high structure cohesiveness, according to existing algorithms. However, Peter obviously does not have common attributes with the vertices in part C. The truth is, B, as one part of A, is the community about tourism and comics, and the other part, C is the community tagged with movie. A is not a cohesive community on query request, but B is. Therefore, loss of attributes results in decrease of community cohesiveness.

Motivated by the above observations, we propose directed attributed community query (DACQ). DACQ aims to retrieve effective communities in directed graphs, of which vertices are closely related to the query vertex in aspects of the

structure and attributes. Furthermore, we can also apply DACQ in the undirected networks by using two directed edges to represent the undirected edge
between two vertices. For example, in the network of DBLP, two vertices denotes
two authors, and the edge between two authors is a co-authorship relationship.
We can use two directed edges to guarantee that the two authors keep reachable
to each other.

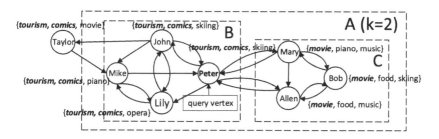

Fig. 2. Tourism subgraph and tourism community (circled).

Specifically, DACQ works on directed attributed graphs. We first get
attributes from LDA model (in most networks) and generate attribute combinations in decreasing order of their set size. Next, we find strongly directed
k-core(k-SCS) with different attribute combinations. We finally retrieve effective communities in terms of the structure and attributes. Figure 2 fully displays
the users, their directed relationships, and their attributes in the real-world
social networks. As shown in Fig. 2, Taylor and part B is the subgraph with the
attribute label of tourism and comics, and a effective community is retrieved from
the subgraph, part B with structure cohesiveness 2 and the maximal attribute
combination.

In addition, we present a method which supplements attributes of vertices
based on topological structure. A new metric is used in DACQ to measure structure cohesiveness and k-SCS (strongly connected subgraph of k-core) as a new
standard for a directed community.
In summary, this paper makes the following contributions.

- We propose DACQ, a novel framework to retrieve effective communities in
  directed attributed graphs, which guarantee strongly connected structure
  cohesiveness and attribute cohesiveness.
- In most cases, attribute sets are deficient and relations between vertices are
  sufficient. DACQ can supplement attributes based on topological structure,
  which makes up for the loss of attributes in the process of LDA and increase
  attribute cohesiveness of the community.
- DACQ can process different attribute combinations of query vertex, so that
  we can find personalized communities with common interest.
- We conduct extensive experiments on large networks, which demonstrate its
  efficiency and effectiveness of retrieved communities.

The remainder of the paper is organized as follows. We briefly review the related work in Sect. 2. We introduce problem definition in Sect. 3 and overview of DACQ in Sect. 4. In Sects. 5, 6 and 7, we describe the algorithm for retrieving communities in directed attributed graphs. In Sect. 8, we report extensive experimental results. Finally, Sect. 9 concludes the paper.

2 Related Work

Our work relates to two main streams of researches, concerning directionality of relationships and attributes of vertices, respectively.

Various solutions to retrieve communities in recent literature, such as k-clique [2], densest subgraph [23], k-truss [8,9], spectral clustering [14,17]. However, due to the CS problem and strong connectivity of community, these solutions are difficult to, even cannot be applied in directed graph. Other algorithms in early years [3,13,20] are based on k-core, but they are used in simplified undirected graphs. Sozio [20] proposed the first algorithm global search to find communities with the technology of k-core containing the query vertex. Cuiet [3] proposed local search, which uses local expansion techniques to enhance the performance of global. We will compare these two solutions in our experiments. Researchers in [6] proposed an algorithm based on query vertex in directed graphs, yet the paper emphasizes importance of relationships between each vertex and the query vertex, not importance of community to the query vertex. In [15], Malliaros presented a method to solve the problem of relationships' directionality, which changes structure of undirected graphs to make up for the loss of directed edges. However, it cannot solve the problem completely and is designed to cluster the graphs, not to search communities.

Some research [1,4,10,11] works on attributed graphs. However, these works are substantially different from the DACQ problem, since they cannot take structure cohesiveness into consideration, besides, the attributes of the outcome communities are not enforced to be a subset of the query vertex's. In [5], Yixiang Fang proposed ACQ, which guarantee both structure and attribute cohesiveness, but he ignores the loss of attributes in the process of generating them, especially for social networks. We will compare ACQ in our experiments. Shang [19] presented a attribute-based method to supplement the topological structure, in which attributes and the topological structure are complementary. However, what we need to supplement is attributes, which is the opposite of the method.

3 Problem Definition

The definitions of community in the area of community discovery are similar, which often refer to a relatively compact graph. For attributed graph, the community should satisfy the condition that the vertices share one attribute set. In this section, we present the definitions of community, structure cohesiveness, and attribute cohesiveness for directed graph (Table 1).

Definition 1. *Given a directed graph G, a **SCS** is a strongly connected subgraph of the graph. **k-SCS** is the largest SCS of G, such that $\forall v \in k\text{-}SCS, deg_{k-SCS}(v) \geq k$.*

Definition 2. *Given a k-SCS, the **core number** of k-SCS is k, and the vertex's **core degree** is the highest order of a $k - SCS$. **Min-degree** is the minimum of v's in-degree value and out-degree value in G.*

Problem 1 (DACQ). Given a directed graph G(V,E), a positive integer k, a vertex $q \in V$ and a set of attributes $S \in Attr(Q)$, it returns a set of graphs, such that $G_q \subseteq G$, the following properties hold:

1. **Strong Connectivity.** $G_q \subseteq G$ is strongly connected and contains q;
2. **Structure cohesiveness.** $v \in G_q$, $mindeg_{G_q}(v) \geq k$;
3. **Attribute cohesiveness.** The size of attribute set is maximal, which is the set of attributes shared in S by all vertices of G_q.

Table 1. Symbols and meanings

Symbol	Meaning
$G(V, E)$	An attributed graph with vertex set V and edges set E
$Attr(v)$	The attribute set of vertex v
$deg_G(v)$	The degree of vertex v in G
$G[S]$	The largest subgraph of G s.t. q$\in G[S]$, and $\forall v \in G[S]$, $S \subseteq (\forall Attr(v)$ in $G[S])$
$G_k[S]$	$G[S]$ s.t. $\forall v \in G_k[S]$, $deg_{G_k[S]}v \geq k$
$CG_k[S]$	$G[S]$ s.t. $\forall G_k[S]$ is strongly connected, $v \in G_k[S]$, $deg_{G_k[S]}v \geq k$
$avgDeg(G)$	The average of in-degree values and out-degree values of $\forall v \in G$

For DACQ problem, strong connectivity and structure cohesiveness guarantee that the vertices are reachable to each other and linked closely in communities. We use min-degree as the measurement of structure cohesiveness in directed graphs. Meanwhile, attribute cohesiveness enable the vertices to share common attribute in the community.

4   Overview of DACQ

We take the social networks as an example, and the phenomenon we demonstrate below also exists in other cases. As shown in Fig. 3(a), given a network and a query vertex, we use DACQ to retrieve communities.

Firstly, we generate and process the attribute sets, according to the attribute set of query vertex. In general, we use the LDA model to generate attributes in social networks. LDA [7,16] model sets bound to guarantee that chosen topics (attributes) are relatively important. In this case, attributes of vertices are limited and relations between vertices are sufficient, therefore, we present a method to supplement attributes based on the topological structure. As shown

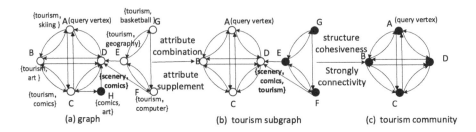

Fig. 3. Process to get communities

in Fig. 3(b), we generate attribute combinations and retrieve the subgraphs with different attribute combinations, $G[S_i]$.

Then, we k-SCSs from the attributed subgraphs and guarantee strongly connected with any core number. If there is a vertex in $G_k[S_i]$ not reachable to the query vertex, then it will be classified to the SCS with lower core number. The communities, whose structure cohesiveness is greater than the threshold, are chosen out with the attribute combination in Fig. 3(c). Finally, we get the community that meet with the demands of strongly connected structure cohesiveness and attribute cohesiveness.

5   Generating Attribute Combinations

As discussed in Sect. 1, attributes are an important aspect for community's cohesiveness. In this section, we supplement attributes according to the topological structure. Besides, we propose methods to get the valid attribute combinations about the query vertex.

5.1   Supplementing Attributes

Consider the case where attributes are deficient and relations between vertices are sufficient, since the attributes tagged or chosen are always in limited quantity. For example, in social networks, we can only generate limited relatively important attributes for the vertex through the LDA model.

DACQ can supplement attributes based on topological structure, which makes up for the loss of attributes in the process of generating attributes and increasing attribute cohesiveness of the community. As shown in Algorithm 1, the method is based on greedy algorithm to find the vertices, which supplements the attributes according to attributes of the query vertex. We first get the subgraph $G[S]$ of $G(V, E)$, of which attribute is S. Then, for each vertex which is the neighbors of $G[S]$, if it is closely correlated with the attributed subgraph $G[S]$, we supplement S to the attribute set of the vertex. The method sets minimum bound $avgDeg(G)$ to guarantee that the vertices not only keep densely connected with the attributed subgraph, but also can bring gain on attribute cohesiveness to the attributed subgraph.

Example 2. In Fig. 3(a), note that D in graph is not tagged by the attribute tourism. However, D is densely connected with other vertices with attribute tourism, besides, D strengthens the relations between other vertices and the tourism community. Hence, we add tourism to the attribute set of D. Then we generate attribute combinations in query vertex A and its neighbors. As shown Fig. 3(b), H is not closely linked with tourism subgraph, so we move away H.

Algorithm 1. Supplement attributes

Input: Graph $G = (V, E)$; attribute sets S
Output: vertices with supplemental attributes;
1: S_i is one attribute in Attr(v), L is the set size of Attr(v);
2: **while** $i \leq L$ **do**
3:     find $G[S_i]$ from the graph G;
4:     Neighbor($G[S_i]$) is the vertex set that contains the neighbors of vertices in $G[S_i]$;
5:     **for** each v∈ Neighbour($G[S_i]$) **do**
6:       **if** $deg_{G[S_i]}[v] > avgDeg(G)$ **then**
7:         attribute(v).add(S_i);
8:       **end if**
9:     **end for**
10: **end while**
11: **return** the set of vertices;

5.2 Candidate Attribute Combinations

A straightforward method to retrieve attributed subgraphs is that we enumerate all the subset of Attr(q), S_i ($1 \leq i \leq 2^L - 1, L = |S|$), and find the subgraphs of all the attribute combinations. In this section, we use frequent pattern mining algorithms to get candidate attribute combinations.

If S is qualified attribute set, then there are at least k of q's neighbors containing set S, since every vertex in $G_k[S]$ must has degree at least k. Consequently, we can prune the attribute sets directly through query vertex q and Neighbor(q) without other vertices. In this paper, we apply FP-growth algorithm to find the frequent attribute combinations, where attributes correspond to item sets. We set the minimum support as k, since our goal is to generate attributes combinations shared by at least k neighbors. As shown in Fig. 4(a), we get query vertex, Lily and her neighbors with attributes. The result of FP-growth shown in Fig. 4(b) are candidate attributes, which we set minimum supports count (k = 3) as minimum structure cohesiveness to generate. The algorithm prunes invalid attribute sets.

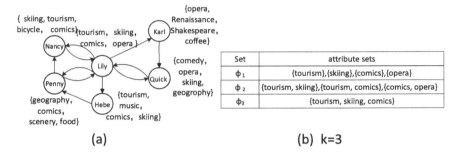

Fig. 4. Process of retrieving frequent attribute combinations

6   Retrieval of k-SCSs

In this section, we demonstrate how to get k-SCSs in the directed attributed graphs and construct index based on k-SCSs and attributes for querying efficiently.

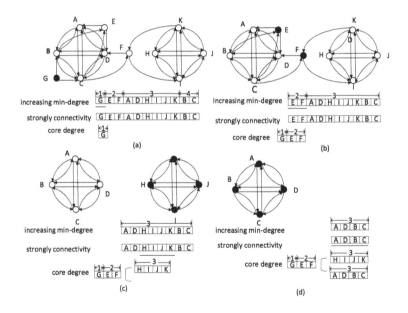

Fig. 5. Process of getting k-SCSs

6.1   Cores Decomposition

For a directed graph G and a query vertex q, we use the notation, $k\text{-}SCS$, to search communities. Common structure cohesiveness metric is the minimum degree [3,5]. For the question of retrieving communities in the directed graph, we define the k-SCS based on min-degree, which is minimum of the in-degree value and out-degree value of the vertices in the directed graph. In [12], Vladimir Batagelj present an algorithm for k-core, which determines the cores hierarchy, for implementing both functions and running in a constant time $(O_{(m)})$. As shown in Algorithm 2, we improve the $O_{(m)}$ algorithm for directed graph based on min-degree, which guarantee that the vertex is closely linked with other vertices in the community, and avoid the effect of a celebrity sa discussed in Sect. 1 .

Algorithm 2. Cores Decomposition

Input: Graph $G = (V, E)$; query vertex q; structure cohesiveness k
Output: strongly connected subgraphs with core number k;
  1: order the set of vertices V in increasing order of their min-degree;
  2: **for** each $v \in V$ in the order **do**
  3:    **if** min-degree[v]=k **then**
  4:      break
  5:    **end if**
  6:    $Q_i := Tarjan(q)$;
  7:    min-degree of vertices:= min-degree[v-1] which not$\in Q_i$
  8:    **for** each u$\in$ in-Neighbour(v) **do**
  9:      **if** in-degree[u]>in-degree[v] **then**
10:        in-degree[u] := in-degree[u]-1;
11:      **end if**
12:    **end for**
13:    **for** each $u \in$ out-Neighbour(v) **do**
14:      **if** out-degree[u]>out-degree[v] **then**
15:        out-degree[u]:=out-degree[u]-1;
16:      **end if**
17:    **end for**
18:    reorder V accordingly
19: **end for**
20: **return** K-SCS

6.2 Strongly Connected Component Retrieval

Strong connectivity guarantees that each member of the community is reachable to others. Tarjans strongly connected components algorithm takes a directed graph as input, and produces a partition of the graph's vertices into the graph's strongly connected components, We apply the Tarjans algorithm to retrieve strongly connected subgraphs with different core numbers. That is, the maximal core number determines the iterative times of algorithm's process. The improved Tarjans algorithm [12] uses several arrays to guarantee that the algorithm runs in linear time.

Example 3. The process of getting k-SCSs is shown in Fig. 5, there is a subgraph $G[S]$ about one attribute set S. We first order the vertices in an increasing order of their min-degrees and verify the strong connectivity. In Fig. 5(a), we move away the G with lowest min-degree and record G with core-degree 1. Then, we reduce the min-degree of $G's$ neighbors and reorder them, accordingly. In Fig. 5(b), we we record E, F with core-degree 2 and verify the strong connectivity again. Next, we known that H, I, J, K and A, B, C, D are two subgraphs,through strong connectivity algorithm. We thus get the core degree of them and record them, as shown respectively in Fig. 5(c) and (d). Finally, we get the 1-SCS, 2-SCS, and two 3-SCSs with attribute of S.

6.3   Index Construction

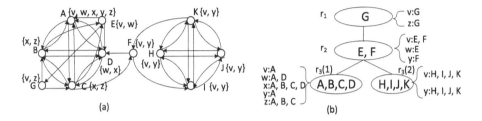

Fig. 6. Process of index construction

We construct a CL-tree (Core Label tree) index to search communities effi-ciently for some queries. First, we generate strongly connected subgraphs and core degrees of all the vertices in the subgraphs. We then construct an index with attribute labels. As shown in Fig. 6, we choose G with lowest core degree as root (r_1) and E, F as its child node (r_2). A, B, C, D is not strongly connected with H, I, J, K, so both of the two nodes are child nodes of r_2, as $r_3(1)$ and $r_3(2)$. If A is the query vertex and structure cohesiveness threshold is 2, we will find communities in the subtree (r_2) and ($r_3(1)$).

Time complexity. The k-core decomposition [12] can be done in $O(m)$ and Tarjans algorithm used to verify strongly connected component costs $O(m + n)$. Besides, the CL-tree could be constructed in $O(l \cdot n)$. We apply Tarjans algorithm in the subgraphs with different core numbers. If maximum of structure cohesiveness is k_{max}, the total time cost is $O(k_{max} \cdot m + l \cdot n)$.

7   Query Algorithm

In this section, we design community query algorithm as shown in Algorithm 3. First, we get candidate attribute sets which are supplemented based on the topological structure in Algorithm 1, and subtree of CL-tree which is constructed in Algorithm 2. In the while loop, we find the subgraphs tagged with an attribute combination, $G[S]$ from the graph. For maximum attribute cohesiveness, S is chosen in decreasing order of attribute combinations' set size, from Φ_c to Φ_1. Next, we find $CG_k[S]$ which satisfies strongly connected structure cohesiveness. Finally, we output all the attributed communities $CG_k[S]$.

Algorithm 3. Query algorithm

Input: Graph $G = (V, E)$; *query vertex q*
Output: communities on directed attributed graphs;
  1: L is the number of attributes, Q is a set of community;
  2: Generate subtree which contains q in the CL-tree and $\Phi_1, \Phi_2, \ldots, \Phi_L$ in order
     of increasing set size
  3: i=L;
  4: **while** $L \geq 1$ **do**
  5:    **for** each $s \in \Phi_i$ **do**
  6:      find $G[S_i]$ from the subtree;
  7:      **if** $CG_k[S_i]$ exists **then**
  8:        $Q.add(CG_k[S_i])$
  9:      **end if**
10:      **if** $(Q\ is\ \emptyset)$ **then**
11:        $L = i - 1$;
12:      **else**
13:        break;
14:      **end if**
15:    **end for**
16: **end while**
17: **return** communities in Q

---

8 Experiments

8.1 Setup

In order to show effectiveness in different networks, we choose three different kinds of datasets, Twitter[1] and Weibo[2], Tencent[3], and DBLP[4]. Twitter and Weibo represent for directed social networks, Tencent for undirected social networks, and DBLP for other undirected networks. For Tencent, we can use two directed edges to represent the bidirectional relationship of two users. Similarly, the edge which represent a co-authorship relationship between two authors in DBLP, can be taken place by two directed edges. We get datasets of Twitter and Weibo by crawling, and obtain graph of Tencent from the KDD contest 2012 (Table 2).

We randomly selected 100 query vertices, of which core numbers are higher than 5. We calculate the averages of the 100 queries. Our methods were implemented on a machine with CPU Inter(R) Core(TM) i7-2600, 8.00 GB memory, 3.40 GHz frequency, 500 GB hard disk. All programs are coded in Java.

---

[1] https://www.twitter.com/.
[2] https://www.weibo.com/.
[3] http://www.kddcup2012.org/c/kddcup2012-track1.
[4] http://dblp.uni-trier.de/xml/.

Table 2. Datasets of the networks

Dataset	Vertices	Edges
Twitter	61,791	4,801,709
Weibo	35,451	3,202,383
Tencent	2,320,895	50,133,369
DBLP	977,288	3,432,273

8.2   Results on Effectiveness

In this part, we conduct experiments of classical algorithm in several different data sets, and compare DACQ with other outstanding CS methods: Local search [20], Global search [3] and ACQ [5].

Given a graph G, a query vertex q and a set of communities obtains by an algorithm $C(q) = \{C_1, C_2, ..., C_\psi\}$, we adopt CMF (community member frequency) and CPJ [5] to measure effectiveness. The higher their value, the more cohesive is a community.

- CMF: $CMF(C(q)) = \frac{1}{\psi \cdot |Attr(q)|} \sum_{i=1}^{\psi} \sum_{h=1}^{|Attr(q)|} \frac{f_{(i,h)}}{|C_i|}$

  $f_{(i,h)}$ is the number of vertices of C_i whose attribute sets contain the h-th attribute of Attr(q). The CMF is the average of this value over all attributes in $Attr(q)$, and all communities in $C(q)$.

- CPJ: $cpj(C(q)) = \frac{1}{\psi} \sum_{i=1}^{\psi} \left[\frac{1}{|C_i|^2} \sum_{j=1}^{|C_i|} \sum_{k=1}^{|C_i|} \left(\frac{|W(C_{(i,j)}) \cap W(C_{(i,k)})|}{|W(C_{(i,j)}) \sqcup W(C_{(i,k)})|} \right) \right]$

  It computes the average similarity over all pairs of vertices of C_i, and all communities of C(q), which is adapted from Jaccard similarity.

Global search and Local search are based on undirected non-attributed graphs, and ACQ is based on undirected attributed graphs. DACQ works on directed attributed graphs. The four methods all adopt minimum degree measurement to guarantee the structure cohesiveness of communities. However, the algorithms and the graphs they work on are different, which result in different effectiveness of retrieved communities.

In Fig. 7, we compare DACQ with other CS methods about cohesiveness of communities specifically, about CMF and CPJ value for the four given datasets. The figure shows that ACQ and DACQ outperform in cohesiveness of communities, because ACQ mainly considers vertex attributes, while Global search and Local search do not. Furthermore, DACQ also show better performance than ACQ in directed networks (Twitter, Weibo), since DACQ works on directed networks without any simplification. As we discuss in Sect. 1.1, using undirected edges to represent unidirectional and bidirectional relationships could lose relationships and further produce wrong results. Besides, DACQ performs better than ACQ in undirected networks (Tencent, DBLP) for supplemental attributes.

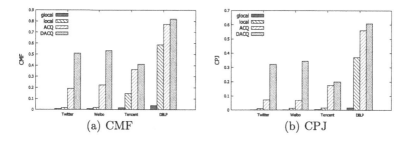

(a) CMF   (b) CPJ

Fig. 7. Effectiveness of the algorithms

8.3   Results on Efficiency

In this part, we compare the query efficiency with other CS methods for the four given datasets, under different k, which is the threshold of community cohesiveness. A lower k renders a larger subgraph of the graphs simplified from networks for all the algorithms. Extensive experiments were conducted to verify the efficiency of DACQ.

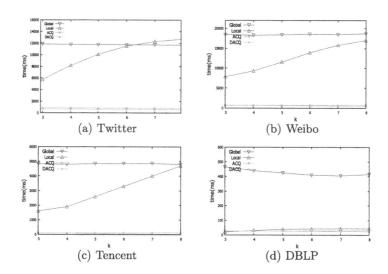

(a) Twitter   (b) Weibo

(c) Tencent   (d) DBLP

Fig. 8. Efficiency of the algorithms about different k

In Fig. 8, we can see Local search outperforms than Global search in general, and it is apparent that DACQ and ACQ execute more efficiently than others because of index construction. Besides, DACQ cost a little more time than ACQ. We apply $O(m)$ strongly connected algorithm for subgraphs with different core numbers in the process of index construction, and ACQ guarantees connectivity for once. We could use the index which are not be reconstructed, to find communities for a large number of queries. Hence, the little additional time could be ignored.

9   Conclusion

In this paper, we investigate the problem of community search in directed attributed graphs and propose a novel framework DACQ to retrieve effective community with strongly connected structure cohesiveness and attribute cohesiveness. To the best of our knowledge, this is the first work on community search in directed graphs. We can also apply DACQ in undirected graphs, which shows its wide applicability. As shown in experiments, DACQ method is efficient and more effective than other methods, for both directed and undirected networks.

References

1. Bhalotia, G., Hulgeri, A., Nakhe, C., Chakrabarti, S., Sudarshan, S.: Keyword searching and browsing in databases using banks. In: 2002 Proceedings of 18th International Conference on Data Engineering, pp. 431–440. IEEE (2002)
2. Cui, W., Xiao, Y., Wang, H., Lu, Y., Wang, W.: Online search of overlapping communities. In: Proceedings of the 2013 ACM SIGMOD International Conference on Management of Data, pp. 277–288. ACM (2013)
3. Cui, W., Xiao, Y., Wang, H., Wang, W.: Local search of communities in large graphs. In: Proceedings of the 2014 ACM SIGMOD International Conference on Management of Data, pp. 991–1002. ACM (2014)
4. Ding, B., Yu, J.X., Wang, S., Qin, L., Zhang, X., Lin, X.: Finding top-k min-cost connected trees in databases. In: 2007 IEEE 23rd International Conference on Data Engineering, ICDE 2007, pp. 836–845. IEEE (2007)
5. Fang, Y., Cheng, R., Luo, S., Hu, J.: Effective community search for large attributed graphs. Proc. VLDB Endow. **9**(12), 1233–1244 (2016)
6. Fang, Y., Chang, K.C.C., Lauw, H.W.: Roundtriprank: graph-based proximity with importance and specificity? In: 2013 IEEE 29th International Conference on Data Engineering (ICDE), pp. 613–624. IEEE (2013)
7. Fortunato, S.: Community detection in graphs. Phys. Rep. **486**(3), 75–174 (2010)
8. Huang, X., Cheng, H., Qin, L., Tian, W., Yu, J.X.: Querying k-truss community in large and dynamic graphs. In: Proceedings of the 2014 ACM SIGMOD International Conference on Management of Data, pp. 1311–1322. ACM (2014)
9. Huang, X., Lakshmanan, L.V., Yu, J.X., Cheng, H.: Approximate closest community search in networks. Proc. VLDB Endow. **9**(4), 276–287 (2015)
10. Kacholia, V., Pandit, S., Chakrabarti, S., Sudarshan, S., Desai, R., Karambelkar, H.: Bidirectional expansion for keyword search on graph databases. In: Proceedings of the 31st International Conference on Very Large Data Bases, VLDB Endowment, pp. 505–516 (2005)
11. Kargar, M., An, A.: Keyword search in graphs: Finding r-cliques. Proc. VLDB Endow. **4**(10), 681–692 (2011)
12. Khaouid, W., Barsky, M., Srinivasan, V., Thomo, A.: K-core decomposition of large networks on a single PC. Proc. VLDB Endow. **9**(1), 13–23 (2015)
13. Li, R.H., Qin, L., Yu, J.X., Mao, R.: Influential community search in large networks. Proc. VLDB Endow. **8**(5), 509–520 (2015)
14. Li, Y., Chen, J., Liu, R., Wu, J.: A spectral clustering-based adaptive hybrid multi-objective harmony search algorithm for community detection. In: 2012 IEEE Congress on Evolutionary Computation (CEC), pp. 1–8. IEEE (2012)

15. Malliaros, F.D., Vazirgiannis, M.: Clustering and community detection in directed networks: a survey. Phys. Rep. **533**(4), 95–142 (2013)
16. Newman, M.E., Girvan, M.: Finding and evaluating community structure in networks. Phys. Rev. E **69**(2), 026113 (2004)
17. Qiu, J., Peng, J., Zhai, Y.: Network community detection based on spectral clustering. In: 2014 International Conference on Machine Learning and Cybernetics (ICMLC), vol. 2, pp. 648–652. IEEE (2014)
18. Ruan, Y., Fuhry, D., Parthasarathy, S.: Efficient community detection in large networks using content and links. In: Proceedings of the 22nd International Conference on World Wide Web, pp. 1089–1098. ACM (2013)
19. Shang, J., Wang, C., Wang, C., Guo, G., Qian, J.: An attribute-based community search method with graph refining. J. Supercomput. pp. 1–28 (2017)
20. Sozio, M., Gionis, A.: The community-search problem and how to plan a successful cocktail party. In: Proceedings of the 16th ACM SIGKDD International Conference on Knowledge Discovery and Data Mining, pp. 939–948. ACM (2010)
21. Tong, Y., Chen, L., Shahabi, C.: Spatial crowdsourcing: challenges, techniques, and applications. Proc. VLDB Endow. **10**(12), 1988–1991 (2017)
22. Tong, Y., She, J., Ding, B., Chen, L., Wo, T., Xu, K.: Online minimum matching in real-time spatial data: experiments and analysis. Proc. VLDB Endow. **9**(12), 1053–1064 (2016)
23. Wu, Y., Jin, R., Li, J., Zhang, X.: Robust local community detection: on free rider effect and its elimination. Proc. VLDB Endow. **8**(7), 798–809 (2015)
24. Xu, Z., Ke, Y., Wang, Y., Cheng, H., Cheng, J.: A model-based approach to attributed graph clustering. In: Proceedings of the 2012 ACM SIGMOD International Conference on Management of Data, pp. 505–516. ACM (2012)

EPAF: An Efficient Pseudonymous-Based Inter-vehicle Authentication Framework for VANET

Fei Wang[1]([⊠]) [iD], Yifan Du[1,2], Yongjun Xu[1], Tan Cheng[1],
and Xiaoli Pan[3]

[1] Institute of Computing Technology, Chinese Academy of Sciences,
Beijing, China
{wangfei,duyifan,xyj,chengtan}@ict.ac.cn
[2] University of Chinese Academy of Sciences, Beijing, China
[3] 93868 Troops, People's Liberation Army, Beijing, China
lavenderpanpan@163.com

Abstract. Road users are now able to retrieve safety information, computing task results and subscribing content through various vehicular ad hoc network (VANET) services. Most commonly used services are safety beacon, cloud computation, and content subscription. Road users concern more about data security than ever. Privacy preserving authentication (PPA) is one main mechanism to secure inter-vehicle messages. However, for historical reasons, PPA for three services are different and therefore hard to be unified and not lightweight enough. To improve the flexibility and efficiency of PPA for various VANET services, it is necessary to securely authenticate messages preserving privacy for individual service, but also to unify PPA processes of various services in one vehicle. Here we propose an Efficient Pseudonymous-based Inter-Vehicle Authentication Framework for various VANET services. Our novel framework employs three methods. Method No. 1 consists of a decentralized certificate authority (CA), which allows vehicles to communicate only if vehicles registering themselves. Method No. 2 adopts a three-stage mutual authenticating process, which adapts to different communicating models in various services. Method No. 3 we design a universal basic module that requires only lightweight hashing and MAC operations to accomplish the signing and verifying processes. To analyze the security performance of our EPAF, we use automated tool under symbolic approach. Our results strongly suggest that EPAF is secure, robust and adaptable in vehicular safety, as well as in content and cloud computation services. To analyze the performance of EPAF, we calculate benchmarks and simulate the network. Our results strongly suggest that EPAF reduces computation cost by 370–3500 times, decreases communication overhead by 45.98%–75.53% and CA need not to manage CRL compared with classical schemes. In conclusion our framework provides insights into how data privacy can be simultaneously protected using our EPAF, while also improving communication and computing speed even in high traffic density.

Keywords: VANET · Privacy preserving · Authentication framework
Cloud computation

© Springer Nature Singapore Pte Ltd. 2018
L. Zhu and S. Zhong (Eds.): MSN 2017, CCIS 747, pp. 252–270, 2018.
https://doi.org/10.1007/978-981-10-8890-2_18

1   Introduction

Various services now depend on vehicular networks like traditional safety service, arising content subscribe/publish service [1] and vehicular cloud computation service [3]. In safety service, VANET is supposed to collect and disseminate useful information through vehicle-to-vehicle (V2V) and vehicle-to-roadside unit (V2R) based on dedicated short-range communications (DSRC), supporting applications like Forward Collision Warning (FCW) and Blind Spot Warning (BSW) [2]. In content service, it on one hand receive content through 4G/5G, on the other store and forward content (road map around, media, POIs) through opportunistic communication. In computation service, a temporary vehicular computation cloud is formed on the fly by dynamically integrating resources from a cluster of vehicles like hundreds in parking lots, helping nearby users especially ones in cheaper cars to accomplish heavy computation tasks and gain actual benefits [6]. No matter what services VANET take on, security issues are inevitable.

Three types of security requirements are considered in this paper. (1) Basic type like resilience to eavesdropping, forgery and modification due to wireless communication. (2) Common type includes service data privacy preserving, unlinkability for multiple anonymous messages and tracking a vehicle (implied by level 3 privacy in [7]) and conditional traceability. (3) Dedicated type for various services. The first is core service data, apart from private identity information and locations, safety service focuses on vehicle motion status and road events, content service focuses on subscribe/publish information, computation service focuses on request, result and vehicle reputation. Unlinkability for identity and location is fundamental. But subscribe/publish information in content service, request/reply and reputation in computation service should be preserved. Apart from above, the performance should be redundant to adapt to arising different services.

Privacy preserving authentication (PPA) keeps an astonishing idea to ensure the security of VANET [3–10]. Some are based on public key infrastructure (PKI) and employs traditional digital signature technique to authenticate messages. Main downsides of such schemes are three: (1) Vulnerable to effortless Denial of Service (DoS) attack. (2) Collapse of scheme caused by high packet loss ratio. (3) Heavy burden on trusted authority (TA) performing certificate updating and revoking. We observe new trends in VANET. On-vehicle computer computes much faster, which leads to that road infrastructure needs not to be responsible for security tasks. As the vehicular network services are developing, the integration of hardware and software for PPA is inevitable rather than separated for different services. Lastly, urban three-dimensional traffic system incurs the need of enough redundant performance.

In this paper, we proposed an Efficient Pseudonymous-based Inter-Vehicle Authentication Framework for various VANET services (EPAF). For each vehicle a telematics device (TD) and a tamper proof device (TPD) are equipped acting as a distributed security proxy. Lightweight basic modules are decoupled and designed, each of which requires only several extreme lightweight operations to accomplish signing and verification. Moreover, the framework is able to adapt to one-way dissemination or a request/reply routine in various services. As we know, EPAF is the first strong-privacy-preserving and dos-resilient authentication framework compatible with various services. Even compared with PPA scheme for safety service, hundreds of times efficiency redundancy is assured.

Followings are the advantages of EPAF:

- Level 3 privacy and strong privacy preservation: EPAF is able to guarantee level 3 privacy. Moreover, TD and TPD devices act like proxy, which leads to strong privacy that adversary is unable to pry into real identities of vehicles even if all RSUs are compromised.
- Reduced certificate overhead: In EPAF, a dynamic pseudo identity and a short MAC is carried within message. All CRL related overhead is eliminated and our EPAF achieves a decrease of 45.98%–75.53% in communication compared with other schemes.
- Compatible with various services: Through a mutual authentication mechanism, EPAF is able to satisfy security requirements which is compatible with one-direction message dissemination or bi-direction request/reply service. EPAF's integrity and unlinkability are compatible with different service data.
- Redundant performance efficiency: In user, message or service authentication, EPAF employs only hash operations coupled with MAC generation to accomplish the signing verification of service message. Subsequently achieving a significant increase of nearly 370–3500 times in computation compared with even safety schemes. This makes EPAF efficient enough for various services even in large traffic density.

Rest of this paper are as follows. Section 2 presents the related work about privacy authentication in VANET. In Sect. 3 system model and adversary model is defined. Then Sect. 4 gives full details of EPAF. In Sect. 5 we analyze the security of the scheme using symbolic approach. Section 6 gives performance analysis of EPAF, and Sect. 7 concludes the paper and look into the future work.

2 Related Work

Bulk of research work has been proposed to improve conditional privacy preservation for VANET in last decades, which is considered as candidate framework design references [5–9, 15, 18–21].

Pseudonymous-based schemes like BP [5], ECPP [7] and PTVC [6] link and update many pairs of private key and pseudonymous certificate to a pseudo identity. However, these schemes suffer from high overhead of certificate management and time window between certificate update (e.g. 1 min). In group based schemes, group members hide their real identities through a group identity. In schemes like [8, 9], CRL item checking needs two paring calculations, which is 104 times high than a string comparison in computation overhead, which makes computational cost for authentication too high to adapt to complex service handshake. Pervasive road side units (RSUs) are usually needed to maintain group, which makes group leader bottleneck. Hybrid schemes are ones which combine pseudonymous authentication protocol, digital signature, MAC and other authentication techniques to make a tradeoff [9]. In [8], group signature CRL checking is still expensive. TESLA++ [9] provides fast authentication and non-repudiation and data integrity. However, it is unable to provide privacy preservation and conditional traceability. Batch verification based schemes are based batch verification. In RAISE and succeeding schemes [15], RSU was utilized as aggregator to verify messages from vehicles. The approach utilizes the IBE cryptography for generating secret keys for pseudo identities and thus avoids the use of certificates. Total computation overhead of vehicles are significantly reduced, but a vehicle still need store and wait for aggregation message from RSU. As for batch verification based ones, on one hand conditional traceability is not effective for replying messages shared back to vehicles, on the other the verification delay are inevitable and hard to deal.

The mentioned schemes have common bottlenecks of relying on infrastructure and not supporting mutual service message authentication. High overhead of signing, verification or certificate management by centered architecture is inevitable.

3 System Model

In this section, system model (network model and attack model), and design goals are presented.

3.1 Network Model

We consider a hybrid VANET scenario in which safety, content and computation services are supported. We divided the network model into two parts: common model for entities and service processing model for services.

In common model, TA is fully trusted by others. It has nearly unlimited computation and storage resources and accomplishes tasks as (1) RSUs and vehicle registration, (2) system key management, (3) conditional tracing. RSU communicates with TA directly through wired channel. It has large storage and powerful communication capability of 1 km to 3 km. It is responsible for message forwarding and distributed RSU aided key updating.

Every vehicle is equipped with an OBU as shown in Fig. 1. In safety service, OBU gathers information from vehicle sensors (e.g., GPS, forward, speed) and Event Data Recorder, packs safety beacon and broadcasts it through dedicated channel [2]. In content service, OBU acquires and provides content. For computation service, OBU helps generate requests and receive results. Telematics Device (TD) and Tamper Proof Device (TPD) cooperate with each other to ensure the security of the services. TPD is hard to hack into and used to store cryptographic materials and process cryptographic operations. Time synchronization is assured for all OBUs.

Different messages exchanging process are as followings:

Safety Service:
$V_i \rightarrow V_j$: *<id, timestamp, motion attribute, events>*
V_j: *consume and make driving decision*
Content Service:
$V_i \rightarrow V_j$: *<id, timestamp, motion attribute, subscribe info>*
V_j: *consume and make routing decision*

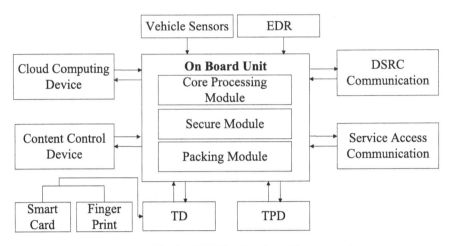

Fig. 1. OBU functional model

Set up a secure channel between V_i and V_j

$V_j \rightarrow V_i$: *<id, timestamp, motion attribute, publish info>*

Computation Service:

$V_i \rightarrow V_j$: *<id, timestamp, motion attribute, computation request, trust threshold>*

$V_j \rightarrow V_i$: *<id, timestamp, motion attribute, computation reply, reputation value>*

In cloud computation service [6], End user (EU) needs to locate the high-reputation computing units (CUs) firstly. V_i sets a threshold trust level, and broadcasts the computation request. After receiving the V_i's requests, V_j verifies the request, calculates the proof and reply to V_i. If the reputation satisfies the trust level requirement, vehicle (EU) outsource its data through secure channel and receive results eventually.

The above processes show that, to achieve a compatible PPA framework, the direct and simple way is bi-direction authentication.

3.2   Adversary Model

Attack model is divided into common and dedicated.

Common Attack Model

Adversary controls communication channel, monitor all the on-the-fly data through these channel and tamper the message. Eavesdropping, RSU or vehicle compromising, privacy prying, identity impersonation and DoS attack (through jamming, injection or high density traffic) are possible. One hypothesis is that materials are kept safe in TPDs.

Special Attack Model for Safety Service

An adversary would forge safety beacon to induce the legitimate vehicles to accept false or harmful messages without being detected, thus abusing the VANET to maximum its gains (e.g., cheating a clear path, snooping users' location).

Special Attack Model for Content Service

Subscribe information is forged to disturb opportunistic networking, or to help adversary obtain more information without being billed. Adversary might also forge high quality content information and cheat on credit. Sub./Pub. message link attack might happen because of embedded interest.

Special Attack Model for Cloud Computation Service

Reputation spoofing attack is one severe attack when CUs impersonate as other CUs and provide fake reputation to obtain more data. Adversary is able to use reputation in several messages to track a vehicle. Vehicular cloud computation is a hot topic. However, in this paper we focus only on privacy-preserving authentication, thus only reputation spoofing attack and reputation message link attack are considered.

3.3 Design Goals

First are basic security goals for wireless communication: *Resilience to forgery or modification* is that every message should be authenticated to ensure that its source legitimate and payload unaltered. Any forged or modified messages shall be detected by vehicle. As service is different, core messages are different. *Non-repudiation* includes three meanings which are (1) not claiming to be other vehicle; (2) not cheating about their position and service data; (3) not denying the actions and the time of generating and sending messages.

Second are goals concerning V2V communications: *Identity privacy preserving (Authentication and Anonymity)* is fundamental because of the broadcasting nature in VANET. Privacy leaking must be prevented in which binding between real identities and information of VANET. *Unlinkability* is part of level 3 privacy. It means that adversaries are never able to find common properties in multiple messages and link them to one particular vehicle. Considering various services, the meanings are different. Location privacy violation problem might be incurred without unlinkability. Subscribe and publish interest privacy leaking also happens. For computation service, reputation linking is considered in this paper. *Strong privacy preservation* is also necessary, which means with all RSUs compromised, the adversary cannot obtain vehicles' private information. *Conditional traceability* means that TA is able to retrieve a vehicle's real identity when the message is in dispute.

Third are goals to achieve efficiency redundancy and flexibility redundancy like DoS resilience and separate user to one vehicle support.

4 Proposed EPAF Framework

4.1 Overview

The proposed framework is based on three methods: (1) Decentralization is implemented by TD and TPD devices which stores secret information like system key, initial pseudo identity, one-way-function result of user's password and help to verify user's or vehicle's identity and to keep or update passwords. (2) To achieve good extendibility for various services, a three stage mutual authentication is designed, which includes user authentication, message authentication and service authentication. (3) EPAF divides modules into four types of basic function modules: modules of registration, modules on TD, modules on TPD for message authentication, modules on TPD for service authentication. This decoupling aims to give a lightweight adaptable pseudonymous-based protocol structure without implementation details. MAC and one-way hash operations are used to implement the modules. Revocation and conditional tracing are also designed.

4.2   Framework Workflow and Modules

In registration and initialization phase, after **System Initialization** of CA, user of the vehicular services drives the vehicle to CA, and uploads his password $pw_{i,u}$ (usually in form of biometrics features like fingerprint and iris scan), identity of vehicle and necessary information of vehicle through **Info. Upload** module. **Info. Upload** module does one-way function to $pw_{i,u}$ and obtain $\gamma_{i,u}$, then uploads $<ID_i, \gamma_{i,u}, Info_i>$ to CA. Through **Pseudo Identity and Param. Generation** module, CA picks initial pseudo identity PID_i and $TDID_i$ for both TPD and TD devices. Then relevant secure parameters are calculated. CA writes $<PID_i, k_m, ts_{key}, [param.]>$ to TPD device and $<TDID_i, ID_i, [param.]>$ to TD device.

In order to handle different application situations, we propose a direct and simple three stage authentication scheme, structure of which is shown in Fig. 2.

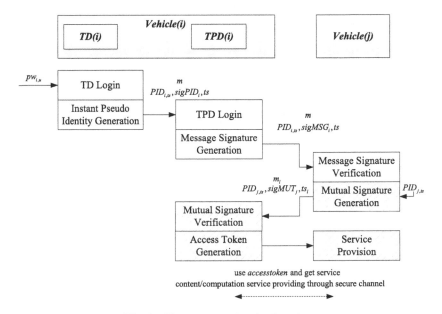

Fig. 2. Three stage authentication phase

User Authentication and TPD Login
User authentication stage is performed by **TD Login** module in telematics device. When new messages come, instant pseudo identity $PID_{i,u}$ and the signature $sigPID_i$ are generated using PID_i by **Instant Pseudo Identity Generation** module. Afterwards, the $<PID_{i,ts}, sigPID_i, ts>$ is delivered to tamper proof device. Two core modules **TPD Login** and **Message Signature Generation** are performed in TPD. With assistance of PID_i pre-installed in TPD, $sigPID_i$ is verified.

Message Authentication Stage
After the verification of **TPD Login module**, **Message Signature Generation** module would generate the signature of message using $PID_{i,ts}$, pre-stored k_m, and current timestamp ts. Then $<m, PID_{i,ts}, sigMSG_i, ts>$ is broadcasted to nearby vehicles. When message is received by another vehicle, **Message Signature Verification** module is performed by $TPD(j)$. If the verification process returns true, message is valid and is available to be consumed.

Service Authentication Stage
This stage aims to support bi-direction communication service and verification of vehicular service provider. **Mutual Signature Generation** module on $TPD(j)$ is performed to take service link information, $PID_{i,ts}$, ts_l as input and generate mutual signature for service link information. Then $<PID_{j,ts}, sigMUT_i, ts_l, m_l>$ is sent back to *Vehicle(i)*. **Mutual Signature Verification** is performed on $TPD(i)$ to verify the identity and the service information from *Vehicle(j)*. If the verification is passed, **Access Token Generation** is performed to output a service *accesstoken* for *Vehicle(j)*, which would sent it to *Vehicle(j)*. After the *accesstoken* is verified valid, *Vehicle(j)* enters into **Service Provision** module and the vehicles communicate through specific secure channels.

4.3 Core Module Implementation

To explain the module implementation of EPAF, we use two vehicles. The correlated modules are shown in Figs. 3 and 4. Each module implementation is shown as followings:

System Initialization and Info. Upload
Suppose **G** be a cyclic additive group of order q, $P \in \mathbf{G}$ a generator of **G** and e: $\mathbf{G} \times \mathbf{G} \rightarrow V$ be a bilinear map which satisfies following conditions [12]: Bilinear, $e(x_1 + x_2, y) = e(x_1, y)e(x_2, y)$ and $e(x, y_1 + y_2) = e(x, y_1 + y_2)$; Non-degenerate, There exists $x \in \mathbf{G}$ and $y \in \mathbf{G}$ such that $e(x, y) \neq 1$. CA randomly picks integer $\alpha \in Z_q^*$ as private key for the vehicular network system, and computes $\beta = \alpha P$ as public key. CA computes $S_{IDCA} = \alpha H(ID_{CA})$ as its identity secret key and generates system key $k_m = \{k_m^1, k_m^2\}$, where $k_m^1 \in \{0, 1\}^a$, a is the key length of $Enc_k(.)$; $k_m^2 \in \{0, 1\}^b$, b is the key length of $h_k^1(.)$. CA publishes $\{\beta, ID_{CA}\}$, and keeps α, k_m, S_{IDCA} secret.

   Vehicle_i along with its user firstly submit real identity ID_i, $\gamma_{i,u} = h(pw_{i,u})$ and *Info_i* (e.g., engine serial number, date of manufacture, vehicle owner, service registration information) to **Info. Upload** through secure channels. **Info. Upload** then outputs $<ID_i, \gamma_{i,u}, Info_i>$.

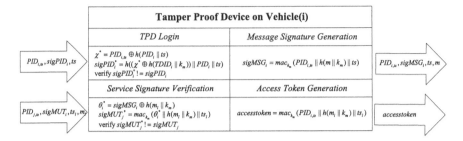

Fig. 3. Modules on TPD(i) of Vehicle(i)

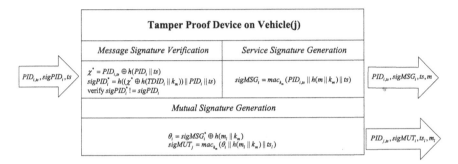

Fig. 4. Modules on TPD(j) of Vehicle(j)

Pseudo Identity and Param. Generation

CA checks the correctness of input $<ID_i, \gamma_{i,u}, Info_i>$ (usually with help of national vehicle management department and the VANET service provider). Then CA randomly picks $PID_i \in \mathbf{Z}_q^*$ and $TDID_i$ for $Vehicle_i$ and $TD_i <ID_i, TDID_i, PID_i, Info_i>$ is then inserted into user and vehicle information table. CA computes parameters like (Table 1):

$$pS_i = h(ID_i||TDID_i||PID_i) \oplus h(TDID_i||k_m), pU_{i,u} = h(ID_i||\gamma_{i,u}||PID_i) \oplus h(TDID_i||k_m),$$
$$pV_{i,u} = h(\gamma_{i,u} \oplus PID_i), pK_{i,u} = PID_i \oplus h(TDID_i \oplus \gamma_{i,u}).$$

Here $pV_{i,u}$ is employed as a user verifier to authenticate driver's identity, $pK_{i,u}$ is employed as a password keeper and $pU_{i,u}$ is used to update the user password through TPD device. Moreover, if user changes the password $pK_{i,u}$ would be updated and all values of $pK_{i,u}$ are kept in a table in TPD device for message tracing use, we call it **pK-table**.

Finally, CA saves $<ID_i, TDID_i, PID_i, Info_i>$ to a user information table, and writes $\{TDID_i, ID_i, pS_i, <pV_{i,u}, pK_{i,u}>\}$ to TD_i, and preloads $\{PID_i, k_m, ts_{key}, <pU_{i,u}, pK_{i,u}>\}$ on TPD_i.

Table 1. Notations used in proposed scheme

Symbol	Description	Symbol	Description
CA	Certificate authority	ID_{CA}	Identity of CA
k_m	System key	$Vehicle_i$	The ith vehicle
ts_{key}	Timestamp of current system key being updated	$h(.)$	Hash function $h : \{0, 1\}^* \times V \rightarrow Z_q^*, Z_q^* = \{x \in \{1, ..., q-1\} \mid \gcd(x, q) = 1\}$
$Info_i$	Vehicle information of $Vehicle_i$	$h_k^1(.)$	Hash function $h_k^1 : \{0, 1\}^* \rightarrow \{0, 1\}^n$
IDi	Real identity of $Vehicle_i$	$TDID_i$	Identity of TD_i
$pw_{i,u}$	Biological password of driver u of $Vehicle_i$	$PID_{i,ts}$	Dynamic pseudo identity of $Vehicle_i$ at ts
$Enck(.)$	Encryption function using k as key, like AES	$Dec_k(.)$	Decryption function using k as key, like AES
$H(.)$	Hash function $H: \{0, 1\}^* \rightarrow G^*$, $G^* = G\backslash\{0\}$	$mac_k(.)$	MAC using k as a key, such as HMAC [11]
PID_i	Initial pseudo identity of $Vehicle_i$	$\|$	Message concatenation operation

TD Login

User firstly plugs the TD_i into the $Vehicle_i$ and input $pw_{i,u}$. Then $<pV_{i,u}, pK_{i,u}>$ is used to verify user as shown in Fig. 4. If the driver is legitimate, the restored PID_i is stored in memory until TD_i is unplugged.

Instant Pseudo Identity Generation

Figure 4 gives the generation process of $PID_{i,ts}$ and $sigPID_i$: $PID_{i,ts} = h(ID_i\|TDID_i\|PID_i) \oplus h(PID_i\|ts)$, $sigPID_i = h(pS_i\|PID_i\|ts)$. Then TD_i sends $\{PID_{i,ts}, sigPID, ts\}$ to TPD_i.

TPD Login

TPD_i would verify the legitimacy of TD_i, if TD_i is legitimate, then OBU is free to use TPD_i to perform further action.

Message Signature Generation

Every time a new message payload m is generated, TD_i redoes the **TPD login** to update dynamic pseudo identity $PID_{i,ts}$. If the **TPD login** is passed, TPD_i would generate: $sigMSG_i = mac_{km}(PID_{i,ts}\|h(m\|k_m)\|ts)$ and packs the message like $\{PID_{i,ts}, sigMSG_i, ts, m\}$ as module output.

Message Signature Verification

After $Vehicle_j$ receives a packet $\{PID_{i,ts}, sigMSG_i, ts, m\}$ from $Vehicle_i$, TPD_j on $Vehicle_j$ would calculate $sigMSG_i^* = mac_{km}(PID_{i,ts}\|h(m\|k_m)\|ts)$ to verify the legitimacy of the message. If $sigMSG_i^*! = sigMSG_i$ returns false, $Vehicle_j$ then accepts the message for application or launches **Mutual Signature Generation** in content or computation service.

Mutual Signature Generation

Mutual signature is generated by vehicle which replies the service request like: $sigMUT_j = mac_{km}(\theta_i||h(m_l||k_m)||ts_l), \theta_i = sigMSG_i^* \oplus h(m_l||k_m)$. The generation process is just simple like *Message Signature Generation* module.

Mutual Signature Verification

TPD_i uses $\{PID_{j,ts}, sigMUT_j, ts_l, m_l\}$ as input and computes $\theta_i^* = sigMSG_i \oplus h(m_l||k_m)$, $sigMUT_j^* = mac_{km}(\theta_i^*||h(m_l||k_m)||ts_l)$ to verify service signature.

Through accesstoken = $mac_{km}(PID_{i,ts}||h(m_l||k_m)||ts_l)$, access token is generated and is used in future service acquisition. *Vehicle$_j$* would verify the access token, if it returns true, then the vehicles enter service provision through secure dedicated channel. The Service provision processing is potential to be realized in many different ways and the corresponding discussion is not included in this paper.

4.4   Revocation and Conditional Tracing Phases

Pseudonym Revocation

In a decentralized framework, it is hard to revoke an invalid vehicle which is judged invalid. EPAF only needs CA to broadcast one revocation message $\{PID_i, sg_{rev}\}$ to all vehicles, in which sg_{rev} is the signature of PID_i calculated by $sg_{rev} = Sign_{SIDCA}(PID_i)$. If *Vehicle$_i$* receives the revocation message and verify the source legitimacy of it, TPD_i deletes all the secret materials preloaded in registration phase including $\{PID_i, k_m, ts_{key}, <pU_{i,u}, pK_{i,u}>\}$. Once the telematics device is plugged in the vehicle, the corresponding preload secret materials $\{TDID_i, ID_i, pS_i, <pV_{i,u}, pK_{i,u}>\}$ would also be erased.

Conditonal Tracing for Vehicle and User

Message tracing process provides the capability of tracing\messages in services. Take $\{PID_{i,ts}, sigMSG_i, ts, m\}$ as an example. CA selects $<ID_i, TDID_i, PID_i, Info_i>$ where $PID_{i,ts} == h(ID_i||TDID_i||PID_i) \oplus h(PID_i||ts)$, from user and vehicle information table. Therefore, *Vehicle$_i$* is found and located through $Info_i$. Through *pK-table* stored on TPD_i, the authority is able to trace the user on vehicle using evidence of $pU_{i,u}$ when the message is being sent.

5   Security Analysis

Preliminaries about symbolic approach is given in this chapter. Then we implement core phases of EPAF using ProVerif and compare the security properties of schemes.

5.1   Preliminaries

The computational approach and the symbolic approach are two major methods to analyze the cryptographic protocols employed in last two decades. Symbolic approach is amenable enough to realize in automatous way due to its algebraic structure. Many automated tools are introduced for the symbolic approach. For example, ProVerif is a tool for applied spi calculus. Yet problems exist: (1) the computational soundness is unclear; (2) the number of participants has to be fixed. (3) the time complexity increases exponentially along with the number of participants. Recently, Canetti et al. [16] has proposed the universally composable symbolic analysis (UCSA) approach, in which it is proved that the security is unrelated with the number of sessions. However, it is only able to deal with two-party cryptographic protocols. Later in [17], the UCSA approach is extended to deal with arbitrary number of participants. Moreover, according to Theorem 2 in [17], symbolic approach implies computational approach. Some important keywords of the pi calculus are as followings:

Query attacker: M means that the attacker may have M in phase (M is not secret). **query ev:f(x1,…, xn) ==> ev:f′(x1,…, xn)** is non-injective agreement: it is true when, if the event f has been executed, then the event f′ must have been executed before f. **choice [<term>, <term>]:** it tries to reconstructs a trace until a program point at which the process using the first argument of choice behaves differently from the one using the second. If a trace is reconstructed, it means the attacker is able to distinguish the first argument from the second one. **!<process>:** it means the replication executes an unbounded number of copies of <process> in parallel: <process> | <process> | <process> | ….

5.2   Experiment and Analysis

In this chapter, we compare the security features of EPAF framework with classical BP, GSIS, VAST and PTVC.

Resilience to Forgery or Modification of Message
The messages in the framework is protected by MAC. The proposed scheme is able to detect the forged or modified messsages with the assistance of tamper proof device. Results in [19] show that if "event endAuthV2V(PID_i_ts, sigMSG_i, ts)" has been executed, then "event beginAuthV2V(PID_i_ts, sigMSG_i, ts)" must have been executed. Thus the adversary is unable to forge or modify {$PID_{i,ts}$, $sigMSG_i$, ts, m} or {$PID_{j,ts}$, $sigMUT_j$, ts_l, m_l}.

Non-repudiation
Each message is integrated with instant pseudo identity, which is generated from ID_i, PID_i, $TDID_i$ and timestamp by **_Instant Pseudo Identity Generation_** module. Non-repudiation is guaranteed because an adversary is never able to deny the action nor time of message.

Identity Privacy Preserving
$PID_{i,ts}$ or $PID_{j,ts}$ is utilized to preserve the ID_i. User need to pass **_TD Login_** module on TD and pass **_TPD Login_** module on TPD to access the vehicular network. Thus identity privacy is preserved even if the telematics device is stolen. As shown in [19], the adversary is unable to obtain any information about ID_i and ID_j.

Unlinkability
In EPAF, $PID_{i,ts}$ differs as time changes, adversary is unable to launch replay attack nor link numerous messages to one vehicle. Moreover, in core modules, key operations of

MAC generation and message authentication are accomplished without knowing the real identity. We use keyword "*choice[PID_i_ts,r0]*", "*choice[PID_j_ts,r0]*" in to test the anonymity. The result is "RESULT Observational equivalence is true (bad not derivable)", as shown in [19], which means $PID_{i,ts}$ is unable to be distinguished from a random number r0. To test the unlinkability, we use "!" before the processes and the result is still true, which means no matter how many commutation processes are running, none of information about vehicle's identity will be revealed. Thus the proposed scheme achieves level 3 privacy: authentication, anonymity, unlinkability.

Mutual Authentication
In proposed framework, a three stage mutual authentication mechanism is provided. In message authentication stage, beacon safety message itself or service request message (Subscribe information message or computation request message) is being verified. In service authentication stage, the service reply message (Publish information or computation reply) is being verified to achieve the PPA along with extendibility for various services.

Compatible with Different Services
EPAF achieves the compatibility which focus on different core data in message integrity, unlinkability and a mutual authentication service hand shake. These are the simplest model to provide unified privacy preserving authentication service. In contrast, BP, GSIS and VAST are designed for safety and PTVC is designed for computation. Other schemes including batched based schemes, hybrid schemes, k-anonymity based schemes and cloud assisted schemes are only able to adapt for one kind of vehicular services and hard to extend.

Apart from above security feature analysis, EPAF also achieves strong privacy preservation and conditional traceability which are fundamental in PPA. As is shown in

Table 2. Security comparision

Schemes		Properties				
		BP	GSIS	VAST	PTVC	EPAF
Data integrity		✓	✓	✓	✓	✓
Non-repudiation		✓	✓	✓	✓	✓
Level3 privacy	Authentication	✓	✓	✓	✓	✓
	Anonymity	✓	✓	✗	✓	✓
	Unlinkability	✗	✓	✗	✓	✓
Strong privacy preserving		✗	✗	✗	✗	✓
Conditional traceability	Vehicle	✓	✓	✗	✓	✓
	User	✗	✗	✗	✗	✓
Mutual authentication		✗	✗	✗	✓	✓
Service compatible		✗	✗	✗	✗	✓
Efficient revocability		✗	✗	✗	✗	✓
Resist to DoS	Computation	✗	✗	✓	✓	✓
	Memory	✓	✓	✓	✗	✓

Table 2, EPAF achieves all the issued security properties and is more practical and extendable than their schemes.

6 Performance Analysis

6.1 Authentication Overhead

Communication overhead of one message consists of attached certificate and signature. For PTVC, request and reply message are 87 bytes and 91 bytes (1 timestamp for request and 2 for réply, proof of reputation is not included), shown in Table 3. In EPAF it includes MAC, pseudo identity and a timestamp. It is evident that EPAF significantly decreases communication overhead by 45.98%–75.53% compared with other schemes.

Table 3. Communication overhead for one message

Schemes	BP	GSIS	VAST	PTVC	EPAF
Request overhead (byte)	105	192	145	87	47
Reply overhead (byte)	–	–	–	91	47

In Table 4 and Fig. 5, it illustrates that EPAF is the second most efficient for request and the most efficient for reply. EPAF significantly reduces request signing cost by near 2000 times compared with other schemes, reply signing by 1800 times compared with PTVC.

Table 4. Message signing cost

Schemes	BP	GSIS	VAST	PTVC	EPAF
Request overhead(s)	T_{mul}	$3T_{par} + T_h$	$T_{mul} + T_{mac}$	$T_h + T_{EXP}$*	$7T_h + T_{mac}$
Reply overhead(s)	–	–	–	$3T_{mul} + 3T_{mod} + 3T_h$	$2T_h + T_{mac}$

*Note: T_{EXP} represents uncertain time cost for exponent computation.

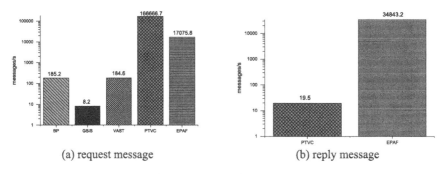

(a) request message   (b) reply message

Fig. 5. Message signing speed

Message verification includes CRL checking, certificate verification and signature verification for BP, GSIS, VAST and PTVC. BP, VAST and PTVC perform CRL checking through string comparison, computation cost is able to be ignored. In GSIS, each CRL item needs two paring operations, which makes total cost $2NcrlT_{par}$. In PTVC, both request and reply message verification need one T_{par}. In comparison, EPAF only needs light MAC and hash operations to accomplish verification and achieves an efficient verification speed as shown in Fig. 6 (Table 5).

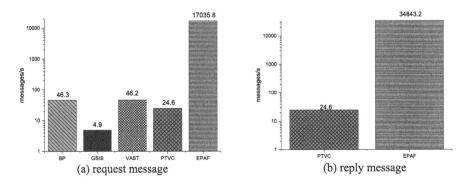

Fig. 6. Message verification speed

Table 5. Message verification cost

Schemes	BP	GSIS	VAST	VAST*	EPAF
CRL checking	0	$2N_{crl}T_{par}$	0	0	–
Certificate verification	$2T_{mul}$	0	$2T^*_{mul}$	0	–
Request signature verification	$2T_{mul}$	$5T_{par} + T_h$	$2T^*_{mul} + 2T_{mac}$	$T_{par} + 2T_h$	$T_h + T_{mac}$
Reply signature verification	–	–	–	$T_{par} + 2T_h$	$2T_h + T_{mac}$
Total	$4T_{mul}$	$2N_{crl}T_{par} + 5T_{par} + T_h$	$4T^*_{mul} + 2T_{mac}$	$2T_{par} + 4T_h$	$3T_h + 2T_{mac}$

*Note: In VAST, certificate and digital signature verification is only performed when non-repudiation is necessary. In this paper, we focus on VAST needing non-repudiation because of service concern.

6.2   Simulations

In this subsection, we use Opportunistic Networking Environment (ONE [13]) to run simulations. We import a part from real map (northeast corner of area surrounded by the No. 2nd Ring Road of Beijing). Parameters are in Table 6.

In simulation, EPAF and PTVC both need request and reply messages and the metrics for each type are the average message delay, average message loss ratio and

Table 6. Simulation configuration

Parameter	Values
Communication range	4000 m
Simulation time	100 s
Channel bandwidth	6 Mbps
Wait time	0–5 s
Buffer size	1M bytes
Broadcast interval	0.3 s
Speed	[20 km/h, 100 km/h] ± 10 km/h

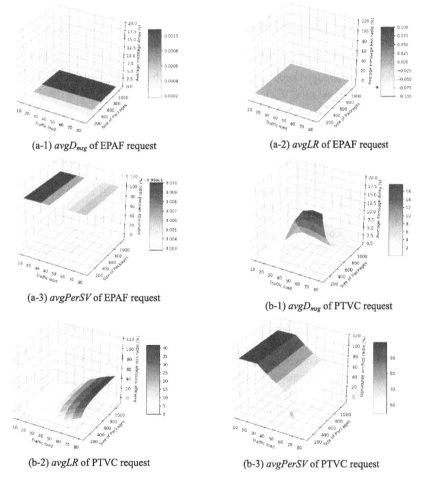

(a-1) $avgD_{msg}$ of EPAF request   (a-2) $avgLR$ of EPAF request

(a-3) $avgPerSV$ of EPAF request

(b-1) $avgD_{msg}$ of PTVC request

(b-2) $avgLR$ of PTVC request   (b-3) $avgPerSV$ of PTVC request

Fig. 7. Traffic load and message size's impact on performance

percentage of signature verified, which are represented as *avgDmsg*, *avgLR* and *avg-PerSV* and stated as same as in our previous work [14].

In Fig. 7 we compare the performance of EPAF with PTVC under different traffic load (vehicles in communication range) and message sizes. Because reply performance is nearly the same as request in both PTVC and EPAF, only figures for request performance are listed.

EPAF achieves low and stable $avgD_{msg}$ below 0.002 s for both request and reply message as shown in Fig. 7(a-1). However, PTVC's $avgD_{msg}$ increases dramatically along with traffic load increasing shown in (b-1). When size of packages increases, PTVC's $avgD_{msg}$ decreases because vehicles' buffer space is filled rapidly, older messages are dropped and are not count. The trend in (b-2) is able to prove it.

Figure 7(a-2) shows, as traffic load growing larger and messages growing bigger, *avgLR* of EPAF is stable at nearly 0%, even with traffic load 80 and size of packages 1000 bytes. For PTVC, with traffic load above 40, *avgLR* increases dramatically as shown in (b-2). Apparently, EPAF achieves good performance in high traffic load and large package size.

Comparisons for *avgPerSV* are shown in (a-3) and (b-3). *avgPerSV* for both EPAF request and reply messages keeps near 100% at all configuration. For PTVC, *avgPerSV* decreases as traffic load growing larger. It is lower than 60% when traffic load is above 80. This is unacceptable in real use.

It is evident that EPAF is DoS resilient and significantly increases availability of PPA, which turns out to have potential extendibility to support various VANET services.

7 Conclusion

In this paper, we proposed an efficient pseudonymous-based inter-vehicle authentication framework for various VANET services. Security analysis based on ProVerif proves that EPAF achieves all designing security features, including 3 level privacy, strong privacy preserving, mutual authentication and other security features. Performance evaluation shows that EPAF has advantage in communication, message signing/verification speed and achieves a significant increase of nearly 370–3500 times in computation compared with safety schemes. This makes EPAF DoS resilient in complex scenarios.

To the best of our knowledge, EPAF is the first PPA framework which achieves both necessary security features and DoS resilience for various VANET services. It would work as a design reference in more vehicular services like navigation, data fusion and unmanned driving, and be implemented using other cryptographic methods. Proposing a unified privacy preserving authentication framework for various services is a new topic. We will focus on the common security problems in different scenarios and make the EPAF framework to a more adaptable version, while maintaining the applicable efficiency.

References

1. Su, Z., Hui, Y., Yang, Q.: The next generation vehicular networks: a content-centric framework. IEEE Wirel. Commun. **24**(1), 60–66 (2007)
2. Harding, J., Powell, G., Yoon, R., Fikentscher, J., Doyle, C., Sade, D., Lukuc, M., Simons, J., Wang, J.: Vehicle-to-vehicle communications: readiness of V2V technology for application. NHTSA, Washington, DC, Technical report, DOT-HS-812-014 (2014)
3. Chim, T.W., Yiu, S.M., Hui, L.C., Li, V.O.: VSPN: VANET-based secure and privacy-preserving navigation. IEEE Trans. Comput. **63**(2), 510–512 (2014)
4. Wang, M., Liu, D., Zhu, L., Xu, Y., Wang, F.: LESPP: lightweight and efficient strong privacy preserving authentication scheme for secure VANET communication. Computing **98**, 1–24 (2014)
5. Raya, M., Hubaux, J.-P.: Securing vehicular Ad hoc networks. J. Comput. Secur. **15**(1), 39–68 (2007)
6. Huang, C., Lu, R., Zhu, H., Hu, H., Lin, X.: PTVC: achieving privacy-preserving trust-based verifiable vehicular cloud computing. In: 2016 IEEE Global Communications Conference (GLOBECOM), Washington, DC, pp. 1–6 (2016)
7. Lu, R., Lin, X., Zhu, H., Ho, P.-H., Shen, X.: ECPP: efficient conditional privacy preservation protocol for secure vehicular communications. In: Proceedings of the INFOCOM 2008, pp. 1903–1911 (2008)
8. Lin, X., Sun, X., Ho, P.-H., Shen, X.: GSIS: a secure and privacy-preserving protocol for vehicular communications. IEEE Trans. Veh. Technol. **56**(6), 3442–3456 (2007)
9. Zhang, L., Wu, Q., Solanas, A., Josep, D.-F.: A scalable robust authentication protocol for secure vehicular communications. IEEE Trans. Veh. Technol. **59**(4), 1606–1617 (2010)
10. Studer, A., Bai, F., Bellur, B., Perrig, A.: Flexible, extensible, and efficient VANET authentication. J. Commun. Netw. **11**, 589–598 (2009)
11. Bellare, M., Canetti, R., Krawczyk, H.: Message authentication using hash functions: the HMAC construction. RSA Laboratories' CryptoBytes **2**(1), 12–15 (1996)
12. Scott, M.: Efficient Implementation of Cryptographic Pairings. http://www.pairing-conference.org/2007/invited/Scott slide.pdf
13. Keränen, A., Ott, J., Kärkkäinen, T.: The ONE simulator for DTN protocol evaluation. In: Proceedings of the 2nd International Conference on Simulation Tools and Techniques (2009)
14. Wang, F., Xu, Y., Zhang, H., Zhang, Y., Zhu, L.: 2FLIP: a two-factor lightweight privacy-preserving authentication scheme for VANET. IEEE Trans. Veh. Technol. **65**(2), 896–911 (2016)
15. Horng, S.J., Tzeng, S.F., Li, T., Wang, X., Huang, P.H., Khan, M.K.: Enhancing security and privacy for identity-based batch verification scheme in VANET. IEEE Trans. Veh. Technol. **66**(4), 3235–3248 (2017)
16. Canetti, R., Herzog, J.: Universally composable symbolic analysis of mutual authentication and key-exchange protocols. In: Halevi, S., Rabin, T. (eds.) TCC 2006. LNCS, vol. 3876, pp. 380–403. Springer, Heidelberg (2006). https://doi.org/10.1007/11681878_20
17. Zhang, Z., Zhu, L., Liao, L., Wang, M.: Computationally sound symbolic security reduction analysis of the group key exchange protocols using bilinear pairings. Inf. Sci. **276**(20), 93–112 (2012)
18. Du, X., Chen, H.H.: Security in wireless sensor networks. IEEE Wirel. Commun. Mag. **15**(4), 60–66 (2008)

19. Du, X., Guizani, M., Xiao, Y., Chen, H.H.: Secure and efficient time synchronization in heterogeneous sensor networks. IEEE Trans. Vehi. Technol. **57**(4), 2387–2394 (2008)
20. Du, X., Xiao, Y., Guizani, M., Chen, H.H.: An effective key management scheme for heterogeneous sensor networks. Ad Hoc Netw. **5**(1), 24–34 (2007)
21. Xiao, Y., Rayi, V., Sun, B., Du, X., Hu, F., Galloway, M.: A survey of key management schemes in wireless sensor networks. J. Comput. Commun. **30**(11–12), 2314–2341 (2007)

CHAR-HMM: An Improved Continuous Human Activity Recognition Algorithm Based on Hidden Markov Model

Chuangui Yang, Zhu Wang, Botao Wang[(⊠)], Shizhuo Deng,
Guangxin Liu, Yuru Kang, and Huichao Men

Northeastern University, Shenyang, China
chuanguiy@163.com, wangbotao@cse.neu.edu.cn

Abstract. With the rapid development of wearable sensor technology, Human Activity Recognition (HAR) based on sensor data has attracted more and more attentions. The Hidden Markov Model (HMM) with perfect performance in speech recognition has a good effect on HAR. However, almost all these techniques train multiple Hidden Markov Models for different classes of activity. For a given activity sequence with multiple activities, the activity corresponding to the HMM with the maximum generating probability is selected as the recognition result, which is not suitable for continuous HAR with multiple activities. For this problem, we propose an improved Hidden Markov activity recognition algorithm where discriminative model and generative model are utilized. The discriminative model SVM is used to produce the observation sequence of HMM, and the generative model HMM is used to generate the final result. Compared with the traditional Hidden Markov HAR model, our proposal has good performance in terms of precision, recall and F1 score.

Keywords: Human Activity Recognition · Hidden Markov Model
Support Vector Machine · Cyber-Physical system · Accelerometer signal

1 Introduction

1.1 A Subsection Sample

With the rapid development of microprocessors and integrated circuits, large amount of sensors and mobile electronic devices have been developed with more powerful computation capability and smaller size. The applications based on sensors and mobile devices play a significant role in daily life, such as smart home, activity monitoring, elderly care and game interaction, etc. The Human Activity Recognition (HAR) based on wearable sensors has become more and more popular for small size, convenient wearing and privacy protection different from other types of data acquisition devices [1–6].

In the field of HAR based on wearable sensors, various machine learning algorithms are utilized to classify different activities. There, Support Vector Machine [7] (SVM), Artificial neural networks [8] or Template matching [9] is used as discriminative model, and Hidden Markov Model (HMM) is used as generative model. Considering the

© Springer Nature Singapore Pte Ltd. 2018
L. Zhu and S. Zhong (Eds.): MSN 2017, CCIS 747, pp. 271–282, 2018.
https://doi.org/10.1007/978-981-10-8890-2_19

outstanding performance of HMM in the field of speech recognition, more and more techniques apply HMM to HAR and have achieved an efficient effect.

However, the existing studies still have limitations for Continuous Human Activity Recognition (CHAR) in which the activities to be recognized are continuously performed in a chronological order and the objective is a continuous sequence. For one hand, the Potential temporal relationship between activities was disregarded. For another hand, most activity recognition algorithms train one model for each activity with assumption that the activity type of the inputted sequence is same. They evaluate the same data sequence with all models, then choose the activity with largest probability as result which is not suitable for the sequence with multiple activities. The computation cost of above algorithms is proportional to the number of activities to be recognized.

In real life, the data sequence to be recognized consists of continuous sub-sequences from sensors, which may contain more than one kind of activity. For example, the sequence of data may contain three activities (walk, fall and lie). There, the fall activity which has a short duration may be dominated (neglected) by other activities which have longer durations. In this case, the existing HMM-based solutions cannot provide users with high-quality services. For this problem, we propose an improved algorithm based on HMM for continuous human activity recognition (CHAR-HMM) where both discriminative model and generative model are utilized. The main contributions of this paper are as follows:

- We propose a model which combines discriminative model (SVM) with generative model (HMM) where only one model is used for continuous human activity recognition.
- We evaluate CHAR-HMM, and the results show that our proposal performs better in precision, recall and F1 compared to the traditional HMM-based solution.

The rest of this paper is organized as follows. Section 2 gives a brief description the research and application of HMM in HAR. Section 3 defines problems and CHAR-HMM proposed in this paper. Section 4 describes the data set and evaluation results. Finally, we conclude the paper in Sect. 5.

2 Related Work

The algorithms used for human activity recognition are mainly divided into two categories: discriminative model and generative model. The algorithms based on discriminative models include Decision Tree [15], Support Vector Machine [16] and so on. Generative models include Gaussian Mixture Model (GMM) [17], Hidden Markov Model (HMM) [18] and so on. As a result of the success of hidden Markov models in the field of speech recognition, more and more researchers utilize this model in HAR.

Piyathilaka et al. applied GMM-HMM to model each activity for the skeleton information in the image sequence of Kinect [10]. Claudia Nickel et al. applied HMM to solve the problem that the boundary of two adjacent windows is not clear [11]. They collected walking data from 48 subjects where one model is trained for one subject and another model is trained for the other 47 subjects. Cheng et al. used three algorithms based on SVM, HMM and NN to recognize five kinds of daily activities [12]. Nickel et al. studied the effect of different combinations of features, sequence lengths and sizes of training data, and compared the performance of SVM and HMM [13]. Wang et al. used GMM and HMM model to recognize six daily routine activities based on wrist acceleration sensor data [14].

For all the works above, the HMM model is built for each activity to be recognized. Then, it calculates the probability of each activity model and chooses the activity with the largest probability as the recognition result. So the different activities in given data sequence would be regarded as same activity potentially, which will lead to incomplete result.

Different from the works above, our proposal builds only one model for multiple activities.

3   HMM-Based Activity Recognition Algorithm

3.1   Hidden Markov Model

A Hidden Markov Model (HMM) is determined by initial probability distribution, transition probabilities and emission probability distribution. It is defined as follows.

The set of states is denoted by Q : $Q = \{q_1, q_2, \ldots, q_N\}$, and the set of observations is denoted by V : $V = \{v_1, v_2, \ldots, v_M\}$, where N is the number of states and M is the number of observations.

The state sequence is denoted by I : $I = \{i_1, i_2, \ldots, i_T\}$, and the observation sequence will be denoted as O : $O = \{o_1, o_2, \ldots, o_T\}$, where T is the length of I.

Transition probability matrix is

$$A = [a_{ij}]_{N \times N},$$

where $a_{ij} = P(i_{t+1} = q_j \mid i_t = q_i)$ is the probability of state q_i at time t transferring to state q_j at time $t + 1$.

The emission probability matrix will be denoted by B:

$$B = [b_j(k)]_{N \times M},$$

where $b_j(k) = P(o_t = v_k \mid i_t = q_j)$ is the probability of the emission of the v_k when state is q_j at time t.

π is the initial state probability vector: $\pi = (\pi_1, \pi_2, \ldots, \pi_N)$, where $\pi(i) = P(i_1 = q_i)$.

The Hidden Markov Model is determined by initial probability vector π, transition probability matrix A and emission probability matrix B. π and A determine the state sequence, and B determines the observation sequence. Therefore we can denote a Hidden Markov Model as a triplet $\lambda = (A, B, \pi)$, where A, B and π are three elements of the Hidden Markov Model.

3.2   Problem Description

We define the HMM-based continuous human activity recognition problem as follows.

The set of activities to be recognized is defined as $A = (a_1, a_2, \ldots, a_N)$, where N is the number of activity categories. For each item in the activity set, its corresponding training data set is $T_1, T_2, \ldots, T_N$. Given a new observation $O(o_1, o_2, \ldots, o_T)$, where T is the length of the observation sequence, and its actual corresponding sequence of the target is $A = (SA_1, SA_2, \ldots, SA_M)$, where M is the actual number of activity categories in the sequence. $SA_1, SA_2, \ldots, SA_M \in A$, and $SA_1, SA_2, \ldots, SA_M$ are different from each other. The goal is to train a Hidden Markov Model by training data and use it to recognize the observation sequence to obtain the correct recognition results $(SA_1, SA_2, \ldots, SA_M)$.

The existing HMM-based activity recognition algorithms (Sect. 2) use training data sets $T_1, T_2, \ldots, T_N$ to build N models $\{HMM_1, HMM_2, \ldots, HMM_N\}$, and use Baum-Welch algorithm [18] to calculate model parameters. The forward algorithm [18] is used to calculate the probabilities of observed sequences using the corresponding model HMM_i, the result is computed by:

$$A = (SA_i) = \arg\max\{P(O|HMM_i)\} \tag{1}$$

If the observed sequence contains more than one type of activity ($M > 1$) the above procedure can only recognize the sequence as only one activity and will result in an incomplete recognition result.

3.3   CHAR-HMM: Improved HMM-Based Human Activity Recognition Algorithm

For the above problem, this paper proposes an improved HMM-based continuous human activity recognition algorithm CHAR-HMM. Different from the existing HMM-based solutions, our proposal builds only one model for multiple activities. So Baum-Welch algorithm cannot be used to determine the model parameters. The main problem is how to determine the initial probability, transition probability matrix and emission probability matrix. In the follows, we introduce a method to get model parameters and the CHAR-HMM in Subsect. 3.3.

Model Parameters. The steps for parameter setting of CHAR-HMM are as follows.

Initial State Probability. According to the definition of initial state probability of Hidden Markov Model in Sect. 3.1, π_i represents the probability of being in state q_i at time $t = 1$. All activity sequence data are divided into data segments with equal size as the input. The first activity in each data segment corresponds the state while $t = 1$. All activities to be recognized have the same probability at the first state of each data segment, so the initial probability is

$$\pi_i = P(i_i = q_i) = 1/N, i = 1, 2, \ldots, N \tag{2}$$

Where N is the number of activity categories. In the following example (Table 1), $\pi_i = 1/5, i = 1, 2, \ldots, 5$.

Transition Matrix. For easy understanding, we use numbers 1 to 5 as the labels of the corresponding activities. As shown in Table 1.

Table 1. Mapping table of activity and label

Activity	Sit	Sit-down	Stand	Stand-up	Walk
Label	1	2	3	4	5

Considering the constraint among 5 activities, the algorithm in this paper uses a self-defined state transition matrix. For example, we set the probability of the transition from activity *Sit-down* to *Walk* to be 0 because *Stand-up* must happen between them. The details of state transition matrix are shown in Table 2, where a_{ij} denotes the transition probability from state i to state j.

Table 2. The transition probability matrix

	1	2	3	4	5
1	0.5	0	0	0.5	0
2	0.4	0.5	0	0.1	0
3	0	0.3	0.4	0	0.3
4	0	0	0.3	0.4	0.3
5	0	0.1	0.4	0	0.5

Emission Probability Matrix. When SVM is used for multi-classification, it is hard to categorize all kinds of activities completely based on the division of feature space, so the soft-interval SVM classifier [16] is proposed. Inspired by this process, our proposal uses SVM to determine the observation set and its division while using HMM. Due to the huge computation amount of SVM on high-dimensional data, we use Linear Discriminant Analysis (LDA) to reduce the data dimension and to accelerate the training process of SVM [19]. Compared with other dimension reduction techniques like Principal Component Analysis (PCA), LDA can increase the class internal and make the data easier to classify. But it is not necessary in the following observed probability calculation procedure.

$U = \{u_1, u_2, \ldots, u_N\}$ denotes both the states set and the observation set, where N is the number of states. The reason is that the number of subspaces obtained by trained SVM for the whole feature space is equal to the number of different labels in training data. Each activity in activity recognition corresponds to a state u_i in Hidden Markov Model, and the training data set for each activity is denoted by $T_1, T_2, \ldots, T_N$. The prediction of SVM for each training data also corresponds to one state in the observation set. R_j represents the result set of the *j-th* activity predicted by SVM, and $NOA_k(R_j)$ represents the number of activity k in R_j.

Computation of the emission probability matrix by SVM mainly consists of the following three steps:

(a) Train SVM on all of the training data set $T_1, T_2, \ldots, T_N$.
(b) For T_j of each activity, SVM trained by step (a) is used to predict and get the result set R_j.
(c) Calculate the emission probability matrix by the following formula:

$$b_j(k) = \frac{NOA_k(R_j)}{NOA_j(T_j)} \tag{3}$$

Laplace smoothing is used on observation probability matrix. There may exist some zeros in emission probability matrix because the training data cannot fully cover the feature space, so we use Laplace smoothing to deal with it. The additive factor in this experiment is 5. Based on the above steps, the triples of Hidden Markov Model can be determined.

The Improved HMM-Based Activity Recognition Algorithm. The procedure of the algorithm is shown in Fig. 1. The left part is the training process of the model, and the right part is the recognition process on the observation data sequence. To be more clear, we also describe this procedure with pseudo code in Program CHAR_HMM.

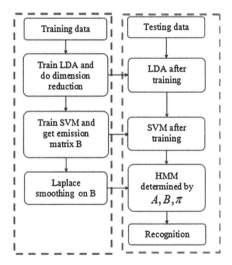

Fig. 1. Procedure of the improved HMM-based algorithm

- Training process

(a) In line 2 of pseudo code list, train LDA with the training data and then use the trained LDA for dimension reduction on training data.
(b) In lines 3–10, train SVM with the data set obtained by step (a), then use the trained SVM to predict on the same data set. The emission probability matrix B is calculated by formula (3).
(c) Set the initial probability by formula (2) and then set the transition probability matrix. Use Laplace smoothing to get the final emission probability matrix in step (b).

The pseudo code of procedure of the improved HMM-based algorithm is shown as following:

```
program CHAR_HMM(Raw, O)
1   // training process
2   P = lda.fit_transform(Raw.data, Raw.target)
3   svm.fit(P.data, P.target)
4   for j = 1 to N:   // for N kinds of activities
5       T = P[P.target == j]
6       Q = svm.predict(T.data)
7       NOATj = T.length   // number of activity j in T
8       for k = 1 to N:   // for N kinds of states
9           NOARk = (Q == k).sum()   // number of  activity
j in R
10          B[j, k] = (NOARk + 1) // (NOATj + N)
11 hmm = HMM(A, B, pi)
12 // recognition process
13 P = lda.transform(O.data)
14 Q = svm.predict(P.data)
15 A = hmm.predict(Q)
```

Through the three steps above, the Hidden Markov Model can be determined.

- Recognition process

(a) Line 13 shows that for a given observation data sequence $O = (o_1, o_2, \ldots, o_r)$, use the trained LDA in training process for dimension reduction, and get result $P = (p_1, p_2, \ldots, p_r)$.
(b) Line 14 shows that use the trained SVM to predict P and get the result $Q = (q_1, q_2, \ldots, q_r)$.
(c) Line 15 shows that predict Q by the trained HMM and Viterbi algorithm. The final result is $A = (SA_1, SA_2, \ldots, SA_M)$.

4   Experimental Evaluation

CHAR-HMM is evaluated on a Dell Inspiron N5110 laptop. The operation system is Ubuntu 14.04 LTS, CPU is Intel(R) Core(TM) i3-2310M@2.10 GHz, Memory is 8 GB DDR RAM. Scikit-learn is used and the programming language is Python.

4.1   Data Set

The evaluation data is from W.Ugulino[1] team with four wearable tri-axial accelerometers. These accelerometers are placed on right arm, left thigh, right ankle and waist. The sampling frequency was 8 Hz.

The subjects consisted of four healthy volunteers, two men and two women. The details are shown in Table 3. Although there are only four people, the subjects' attributes are well established: different genders (men and women), different ages (young, middle-aged and old). Moreover, the distribution of height and weight are also reasonable.

Table 3. Information table of subjects

Subject	Gender	Age	Height	Weight	Sample size
Debora	Female	46	1.62 m	67 kg	51577
Katia	Female	28	1.58 m	53 kg	49797
Wallace	Male	31	1.71 m	83 kg	51098
Jose	Male	75	1.67 m	67 kg	13161

The types of activity include *sit, sit down, stand, stand up and walk*. In the evaluation, each subject wearing sensor performs five kinds of activities. Each activity lasts for 2 h, and each accelerometer measures the acceleration of three directions of *(X, Y, Z)*. The dimension of feature vector is 12 as there are 4 accelerometers.

To prove the effectiveness of the algorithm comparing with [12], the number of data sets in our evaluation is set to the same with that in [12]. The subject (Wallace in this paper) had 1,000 samples selected for each activity, and 5000 samples in total are used for training and testing.

4.2   Evaluation Result

We calculate the confusion matrix, precision, recall and F1 score of the two algorithms using 5 fold cross-validation. The confusion matrices are shown in Tables 4 and 5 where the row represents the actual label and the column represents the result of prediction. The precision, recall and F1 score are shown in Figs. 2, 3 and 4.

Here we extract samples from the test data to simulate the real scenario *stand-> sit down -> sit -> stand up -> walk*. The result is shown in Table 4.

---

[1] https://archive.ics.uci.edu/ml/datasets/Wearable+Computing%3A+Classification+of+Body+Postures +and+Movements+(PUC-Rio).

Table 4. Confusion matrix of HMM

	1	2	3	4	5
1	969	0	0	29	2
2	0	969	3	21	7
3	0	54	936	10	0
4	0	110	0	866	24
5	0	1	0	1	993

Table 5. Confusion matrix of improved HMM

	1	2	3	4	5
1	1000	0	0	0	0
2	0	980	1	11	8
3	0	36	955	1	8
4	0	99	1	885	15
5	0	2	34	7	957

4.3   Results Analysis

As shown in Figs. 2, 3 and 4, the performance of CHAR-HMM is better than that of the existing solution [12].

In Fig. 2, the precision of improved algorithm is higher than the that of [12] except activity stand. Figure 3 shows that the recall of CHAR-HMM is higher except activity walk. F1-value of CHAR-HMM is higher on three kinds of activity in Fig. 4.

For a given data segment which contains more than one kind of activity, the performance of CHAR-HMM is obviously better. As is shown in Table 6, the sub-sequence marked in bold lasts a very short time while activity transition. For example, the transition action sit-up is very short while transmitting from stand to sit. Obviously, the CHAR-HMM can recognize it exactly while the existing solution.

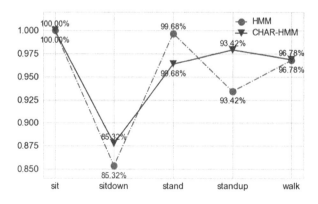

Fig. 2. Precision

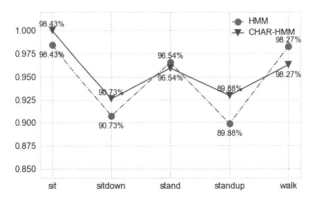

Fig. 3. Recall

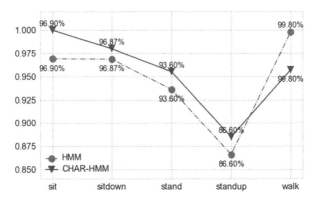

Fig. 4. F1-score

Table 6. Comparison of recognition results between HMM and CHAR-HMM

Actual activity sequence	3->3->3->3->3->3->3->3->3->**3->2->1**->1->1->1->1->1-> 1->1->1->1->**1->4->5**->5->5->5->5->5->5->5->5->5
Recognition results of HMM	3->3->3->3->3->3->3->3->3->**4->4->4**->1->1->1->1->1-> 1->1->1->1->**5->5->5**->5->5->5->5->5->5->5->5->5
Recognition results of CHAR-HMM	3->3->3->3->3->3->3->3->3->**3->2->1**->1->1->1->1->1-> 1->1->1->1->**1->4->5**->5->5->5->5->5->5->5->5->5

5   Conclusion and Future Work

For the problem that the existing HMM-based HAR solutions cannot recognize the multiple activities in the continuous observed sequence effectively, this paper proposes an improved HMM-based algorithm CHAR-HMM considering the constraints among different activities. With a self-defined transition probability matrix, we use SVM to determine the emission probability matrix. Compared with traditional HMM where different HMM models are trained for different activities, our propose CHAR-HMM uses only one HMM for all activities. CHAR-HMM performs better in precision, recall and F1 score while the various activities contained in a given data sequence can be recognized correctly.

In the future, firstly we would like to improve our algorithm to recognize more complicated continuous activities with larger dataset. Secondly we would like to improve the performance of HMM in the case that the quality of the emission matrix produced by SVM is low.

Acknowledgment. The corresponding author Botao Wang is supported by the NSFC (Grant No. 61173030).

References

1. Khan, A.M., Lee, Y.K., Lee, S.Y., et al.: A triaxial accelerometer-based physical-activity recognition via augmented-signal features and a hierarchical recognizer. IEEE Trans. Inf. Technol. Biomed. **14**(5), 1166–1172 (2010)
2. Alaqtash, M., Yu, H., Brower, R., et al.: Application of wearable sensors for human gait analysis using fuzzy computational algorithm. Eng. Appl. Artif. Intell. **24**(6), 1018–1025 (2011)
3. Cheung, V.H., Gray, L., Karunanithi, M.: Review of accelerometry for determining daily activity among elderly patients. Arch. Phys. Med. Rehabil. **92**(6), 998–1014 (2011)
4. Joshua, L., Varghese, K.: Accelerometer-based activity recognition in construction. J. Comput. Civil Eng. **25**(5), 370–379 (2010)
5. Lee, M.W., Khan, A.M., Kim, T.S.: A single tri-axial accelerometer-based real-time personal life log system capable of human activity recognition and exercise information generation. Pers. Ubiquit. Comput. **15**(8), 887–898 (2011)
6. Peng, J.X., Ferguson, S., Rafferty, K., et al.: An efficient feature selection method for mobile devices with application to activity recognition. Neurocomputing **74**(17), 3543–3552 (2011)
7. Beily, M.D.E., Badjowawo, M.D., Bekak, D.O., et al.: A sensor based on recognition activities using smartphone. In: 2016 International Seminar on Intelligent Technology and Its Applications (ISITIA), pp. 393–398. IEEE (2016)
8. Kurban, O.C., Yildirim, T.: Neural network based daily activity recognition without feature extraction. In: 2014 22nd Signal Processing and Communications Applications Conference (SIU), pp. 567–570. IEEE (2014)
9. Margarito, J., Helaoui, R., Bianchi, A.M., et al.: User-independent recognition of sports activities from a single wrist-worn accelerometer: a template-matching-based approach. IEEE Trans. Biomed. Eng. **63**(4), 788–796 (2016)

10. Piyathilaka, L., Kodagoda, S.: Gaussian mixture based HMM for human daily activity recognition using 3D skeleton features. In: 2013 8th IEEE Conference on Industrial Electronics and Applications (ICIEA), pp. 567–572. IEEE (2013)
11. Nickel, C., Busch, C., Rangarajan, S., et al.: Using hidden markov models for accelerometer-based biometric gait recognition. In: 2011 IEEE 7th International Colloquium on Signal Processing and its Applications (CSPA), pp. 58–63. IEEE (2011)
12. Cheng, L., Guan, Y., Zhu, K., et al.: Recognition of human activities using machine learning methods with wearable sensors. In: 2017 IEEE 7th Annual Computing and Communication Workshop and Conference (CCWC), pp. 1–7 (2017)
13. Nickel, C., Brandt, H., Busch, C.: Benchmarking the performance of SVMs and HMMs for accelerometer-based biometric gait recognition. In: 2011 IEEE International Symposium on Signal Processing and Information Technology (ISSPIT), pp. 281–286. IEEE (2011)
14. Wang, J., Chen, R., Sun, X., et al.: Generative models for automatic recognition of human daily activities from a single triaxial accelerometer. In: The 2012 International Joint Conference on Neural Networks (IJCNN), pp. 1–6. IEEE (2012)
15. Quinlan, J.R.: Induction of decision trees. Mach. Learn. **1**(1), 81–106 (1986)
16. Cortes, C., Vapnik, V.: Support-Vector Networks. Kluwer Academic Publishers, Boston (1995)
17. Stauffer, C., Grimson, W.E.L.: Adaptive background mixture models for real-time tracking. In: IEEE Computer Society Conference on Computer Vision and Pattern Recognition, vol. 2, p. 252. IEEE Xplore (1999)
18. Rabiner, L.R., Juang, B.H.: An introduction to hidden Markov models. IEEE ASSP Mag. **3**(1), 4–16 (1986)
19. Fisher, R.A.: The use of multiple measurements in taxonomic problems. Ann. Eugen. **7**(2), 179–188 (1936)

A Prediction Method Based on Complex Event Processing for Cyber Physical System

Shaofeng Geng[1,2], Xiaoxi Guo[1(✉)], Jia Zhang[1], Yongheng Wang[2], Renfa Li[2], and Binghua Song[2]

[1] Jimei University, Xiamen 361021, China
gxxamy@163.com
[2] Hunan University, Changsha 410082, China

Abstract. For flow prediction in intelligent traffic system, one certain model cannot get excellent performance under different environments. Predicting models should also be updated according to data stream. In order to resolve these problems, a prediction method based on complex event processing was proposed. With fuzzy ontology to model historical event context and context clustering to partition events, this method could learn Bayesian network models according to different data during complex event processing. Appropriate Bayesian network model or combination of Bayesian network models could be provided by this method for real-time prediction and analysis of current context of events. The experimental result shows that this method can process events stream of Cyber Physical System (CPS) effectively and has favorable prediction performance.

Keywords: Cyber Physical System · Big data · Complex event processing
Bayesian network

1 Introduction

In recent years, how to effectively process a large amount of data in real-time is the main problem for CPS applications. Complex Events Processing (CEP) [1, 3] is an important technique in real-time processing of big data streams. Based on some models, CEP can interpret and combine these huge numbers of simple primitive events in real-time to obtain valuable high-level complex events.

Predictive Analytics (PA) based on complex event data can build the predict model according to the observed complex event. This model can predict certain properties of the observed system based on the historical event data which has great significance to CPS application. In recent years, Bayesian Network (BN) [8–10] and Neural networks (especially deep neural networks) are major approaches for prediction modeling. Among them, BN and its variants can integrate domain knowledge and data, and support incomplete data processing and causal analysis.

At present, there are some challenges in integration of complex event processing and predictive analysis. First of all, the system can only process data of one time fragment and cannot control the time order of samples' arrival in CEP. Secondly, a certain model cannot have favorable predictive performance in different environments [4]. In addition,

© Springer Nature Singapore Pte Ltd. 2018
L. Zhu and S. Zhong (Eds.): MSN 2017, CCIS 747, pp. 283–292, 2018.
https://doi.org/10.1007/978-981-10-8890-2_20

with the development of CPS and mobile computing technologies, the information of multiple environments context can be obtained in real-time. However, the existing prediction methods can only perform based on limited information, and do not take various real-time context into consideration comprehensively.

In order to solve the above problems, this paper presents a Context-aware Prediction Method (CPM) based on complex event processing technology for indeterminate event flows in CPS [13]. This method could learn corresponding BN models according to different data during complex event processing. Appropriate BN model or combination of BN models could be adopted by this method for real-time prediction and analysis of current context of events.

2   Architecture of Prediction System

The architecture of prediction system is shown in Fig. 1. The raw data stream is processed by a probabilistic complex event processing engine to obtain meaningful high-level complex events [13]. Probabilistic Event Processing Agent (PEPA) [2] is responsible for processing the raw data stream generated by the underlying device, then generating probabilistic events and saving them in the historical database. The historical data is divided into time slices, and then clustered according to the event context. The corresponding BN structure and parameters are learned for each cluster. And the BN model or model combination is selected according to the current context adaptability for real-time prediction.

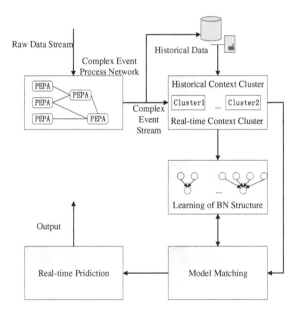

Fig. 1. System architecture

3   Event Context Clustering

For event processing, the context can be defined as some special conditions. Based on these conditions, the event instance is divided and associated for further processing. The representation of context in the real world is often fuzzy. For example, "a blue car with fast driving speed", in which "fast speed", "blue" and "car" are all fuzzy concepts. Therefore, this paper uses fuzzy ontology method to model the context [5]. For the same type of event data, it is highly possible that different models should be applied under the circumstance of different context. The traditional FCM algorithm requires the number of clusters to be determined in advance. However, in some application environments such as road traffic monitoring system, it is unpractical to pre-determine the number of types of context clusters. If the number of clusters is not accurate, the algorithm would be wrongly conducted. In this paper, an improved FCM algorithm was proposed. First, the cluster centers are determined by fast search and find of density peaks [6], and then the FCM is used to cluster the historical data.

For any data points xi in the context data set $S = \{x_1, x_2, \ldots x_n\}$ to be clustered, two parameters can be defined as: the local density ρ_i and the distance δ_i.

3.1   Local Density ρi: Including the Cut-off Kernel and the Gaussian Kernel

- Cut-off kernel:

$$\rho_i = \sum_{j \in I_S\{I\}} x(d_{ij} - d_c) \tag{1}$$

$x(x)$ can be defined as:

$$x(x) = \begin{cases} 1, & x < 0; \\ 0, & x \geq 0, \end{cases} \tag{2}$$

Where d_{ij} represents the distance between data points x_i and x_j, and d_c is the cutoff distance which needs to be specified in advance. The context represented in fuzzy ontology has a hierarchical structure and the distance between data points is defined based on their distance in the structure:

$$D(C_i, C_j) = \frac{\alpha_i \alpha_j}{O_{ij}} \tag{3}$$

Where α_i and α_j are the weights of two contexts C_i and C_j, and O_{ij} is the distance of C_i and C_j in ontology structure. An event can correspond to multiple contexts. In order to compare the distance between event context sets, let the context of event x be $C_x = (c_{x1}, \ldots, c_{xm})$ and the context of event y is $C_y = (c_{y1}, \ldots, c_{ym})$. For each $c_{xi} \in C_x$, a c_{yj} is found to satisfy $\min_{C_{yi}} (D(C_{xi}, C_{yj}))$. Then the distance from C_x to C_y can be defined as:

$$Q(C_x, C_y) = \sum_{i=1}^{m} r(C_{xi}) D(C_{xi}, C_{yj}) \tag{4}$$

Where function r is the weight of the distance, and the distance of C_y to C_x is:

$$Q(C_y, C_x) = \sum_{j=1}^{m} r(C_{yj}) D(C_{yj}, C_{xi}) \tag{5}$$

Finally, the distance from C_x to C_y is:

$$D(C_x, C_y) = \frac{Q(C_x, C_y) + Q(C_y, C_x)}{2} \tag{6}$$

- Gaussian kernels:

$$\rho_i = \sum_j e^{-(d_{ij}/d_c)^2} \tag{7}$$

Gaussian kernels are similar to Gaussian kernel functions in spectral clustering. Gaussian kernel functions are commonly used to calculate the similarity between two points in spectral clustering. Relative to the cut-off kernel, the Gaussian kernel generates a smaller probability of collision, thus improving the robustness of the entire cluster.

3.2 Minimum Distance δ_i

Let $\{q_1, q_2, \ldots, q_n\}$ denote a descending order of $\{\rho_1, \rho_2, \ldots, \rho_n\}$, δ_i can be defined as:

$$\delta_i = \begin{cases} \min_{j:q_j > q_i}(d_{ij}) & i \text{ is the point without largest density} \\ \max_j(d_{ij}) & i \text{ is the point with largest density} \end{cases} \tag{8}$$

(ρ_i, δ_i) is calculated for each data point in S, and then all the data points are identified in a two-dimensional decision graph with ρ as the horizontal axis and δ as the vertical axis. The data point with a larger density and distance is found to be the initial cluster center of S.

The initial cluster center determined by qualitative analysis is influenced by subjective factors. Therefore, it may not be the optimal result. Based on the initial cluster centers and historical data, the clustering centers are corrected through an iterative process to achieve the result that minimizes the following objective function:

$$J_m(U, V_1, \ldots, V_c) = \sum_{i=1}^{c} \sum_{j=1}^{n} u_{ij}^m d_{ij}^2 \tag{9}$$

Where $V = [V_1, \ldots, V_c]$ is the cluster center, u_{ij} represents the membership degree of the j-th data to the i-th class, and m is a fuzzy weighted index with the range of $[1, +\infty)$ which controls the fuzzy degree of membership matrix $U = [\mu_{ij}]_{c \times n}$. $d_{ij} = \|V_i - x_j\|$ denotes the distance between the i-th cluster center and the j-th data point. Using Lagrange multiplication to solve (9), the objective function is constructed as:

$$\overline{J_m}(U, V_1, \ldots, V_c, \lambda_1, \ldots, \lambda_n) = \sum_{i=1}^{c} \sum_{j=1}^{n} u_{ij}^m d_{ij}^2 + \sum_{j=1}^{n} \lambda_j \left(\sum_{i=1}^{c} u_{ij} - 1 \right) \qquad (10)$$

$\lambda_j (j = 1, 2, \ldots, n)$ is a constrained Lagrange multiplier, which is used to differentiate the input parameters. The necessary condition to minimize (9) is:

$$V_i = \frac{\sum_{j=1}^{n} u_{ij}^m x_j}{\sum_{j=1}^{n} u_{ij}^m} \qquad (11)$$

$$u_{ij} = \frac{1}{\sum_{k=1}^{c} \left(\dfrac{d_{ij}}{d_{kj}} \right)^{2/(m-1)}} \qquad (12)$$

According to (11) and (12), the cluster center and membership matrix are adjusted appropriately after each iteration. When the change between two adjacent cluster centers is smaller than the preset threshold ε, the best cluster center and membership matrix are obtained.

4   Principles of Prediction Method

Structure Varying Dynamic Bayesian Network is represented as <G(t), Θ(t), C(t), F>, where G(t) and Θ(t) denote a directed acyclic graph representing the BN structure and parameters (mainly a conditional probability table) of the BN at time t respectively. C(t) ∈ C is the context category at time t, C is the set of context categories and F is the mapping of G(t) and Θ(t) to C(t).

Applied in the field of traffic flow prediction, BN structure is shown in Fig. 2. This figure has two dimensions: position and time. Assuming that the vehicle travels at N intersections, s(i, t) is the congestion state of a node (i, t) in the graph depending on its parent nodes, denoted as pa(i, t). The nodes with directed edge connected to node (i, t) are its parent nodes. The state of pa(i, t) can be expressed as Spa(i, t) = {sj, s | (j, s) ∈ pa(i, t)}.

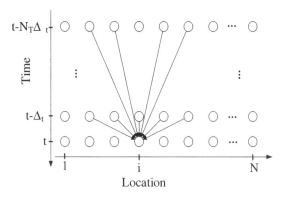

Fig. 2. The BN structure

According to Bayesian theory, the joint distribution of node states in this BN can be expressed as:

$$p(S) = \prod_{i,t} p(s_{i,t} | S_{pa(i,t)}) \tag{13}$$

The conditional probability p(si, t | Spa(i, t)) can be calculates as:

$$p(f_{i,t} | S_{pa(i,t)}) = p(s_{i,t} | S_{pn(i,t)}) / p(S_{pa(i,t)}) \tag{14}$$

The joint distribution p(si, t, Spa(i, t)) is modeled with Gaussian Mixture Model [12]:

$$p(s_{i,t}, S_{pa(i,t)}) = \sum_{m=1}^{M} \alpha_m g_m(s_{i,t}, S_{pa(i,t)} | \mu_m, C_m) \tag{15}$$

Where M is the number of nodes, gm($\cdot$|μm, Cm) is the m-th Gaussian distribution model, μm is the mean vector, Σm is the covariance matrix, and αm is the coefficient of the m-th Gaussian model. Using the EM algorithm [7], the parameters $\{\alpha_m, \mu_m, C_m\}$ can be learned from the sample data. p(si, t(Spa)) is calculated from the obtained parameters and then the distribution p(si, t, Spa(i, t)) can be determined.

Search-and-score algorithm [12] is used to learn the structure of BN. The main idea of this algorithm is to maximize the score function in order to achieve the best fitting BN structure for sample data.

Since the current state of the node in BN is related to the historical state over a period of time, the event flow is firstly divided based on a time-span parameter δ, and each segment is called a slice. The data of slice is clustered according to the event context. And for each clustering result, the structure and parameters of corresponding BN are studied.

Due to the complexity of the event context, it is possible that sample points are divided into multiple clusters. In order to make the distribution of samples among the clusters more reasonable for BN learning, the partitioning adjustment for those samples classed into multiple clusters is based on the following library guidelines.

Librarian criterion 1. Compactness: Copies of the same book might be placed in different shelves. However, to reduce cost, the book placing method should be designed to minimize the need for multiple copies.

Librarian criterion 2. Even dimensionality: Books should be more or less evenly distributed in various shelves.

For compactness criterion, the probability of the event context ci to the clustered Vc is calculated based on Eq. (16):

$$\hat{p}(V_c | c_i) = 1/D(c_i, V_c) \sum_j 1/D(c_i, V_j) \tag{16}$$

Assuming that ci has been classed into k clusters initially, the normalized entropy is calculated as follows:

$$H_{norm}(c_i) = -\sum_{h-1}^{k} \hat{p}(V_c | c_i) log_2 \hat{p}(V_c | c_i) / log_2 k \tag{17}$$

According to the principle of compactness, the normalized entropy Hnorm(ci) should be as close to 0 as possible. Adding the Hnorm(ci) value for all ci, the best partition is achieved when Hnorm(ci) reach the minimum value.

For even dimensionality criterion, p(ci|Vc) can be calculated by Bayesian theory:

$$p(c_i|V_c) = p(V_c|c_i)p(c_i)/p(V_c) \tag{18}$$

This conditional probability satisfies $\sum_{i=1}^{N} p(c_i|V_c) = 1$. Assume p(ci) = 1/N, then:

$$\sum_{i=1}^{N} p(c_i|V_c) = \sum_{i=1}^{N} p(c_i|V_c)p(c_i)/p(V_c) \tag{19}$$

$p(V_c)$ can be calculated by:

$$p(V_c) = \sum_{i=1}^{N} p(V_c|c_i)/n \tag{20}$$

Finally the normalized entropy can be defined as:

$$H_{norm}(V_c) = - \sum_c p(V_c)log_2 p(V_c)/log_2 k \tag{21}$$

The average of all Hnorm(Vc) is calculated for each partition. The larger the average value is, the more reasonable it is.

For real-time updating the BN structure, the strategy is described as follows: first of all, for the new sample D in clusters, the node set V and edge set E that would be influenced by D need to be determined. And then, for each node in V, the edges with all parent nodes should be included into E if the new edge maximize the BIC score or be removed from E if the edge does not reduce the BIC score.

In real-time prediction, if the current context is similar to multiple clusters (the difference is less than a certain threshold δ), all the available clusters should be selected. The corresponding models are predicted by Bayesian Combination Method (BCM) [4].

When using the EM algorithm to study the parameters of a Gaussian mixture model, the final values of the parameters and the intermediate results would be retained in memory. In order to update the parameters of the Gaussian mixture model, the current parameters of αm, μm, Σm are used to calculate the distribution of the hidden variables for the changed samples. Then the new parameters of αm, μm, Σm are calculated according to the method of maximum likelihood based on the distribution of the hidden variables. There is no need to update the online parameters if there is no significant change in the parameters or log-likelihood convergence. Otherwise, repeat the above steps until convergence and update the online model parameters.

5   Experimental Evaluations

In this paper, two kinds of event sources are chosen: real data and traffic simulation system. The real data comes from the PeMS Traffic Surveillance Network, which collects real-time traffic flow data of Los Angeles 101 Highway at various time intervals.

The context of traffic networks and events in real data is relatively simple, so the open source traffic simulation system SUMO is used as event source [11]. 15 × 15 junctions and 80,000 cars are set in the simulation map. In order to be more like the real situation, a set of rules is defined: Each car has a home location and an office location. The probability that vehicle Vi runs between home and office is pi. These vehicles have certain probability to go to other locations. The experiment used three Xeon processors and 16 GB of memory as servers for data processing.

The parameter m of FCM is 2, the threshold ε is 0.001, and the model number M of GMM is 25–30 in the experiment. The traffic flow data from an observatory on I-405 road in PeMS from March 7, 2016 to March 13, 2016 was selected as a model training sample. The experiment selected the traffic condition as the events context. Flow rate, speed and occupation [15] are the input variables for traffic status evaluation. For SUMO simulation data, various types of context were firstly obtained by running the system multiple times, and then the historical data was saved and the model was trained offline.

After getting the context of real and simulated data events, this paper compares CPM with the Adaptive Bayesian Network (ABN) [9] adopted by Pascal et al. and the deep belief network (DBN) [14] used by Huang et al. The real data is predicted at 30-min intervals and the results are shown in Fig. 3. It can be seen from the results that CPM has better accuracy than most other methods for most of the time, but without much difference. The reason is that the traffic flow was relatively stable after 6.5 h, and the context of the event had not changed much, hence the advantages of CPM was not fully presented. The simulation data was predicted at intervals of 1 min, and the result is shown in Fig. 4. Compared with the real data, the traffic of simulated data is larger and the change is more dramatic. The most important context here is the change of road states between smoothness and congestion. The accuracy of these three methods has declined. However, the CPM approach gives better results than BN and DBN because CPM uses a combination of multiple BN models for different event contexts.

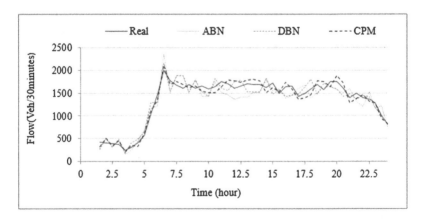

Fig. 3. Prediction result of PEMS data

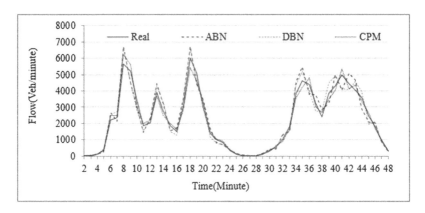

Fig. 4. Prediction result of SUMO data

6   Discussions and Conclusion

This paper presents a prediction method based on complex event processing techniques. This method uses fuzzy ontology to model the context of historical events and then divides the data by context clustering. According to the different BN model of data learning, the predicting system can select the appropriate model or combination of models for predictive analysis according to the context of current events. Experimental evaluation shows that this method can effectively handle event data flow and has good predictive performance. There are some shortcomings in this paper. First, the choice of context clustering centers uses qualitative analysis, which lacks of an effective automatic learning method. Second, parallel and distributed predictive processing are not considered. How to solve the above problems is our major work in the future.

Acknowledgment. The work of this paper is sponsored by the National Natural Science Foundation of China (Grant No. 61371116) and Natural Science Foundation of Fujian Province (Grant No. 2015J01264).

References

1. Luckham, D.C.: The Power of Events: An Introduction to Complex Event Processing in Distributed Enterprise Systems. Addison Wesley, Boston (2002)
2. Wang, Y.H., Cao, K., Zhang, X.M.: Complex event processing over distributed probabilistic event streams. In: Proceedings of the International Conference on Fuzzy Systems and Knowledge Discovery, China, pp. 1808–1821. IEEE (2012)
3. Etzion, O., Niblett, P.: Event Processing in Action. Manning Publications, Greenwich (2010)
4. Wang, J., Deng, W., Guo, Y.: New Bayesian combination method for short-term traffic flow forecasting. Transp. Res. Part C Emerg. Technol. **43**, 79–94 (2014)
5. Cao, K., Wang, Y., Li, R., et al.: A distributed context-aware complex event processing method for Internet of Things. J. Comput. Res. Develop. **50**(6), 1163–1176 (2013)

6. Rodriguez, A., Alessandro, L.: Clustering by fast search and find of density peaks. Science **344**(6191), 1492–1496 (2014)
7. Verbeek, J., Vlassis, N., Kröse, B.: Efficient greedy learning of Gaussian mixtures. Neural Comput. **15**(2), 469–485 (2003)
8. Castillo, E., Menéndez, J.M., Sánchez-Cambronero, S.: Predicting traffic flow using Bayesian networks. Transp. Res. Part B Methodological **42**(5), 482–509 (2008)
9. Pascale, A., Nicoli, M.: Adaptive Bayesian network for traffic flow prediction. In: Proceedings of the Statistical Signal Processing Workshop, France, pp. 177–180. IEEE (2011)
10. Sun, S., Zhang, C., Yu, G.A.: Bayesian network approach to traffic flow forecasting. IEEE Trans. Intell. Transp. Syst. **7**(1), 124–132 (2006)
11. Behrisch, M., Bieker, L., Erdmann, J., et al.: Sumo - simulation of urban mobility: an overview. In: Proceedings of the Third International Conference on Advances in System Simulation, SIMUL, Spain, pp. 63–68 (2011)
12. Samaranayake, S., Blandin, S., Bayen, A.: Learning the dependency structure of highway networks for traffic forecast. Mol. Pharmacol. **62**(1), 5983–5988 (2011)
13. Geng, S., Wang, Y., Li, R.: The research of a proactive complex events processing method. J. Commun. **37**(9), 111–120 (2016)
14. Huang, W., Song, G., Hong, H., et al.: Deep architecture for traffic flow prediction: deep belief networks with multitask learning. IEEE Trans. Intell. Transp. Syst. **15**(5), 2191–2201 (2014)
15. Kerner, B.S.: Three-phase traffic theory and highway capacity. Phys. A **333**(1), 379–440 (2004)

A Fast Handover Scheme for SDN Based Vehicular Network

Xing Yin[1,2] and Liangmin Wang[2(✉)]

[1] School of Electrical and Information Engineering, Jiangsu University, Zhenjiang, China
staryin@126.com
[2] School of Computer Science and Communication Engineering,
Jiangsu University, Zhenjiang, China
Wanglm@ujs.edu.cn

Abstract. Vehicular network can provide Internet connectivity for mobile vehicle by handover mechanism. However, existing handover schemes still face poor handover performance when they are applied in vehicular network. Software Defined Network (SDN) is a new architecture which can be used to optimize vehicular network by making network devices to be programmable. In this paper, we propose a new fast handover scheme for SDN based vehicular network to improve handover performance. SDN controllers of our scheme predict movement of vehicles by detecting port status of SDN switches, and then they start to perform the proactive handover procedure based on prediction results. Evaluation results show that the handover delay and packet loss of our scheme are lower than the contrast schemes. Simulation results prove that our handover scheme is more fit for delay sensitive vehicular network.

Keywords: Vehicular network · Software Defined Network (SDN) · Handover
Predict · Delay

1 Introduction

As an important application area of Internet of Things and mobile Internet technologies, vehicular network is becoming increasingly attractive to researchers in academia and industry during these years. One of the main aims of vehicular network is to allow any vehicle access to the Internet whenever it is traveling on a road, that is, to provide Vehicle-to-Infrastructure (V2I) connectivity [1, 2].

Although Mobile IPv6 (MIPv6) [3] and its derivatives [4] can realize V2I connection, these protocols still have some shortcomings such as high handover delay and packet loss rate [5]. Handover performance is critical to vehicular network since there are many delay sensitive applications which are running on vehicles. Fast mobile IPv6 (FMIPv6) [6] protocol and some extended schemes [7–10] were proposed by using proactive handover mechanism to optimize handover performance of vehicular network to some extend. However, handover delay of these schemes are still high for vehicular communications. Furthermore, the control function and data forwarding are tightly coupled in

© Springer Nature Singapore Pte Ltd. 2018
L. Zhu and S. Zhong (Eds.): MSN 2017, CCIS 747, pp. 293–302, 2018.
https://doi.org/10.1007/978-981-10-8890-2_21

network devices in traditional vehicular network [11], which makes it difficult for these devices to be programmable to improve handover performance.

Software Defined Network (SDN) is a promising network paradigm which can overcome the inflexibility of traditional network by separating the control plane from the data plane [12]. All network devices in data plane are regarded as SDN switches and they are only responsible for data forwarding according to their flow tables. All control functions of these devices are abstracted to a logically centralized SDN controller, which has a global view of the whole network and manages SDN switches by downloading flow entries to their flow tables through the famous south bound interface protocol, i.e. OpenFlow [13]. These characteristics of SDN can make network devices to be more programmable and controllable.

Due to the significant improvements in programmability and flexibility provided by SDN, many researchers try to propose handover schemes based on SDN network to optimize handover performance [14]. Wang et al. [15] proposed a mobility scheme, which we name as SDMA, to provide basic handover function for a mobile nodes in SDN based network. Since SDMA dose not provide a handover optimize method, its handover performance is still not be improved. Yang et al. [16] proposed a handover scheme to provide seamless handover in SDN based satellite network. Their scheme has improved the handover performance for satellite network, but it was not fit for vehicular network.

From the above analysis, we can conclude that existing handover schemes have the following drawbacks:

- Some of them do not make full use of the specially features of vehicular network, such as predictable movement of vehicles, to optimize handover procedure.
- Some of them are based on traditional network, which leads to the inflexibility of their scheme. This drawback will hinder further improvement of handover performance.
- Some of them have complex handover procedures, which leads to high handover delay.

To overcome the above shortcomings of the existing related works, this paper presents a novel fast handover scheme to improve the handover performance of SDN based vehicular network. The main contributions of our proposal is listed as follows:

1. By taking advantage of the predictable characteristic of vehicular network, we propose a proactive handover procedure to optimize handover performance. SDN controllers in our scheme can predict movement direction of vehicles and then perform some handover steps beforehand.
2. By simplifying the handover procedure of our scheme, the handover performance is further improved.

The rest of this paper is organized as follows. In Sect. 2, we give a typical SDN based vehicular network topology. Then we design a new handover procedure based on this topology. In Sect. 3, handover performance such as handover delay and packet loss of our scheme are evaluated and compared with some typical comparatives. In Sect. 4, we conclude our work.

2   Proposed Scheme

In this section, we construct a SDN based vehicular network topology. Then based on the topology, we propose a handover procedure by using prediction mechanism to optimize the handover performance.

2.1   Network Topology

A typical SDN based network topology for V2I communication in vehicular network is shown in Fig. 1. We assume that access points (AP) are distributed evenly along one side of the road. Wireless signal of these APs can cover the entire road to ensure that every vehicle can connect to one or more APs. Each AP can connect to the Internet through SDN switches. These network devices and their controller compose a district, which we call it as a domain. Figure 1 shows that AP11, AP12, AP13 and S11, S12 of SDN switches, are all controlled by SDN controller C1. The left domain consists of these devices. The right domain consists of AP21, AP22, AP23, and S11, S12 of SDN switches, which are all controlled by C2.

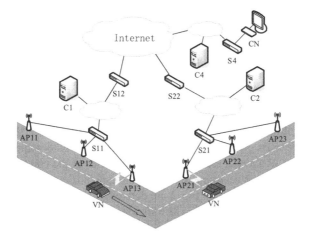

Fig. 1. Typical topology of SDN based vehicular network

In Fig. 1, each vehicle is defined as a vehicular node (VN). Just like a mobile node defined in MIPv6, VN can change its point of attachment to different access points through wireless link when it drives along a road. VN can keep its session with a correspondent node (CN) by applying some mobility management protocols (e.g. MIPv6). However, VN in vehicular network has some special mobility characteristics which are different from that of mobile nodes in broadly defined mobile network. This is because the trajectory of VN is always along a certain road and the direction of movement can be predicted in most cases.

In order for the controllers to have the functionality of predicting the handover of VN, each SDN controller maintains a port status table which is shown as Table 1. This table lists the information of the ports of switches directly connected to access points. Every SDN switch is responsible for reporting the attachment and detachment events to their controller to update the port status table.

Table 1. Port status table

Port ID	Switch	AP ID	Location	List of VN
1001	S11	AP11	Edge	-
1002	S11	AP12	Intermediate	-
1003	S11	AP13	Edge	PIP
2001	S21	AP21	Edge	-
2002	S21	AP22	Intermediate	-
2003	S21	AP23	Edge	-

Items of Table 1 are explained as follows:

- Port ID: Identification number of different port of each SDN switch. Port ID is allocated by the controller of current domain, and the value is unduplicated.
- Switch: The identification of the SDN switch, which the current port belongs to.
- AP ID: The identification of the access point which is connecting to the current port.
- Location: The location of the AP current port connecting to. This attribute has two types of values. The value Edge indicates that the AP is located in the end of current domain (i.e. current road) and the value Intermediate indicates that the AP is not at the two end sides of the current road.
- List of VN: List of up-to-data IP addresses of VNs which are currently connect to this port.

In order to facilitate our analysis, we use the original IP address IP_VN, which is obtained when VN starts up in its home network, as its identity identifier. Furthermore, we use the routable IP address assigned by the controller of the current domain as the location identifier of VN. We assume that the location identifiers of VN when it is in the left domain and the right domain in Fig. 1 are defined as PIP and NIP respectively. The IP address of CN is defined as CN_IP. The following designation and analysis are based on the network topology illustrated in Fig. 1.

2.2   Handover Procedure

Based on the above network topology, we design a handover procedure when a vehicle travels along a road. Since AP11, AP12 and AP13 are connected to the same SDN switch, i.e. S11, the handover procedure that VN moves from AP12 to AP13 is easy to be handled by controller C1. In this situation, C1 makes routing decision according to the status report message from AP13 and then downloads a flow entry to S11 to redirect data flow from one port to another. As for the handover when VN moves from AP13 to AP21, this procedure is a cross domain movement and it is much more complex than the former handover.

In our proposal, we use a predict mechanism to design and optimize handover procedure for vehicular network. The handover procedure of our scheme, which is shown in Fig. 2, is depicted as follows.

1. When VN moves along the road and it will move from the left domain to the right one, VN will detach from AP13 and attach to AP21. S11 detects the change of wireless signal strength. Then S11 sends an extended Port Status (Ext-PS) message containing PIP and the port ID to its controller C1 to report this movement event.

2. After receiving the Ext-PS message, C1 looks up its port status table with the port ID and PIP to predict where VN will move to and which kind of handover will take place. For example, the look up result shows that the previous and the current access point of VN are AP12 and AP 13 respectively and AP13 is an Edge access point of the current road. Therefore, C1 can predict that VN will move from AP13 to AP 21 in the left domain and perform a handover. Then C1 sends a Notify message including IP_VN to C2 to notify the incoming of VN proactively.

3. When receiving the Notify message, C2 generates a new routable IP address (i.e. NIP) for VN as its new location identifier in advance. C2 creates a binding which contains IP_VN and NIP, and then stores this binding in its binding cache. After that, C2 sends binding update (BU) messages to C1 and C4 at the same time. If VN has a home network, C2 also sends a BU message to the controller of VN's home network. Furthermore, C2 sends a Flow-Mod message to S22 to inform it to cache all data packets which take NIP as the destination address.

4. After receiving the BU message form C2, C1 downloads flow entry to S12. After that, S12 will cache all the packets which destination address is PIP and rewrite the destination address to NIP, and then redirects these packets to S22.

5. C4 updates its binding cache (BC) and sends a Flow-Mod message to S4 to add a flow entry about VN in the flow table of S4 when C4 receives the BU message from C2. After that, S4 rewrites the destination address of data packets which send from CN to VN. These packets are routed to the new IP address of VN.

6. Owing to the transparent character of our handover scheme, VN can perform link layer (i.e. Layer 2, L2) handover at any time when it detects the signal of AP21. Note that the step 3, 4, 5, or even 6 can be performed at the same time.

7. After L2 handover is finished and VN attaches to AP21, VN sends a route solicitation (RS) message to S21 to notify the attachment event.

8. When detecting the attachment of VN, S22 sends a Ext-PS message to it controller C2 to report VN's attachment.

9. C2 updates its port status table and send a Flow-Mode message to S21 and S22 respectively for updating their flow tables.

10. When S22 receiving the Flow-Mode message, it updates its flow table and forwards all the packets which destined to NIP to S12. At the same time, S12 updates it flow table according to the Flow-Mod message it has received. Finally, S21 rewrites the destination IP address of these packets to IP_VN and then delivers them to VN.

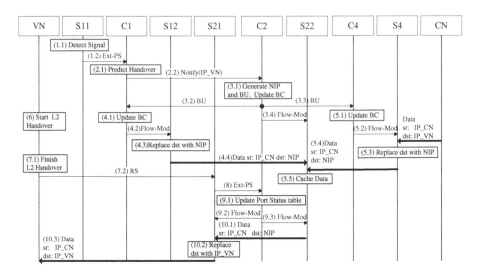

Fig. 2. Handover procedure of our scheme

After the above handover procedure is completed, the communications between CN and VN can be recovered. It should be explained that the above procedures are based on the assumption that CN is stationary. If CN is a mobile node, it can be treated as VN too, and the handover procedure of a mobile CN is the same to that of VN mentioned above.

3   Performance Evaluation

In this section, we evaluated and compared the performance of our proposed scheme, SDMA and FLBH. SDMA is a typical mobility management scheme based on SDN architecture, and FLBH is a representative of handover schemes based on traditional vehicular network.

Handover delay and packet loss number are important metrics to measure the performance of a handover scheme. Handover delay can directly reflect the length of communication interruption during handover procedure. This metric is critical factor for delay sensitive applications. Packet loss is critical for important data transmission. We analyze these two metrics of different handover schemes through the following simulation.

We carry out our simulation based on the famous SDN simulator, i.e. Mininet 2.2.1 [17]. We use Virtual Box, Pox and Open vSwitch (OvS) as virtual machine, SDN controller and virtual SDN switch respectively in our experiment. We have implemented handover procedures of our scheme and the above two schemes in controllers.

For convenient of experiment, we assume that CN sends data packets to VN contin-uously during the whole simulation time, and all packets will not be lost in wired and wireless links. Length of data packet is 56 bytes and packet sending rate is 100 packets per second. We ignore the processing delay of data and signaling message in our experiment. Parameters required for simulation are listed in Table 2. The values of these parameters are referred to literature [18, 19].

Table 2. Simulation parameters

Perimeter	Value
Average delay of one hop wire link (ms)	2
Average delay of one hop wireless link (ms)	10
Average delay of Layer 2 handover (ms)	50
Average bandwidth of wire link (Mbps)	100
Average bandwidth of wireless link (Mbps)	10

The changes of packet sequence numbers with the simulation time are shown in Fig. 3. The abscissa represents the simulation time T, and the ordinate represents the sequence number N. Each point in Fig. 3 represents the sequence number of the data packet received by the VN at time T. The length of the abscissa section corresponding to the blank area in Fig. 3 indicates the handover delay of once handover from AP13 to AP21, and the length of the corresponding ordinate section indicates the total number of packets which have lost during the handover.

As we can see in Fig. 3(a), the handover delay of SDMA is largest, and all the data packets transmitted during the handover time are lost. This is because SDMA does not provide any proactive handover mechanism to optimize handover performance, even if SDMA can support a simple handover function in SDN based network. Figure 3(b) shows that the handover delay of FLBH is lower than SDMA, this is because FLBH proposes a fast location-based handover to drop the handover delay. However, data loss still takes place in FLBH, which is owing to the luck of data caching and forwarding mechanism. Figure 3(c) indicates that our scheme has the lowest handover delay, and data loss problem does not appear in our simulation. This is because we utilize the prediction method to design a optimized handover procedure based on SDN architecture.

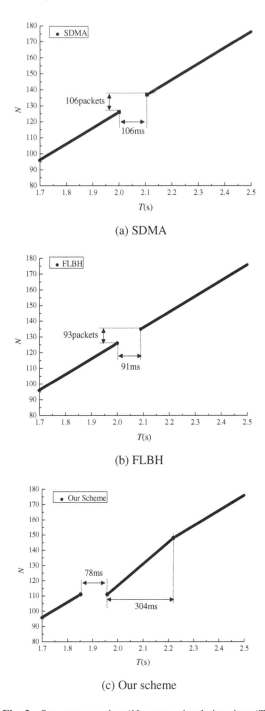

(a) SDMA

(b) FLBH

(c) Our scheme

Fig. 3. Sequence number (N) versus simulation time (T)

4 Conclusion

In this paper, we proposed a new fast handover scheme based on SDN paradigm by using the characteristic of predictable movement in vehicular network. Simulation result demonstrates that our proposed handover scheme has lower handover delay than the contrastive schemes. Besides, packet loss problem does not occurred in our simulation also. The experiment illustrates that our handover scheme is more suitable for vehicular network environment.

Acknowledgements. This research is supported by the National Natural Science Foundation of China Grants (61472001, 61272074, U1736216, U1405255) and the Key research and development plan project of Jiangsu Province (BE2015136).

References

1. Jarupan, B., Ekici, E.: Prompt: a cross-layer position-based communication protocol for delay-aware vehicular access networks. Ad Hoc Netw. **8**, 489–505 (2010). https://doi.org/10.1016/j.adhoc.2009.12.006
2. Ma, S., Jiang, H., Han, M., Chen, L.: Survey of information security research for vehicle electronic control system in vehicle internet environment. Jiangsu Daxue Xuebao **35**, 635–643 (2014). https://doi.org/10.3969/j.issn.1671-7775.2014.06.003
3. Perkins, C., Johnson, D., Arkko, J.: Mobility Support in IPv6. RFC 6275, IETF (2011)
4. Bernardos, C.J.: Proxy Mobile IPv6 Extensions to Support Flow Mobility. RFC 7864, IETF (2016)
5. Gladisch, A., Daher, R., Tavangarian, D.: Survey on mobility and multihoming in future internet. Wirel. Pers. Commun. **74**, 45–81 (2014). https://doi.org/10.1007/s11277-012-0898-6
6. Koodli, R.: Mobile IPv6 fast handovers. RFC 5568, IETF (2009)
7. Schmidt, T., Waehlisch, M., Koodli, R., Fairhurst, G., Liu, D.: Multicast Listener Extensions for Mobile IPv6 (MIPv6) and Proxy Mobile IPv6 (PMIPv6) Fast Handovers. RFC 7411, IETF (2014)
8. Kim, M.S., Lee, S.K., Golmie, N.: Enhanced fast handover for proxy mobile IPv6 in vehicular networks. Wirel. Netw. **18**, 401–411 (2012). https://doi.org/10.1007/s11276-011-0407-y
9. Almulla, M., Wang, Y., Boukerche, A., Zhang, Z.: Design of a fast location-based handoff scheme for IEEE 802.11 vehicular networks. IEEE Trans. Veh. Technol. **63**, 3853–3866 (2014). https://doi.org/10.1109/TVT.2014.2309677
10. Yin, X., Wu, G., Dong, Y.: A proactive handover scheme for high-speed network mobility. J. Southeast Univ. (Nat. Sci. Ed.) **45**, 1038–1045 (2015). https://doi.org/10.3969/j.issn.1001-0505.2015.06.003
11. Xia, W., Wen, Y., Foh, C.H., Niyato, D.: A survey on software-defined networking. IEEE Commun. Surv. Tutorials **17**, 27–51 (2015). https://doi.org/10.1109/COMST.2014.2330903
12. Open Networking Fundation: Software-Defined Networking: The New Norm for Networks (2012). http://www.opennetworking.org/component/content/article/46-sdn-resources/sdn-library/whitepapers/816-software-defined-networking-the-new-norm-for-networks
13. Mckeown, N., Anderson, T., Balakrishnan, H., Parulkar, G., Peterson, L., Rexford, J.: OpenFlow: enabling innovation in campus networks. ACM Sigcomm Comput. Commun. Rev. **38**, 69–74 (2008). https://doi.org/10.1145/1355734.1355746

14. Liyanage, M., Gurtov, A., Ylianttila, M.: Software Defined Mobile Networks - SDMN: Beyond LTE Network Architecture, pp. 9–10. Wiley Publishing (2015)

15. Wang, Y., Bi, J., Zhang, K.: Design and implementation of a software-defined mobility architecture for IP networks. Mob. Netw. Appl. **20**, 40–52 (2015). https://doi.org/10.1007/s11036-015-0579-2

16. Yang, B., Wu, Y., Chu, X., Song, G.: Seamless handover in software-defined satellite networking. IEEE Commun. Lett. **20**, 1768–1771 (2016). https://doi.org/10.1109/LCOMM.2016.2585482

17. Mininet: An Instant Virtual Network on your Laptop (or other PC). http://mininet.org

18. Makaya, C., Pierre, S.: An analytical framework for performance evaluation of IPv6-based mobility management protocols. IEEE Trans. Wirel. Commun. **7**, 972–983 (2008). https://doi.org/10.1109/TWC.2008.060725

19. Lee, C.W., Chuang, M.C., Chen, M.C., Sun, Y.S.: Seamless handover for high-speed trains using femtocell-based multiple egress network interfaces. IEEE Trans. Wirel. Commun. **13**, 6619–6628 (2014). https://doi.org/10.1109/TWC.2014.2364179

Secret-Sharing Approach for Detecting Compromised Mobile Sink in Unattended Wireless Sensor Networks

Xiangyi Chen$^{(\boxtimes)}$ and Liangmin Wang

School of Computer Science and Telecommunication Engineering,
Jiangsu University, Zhenjiang, China
{chenxyzj,wanglm}@ujs.edu.cn

Abstract. In unattended wireless sensor networks (UWSNs), static sensor nodes monitor environment, store sensing data in memory temporally. Mobile sink patrols and collects the sensors' data itinerantly. Mobile sink is granted with more permissions than static sensor nodes, rendering it more attractive to the adversary. By compromising the mobile sinks, the adversary can not only seek the sensing data, but it also can steel all kinds of keys and access permissions, which may be abused to undermine other benign sensor nodes, even worse to upset the whole network. Currently, many related works focus on key management, permission management to restrict the compromised mobile sink or authentication to guarantee data reliability. However, the issue of compromised mobile sinks attracts little attention, and gradually become one obstacle to the application of UWSNs.

In this paper, we proposed a secret-sharing method for detecting compromised mobile sink in UWSNs. Before the sensing data are collected by the mobile sink, every sensor node splits the digest of its data into shares by using a polynomial secret sharing algorithm, and dispatches these secret shares to randomly chosen neighbor nodes, which thereafter send to the base-station through different routes. After enough shares are gathered, the base-station recovers the original data digest, which will be used to validate the sensing data submitted by the mobile sink. If the validation fails, it reveals a compromised mobile sink. Theoretical analysis and evaluation indicate the effectiveness and efficiency of our method. Also, we proposed two types of attacking model of the mobile adversary, and obtained the respective detection probability.

Keywords: Detecting · Compromised mobile sink · Secret sharing
Unattended wireless sensor networks

1 Introduction

Unattended wireless sensor networks [1–3] are deployed in monitoring environment or inaccessible enemy areas, such as volcanoes, battlefield, national borders and other places, for disaster monitoring, military espionage and tracking, intrusion early warning, etc. In an UWSN, static nodes accomplish tasks like sensing the environment and storing the monitoring data, the mobile sink (MS) periodically visits and gathers data from static

© Springer Nature Singapore Pte Ltd. 2018
L. Zhu and S. Zhong (Eds.): MSN 2017, CCIS 747, pp. 303–317, 2018.
https://doi.org/10.1007/978-981-10-8890-2_22

nodes. And finally the mobile sink reports these data to the base-station (BS). Accordingly, the mobile sink can also help the base-station carry out other important tasks, such as time synchronization, session key update, network maintenance, etc.

The unattended nature makes UWSNs vulnerable to various kinds of attacks. Especially, the mobile sink is authorized to gather data, update session key, and other critical missions, therefore is the focus of attackers. With the compromised mobile sink, the adversary can grab, expurgates, falsifies, and even forge all the monitoring data, further can launch other more threatening attacks, such as, revoking the benign sensor nodes, desynchronizing network time, forging network routes and causing network topology division, etc. Besides, the adversary can also launch other insider attacks, for example eavesdropping, denial-of-sleep attack [4], sybil attack [5], sinkhole attack [6], replication attack [7–12], etc.

Although a few studies [13, 14] proposed some strategies to curtail the power of mobile sink in UWSN. Once the mobile sink was found compromised, the base-station limits or revokes the authorized permissions, preventing its subsequent destruction. However, there is little research on the detection of mobile sink. At present, current UWSN research mainly focus on the defense of compromised mobile sink and detection of compromised static nodes, leaving the detection of compromised mobile sink an open problem.

Focusing on the detection of the mobile sink in UWSN, this article proposed a method for detecting the compromised mobile sink based on secret sharing. As shown in Fig. 1, during every data collecting round of the mobile sink, every static node calculates the digest of its sensing data, splits the digest into multiple shares by using a polynomial secret-sharing algorithm. Then, these secret shares are sent to some randomly selected neighbor nodes, which will thereafter forward these secret shares to the central base-station. The base-station can recover the original data digest using the secret-sharing algorithm after receiving enough shares. At the end of the data aggregation round when the mobile sink submits the aggregated data to the base-station, the aggregated data and the data digest can be used to validate whether the mobile sink has ever tampered the sensors' data. If the validation fails, then the compromised mobile sink is detected.

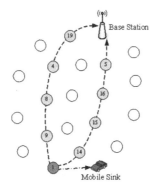

Fig. 1. Compromised mobile sink detection by using secret sharing

The rest of this article is organized as follows: Sect. 2 overviews some relevant works in the literature. In Sect. 3, the network model and security hypothesis are introduced. Further, Sect. 4 presents our detection method of the compromised mobile sink based on secret sharing. Section 5 analyzes and evaluates the performance of our method. Finally, Sect. 6 summarizes the whole work.

2 Related Works

Currently there are many works related to node compromise in wireless sensor networks, such as replication attack detection [7–12], node compromise detection [15–20] and physical capture detection [21–24].

2.1 Replication Attack Detection

Yu et al. [10] proposed XED method to detect replication attack in mobile sensor network. When two mobile sensor nodes meet they exchange two random numbers as their encounter evidence, which will be used as passphrases in their next meeting. If the passphrases authentication fails, replication attacks are detected. Although this approach is simple and effective, but it does not consider the collusion of multiple replica nodes. Kai et al. [11] proposed to detect replication attacks in MANETs, by means of conflicting nodes' location and time after local information interchange between mobile nodes in their meeting. Wang et al. [12] proposed to use mobile patroller to detect replication attacks. These studies [10–12] deal with the node replication issue instead of compromised mobile sink problem in UWSNs.

2.2 Compromised Static Nodes Detection

Taejoon et al. [15] proposed to detect compromised sensor nodes by verifying the node's program code. References [16–20] uses the message passing to verify node's program to detect the compromised node by the adversary.

2.3 Physical Capture Attacks Detection

Most studies assume that node capture is easy to implement and difficult to detect. However, Becher et al. [21] overturn this assumption by experiments, they found that it's not easy to conduct the physical capture attack. Apart from enough indispensible professional knowledge and expensive equipment, the sensor node must be taken offline for a period of time that cannot be ignored. Short attacks involve in creating plug-in connections and make data transfers takes about 5 min, the medium duration attacks involving welding or de-welding device consume more than 30 min, and the long duration attacks involving erasing the program security protection and modifying the code require at least several hours.

Based on Becher et al.'s work [21], Mauro et al. [22, 23] proposed to detect node capture attacks in MANETs by using mobility and collaboration, if the meeting interval exceeds a preset threshold, then the physical capture attacks is detected with large probability. But this method is not applicable in sensor networks with static nodes. Ding et al. [24] proposed to determine whether the neighbor is online to detect physical capture attack by response messages after periodically sending hello message.

3 Network Model and Assumptions

In this section, we presents our network model and security assumptions. First, Table 1 lists the notations used in this article and their corresponding meaning.

Table 1. Notations and descriptions

Notation	Meaning
Z	The identifiers set of static sensor nodes in network, $Z = \{1, 2, 3,..., N\}$
N_i	The neighbor nodes set of sensor node s_i
$|N_i|$	The neighbors number of sensor node s_i
U_i	The neighbors set chosen by sensor node s_i for sharing the secret
$|U_i|$	The number of the set U_i
d_i^r	Sensing data by node s_i in the r-th round
D_i	$\{d_i^r | 1 \leq r \leq \tau\}$, sensing data by node s_i in τ rounds
$h(.)$	One way hash function
τ	The hop count from secret share holder to the base-station
t_i	The threshold parameter in secret sharing chosen by node s_i
n_i	The total number of the secret shares split by node s_i
p_i	The prime number chosen by node s_i
Z_{p_i}	A finite field with order p_i
a_{ij}	$1 \leq j \leq t_i - 1, 0 \leq a_{ij} < p_i$, the j-th coefficient in node s_i's polynomial
M_i	Secret to be shared by node s_i
z_i	$z_i = h(M_i)$, the hash value of the secret of node s_i
$f_i(x)$	The secret-sharing polynomial of node s_i

3.1 Network Model

The unattended wireless sensor network consists of N static nodes, a mobile sink and one central base-station. The mobile sink periodically patrols around the network, collects the sensing data from every static sensor node and temporarily stores in its memory. At the end of one patrol round, the mobile sink submits all the data to the base-station.

3.2 Security Assumptions

It is assumed that the base-station and the mobile sink both have strong computing and storage capabilities, the public key algorithm between mobile sink and BS is used to implement encryption and signature to ensure confidentiality and integrity of data.

While, the static nodes have limited computing and storage capabilities, symmetric key algorithms are used for session keys between the base-station and the static nodes, between the mobile sink and the static nodes.

Also, we assume that the trusted central base station is located in a secure location, it will not be captured by the attacker, and however, both the mobile sink and the static nodes could be captured by the attacker. Once the mobile sink or any static node is captured, the attacker can acquire the node ID, the key, and the sensor data. The mobile sink, compared to the static sensor node, owns more credentials and aggregates the sensing data, attracts much more attention from the attacker. Therefore, the mobile sink will be the first target of the attacker. Thus, we focus on the detection of compromised mobile sink in this work.

In order to avoid triggering nodes offline defense mechanism [22–24], the captured sensor nodes will be released back into the network by the attacker, allowing the compromised nodes to participate in the network as if they are benign nodes. In addition, it is assumed that the number of nodes that the attacker can capture at a time is less than the total number of nodes of the network; otherwise all security mechanisms will fail.

4 Compromised Mobile Sink Detection by Using Secret Sharing

In this section, we first present the method to share secrets among static nodes. Then, the approach for the base-station to detect compromised mobile sink is proposed.

4.1 Secret Partition and Distribution

At the τ-th round, the static node acquires its sensing data, then it shares the secrets among its neighbors, which can be described as six steps in the following.

(1) Parameters selection

Sensor node s_i randomly chooses parameters t_i and n_i, which also meet $1 < t_i \leq n_i < |N_i|$. Then, it randomly chooses n_i neighbors as a subset, denoted by U_i, from its neighbors set N_i.

(2) Secret generation

Sensor node s_i calculate the secret to be shared M_i as Eq. (1).

$$M_i = h(t_i \| k_1 \| \ldots \| k_l \| k_{l+1} \| \ldots \| k_{n_i} \| d_i^0 \| d_i^1 \| \ldots \| d_i^\tau)$$
$$(k_l \in Z, k_l < k_{l+1}) \tag{1}$$

(3) Secret polynomial

Sensor node s_i selects a prime p_i which satisfies $p_i > \max(n_i, M_i)$. Then, $(t_i - 1)$ independent coefficients in the finite field Z_{p_i} are chosen at random, which is denoted by the set $\{a_{ij} | (1 \leq j \leq t_i - 1) \wedge (0 \leq a_{ij} < p_i)\}$, which are used to produce a $(t_i - 1)$-order secret sharing polynomial $f_i(x)$ as Eq. (2).

$$f_i(x) = \left(\sum_{j=1}^{t_i-1} a_{ij}x^j + M_i\right) \bmod p_i \tag{2}$$

(4) Secret splitting

In Eq. (2), x respectively takes the identifiers in the chosen neighbor subset U_i. After calculations, the identifiers and the respective secret shares can be expressed as a set $\{(k, y_{ik})|y_{ik} = f_i(k), k \in U_i\}$.

(5) Secret shares dispatching

Sensor node s_i sends the secret share y_{ik} to sensor node s_k, which would independently forwards such secret share to the base-station.

(6) Secrets deletion

Sensor node s_i deletes secret M_i, parameters t_i and n_i, as well as the coefficients set $\{a_{ij}\}$ and the polynomial $f_i(x)$, while it stores the prime number p_i and all its sensing data. The neighbor node will delete the secret share after sending it to the base station.

4.2   Compromised Mobile Sink Detection

(1) Mobile sink submits data to base-station

The mobile sink patrols around the network for collecting sensing data from the static nodes. For each node $s_i(1 \le i \le N)$, the mobile sink collects the sensing data D_i and the stored prime number p_i. Then, the sensor node removes such data from its memory and begins next sensing round. After all sensor nodes have been patrolled and data have been collected, the mobile sink submits the result $\{(D_i, p_i)|i \in Z\}$ to the base-station.

(2) Secret recovery

After receiving all the secret shares of sensor s_i, the base-station counts and gets the number n_i of total shares. Then, it recovers the secrets by means of polynomial interpolation.

As shown in Eq. (3), polynomial interpolation can be conducted in the point set $\{(k, y_{ik})|y_{ik} = f_i(k), k \in U_i\}$, which was composed by the secret shares from sensor s_i.

$$f_i(x) = \sum_{k \in U_i} y_{ik} \prod_{l \in U_i \wedge l \ne k} \frac{x-k}{l-k} \bmod p_i \tag{3}$$

Further, the base-station can restore the original secret as in Eq. (4). The secret sharing parameter t_i equals the highest exponent of polynomial (4) plus one.

$$M_i = f_i(0) = \sum_{k \in U_i} y_{ik} \prod_{l \in U_i \wedge l \ne k} \frac{k}{k-l} \bmod p_i \tag{4}$$

(3) Detecting the compromised mobile sink

With the identifier ID, the parameter t_i^r and the sensors' data submitted by the mobile sink, $h(t_i\|k_1\|\ldots\|k_l\|k_{l+1}\|\ldots\|k_{n_i}\|d_i^0\|d_i^1\|\ldots\|d_i^\tau)(k_l \in D, k_l < k_{l+1})$ is calculated by the base-station. After comparing this digest with the restored corresponding value enclosed in the secret M_i, the base-station could judge whether the mobile sink has been compromised or not. If this verification fails, it implies the compromise of the mobile sink.

5 Analysis and Evaluation

In this section, we will analyze and calculate the detection overheads in computation, memory, communication and the detection efficiency. Also, the parameters selection and how these parameters affect the detection results will be discussed in details.

5.1 Detection Overheads

(1) Computation overhead

The main computation overhead of static sensor nodes is the modular exponential algorithm of the polynomial $f_i(x) = (\sum_{j=1}^{t_i-1} a_{ij}x^j + M_i) \bmod p_i$ in finite field. Since multiplication is more complex and computationally intensive than addition, the overall computation overhead can be approximated using the number of total multiplications. In the polynomial $f_i(x)$, there are total $(2t - 3)$ multiplications, which involve $(t - 2)$ multiplications in the modular exponentiation, and $(t - 1)$ multiplications in the products between the exponentiations and the coefficients. Therefore, the total computation cost is $O(n(2t - 3))$.

(2) Memory overhead

Every static sensor node splits its secret into n shares, and sends to randomly selected neighbors. Thus, the average memory overhead is $O(n)$.

(3) Communication overhead

The n secret shares are forwarded to the base-station through different routes by the randomly selected neighbors. The average number of hops in those routes is $O(\sqrt{N})$ [25], so the communication cost of every sensor node are $O(n\sqrt{N})$.

5.2 Performance Analysis and Parameters Setting

We first consider an adversary that can only compromise one sensor node during the period of the share forwarding between two neighbors. Based on this attacking model, analysis and evaluations are detailed as to the detection efficiency. we analyze and discuss how to increase the detection efficiency and lower the detection overheads. Finally, we consider the more powerful adversary which can compromise more than one sensor nodes in one-hop communication interval. The detection efficiency against such adversary is deduced and discussed with different parameters.

(1) Only one static sensor node compromised in one round

We supposed an adversary with the knowledge of the network topology, the defense strategy and the intrusion detection methods. But the adversary is unaware of the secret sharing parameters t and n due to the randomness. As a consequence, in order to compromise the original secret, the adversary would have to recovery the secret after compromising as much secret shares as possible.

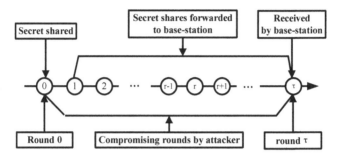

Fig. 2. Node compromised by adversary

In Fig. 2, we assume the average forwarding hops from the static sensor nodes to the base-station is τ. Also, it is assumed that the adversary can only compromise one sensor node in one hop communication. Then before the secret shares of the message digest reach the base-station, there are τ rounds for the adversary to compromise static sensor nodes.

Definition 1. $S = \{s, f\}$ is a sample set with only two elements, s indicates that the compromised sensor node is a secret shareholder, while f indicates that the compromised sensor node does not own a secret share.

Definition 2. X is a random variable with (0–1) distribution defined in the sample space. It represents the result after one round attack by the adversary, just as in Eq. (5).

$$X = X(e) = \begin{cases} 0, when & e = f \\ 1, when & e = s \end{cases} \tag{5}$$

In one round of compromise, the adversary captures one sensor node. This can be regarded as one random experiment with two possible results: the sensor node has the secret share holder or not. Before the secret shares are forwarded to the base-station, there are τ attempts for the adversary to compromise.

Let Y denotes the number of experiments with result $\{X = 1\}$ in τ rounds random experiments. That is, the number of total secret shares compromised by the attacker in τ

rounds. The domain of Y should be $[\max(0, \tau + n - N), \min(n, \tau)]$, and the probability of the event $\{Y = k\}$ can be expressed as Eq. (6).

$$P\{Y = k\} = p_k, k \in [\max(0, \tau + n - N), \min(n, \tau)] \tag{6}$$

Equation (6) is the probability distribution of the random variable Y. If the compromised sensor node doesn't hold the desired secret share, then it will be released to the network by the attacker lest this attack alarms the off-line intrusion detection mechanism. Later, the adversary chooses other compromising sensor node from the remaining sensor nodes. This attacking model can be modeled as sampling without replacement, or the "urn problem". In a network whose total number of sensor nodes is N, the number of the desired secret shares is n, while only t shares are needed to recover the original desired secret. There are τ attempts for the adversary to compromise. The event that the number of the success compromise equals k is denoted by $\{Y = k\}$. Let $P\{Y = k\}$ be the probability of this event. Then the random variable Y obeys the hyper geometric distribution with parameters (N, n, τ). The distribution law can be expressed as Eq. (7).

$$P\{Y = k\} = \frac{C_n^k C_{N-n}^{\tau-k}}{C_N^{\tau}}, k \in [\max(0, \tau + n - N), \min(n, \tau)] \tag{7}$$

Figure 3 illustrates how $P\{Y = k\}$ changes in two cases with different parameter setting. In Fig. 3(a), $N = 100$ and $n = 8$, when parameter t changes from 2 to 8, the probability that the adversary compromises k secret shares decreases gradually. However, if the number of compromised sensor nodes increases from 0 to 100, the probability will gradually become larger. Figure 3(b) reveals a similar trend.

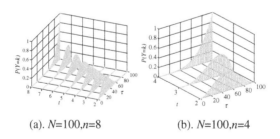

(a). $N=100, n=8$ (b). $N=100, n=4$

Fig. 3. $P\{Y = k\}$ varies with parameter t and τ

If the adversary wants to tamper the sensing data by compromising the mobile sink, he must compromise at least t sensor nodes which also own t secret shares. Therefore, we can define the false negatives of compromised mobile sink as follows.

Definition 3. The false negative of compromised mobile sink detection is defined as an event that the compromised mobile sink is not detected (**CMU: Compromised Mobile sink Undetected**), that is the adversary compromised at least t sensor nodes which own the respective secret shares. The probability is defined as false negative of the detection.

Let $\mathbf{CMU} = \{Y >= t\}$ be the false negative event, and $\boldsymbol{P_{cmu}}$ be the false negative, and then we obtain Eq. (8).

$$
\begin{aligned}
P_{cmu} &= P\{Y > = t\} \\
&= P\{Y = t\} + P\{Y = t+1\} + \ldots + P\{Y = \min(n,\tau)\} \\
&= \sum_{j=t}^{\min(n,\tau)} P\{Y = j\}
\end{aligned}
\tag{8}
$$

In Eq. (8), when $j > \min(n, \tau)$, then we have $P\{Y = j\} = 0$. So, Eq. (8) can be further regarded as Eq. (9).

$$
\begin{aligned}
P_{cmu} &= P\{Y \geq t\} \\
&= P\{Y = t\} + P\{Y = t+1\} + \ldots + P\{Y = \min(n,\tau)\} + \ldots \\
&= \sum_{j=t}^{\infty} P\{Y = j\} \\
&= \frac{C_\tau^t C_{N-\tau}^{n-t}}{C_N^n} {}_3F_2 \left[\begin{matrix} 1, n-t, \tau-t \\ t+1, N+t+1-n-\tau \end{matrix} ; \ 1 \right]
\end{aligned}
\tag{9}
$$

In Eq. (9), ${}_3F_2 \left[\begin{matrix} 1, n-t, \tau-t \\ t+1, N+t+1-n-\tau \end{matrix} ; \ 1 \right]$ is a hyper geometrical series.

When N and τ are fixed, the false negatives are determined by parameter t and n. Figure 4 shows the false negatives of our detection method in two scenarios. In Fig. 4 (a) with $N = 100$, $n = 8$, and the average hops of the network $\tau = \sqrt{N} = 10$, the false negatives will be less than 5% when $t \geq 3$; while in Fig. 4(b) with $N = 10000, n = 8$, and the average hops of the network $\tau = \sqrt{N} = 100$, the false negatives will be less than 0.3% when $t = 2$.

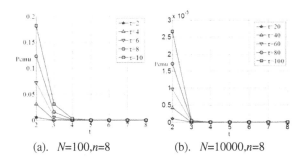

(a). $N=100, n=8$ (b). $N=10000, n=8$

Fig. 4. False negatives in two scenarios

If after τ rounds of attacks, the count of the compromised sensor nodes which own the secret shares is less than t, then the compromised mobile sink would be detected. So, we can define the compromised mobile sink detected event and its probability as follows.

Definition 4. The compromised mobile sink detected event is defined as **CMD** (compromised-mobile sink-detected), that is the adversary compromised less than t sensor nodes which own the secret shares.

Let **CMD** $= \{Y < t\}$ be the detection event, and P_{cmd} be the probability, and then we obtain the Eq. (10).

$$
\begin{aligned}
P_{cmd} &= P\{Y < t\} = P\{Y = 0\} + P\{Y = 1\} + \ldots + P\{Y = t - 1\} \\
&= \sum_{j=0}^{t-1} P\{Y = j\} = 1 - P\{Y \geq t\} \\
&= 1 - \frac{C_\tau^t C_{N-\tau}^{n-t}}{C_N^n} \, {}_3F_2 \left[\begin{matrix} 1, n - t, \tau - t \\ t + 1, N + t + 1 - n - \tau \end{matrix} \; ; \; 1 \right]
\end{aligned}
\tag{10}
$$

When N and n are fixed, the detection probability P_{cmd} is determined by secret sharing parameters t and τ. Figure 5 shows four cases of detection probability with parameters t and τ.

As shown in Fig. 5, if N is fixed, the average hops of the network are $\sqrt{N}$, so $1 \leq \tau \leq \sqrt{N}$. In Fig. 5(a), the detection probability is greater than 80% when $N = 100$ and $n = 8$. Figure 5(b) shows the detection probability exceeds 95% even if n is reduced to 4 with $N = 100$. Similarly, in Fig. 5(c) and (d) with total sensor number $N = 10000$, the detection probabilities are both greater than 99% for $n = 8$ and $n = 4$. Also, it is shown that the secret sharing parameters n and t have little influence on the

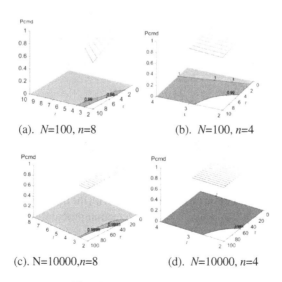

(a). $N=100, n=8$ (b). $N=100, n=4$

(c). N=10000,n=8   (d). $N=10000, n=4$

Fig. 5. Detection probability

detection probability when $N \gg \tau$. Therefore, under such circumstances, in order to decrease the detection overheads, parameters t and n should take smaller values.

(2) **More than one node captured in one round**

In this subsection, we consider a more powerful adversary, which can compromise ρN nodes; ρ is a proportional factor between 0 and 1.

If in the r-th round, the probability that all the secret shares are acquired by the adversary is P_r, then the probability that the adversary couldn't obtain the secret until the r-th round can be calculated in Eq. (11).

$$P = (1 - P_1)(1 - P_2)\ldots(1 - P_{r-1})(1 - P_r) = \prod_{i=1}^{r} (1 - P_i) \tag{11}$$

The secret shares owned by the sensors in the $(r - 1)$-th round are forwarded to the its' next-hop sensors in the r-th round. If all the secret shares are not grabbed in the $(r - 1)$-th round, the adversary has to carry out the same capture attack in the r-th round. So, the probability that all secret shares are grabbed by the adversary is equal in every round, as shown in the Eq. (12).

$$P_1 = P_2 = \ldots = P_{r-1} = P_r \tag{12}$$

The probability in the Eq. (12) can be calculated as Eq. (13).

$$\begin{aligned} P_1 &= \frac{C_n^n C_{N-n}^{\rho N-n}}{C_N^{\rho N}} = \frac{C_{N-n}^{\rho N-n}}{C_N^{\rho N}} \\ &= \frac{(N-n)!}{(\rho N - n)!(N - \rho N)!} \times \frac{\rho N!(N - \rho N)!}{N!} \\ &= \frac{\rho(\rho N - 1)\ldots(\rho N - n + 1)}{(N - 1)\ldots(N - n + 1)} \end{aligned} \tag{13}$$

When $N \gg n$, Eq. (13) can be approximated as Eq. (14).

$$P_1 \approx \frac{\rho(\rho N)\ldots(\rho N)}{N\ldots N} = \rho^n \tag{14}$$

Finally, we obtain the approximation Eq. (15) about the Eq. (11).

$$P = (1 - P_1)^r \approx (1 - \rho^n)^r \tag{15}$$

Figure 6 shows this detection probability varies with the three parameters n, τ and ρ. In Fig. 6(a), N is fixed to 400 and $\rho = 20\%$, the detection probability approximates 100% when n is greater than 5. Figure 6(b) shows that when $\tau = 20$, even if half of the sensor nodes are compromised ($\rho = 20\%$), the detection probability still approximates 100% as long as $t = n > 10$. As illustrated in Fig. 6(c), if $t = n = 10$, the detection probability approaches 100% even if the adversary compromises $\rho = 50\%$ sensor nodes.

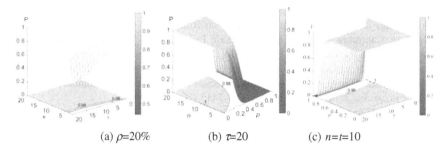

(a) ρ=20%   (b) τ=20   (c) n=t=10

Fig. 6. Detection probability

6   Conclusion

In this paper, we proposed a compromised mobile sink detection scheme by using secret sharing. Every sensor node first splits the digest of its sensing data into shares by using a polynomial secret sharing algorithm, and then the secret shares are sent to the base-station through different routes by the sensor's neighbors. Finally, the base-station receives the shares, and then recovers the original data digest, compares with the data submitted by the mobile sink. Any difference reveals the compromised mobile sink, results in the detection by the base-station. Theoretical analysis and evaluation shows the effectiveness and efficiency of our method, the detection overheads are small. Also, the upper limit of detection probability was computed with the proposed compromise model of the mobile adversary.

Acknowledgment. This work is supported by the National Natural Science Foundation of China under Grant No. 61272074 and No. U1405255, the Key Research & Development Project of Jiangsu Province under Grant No. BE2015136, and the Industrial Science and Technology Foundation of Zhenjiang City under Grant No. GY2013030.

References

1. Khan, A.W., Abdullah, A.H., Anisi, M.H., Bangash, J.I.: A comprehensive study of data collection schemes using mobile sinks in wireless sensor networks. Sensors **2014**(14), 2510–2548 (2014)
2. Di Pietro, R., et al.: Data security in unattended wireless sensor networks. IEEE Trans. Comput. **58**(11), 1500–1511 (2009)
3. Reddy, S.K.V.L., Ruj, S., Nayak, A.: Distributed data survivability schemes in mobile unattended wireless sensor networks. In: Global Communications Conference (GLOBECOM 2012), Anaheim, California, USA, pp. 979–984. IEEE Press (2012)
4. Chen, C., Gao, X.B., Pei, Q.Q., et al.: A tactics to alleviate influence of denial-of-sleep attack in WSN. J. Jiangsu Univ. Nat. Sci. Ed. **31**(5), 570–575 (2010)
5. Douceur, J.R.: The sybil attack. In: Druschel, P., Kaashoek, F., Rowstron, A. (eds.) IPTPS 2002. LNCS, vol. 2429, pp. 251–260. Springer, Heidelberg (2002). https://doi.org/10.1007/3-540-45748-8_24

6. Culpepper, B.J., Tseng, H.C.: Sinkhole intrusion indicators in DSR MANETs. In: Proceedings of 1st International Conference on Broadband Networks (Broad-Nets 2004), San Jose, California, USA, pp. 681–688. IEEE Press (2004)

7. Khan, W.Z., Aalsalem, M.Y., Saad, N.M.: Distributed clone detection in static wireless sensor networks: random walk with network division. PLoS One 10(5), e0123069 (2015)

8. Mishra, A.K., Turuk, A.K.: Node coloring based replica detection technique in wireless sensor networks. Wirel. Netw. 20(8), 2419–2435 (2014)

9. Contia, M., Pietro, R., Di Spognardic, A.: Clone wars: distributed detection of clone attacks in mobile WSNs. J. Comput. Syst. Sci. 80(3), 654–669 (2014)

10. Yu, C.M., Lu, C.S., Kuo, S.Y.: Mobile sensor network resilient against node replication attacks. In: Proceedings of the 5th Annual IEEE Communications Society Conference on Sensor, Mesh and Ad Hoc Communications and Networks (SECON 2008), San Francisco, USA, pp. 597–599. IEEE Press (2008)

11. Xing, K., Cheng, X.: From time domain to space domain: detecting replica attacks in mobile ad hoc networks. In: Proceedings of the IEEE INFOCOM 2010, San Diego, CA, USA, pp. 1–9. IEEE Press (2010)

12. Wang, L.M., Shi, Y.: Patrol detection for replica attacks on wireless sensor networks. Sensors 2011(11), 2496–2504 (2011)

13. Song, H., Zhu, S., Zhang, W., et al.: Least privilege and privilege deprivation: toward tolerating mobile sink compromises in wireless sensor networks. ACM Trans. Sens. Netw. (TOSN), 4(4) (2008). Article 23

14. Liu, Z., Ma, J., Park, Y., et al.: Data security in unattended wireless sensor networks with mobile sinks. Wirel. Commun. Mob. Comput. 12(13), 1131–1146 (2012)

15. Park, T., Shin, K.G.: Soft tamper-proofing via program integrity verification in wireless sensor networks. IEEE Trans. Mob. Comput. 4(3), 297–309 (2005)

16. Du, X.: Detection of compromised sensor nodes in heterogeneous sensor networks. In: Proceedings of the IEEE 2008 International Conference on Communications (ICC 2008), Beijing, China, pp. 1446–1450. IEEE Press (2008)

17. Yang, Y., Wang, X., Zhu, S., et al.: Distributed software-based attestation for node compromise detection in sensor networks. In: Proceedings of 26th IEEE International Symposium on Reliable Distributed Systems, Beijing, China, pp. 219–230. IEEE Press (2007)

18. Krauß, C., Stumpf, F., Eckert, C.: Detecting node compromise in hybrid wireless sensor networks using attestation techniques. In: Stajano, F., Meadows, C., Capkun, S., Moore, T. (eds.) ESAS 2007. LNCS, vol. 4572, pp. 203–217. Springer, Heidelberg (2007). https://doi.org/10.1007/978-3-540-73275-4_15

19. Jin, X., Putthapipat, P., Pan, D., et al.: Unpredictable software-based attestation solution for node compromise detection in mobile WSN. In: Proceedings of the IEEE 2010 GLOBECOM Workshops (GC Wkshps), Miami, Florida, USA, pp. 2059–2064. IEEE Press (2010)

20. Sei, Y., Ohsuga, A.: Need only one bit: light-weight packet marking for detecting compromised nodes in WSNs. In: Proceedings of the 7th International Conference on Emerging Security Information, Systems and Technologies (SECURWARE 2013), Barcelona, Spain, pp. 134–143. IARIA (2013)

21. Becher, A., Benenson, Z., Dornseif, M.: Tampering with motes: real-world physical attacks on wireless sensor networks. In: Clark, J.A., Paige, R.F., Polack, F.A.C., Brooke, P.J. (eds.) SPC 2006. LNCS, vol. 3934, pp. 104–118. Springer, Heidelberg (2006). https://doi.org/10.1007/11734666_9

22. Conti, M., Di Pietro, R., Mancini, L.V., et al.: Emergent properties: detection of the node-capture attack in mobile wireless sensor networks. In: Proceedings of the First ACM Conference on Wireless Network Security, Alexandria, Virginia, USA, pp. 214–219. ACM (2008)

23. Conti, M., Di Pietro, R., Mancini, L.V., et al.: Mobility and cooperation to thwart node capture attacks in manets. EURASIP J. Wirel. Commun. Network. **2009**(1), 945943 (2009)

24. Ding, W., Yu, Y., Yenduri, S.: Distributed first stage detection for node capture. In: Proceedings of 2010 IEEE GLOBECOM Workshops (GC Wkshps), Miami, USA, pp. 1566–1570. IEEE Press (2010)

25. Dimitriou, T., Sabouri, A.: Pollination: a data authentication scheme for unattended wireless sensor networks. In: Proceedings of the 10th IEEE International Conference on Trust, Security and Privacy in Computing and Communications (TrustCom 2011), Changsha, China, pp. 409–416. IEEE Press (2011)

Understanding Trajectory Data Based on Heterogeneous Information Network Using Visual Analytics

Rui Zhang[1,2,3], Wenjie Ma[3], Luo Zhong[3(✉)], Peng Xie[3], and Hongbo Jiang[4]

[1] Hubei Key Laboratory of Transportation Internet of Things, Wuhan University of Technology,
Wuhan, Hubei, China
zhangrui@whut.edu.cn
[2] Hubei Key Laboratory of Inland Shipping Technology, Wuhan University of Technology,
Wuhan, Hubei, China
[3] School of Computer Science and Technology, Wuhan University of Technology,
Wuhan 430072, Hubei, China
15827182791@163.com, zhongluo@whut.edu.cn, xiepeng0715@gmail.com
[4] School of Electronic Information and Communications,
Huazhong University of Science and Technology, Wuhan 430074, Hubei, China
hongbojiang2004@gmail.com

Abstract. With its continuous development, location information acquisition technology is able to collect more and more trajectory data, and the rich information contained therein is gradually attracting attention from researchers. Trajectory data involves complex relationships among moving objects, time, space, which are hard to understand and be used directly. Nowadays, visual analysis of trajectory data is mainly focus on its representation and interaction, but fails to address the complex correlation contained in trajectory data. Hence, we propose TrajHIN, a heterogeneous information network model built on trajectory data, measure the meta path-based similarity and centrality, and use a visual analytics method to deeply understand trajectory data. The example of visual analysis of real trajectory data has been interpreted and given feedback from domain experts, which proves effectiveness of TrajHIN and feasibility of mining implicit semantic information from trajectory data.

Keywords: Trajectory · Heterogeneous information network · Visual analysis

1 Introduction

Nowadays, with the continuous progress of location information acquisition technology, trajectory data has gradually received public attention and concern. Trajectory data plays an important role in behavioral patterns mining, traffic flow prediction, and POI recommendation, etc. However, trajectory data involves complex relationships between moving objects, time and space, making it difficult to be understood intuitively. Most existing research regards trajectory data as homogeneous information networks.

© Springer Nature Singapore Pte Ltd. 2018
L. Zhu and S. Zhong (Eds.): MSN 2017, CCIS 747, pp. 318–327, 2018.
https://doi.org/10.1007/978-981-10-8890-2_23

However, moving objects are related to locations, environment and other things in real-life scenarios, so homogeneous information networks are not suitable for analyzing trajectory data.

Han et al. proposed Heterogeneous Information Networks [1, 2], which are the logical networks involving multiple typed objects or multiple typed links denoting different relations, such as bibliographic networks, social media networks. Heterogeneous information networks can be used to model complex interaction data.

By analyzing trajectory data based on heterogeneous information network, we can get the semantics and information that cannot be mined by many homogeneous information networks. For instance, a meta path of region → car → region suggests the most frequently used region of taxi, and that the region may be the traffic center during this period. In order to further analyze the underlying relevance in trajectory data, we measure the meta path-based similarity and centrality.

Visualization is desired since it allows the domain users to incorporate their domain knowledge and human intelligence in the exploratory analysis process. However, the scale and complexity of the trajectory data make interactive visualization a challenging task. Some researchers also introduce graph into visual analysis of trajectory data [8], but they fail to pay sufficient attention to the various types of objects and relationships involved in trajectory data, and visualize the high dimensional features of trajectory data. We hope that the implicit correlation information in trajectory data can be displayed to users more clearly. We integrate visualization methods with trajectory data analysis based on heterogeneous information networks so that the information obtained from analysis can be fully utilized.

The main contributions of this paper are as follows:

- We build TrajHIN, a heterogeneous information network model based on trajectory data, it is constructed to model complex correlation of trajectory data and express trajectory data more clearly.
- With TrajHIN, we measure the meta path-based similarity and centrality.
- We integrate the heterogeneity information network model TrajHIN with visual analysis so that users can easily understand and analyze the relationship between corresponding objects and mine correlation information in trajectory data.

The respect of this paper is organized as follows. Section 2 describes the related work. The third section gives the definition and description of our model. The fourth section presents the visualization and some experiments about the method. Section 5 concludes the paper.

2   Related Work

In this section, we explain some other work related to our research, including others' work in trajectory data, brief introduction of heterogeneous information networks and some work in visual analysis.

2.1 Trajectory Data

Many scholars have mined behavior patterns through analyzing and understanding trajectory data. For example, Hirokazu Madokoro modeled trajectory data by using hidden markov model and used behavior patterns in an interest-recommending website [3]. Also, Mahdim Kalayeh proposed a dynamic model of mining behavior patterns from trajectory data [4]. Trajectory data was studied in behavior and path planning that Bucher et al. proposed a path planning algorithm which required less computation based on individual user trajectory log [5]. There are also some research on trajectory data for predicting location, such as taxi status inquiry and waiting time forecasting based on taxi trajectory data [6, 7]. According to current position and historical trajectories of a moving object, predicting location is able to forecast the location of this object [8]. On the other hand, there are some other research on semantic information mining of trajectory data as well. For instance, Liu et al. analyzed the best location for setting up billboard from urban taxi trajectory data [9]. By regarding trajectory data as link relation, Huang et al. constructed an urban road network relationship and analyzed the traffic condition of roads in urban center by the link relations between road sections [10].

2.2 Heterogeneous Information Networks

There are some research on the similarity measurement of heterogeneous information networks. After Han et al. proposed the meta paths for DBLP, the concept of meta paths was widely introduced into similarity measurement on heterogeneous information networks. Subsequently, Han et al. proposed Pathsim, a novel similarity measurement method based on meta path which is able to find peer objects in the network, making it possible to accurately distinguish different latent semantics in heterogeneous information networks [11, 12]. Also, there are some other research on clustering analysis of heterogeneous information networks. For example, Aggarwal et al. used local optimal features to balance heterogeneous information networks which can achieve clustering [13]. In link prediction of Heterogeneous Information Networks, some studies predicted possible relationship between two nodes by using observed links and node attributes [14–16].

2.3 Visual Analysis

Visual analysis related to our work is often focused on two primary aspects. The first aspect is analysis related to graph. For example, Pienta et al. designed a locally adaptive exploration model for it, which is of data graph [17]. Chau et al. developed an interactive visualization system and iteratively improved it to interpret large-scale deep learning models and results [18]. They even presented a novel interactive visual analytics system to explore and comprehend them completely [19]. Another aspect in visual analysis is related to trajectory. One of the most classic applications is proposed by Huang et al. [10], in which they used taxi trajectory data and graph-based visual analysis to study urban network centers. Al-Dohuki et al. put forward SemanticTraj as well, which can be used to link the map and users' semantic information, make users querying much more efficient than before [20]. However, visual analysis neither related to graph nor trajectory has considered the various types of objects and relationships involved in trajectory data, which may make it not much suitable when dealing with complex relationships. Therefore, our method should take good care of this.

3   TrajHIN Model

In this section, we first constructed a heterogeneous information networks model based on trajectory data. We then described the Pathsim algorithm and measured the meta path-based similarity in Sect. 3.2. In Sect. 3.3, we designed a new degree centrality measure of trajectory data and evaluated meta path-based degree centrality.

3.1   TrajHIN Construction

Trajectory data is data information formed by sampling the movements of a moving object. A trajectory can be seen as a sequence of time-stamped positions. In this paper, the trajectories of ships are used as an example of visual analysis. Specifically, ship trajectories are taken from AIS equipment and include information such as unique identification, position, course, and speed, name of ship, type of ship, destination and timestamp.

Heterogeneous information networks can be denoted by $G = (V, E)$, while V, E are object and link respectively [1]. Each V has a function: $\Psi:V \rightarrow T$, for T is a set of a kind of objects; Each E has a function: $\Phi:E \rightarrow R$, for R is a set of a kind of links. In heterogeneous information networks, $|T| > 1$ or $|R| > 1$. TrajHIN is constructed by extracting the moving objects in trajectory data and related concepts such as time, space and inter-relationship. In this paper, the set of object types includes region, ship and destination while the adjacent, contained and included form the set of relationship types. Region is obtained from geographical coordinates converted by anti-geocoding after trajectory data is de-noised and compressed. TrajHIN model construction is shown in Fig. 1.

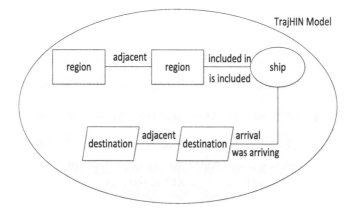

Fig. 1. TrajHIN model.

TrajHIN treats region, ship and destination as different types of objects respectively. In this paper, we mainly examine the following meta paths where a meta path is a path consisting of a sequence of relations defined between different object types:

- *ASDSA* (region *A*, ship *S*, destination *D*)
- *DSASD* (destination *D*, ship *S*, region *A*)
- *SAS* (ship *S*, region *A*, ship *S*)
- *SDS* (ship *S*, destination *D*, ship *S*)

Both similarity and centrality measures use the above meta paths as one of their factors.

3.2 Measuring Similarity in TrajHIN

The settings of heterogeneous information network model TrajHIN and meta paths generate semantic meaning of similarity between objects in trajectory data. For example, similarity of two trajectories is no longer limited to the shape and so on, and we can also mine semantic information through meta path *ASDSA* and measure similarity by analyzing meta path between two objects. Pathsim proposed by Sun [15] can well measure the similarity between nodes in heterogeneous information networks. For example, given a symmetric meta path $P = ASDSA$, Pathsim measures in areas a and b as below:

$$S(a, b) = \frac{2 \times \left|\{P_{a \to b} : P_{a \to b} \in P\}\right|}{\left|\{P_{a \to a} : P_{a \to a} \in P\}\right| + \left|\{P_{b \to b} : P_{b \to b} \in P\}\right|} \tag{1}$$

$Pa \to b$ refers to a path instance between a and b, $Pa \to a$, $Pb \to b$ also represent the paths from a to a and b to b, respectively.

3.3 Measuring Centrality in TrajHIN

Centrality demonstrates a degree that whether a node is in the center of the information network. If a node has directly link with many other nodes, it is more like a center than those nodes which don't have so many links. We studied trajectory data according to measuring meta path-based centrality and designed a new centrality measure of trajectory data in the basis of the heterogeneous network. Given a meta path $P(ASA)$, degree centrality of a node v is the number of entries back to this node along path P. Then, when comparing different graphs, we need to normalize degree centrality. From meta path P, we can see that if the first and the last nodes of the path are in same type, it can be divided by maximum number of possible connections $Num(A) - 1$, where A is the set of points of the same type as point v and $Num(A)$ described those points generated by path P.

4   Visualization

Through the model TrajHIN we constructed and measured the meta path-based simi-larity and centrality above. Next we conduct visualization of our method. We first designed a interface by integrating TrajHIN with visual analysis in section A and B. In section C and D, we used real trajectory data to explore similarity and centrality in TrajHIN. Then, we interpreted visual analysis of real trajectory data and compared it with feedback from domain experts.

4.1   Interface

We integrate heterogeneous information network based on trajectory data with visual analysis to analyze trajectory data. Functions include: map matching, region selection, graph visualization, similarity query and centrality query, the interface is shown in Fig. 2. Module (1) shows the map; Module (2) displays the trajectory data graph; Module (3) shows the results of measuring meta paths-based similarity and centrality. (4) represents the trajectory data information search module.

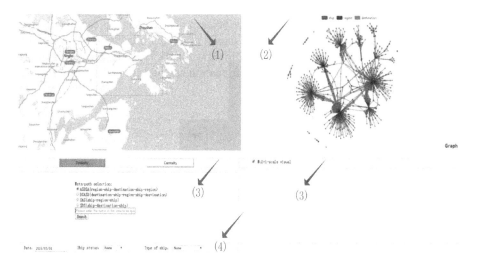

Fig. 2.   Visual analysis interface.

4.2   Visualizing TrajHIN

The module shows a graph of heterogeneous information network model constructed on trajectory data, which contains three types of objects: region, ship, destination and different types of edges. In Fig. 3, ship GANGFENG8 is connected to region Ningbo-Ninghai. The graph in this module also has the function of dragging zooming, where different colors of nodes are used to distinguish different types of objects and links.

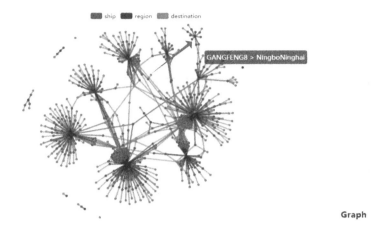

Fig. 3. Graph (Color figure online).

4.3 Exploring Similarity in TrajHIN

By selecting the meta path and inputting the object to be studied, we can display the top-4 objects in the form of histogram. The names of similar objects are shown in the abscissa and similarity measurement scores are shown in the ordinate. The histogram is shown in Fig. 4. The local heterogeneous information network formed by top4 and the object to be studied are shown in Fig. 5.

Fig. 4. Histogram of similarity analysis.

Fig. 5. Similarity analysis graph.

In this example, area is Dinghai, and the research meta path is *ASDSA*. The histogram shows that the similarity between Dinghai and Putuo is the highest by measuring similarity through *ASDSA*. It can also be seen from graph that the number of meta paths of Dinghai → Putuo will be greater than other areas. Through the meta path analysis like *ASDSA*, it can be inferred that the reachability of Dinghai and Putuo is the most similar for some destinations. As confirmed by domain experts, many ships sail through common channels in Dinghai and Putuo, so the two areas are similar.

4.4   Exploring Centrality in TrajHIN

By setting the region and time threshold, the user can draw a line chart reflect the degree centrality with the change of time. Figure 6 shows degree centrality of the area Dinghai on March 1, 2015. By analyzing the meta path *ASA*, we can understand that degree centrality actually refers to the navigation of ships in the area within time threshold. We can draw the semantic result that centrality of the area is the highest in early morning when the time threshold for Dinghai area is set to one hour. This means that Dinghai is the area where fishing vessels work. After doing a field investigation, we find that Dinghai is indeed the scope of fishing vessels activities on that day. It is shown that the improved centrality method can be applied to heterogeneous information networks and obtain semantic information.

Fig. 6.   Centrality Results.

4.5   Case Study

We choose Dinghai as the area and observe trajectory data of fishing vessels. Through similarity analysis of Dinghai based on meta path *ASDSA*, it can be inferred that Dinghai and Putuo have the highest reachability on some destinations. By setting time threshold and meta path *ASA*, the degree centrality of Dinghai within a specific day was analyzed. We found that degree centrality of Dinghai was the highest and the area was the most active from 0:00 to 2:00 and 21:00 to 24:00. Therefore, the conclusion is that this area is the scope of fishing vessels activities, which was confirmed by a field investigation. From the results above, we can conclude that the integration of TrajHIN and visual analysis makes it easy for users to understand and analyze relationship between corresponding objects in trajectory data, where semantic information can be mined from trajectory data at the same time.

5   Conclusion

The rapid development of location logging has led to the explosive growth of trajectory data. Meanwhile, the abundant information hidden in trajectory data has drawn a lot more attention. Based on AIS navigation trajectory data, a heterogeneous information network model TrajHIN is constructed and combined with visual analysis. Experimental results have validated the effectiveness of TrajHIN and visual analysis. In the future, we will expand the scale of trajectory data and incorporate the idea of parallel computing into the model to iterate the visual analysis model so that it can be used for visual analysis of large-scale trajectory data.

Acknowledgements. This work was supported in part by the National Natural Science Foundation of China under Grants 61572219, 61502192, 61671216, 61471408 and 51479157; by the China Postdoctoral Science Foundation under Grants 2017T100556; and by the Fundamental Research Funds for the Central Universities under Grant 2015QN073, 2016YXMS297, 2016JCTD118 and WUT:2016III028; by fund of Hubei Key Laboratory of Inland Shipping Technology under Grant NHHY2015005.

References

1. Sun, Y., Han, J.: Mining heterogeneous information networks: a structural analysis approach. ACM SIGKDD Explor. Newsl. **14**(2), 20–28 (2013)
2. Deng, H., Han, J., Lyu, M. R., King, I.: Modeling and exploiting heterogeneous bibliographic networks for expertise ranking. In: Proceedings of the 12th ACM/IEEE-CS joint conference on Digital Libraries, pp. 71–80. ACM, June 2012
3. Madokoro, H., Honma, K., Sato, K.: Classification of behavior patterns with trajectory analysis used for event site. In: International Joint Conference on Neural Networks (IJCNN), pp. 1–8. IEEE, June 2012
4. Kalayeh, M.M., Mussmann, S., Petrakova, A., Lobo, N.D.V., Shah, M.: Understanding Trajectory Behavior: A Motion Pattern Approach (2015). arXiv preprint arXiv:1501.00614
5. Bucher, D., Jonietz, D., Raubal, M.: A heuristic for multi-modal route planning. In: Gartner, G., Huang, H. (eds.) Progress in Location-Based Services 2016. LNGC, pp. 211–229. Springer, Cham (2017). https://doi.org/10.1007/978-3-319-47289-8_11
6. Luo, W., Tan, H., Chen, L., Ni, L.M.: Finding time period-based most frequent path in big trajectory data. In: Proceedings of the 2013 ACM SIGMOD international conference on management of data, pp. 713–724. ACM, June 2013
7. Su, H., Zheng, K., Huang, J., Jeung, H., Chen, L., Zhou, X.: Crowdplanner: a crowd-based route recommendation system. In: IEEE 30th International Conference on Data Engineering (ICDE), pp. 1144–1155. IEEE, March 2014
8. Xue, A.Y., Zhang, R., Zheng, Y., Xie, X., Huang, J., Xu, Z.: Destination prediction by sub-trajectory synthesis and privacy protection against such prediction. In: IEEE 29th International Conference on Data Engineering (ICDE 2013), pp. 254–265. IEEE, April 2013
9. Liu, D., Weng, D., Li, Y., Bao, J., Zheng, Y., Qu, H., Wu, Y.: SmartAdP: visual analytics of large-scale taxi trajectories for selecting billboard locations. IEEE Trans. Visual Comput. Graphics **23**(1), 1–10 (2017)

10. Huang, X., Zhao, Y., Ma, C., Yang, J., Ye, X., Zhang, C.: TrajGraph: a graph-based visual analytics approach to studying urban network centralities using taxi trajectory data. IEEE Trans. Visual Comput. Graphics **22**(1), 160–169 (2016)
11. Shang, J., Qu, M., Liu, J., Kaplan, L.M., Han, J., Peng, J.: Meta-Path Guided Embedding for Similarity Search in Large-Scale Heterogeneous Information Networks (2016). arXiv preprint arXiv:1610.09769
12. Yu, X., Sun, Y., Norick, B., Mao, T., Han, J.: User guided entity similarity search using meta-path selection in heterogeneous information networks. In: Proceedings of the 21st ACM International Conference on Information and Knowledge Management, pp. 2025–2029. ACM, October 2012
13. Gupta, M., Aggarwal, C., Han, J., Sun, Y.: Evolutionary Clustering and Analysis of Heterogeneous Information Networks. IBM Research Report, 1006-064 (2010)
14. Zhang, J., Yu, P.S., Zhou, Z.H.: Meta-path based multi-network collective link prediction. In: Proceedings of the 20th ACM SIGKDD international conference on Knowledge discovery and data mining, pp. 1286–1295. ACM, August 2014
15. Kong, X., Zhang, J., Yu, P.S.: Inferring anchor links across multiple heterogeneous social networks. In: Proceedings of the 22nd ACM international conference on Information & Knowledge Management, pp. 179–188. ACM, October 2013
16. Zhang, J., Kong, X., Yu, P.S.: Transferring heterogeneous links across location-based social networks. In: Proceedings of the 7th ACM international conference on Web search and data mining, pp. 303–312. ACM, February 2014
17. Pienta, R., Lin, Z., Kahng, M., Vreeken, J., Talukdar, P.P., Abello, J., Chau, D.H.: Seeing the Forest through the Trees: Adaptive Local Exploration of Large Graphs (2015). arXiv preprint arXiv:1505.06792
18. Kahng, M., Andrews, P.Y., Kalro, A., Chau, D.H.P.: ActiVis: visual exploration of industry-scale deep neural network models. IEEE Trans. Visual Comput. Graphics **24**(1), 88–97 (2018)
19. Pienta, R., Hohman, F., Endert, A., Tamersoy, A., Roundy, K., Gates, C., Chau, D.H.: VIGOR: Interactive Visual Exploration of Graph Query Results. IEEE Trans. Visual. Comput.graphics **24**(1), 215–225 (2018)
20. Al-Dohuki, S., Wu, Y., Kamw, F., Yang, J., Li, X., Zhao, Y., Wang, F.: SemanticTraj: A new approach to interacting with massive taxi trajectories. IEEE Trans. Visual. Comput. Graphics **23**(1), 11–20 (2017)

Automatic Prediction of Traffic Flow
Based on Deep Residual Networks

Rui Zhang[1,2,3(✉)], Nuofei Li[3], Siyuan Huang[3], Peng Xie[3], and Hongbo Jiang[4]

[1] Hubei Key Laboratory of Transportation Internet of Things, Wuhan University of Technology,
Wuhan 430072, Hubei, China
zhangrui@whut.edu.cn
[2] Hubei Key Laboratory of Inland Shipping Technology, Wuhan University of Technology,
Wuhan 430072, Hubei, China
[3] School of Computer Science and Technology, Wuhan University of Technology,
Wuhan 430072, Hubei, China
linuofeirz@126.com, yinshu@whut.edu.cn, xiepeng0715@gmail.com
[4] School of Electronic Information and Communications,
Huazhong University of Science and Technology, Wuhan 430074, Hubei, China
hongbojiang2004@gmail.com

Abstract. Traffic flow often contains massive amounts of information that is related to location and shows some regularity. And the traffic flow analysis based on trajectory data has become one of the most popular research topics in recent years. With the wide application of deep learning and for its higher accuracy than other approaches, methods such as convolution neural network and deep residual network have been introduced in traffic flow research and achieve good results. However, these methods usually require the training of a large number of parameters, which leads to some problems. For example, frequent manual adjustment is needed, and some parameters cannot be dynamically adjusted with the training process. We find that learning rate plays a crucial role in all parameters, which has important influence on the training speed of the residual network. In other words, the soundness of traffic flow predication results depends on the learning rate. Hence, we propose G4 algorithm to automatically determine the learning rate. It can be adjusted automatically in the process of trajectory data mining, and therefore solve the traffic flow prediction problem. Experiments on real data sets show that our method is effective and superior over some traditional optimizing methods of traffic flow analysis.

Keywords: Automatic prediction · Traffic flow · Trajectory
Deep residual network · Fourier series

1 Introduction

Trajectory data contains large amounts of information, has close relations with geographic location or point of interest (POI), and can reflect general regularity. Therefore, analyzing traffic flow based on trajectory data has become a hot research direction in recent years. For example, Masahiro et al. found that the frequency of car travel will

© Springer Nature Singapore Pte Ltd. 2018
L. Zhu and S. Zhong (Eds.): MSN 2017, CCIS 747, pp. 328–337, 2018.
https://doi.org/10.1007/978-981-10-8890-2_24

not change with the season through the analysis of the GPS data of Hakodate city, while the frequency of the cycling and hiking is severely affected by the change of season [1]. Through the analysis of MIT trajectory data set of vehicles and pedestrians, Dheeraj et al. successfully found out the representatively abnormal phenomena [2]. At the same time, some deep learning methods are introduced in the field of trajectory data mining and achieve high accuracy and small error. For example, for the same topic of traffic flow and pedestrian flow analysis in the center of the city, Stefan et al. managed to use the convolutional neural network to largely accelerated the speed of training [3]. Xiao et al. even proposed the concept of ensemble learning to better study hybrid transportation modes [4].

However, despite their good performance in the field of trajectory data mining, existing deep learning methods still face some problems, especially a large number of parameters and hyper parameters relying heavily on manual adjustment. Zheng et al. used three convolution neural networks to analyze the GPS data in Beijing, predicted the traffic and pedestrian flow at a certain spot, and achieved good results, but there were over a dozen parameters relying on manual adjustment such as smoothness, periodicity and trend which had a direct bearing on the final results [5]. In addition, certain parameters may need to change with the learning process. Song et al. proposed the model of DeepMob to analyze GPS data to help humans avoid natural disasters [6]. According to our research, whether parameters such as learning rate change with the process will greatly influence traffic flow analysis results, in this case, i.e., will affect the final outcome of disaster analysis. The reason is that the prediction of any flow is indispensable to the learning of the existing data, and the learning rate affects the learning speed, thus affecting the final effect.

To solve these problems, our goal is to develop methods that allow the parameters of some deep learning methods to adapt to the learning process automatically and reduce human intervention. To achieve this goal, we consider the following aspects. First, the parameters we study should be applicable to many different methods, rather than individual, specific parameters in certain methods so that a greater variety of traffic flows can be analyzed. Second, our method should be able to adjust parameters spontaneously, thus reducing human intervention and improving analysis performance. Third, our method should be superior to some un-optimized methods and achieve the task without compromising the effect. Therefore, we propose G4 (Gradient FOURier series) algorithm to automatically determine the learning rate so that it can be adjusted automatically in the process of trajectory data mining and solve traffic flow prediction problems. We were first inspired by the Fourier series of signal processing, then built connections between learning rate adjustment and some parameters in the model through Fourier series, and applied it in the deep residual network, finally to address practical problems such as traffic flow. Our main contributions are as follows:

- We proposed G4 algorithm to automatically determine the learning rate of a series of deep learning methods.
- We integrated the algorithm into the deep residual network model, and reduced human intervention in the process of trajectory data analysis.
- According to experiments on real data sets, our method outperforms some traditional analysis methods.

The respect of this paper is organized as follows. Section 2 describes the related work. The third section gives the definition of problem and its mathematical description. The fourth section presents the framework and detailed implementation of the method. Section 5 evaluates our method through experiments. Section 6 concludes the paper.

2 Related Work

In this section, we explain some other work related to our research, including a brief introduction to Fourier series and some improvements achieved by other scholars in traffic flow analysis.

2.1 Fourier Series

In electronic technology, Fourier series is used for signal transformation, so that it can be restored with some simple signals. The single entry form of the Fourier series is:

$$f(x) = c_n e^{i\frac{n\pi x}{l}} \tag{1}$$

where c_n, x, l, i represent coefficient, time (signal changes over time), half period, and imaginary unit, respectively. Note that if a certain time and a certain semi-cycle are given, the size of a signal can be determined. In practice, signals produced by electronic devices are often very complicated and cannot be described with simple mathematical laws. The Fourier series describes a way that can transform any form of signal into a summary of several simple periodic functions.

2.2 Other Work

Many scholars have analyzed traffic flow by improving the learning rate. For example, Sun et al. learnt human walking trajectories using RMSProp, and then predicted human trajectory [7]. Gang et al. even made clear that the deep learning model has greatly improved the analysis of group movement behaviors with the use of RMSProp. However, although methods such as RMSProp and Adam have performed very well, yet they require manual adjustment of the decay rate. When using Adam, the user must adjust two different decay rates. These parameters must be configured manually. In other words, this type of methods actually replaces the adjustment of learning rate with the adjustment other parameters, and has not solved the problem fundamentally. Even the number of parameters that need to be adjusted may increase rather than decrease. On the other hand, although some approaches used by researchers do not increase the number of parameters requiring manual adjustment, these methods often achieve general improvements for learning rate, rather than for the unique model or approach for the analysis of traffic flow. In other words, these methods may fail to take into account the characteristics of trajectory itself. For example, Tong et al. used Adagrad to optimize the simple linear model, and then directly realized the prediction of taxi route [8]. However, this optimization ignored some features of trajectory. For example, will the number of taxis on this route between adjacent intervals (for example, half an hour or an hour) affect the number of current intervals? Could there be a time interval yesterday affect the same interval today? None of these questions can be answered by such an optimization. Therefore, our approach should strive to avoid these problems.

3   Proposed Method

In this section, we give relevant definitions and mathematical descriptions of our methods, and then explain some of the concepts applied to traffic flow analysis.

3.1   Gradient Fourier Series

Considering the time of the signal, as each neutral unit can exist independently, and almost all properties of the unit in the learning process keep changing, we set up a parameter as time in Fourier transformation. For a single unit, the gradient of its weight plays a key role in its learning process, and it changes with the number of iterations, which is similar to the structure of time. Therefore, we have the following definitions:

Definition 1 (Gradient Instant). The gradient of the weight which connecting two neural units at any instant is called a gradient instant.

Definition 2 (Gradient Time). For each individual neural unit, the summary of the gradient of the weight connecting it to any other unit is called gradient time. Each gradient time consists of multiple gradient instants.

Considering the half period. The half period describes the time degree of harmonic transformation. In other words, this parameter determines the duration of the change. It is obvious that the number of iterations in the trajectory data mining determines the length of learning time. (We normally do not consider the scenario where the iteration is terminated when the loss function is lower than the threshold). Therefore, we have the following definition:

Definition 3 (Period). The number of iterations is the period of the current harmonic transformation.

Considering the coefficient. As the initial learning rate never changes, and the change only happens in the process of learning, so the initial learning rate can be seen as a coefficient which remains the same despite the change of gradient instant and gradient time. We have the following definition:

Definition 4 (Coefficient). Initial learning rate is the coefficient.

Assume that the initial learning rate, the weight matrix, the loss function and the current iteration are α, w, $E(w)$, t respectively. According to the definition, gradient instant is $\partial E(w)$, therefore gradient time is $\sum_{i=1}^{t} \partial E(w)$, and period is t. In addition, because i is an imaginary unit, in trajectory data mining we convert it back to the real unit. Therefore, we get the equation of harmonic transformation of learning rate:

$$\alpha: = \alpha e^{\sqrt{\dfrac{\sum\limits_{i=1}^{t} \partial E(w)}{t}}} \tag{2}$$

where α, $\sum_{i=1}^{t} \partial E(w)$, t are c_n, x and l, respectively. The reason of introducing the square is to make the transformation smoother. The harmonic transformation of learning rate is applied to the learning process of the deep residual network to optimize learning rate.

3.2 Trajectory Deep Residual Networks

Considering other features of traffic flow, we need to handle some other settings. Referring to the settings used by Zheng et al. on their research of traffic flow [5], we have following definitions.

Definition 5 (Interval). Trajectory data may undergo a very long time. The basic unit we study is called an interval. Usually, the interval can be one hour, half an hour, etc.

Definition 6 (Closeness). If the adjacent n intervals ($n \geq 1$, similarly hereinafter) have an effect on the current interval of the trajectory, then this effect is called closeness.

Definition 7 (Cycle). If the same intervals in the adjacent n days have an effect on the current interval, then the effect is called cycle.

Definition 8 (Trend). If the same intervals in the same week m, ($m = Mon., Tue., \dots, Sun.$) among the adjacent n weeks have an effect on the current interval, then the effect is called trend.

With these characteristics, we can better analyze trajectory data by catering to trajectory patterns.

4 Harmonic Transformation

The framework of our method is shown in Fig. 1. Firstly, we initialize the learning rate which can be set manually or randomly. Randomly generate the weight matrix of the deep residual network (DRN). Then, set the characteristics associated with traffic flow data. After the initialization is completed, the flow data is taken into the DRN, and the learning rate is adjusted dynamically during the training process. Then, train the flow data and their residual according the learning rate, and feed return the learning results back to the DRN for iterative training. When the training is complete, the test set is brought into the network for further adjustment. Finally, the results are compared against other methods. We emphasize that we analyze traffic flow model for the DRN, which combines the weights during activation function of neural units with flow itself to learn flow rules and separate from other network methods.

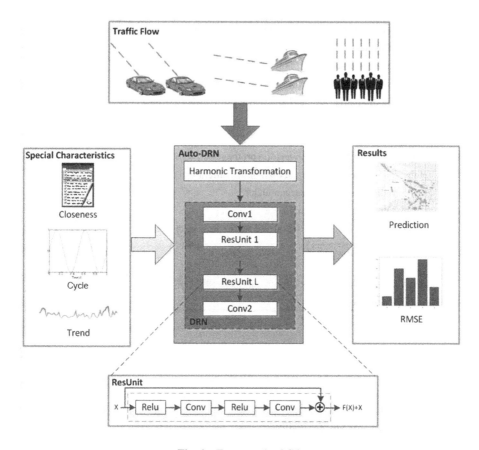

Fig. 1. Framework of G4.

The algorithm is show in Algorithm 1. The calculation of the time complexity of the algorithm is very simple. Assume through m iterations end training, through n iterations end testing. Because of harmonic transformation occurred and only occurred once in each iteration, in terms of G4 algorithm, the time complexity must be $O(m + n)$. Note here that the time complexity we're talking about is only for our algorithms, not include the time complexity for the structures of convolutional neural network and deep residual network respectively.

Algorithm 1 (G4: automatically adjust the learning rate and analyze the traffic flow)

Input: Traffic flow data, DRN

Output: Automatic learned DRN model

(01) initialize learning rate;

(02) initialize weight matrix, set the characteristics of **traffic flow data**;

(03) $t = 1$;

(04) **while** $t < iterations$ or $E(w) > 0$:

(05)   calculate the flow and its MSE and import them into the **DRN**;

(06)   get the gradient corresponding to each of the current weights;

(07)   get the gradient time through accumulator;

(08)   perform harmonic transformation, see equation (2);

(09)   feedback to DRN based on residual and **traffic flow data** itself;

(10) $t++$;

(11) **end while**

(12) import the test set into **DRN** and follow the steps (04)-(10);

(13) **return DRN model**;

---

5   Experiments

In this section, we conduct some experiments based on real data sets to evaluate our method. First, we describe the data sets, then explain the parameters settings of some models, and finally present the results.

5.1   Datasets

We use AIS data to validate our approach. The AIS data records the location information and other information of the ship over time. We select the AIS data recorded from March 2, 2015 to June 30, 2015 in Zhoushan port, China. Since we are forecasting regional activities or traffic flow of ships, we adopt the following methods to carry out the experiment. We divide the research area into 16*8 grids and use *interval* as the basic unit to count the number of signals emitted by ships in each region as the basis for predicting traffic flow. The schematic diagram is shown in Fig. 2. For a specific grid, the existence of ship signal in a grid in an *interval* indicates that the ship is located in this grid in that interval. If in the next *interval* this ship signal is not in the grid, but in an adjacent grid, it means that the ship has moved to the next grid from the current grid, so that the AIS trajectory data can be converted to the grid's data format, which can be imported to the DRN.

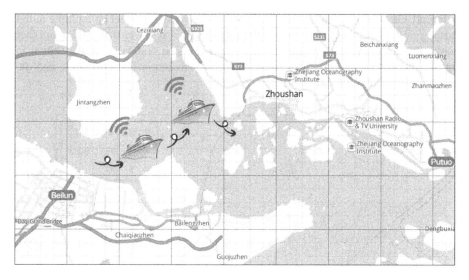

Fig. 2. Trajectory data can be transformed into the grid's data format, which can be imported to the DRN.

5.2 Parameters Settings

Next, we describe some parameter settings. The number of iterations for the validation set and the test set are set to 50 and 100, respectively. The number of iterations for the validation set can be set to be smaller, because the validation set comes from the training set. Therefore, its training speed will be faster than the test set which is not from the training set. *Interval* is set to half an hour, i.e. 48 *intervals* a day. Closeness is set to 3, that is, considering a total of three *intervals* from (*interval − 3*) to (*interval − 1*) have an impact on the current *interval*. Both cycle and trend are set to 1, which means that the same *interval* yesterday and the same *interval* last week have an impact on the current *interval*. The residual units are set to 2, that is, two DRNs analyze the flow simultaneously. Special emphasis, there are two identical matrices of flow, but the data of them are different, meaning that one of them saves how much flow for each grid in each interval more than the former interval, and vice versa.

5.3 Results

For the ease of comparison, we use the traditional stochastic gradient descent (SGD) and our methods to predict the traffic flow. Figure 3 demonstrates a comparative experiment, where the initial learning rate of best-SGD is set to the best, i.e. the learning rate has the best performance after we choose from manual debugging, and the initial learning rate of rand-SGD method and our method are randomly set. The x-coordinate shows the number of iterations, and the y-coordinate represents the loss function, which is set to mean squared error (MSE). It can be seen that even for an appropriate learning rate that has been fixed for a long time, our method still outperforms best-SGD from the beginning to the end. On the other hand, in terms of prediction accuracy, we set up multiple initial learning rates to start together, but all the RMSE of G4 is lower than SGD,. In other words, the accuracy of flow prediction is higher. Some comparisons are shown in Fig. 4. The horizontal coordinate represents different initial learning rates, and the vertical coordinate represents RMSE.

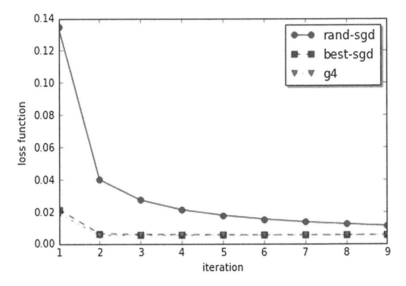

Fig. 3. The loss function changes with the iterations.

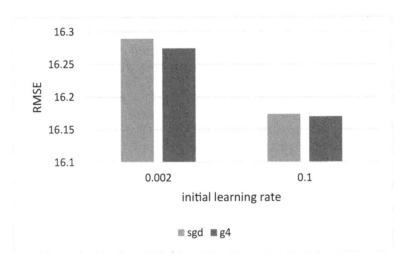

Fig. 4. The loss function changes with the iterations.

6   Conclusions

In this paper, G4 algorithm is proposed to automatically determine the learning rate and predict the traffic flow. Experiments on real data sets show that our algorithm reduces the tedious manual adjustment of parameters, and outperforms some traditional methods. Even the classic method with the optimal parameter settings is still slower than our approach in training. Future work will also include automation research and applications in the field of trajectory data for other parameters of DRN or other deep learning methods.

References

1. Araki, M., Kanamori, R., Gong, L., Morikawa, T.: Impacts of seasonal factors on travel behavior: basic analysis of GPS trajectory data for 8 months. In: Sawatani, Y., Spohrer, J., Kwan, S., Takenaka, T. (eds.) Serviceology for Smart Service System, pp. 377–384. Springer, Tokyo (2017). https://doi.org/10.1007/978-4-431-56074-6_41
2. Kumar, D., et al.: A visual-numeric approach to clustering and anomaly detection for trajectory data. Vis. Comput. **33**(3), 265–281 (2017)
3. Hoermann, S., Bach, M., Dietmayer, K.: Dynamic Occupancy Grid Prediction for Urban Autonomous Driving: A Deep Learning Approach with Fully Automatic Labeling. arXiv preprint arXiv:1705.08781 (2017)
4. Xiao, Z., et al.: Identifying different transportation modes from trajectory data using tree-based ensemble classifiers. ISPRS Int. J. Geo-Inf. **6**(2), 57 (2017)
5. Zhang, J., Zheng, Y., Qi, D.: Deep spatio-temporal residual networks for citywide crowd flows prediction. In: AAAI (2017)
6. Song, X., et al.: DeepMob: learning deep knowledge of human emergency behavior and mobility from big and heterogeneous data. ACM Trans. Inf. Syst. (TOIS) **35**(4), 41 (2017)
7. Sun, L., et al.: 3DOF Pedestrian Trajectory Prediction Learned from Long-Term Autonomous Mobile Robot Deployment Data. arXiv preprint arXiv:1710.00126 (2017)
8. Tong, Y., et al.: The simpler the better: a unified approach to predicting original taxi demands based on large-scale online platforms. In: Proceedings of the 23rd ACM SIGKDD International Conference on Knowledge Discovery and Data Mining. ACM (2017)

Trust Mechanism Based AODV Routing Protocol for Forward Node Authentication in Mobile Ad Hoc Network

Muhammad Sohail[1(✉)] ⓘ, Liangmin Wang[1], and Bushra Yamin[2]

[1] School of Computer Science and Communicatoin Engineering,
Jiangsu University, Zhenjiang 212013, People's Republic of China
engrsohailaslam@yahoo.com, Wanglm@ujs.edu.cn
[2] School of Library and Archive management, Jiangsu University, Zhenjiang 212013,
People's Republic of China
bushrasohail@yahoo.com

Abstract. Ad hoc networks due to its open and dynamic nature are susceptible to a variety of security threats. Recently trust management emerged as the promising candidate to provide less computational and secure solutions. This paper based on novel idea i.e. trust mechanism based AODV (Ad hoc On-demand Distance Vector) routing protocol in the network layer of MANET to enhance network security. In our proposed scheme trust among nodes is represented by opinions, which is an item derived from three Valued subjective logic (3VSL). The opinions are dynamic, therefore judged, combined and updated frequently. In 3VSL the theoretical capabilities are based on Dirichlet distribution by considering prior and posterior uncertainty of the said event. Meanwhile, using advised and personal trust, a node can make relative judgment for forward node authenticity. The simulated results validate the accuracy of our proposed scheme.

Keywords: AODV · Trust management
Three valued subjective logic · MANET

Ad hoc network is a special kind of communication, where users rely on each other to acquire services. This open and dynamic nature makes ad hoc networks unique and challenging. These networks impose many security threats due to decentralized nature. Adversaries in MANET can cause huge damage, therefore requires urgent solution. Many security solutions in the literature have been proposed like cryptographic and public key infrastructure [1]. These techniques are complex and increase computation overhead. In contrast the solution with trust, trust management come up as lightweight solutions to enhance ad hoc network security [2]. The concept of putting trust in the field of networks has taken from the social world which defines it "The expected behavior of an object according to the will of a trustee in particular context" [3].

© Springer Nature Singapore Pte Ltd. 2018
L. Zhu and S. Zhong (Eds.): MSN 2017, CCIS 747, pp. 338–349, 2018.
https://doi.org/10.1007/978-981-10-8890-2_25

In ad hoc networks, number of trust management techniques are proposed, but they rarely count ignorance (uncertainty) management in between these distributed networks. This ignorance before and during nodes interaction needs careful handling through proper mechanism. One solution is the probabilistic-based subjective logic proposed by Josang in [4], but the pioneer subjective logic is only able to define prior uncertainty while ignoring uncertainty generated as result of trust propagation. After that Liu et al. [5] came up with a 3VSL idea ·that defines both prior and posterior uncertainty precisely.

In this article, we apply the trust mechanism idea into the security solutions of MANET to authenticate forward node selection. Our trust model is derived and modified from 3VSL, which qualitatively defines the representation, calculation, and combination of trust. Trust models have found many security applications in social, peer-to-peer and some other distributed networks [6,7]. Some research work is conducted to apply trust models into the security solutions of MANET [8]. However, we still need concrete and application design for security solutions of MANET. The contribution of this paper can be summarized as

- A trusted AODV routing is proposed using 3VSL as trust model to the network layer of MANET as efficient multi-hop trust assessment technique. This trust model is capable of assessing trust between multi path, arbitrary and bridge topologies.
- In our scheme, nodes perform trusted routing behavior mainly according to the trust relationship between them, a node that will behave malicious eventually denied from the network.
- System performance is improved by means of trusted AODV that avoid verifying and requesting certificate exchange at each step.
- Forward Node is authenticated by using trusted AODV, which is quite capable of handling malicious intentions like, Gray and Black hole attacks.
- The proposed trust mechanism is also able to handle topology based vehicular ad hoc network under some specific network parameters.

The rest of the paper sectioned as, In Sect. 1, three valued subjective logic and AODV routing are briefly introduced. In Sect. 2, we briefly recall the network model and assumptions also with our proposed trust mechanism. In Sect. 3, 3VSL, defined as a kind of trust model, which operates on subjective beliefs about the world. In Sect. 4, trusted routing operation is revealed in detail. Experimental setup with some important evaluation parameter is discussed in Sect. 5. Finally, we draw conclusions in Sect. 6.

1   Background

1.1   Three Valued Subjective Logic 3VSL

3VSL is a kind of algebraic trust model proposed by Liu [9]. It is a logic, which operates on subjective beliefs about the world, and uses the term opinion to denote the representation of a subjective belief". The reason behind choosing

3VSL is that it assess the credibility of the user by adapting the multivalued Dirichlet distribution function to deal with the prior and posterior uncertainty of an event. In MANET, nodes may experience random topologies with unknown entities time being. A node may be uncertain about another node's trustworthiness because it does not collect enough evidence. This uncertainty is a common phenomenon in a distributed environment and therefore, needs careful treatment. It need trust model to represent such uncertainty accordingly. Traditional probability models cannot express these uncertainties properly. In contrast, an opinion in 3VSL comprised of belief, disbelief, prior and posterior uncertainties, which gracefully meets our demands. For more details about 3VSL please refer Sect. 3.

1.2   Ad Hoc On-Demand Distance Vector (AODV) Routing

AODV is widely used reactive routing protocol for ad hoc networks as paths are made on fly. In AODV paths are made on demand and remain active until two users require each other services.

When a source node S broadcast RREQ packet in search of destination node each recipient of the RREQ packet looks up in its routing table. If receiving node doesn't contain any information about the destination. It will create a reverse path towards RREQ packet originator and rebroadcast the routing request. Intermediary node receiving this RREQ will generate a RREP message either if it has fresh route request information to satisfy or itself a destination. Then this intermediary or destination node will generate a RREP packet and will forward it to the next hop towards RREQ generating intermediary node, as indicated by source node routing entry table. When a node receives RREP packet it update some fields in the routing table of RREP packet, and then forward it to the originator (source node). After that a bidirectional path is setup between source and required destination node and it is maintained as long they required each other services [10].

Route maintenance is performed by either sending hello messages which acknowledge about the positive connectivity about the nodes and sender can listen these hello messages. Route maintenance can also be achieved using packet acknowledge in which nodes are in promiscuous mode and can overhear the packet transmission and easily detect malicious attacks [11].

1.3   Dirichlet Distribution

A Dirichlet distribution is based on initial belief of an unknown event according to prior distribution. It provides a solid mathematical foundation for measuring the uncertainty of recommendation based on historical data. Compared with Beta distribution, which is more appropriate in a binary satisfaction level [12]. Dirichlet distribution is more appropriate for multivalued satisfaction levels. In our case, the evaluation trustworthiness of node is described by continuous trust values. Therefore, we will use Dirichlet distribution [13] to estimate opinion space of user vehicle recommended in the future and then build our trust model accordingly.

The Dirichlet distribution is a continuous sequence of observation having multiple outcomes with k positive real parameters $\alpha(x_i), i = 1....k$, in the form of compact vector notation $\boldsymbol{p} = p(x_i|1 \leq i \leq k)$ denotes the k-component random probability variable and a vector $\boldsymbol{\alpha} = (\alpha_i|1 \leq i \leq k)$, denotes random observation variable of k components such that $[\alpha(x_i)]_i^k$. The general form of Dirichlet distribution is as

$$f(\boldsymbol{p} \mid \boldsymbol{\alpha}) = \frac{\Gamma\left(\sum_{i=1}^k \alpha(x_i)\right)}{\prod_{i=1}^k \Gamma\alpha(x_i)} \prod_{i=1}^k p(x_i)^{\alpha(x_i)-1}$$

In 3VSL as evidences in opinion space have three factors i.e. trust, distrust and neutral so, modifying three valued evidence space to Dirichlet distribution as

$$f(P_b, P_d, P_n \mid \alpha, \beta, \gamma) = \frac{\Gamma(\alpha + \beta + \gamma)}{\Gamma_{(\alpha)} + \Gamma_{(\beta)} + \Gamma_{(\gamma)}} . P_b^{\alpha-1} . P_d^{\beta-1} . P_n^{\gamma-1} \tag{1}$$

Where (α, β, γ) is the controlling vector and $P(b, d, n)$ shows probability of belief, disbelief, and neutral respectively. Let r, s and o denote observed number of evidences that a node is trustworthy, untrustworthy or neutral. According to Dirichlet distribution we have $(\alpha = r + 1, \beta = s + 1, \gamma = o + 1)$.

Let us assume that neighboring node had one prior evidence of each event (b, d, n). The assumption is reasonable because the Dirichlet distribution still works even when no event is observed, i.e. $(\alpha = 1, \beta = 1, \gamma = 1)$ and probability of each event will be $1/3$, these three events are prior uncertainties. The opinion space in 3VSL can be expressed as following after having Dirichlet distribution

$$b_X^A = \frac{r}{r+s+o+3}, \quad d_X^A = \frac{s}{r+s+o+3}$$
$$n_X^A = \frac{o}{r+s+o+3}, \quad e_X^A = \frac{3}{r+s+o+3} \tag{2}$$

Here, prior evidences is set to 3, its ratio to the number of observed event is e_X^A. it is worth noting that uncertainty u defined in subject logic is actually the prior evidence in 3VSL. Since in 3VSL, the expected probability of each event can be determined by using the following equation.

2   Overview of Trusted AODV

2.1   Network Model and Assumptions

Here, we made some assumptions for specific roles of entities, further we argue that we are mainly focused on security solution to the routing behavior at the network layer. Also, we do not concern with the security problem impose due to the instability of physical or data link layer.

- Each user in the network layer can access to all its neighbor and broadcast some essential trusted information.
- Every user possess unique ID like physical network interface address, that can be distinguished from others.
- We also suppose that system is equipped with some monitoring mechanism in either network or application layer for node observation.
- Another secure routing protocol based on some cryptographic or public key infrastructure is recommended to take effect before users in TAODV establish the trust relationship with each other.
- In the network layer a new node model is designed based on our trust mechanism by adding some trust fields to the node routing table.

2.2 Trusted Mechanism

Trust mechanism include three modules first is basic AODV routing protocol. Second module is trust model i.e. this stage consider general behavior and forward node authentication using three valued subjective logic. Finally, the third module produce trust mechanism based AODV routing. The general procedure for establishing trust relationships among nodes and for performing routing discovery is described as follows.

Let us consider the beginning stage when new nodes initiates communication with the network but they are uncertain about each other. Let node A has opinion about node B which is $(0,0,0,1)$ that is fully uncertain about B's trustworthiness. At the start of the network assigning high trust value to new joining nodes can be harmful, especially with black hole and gray hole attacks. After this initial activity, having some successful or failed communication node A can change its opinion about node B's behavior using trust update with the time $[0,t]$. After establishing bidirectional communication paths nodes can use our trusted routing protocol for secure operation. As trust is asymmetric, mobile nodes uses second hand observation given by its neighbors, and finally combines them into a single trust value. Notice that a node can join the existing MANET through many ways and several security algorithms can be used to run this operation. In this frame work trust establishment and the route discovery are all treated by node's cooperation without any third or central party.

3 Trust Model

3.1 Trust Representation

The major difference in 3VSL is the use of neutral element in the opinion space, which makes difference from the prior probability value. So opinion space in 3VSL is

$$\begin{cases} \omega_B^A = \left(b_B^A, d_B^A, n_B^A, e_B^A\right) \mid a_B^A \\ b_B^A + d_B^A + n_B^A + e_B^A \implies \left(b_j^i + d_j^i + n_j^i + e_j^i\right) \mid a_j^i = 1 \end{cases} \tag{3}$$

Where $b_B^A, d_B^A, n_B^A, e_B^A$ represents belief, disbelief, posterior and prior uncertainty values. The base rate a_B^A, which is minimal probability value before start of the operation between A and B.

Mapping. The mapping from evidence to opinion space is done through Dirichlet distribution in 3VSL. Let r, s and o denotes observed number of evidences that a node is trustworthy, untrustworthy or neutral. The four components in 3VSL opinion vector can be express as following after having Dirichlet distribution evidence spaces

$$
b_X^A = \frac{r}{r+s+o+3}
$$
$$
d_X^A = \frac{s}{r+s+o+3}
$$
$$
n_X^A = \frac{o}{r+s+o+3}
$$
$$
e_X^A = \frac{3}{r+s+o+3}
$$

(4)

3.2 Trust Combination

In our trust mechanism, a node will collect all its neighbors opinions about targeted node and combine them together using consensus and discounting operations.

Discounting Combination. The purpose of discounting combination is to judge multi-hop users within a MANET. We first introduce how to discount one opinion from another, and then generalize it to support multiple opinions. Considering a simple case where user A trusts B who trusts C, the discounting operation allows A to discount B's opinion over C to obtain her own opinion on C. Suppose A and B are two users where $w_B^A = (b_1, d_1, n_1, e_1)$ is A's opinion on user B trustworthiness. Let C is another user where $w_C^B = (b_2, d_2, n_2, e_2)$ is B's opinion about user C trustworthiness. Then the discounting operation $\triangle(w_B^A, w_B^A)$ is carried out as follows:

$$
\triangle\left(w_B^A, w_C^B\right) = \begin{cases} b_{12} = b_1 b_2 \\ d_{12} = b_1 d_2 \\ n_{12} = 1 - b_1 - d_2 - e_2 \\ e_{12} = e_2 \end{cases}
$$

(5)

$\triangle(w_B^A, w_C^B)$ is A's opinion on C after B's advice to A, also called A's second hand observation about C.

Consensus Combination. In a parallel topology opinions from parallel paths should be combined or fused in a fair and equal way so that the resulting opinion reflects all opinions. if we have $w_C^A = (b_1, d_1, n_1, e_1)$ and $w_C^B = (b_2, d_2, n_2, e_2)$ are

DestinationIP	DestinationSeq	· ·	HopCount	...	Lifetime	Positive Events	Negative Events	Opinion

Fig. 1. Extended routing table for Trusted AODV

two opinion in parallel paths between two users then combining operation can be expressed by using below equation

$$\Theta(\omega_C^A, \omega_C^B) = \begin{cases} b_{12} = \dfrac{e_2 b_1 + e_1 b_2}{e_1 + e_2 - e_1 e_2} \\ d_{12} = \dfrac{e_2 d_1 + e_1 d_2}{e_1 + e_2 - e_1 e_2} \\ n_{12} = \dfrac{e_2 n_1 + e_1 n_2}{e_1 + e_2 - e_1 e_2} \\ e_{12} = \dfrac{e_1 e_2}{e_1 + e_2 - e_1 e_2} \end{cases} \tag{6}$$

$\Theta(\omega_C^A, \omega_C^B)$ shows A's and B's first observation on node C.

4   Trusted Routing Operation in AODV

4.1   Node Model

In our trust model, we have added trust field to the AODV routing table i.e. positive and negative events which take place between the neighboring nodes and trust repository counter is updated with increase of trust value and vice versa as can be seen in Fig. 1.

4.2   Trust Judging Rules

For trust judgment, we have set the threshold $= 0.5$. This threshold value can be changed depending upon one's system design and security level.

– If a node A wants to communicate with node B and in ω_B^A if believe of A in B is $>= 0.5$ then A will trust B and start to route packet to node B
– If disbelieve opinion of A in node B i.e > 0.5 A will not trust node B and will not route packet and ask for signature verification or try to find alternate route for communication.
– If uncertainty of node A in node B is > 0.5 A will ask for digital signature for node B and waits for the verifying. If A successfully verifies B's signature then A will start communication with B.

4.3   Trust Updating Rule

When we talk about trust assessment then information update is very important because we need fresh information about a particular node. We keep updating our repository due to dynamic nature of mobile ad hoc networks.

– If node A had successful communication with node B then its update the trust value by incrementing trust in that node by successful communication. We mean normal packet forward or RREP with in the time $[0, t]$.
– If node A had failed communication with node B by number of means then it degrades trust values by decrement the update counter.
– Every time field of successful or failed event is changed, opinion space values are recalculated using Eq. (4).
– If node $B's$ routing entry is deleted from node $A's$ routing table due to expiry, then new opinion will be $\omega_B^A = (0, 0, 0, 1)$.

4.4   Trusted Information Exchange

Our trust mechanism includes three kinds of recommendation messages, which are TREQ (Trusted Route Request), TREP (Trusted Route Reply), TWARN (Trusted Route Warning). These messages help us to reduce extra routing head by attaching the trust value with the RREQ and RREP.

4.5   Node Authentication

At the start of the network usually, nodes are uncertain about each other behavior. This is called the beginning stage and the opinion space at this stage between user A and B is $\omega_B^A = (0, 0, 0, 1)$. With the opinions being updated with the time $[0, t]$, the third component uncertainty of opinion space will be decreased and the trust relationships among nodes are formed. Nodes will thus employ the combination of different opinions to authenticate one another. The combination method is derived from the 3VSL introduced in Sect. 3.

   The general procedure when performing trusted routing discovery, which can be seen in Fig. 2. The route path from the source node S to the target node T is totally uncovered. Node N_2 is the most important intermediate node during the establishment of a route path from S to T. Further to know the behaviors of N_2, we assumed that intermediate nodes perform some initial authentication and that is true. After that the node is judged using Algorithm 1. The minimum threshold for node authentication is set to be 0.5, which has flexibility depending one's system design and security level.

4.6   Trusted Route Maintenance

Route maintenance is analogous to trusted route discovery. Nodes use trust information exchange rule to evaluate node trustworthiness and forward node authentication. So here extra detailed about route maintenance algorithm is not mentioned.

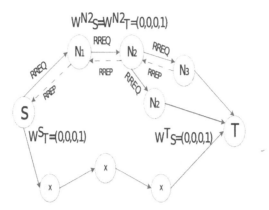

Fig. 2. An example of Trusted routing discovery.

5 Numerical Analysis

For simulation, we have used NS-2.35 developed by monarch research group (https://www.isi.edu/nsnam/ns/). NS-2 is IP based discrete event simulator and has good support for simulating complete wireless network protocol. Data rate is set to 2 Mb/sec having 250 m transmission range. The MAC layer is implemented according to IEEE 802.11 Distributed Coordination Function (DCF). The basic parameters of our simulation are as we considered 20 nodes movement in a 1000 m * 1000 m field according to random way point model with a uniformly distributed velocity starting from 0 and 20 m/s. Each of the node initially moves to a randomly chosen location. After reaching the target node, the node will stop for a pause time then move to next destination. The traffic source sends 4 data packets of 512 bytes per second using CBR (Constant Bit-Rate). The simulation runs maximum for 200 s.

Algorithm 1. Node's authentication

Require: Exchange opinions about N_2 with its neighbors N_1 using the trusted information exchange rule.

Ensure: /* $\omega_{N_1}^{N_2} \neq U$ */

    if $u_{N_1}^{N_2} \geq 0.5$ **then**

      request and verify digital certificate

    else if $d_{N_1}^{N_2} \geq 0.5$ **then**

      distrust N_1 for expiry time

    else if $b_{N_1}^{N_2} \geq 0.5$ **then**

      trust N_1 and forward RREQ/RREP

    else

      /* the confidence about trustworthiness is decreased*/ request and verify N_1 certificates, by default

    end if

5.1   Forward Node Authentication

The minimum threshold for forward node authentication is set to be 0.5. From Fig. 3, we can see that nodes $(10, 8, 4, 3, 2, 14, 17, 19)$ are authenticated and selected for communication. Also in Fig. 3, node 10 is the sender and node 19 is receiver, so a benevolent path from source to destination is made and other nodes are ignored. The calculated value of final trust score of these selected nodes can be seen in Appendix (Figs. 4 and 5).

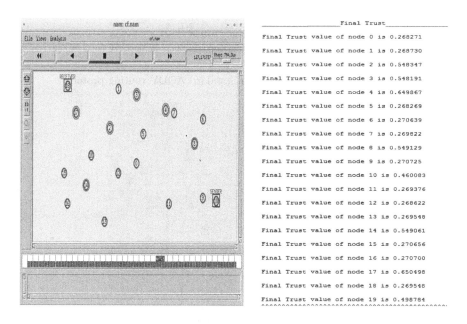

Fig. 3. Nodes having trust value > 0.5 are selected for communication.

5.2   Throughput

The first performance evaluated in term of packet throughput. This value is calculated by dividing the overall number of messages received at destination node by the total messages sent from source nodes according to the following equation:

$$Throughput = \frac{\sum Total\,packets\,received}{\sum Total\,packets\,sent}$$

5.3   Delay

This is one of the important and critical parameters that measured the overall system performance. It can be defined as the packets per unit time interval

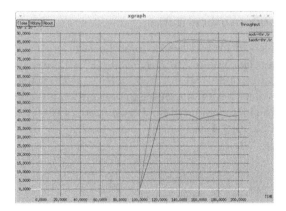

Fig. 4. Throughput of Trusted vs Standard AODV routing protocol.

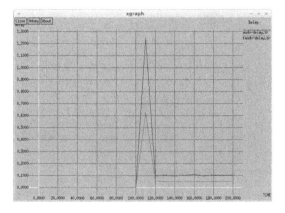

Fig. 5. Delay between Trusted vs Standard AODV routing protocol.

length. On the other hand, delay represents the time period that needs to route a packet from the source to the desired destination which depends on PDR value in the system and can be calculated as the following equation

$$Delay = \frac{Number\,of\,sending\,bits\,in\,the\,packet}{Throughput}$$

6   Conclusions

This paper highlight the trust mechanism based AODV using three valued subjective logic into the security solution of MANET. Trust among nodes can be represented, combined and calculated using an item opinion. In our proposed routing protocol nodes can cooperate with each other to judge other nodes trustworthiness. They can also highlight posterior uncertainty generated during propagation and capable to accurately assess trust even in random and arbitrary topologies. In our scheme nodes perform trusted routing behavior according to the trust relationship among them. In addition, the extra routing overhead is reduced due to the exchange of trust recommendation messages, without asking certificate verification all the time. In summary, our trust mechanism based AODV routing protocol is more lightweight and flexible than other cryptographic and authentication designs.

References

1. Jiang, S., Zhu, X., Wang, L.: An efcient anonymous batch authentication scheme based on HMAC for vanets. IEEE Trans. Intell. Transp. Syst. **17**(8), 2193–2204 (2016)
2. Movahedi, Z., Hosseini, Z., Bayan, F., Pujolle, G.: Trust-distortion resistant trust management frameworks on mobile ad hoc networks: a survey. IEEE Commun. Surv. Tutorials **18**(2), 1287–1309 (2016)
3. Cook, K.S.: Trust in Society. Russell Sage Foundation Series on Trust, vol. 2, February 2003
4. Josang, A.: A logic for uncertain probabilities. Int. J. Uncertain. Fuzziness Knowl. Based Syst. **09**(03), 279–311 (2001)
5. Liu, G., Yang, Q., Wang, H., Lin, X., Wittie, M.P.: Assessment of multi-hop interpersonal trust in social networks by three-valued subjective logic. In: IEEE INFOCOM 2014 - IEEE Conference on Computer Communications, pp. 1698–1706 (2014)
6. Liu, G., Chen, Q., Yang, Q., Wang, H., Zhu, B., Wang, W.: Opinionwalk: an efficient solution to massive trust assessment in online social networks. In: IEEE INFOCOM 2017 - IEEE Conference on Computer Communications (2017)
7. Awasthi, S.K., Singh, Y.N.: Generalized analysis of convergence of absolute trust in peer-to-peer networks. IEEE Commun. Lett. **20**(7), 1345–1348 (2016)
8. Nguyen, D.Q., Toulgoat, M., Lamont, L.: Impact of trust-based security association and mobility on the delay metric in MANET. J. Commun. Networks **18**(1), 105–111 (2016)
9. Liu, G., Yang, Q., Wang, H., Wu, S., Wittie, M.P.: Uncovering the mystery of trust in an online social network. In: 2015 IEEE Conference on Communications and Network Security (CNS), Florence, pp. 488–496 (2015)
10. Perkins, C.E., Royer, E.M.: Ad-hoc on-demand distance vector routing. In: Proceedings of the Second IEEE Workshop on Mobile Computing Systems and Applications, WMCSA 99, pp. 90-100 (1999)
11. Xia, H., Jia, Z., Li, X., Ju, L., Sha, H.M.: Trust prediction and trust-based source routing in mobile ad hoc networks. Ad Hoc Netw. **11**(7), 2096–2114 (2013)
12. Jsang, A., Ismail, R.: The beta reputation system. In: Proceedings of the 15th Bled Electronic Commerce Conference, pp. 2502–2511 (2002)
13. Fung, C.J., Zhang, J., Aib, I., Boutaba, R.: Dirichlet-based trust management for effective collaborative intrusion detection networks. IEEE Trans. Netw. Serv. Manage. **8**(2), 79–91 (2011)

Hybrid Quantum-Behaved Particle Swarm Optimization for Mobile-Edge Computation Offloading in Internet of Things

Shijie Dai[1], Minghui Liwang[1], Yang Liu[1], Zhibin Gao[1(✉)],
Lianfen Huang[1], and Xiaojiang Du[2(✉)]

[1] School of Information Science and Engineering, Xiamen University,
Xiamen 361005, China
xmu_dsj@sina.com, minghuilw@stu.xmu.edu.cn,
liuyangxmuce@126.com, {gaozhibin,lfhuang}@xmu.edu.cn
[2] Department of Computer and Information Sciences, Temple University,
Philadelphia, PA 19122, USA
dux@temple.edu

Abstract. Mobile edge computing (MEC) is a technology that transfers resource to the edge of network, which spares more attention to giving users easier access to network and computation resources. Due to the large amount of data computation needed for devices in Internet of Things, MEC technology is applied to improve computing efficiency. Though MEC can be applied to the Internet of Things, it needs further consideration on how to efficiently and reasonably allocate computing resources, and how to minimize the computing time of all users. This paper proposes a computing resources allocation scheme based on hybrid quantum-behaved particle swarm optimization. Simulation experiments with the network environment based on the Internet of Things is carried out. The results show that this algorithm can accelerate the whole computing process and reduce the number of iterations.

Keywords: Internet of Things · Mobile edge computing · Offloading

1 Introduction

With the rapid development of information technology and information industry, the Internet of Things (IoT), supported by big data mining, cloud computing and machine learning, has been applied to various fields. And the appearances of newly-developing technology, cloud computing, bid data, AR and other technologies, promote the industry IoT upgrading. A recent study by NCTA in United States assumes that about 5.01 million Internet of Things will be connected to the Internet by 2020 [1].

The future era will rely on Internet technology to achieve the intelligent life, covering the fields in home security, environmental testing, energy, car networking, industrial intelligence manufacturing and other. IoT transforms itself from simple mode of things to the intelligent mode. IoT typically involve a large number of smart sensors that sense information from the environment and share it with the cloud service for processing. IoT application services can be divided into two types: one is a post hoc

© Springer Nature Singapore Pte Ltd. 2018
L. Zhu and S. Zhong (Eds.): MSN 2017, CCIS 747, pp. 350–364, 2018.
https://doi.org/10.1007/978-981-10-8890-2_26

analysis, which collects data through the IoT terminal. And it upload to the cloud through the IoT private network or public network. Then the information will combine with bid data to be filtered and analyzed in the cloud. This application is often one-way. In other words, to capture and analysis do not need feedback data transmission. The other one is a real-time feedback type, which is making data acquisition and analysis not only through the IoT terminal, but also through the reverse real-time feedback. Such applications have higher requirements for latency and reliability.

Currently the IoT architecture is still cloud-centric architecture. Its main feature is that the communication exists between terminal and the cloud, and the main type of application services is a post hoc analysis. With the development of IoT, real-time feedback application requirements will increase more and more. And the IoT current architecture, cloud-centric architecture, is clearly unable to meet the needs of such applications. The main problems caused by generate data from IoT are: (1) IoT application processing time may be limited by the network delay in offloading data to the cloud. (2) the generation and upload of a large amount of IoT data causes network congestion resulting in further network delay.

To address the network problems designed in the Internet of Things and similar applications, researchers have proposed to bring computing closer to data generators and consumers. One suggestion is the fog computation [2], which enables the device to run the cloud application on its native architecture. The purpose of the fog is to perform low latency calculations/aggregations on the data while routing it to the central cloud for a large amount of calculation [3, 4]. On the other hand, the edge-centric computing cloud (mobile edge computing) [5] is inspired by projects such as SETI @ Home, Folding @ Home [6, 7], and the integration of voluntary human resources are proposed, such as desktop PC, Tablet, smartphone, nanometer data center as cloud. Since the resources in the Edge cloud are usually located near the hop of the Internet of Things sensors, processing the data at the edges can significantly reduce network latency [8, 9]. In addition, several papers (e.g., [10–20]) have studied the related wireless and IoT issues.

The essence of fog calculation/MEC is "near-service" and "segmental intelligence". The traditional IoT uses a three-tier architecture, about the perceived layer, the network layer, and the platform layer. As shown in the figure, through the Internet of Things gateway equipped with MEC service platform, IoT gateway not only has the router function, but also obtain the abilities in storage and computing capacity in some actual application scenarios. Gateway nodes have the full ability to achieve the edge of intelligent networking. However, due to the wireless network resources provided by the nodes and the computation resource provided by the MEC server is limited, the problem of wireless and computation resource allocation problem is appeared. Therefore, how to choose access devices to provide computation offloading service under limited resources is a decision-making process.

In this paper, the MEC calculation offloading decision algorithm is studied. Firstly, the scene of wireless communication system with MEC calculation offloading technology under microcell is introduced. Then the content of the scene was mathematical modeling. It sums up the corresponding mathematical expression and establishes the problem model. Then the quantum-behaved particle swarm optimization algorithm is introduced to optimize the MEC calculation offloading decision, and the water injection algorithm is mixed into the above optimization algorithm. Based on this, a quantum-behaved particle swarm optimization algorithm with water injection algorithm is proposed to solve the above problems. And the algorithm is simulated. The simulation results show that the result of the algorithm approximates the optimal solution, which can effectively reduce the task's completion time.

The remainder of the paper is organized as follows. In Sect. 2, we describe the Edge-computation architecture and we propose our approach for deploying compute application tasks on the Edge-computation in efficient manner. In Sect. 3 we evaluate the effectiveness of our HQPSO algorithm by some simulation. Section 4 concludes the paper.

2 System Model

2.1 Systems Background

As shown in the Fig. 1, the IoT devices connect to the MEC server through a wireless network access node(AN). The AN is responsible for scheduling the time-frequency resource when the device communicates with the AN and is responsible for forwarding the data and related information of the device's calculation task to the Edge-Computation server. And the Edge-Computation server is responsible for scheduling the corresponding computing resources and storage resources for the device tasks to be evaluated. And it helps the devices to completes the calculation task and returns the calculated result to the AN. The AN then returns the result to the device via the wireless access network.

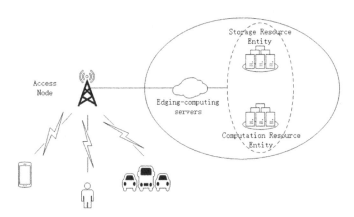

Fig. 1. The architecture of mobile edge computation offloading

Based on the above scenario, we model the radio access network as an OFDM system. And the minimum scheduling unit is a subcarrier (each subcarrier width is 15 kHz). When the device has a calculating task to upload, the AN schedules some subcarrier resources for the device. Edge-computation server, the cloud computing virtualization management server, manages many computing resources and storage resources. And in our simulation,

We simplify the Edge-computation server. At a random point, multiple device's calculation task requests are uploaded to the AN. AN and Edge-computation server make joint decision, which is to assign all or many tasks to some computing resource. The order of assigning is following the principle named first-come-first-served (FCFS).

In our paper, we propose an algorithm to optimal the time for completing all calculation task by reasonably assigning computing resource.

2.2   System Parameters and Model

As mentioned in the previous section, we consider that the AN has a total of N subcarriers scheduled to M devices. The CPU of the computing resource, which is single-core single-threaded, execute by the principle of the first-come-first-served (FCFS).

Each device has only one calculation task to perform. They could choose to calculate locally or offloading to MEC for calculation. Some arguments are introduced in Table 1.

Table 1. The arguments of system

Arguments	Significance
f	The frequency of the CPU
$C = (1, 2, \ldots, N)$	The set of scheduled carriers
$U = \{1, 2, \ldots, M\}$	The device
B	The bandwidth of each carrier
$task_m = \{I_m, T_{max}^m\}, m \epsilon U$	The m-th device's calculation task
I_m	The number of m-th device's data bits
T_{max}^m	The maximum completion time allowed by the m-th calculation task
f_L^m	The CPU frequency of each device
P_{max}	The maximum transmit power
κ	The number of CPU clock cycles required to process each bit of data
R_m	The m-th device can upload rate

The time of computational tasks performed locally is defined as:

$$T_C^m = \frac{KI_m}{f_m} \tag{1}$$

Define $\exists! m : \eta(m, n) = 1, \forall m \epsilon U, \forall n \epsilon C$, which indicates whether the n-th carrier is assigned to the m-th device or not. $\eta(m, n) = 1$ indicates that the n-th carrier is assigned to the m-th device, and vice versa.

Define $\eta(m, n) = \{0, 1\}, \forall m \epsilon U, \forall n \epsilon C$, represents the power value on the n-th carrier of m-th device.

The total power of the device is limited, so we define:

$$P_m = \sum_{n=1}^{N} \eta(m,n)P(m,n) \leq P_{max}, \forall m\epsilon U \tag{2}$$

which constrains the power of m-th device on all subcarriers. It is meant that the power of m-th device on all subcarriers shall not exceed the maximum transmit power of the device.

By the Shannon formula, the m-th device can upload the total rate is as:

$$R_m = B\sum_{n=1}^{N} \eta(m,n)\log(1+P(m,n)H(m,n)), \tag{3}$$
$$\forall m\epsilon U$$

Where $H(m,n)$ represents the channel gain for noise on the n-th carrier of device m.

Offloading calculation time includes the task's upload time, queuing time, execution time and download time.

Therefore, the device to calculate the task data upload time is:

$$T_U^m = \frac{I_m}{R_m} \tag{4}$$

The calculation execution time in MEC is:

$$T_C^m = \frac{KI_m}{f_m} \tag{5}$$

Since the schedule for assigning CPU of MEC is FCFS, the queuing time of the device is determined by its upload time and the execution time of the MEC calculation. Here, it is assumed that the MEC server provides the sufficient memory to store the upload data. Since the number of carriers per device is not necessarily same and the channel quality is different, the time for each device uploading and calculate the task data is different. According to the upload time is not of uniform size, we could get the order of the task reaching the MEC. Therefore, the tasks should be executed orderly.

Define $A = \{a_i | a_i = 1, 2, \ldots, M, i \neq j, i, j\epsilon U\}$, which represents each tasks' order of arrival, and the order of each task executing is a unique value.

The work of the preceding article got the task's upload time, arrival order and computing resources for the task calculation time. We can define the task's queuing time:

$$Q_{wait}^{a_i} = \begin{cases} 0, & a_i = 1 \\ max(0, T_U^j + T_C^j + Q_{wait}^{a_j} - T_U^i, a_j = a_i - 1, a_i \neq 1) \end{cases} \tag{6}$$

If the task is the first one arriving, then his waiting time must be equal to 0. If the task is not the first to arrive, the second formula is calculated. If the value is equal to 0, then the previous task has been completed, before the arrival of this task. Otherwise, the waiting time should be the above time difference.

After the task is executed by the MEC, the calculation result is returned to the device. The amount of result's data is very small, and the time to download it to the device is considered negligible.

Therefore, the completion time of the task for the device performing the calculation offloading is:

$$T_{MEC}^m = T_U^m + Q_{wait}^{a_i} + T_C^m \tag{7}$$

At this point, the minimum time to complete the task is calculated from follow equation set:

$$\min_{\eta, P, K_1, K_2} \sum_{k_1=1}^{k_1 \in K_1} T_L^{k_1} + \sum_{k_2=1}^{k_2 \in K_2} T_{MEC}^{k_2} \tag{8}$$

subject to

$$\exists! m : \eta(m, n) = 1, \forall m \in U, \forall n \in C \tag{9}$$

$$\eta(m, n) = \{0, 1\}, \forall m \in U, \forall n \in C \tag{10}$$

$$\sum_m^M \sum_n^N \eta(m, n) = N, \forall m \in U, \forall n \in C \tag{11}$$

$$P(m, n) \geq 0, \forall m \in U, \forall n \in C \tag{12}$$

$$P_m = \sum_{n=1}^N \eta(m, n) P(m, n) \leq P_{max}, \forall m \in U \tag{13}$$

$$R_m = B \sum_{n=1}^N \eta(m, n) \log(1 + P(m, n) H(m, n)), \forall m \in U \tag{14}$$

$$K_1 \cup K_2 = U, K_1 \cap K_2 = \varnothing \tag{15}$$

$$T_{MEC}^{k_2} = T_U^{k_2} + Q_{wait}^{a_i} + T_C^{k_2} \leq T_L^{k_2}, \forall k_2 \in K_2 \tag{16}$$

2.3 Hybrid Quantum-Behaved Particle Swarm Optimization

The model with the smallest completion time established by (7)–(16) is a mixed integer nonlinear programming. The complexity of the problem is very high because its constraints contain integer terms and the nonlinearity of the objective function. And it is difficult to find the optimal solution of the objective function. Therefore, a feasible method is proposed based on the evolutionary algorithm.

First, we decompose the optimization problem established by (7)–(16) into sub-problems 1 and sub-problem 2. The mathematical model of Sub-problem 1 consists of (16)–(18).

The restriction condition is that the total number of subcarriers is limited and whether the condition for the device offloading calculation satisfies that the total time of the MEC calculation is less than the local calculation time or not. The optimization goal is to maximize the time saved.

$$\max_{\eta, K_2} \sum_{k_2=1}^{k_2 \in K_2} T_L^{k_2} - T_{MEC}^{k_2} \tag{16}$$

subject to

$$\sum_m^M \sum_n^N \eta(m, n) = N, \forall m \epsilon U, \forall n \epsilon C \tag{17}$$

$$T_{MEC}^{k_2} = T_U^{k_2} + Q_{wait}^{a_i} + T_C^{k_2} \leq T_L^{k_2}, \forall k_2 \epsilon K_2 \tag{18}$$

The mathematical model of sub-problem 2 consists of (19)–(24), which mainly solves the calculation of subcarrier and power allocation and the total uploading rate.

$$\max_{\eta, P_2} R_m \tag{19}$$

subject to

$$\exists! m : \eta(m, n) = 1, \forall m \epsilon U, \forall n \epsilon C \tag{20}$$

$$\eta(m, n) = \{0, 1\}, \forall m \epsilon U, \forall n \epsilon C \tag{21}$$

$$P(m, n) \geq 0, \forall m \epsilon U, \forall n \epsilon C \tag{22}$$

$$P_m = \sum_{n=1}^N \eta(m, n) P(m, n) \leq P_{max}, \forall m \epsilon U \tag{23}$$

$$R_m = B \sum_{n=1}^N \eta(m, n) \log(1 + P(m, n) H(m, n)), \tag{24}$$
$$\forall m \epsilon U$$

It is not difficult to find that the device waiting time in sub-problem 1 needs to be solved by the device upload rate obtained from sub-problem 2. Therefore, solving sub-problem 1 needs to solve sub-problem 2 first, and then solve sub-problem 1 to get the solution of modeling problem. However, it is necessary to determine the allocation of the K_2 carriers in sub-problem 1 to solve sub-problem 2. For the above analysis, we propose a quantum behavior particle swarm optimization algorithm that combines the water-filling algorithm to solve the sub-problem 1 and the sub-problem 2, so that the optimization problem established by (7)–(15) is also solved.

First, we apply the quantum-behaved particle swarm algorithm to solve sub-problem 1 and initialize K particles to represent the initialization of M devices in sub-problem 1. The k-th particles are initialized as $X_k = \left(X_k^1, X_k^2, \ldots, X_k^m, \ldots, X_k^M\right)$. Unlike the previous section, where X_k^m represents only the subcarrier allocation of the m-th device, but no more parameters on the allocation of power on the subcarriers are involved. Thus, the dimensions of the solution are reduced.

$$X_k^m = (\eta(m, 1), \ldots, \eta(m, n), \ldots, \eta(m, N)) \tag{25}$$

Similarly, $\eta(m, n)$ is 0 or 1, indicating whether the n-th carrier is allocated to the m-th device or not.

When the particle swarm is initialized, it means that the initial subcarrier allocation has been determined. In this case, sub-problem 2 can be simplified as shown in Eqs. (26)–(28). By solving sub-problem 2, the maximum uplink transmission rate of the device can be calculated. Where C_m is the set of subcarriers in each column of X_k^m equal to 1, and J is the total number of elements equal to 1 in row vector X_k^m, which is the total number of subcarriers allocated to device m.

$$\max_P R_m = B \sum_{j=1}^{J} \log(1 + P(m, j)H(m, j)), \tag{26}$$
$$\forall j \epsilon C_m$$

subject to

$$P(m, j) \geq 0, \forall j \epsilon C_m \tag{27}$$

$$\sum_{j=1}^{J} P(m, j) \leq P_{max} \tag{28}$$

At this point, solving sub-problem 2 can be understood as the maximum uplink transmission rate of the device when the total power of the device equipment transmitted is invariable.

To solve sub-problem 2, we establish the Lagrangian equation for (26)–(28) according to the Karush-Kuhn-Tucker (KKT) condition as (28):

$$L(P, \mu) = B \sum_{j=1}^{J} \log(1 + P(m, j)H(m, j))$$
$$- \mu \left(\sum_{j=1}^{J} P(m, j) - P_{max} \right) \tag{29}$$

Where μ is the Lagrangian multiplier, which is a constant.

Next, to solve the optimal transmission power of the device m on each carrier, the transmission power of the m-th device in the Eq. (29) is subjected to calculate its partial derivative:

$$
\begin{cases}
\frac{\partial L(P,u)}{\partial P(m,1)} = 0 \\
\frac{\partial L(P,u)}{\partial P(m,2)} = 0 \\
\quad . \\
\quad . \\
\frac{\partial L(P,u)}{\partial P(m,J)} = 0
\end{cases}
\tag{30}
$$

Solve Eq. (30), and we could get the equation J shown equation.

$$
P(m,j) = \max\left\{0, \frac{B}{\ln 2 \cdot \mu} - H(m,j)^{-1}\right\}, \\
\forall j \epsilon C_m
\tag{31}
$$

From the Eq. (31) we can see that if the sub-carrier's gain-to-noise ratio is bigger, which means that the better channel quality of the subcarrier, the assigned transmit power of the subcarrier should be larger. The idea of power allocation above is the principle of water-filling algorithm.

In the following, we use the water-filling algorithm proposed in [22] to solve the sub-problem 2 that the subcarrier transmit power is allocated under the condition that the total transmit power is limited to maximize the total rate of the device. Compared with the classical binary search water-filling algorithm, the water-level algorithm reduces the complexity of the algorithm because it does not solve the Lagrangian factor directly by iterative method, but by using the iterative factors for the inconvenient adjustment of the iterative adjustment until all the power distribution is completed in power limited and initial water-filling line assumed conditions.

Then, back to the analysis of sub-problem 1, after get the device's upload rate, we can calculate the time of task uploading and calculating. According to the upload time, we could get the order of the tasks reach the AN for getting the execution order and the waiting time of tasks.

In Sub-problem 1, the goal of solving the problem is to maximize the difference between the completion time of the offloading task calculation task and the completion time of the local task calculation. Previously, by initializing the M particles representing the subcarrier assignment of K devices in sub-problem 1, there is a certain degree of randomness. Because the device's subcarrier allocation determines whether the device can perform the offloading calculation. And we can get all the possible distribution and device uninstall calculation.

Due to adopting the method of split solution, we need to modify penalty coefficient function of the fitness function. In the sub-problem 2, the water-filling algorithm has been applied to solve the power-related constraints, so the penalty function is the function (32) term.

$$\sum_{n=1}^{N} \left(\sum_{m=1}^{M} \eta(m,n) - 1 \right)^2 \tag{32}$$

Thus, the final fitness function is shown in (33), where α is the penalty factor.

$$f(X) = \sum_{k_2=1}^{k_2 \epsilon K_2} (T_L^{k_2} - T_{MEC}^{k_2}) - \alpha \cdot \sum_{n=1}^{N} \left(\sum_{m=1}^{M} \eta(m,n) - 1 \right)^2 \tag{33}$$

In addition, the device needs the data size of the computing task, the calculation rate of their own equipment and other information reported to the AN. these all are a priori information. In the premise of obtaining these information, the AN solve the decision problem to get the final subcarrier allocation results through the proposed algorithm, and reply to the device. And the device will decide to choose the offloading calculation or local calculation according to the results of the answer.

3 Simulation Setting and Result

3.1 Simulation Parameter Setting

Table 1 shows the simulation parameters of the MEC calculation unloading decision algorithm based on the hybrid quantum-behaved particle swarm optimization algorithm proposed in the mobile communication macro cellular network.

The simulation scene is a hexagonal area (500 * 500 m), and the user's cellular terminal equipment evenly distributed in the network. The simulation scene is shown in Fig. 2. The small red dots represent devices, and the blue point represents the macro base station, the devices' location in the figure is randomly generated. To ensure the

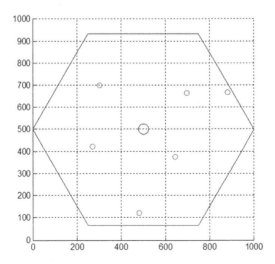

Fig. 2. The paper's simulation scene

generalization of the simulated devices' position, we compare the average of the solution obtained by solving the algorithm with 100 devices randomly generated and the average of the 100 optimal solutions Values. The path loss mainly considers large-scale fading. The channel model refers to the LTE COST231-HaTa propagation model proposed by 3GPP [23]. And the MEC calculation speed reference to [21]. And the rest of the simulation parameters are shown in Table 2. Through repeated experiments, the value of the penalty factor α of the penalty function in the fitness function is set to be 0.05, can get the better simulation result.

Table 2. Simulation parameters

Parameters	Values
Area of simulation Scene	Regular hexagon (length of side: 600 m)
Working frequency	2.4 GHz
MEC rate of computing	8×10^8 cycle/s
The amount of task data	(5–20) KB
Value of κ	200
Subcarrier bandwidth	15 kHz
BS coverage	500 m
Maximum transmit power	24 dBm
Thermal noise power density	−174 dBm/Hz
Number of iterations	300

3.2   Simulation Result

In the simulation, we compare the performance of the proposed algorithm with the average calculation completion time of the optimal solution introduced. Figure 3 shows the average time of completing the calculation and obtaining the optimal solution by the offloading decision algorithm in different situations with the different number of subcarriers. As is shown in the figure, with the increasing of the total number of subcarriers, the average time at which the user completes the computational task is reduced. In addition, it can be seen from the figure that the performance of proposed HQPSO algorithm is close to the one of optimal solution. In the hybrid quantum-behaved particle swarm optimization algorithm, the allocation of subcarriers is randomly initialized firstly, and the penalty function is introduced to modify the fitness function to solves the optimization target problem. This not only considers the sub-carrier resources that may be wasted due to the long offload time, but also the situation in which the user's task is queued after offloading. It effectively allocate all available subcarriers to the devices who uploaded the calculation. It can be seen from Fig. 3 that the solution result based on the hybrid quantum-behaved particle swarm optimization algorithm is very small and the difference is less than 5%.

Figure 4 shows the number of different users, by selecting some devices to offloading the calculation, we can optimize the calculation of the completion of the time value. It can be seen from the figure that the performance of the random allocation algorithm is very poor because it does not consider the devices' situation. However, the

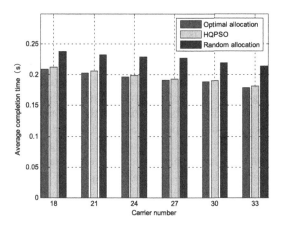

Fig. 3. The average time for computational task

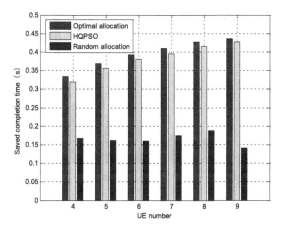

Fig. 4. The total time saved by each algorithm

results of the HQPSO algorithm we proposed and the optimal solution increase with the increase in the number of devices. And the calculation time is also increasing. This is because that the greater the number of selectable devices, the greater the likelihood of a better allocation scheme in the case of allocating the same number of subcarriers. It can be seen from Fig. 3 that the results of the proposed HQPSO algorithm are still close to those of the optimal solution.

Figure 4 shows the reduction in the completion time of the unloading calculation with the total transmission power of the different devices. As is seen from the figure, with the increase of the total transmission power of the device terminal equipment, the optimization of the equipment offloading computation time is increased, which is meant that the user can complete the task calculation in a shorter time. This is mainly due to the increase in allocable power resulting in an increase in user upload rates. So, the calculation time for each task is decreasing

Figure 5 is the calculated time reduction for HQPSO in the case of 6 devices assigned 30 carriers. The result is averaged by 100 iterations of randomly generated device simulations. The optimal solution value is the value of the fitness function obtained when the optimal subcarrier is allocated. The final value of HQPSO is the global optimal value of the fitness function obtained by iterative convergence. It can be observed from the figure that the proposed algorithm can quickly reach the convergence of the iteration. In addition, the accuracy of the algorithm is relatively high, it usually could be achieved with the optimal value of less than 10% within 50 iterations. This is because we have incorporated the water-filling algorithm into the iterative solution of the quantum-behaved particle swarm optimization, which reduces the dimension of the feasible solution, accelerates the speed of the iterative convergence and improves the accuracy of the solution.

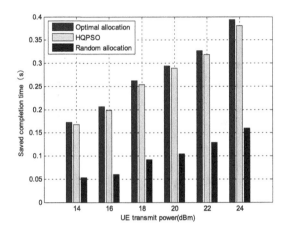

Fig. 5. The calculated time reduction for HQPSO in the case of 6 devices assigned 30 carriers

4 Conclusion

This paper first introduces the research progress of Internet of Things (IoT) and mobile edge computing. And the mathematical modeling is carried out on this basis, and the corresponding optimization problem model is put forward. Then, to reduce the complexity of iterative computation, this paper proposes a hybrid quantum behavior particle swarm optimization algorithm to solve the optimization problem. Finally, we verify the performance of the proposed algorithm, and analyze the performance of the proposed algorithm. And experimental results prove that this algorithm can accelerate the whole computing process and lessening the iterations.

Acknowledgment. The work presented in this paper was partially supported by the 2015 National Natural Science Foundation of China (Grant number 61401381).

References

1. Cremer, D., Bang, N., Simkin, L.: The integrity challenge of the Internet-of-Things (IoT): on understanding its dark side. J. Mark. Manage. **33**(1–2), 145–158 (2017)
2. Bonomi, F., Milito, R., Natarajan, P., Zhu, J.: Fog computing: a platform for internet of things and analytics. In: Bessis, N., Dobre, C. (eds.) Big Data and Internet of Things: A Roadmap for Smart Environments. SCI, vol. 546, pp. 169–186. Springer, Cham (2014). https://doi.org/10.1007/978-3-319-05029-4_7
3. Yannuzzi, M., Milito, R., Serral-Gracià, R., et al.: Key ingredients in an IoT recipe: fog computing, cloud computing, and more fog computing. In: 2014 IEEE 19th International Workshop on Computer Aided Modeling and Design of Communication Links and Networks (CAMAD), pp. 325–329. IEEE (2014)
4. Hong, K., Lillethun, D., Ramachandran, U., et al.: Mobile fog: a programming model for large-scale applications on the internet of things. In: Proceedings of the Second ACM SIGCOMM Workshop on Mobile Cloud Computing, pp. 15–20. ACM (2013)
5. Lopez, P.G., Montresor, A., Epema, D., et al.: Edge-centric computing: vision and challenges. ACM SIGCOMM Comput. Commun. Rev. **45**(5), 37–42 (2015)
6. Korpela, E., Werthimer, E., Anderson, D., et al.: SETI@HOME—massively distributed computing for SETI. Comput. Sci. Eng. **3**(1), 78–83 (2001)
7. Beberg, A.L., Ensign, D.L., Jayachandran, G., et al.: Folding@home: lessons from eight years of volunteer distributed computing. In: IEEE International Symposium on Parallel & Distributed Processing, IPDPS 2009, pp. 1–8. IEEE (2009)
8. Islam, S., Grégoire, J.C.: Giving users an edge: a flexible cloud model and its application for multimedia. Future Gener. Comput. Syst. **28**(6), 823–832 (2012)
9. Chandra, A., Weissman, J., Heintz, B.: Decentralized edge clouds. IEEE Internet Comput. **17**(5), 70–73 (2013)
10. Yao, X., Han, X., Du, X., Zhou, X.: A lightweight multicast authentication mechanism for small scale IoT applications. IEEE Sens. J. **13**(10), 3693–3701 (2013)
11. Du, X., Wu, D., Liu, W., Fang, Y.: Multi-class routing and medium access control for heterogeneous mobile ad hoc networks. IEEE Trans. Veh. Technol. **55**(1), 278–285 (2006)
12. Hei, X., Du, X.: Biometric-based two-level secure access control for implantable medical devices during emergency. In: Proceedings of IEEE INFOCOM 2011, Shanghai, China, April 2011
13. Du, X., Xiao, Y., Chen, H.H., Wu, Q.: Secure cell relay routing protocol for sensor networks. Wirel. Commun. Mobile Comput. **6**(3), 375–391 (2006)
14. Xiao, Y., Rayi, V., Sun, B., Du, X., Hu, F., Galloway, M.: A survey of key management schemes in wireless sensor networks. J. Comput. Commun. **30**(11–12), 2314–2341 (2007)
15. Du, X., Xiao, Y., Guizani, M., Chen, H.H.: An effective key management scheme for heterogeneous sensor networks. Ad Hoc Netw. **5**(1), 24–34 (2007)
16. Hei, X., Du, X., Wu, J., Hu, F.: Defending resource depletion attacks on implantable medical devices. In: Proceedings of IEEE GLOBECOM 2010, Miami, Florida, USA, December 2010
17. Du, X., Guizani, M., Xiao, Y., Chen, H.H.: A routing-driven elliptic curve cryptography based key management scheme for heterogeneous sensor networks. IEEE Trans. Wireless Commun. **8**(3), 1223–1229 (2009)
18. Xiao, Y., Du, X., Zhang, J., Guizani, S.: Internet protocol television (IPTV): the killer application for the next generation internet. IEEE Commun. Mag. **45**(11), 126–134 (2007)
19. Du, X., Chen, H.H.: Security in wireless sensor networks. IEEE Wirel. Commun. Mag. **15**(4), 60–66 (2008)

20. Du, X., Guizani, M., Xiao, Y., Chen, H.H.: Secure and efficient time synchronization in heterogeneous sensor networks. IEEE Trans. Veh. Technol. **57**(4), 2387–2394 (2008)
21. Munoz, O., Pascual-Iserte, A., Vidal, J.: Optimization of radio and computational resources for energy efficiency in latency-constrained application offloading. IEEE Trans. Veh. Technol. **64**(10), 4738–4755 (2015)
22. Liu, Y., Tan, X., et al.: Research on spectrum allocation algorithms based on game theory in cognitive radio networks, Harbin Institute of Technology
23. TR25 G. 996, 3GPP SCM channel models, 3GPP TR25.996, vol. v6.1 (2003)

Enhancing Software Reliability Against Soft Error Using Critical Data Model

Li Wei$^{1(\boxtimes)}$ and Mingwei Xu^2

^{1} Beijing University of Posts and Telecommunications, Beijing, China
weili@bupt.edu.cn
^{2} Tsinghua University, Beijing, China
xmw@cernet.edu.cn

Abstract. In modern life, software plays an increasingly important role and ensuring the reliability of software is of particular importance. In space, a Single Event Upset occurs because of the strong radiation effects of cosmic rays, which can lead to errors in software. In order to guarantee the reliability of software, many software-based fault tolerance methods have been proposed. The majority of them are based on data redundancy, which duplicates all data to prevent data corruption during the software execution. But this fault tolerant approach will make the data redundant and increase memory overhead and time overhead. Duplicating critical variables only can significantly reduce the memory and performance overheads, while still guaranteeing very high reliable results in terms of fault-tolerance improvement. In this paper, we propose an analysis model, named CDM (Critical Data Model), which can compute the critical of variables in the programs and achieve the purpose of reducing redundancy for the reliable program. According to the experimental results, the model proposed in this paper can enhance the reliability of the software, reduce the time and memory cost, and improve the efficiency of the reliable program.

Keywords: Reliability · Redundancy · Critical data · Fault tolerance

1 Introduction

Software errors, also called single-event upsets (SEUs), are transient faults caused by external radiation or electrical noise, such as high energy neutrons from cosmic rays, power glitches, electromagnetic interference and etc. [1–3]. In space, SEU errors are regarded as a major concern for space applications. According to statistics, the router restarts about 20 times a day. Software errors can flip the bits stored in storage cells, thus change the value computed by logic elements. The reliability of programs is essential to space applications.

Various approaches have been proposed to reply the software errors. These techniques can be mainly divided into two types: hardware redundancy and software redundancy. The methodologies of hardware redundancy are high priced, since it requires replicating hardware modules or developing custom hardware. Although they are effective in enhancing the reliability and protecting against transient faults, because of the huge cost, they are not widely used. The methodologies of software redundancy

© Springer Nature Singapore Pte Ltd. 2018
L. Zhu and S. Zhong (Eds.): MSN 2017, CCIS 747, pp. 365–376, 2018.
https://doi.org/10.1007/978-981-10-8890-2_27

are a more attractive approach, because it does not incur the high costs. Furthermore, the SHIFT (Software Implemented Hardware Fault Tolerance) techniques are more universal and easy to implement [4, 5].

Data duplication technique is the most popular way for SHIFT, which exploits the characteristic that soft errors are a random phenomenon with very low probability, and the same error does not occur repetitively. The basic concept for data duplication technique is to duplicate the data and keep two versions of data during a program's runtime. A master version is the original data in the source code and a shadow version is the duplicated data. When a read operation occurs for the master version, a consistent checking operation has to be made. When a write operation occurs for the master version, the new value has to be written into the shadow version. Thus data duplication techniques keep the two versions consistent. These techniques have been used widely for its advantage on flexible, effective, and general implementation.

However, data duplication will inevitably provoke memory overhead and performance degradation because of the duplication. On one hand, the full duplication of data may result in double memory occupation, on the other hand, the performance declines significantly when considerable consistency check instructions are introduced. The overhead will be unacceptable in some situations, especially for real-time systems and embedded applications. On the other hand, the duplication of a lower percentage of data may incur worse error coverage. Moreover, in some space conditions, safety-critical applications have strict constraints in terms of memory occupation and system performances. The tradeoff between reliability, performance and memory overhead must be carefully considered. One possible solution is to only duplicate the most critical variables, which improve the capacity of fault-tolerance significantly, while keeping an acceptable memory and performance overheads.

This paper proposes CDM (Critical Data Model). The reliable weight for variables is computed by CDM. The model has been implemented based on RECCO [6], which can transform any input source code into an output reliable code, properly modified to increase its dependability characteristics. Using CDM, we are able to access the reliable weight for every variable. Based on the reliable weight, we can only duplicate critical data. To illustrate the effectiveness of our method, we perform several fault injection experiments and performance evaluations on a set of simple benchmark programs through the Simple Scalar tool set.

The paper is organized as follows: Sect. 2 describes related work in this area while Sect. 3 introduces the Critical Data Model, including error generation model, error propagation model and calculating the critical weight. In Sect. 4, the experimental results are discussed. Conclusions are summarized in Sect. 5.

2   Related Works

Researchers have showed that, in software systems, a lot of software errors cause a Fail Silent Violation (FSV), which means the system produces incorrect result while the program seems to terminate correctly [7]. Aiming at achieving high reliable codes, errors and mistakes should be reduced even eliminated in the program. Also, critical data of programs should be identified so that they should be protected against software errors. Data duplication techniques have been well investigated in the past. There have been numerous available techniques in this area. In the followings, some of the recent research studies conducted in this filed are overviewed.

In [8], the researchers have found that for achieving a high level of software reliability in average computers with error detection mechanisms, a series of effective software approaches for error detection have been proposed. These methods include ABFT (algorithm-based fault tolerance), Time redundancy, Expressions, and Control Flow checking [9–12]. ABFT is a highly effective method but it lacks generality. It is useful for application programs with regular structures. However, it only can be used for a limited number of problems [8].

Oh et al. proposed EDDI [10], an instruction-level method. The method duplicates both data and instruction for achieving a high degree reliability. The proposed approach boosts the program reliability against soft errors by introducing data duplication and data redundancy. Before the store instructions and control flow instructions are executed, the consistency checking instructions are inserted, thus ensuring the correctness of values written into memory.

In [13], Xu proposed an analysis model named PRASE. PRASE is able to compute its reliability under the occurrence of soft error. Based on PRASE, Xu introduced an ODD (Optimum Data Duplication) approach, which can provide the optimum error coverage under system performance constraints. However, the paper didn't explain how to compute the reliability of variables in detail.

In [14], Saeid proposed a approach, based on class diagram and formula. The proposed method protects the program data by applying minimum redundancy. The evaluation of the operation of the propose method on program indicated that it can improve reliability, reduce efficiency overhead, redundancy and complexity. Though the formula can detect and mark vulnerable data, it is an empirical analysis. Besides, it doesn't take dependence relations into count.

In [6], Benso et al. proposed a source-to-source compiler for enhancing the reliability of application programs, named RECCO, which is able to detect data errors and improve the reliability through code re-ordering and variable duplication. RECCO propose the concept of reliability weight to measure the criticality of the variables. However, the technique is mainly empirical and lack of a more precise analysis. The augmented work is proposed in [15]. In this model, the authors introduced a formal model and defined the criticality function of variables with parameters initialized through fault injection experiment. However, the parameters are determined by the golden application and lack of conviction. Moreover, the probability of errors occurring in a variable should not be constant [13].

3   Critical Data Model

FSV could be a big concern for safety critical applications. Both data and code can be affected by soft errors during a program's runtime. In this paper, we only consider soft errors occurring in data segment. The error occurring in code segment is not in the scope of this article. And human incurred errors are not considered. For space applications, that means the applications only occur SEU error.

The concrete Critical Data Model consists of the following three parts: (1) Error generation model, (2) Error propagation model, (3) Calculate reliable weight

3.1   Error Generation Model

The error generation model is based on the following two reasonable hypothesis: (1) The radiation on register or memory in space is well-distribute; (2) Only SEU errors are considered. According to the two hypothesis, we have the following two sequiturs: (1) The transient state probability of SEU error should be constant because of the radiation; (2) With the increase of survival time of variables, the probability of SEU error for storage cell also increases.

Because of the strong radiation in space, program will incur SEU error. For a basic a single-bit cell b, we define the probability of b incurs a raw soft error during time t as $P_f(b)$ and the probability of u keeping correct during t as $P_t(b)$. Obviously, we can get this equation: $P_f(b) + P_t(b) = 1$. It is widely accepted that raw soft errors for the storage structure follow exponential time-to-failure distribution. We denote the raw software error rate (SER) as λ. Then the probability that a single-bit cell b will incur a raw soft error during time t, $P_f(b) = 1 - e^{-\lambda t}$. So, the probability of u keeping correct during t, $P_t(b) = e^{-\lambda t}$. For a single-bit cell, it is an independent event whether the storage bit incurs SEU error or not. Therefore, it is still an independent event whether multiple-bits incur SEU error or not. Thus, for a storage unit u, u has multiple bits. Since the errors in every bit of u are independent, so do the events for every bit of u keeping correct. We have:

$$P_t(u) = P_t(b_1 b_2 \ldots b_l) = e^{-\lambda l t} \tag{1}$$

$$P_f(b) = 1 - e^{-\lambda t} \tag{2}$$

Among them, u is the storage cell and is the bit-length of u. And t is the survival time of data. The raw SER, λ is determined by the circuit's characteristic of storage structure, and environmental parameters, which has been well studied.

Based on the above analysis, we can calculate the critical weight. In actual calculation, the parameter, t, means the number of lines between birth and death. Birth represents the declaration of the variable in the program while death means the variable is removed from the memory. For example, if a 32-bit variable named v, the birth-line is m and the death-line is n, then, the $t = n - m$, $P_f(v) = 1 - e^{-32\lambda(n-m)}$.

3.2   Error Propagation Model

A program is made up of a series of instructions. The output of the previous instruction may be used as the input of subsequent instructions. This state of output to input means that Raw Soft Error may be passed to other data. Considering the dependency relation of variables, the error propagation model is proposed. When programs run, the value of a variable can pass on to others. Once the value is not correct, it will influence the others.

In Fig. 1, $v_i(i = 1, 2, 3)$ represents the set of variables and $e_i(i = 1, 2, 3)$ represents the set of error events. Figure 2 shows how the errors propagate. The error event of v_1, e_1 is passed to v_3 and the error event of v_2, e_2 is also passed to v_3. Finally, through error propagation, all events are propagated into the top value. The arrow starts from parent variable and points to the descendant variables.

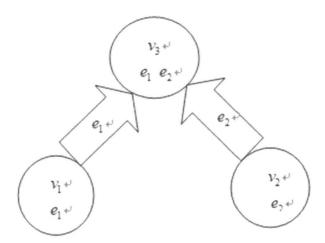

Fig. 1. Error propagation model

When parent node incurs errors, the error probability of descendants will greatly increase. As we know, the variables with high error probability should be protected. Because of the error propagation, the error probability of descendants increases greatly. However, the critical element is parent data which pass the errors to descendants. Actually, parent node is critical than the descendants. Taking this into account, an IDFG (Invert of Data Flow Graph) method is proposed.

The IDFG method will invert the direction of the data flow graph. For more critical than descendants, the weight of descendants will be distributed to parents averagely. In Fig. 1, the initial critical weight of v will be divided averagely in two parts and the parents of v, v3 and v4, will get the value passing from v. That means the critical weight v3 and v4 will add the half of the critical weight of v. Thus, the critical weight of all parent elements will raise.

3.3   Calculate Reliable Weight

The reliability weight of a data segment is determined by two factors: (1) the survival time of variable; (2) the dependency relation among variables. Thus, the critical weight of the variable is first determined by survival time. Based on the error generation model, initial weights can be calculated. Then the IDFG method take effects. According to the IDFG method, we can calculate the dependency weight. Finally, by adding the initial critical weight and the dependency weight, we can calculate the final critical weight of the variable.

For a variable v, stored in basic cell u, when the cell is exposed to strong radiation, the variable may incur SEU errors. We define probability of b incurs a raw soft error during time t as $P_f(u) = 1 - e^{-\lambda t}$.

In [13], $\lambda = 5 * 10^{-14} \text{cm}^2/\text{bit}$. So, λ is a very small value. According to the mathematical knowledge, the following approximate calculation can be obtained:

$$P_f(u) = 1 - e^{-\lambda lt} = \lambda lt \qquad (3)$$

We define a function $W_s(u)$. For a variable v, stored in basic cell u, the initial critical weight is $W_s(u)$. Moreover, we need to know the order of critical weight among variables in the program. However, we needn't to compute the precise critical weight value for the variables in the same program. Considering this, we have:

$$W_s(u) = lt \qquad (4)$$

So, we get the initial critical weight for a variable in program. As for dependency weight, we define a function $W_d(u)$. For a parent variable v, stored in basic cell u, the critical weight passing from the descendants is $W_d(u)$.

In Fig. 2, we have:

$$W_d(v_1) = W_d(v_2) = W_s(v_3)/2 \qquad (5)$$

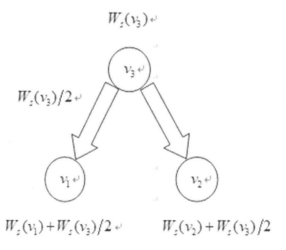

Fig. 2. Invert of data flow graph

Thus, we can get the final critical weight for a variable:

$$W(v) = W_s(v) + W_d(v) \qquad (6)$$

$W(v)$ represents the final critical weight for a variable v.

Finally, we can get the function for calculating the weight of critical variables. It is a reasonable and analytical function. The weight is determined by the time of the data storing in the register or memory and the dependency relation. When the data increases, the circular reference can incur easily. Our method for circular reference is to define a new variable rather than to refer to the original data.

4 Experiments

In order to evaluating the effectiveness of the proposed model in identifying the critical data and improving the reliability, a series of the fault injection experiments have been performed the benchmark programs. In reliability experiments, we first demonstrate the efficiency of the CDM, which is conducted on the SimpleScalar tool set. After that, another fault injection experiments are performed for the sake of comparing with the empirical model of RECCO. In our experiments, the concrete version of SimpleScalar is 3.0, which runs under Ubuntu 10.10.

4.1 Reliability Experiments

Before the first reliability experiments, the benchmarks have been transform to reliable code through the RECCO. Our critical data model has been implemented on the RECCO. During the runtime of RECCO, the critical weight of every variable in the benchmark program will be calculated and sorted according to the value of weight. We test five versions for each benchmark program, i.e. 0%, 25%, 50%, 75%, and 100%. Each different version means the different percentage of data duplication rate. Every time, the input benchmark program chosen the critical data using CDM perform data duplication.

To evaluate the performances, we perform the first fault injection experiments in the sim-safe simulator for every program. The simulator emulates the appearance of data faults corrupting memory locations storing data. The adopted fault model is the Single Event Upset (SEU), consisting in bit flip in one data memory locations storing data. SEU errors are transient faults, affecting data without physically damaging the memory: the fault effect therefore disappears when the fault location is overwritten. The tool set includes several simulators ranging from a fast functional simulator to a detailed performance simulator [17]. The fault injection results have been classified in four categories: Fail Silent (FS), Fail Silent order to Violation (FSV), Error Detected (ED) and Exception (EX). Besides, each program has been injected 1000 errors.

The fault injection experiments results are showed in Table 1. FS means the program terminates without any error. And the FSV means the program outputs the wrong answer but terminates normally. From Table 1, we can find that the reliability of the benchmarks increases along with the increasing of the data duplication percentage. When the rates range from 0% to 25%, the reliability of each program improves a lot. However, when the rates range from 25% to 100%, the reliability of each program still increases but a little. This fact shows that we can surely enhancing the software reliability by using CDM. And it is an effective method for improving the reliability.

Table 1. Fault injection experiments on Sim-Safe simulator

Rate	State	fib	bsort	mm	shuf
0%	FS	589	138	273	478
	EX	313	246	11	62
	FSV	98	616	716	460
	ED	0	0	0	0
	Realibillity	58.9%	13.8%	27.3%	47.8%
25%	FS	147	126	342	198
	EX	41	54	7	9
	FSV	5	37	4	5
	ED	807	783	647	788
	Realibillity	95.4%	90.9%	98.9%	98.6%
50%	FS	165	143	317	186
	EX	18	14	6	2
	FSV	4	10	3	5
	ED	813	833	674	807
	Realibillity	97.8%	97.6%	99.1%	99.3%
75%	FS	159	197	327	213
	EX	4	11	1	5
	FSV	2	7	4	0
	ED	835	785	668	782
	Realibillity	99.4%	98.2%	99.5%	99.5%
100%	FS	142	183	289	194
	EX	2	1	1	2
	FSV	0	5	3	1
	ED	856	811	707	803
	Realibillity	99.8%	99.4%	99.6%	99.7%

Our model has been embedded into the RECCO program. In order to compare with the original RECCO, another fault injection experiments were performed. And the benchmark programs are showed in Table 2 [6].

Table 2. Benchmarks characteristics

Benchmark	Code lines	Number of variables	Type of variables	Characteristics
Matrix product	10	3	int	Strong read-write dependencies
Elliptic filter	40	45	Long int	Medium read-write dependencies

Each of the benchmark programs includes a lot of variables and a large number of arithmetic operations executed on them. Our experimental cases comprise a matrix product and an elliptical filter.

RECCO is a reliable code compiler, which provides two ways for duplication: all duplication and random duplication. Though RECCO can improve the reliability for a program, it is lack of precise analysis and proper model. In [6], RECCO uses the four benchmarks to evaluate the performance. Table 2 summarizes the main characteristics of the four benchmarks in this experiment. For each of them, the table showed the number of variables and the code length and the type of variables [6]. The four benchmarks are adopted by RECCO and the result will be compared with RECCO. Since our approach mainly aims at increasing data reliability, the four benchmarks are data dominated, which include a large number of variables and a lot of arithmetic operations. The RECCO proposed code re-ordering method and duplicated variables. The core of RECCO is to reduce the survival time for variables. Then all variables or part of the variables randomly are duplicated. Thus, it can increase the reliability.

The fault injection experiment results on all duplication are showed in Table 3. The results show that our model can reduce FSV and it is clearly that with our new methodology can reach a higher reliable level by using CDM. However, in this experiment, RECCO duplicates all the variables. Thus, the reliability of RECCO is higher than our CDM. The results reflect that our critical data model still needs to improve.

Table 3. Original RECCO duplicates all variables

	Original RECCO (duplicate all varibales)		CDM RECCO	
Benchmark	FSV	Rate	FSV	Rate
Matrix product	249	24.9%	323	32.3%
Elliptic filter	41	4.1%	76	7.6%

The fault injection experiment results on the random duplication are showed in Table 4. The benchmark for this experiment is FFT program. FFT is a golden application which is a Fast Fourier Transfer calculation routine. Fault injection experiments are performed on the FFT for contrast to the random duplication of RECCO. The results show that our critical data model is more reliable than the random duplication. In other words, out model is able to reach a higher reliability levels but using a lower amount of redundancy.

Table 4. Original RECCO randomly duplicates variables.

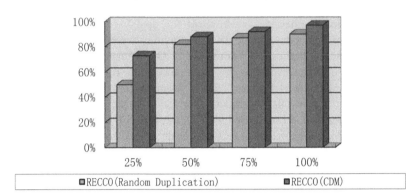

4.2 Performance Evaluation

We do performance evaluations through the sim-out order simulator, which is the most complicated and detailed micro-architectural simulator. This tool models in detail and out-of-order microprocessor with all of the bells and whistles, including branch prediction, caches, and external memory. This simulator is highly parameterized and can emulate machines of varying numbers of execution units. In this simulator, timing statistics are generated for a very detailed out-of-order issue superscalar processor core with a two-level cache memory hierarchy. The simulator also implements the branch predictor and the pipeline, tracking the latency of all pipeline operation. Therefore, it is appropriate for our performance evaluations [13].

In Fig. 3, it deeply shows the relations between different duplication rates and the costs in memory overhead and performance degradation. During the experiments, we first run the original benchmark program for several times and calculate the average running time which is regarded as the basic criteria. Then we run the four benchmark programs in Table 1 for several times and calculate the average time. These results are presented in Fig. 3.

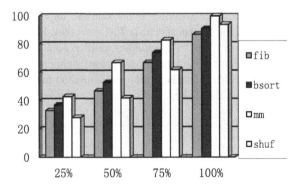

Fig. 3. Performance evaluations

From the Fig. 3, we can know that because of the data duplication, the program can inevitably cause the performance degradation. When we duplicate 25% of variables, the average percentage of performance degradation is 35.5%. Data duplications will bring the comparison instructions and the store operation for shadow version. Every time, read operation to original version will incur the compare with shadow version while write operation to original version will incur the store instruction to the shadow version. However, the performance degradation is acceptable for only duplicating the 25% of variables.

5 Conclusion

In this paper, we propose the critical data model (CDM), a model able to calculate the reliability of the variables. Based on the CDM, we can analyze the vulnerable and critical data. Thus, data duplication can be applied to the critical data or vulnerable data. The reliability of the variable is determined by the survival time and the dependency relation. Our critical data model is implemented on the RECCO, which is a reliable code compiler. The modifications introduced by the tool are completely transparent to the input source code and it will output the reliable code enhanced by using CDM. A series of fault injection experiments have been conducted. Experimental results show that our model can significantly improve the reliability of the program with performance degradation slightly. Comparing with duplicating all data, the reliability of programs decreases a little by using critical data model. In contrast to the memory and performance overhead, the slightly diminution on the reliability can be acceptable.

References

1. Ziegler, J.F., et al.: IBM experiments in soft fails in computer electronics (1978–1994). IBM J. Res. Dev. **40**(1), 318 (1996)
2. Clerk Maxwell, J.: A Treatise on Electricity and Magnetism, vol. 2, 3rd edn, pp. 68–73. Clarendon, Oxford (1892)
3. Baumann, R.C.: Soft errors in advanced semiconductor devices-part I: the three radiation sources. IEEE Trans. Device Mater. Reliab. **1**(1), 17–22 (2001)
4. Shirvani, P.P., Oh, N., McCluskey, E.J., Wood, D.L., Lovellette, M.N., Wood, K.S.: Software-implemented hardware fault tolerance experiments: COTS in space. In: International Conference on Dependable Systems and Networks (FTCS-30 and DCCA-8), New York, NY, pp. B56–B57. Elissa (2000). Title of paper if known, unpublished
5. Shirvani, P.P., Saxena, N.R., McCluskey, E.J.: Software-implemented EDAC protection against SEUs. IEEE Trans. Reliab. **49**(3), 273–284 (2000)
6. Benso, A., Chiusano, S., Prinetto, P., Tagliaferri, L.: C/C++ source-to-source compiler for dependable applications. In: International Conference on Dependable Systems and Networks, (FTCS-30 and DCCA-8), New York, NY, pp. 71–78 (2000)
7. Silva, J.G., Carreira, J., Maderia, H., Costa, D., Moreira, F.: Experimental assessment of parallel systems. In: Proceedings of FTCS-26, Sendaj (J), pp. 415–424 (1996)

8. Zenha Rela, M., Maderia, H., Silva, J.G.: Experimental evaluation of the fail-silent behavior in programs with consistency checks. In: Proceedings of FTCS-26, Sendaj (J), pp. 394–403 (1996)
9. Hiller, M.: Executable assertions for detecting data errors in embedded control systems. In: Proceedings of International Conference on Dependable Systems and Networks, p. 24 (2000)
10. Oh, N., Shirvani, P.P., McCluskey, E.J.: Control-flow checking by software signatures. IEEE Trans. Reliab. **51**, 111–122 (2002)
11. Li, A., Hong, B.: Software implemented transient fault detection in space computer. Aerosp. Sci. Technol. **11**(2–3), 245–252 (2007)
12. Reis, G.A., Chang, J., Vachharajani, N., et al.: SWIFT: software implemented fault tolerance. In: Proceedings of International Symposium Code Generation and Optimization (2005)
13. Xu, J., Shen, R., Tan, Q.: PRASE: an approach for program reliability analysis with soft errors. In: Proceedings of Pacific Rim International Symposium on Dependable Computing (2008, to appear)
14. Keshtgar, A., Araste, B.: Enhancing software reliablity against soft-error using minimum redundancy on Criticalata. Int. J. Comput. Netw. Inf. Secur. **9**(5), 21 (2017)
15. Benso, A., Di Carlo, S., Di Natale, G., Prinetto, P., Tagliaferri, L.: Data criticality estimation in software applications. In: International Test Conference (2003)
16. Xu, J., Shen, R., Tan, Q.: A novel optimum data duplication approach for soft error detection. In: Proceedings of Pacific Rim International Symposium on Dependable Computing (2008, to appear)
17. Burger, D., Austin, T.M., Bennett, S.: Evaluating future microprocessors: the SimpleScalar tool set. UW Madison CS Technical report #1342 (1997)

APDL: A Practical Privacy-Preserving Deep Learning Model for Smart Devices

Xindi Ma[1](✉), Jianfeng Ma[1], Sheng Gao[2], and Qingsong Yao[1]

[1] School of Cyber Engineering, Xidian University, Xi'an, China
xdma1989@gmail.com
[2] School of Information, Central University of Finance and Economics,
Beijing, China

Abstract. With the development of sensors on smart devices, many applications usually learn an accurate model based on the collected sensors' data to provide new services for users. However, the collection of data from users presents obvious privacy issues. Once the companies gather the data, they will keep it forever and the users from whom the data is collected can neither delete it nor control how it will be used.

In this paper, we design, implement, and evaluate a practical privacy-preserving deep learning model that enables multiple participants to jointly learn an accurate model for a given objective. We introduce a light-weight data sanitized mechanism based on differential privacy to perturb participant's local training data. After that, the service provider will collect all participants' sanitized data to learn a global accurate model. This offers an attractive point: participants preserve the privacy of their respective data while still benefitting from other participants' data. Finally, we theoretically prove that our APDL can achieves the ε-differential privacy and the evaluation results over a real-word dataset demonstrate that our APDL can perturb participant data effectively.

1 Introduction

Over the past years, by virtue of the rapid advances in the development of sensors on smart devices, the applications based on sensors have become an essential and inseparable part of our daily lives. Majority of applications are free, relying on information collected from user's device sensors for targeted service. As the bases, the collected data will be trained to learn an accurate model, which is usually called deep learning. After that, they will use the trained model as a foundation of their new services and applications, including accurate image and speech recognition [1] which surpassing humans [2].

However, the collection of data from users always has a number of privacy concerns for the data contributors. Nowadays, many companies collect photos, video, and speech information from individuals with privacy risks. Once the companies gather the data, they will keep it forever and the users from whom the data is collected can neither delete it nor control how it will be used [3]. What is worse, the collected voice recordings and images always contain many

© Springer Nature Singapore Pte Ltd. 2018
L. Zhu and S. Zhong (Eds.): MSN 2017, CCIS 747, pp. 377–390, 2018.
https://doi.org/10.1007/978-981-10-8890-2_28

accidentally captured sensitive information, for example, the sound of others speaking, ambient noises, computer screens, people faces, and other sensitive items [4]. After processing the above information, the companies can analyze and obtain users' live environments and social relationships which are also considered as privacy information for users.

In many domains, especially those related to medicine, the privacy and confidentiality worries may prevent hospitals and research centers from share their medical datasets by the law or regulation. As a result, the medical researchers can only perform the deep learning on the datasets which belong to their own institutions. However, it is well known that the deep learning model will be trained more accurately as the training datasets grow bigger and more diverse. Since the training data is simplex, the researchers may obtain worse models which can not be used for other datasets. For example, the training dataset which is owned by a single organization may be homogeneous, the trained model will be overfitted which produce inaccurate results when used on other inputs. In this case, the utility of datasets will be reduced significantly resulted by privacy restriction.

The goal of this paper is to design a privacy-preserving collaborative deep learning model that offers an attractive tradeoff between utility and privacy. To achieve the goal, we propose a practical privacy-preserving deep learning model based on differential privacy, named APDL. In APDL, we introduce differential privacy mechanism to perturb participant local training data and then upload perturbed data to service provider to train a global deep learning model. The main contributions of this paper are summarized as follows:

- We propose a novel privacy-preserving collaborative deep learning model (APDL) which perturb participant data based on differential privacy. The advantages of APDL are that it not only achieves participant data privacy preservation but also enables multiply participants to learn deep learning models on their own inputs collaboratively. As a result, the participant can benefit from other participants who are concurrently learning similar models.
- To protect participant local training data, we introduce the state-of-the-art differential privacy notions. We quantify the participant privacy level by optimizing the utility based on the local training model and then develop a lightweight data sanitized mechanism to preserve the privacy of local training data. In this manner, using the perturbed training data, the service provider can efficiently train a global deep learning model to provide service for all participants without leaking private information of participants.
- We conduct the analysis of APDL in both theory and practice. The results indicate that our APDL achieves ε-differential privacy and can perturb participant data effectively.

The rest of this paper is organized as follows. Section 2 presents some related works. In this Sect. 3, we present some preliminaries and the system overview, followed by the details of APDL in Sect. 4. Section 5 presents the theoretical analysis of privacy. In Sect. 6, we empirically evaluate the performance of our APDL. Finally, we conclude this paper in Sect. 7.

2   Related Work

In the past few years, deep learning has been considered to be a significant application in big data era. However, most of existing studies has faced an enormous challenge, that is how to protect user privacy while training a accurate deep learning model. In this section, we review the current research status of deep learning and privacy preservation in machine learning.

2.1   Deep Learning

Deep learning is researched to train the nonlinear features and functions from big data. The authors in [5,6] has given some surveys for deep-learning architectures, algorithms, and applications. And in some aspects, the deep learning has been shown to outperform traditional techniques, such as image recognition [7], speech recognition [1,8], and face detection [9]. In the domain of medical research, deep learning has been demonstrated its effective for analyzing biomedical data related to genetics [10] and cancer [11,12].

2.2   Privacy in Machine Learning

Privacy has attracted an increasing concern. A number of approaches have been proposed to address identity privacy [13–15], location privacy [16–20] and search privacy [21,22]. Simultaneously, there are many existing works to research the privacy preservation in machine learning. All of them are try to address the following three objectives: privacy of data used for learning a model or as input to an existing model, privacy of the model, and privacy of the model's output.

Addressing the privacy preservation of training data, the authors in [23–27] proposed some models based on encryption scheme. They encrypted the training data with homomorphic encryption and designed some protocols to train the deep learning model. However, these mechanisms usually had the lower efficiency and can not be used as a practical solution. In [28], Abadi et al. developed new algorithmic techniques for deep learning and a refined analysis of privacy costs within the framework of differential privacy. As a directly related work, Shokri and Shmatikov [3] presented a system for privacy-preserving deep learning, allowing local datasets of several participants staying home while the learned model for the neural network over the joint dataset can be obtained by the participants. Phan et al. [29] also proposed a novel mechanism to preserve differential privacy in deep neural networks. They intentionally added more noise into features which are less relevant to the model output, and vice-versa. Yet, most of these works still suffer from the low learning accuracy and efficiency. In comparison, out APDL perfectly protects participants' privacy by utilizing differential privacy while providing a high-quality learning accuracy.

3   System Overview

As discussed above, massive data collection may invoke unexpected privacy issues, which is a key bottleneck for the development and widespread of deep

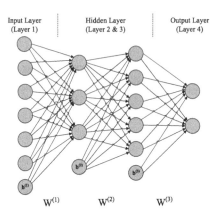

Fig. 1. Neural network mode

learning. To this end, we design APDL based on differential privacy. In this section, we first present some preliminaries that serve as the basis of our APDL, and then present the system model and threat model.

3.1 Preliminaries

Differential Privacy. In our privacy-preserving model, we use the state-of-the-art privacy notion, *Differential Privacy* [30], which can not only provides strong privacy protection but also resist any background knowledge attack from adversaries. Informally, an algorithm A is differentially private if the output is indistinguishable to any particular record in the dataset.

Definition 1 (ε-Differential Privacy [30]). *Let $\varepsilon > 0$ be the privacy budget. A randomized algorithm $\mathcal{A}$ is ε-differentially private if for all data sets D_1 and D_2 differing on at most one element, i.e., $d(D_1, D_2) = 1$, and all $\mathcal{S} \in Range(\mathcal{A})$,*

$$Pr[\mathcal{A}(D_1) \in \mathcal{S}] \leq exp(\varepsilon)Pr[\mathcal{A}(D_2) \in \mathcal{S}] \tag{1}$$

Privacy budget $\varepsilon > 0$ is a small constant, which specifies the desired privacy level. The smaller of ε, the stronger of privacy preservation, leading to more limit on the influence of items. Typically, ε is small (e.g., $\varepsilon \leq 1$).

To achieve the differential privacy, there are two well-established techniques: the Laplace mechanism [31] and the exponential mechanism [32], which are both based on the concept of global sensitivity [31] to compute over a dataset.

Deep Learning. Deep learning can be seen as a set of techniques applied to neural networks. Figure 1 is a neural network with 6 inputs, 2 hide layers, and 2 outputs. The neuron nodes are connected via weight variables. In a typical multi-layer network, each neuron receives the output of the neuron in the previous layer plus a bias signal from a special neuron, such as $b^{(1)}, b^{(2)}$, and $b^{(3)}$. In a deep learning structure of neural network, there can be multiply layers each with thousands of neurons.

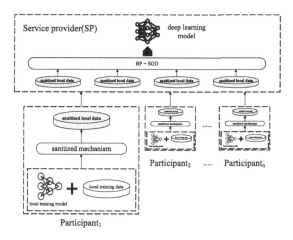

Fig. 2. System model of APDL

Each neuron node (except the bias node) is associated with an activation function f. Examples of f in deep learning are $f(x) = max\{0, x\}$ (rectified linear), $f(x) = \frac{e^x - e^{-x}}{e^x + e^{-x}}$ (hyperbolic tangent), and $f(x) = (1 + e^{-x})^{-1}$ (sigmoid). The output at layer $l+1$, denoted as $a^{(l+1)}$, is computed as $a^{(l+1)} = f(W^{(l)}a^{(l)} + b^{(l)})$, in which $(W^{(l)}, b^{(l)})$ is the weights connecting layers l and $l + 1$, $b^{(l)}$ is the bias term at layer l, and $a^{(l)}$ is the output at layer l. In APDL, we assume that the deep learning model has k layers and the i-th layer owns $n^{(i)}$ nodes.

The learning task is, given a training dataset, to determine these weight variables to minimise a pre-defined cost function such as the cross-entropy or the squared-error cost function [33]. In our model, we consider each participant has trained his own deep learning model using his dataset, expressed as $\overline{Y} = M(X)$, in which X is the input dataset, M is the deep learning model, and $\overline{Y}$ is the computed output of the network.

3.2 System Model

Our APDL is designed to protect participants' data privacy without changing the existed deep learning model. Before describe the details, we derive the basic components in our APDL in Fig. 2.

- **Participants**. In APDL, we consider all participants has the same training objective and each participant has his local training data and local training model. However, his data maybe very homogeneous and training an overfitted model which will be inaccurate when used on other inputs. So we design a service provider (SP) to collect all participants' local training data and train a global deep learning model. Before sharing their local data, participants will sanitize the data using sanitized mechanism (e.g., differential privacy in APDL) to protect the privacy of data owners.

– **Service Provider (SP).** To train the accurate deep learning model, SP collects the sanitized training data from participants. After that, the global accurate model is trained based on back propagation (BP) and stochastic gradient descent (SGD).

3.3 Threat Model

In APDL, malicious attackers may exist around the participants and steal information during uploading training data. Then, we consider the SP to be curious-but-honest. During the training process, SP may be curious about participants' local data. So SP may be strictly follow the training protocol but also violate and disclose participants' privacy information.

3.4 Design Goals

As a privacy-preserving deep learning model, APDL should fulfill the following requirements.

– **Learning accuracy:** The proposed mechanism should train an accurate deep learning model to suit for all participants' data.
– **Security goals:** The proposed mechanism should keep the privacy of participants' training data. In more details, no sensitive information about the data will be leaked to SP and other participants.

4   Design of Sanitized Mechanism

In this section, we design the sanitized mechanism based on the differential privacy. As described above, one of the most widely used mechanism to achieve ε-differential privacy is Laplace mechanism [31] (Theorem 1), which adds random noises to the numeric output of a query, in which the magnitude of noises follows Laplace distribution with variance $\frac{\Delta f}{\varepsilon}$ where Δf represents the global sensitivity of function f.

Theorem 1 (Laplace Mechanism [31]). *For function $f : \mathcal{D} \to \mathbb{R}^n$, a randomized algorithm $\mathcal{A}_f = f(D) + Lap(\frac{\Delta f}{\varepsilon})$ is ε-differential private, where $Lap(\frac{\Delta f}{\varepsilon})$ is generated from the Laplace distribution with parameter $\frac{\Delta f}{\varepsilon}$. That is:*

$$Pr[Lap(\frac{\Delta f}{\varepsilon}) = z] \propto exp(-z \cdot \frac{\varepsilon}{\Delta f}) \tag{2}$$

Given two neighboring datasets $\mathcal{D}_1$ and $\mathcal{D}_2$, we present the global sensitivity of function f as follow:

$$\Delta f = \max_{d(D_1, D_2)=1} \|f(D_1) - f(D_2)\|_1 \tag{3}$$

Unfortunately, the naive application of Laplace mechanism results in the significantly large noise magnitude and uselessness of perturbed data because of large global sensitivity. So we adopt a practical differentially private method [34] to sanitize the local training data. In the following, we divide the sanitized mechanism into two phases: *noise calibration*, focuses on selecting the magnitude (denoted as $z_i^{(k)}$) for each output neuron node using local training model; *data sanitization*, aims to generate the useful sanitized training data based on the local training model.

4.1   Noise Calibration for Local Training Model

Based on the pre-defined cost function and local training model, the noise magnitude can be determined by optimizing the cost. In our model, we assume that each local training model has $n^{(1)}$ input neuron nodes and select the average sum-of-squares error between computed output $\overline{Y}$ and true value Y as the cost function. The sanitized noise injected to input neuron nodes is denoted as $Z = (z_1^{(k)}, z_2^{(k)}, \dots, z_{n^{(k)}}^{(k)})$ in which $z_i^{(k)}$ is the magnitude of Laplace noise for output node i in output layer k. For simplicity, we denote the reciprocal of Z as $Z_r = (1/z_1^{(k)}, 1/z_2^{(k)}, \dots, 1/z_{n^{(k)}}^{(k)})$. After that, we can determine the magnitude of Laplace noise on each input neuron node via the following programming:

$$
\begin{aligned}
minimize \quad & \|Z\|_1 \\
subjective\ to \quad & [M(X) - M(X_p)] \cdot Z_r \leq \varepsilon \\
& Z, Z_r \geq 0 \\
& d(X, X_p) = 1
\end{aligned}
\tag{4}
$$

Through the above equations, we can obtain the minimized expected error of all injected noises onto input neuron nodes since the Laplace noises are independent and each of them satisfies $E[|Lap(z_i^{(k)})|] = z_i^{(k)}$. Since the first constrain, we can guarantee the ε-differential privacy for the sanitized local training data. Then, another purpose of the first constrain is to capture the correlation between local training model and neighbouring local data. The noise magnitude Z and Z_r also be ensured non-negative by the second constrain.

Since the above formulation (4) is non-convex, it must be transformed into a convex one to obtain a global optimal solution. For simplicity, we introduce another two variables Z_1 and Z_2 and set $Z_1 = Z, Z_2 = Z_r$. As described above, we can get $z_i^{(k)} \cdot z_{ri}^{(k)} = 1$. Thus, another additional constraint can be added to ensure the reciprocal relationship for each $i \in [1, n^{(k)}]$. Moreover, the constraint can be relaxed to $Z_1 \cdot Z_2^T \geq I$. So we can transform the formulation (4) into the following programming:

$$
\begin{aligned}
minimize \quad & \|Z_1\|_1 \\
subjective\ to \quad & [M(X) - M(X_p)] \cdot Z_2 \leq \varepsilon \\
& Z_1, Z_2 \geq 0 \\
& Z_1 \cdot Z_2^T \geq I \\
& d(X, X_p) = 1
\end{aligned}
\tag{5}
$$

After that, we first solve the convex formulation in programming (5). Then, we set $Z_r = Z_2$ such that our sanitized mechanism also satisfy ε-differential privacy and set Z by letting each item $z_i^{(k)}$ be the reciprocal of the i-th item in Z_r. Since the formulation (5) is convex, we can ensure that our noise calibration algorithm is outperform the traditional Laplace algorithm.

4.2   Adding Noise to Local Training Data

In this section, a noise vector is generated to sanitize the local training data. We take the above noise magnitude output Z as input and generate the Laplace noise to form a useful sanitized local training data. The usefulness of sanitized data is qualified by minimizing the error between local model output based on the sanitized training data and the noisy local model output. Specifically, two error vectors $\{R, L\}$ are also introduced and the utility is qualified by their root mean square error (RMSE): $\frac{1}{2}\|R + L\|_2^2$. Then, the optimization formulation is given as follows:

$$
\begin{aligned}
minimize \quad & \frac{1}{2}\|R + L\|_2^2 \\
subjective\ to \quad & O_z - L \leq M(X_p) \leq O_z + R \\
& X_p \in \{0, 1\}^{n^{(1)}}
\end{aligned}
\tag{6}
$$

where O_z is the noise local model output vector and $O_z(i) = v_i^{(k)} + Lap(z_i^{(k)})$, $i \in [1, n^{(k)}]$, $v_i^{(k)}$ is the deep learning model output of node i in layer k.

However, we can easily find that solving formulation (6) is **NP**-hard by reducing it from Exact Cover problem (The proof is omitted because of the limited space and it is similar to that in [35]). So we replace the X_p with X_p^r, $X_p^r \in [0, 1]^{n^{(1)}}$, to solve the relaxed formulation (6) in our data sanitized algorithm. After that, we can obtain X_p by rounding each item x_{pi}^r to 1 with probability x_{pi}^r.

After the process described above, the participants can generate the sanitized local training data. Then, the participants will upload the sanitized data to SP and SP trains the global deep learning model based the uploaded data. The details of the process are listed in Algorithm 1.

5   Theoretical Analysis

In this section, we theoretically analyze the privacy preservation which APDL satisfies, which is described above that our APDL is ε-differential privacy.

Theorem 2. *Based on the local training data perturbation, APDL satisfies ε-differential privacy.*

Algorithm 1. Process of APDL for Deep Learning Model

Input: Local training data X, local training model M, privacy budget ε.
Output: Sanitized local training data X_p.
1: Solve mathematical formulation (5);
2: Set $Z_r = Z_2$;
3: Set Z be the reciprocal of each item in Z_r;
4: Generate noise according to $Lap(z_i^{(k)})$ for each output node $i, i \in [1, n^{(k)}]$;
5: **for** each node i in output layer k **do**
6:     Set $O_z(i) = v_i^{(k)} + Lap(z_i^{(k)})$;
7: **end for**
8: Relax the constrains in formulation (6);
9: Replace X_p with $X_p^r \in [0,1]^{n^{(1)}}$ to solve the relaxed (6);
10: **for** each node i in input layer **do**
11:     Randomly generate a number ρ in $[0,1]$;
12:     **if** $\rho \leq x_{pi}^r$ **then**
13:         Set $x_{pi} = 1$;
14:     **else**
15:         Set $x_{pi} = 0$;
16:     **end if**
17: **end for**
18: Send perturbed local training data X_p to SP;

Proof. Since the data sanitization in Sect. 4.2 is considered as post-processing on differentially privacy without the access of local training data, we consider that there is no privacy loss in this phase. Hay et al. [36] had shown that any post-processing of the answers cannot diminish the rigorous privacy guarantee, so we only need to focus on analyzing the privacy guarantee in Sect. 4.1.

Let $M(D_i)$ be the output of local training model with input dataset D_i, $\mathcal{A}$ be the sanitized mechanism, and D_1, D_2 be the neighboring datasets. For any $S = (s_1, s_2, \ldots, s_n{}^{(k)}) \in Range(A)$, the following formulation can be established:

$$\frac{Pr[\mathcal{A}(D_1)] = S}{Pr[\mathcal{A}(D_2)] = S} = \prod_{i=1}^{n^{(k)}} \frac{Pr[\mathcal{A}(D_1)_i = r_i]}{Pr[\mathcal{A}(D_2)_i = r_i]}$$

$$\geq \exp\left(-\sum_{i=1}^{n^{(k)}} \frac{1}{z_i^{(k)}} |M(D_1)_i - M(D_2)_i|\right) \quad (7)$$

$$\geq \exp\left(-\max_{d(D_1, D_2)=1} \sum_{i=1}^{n^{(k)}} \frac{1}{z_i^{(k)}} |M(D_1)_i - M(D_2)_i|\right)$$

$$\geq \exp(-\varepsilon)$$

The first step is established because of the noises is injected independently on each model output; the second step is obtained from the introduced Laplace noises and triangle inequality, and the last step is derived from the first constraint in formulation (5).

The proof is complete.

Utility Analysis. The expected Mean Absolute Error (MAE) is used to measure the deviation between participant's raw and perturbed training data, which is formally defined as following [35].

$$MAE(X, X_p) = E[\frac{1}{n^{(k)}} \sum_{j=1}^{n^{(k)}} |x_j - x_{pj}|] \tag{8}$$

Let $z_j^{(k)}, l_j, r_j$ be the j_{th} entry in vector Z, R, L.

$$\begin{aligned}
\text{MAE} &= \frac{1}{n^{(k)}} E[\sum_{j=1}^{n^{(k)}} |x_j - x_{pj}|] \\
&\leq \frac{1}{n^{(k)}} (E[\sum_{j=1}^{n^{(k)}} |Lap(z_j^{(k)})|] + E[\sum_{j=1}^{n^{(k)}} |max\{l_j, r_j\}|]) \\
&\leq \frac{1}{n^{(k)}} (\sum_{j=1}^{n^{(k)}} E[|Lap(z_j^{(k)})|] + E[\sum_{j=1}^{n^{(k)}} |l_j + r_j|]) \\
&= \frac{1}{n^{(k)}} (||Z||_1 + E[||R + L||_1])
\end{aligned} \tag{9}$$

6   Experimental Evaluation

In this section, we present a series of empirical results of APDL conducted over MINIST dataset [37] which is composed of 60,000 training handwritten digits and 10,000 test ones. Then, we use Torch7 [38] and Torch7 nn packages to construct and train the deep learning model. During the training, we use LeNet neural network as the training model.

While evaluating the local training data perturbation in APDL, we mainly focus on analyzing the influence of participants for model accuracy and the perturbation quality of APDL. We also compare the accuracy of APDL with the non-privacy-preserving scheme (NPP). We assume that there are three participants contributing their local training data and each participant have 20,000 examples. In the evaluation, we use the probabilistic method to measure the learning accuracy: $P = sum\{x = x_p\}/total$, where x is the true value, x_p is the output of the learning model, and $total$ is the number of test examples.

First of all, we carry out the analysis on the training model accuracy influenced by the number of participants. As shown in Fig. 3, the model accuracy increase with the number of epoch. As the increase of epoch, our APDL can train a more accurate deep learning model. So the process of test will be more accurate. Additionally, with more participants joining the training process, the SP has more training data to learn the model. As described above, the deep learning model will be trained more accurately as the training datasets grow bigger and more diverse. So the trained model which has 3 participants has a better model accuracy than that with 1 or 2 participants.

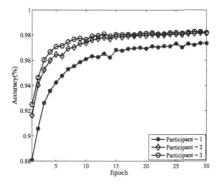

Fig. 3. Model accuracy influenced by participants

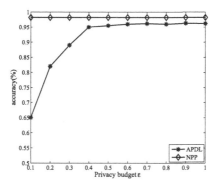

Fig. 4. Model accuracy influenced by privacy budget

Then, we plot the model accuracy by varying the privacy budget ε in differential privacy and compare the accuracy of our APDL with NPP in Fig. 4. As the simulation result shows, the accuracy of our APDL increases with the privacy budget ε. With the increasing of ε, APDL will generate less noise to sanitize the local training data to guarantee the utility. So our APDL will train a more accurate model. However, the accuracy of our APDL has not reached the NPP resulted by the added noise.

7   Conclusion

The disclosure of training data in a union deep learning system seriously threatens participants privacy, especially when participants send their raw data to SP. In this paper, we propose a novel solution, called APDL, to address the privacy issues in deep learning model. In APDL, we introduce differential privacy as the sanitized mechanism to perturb participant's local training data. Our methodology works for any type of neural network. Therefore, it can help bring the benefits of deep learning to domains where data owners are precluded from sharing their data by confidentiality concerns.

Acknowledgment. This work was supported by the National Natural Science Foundation of China (Grant Nos. U1405255, 61672413, 61602537, 61602357, 61303221), National High Technology Research and Development Program (863 Program) (Grant Nos. 2015AA016007), Shaanxi Science & Technology Coordination & Innovation Project (Grant No. 2016TZC-G-6-3), Shaanxi Provincial Natural Science Foundation (Grant Nos. 2015JQ6227, 2016JM6005), China 111 Project (Grant No. B16037), Beijing Municipal Social Science Foundation (Grant No. 16XCC023).

References

1. Hannun, A.Y., Case, C., Casper, J., Catanzaro, B., Diamos, G., Elsen, E., Prenger, R., Satheesh, S., Sengupta, S., Coates, A., Ng, A.Y.: Deep speech: scaling up end-to-end speech recognition, CoRR, vol. abs/1412.5567 (2014)
2. He, K., Zhang, X., Ren, S., Sun, J.: Delving deep into rectifiers: surpassing human-level performance on imagenet classification. In: 2015 IEEE International Conference on Computer Vision, ICCV 2015, Santiago, Chile, 7–13 December 2015, pp. 1026–1034 (2015)
3. Shokri, R., Shmatikov, V.: Privacy-preserving deep learning. In: Proceedings of the 22nd ACM SIGSAC Conference on Computer and Communications Security, Denver, CO, USA, 6–12 October 2015, pp. 1310–1321 (2015)
4. Shultz, D.: When your voice betrays you (2015)
5. Bengio, Y.: Learning deep architectures for AI. Found. Trends Mach. Learn. **2**(1), 1–127 (2009)
6. Deng, L.: A tutorial survey of architectures, algorithms, and applications for deep learning. APSIPA Trans. Sig. Inf. Process. **3**, 1–29 (2014)
7. Krizhevsky, A., Sutskever, I., Hinton, G.E.: Imagenet classification with deep convolutional neural networks. Commun. ACM **60**(6), 84–90 (2017)
8. Graves, A., Mohamed, A., Hinton, G.E.: Speech recognition with deep recurrent neural networks. In: IEEE International Conference on Acoustics, Speech and Signal Processing, ICASSP 2013, Vancouver, BC, Canada, 26–31 May 2013, pp. 6645–6649 (2013)
9. Taigman, Y., Yang, M., Ranzato, M., Wolf, L.: DeepFace: closing the gap to human-level performance in face verification. In: 2014 IEEE Conference on Computer Vision and Pattern Recognition, CVPR 2014, Columbus, OH, USA, 23–28 June 2014, pp. 1701–1708 (2014)
10. Xiong, H.Y., Alipanahi, B., Lee, L.J., Bretschneider, H., Merico, D., Yuen, R.K., Hua, Y., Gueroussov, S., Najafabadi, H.S., Hughes, T.R., et al.: The human splicing code reveals new insights into the genetic determinants of disease. Science **347**(6218), 1254806 (2015)
11. Fakoor, R., Ladhak, F., Nazi, A., Huber, M.: Using deep learning to enhance cancer diagnosis and classification. In: Proceedings of the International Conference on Machine Learning (2013)
12. Liang, M., Li, Z., Chen, T., Zeng, J.: Integrative data analysis of multi-platform cancer data with a multimodal deep learning approach. IEEE/ACM Trans. Comput. Biol. Bioinform. **12**(4), 928–937 (2015)
13. Jiang, Q., Zeadally, S., Ma, J., He, D.: Lightweight three-factor authentication and key agreement protocol for internet-integrated wireless sensor networks. IEEE Access **5**, 3376–3392 (2017)

14. Jiang, Q., Ma, J., Yang, C., Ma, X., Shen, J., Chaudhry, S.A.: Efficient end-to-end authentication protocol for wearable health monitoring systems. Comput. Electr. Eng. **63**, 182–195 (2017)
15. Ma, X., Ma, J., Li, H., Jiang, Q., Gao, S.: ARMOR: a trust-based privacy-preserving framework for decentralized friend recommendation in online social networks. Fut. Gener. Comput. Syst. **79**, 82–94 (2018)
16. Gao, S., Ma, J., Sun, C., Li, X.: Balancing trajectory privacy and data utility using a personalized anonymization model. J. Netw. Comput. Appl. **38**, 125–134 (2014)
17. Gao, S., Ma, J., Shi, W., Zhan, G., Sun, C.: TrPF: a trajectory privacy-preserving framework for participatory sensing. IEEE Trans. Inf. Forensics Secur. **8**(6), 874–887 (2013)
18. Ma, X., Li, H., Ma, J., Jiang, Q., Gao, S., Xi, N., Lu, D.: APPLET: a privacy-preserving framework for location-aware recommender system. Sci. Chin. Inf. Sci. **60**(9), 092101 (2017)
19. Ma, X., Ma, J., Li, H., Jiang, Q., Gao, S.: AGENT: an adaptive geo-indistinguishable mechanism for continuous location-based service. Peer-to-Peer Netw. Appl. **11**(3), 473–485 (2017)
20. Gao, S., Ma, X., Zhu, J., Ma, J.: APRS: a privacy-preserving location-aware recommender system based on differentially private histogram. Sci. Chin. Inf. Sci. **60**(11), 119103 (2017)
21. Fu, Z., Huang, F., Sun, X., Vasilakos, A., Yang, C.-N.: Enabling semantic search based on conceptual graphs over encrypted outsourced data. IEEE Trans. Serv. Comput. **12**(8), 1874–1884 (2016)
22. Fu, Z., Wu, X., Guan, C., Sun, X., Ren, K.: Toward efficient multi-keyword fuzzy search over encrypted outsourced data with accuracy improvement. IEEE Trans. Inf. Forensics Secur. **11**(12), 2706–2716 (2016)
23. Zhang, Q., Yang, L.T., Chen, Z.: Privacy preserving deep computation model on cloud for big data feature learning. IEEE Trans. Comput. **65**(5), 1351–1362 (2016)
24. Mohassel, P., Zhang, Y.: SecureML: a system for scalable privacy-preserving machine learning. In: 2017 IEEE Symposium on Security and Privacy, SP 2017, San Jose, CA, USA, 22–26 May 2017, pp. 19–38 (2017)
25. Li, P., Li, J., Huang, Z., Li, T., Gao, C., Yiu, S., Chen, K.: Multi-key privacy-preserving deep learning in cloud computing. Future Gener. Compt. Syst. **74**, 76–85 (2017)
26. Gilad-Bachrach, R., Dowlin, N., Laine, K., Lauter, K.E., Naehrig, M., Wernsing, J.: CryptoNets: applying neural networks to encrypted data with high throughput and accuracy. In: Proceedings of the 33rd International Conference on Machine Learning, ICML, New York City, NY, USA, pp. 201–210 (2016)
27. Bost, R., Popa, R.A., Tu, S., Goldwasser, S.: Machine learning classification over encrypted data. In: 22nd Annual Network and Distributed System Security Symposium, NDSS, San Diego, California, USA (2015)
28. Abadi, M., Chu, A., Goodfellow, I., McMahan, H.B., Mironov, I., Talwar, K., Zhang, L.: Deep learning with differential privacy. In: Proceedings of the 2016 ACM SIGSAC Conference on Computer and Communications Security, pp. 308–318. ACM (2016)
29. Phan, N., Wu, X., Hu, H., Dou, D.: Adaptive laplace mechanism: differential privacy preservation in deep learning, CoRR, vol. abs/1709.05750 (2017)
30. Dwork, C.: Differential privacy. In: Bugliesi, M., Preneel, B., Sassone, V., Wegener, I. (eds.) ICALP 2006. LNCS, vol. 4052, pp. 1–12. Springer, Heidelberg (2006). https://doi.org/10.1007/11787006_1

31. Dwork, C., McSherry, F., Nissim, K., Smith, A.: Calibrating noise to sensitivity in private data analysis. In: Halevi, S., Rabin, T. (eds.) TCC 2006. LNCS, vol. 3876, pp. 265–284. Springer, Heidelberg (2006). https://doi.org/10.1007/11681878_14

32. McSherry, F., Talwar, K.: Mechanism design via differential privacy. In: Proceedings of the 48th Annual IEEE Symposium on Foundations of Computer Science FOCS, Providence, RI, USA, pp. 94–103 (2007)

33. Murphy, K.P.: Machine Learning - A Probabilistic Perspective. Adaptive Computation and Machine Learning Series. MIT Press, Cambridge (2012)

34. Shen, Y., Jin, H.: EpicRec: towards practical differentially private framework for personalized recommendation. In: Proceedings of the ACM SIGSAC Conference on Computer and Communications Security, Vienna, Austria, pp. 180–191 (2016)

35. Shen, Y., Jin, H.: Privacy-preserving personalized recommendation: an instance-based approach via differential privacy. In: IEEE International Conference on Data Mining, ICDM, Shenzhen, China, pp. 540–549 (2014)

36. Hay, M., Rastogi, V., Miklau, G., Suciu, D.: Boosting the accuracy of differentially private histograms through consistency. PVLDB **3**(1), 1021–1032 (2010)

37. LeCun, Y., Bottou, L., Bengio, Y., Haffner, P.: Gradient-based learning applied to document recognition. Proc. IEEE **86**(11), 2278–2324 (1998)

38. Collobert, R., Kavukcuoglu, K., Farabet, C.: Torch7: a Matlab-like environment for machine learning. In: BigLearn, NIPS Workshop, no. EPFL-CONF-192376 (2011)

Barrier Coverage Lifetime Maximization in a Randomly Deployed Bistatic Radar Network

Jiaoyan Chen[1(✉)], Bang Wang[2], and Wenyu Liu[2]

[1] School of Information Engineering, Nanchang University, Nanchang, China
chenjiaoyan@ncu.edu.cn
[2] School of Electronic Information and Communications,
Huazhong University of Science and Technology, Wuhan, China
{wangbang,liuwy}@hust.edu.cn

Abstract. Maximizing the lifetime of barrier coverage is a critical issue in randomly deployment sensor networks. In this paper, we study the barrier coverage lifetime maximization problem in a bistatic radar network, where the radar nodes follow a uniform deployment. We first construct a coverage graph to describe the relationship among different bistatic radar pairs. We then propose a solution to maximize the barrier lifetime: An algorithm is first proposed to find all barriers based on coverage graph and then determines the operation time for each barrier by using linear programming method. We also propose two heuristic algorithms called greedy algorithm and random algorithm for large-scale networks. Simulation results validate the effectiveness of the proposed algorithms.

1 Introduction

Barrier coverage of wireless sensor network has been widely used as an effective tool in security applications, such as international boundary surveillance and critical infrastructure protection [1]. Wireless sensors usually operate in unattended environments with limited power supply by small-sized batteries. How to ensure network work beyond single sensor lifetime is a critical issue for barrier coverage. Recently, many algorithms that schedule the sensor working states have been proposed for maximizing the barrier coverage lifetime [2–4], however, they are based on the *disk sensing model* or *sector sensing model*. In the disk sensing model, the covered area of sensor is a disk centered at its location with radius as the sensing range. While in the sector sensing model, the covered area of sensor is a sector region of a disk [5].

For the disk model, Kumar et al. [6] first propose an Randomized Independent Sleeping (RIS) algorithm, where each sensor independently determines whether to be activated with a predefined probability. Chen et al. [7] propose a localized

This paper is supported in part by the National Natural Science Foundation of China (No. 61760929, 61461030, 61371141).

L. Zhu and S. Zhong (Eds.): MSN 2017, CCIS 747, pp. 391–401, 2018.
https://doi.org/10.1007/978-981-10-8890-2_29

algorithm called Localized Barrier Coverage Protocol (LBCP) for ensuring local barrier coverage and show that the LBCP outperforms RIS by up to six times. Kumar et al. [8] propose an optimal solution to the problem of how to maximize the total barrier coverage lifetime in homogeneous or heterogeneous networks. Kim et al. [9] identify a new security problem of the proposed algorithms in [8] and propose two remedies for the barrier coverage problem. For the sector sensing model, Zhao et al. [4] propose an efficient algorithm to solve the barrier coverage lifetime maximization problem based on sector sensing model.

Recently, coverage problem based on radar sensors has become a new research focus. Radar sensor emits radio and collects echo reflected from target. Radar determines whether the target exists or not by analyzing the difference between the original radio and collected echo [10]. There are two types of radar sensors according to the location of the transmitter and receiver. Transmitter and receiver co-locate in the monostatic radar. Transmitter and receiver are deployed separatively in the bistatic radar [11]. Much unlike the disk coverage model of monostatic radar, the coverage area of bistatic radar pair can be characterized by the Cassini oval with foci at transmitter and receiver location. Previous studies about coverage problem of bistatic radar focus on the nodes deployment for constructing target coverage and barrier coverage [12,13].

In this paper, we study the barrier coverage lifetime problem for bistatic radar sensor networks. We first construct a coverage graph based on the connected coverage region of bistatic radar pairs. We then propose an algorithm to find barriers in the network and apply the linear programming method to assign operation time slots for each barrier such that the total barrier lifetime can be maximized. We also propose two heuristic algorithms called Greedy Algorithm and Random Algorithm for large-scale networks. As far as we know, the work most similar to ours is [14]. Compared to [14], our work in this paper have several distinct differences: First, the initial energy of radar nodes and the energy consumption rate of transmitter and receiver are considered as different in our work; While there are set the same in [14]. Second, the work [14] does not consider the bistatic radar sensor when their coverage region is disjoint, but our work have considered this issue. Third, each barrier found in this paper satisfies the condition that each receiver only couple with one transmitter while the barrier in [14] does not have such a constraint.

The rest of this paper is organized as follows. We present the network model and problem description in Sect. 2. Section 4 provides our solutions, and simulation results are given in Sect. 5. Finally, Sect. 6 concludes the paper.

2   Network Model and Problem Description

We consider a bistatic radar sensor network consisting of M transmitters and N receivers randomly deployed in a $W \times H$ rectangle region. For a transmitter-receiver pair $T_i R_j$, the *Signal-to-Noise Ratio* (SNR) of R_j due to a target located at z can be computed by [15]:

$$SNR_z(T_i, R_j) = \frac{C}{\|T_i z\|^2 \|R_j z\|^2}, \tag{1}$$

where C is a constant reflecting the physical characteristics of the bistatic radar such as the antenna gain of the transmitter and receiver. $\|T_i z\|$ denotes the Euclidean distance between T_i and z. Given the detection requirement SNR_{th}, a target can be detected by the (T_i, R_j) pair, if $SNR_z(T_i, R_j) \geq SNR_{th}$.

We assume that transmitters can use orthogonal frequencies to avoid interference at receivers [16,17]. Thus a receiver can potentially couple with different transmitters by changing the working frequency at different time slot. However, a receiver can only couple with one transmitter at a time slot since a receiver cannot work with two different frequencies at the same time. For ease of presentation, in this paper, we define the *vulnerability* of the target located at z as:

$$l(z) \doteq \sqrt{\|T_i z\| \cdot \|R_j z\|} \tag{2}$$

The vulnerability contour can be characterized by Cassini oval with foci at the transmitter and receiver location. Given the SNR threshold γ, we define the *maximum vulnerability* as:

$$l_{max} = \sqrt[4]{\frac{C}{SNR_{th}}}. \tag{3}$$

A target located at z can be detected by the (T_i, R_j) pair, if $l(z) \leq l_{max}^2$. In this regard, we also say that the point z can be covered by the (T_i, R_j) pair.

Let two virtual nodes s and t denote the left boundary and right boundary, respectively. We say that a bistatic radar pair (T_i, R_j) form a sub-barrier with s and t, if the coverage region of (T_i, R_j) overlaps with the left and right boundary. A barrier consists of a chain of bistatic radar pairs starting at s and ending at t, where the coverage regions of adjacent radar pairs overlap with each other. Since a receiver can only couple with one transmitter at a time, in one barrier a receiver can only appear at most once. On the other hand, a transmitter can couple with different receivers, and in one barrier a transmitter may appear in different bistatic radar pairs.

Let E_{T_i} and E_{R_j} denote the initial energy of the T_i and R_j, respectively. We assume that both transmitters and receivers consume the energy at a flat rate in the working state. Let α_t and α_r denote the energy consumption rate of an active transmitter and an active receiver, respectively. We assume $\alpha_t \geq \alpha_r$, since in general signal transmission consumes more energy than signal reception. The lifetime of T_i and R_j can be computed by $\frac{E_{T_i}}{\alpha_t}$ and $\frac{E_{R_j}}{\alpha_r}$, respectively.

3   Constructing a Barrier Coverage Graph

In this section, we construct a *barrier coverage graph* (BCG) based on the connected coverage areas of bistatic radars. Without loss of generality, we index the transmitters and receivers according to their x-coordinate from the left boundary to the right boundary of the network. For each bistatic transmitter-receiver pair (T_i, R_j), the shape of its coverage region depends on the relation between l_{max} and $d(T_i, R_j)$, and can be divided into two types:

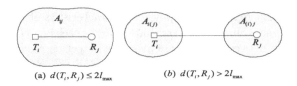

(a) $d(T_i, R_j) \leq 2l_{max}$ (b) $d(T_i, R_j) > 2l_{max}$

Fig. 1. Coverage region of bistatic radar $T_i R_j$

(a1) When $d(T_i, R_j) \leq 2l_{max}$, the coverage region of a (T_i, R_j) pair is a connected region, as shown in Fig. 1 (a); In this case, we denote the connected coverage region of (T_i, R_j) as A_{ij}. Note that A_{ij} contains both T_i and R_j.

(a2) When $d(T_i, R_j) > 2l_{max}$, the coverage region of a (T_i, R_j) pair contains two disconnected ellipse regions, as shown in Fig. 1 (b). In this case, we let $A_{i(j)}$ and $A_{(i)j}$ to denote the two disconnected coverage regions, respectively. Note that $A_{i(j)}$ contains T_i; but does not contain R_j. And $A_{(i)j}$ contains R_j, but not T_i.

It can be shown that when $d(T_i, R_j)$ increases, both the coverage region of $A_{i(j)}$ and $A_{(i)j}$ reduce. When the distance is larger than some threshold, the two coverage regions do not contribute much in barrier construction. So we do not consider a (T_i, R_j) pair when $d(T_i, R_j) > D_{max}$.

In this paper, we use the connected coverage regions from all bistatic radar pairs to search potential barriers. For simplicity, we use the coverage region to denote the covered area of a pair of transmitter and receiver, which might be in the form of A_{ij}, or $A_{i(j)}$ and $A_{(i)j}$. We construct a barrier coverage graph $G = (V, E)$ as follows. In the graph, V is the set of all coverage regions plus two virtual nodes s and t. There are M transmitters and N receivers in the network. So there are in total MN candidate bistatic transmitter-receiver pairs.

In the first step, we determine the shape of bistatic radar coverage region. If its coverage region is a connected region A_{ij}, we use only one vertex A_{ij} in the graph to represent this (T_i, R_j) pair. Otherwise, two vertices $A_{i(j)}$ and $A_{(i)j}$ are used to represent this bistatic radar pair. Therefore, the vertex set V consists of $(2 \times M \times N + 2)$ elements at most.

The set of edges E is constructed as follows:

(b1) An edge connects the virtual node s and a vertex, if the coverage region of the vertex overlaps with the left boundary.

(b2) An edge connects the virtual node t and a vertex, if the coverage region of the vertex overlaps with the right boundary.

(b3) There exists an edge between two vertices, if the coverage regions of the two vertices who is constructed by different receivers overlap with each other.

Furthermore, an edge does not exist in between two vertices in the following cases:

(c1) Two vertices represent the same bistatic radar pair, which happens when the coverage region of bistatic radar contains two disconnected regions. That is, no edge exists in between the two vertices $A_{i(j)}$ and $A_{(i)j}$.

(c2) Two vertices represent two bistatic radar pairs of using different transmitters but the same receiver. That is, no edge exists in between A_{ij} and $A_{i'j}(A_{(i')j}, A_{i'(j)})$. This due to the constraint that one receiver can only couple with one transmitter at a time.

In the edge construction process, we need to determine whether or not two coverage regions overlap with each other. There are two cases when two coverage regions overlap:

(d1) One of the coverage regions is not totally contained in another coverage region, as illustrated in Fig. 2 (a)−(d) and Fig. 3 (a)−(d). In this case, the two coverage regions can expand the barrier coverage region, and an edge should be added to connect the two respective vertices. Furthermore, the perimeter of two coverage regions have at least one intersection point.

(d2) One of the coverage regions is totally contained in another coverage region, as illustrated in Fig. 2 (e) and Fig. 3 (e) and (f). In this case, the contained coverage region cannot help to expand the barrier coverage. We do not add an edge in between the two respective vertices. Therefore, we can compute the intersection point between the perimeter of two coverage regions to determine whether the coverage regions of two vertices overlap with each other or not.

We next use an example to show how to determine whether two coverage regions overlap with each other. We first consider the case of two bistatic radar pairs consist of different transmitters and receivers, e.g., (T_1, R_1) and (T_2, R_2). All possible relations of their coverage regions are shown in Fig. 2 (a)−(e). Assume there is a point $P(x, y)$ on the perimeter of the coverage region of (T_1, R_1), and P is also covered by the (T_2, R_2) pair. Then its location (x, y) can be computed by:

$$\begin{cases} [(x - x_{T_1})^2 + (y - y_{T_1})^2] \cdot [(x - x_{R_1})^2 + (y - y_{R_1})^2] = l_{max}^4 \\ ((x - x_{T_2})^2 + (y - y_{T_2})^2) \cdot [(x - x_{R_2})^2 + (y - y_{R_2})^2] = l_{max}^4 \end{cases} \quad (4)$$

If Eq. (4) exists at least one real root, we say that their coverage regions overlap with each other. Otherwise, their coverage regions are not overlapped.

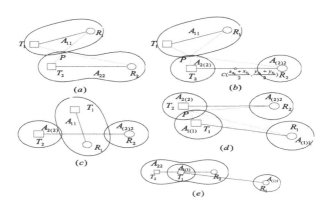

Fig. 2. Illustration of coverage regions by (T_1, R_1) and (T_2, R_2).

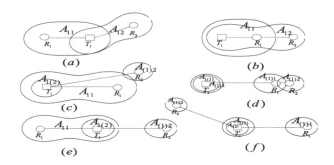

Fig. 3. Illustration of coverage regions by (T_1, R_1) and (T_1, R_2).

For the case that a radar pair (T_2, R_2) contains two disconnected coverage regions, as shown in Fig. 2 (b) and (c), we first use the above method to determine whether there exists an intersection point between the coverage region of (T_1, R_1) and the coverage regions of (T_2, R_2). If at least one intersection point exist and let IP denote the intersection points set. We further determine which coverage region $A_{2(2)}$ or $A_{(2)2}$ of the pair (T_2, R_2) intersects with A_{11} or both two regions intersect with A_{11}.

We solve this problem by using following method. Compute the midpoint C of the line $\overline{T_2 R_2}$ connecting T_2 and R_2. Denote its coordinate as $(\frac{x_{R_2}+x_{T_2}}{2}, \frac{y_{T_2}+y_{R_2}}{2})$. We compare the horizontal ordinate of each intersection point in IP with $\frac{x_R+x_T}{2}$. An edge exists between the vertex A_{11} and $A_{2(2)}$ in the coverage graph, if all the horizontal ordinate of intersection points are smaller than $\frac{x_{R_2}+x_{T_2}}{2}$. And an edge exists between A_{11} and $A_{(2)2}$, if all the horizontal ordinate of intersection points are larger than $\frac{x_{R_2}+x_{T_2}}{2}$. Otherwise, there are two edges connect A_{11} with $A_{2(2)}$ and $A_{(2)2}$, respectively.

We next consider the case that two bistatic radar pairs consist of a same transmitter, e.g., (T_1, R_1) and (T_1, R_2). All possible relations of their coverage regions are shown in Fig. 3. According to the above analysis, we know that there exists an edge between the vertices A_{11} and A_{12} in Fig. 3 (a) and (b). For the cases in Fig. 3 (c) and (d), there exist an edge between the vertices between A_{11} and $A_{(1)2}$, $A_{(1)1}$ and $A_{(1)2}$, respectively. There is no edge between the vertices in Fig. 3 (e) and (f).

4   Solution to the Barrier Coverage Lifetime Maximization Problem

4.1   Finding Barriers Algorithm

Based on the constructed coverage graph G, we propose an algorithm to find barriers in the network. First, we label the vertices in the coverage graph G. Recall that we index the transmitters and receivers according to their x-coordinate from the left boundary to the right boundary, thus:

$$x_{T_1} \leq x_{T_2} \leq ... \leq x_{T_M}$$
$$x_{R_1} \leq x_{R_2} \leq ... \leq x_{R_N}$$

The vertices V in the coverage graph G represent the connected coverage area of each bistatic radar pair. For ease of description, we index the vertices according to the x-coordinate of the transmitter and receiver constructing such vertex. The indexing way is as follows. Assume there are totally U_1 vertices constructed by node T_1, we index those U_1 vertices from v_1 to v_{U_1} according to the receiver's x-coordinate constructing such vertex. If two vertices (such as $A_{1(j)}$ and $A_{(1)j}$) corresponding to the same bistatic radar, we use two successive number to represent those two vertices. We then index the vertices constructed by T_2 from v_{U_1+1} by using the same way until all vertices are indexed.

For two vertices in the graph, we say their are neighbour if there exist an edge between them. An algorithm is proposed to find barriers in the network. The main idea of algorithm is that call function $findpath$ to iterate through the neighbours of vertex. The input parameters for the function $findpath$ include: (e1): coverage graph G; (e2): P is the found path in the previous iteration and its structure is like $P = \{s, v_1, v_3, ..., v_l\}$. (e3) the set Q whose elements are the receiver number already used by vertices in found path P; (e4) the elements in the set U are the vertices that may be the vertex that can't reach the destination or is constructed by the same receiver as that vertices in found path P; (e5) we will explain function of set C in the following paragraph.

In each iteration, we first find the final vertex in the found path P and denote it as L, and then find all neighbour vertices set $Next$ of L. Before go to the next step, we filter the vertices in set $Next$, three types vertices are excluded from the set $Next$: the vertices whose corresponding bistatic radar pair is constructed by the receivers in the set Q, the reason is that one receiver can't couple with different transmitters in one barrier; The vertices belong to the set U and the set C. After the filter process, if the set $Next$ is not empty, we first check whether the virtual node t is in the set $Next$, if it does, one barrier found. The algorithm records the barrier and returns back to the previous (last) iteration to find another path. Otherwise, the algorithm calls the function $findpath$ to lengthen the found path P by visiting each element in the set $Next$.

The vertex set V consists of $(2 \times M \times N + 2)$ elements at most and the total number of all possible paths from s to t is in the order of $O((2 \times M \times N)!)$.

The structure of found path of Algorithm 1 is $B_k = (s, T_i R_j, ..., T_m R_n, t)$. Assume there are K paths in the network, the lifetime of each barrier is determined by the residual energy of radar sensors constructing such barrier. Thus:

$$L(B_k) = \min_{\substack{1 \leq i \leq m \\ 1 \leq j \leq n}} \{\frac{e_{T_i}}{\alpha_T}, \frac{e_{R_j}}{\alpha_R}\}, \{T_1, ..., T_m, R_1, ..., R_n\} \in B_k \qquad (5)$$

4.2   Linear Programming Method

Recall that a same bistatic radar node can appear in more than one barrier. If a barrier is scheduled to work till one of node dies, some other barriers containing

Algorithm 1. function $[b, DC] = findpath(P, Q, U, C)$

1: $b = false$;
2: $DC = C$;
3: Find the last node L in P;
4: $Next = findNeighbour(G, L)$;
5: $Next = Next \setminus U$; $Next = Next \setminus C$
6: Exclude the elements whose corresponding bistatic radar
   pairs are constructed by the receiver in Q from $Next$
7: **if** t is in the set $Next$; **then**
8:    Put the barrier into set $\mathcal{B}_N$; Set $b = true$
9: **else**
10:   $TU = \emptyset$
11:   **for** each $n_i \in Next$
12:      $R_i = findR(n_i)$
13:      $TP = [P, n_i]; TQ = [Q, R_i]$
14:      $[bfind, TC] = findpath(TP, Q, TU, DC)$
15:      **if** $bfind$ **then** $DC = [DC, n_i]$
16:      **else** $TU = [TU, n_i]$ **end if**
17:   **end for**
18: **end if**

this dead node also cannot work any more. On the other hand, we can schedule the working interval for each of these barriers, such that the total working intervals can be maximized. Suppose there are K barriers in $\mathcal{B}_N$, each working for $t_k, k = 1, ..., K$ time slots. The problem of maximizing network lifetime for $\mathcal{B}_N$ can be formulated as the following optimization problem.

$$\text{maximize} \quad L(\mathcal{B}_N) = t_1 + t_2 + ... + t_K$$
$$s.t. \begin{cases} \sum_{k=1}^{K} \alpha_t t_k \leq E_{T_i}; & \text{for all } 1 \leq i \leq M, \\ \sum_{k=1}^{K} \alpha_r t_k \leq E_{R_j}; & \text{for all } 1 \leq j \leq N, \end{cases} \quad (6)$$

where the constraints indicate that the consumed energy of each node in all barriers should not exceed its initial energy. We apply the linear programming method solve the Eq. (6).

4.3   Greedy Algorithm and Random Algorithm

The main idea of these two algorithms are summarized as follows: Firstly, based on the coverage graph G, starting from the virtual s, we choose a neighbour as a sub-node to construct one barrier: In the Greedy algorithm, we choose the neighbour with maximal residual lifetime; While in the random algorithm, we choose a neighbour randomly. Secondly, based on the constructed barrier B_s, we activate the barrier t_g unit time ($t_g = \epsilon$ if $L(B_s) \geq \epsilon$; $t_g = L(B_s)$ if $L(B_s) < \epsilon$, where ϵ is called activation granularity). Thirdly, after t_g time, update the residual energy of the bistatic radar nodes. If the energy of a node is exhausted, this node will not be selected in the next iteration. The barrier finding process continues, until not barriers can be found.

5   Simulation Results

We consider a network with M transmitters and N receivers randomly deployed in a rectangle region with size of 40×10. In all simulations. We set the maximum vulnerability of network as $l_{max} = 5$, and the detection energy consumption rate of transmitter and receiver are $\alpha_t = 1.5$ and $\alpha_r = 1$, respectively. We also set the maximum distance threshold between transmitter and receivers as $D_{max} = 20$. The initial energies are uniformly distributed in $[1, 10]$. We use the optimization toolbox in Matlab to solve the linear programming. All results are the average of 100 different deployments.

Figure 4 compares the barrier coverage lifetime achieved by our proposed algorithms (Linear Programming, Greedy Algorithm and Random Algorithm) and the lifetime achieved by activating all bistatic radar nodes until there is no barrier in the network. We can observe that the proposed algorithms can prolong the barrier coverage lifetime and the lifetime increases with the increase of deployed transmitters. It can also be seen that the lifetime by the Greedy Algorithm is close to that by linear programming method. However, we note that the linear programming method cannot be applied to large-scale networks due to its high computation complexity.

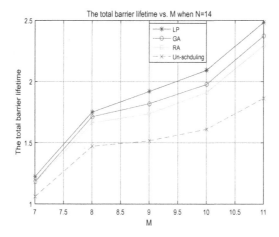

Fig. 4. Comparison of the barrier coverage lifetime.

Figure 5 compares the lifetime for the Greedy Algorithm and Random Algorithm when the transmitters are more than eleven. Note that the linear programming solution could take days for computation, so we do not include them

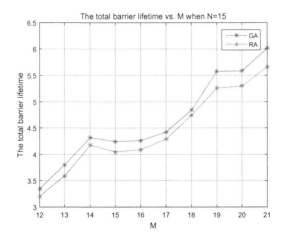

Fig. 5. Comparison of the barrier coverage lifetime.

into comparison. The results indicate that the next nodes selection strategy in the barrier finding step has great impact on the total barrier coverage lifetime: The Greedy Algorithm can achieve better results compared to the Random Algorithm, since it achieves local optima by choosing the next node with the maximal residual lifetime.

6   Conclusion

We have studied the barrier coverage lifetime maximization problem in a randomly deployed bistatic radar network. We first constructed a coverage graph based on the connected coverage region of bistatic radar pairs. We have also proposed an algorithm to find all barriers based on the coverage graph. The linear programming method as well as two heuristic algorithms have been used to determine the operation time for each barrier whiling maximizing the barrier coverage lifetime.

References

1. Wang, B.: Coverage problems in sensor networks: a survey. ACM Comput. Surv. **43**(4), 1–56 (2011)
2. Kumar, S., Lai, T.H., Posner, M.E., Sinha, P.: Optimal sleep-wakeup algorithms for barriers of wireless sensors. In: IEEE International Conference on Broadband Communications, Networks and Systems, pp. 327–336 (2007)
3. Wang, C., Wang, B., Xu, H., Liu, W.: Energy-efficient barrier coverage in WSNs with adjustable sensing ranges. In: IEEE Vehicular Technology Conference Spring, pp. 1–5 (2012)
4. Zhao, L., Bai, G., Jiang, Y., Shen, H., Tang, Z.: Optimal deployment and scheduling with directional sensors for energy-efficient barrier coverage. Int. J. Distrib. Sens. Netw. **10**, 596983 (2014)

5. Tao, D., Wu, T.-Y.: A survey on barrier coverage problem in directional sensor networks. IEEE Sens. J. **15**(2), 876–885 (2015)
6. Kumar, S., Lai, T.H., Arora, A.: Barrier coverage with wireless sensors. Wirel. Netw. (Springer) **13**(6), 817–834 (2007)
7. Chen, A., Kumar, S., Lai, T.H.: Local barrier coverage in wireless sensor networks. IEEE Trans. Mob. Comput. **9**(4), 491–504 (2010)
8. Kumar, S., Lai, T.H., Posner, M.E., Sinha, P.: Maximizing the lifetime of a barrier of wireless sensors. IEEE Trans. Mob. Comput. **9**(8), 1161–1172 (2010)
9. Kim, D., Kim, J., Li, D., Kwon, S.-S., Tokuta, A.O.: On sleep-wakeup scheduling of non-penetrable barrier-coverage of wireless sensors. In: IEEE Global Telecommunications Conference (Globecom), pp. 321–327 (2012)
10. Skolnik, M.: Introduction to Radar Systems. McGraw-Hill, New York (2002)
11. Willis, N.: Bistatic Radar. SciTech Publishing, Raleigh (2005)
12. Gong, X., Zhang, J., Cochran, D., Xing, K.: Optimal placement for barrier coverage in bistatic radar sensor networks. IEEE/ACM Trans. Network. **24**, 259–271 (2016)
13. Tang, L., Gong, X., Wu, J., Zhang, J.: Target detection in bistatic radar networks: node placement and repeated security game. IEEE Trans. Wirel. Commun. **12**(3), 1279–1289 (2013)
14. Wang, R., He, S., Chen, J., Shi, Z., Hou, F.: Energy-efficient barrier coverage in bistatic radar sensor networks. In: IEEE ICC 2015 - Ad-hoc and Sensor Networking Symposium, pp. 6743–6748 (2015)
15. Baker, C., Griffiths, H.: Bistatic and multistatic radar sensors for homeland security. Adv. Sens. Secur. Appl. **2**, 1–22 (2006)
16. Liang, J., Liang, Q.: Orthogonal waveform design and performance analysis in radar sensor networks. In: IEEE Military Communications Conferences, pp. 1–6 (2006)
17. Liang, J., Liang, Q.: Design and analysis of distributed radar sensor networks. IEEE Trans. Parallel Distrib. Syst. **22**(11), 1926–1933 (2011)

On Secrecy Performance of Multibeam Satellite System with Multiple Eavesdropped Users

Yeqiu Xiao[1], Jia Liu[2], Jiao Quan[1], Yulong Shen[1(✉)], and Xiaohong Jiang[3]

[1] School of Computer Science and Technology, Xidian University,
Xi'an 710071, China
ylshen@mail.xidian.edu.cn
[2] Center for Cybersecurity Research and Development,
National Institute of Informatics, Tokyo 101-8430, Japan
[3] School of System Information Science, Future University Hakodate,
Hakodate 041-8655, Japan

Abstract. Satellite communication system is expected to play an important role in wireless networks because of its appealing contributions to ubiquitous coverage, content multicast and caching, reducing user expenditure, and so on. However, due to the inherent broadcasting nature and serious channel conditions, satellite communication system is highly vulnerable to eavesdropping attacks. As an initial step towards this end, this paper focuses on the physical layer security technique and explores the secrecy performance of a multibeam satellite system, where multiple legitimate users are served and each user is exposed to an eavesdropper located in the same beam. With perfect channel state information at the satellite and adopting the complete zero-forcing approach for signal processing, we first derive the optimal beamforming vectors to maximize the achievable secrecy rate. Based on this, we further calculate the secrecy outage probabilities of an individual user and the whole system, respectively. Finally, simulation and numerical results are provided to show the secrecy performance of the multibeam satellite system.

Keywords: Multibeam satellite system · Physical layer security
Beamforming · Secrecy outage probability

1 Introduction

Due to the advantages of ubiquitous coverage, no limitation on user geographic position and low user expenditure, satellite communication (SATCOM) system is expected to play a significant role in facilitating the application and commercialization of wireless networks. However, compared with terrestrial communication systems, SATCOM system is much more vulnerable to eavesdropping and jamming attacks, caused by its inherent openness and bad communication conditions

© Springer Nature Singapore Pte Ltd. 2018
L. Zhu and S. Zhong (Eds.): MSN 2017, CCIS 747, pp. 402–412, 2018.
https://doi.org/10.1007/978-981-10-8890-2_30

(i.e., precipitation attenuation, sky noise, gaseous absorption) [1]. As a result, improving the secrecy performance for SATCOM system is of great importance.

In the past, security in space missions mainly depends on upper layers by cryptographic encryption and decryption mechanisms [2]. However, the features of SATCOM networks, such as the high mobility and limited resources carried by satellites, lead to great difficulties in secret key distribution and management [3,4]. Hence, cryptographic methods cannot completely meet the security demands of satellite communication systems.

Conversely, physical layer (PHY) security based on information-theoretic security [5] has been commonly recognized as the strictest form of security by exploiting the inherent randomness of wireless channels. A basic framework of PHY security, the wiretap channel, was pioneered by Wyner [6] and extended to broadcast channels by Csiszár and Körner [7]. Later, there has been an increasing attraction on physical layer security to guarantee secure terrestrial wireless communication. The concept of secrecy rate is referred to as a rate at which the message can be reliably transmitted but eavesdroppers get no information about the message [3]. To guarantee positive secrecy rate, the legitimate users should have better signal-to-noise ratios (SNRs) than the unintended users. The techniques of multiple-input multiple-output (MIMO) antennas are helpful to improve the security of communication even when legitimate receivers have bad SNRs [3,8,9]. Different secrecy metrics are proposed to evaluate system security under various terrestrial communication scenarios, such as secrecy capacity and secrecy outage probability (SOP) [10–13].

However, there are few works focusing on the PHY security for satellite communication systems with multiple legitimate users. Some of the existed researches are interested in land mobile satellite communication systems or hybrid satellite-terrestrial networks based on Shadowed-Rician model [14–17], while others mainly pay attention to the secrecy transmission of multibeam SATCOM systems [2,18,19]. Multibeam satellite can enhance the channel qualities of intended receivers by generating beams through multiple antenna feeds. In this paper, for the first time, we explore the security performance for a multibeam satellite system with multiple receivers subjected to co-channel inference. A method originating from null-steering beamforming technique [20] is adopted to improve the secrecy rate of each intended user and then we also give out the corresponding derivation of beamforming vector. Finally, simulation and numerical results are carried out to show the secrecy performance of multiform SATCOM systems.

The remainder of this paper is structured as follows. The multibeam satellite system model and problem formulation are introduced in Sect. 2. The beamforming scheme as well as secrecy outage analysis is shown in Sect. 3. Section 4 presents the numerical results, and we conclude the paper in Sect. 5.

Throughout this paper, a number of notations will be adopted. Bold uppercase letters and bold lowercase letters denote matrices and vectors, respectively. $|\cdot|$ represents the modulus of a scalar. $||\cdot||$ is the Euclidean norm for a vector. The mean of a random variable is represented by $\mathbb{E}[\cdot]$. Hermitian transpose and inverse are represented by $(\cdot)^\dagger$ and $(\cdot)^{-1}$, respectively. $\mathbf{A} \odot \mathbf{B}$ denotes Hadamard product of two matrices. $\mathbf{I}_N$ is an $N \times N$ identity matrix. $\mathcal{N}(\mu, \sigma^2)$ denotes the Gaussian distribution with mean μ and variance σ^2. J_k represents the first kind Bessel function of order k.

2   System Model

We consider the downlink of a multibeam satellite communication system with a geostationary satellite, which generates N co-channel beams on the ground via N corresponding antenna feeds (single-feed per beam) leading to a frequency reuse of one, as shown in Fig. 1. There are M ($M < N$) active fixed legitimate users receiving independent data streams from the satellite. The transmit power allocated to each beam is no more than P_0 and it is assumed that at any given time, each beam only serves one legitimate receiver at most. Moreover, we consider that there is a single eavesdropper located in the beam of each legitimate receiver. The overall channels of legitimate users and eavesdroppers can be expressed as

$$\mathbf{H} = [\mathbf{h}_1, \mathbf{h}_2, \ldots, \mathbf{h}_M] \tag{1}$$

and

$$\mathbf{G} = [\mathbf{g}_1, \mathbf{g}_2, \ldots, \mathbf{g}_M], \tag{2}$$

where $\mathbf{h}_k$ is an $N \times 1$ vector and presents the channel of legitimate user k, and $\mathbf{g}_k$ is an $N \times 1$ vector and presents the channel of the corresponding eavesdropper in the same beam k.

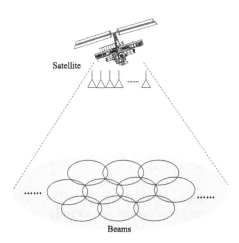

Fig. 1. Multibeam satellite communication scenario.

2.1 Channel Model

Unlike terrestrial communication systems, the satellite systems applying Ka band are subjected to various atmospheric fading mechanisms originating in the troposphere, which heavily affects system performance and availability [1]. Hence, it is essential to take the impact of the troposphere, especially, rain attenuation into consideration. Since rain attenuation is a long term effect, we assume that receivers will suffer from the same fading if located within the same beam but independent fading among different beams.

Rain Attenuation. To predict the rain attenuation effect, this paper employs the empirical model proposed in ITU-R Recommendation P.618-12 [21]. The final power gain in dB ($\xi_{dB} = 20 \log_{10}(\xi)$) is modeled as a lognormal random $\ln(\xi_{dB}) \sim \mathcal{N}(\mu, \sigma)$, where μ and σ rely on the location of the receiver and the state of the satellite. The corresponding $N \times 1$ rain fading vector from all antenna feeds towards a single terminal antenna is given by [2,22]

$$\mathbf{a} = \xi^{-\frac{1}{2}} e^{-j\Phi}, \tag{3}$$

where Φ denotes an $N \times 1$ phase vector following uniform distribution over $[0, 2\pi)$.

Beam Gain. The beam gain matrix describes the average signal to interference-plus-noise ratios (SINR) at each user. It mainly relies on the satellite antenna beam pattern and the receiver position. We consider a radiation pattern given by [23]:

$$b_k(u) = B_k^{max} \cdot \left(\frac{J_1(u)}{2u} + 36 \frac{J_3(u)}{u^3} \right)^2, \tag{4}$$

where $u = 2.07123 \sin \theta_k / \sin(\theta_{3dB})_k$, θ_k represents the angle between the receiver location and the k-th beam center as seen from the satellite and the coefficient, B_k^{max} is the maximum beam gain, J_1 and J_3 denote, respectively, the first kind Bessel functions of order 1 and 3.

Consequently, the overall channel for a certain user can be expressed as

$$\widetilde{\mathbf{h}} = \mathbf{a} \odot \mathbf{b}, \tag{5}$$

where $\mathbf{b}$ is an $N \times 1$ vector and represents the beam gain of the user collected from all transmit antennas.

2.2 Signal Model

Let s_k be the data for user k with unit average power $\mathbb{E}\left[s_k^2\right] = 1, \forall k$. Before transmission, the satellite employs transmit beamforming to communicate with legitimate receivers, and the corresponding beamforming vector is denoted by $\mathbf{w}_k \in \mathbb{C}^{N \times 1}$. Hence, the on board transmitted signal can be expressed as

$$\mathbf{x} = \sum_{k=1}^{M} \mathbf{w}_k s_k. \tag{6}$$

The received signal at the m-th legitimate receiver is given by

$$y_m = \mathbf{h}_m^\dagger \mathbf{w}_m s_m + \mathbf{h}_m^\dagger \sum_{k=1,k\neq m}^{M} \mathbf{w}_k s_k + n_m, \tag{7}$$

and the signal received by its corresponding eavesdropper is determined as

$$y_m^e = \mathbf{g}_m^\dagger \mathbf{w}_m s_m + \mathbf{g}_m^\dagger \sum_{k=1,k\neq m}^{M} \mathbf{w}_k s_k + n_e, \tag{8}$$

where n_k and n_e are the additive Gaussian noises at the m-th legitimate user and the eavesdropper surrounding it, which respectively satisfy $n_m \sim \mathcal{N}(0, \sigma_D^2)$ and $n_e \sim \mathcal{N}(0, \sigma_E^2)$. The term $h_m^\dagger \mathbf{w}_m s_m$ is the desired signal at the m-th legitimate user, while $h_m^\dagger \sum_{k=1,k\neq m}^{M} \mathbf{w}_k s_k$ is the co-channel interference.

Hence, the achievable secrecy rate [24] of the legitimate receiver m can be calculated as

$$C_m^s = \log_2 \left(1 + \frac{\left| \mathbf{h}_m^\dagger \mathbf{w}_m \right|^2}{\sum_{k=1,k\neq m}^{M} \left| \mathbf{h}_k^\dagger \mathbf{w}_k \right|^2 + \sigma_D^2} \right)$$

$$- \log_2 \left(1 + \frac{\left| \mathbf{g}_m^\dagger \mathbf{w}_m \right|^2}{\sum_{k=1,k\neq m}^{M} \left| \mathbf{g}_k^\dagger \mathbf{w}_k \right|^2 + \sigma_D^2} \right). \tag{9}$$

2.3   Problem Formulation

In this paper, we are interested in maximizing the achievable secrecy rate for each intended user, while subjecting to the transmit power constraint P_0 for each individual transmit signal, which can be formally formulated as the following optimization problem:

$$\arg\max_{\mathbf{w}} \quad C_m^s$$

$$s.t. \qquad \|\mathbf{w}_m\| < P_0. \tag{10}$$

3   Beamforming Vectors and Secrecy Outage Analysis

3.1   Complete Zero-Forcing

In this section, we consider a beamforming design in [18], named complete zero-forcing, to maximize the achievable secrecy rate C_m^s. By use of complete ZF, not only signals at all eavesdroppers are nulled out, but co-channel interference among all users is also completely eliminated. Then we have

$$\mathbf{w}_m^\dagger \mathbf{h}_k = 0, \forall k \neq m \quad \text{and} \quad \mathbf{w}_m^\dagger \mathbf{g}_m = 0, \forall m, \tag{11}$$

which makes the achievable secrecy rate of the legitimate receiver m simplified to

$$C_m^s = \log_2 \left(1 + \frac{\left| \mathbf{h}_m^\dagger \mathbf{w}_m \right|^2}{\sigma_D^2} \right). \tag{12}$$

3.2   Problem Solution

The optimization problem in (10) can be reformulated as

$$\arg\max_{\mathbf{w}} \quad C_m^s$$
$$s.t. \quad \mathbf{w}_m^\dagger \mathbf{h}_k = 0, \quad \forall k \neq m$$
$$\mathbf{w}_m^\dagger \mathbf{g}_m = 0$$
$$\mathbf{w}_m^\dagger \mathbf{w}_m = P_0 \tag{13}$$

and further formulated as

$$\arg\max_{\mathbf{w}} \quad C_m^s$$
$$s.t. \quad \mathbf{\Delta}^\dagger \mathbf{w}_m = \mathbf{0}_{1 \times M}, \tag{14}$$
$$\mathbf{w}_m^\dagger \mathbf{w}_m = P_0$$

where

$$[\mathbf{\Delta}]_{ij} = \begin{cases} [\mathbf{H}]_{ij} & j \neq m \\ [\mathbf{G}]_{ij} & j = m \end{cases}. \tag{15}$$

Here, $\mathbf{H}$ and $\mathbf{G}$ describes the overall channel of all legitimate users and all eavesdroppers mentioned in Sect. 2, respectively.

The problem in (14) could be obtained by the knowledge of null-steering beamformer and its optimal solution is given by as [25]

$$\mathbf{w}_m = \frac{\sqrt{P_0}}{\|(\mathbf{I}_N - \mathbf{F}) \mathbf{h}_m\|} (\mathbf{I}_N - \mathbf{F}) \mathbf{h}_m, \tag{16}$$

where $\mathbf{F} = \mathbf{\Delta} \left(\mathbf{\Delta}^\dagger \mathbf{\Delta} \right)^{-1} \mathbf{\Delta}^\dagger$ and $\mathbf{I}_N$ is an $N \times N$ identity matrix.

3.3   Secrecy Outage Analysis

In order to evaluate the secrecy performance of the satellite system in this paper, secrecy outage probability is introduced. It expresses the probability that secrecy outage event occurs. Secrecy outage event of an intended user m will occur in the case that its achievable secrecy rate falls below a predefined confidential information rate ε_m. The secrecy outage probability is expressed as

$$P_m^{out} = Pr\left(C_m^s < \varepsilon_m \right). \tag{17}$$

Substituting achievable secrecy rate C_m^s from (12) into (17), the secrecy outage probability (SOP) of the legitimate user m can be rewritten as

$$P_m^{out} = Pr\left(\left|\mathbf{h}_m^\dagger \mathbf{w}_m\right|^2 < \sigma_D^2 \left(2^{\varepsilon_m} - 1\right)\right). \tag{18}$$

For the whole multibeam satellite system, we introduce two secrecy performance metric measurements in this paper. The first one is a statistic value based on the average SOP of all legitimate receivers

$$P_{average}^{out} = \frac{1}{M}\sum_{k=1}^{M} P_m^{out}, \tag{19}$$

and the second one describes the probability that the system will be secrecy outaged once an intended user cannot keep secure communication with the satellite,

$$P_{strict}^{out} = 1 - \prod_{k=1}^{M}(1 - P_m^{out}), \tag{20}$$

which is a much strict standard.

4   Simulation Results Analysis

In this section, we investigate the secrecy outage probability (SOP) of the multi-beam satellite communication (SATCOM) system with complete zero-forcing technique. For simplicity, we consider a system with $M = 3$ active beams and assume that all receivers set the same secrecy rate constraint $\varepsilon_m = \varepsilon_0, \forall m$. Each legitimate user is supposed to be located in the beam center while the distance between an unintended receiver and the corresponding legitimate receiver is randomly ranging from $[0.15R, R)$, where R is the beam radius, as shown in Fig. 2. Some significant parameters of the multibeam SATCOM system in this paper are given in Table 1. We will present the secrecy performance of all legitimate users and the whole system, respectively and explore the factors that affect the secrecy performance. Note that aiming at evaluating the secrecy outage probability, this paper performs Monte Carlo experiments consisting of 10000 independent trials to obtain the average results.

Figure 3 depicts the results for the SOP of each user and the whole system against the secrecy rate constraint in the case that satellite only generates 4 beams. In Figs. 3 and 4, SOP_a and SOP_s correspond to $P_{average}^{out}$ and P_{strict}^{out} mentioned in Sect. 3. It is observed that user 2 (the legitimate receiver in the 2nd beam) would be less likely secrecy outaged compared with others. Taking note that the distance between the legitimate receiver in the 2nd beam and the 4th beam center is larger, communication of user 2 suffers less co-channel interference from the 4th beam. Otherwise, we illustrate that in the view of P_{strict}^{out}, the performance of system secrecy is mainly affected by those users with the worst performance.

Table 1. Main parameters of the multibeam satellite system.

Parameter	Value
Satellite orbit	Geostationary
Number of active beams	$M = 3$
Beam radius	$R = 250$ km
3 dB angle	$\theta_{3dB} = 0.4°$
Rain fading statistics	$\{\mu; \sigma\} = \{-3.125; 1.591\}$
Transmit power constraint	$P_0 = 1$ dB

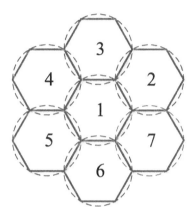

(a) Geographic distribution of beams.

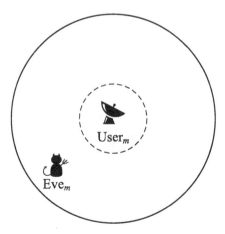

(b) Eavesdropping scenario in a beam.

Fig. 2. A specific multibeam SATCOM scenario.

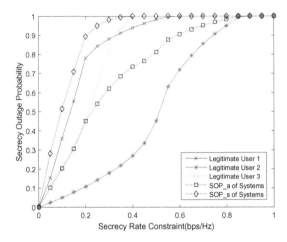

Fig. 3. Secrecy outage probability vs. secrecy rate constraint.

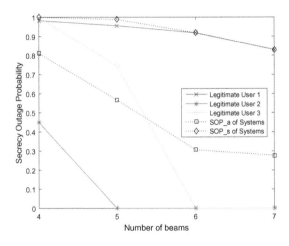

Fig. 4. Secrecy outage probability vs. number of beams.

Figure 4 shows the secrecy outage probability of the system according to the number of beams generated by the satellite. The secrecy rate constraints are randomly selected as $[0.10\ 0.34\ 0.39]^T$. We can notice that two kinds of system SOP both decrease as the number of beams increases. And P_{strict}^{out} of the system is mainly dependent upon the user performing badly.

5   Conclusion

In this paper, we investigated the secrecy performance of a multibeam satellite communication system subject to transmit power constraint. Complete zero-forming technique, a kind of null-steering beamforming method, was adopted to eliminate co-channel interference. By analyzing the secrecy outage performance of both individual user and the whole system, we found that the secrecy outage probability will decrease as the active beam number increases but the secrecy rate constraint decreases. Simulation results have also shown the fact that the strict standard of system SOP is mainly affected by users with low channel quality.

Acknowledgments. This work was supported in part by the Natural Science Foundation of China (NSFC) under Grant U1536202, Grant 61373173, and Grant 61571352; in part by the Project of Cyber Security Establishment with Inter-University Cooperation; and in part by the Secom Science and Technology Foundation.

References

1. Arapoglou, P.D., Liolis, K., Bertinelli, M., Panagopoulos, A., Cottis, P., De Gaudenzi, R.: MIMO over satellite: a review. IEEE Commun. Surv. Tutor. **13**(1), 27–51 (2011)
2. Zheng, G., Arapoglou, P.D., Ottersten, B.: Physical layer security in multibeam satellite systems. IEEE Trans. Wirel. Commun. **11**(2), 852–863 (2012)
3. Hong, Y.W.P., Lan, P.C., Kuo, C.C.J.: Enhancing physical-layer secrecy in multi-antenna wireless systems: an overview of signal processing approaches. IEEE Signal Process. Mag. **30**(5), 29–40 (2013)
4. Schneier, B.: Cryptographic design vulnerabilities. Computer **31**(9), 29–33 (1998)
5. Shannon, C.E.: Communication theory of secrecy systems. Bell Labs Tech. J. **28**(4), 656–715 (1949)
6. Wyner, A.D.: The wiretap channel. Bell Labs Tech. J. **54**(8), 1355–1387 (1975)
7. Csiszár, I., Korner, J.: Broadcast channels with confidential messages. IEEE Trans. Inf. Theor. **24**(3), 339–348 (1978)
8. Zou, Y., Zhu, J., Wang, X., Leung, V.C.: Improving physical-layer security in wireless communications using diversity techniques. IEEE Netw. **29**(1), 42–48 (2015)
9. Foschini, G.J., Gans, M.J.: On limits of wireless communications in a fading environment when using multiple antennas. Wirel. Pers. Commun. **6**(3), 311–335 (1998)
10. Barros, J., Rodrigues, M.R.: Secrecy capacity of wireless channels. In: 2006 IEEE International Symposium on Information Theory, pp. 356–360. IEEE (2006)
11. Koyluoglu, O.O., Koksal, C.E., El Gamal, H.: On secrecy capacity scaling in wireless networks. IEEE Trans. Inf. Theor. **58**(5), 3000–3015 (2012)
12. Romero-Zurita, N., Ghogho, M., McLernon, D.: Outage probability based power distribution between data and artificial noise for physical layer security. IEEE Signal Process. Lett. **19**(2), 71–74 (2012)
13. Zou, Y., Zhu, J., Wang, G., Shao, H.: Secrecy outage probability analysis of multi-user multi-eavesdropper wireless systems. In: IEEE/CIC International Conference on Communications in China (ICCC), pp. 309–313. IEEE (2014)
14. An, K., Lin, M., Liang, T., Ouyang, J., Chen, H.: Average secrecy capacity of land mobile satellite wiretap channels. In: 8th International Conference on Wireless Communications & Signal Processing (WCSP), pp. 1–5. IEEE (2016)
15. An, K., Lin, M., Liang, T., Ouyang, J., Yuan, C., Lu, W.: Secrecy performance analysis of land mobile satellite communication systems over Shadowed-Rician fading channels. In: 25th Wireless and Optical Communication Conference (WOCC), pp. 1–4. IEEE (2016)

16. Yan, Y., Zhang, B., Guo, D., Li, S., Niu, H., Wang, X.: Joint beamforming and jamming design for secure cooperative hybrid satellite-terrestrial relay network. In: 25th Wireless and Optical Communication Conference (WOCC), pp. 1–5. IEEE (2016)

17. An, K., Lin, M., Liang, T., Ouyang, J., Yuan, C., Li, Y.: Secure transmission in multi-antenna hybrid satellite-terrestrial relay networks in the presence of eavesdropper. In: International Conference on Wireless Communications & Signal Processing (WCSP), pp. 1–5. IEEE (2015)

18. Lei, J., Han, Z., Vazquez-Castro, M.Á., Hjorungnes, A.: Secure satellite communication systems design with individual secrecy rate constraints. IEEE Trans. Inf. Forensics Secur. **6**(3), 661–671 (2011)

19. Yuan, C., Lin, M., Ouyang, J., Bu, Y.: Joint security beamforming in cognitive hybrid satellite-terrestrial networks. In: IEEE 83rd Vehicular Technology Conference (VTC Spring), pp. 1–5. IEEE (2016)

20. Friedlander, B., Porat, B.: Performance analysis of a null-steering algorithm based on direction-of-arrival estimation. IEEE Trans. Acoust. Speech Signal Process. **37**(4), 461–466 (1989)

21. Series, P.: Propagation data and prediction methods required for the design of earth-space telecommunication systems. Recommendation ITU-R, 618-12 (2015)

22. Zheng, G., Chatzinotas, S., Ottersten, B.: Generic optimization of linear precoding in multibeam satellite systems. IEEE Trans. Wirel. Commun. **11**(6), 2308–2320 (2012)

23. Díaz, M.A., Courville, N., Mosquera, C., Liva, G., Corazza, G.E.: Non-linear interference mitigation for broadband multimedia satellite systems. In: International Workshop on Satellite and Space Communications (IWSSC 2007), pp. 61–65. IEEE (2007)

24. Liang, Y., Kramer, G., Poor, H.V., Shamai, S.: Compound wiretap channels. EURASIP J. Wirel. Commun. Netw. **2009**, 5 (2009)

25. Dong, L., Han, Z., Petropulu, A.P., Poor, H.V.: Improving wireless physical layer security via cooperating relays. IEEE Trans. Signal Process. **58**(3), 1875–1888 (2010)

Gesture Recognition System Based on RFID

Xuan Wang, Xin Kou, Zifan Wang, Lanqing Wang, Baoying Liu$^{(\boxtimes)}$,
and Feng Chen

School of Information Science and Technology, Northwest University, Xi'an, China
wxkate@stumail.nwu.edu.cn, 1793718532@qq.com, 418026716@qq.com,
757813916@qq.com, 363739293@qq.com, xdcf@nwu.edu.cn

Abstract. Gestures recognition as the main technology of human-computer interaction draws a great amount attention of researchers. Comparing to existing methods, the RFID-based passive gesture recognition requires no specialized equipment which makes it much easier to be used. To achieve the goal, we build a priori gesture database according to signal features caused by perturbation of different gestures. Then, the modified dynamic time warping (DTW) algorithm has been used to match with the priori fingerprint database. Besides, we propose a wireless phase calibration algorithm by utilizing the theory that the noise subspace and the signal subspace is orthogonal in multiple signal classification (MUSIC) algorithm to estimate and remove phase errors that may caused by equipment differences so that we can ensure the accuracy of angle of arrival (AoA) estimation. To evaluate the effectiveness of our gesture recognition system, the experiments in a real scene were carried out. And the experimental results show that we can achieve about 92% accuracy.

Keywords: Gesture recognition · Feature extraction
Phase calibration · AoA estimation · DTW

1 Introduction

In the 21st century, smart devices are gathered and the way of interaction is getting richer and more humane. Therefore, as an important part of human-computer interaction, gesture recognition has drawn extensive attention and become a hotspot of research [1–5]. Gesture recognition makes many operations that used to be hard to achieve become reality. For instance, users can write, pay, and even control the electrical appliances in smart home by gesture with our smart phones, tablets, laptops etc. Moreover, literatures [3,6] can even realize writing in the air by interacting with the smart devices. Obviously, our life become much more convenient if we can control the volume or answer the phone in a second.

© Springer Nature Singapore Pte Ltd. 2018
L. Zhu and S. Zhong (Eds.): MSN 2017, CCIS 747, pp. 413–425, 2018.
https://doi.org/10.1007/978-981-10-8890-2_31

Nowadays, the RF signals that have been mentioned by many papers as they can pass through the walls and won't be affected by smoke, fog and light [7]. So device-free gesture recognition based on RF signals has become a hotspot [3,8–10]. The common device-free wireless gesture recognition technology mostly by using the CSI [11] or RSS [12] to estimate the angle that the signal arrives at the receiver, which always require dedicated equipment [12]. Moreover, RSS value and CSI amplitude of the RF signal are severely affected by the multipath when deployed in real environment, which will decrease the accuracy and the robustness of the gesture recognition technologies severely.

To reduce the impact of multipath on the RF signal, the previous method is to minimize the impact of multipath. But if we can implement gesture recognition by combining the fine-grained phase information of RF signals with the signal strength information and use the gesture influence on the multipath signal to increase the difficulty in the matching part of the recognition, the accuracy of the gesture recognition can be improved.

In the main while, the RFID can not only obtain the characteristic information of the signal easily, but have a broad industrial prospect as well because it can be easily popularized and deployed. As RFID positioning technology [13–15] becoming more and more mature, many researchers began to study how to use RFID technology for gesture recognition. Moreover, RFID-based gesture recognition is cheaper than the Wi-Fi-based gesture recognition methods [3,16,17]. RFID tags are passive nodes, which generate signals by the energy carried by the radio waves. The internal structure of the RFID tags is simple. Its data storage capacity is large and the volume is small. What's more, the price of it is about 0.5 yuan for each, while each Wi-Fi device is mostly at 100 yuan of the above.

Therefore, this paper proposes a device-free gesture recognition system based on RFID, which utilizes impact of gesture on multipath to improve the resolution of gesture recognition with minimal deployment cost. The main idea is utilizing the fact that each moment of the gesture will interfere with the signal differently, so that we can use the feature information of the signal perturbed by the gesture as the fingerprint to recognize gestures. To achieve the RFID-based gesture recognition system well, we have to handle the following key challenges:

- In actual wireless positioning, there are phase errors caused by hardware differences. The introduction of unknown phase offset to the received signal may cause array uncertainty and low accuracy of MUSIC direction finding technology so that estimate an incorrect AoA value. For this reason, this paper introduces a wireless phase calibration algorithm that does not require special equipment. In this algorithm, we will firstly construct an objective function by utilizing the orthogonal theory of signal subspace and noise subspace. After that, we can solve the phase error estimation value by Genetic algorithm.
- Since there are differences of starting time and speed among different users, the length of those two time-series which need to be matching in similarity may not be aligned on the time axis. Therefore, this paper utilizes the modified DTW algorithm which was used for speech recognition to compare and regulate two time-series and then judge the similarity between them.

To verify the performance of the proposed method, this paper carried out the corresponding experiment. We set up the experimental platform in a 7 m × 10 m classroom. The main devices are a 8-antenna linear array, a reader with a frequency of 920.875 MHz and 6 RFID tags. We first make 10 gestures as priori fingerprint database. After that do gesture to identify freely. The experimental results show that this method can achieve a correct recognition probability of about 92%, which shows that the proposed method is highly feasible.

2 Related Work

The existing gesture recognition methods are mainly divided into three categories, which are method based on the sensor technology, the image recognition technology and method based on the RF signal.

Gesture recognition based on sensor mainly relies on MEMS (micro-electromechanical systems) sensors (accelerometers, gyroscopes, magnetometers, etc.) to extract the acceleration and angular velocity signal characteristics of the gesture, which requires users to wear sensors and other equipment. This method is inconvenient for users and has a limited application.

Gesture recognition based on image technology [18] mainly relies on the camera to capture real-time images of users with high precision, but the algorithm is computationally intensive and requires high light intensity and shooting angle.

Gesture recognition based on the RF signal mainly use the ubiquitous WiFi to recognize gesture. For example, WiSee [8] performs gesture recognition based on the Doppler shift caused by human motion measured by a WiFi signal. Since the RF signal can penetrate the wall, WiSee can break out the restriction on line-of-sight. However, this method requires the special equipment USRP, which has good effect but costs a lot and is not suitable for wide applications.

Gesture recognition based on RFID depends on the RFID tags mainly carried by targets to work. Receivers recognize the gesture by analyzing the change of amplitude or phase of the RFID tags. D.Katabi's RF-IDraw virtual writing [6], the recognition rate of which achieves 96.8%, is the most representative achievement of RFID gesture recognition. This achievement need users to wear RFID tags, and write English words or letters, then the receivers can analyze the tracks of spatial location and reconstruct the words.

In order to let users get rid of sensors and special equipment and obtain better experience, in this paper, we use machine learning method to recognize gestures. We obtain feature vector corresponding to every gesture by utilizing the gestures interference on signal obtained by reader. Then we match the database and utilize influence of the multi-path signal to increase the difficulty of matching to improve the identification accuracy.

Unlike Grfid [19], which is also a device-free gesture recognition system based on RFID phase information, we calibrate the phase error caused by hardware difference before feature extraction to improve the identification accuracy. Specifically, we firstly construct an objective function by using the orthogonal theory of signal subspace and noise subspace, estimating and removing phase error caused by equipment differences to ensure the accuracy of AoA estimation.

3 System Design

The critical techniques of our gesture recognition system are shown in Fig. 1. Establishing priori fingerprint database contains data preprocessing module and feature information extraction module. The data preprocessing module calibrates the obtained phases and then processes the collected data into frames, that is processing one gesture at multiple sampling points. Extracting feature information module is to estimate AoA (angle of arrival) utilizing MUSIC algorithm, and a feature matrix is obtained for gesture recognition. The feature information matching module uses the improved DTW algorithm in this paper to compare and sort two time series to optimal the sum of costs to match gestures. Difficulty of matching is increased by the influence of the multi-path so that we can improve the recognition accuracy.

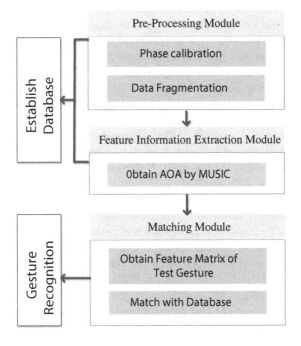

Fig. 1. Overview of the system.

3.1 Get RFID Signal Characteristics

RFID working under UHF has the farthest communication distance, so it is used for our gesture recognition. RFID uses 920 MHz electromagnetic carrier to communicate, and its communication signal as the ordinary wireless communication signal, which has three basic properties, namely, phase (ϕ), amplitude (A), frequency (f). The frequency is known, so the characteristics of the entire carrier signal can be known as long as the phase (ϕ) and the amplitude (A) of the signal are known.

The data obtained by the RFID reader are: phase (ϕ), amplitude(A), tag number (ID), time (T), then the obtained information can be expressed as:

$$antenna_i = (\phi_r, A_r, ID_r, T_r)$$

Here $r = 1, 2, \ldots, N$. $j = 1, 2, \ldots, M$. r is the packet number and j is the antenna number.

3.2   Extract Gesture Fingerprints

Create a priori fingerprint database and match the being recognized gestures with it. First, divide the phase and amplitude for gestures according to disturbance of RFID signal caused by gestures. Then split data into frames and calculate the eigenvectors corresponding to each frame to form the feature matrix of the gesture. Similarly, the feature matrices of other gestures can also be obtained, and then the feature matrixex of all the gestures constitutes a priori fingerprint databases.

Data Division. Because RFID communication is discrete in the time domain, there is no guarantee that there is a continuous signal for each gesture. If the matching is performed directly, errors may occasionally occur, so traditional identification methods based on continuously varying signal characteristics cannot be used. Inspired by the concept of frames in image recognition methods, this paper divide the data into frames in chronological order when analyzing the data. The number of frames depends on the number of sampling points of a gesture. This process is equivalent to dividing one gesture into several discrete moments that describes the gesture.

The data are collected in $Antenna_j$ is chronologically ordered. Divide it into equal parts of n copies, then the amount of data for each copy is $k = \frac{N}{n}$, so divide the data into n frames:

$$Frame_q = (Antenna_{1q}, Antenna_{2q}, \ldots, Antenna_{jq})$$

Here, $q = 1, 2, \ldots, n$.

In this method, multiple tags be used as the signal. That is to separate and classify each $Antenna$ data in $Frame_q$ according to the $TagID$ to obtain the data corresponding to each tag:

$$Tag_d = (Antenna_{1d}, Antenna_{2d}, Antenna_{jd})$$

d is $TagID$ number, so $Frame_q$ is changed to :

$$Frame_q = (Tag_{1_q}, Tag_{2_q}, \ldots, Tag_{d_q})$$

Tag_{d_q} represents the data corresponding to the tag with the data number d in the q frame.

Calculate the Feature Matrix Corresponding to the Gesture. After dividing the data obtained by each antenna into frames, we need to separate the corresponding data information for each tag. It is necessary to analyze the corresponding signal characteristics of each tag data of $Frame_q$. In this paper, the signal characteristics are obtained by using the method of AoA estimation. The method steps are as follows:

(i) Calculate the phase that arrives on each antenna.
   The data processed in this step is a frame of data for each tag. The first column of data in $Antenna_j$ is the phase. Due to the environmental noise, the data may fluctuate. In order to make the data statistically representative, The highest frequency data is considered as real data, that is:

$$\phi_{antenna_j} = \phi \mid max(frequence_{\phi_r}) \tag{1}$$

(ii) Calculate the signal expression received for each antenna.
   We have obtained the phase information of each antenna received data, according to the characteristics of the sine wave, the signal at time t can be expressed as:

$$S_{Antenna_j} = A_{Antenna_j} \cdot exp(i \cdot (2\pi ft + \phi_{Antenna_j})) \tag{2}$$

   Calculate the signal received by each antenna to form the signal S.
(iii) AoA estimation.
   Using the MUSIC algorithm to compute the matrix S, we can get AoA. The parameters are: antenna spacing Xd and step of angle value $\Delta\lambda$ (in degrees). The output data is

$$B = (P_m), \quad m = \Delta\lambda, 2\Delta\lambda, \ldots, \frac{180}{\Delta\lambda}$$

P is the AoA estimation.

3.3   Establish a Priori Fingerprint Database

Each gesture has data of l tags, so each gesture corresponds to 1 vector B, which forms a group, that is, the feature matrix corresponding to one gesture in the qth frame is formed:

$$Action = (B_1, B_2, \ldots, B_l)$$

Doing the above operations on the n frames of data respectively, we can obtain the feature matrix of a certain gesture:

$$W = (Action_1, Action_2, \ldots, Action_n)$$

Enter the data corresponding to all the gestures to build the feature matrix of collected gestures, then the feature matrices of all gestures constitute a knowledge database DB for gesture matching.

3.4 Use RFID Feature Comparison for Gesture Recognition

When recognizing the gesture x, the data of M antennas are acquired and processed according to the method of Sect. 3.2 to obtain the feature matrix Wx corresponding to B_x, $Action_x$.

Recognizing gestures, that is, to find out a feature matrix W which has the best matching rate with Wx in the DB. In the practical application of hand gesture recognition, due to different personal habits, different users have different gesture duration and starting time when making the same gesture, which has the same problem with speech recognition. Therefore, DTW is a good solution to solve this problem. The key idea of DTW algorithm is to compare and regress the time series of the data to be recognized on the time axis, map the input time axis of the gesture to be recognized to the time axis of the prior knowledge base nonlinearly, minimize the alignment cost of all the elements, using which to judge the similarity between the two series.

Using the DTW algorithm to calculate the matrix of two curves to be matched, the similarity of the curves can be output. For any element in the sequence pair, the Euclidean distance between $Action(\alpha)$ and $Action_x(\beta)$, $\alpha \in [1,\mu], \beta \in [1,\nu]$, is the alignment cost, that is:

$$C_{\alpha,\beta} = \mid Action(\alpha) - Action_x(\beta) \mid \tag{3}$$

Matrix with regular sequence and the sum of the cost C is $\mu \times \nu$. Let Z be the aligned arrangement of element pairs in matrix C, $Z = (z_1, \ldots, z_h, \ldots, z_H)$ where $max(\mu, \nu) \le H \le \mu + \nu - 1$ and $z_h = (\alpha_h, \beta_h)$. DTW algorithm is to find the arrangement of Z which make the cost of C smallest, that is:

$$\min_z \sum_{h=1}^{H} Z_h = \sum_{h=1}^{H} C_{\alpha_h, \beta_h} \tag{4}$$

Futher, we take the derivative of each pair of sampling point of the sequence as the second evaluation criteria. After we obtain the derivative of all pairs of samples $D = \{\frac{d\alpha}{dt}\}$, we need to calculate the cost of them C' based on the method described above. Therefore, matching cost here refer to the C' and C.

The sequence W_x of the gesture to be recognized with the characteristic matrix corresponding to each gesture in the DB. If each column in the characteristic matrix W_x has a smaller matching cost with the corresponding column of a gesture characteristic matrix W_y in the fingerprint database DB and the sum of the cost is the smallest, it is considered that the gesture is same as the corresponding gesture in the knowledge base, that is, the recognition is successful.

When the user makes a gesture, the user's limb may block a portion of the path from tag to reader or may reflect the signal to create a new multi-path. Figure 2 shows the AoA estimated characteristic curves generated from five data frames of the same gesture. The curve of Frame 2 shows that the tag forms a new signal path under the influence of the user's body. Therefore, in the matching process, multi-path will increase the difficulty of matching information, thereby improving the recognition accuracy.

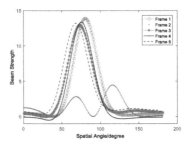

Fig. 2. Characteristic curve of AoA estimation.

3.5   Wireless Phase Calibration

Currently, there are multiple signal processing (MUSIC) algorithms [20,21], minimum variance non-distortion response (MVDR) adaptive beamforming algorithms [22], and ESPRIT algorithms [23] for array AoA estimation. Among them, the MUSIC algorithm has the advantage of high accuracy. Therefore, the MUSIC algorithm is widely used. However, the phase error caused by hardware differences often occur in actual wireless positioning, and an unknown phase offset is introduced into the received signal, which may causes array uncertainty. RFID positioning systems use MUSIC algorithm which assume that the array manifold matrix consists of all possible directions of the received signal. Due to the actual phase error caused by the hardware of the RFID system can not be ignored, such as cables, readers and antennas, signal transmission will have some loss. Literature [24] introduces a wired calibration method, and the traditional calibration method is through manual means, using special equipment, such as the Universal Software Radio Peripheral (USRP), a continuous wave is generated and input to the device to be calibrated as a reference source, and a group of devices including all the cables are measured at a time. The signal of the USRP passes through the device and the connection Line to reach the array. The hardware phase error can be directly estimated by observing the phase difference between the antennas, and then subtracting the phase error from the received signal, the influence of unknown hardware differences on AoA estimation can be eliminated.

However, this conventional method requires the use of a dedicated device, with the disadvantage of high hardware costs, and requiring an additional measurement of a set of data before the experiment to estimate the hardware error and then switch to the general-purpose device, which causes the operability poor.

So in this section we propose a wireless phase calibration method. As shown in Fig. 3, we assume the first antenna as a reference, in addition to the internal error, the i th antenna phase difference should also include the phase error caused by external hardware. Assuming that the phase error introduced by the first antenna is 0, the i th antenna phase error caused by the hardware difference relative to the first antenna is β_{i-1}, the antenna array is composed of the phase error vectors $\beta = \left[1, e^{-i\beta_1}, e^{-i\beta_2}, \cdots, e^{-i\beta_{M-1}}\right]^T$.

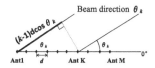

Fig. 3. Array signal model.

Let $\mathbf{B} = diag\{\beta\}$, the real measured signal should be $Rs = \mathbf{AB}x(n) + e(n)$, $\mathbf{U}_n$ is the noise subspace of Rs, $\mathbf{U}_s$ is the signal subspace of Rs, According to the above MUSIC algorithm, we know that the $\mathbf{U}_s$ and $\mathbf{U}_n$ of the actual measured signal are orthogonal, and $\mathbf{U}_n$ is the same as the subspace formed by the direction matrix $\mathbf{B}$, it can be seen that $(\mathbf{AB})^H$ is orthogonal to $\mathbf{U}_n$, that is $J = \left\| (\mathbf{A} \odot \mathbf{B})^H \mathbf{U}n \right\|^2$.

The optimization process has two main points: first, using the information of one of the tags, to obtain the hardware error value that minimizes the objective function J; second, using the MUSIC algorithm to estimate the AoA values of other tags. Calibration algorithm specific process described as follows:

Step 1: Take the first tag for optimization, the parameter information is known (real AoA, phase, RSSI value), and then the signal s received by each antenna can be obtained. Find the autocorrelation matrix of $\mathbf{S}$, $\mathbf{R} = \mathbf{S} * \mathbf{S}'$. According to the above method, decomposing the eigenvalue of R can obtain the noise eigenvector $\hat{\mathbf{U}}_n$ and the direction vector $\hat{a}$;

Step 2: Constructed the objective function for the phase error β as $Obj_\beta = \left(\hat{a} \odot e^{-i\beta}\right)^H \times \hat{\mathbf{U}}_n \times \hat{\mathbf{U}}_n^H \times \left(\hat{a} \odot e^{-i\beta}\right)$.

Through the genetic algorithm to obtain the initial value of β, the one-dimensional search is used to obtain the optimal solution β_{opt} of β which minimizes the objective function;

Step 3: According to β_{opt}, the signal that the other tags arrive at the array after removing the hardware phase error can be obtained as $\mathbf{Rs} = e^{+i\beta_{opt}} \times \mathbf{S}$;

Step 4: The MUSIC algorithm is used to obtain the spatial spectrum. According to the value of the x-axis corresponding to the peak of the curve, the angle-of-arrival AoA can be obtained. Finally, the error can be obtained compared with the real measured AoA.

Step 5: By repeating the above operation, the error between the estimated AoA value and the true measured value can be obtained when each tag is used as a calibration source.

4   Experiment and Analyses of Result

4.1   The Construction of Experimental Scene

We deploy the experimental setting in a $7\,\text{m} \times 10\,\text{m}$ classroom. To obtain data, we use the ImpinJ RFID reader with the with the frequency of 920.875 MHz. The actual transmission distance is about 5m. In the experiment, we choose these parameters: the amount of antenna $m = 8$, the amount of tag $l = 6$, the amount of data frame $n = 5$. A linear array, which is made up of 8 antennas, connects with the reader, the two with a distance of 4 cm. We choose 6 tags in front of the array, and make the tags face the array straightly to the greatest extent, and put them in the range of reader's readable area dispersedly as signal sources. The experimental equipment was shown in the Fig. 4, and the deployment was shown in the Fig. 5.

4.2 The Establishment of Fingerprint Database

We do each gesture circularly, and then we choose the data group which has highest similarity with other groups as the fingerprint for one gesture. In our experiment, we totally display 10 gestures which have been set in advance, as shown in the Fig. 6. So that we can obtain the priori fingerprint base.

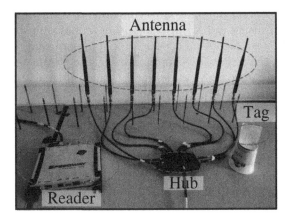

Fig. 4. Experiment equipment.

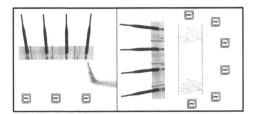

Fig. 5. Experiment deployment.

4.3 The Recognition of Gestures

User make gestures randomly. We use the algorithm introduced in the Sect. 3.2 to get each eigenvector of the tags corresponding to the gesture.

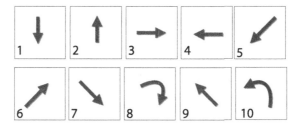

Fig. 6. Priori database of gestures set.

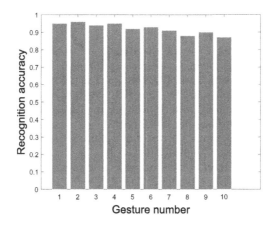

Fig. 7. Accuracy of our gesture recognition system.

In order to quantify similarity and diversity further, we input the data into our modified DTW algorithm to calculate regularly, the output data can quantify distance of each pair of corresponding points. From its output image we can explicitly see the matching rate.

4.4   The Analyses of Performance

In order to evaluate the system proposed in this paper, we repeat our each gesture 10 times. In this way we can get corresponding data. According to the aforementioned method, we obtain the gesture recognition results. Figure 7 shows that the correct recognition probability of our system can reach about 92%, it proves that this method has a quite high feasibility.

5   Conclusion

Gesture recognition is an important part of human-computer interaction. It has great application prospects in the fields of smart home and somatosensory games, which brings convenience to our life. The proposed gesture recognition technology is based on RFID, which is low cost, and easy to be deployed. This method preprocess the data by dividing data into fragment, and calibrates the phase to eliminate the phase difference caused by the hardware difference to improve precision. Then the MUSIC algorithm is used to obtain the eigenvector of each gesture. Finally, modified DTW algorithm is used to recognize the high resolution gesture. The experiment shows that the method proposed in this paper can realize gesture recognition well.

References

1. Kellogg, B., Talla, V., Gollakota, S.: Bringing gesture recognition to all devices. In: Usenix Conference on Networked Systems Design and Implementation, pp. 303–316 (2014)
2. Ziaie, P., Muller, T., Knoll, A.: A novel approach to hand-gesture recognition in a human-robot dialog system. In: First Workshops on Image Processing Theory, Tools and Applications, 2008, IPTA 2008, pp. 1–8 (2008)
3. Sun, L., Sen, S., Koutsonikolas, D., Kim, K.H.: Widraw: Enabling hands-free drawing in the air on commodity wifi devices. In: International Conference on Mobile Computing and Networking, pp. 77–89 (2015)
4. Badi, H.S., Hussein, S.: Hand posture and gesture recognition technology. Neural Comput. Appl. **25**(3–4), 871–878 (2014)
5. Blum, M.: After the kinect, what's next for gesture-recognition technology? Pak. J. Biol. Sci. PJBS **13**(14), 691–698 (2011)
6. Wang, J., Vasisht, D., Katabi, D.: RF-IDRAW: virtual touch screen in the air using RF signals. In: ACM Conference on SIGCOMM, pp. 235–246 (2014)
7. Youssef, M., Mah, M., Agrawala, A.: Challenges: device-free passive localization for wireless environments. In: ACM International Conference on Mobile Computing and Networking, pp. 222–229 (2007)
8. Pu, Q., Jiang, S., Gollakota, S.: Whole-home gesture recognition using wireless signals (demo). In: ACM SIGCOMM 2013 Conference on SIGCOMM, pp. 485–486 (2013)
9. Wang, Y., Liu, J., Chen, Y., Gruteser, M., Yang, J., Liu, H.: E-eyes: Device-free Location-oriented Activity Identification Using Fine-grained WiFi Signatures (2014)
10. Joshi, K., Bharadia, D., Kotaru, M., Katti, S.: Wideo: fine-grained device-free motion tracing using RF backscatter. In: Usenix Conference on Networked Systems Design and Implementation, pp. 189–204 (2015)
11. Tan, S., Yang, J.: Wifinger: leveraging commodity wifi for fine-grained finger gesture recognition. In: ACM International Symposium on Mobile Ad Hoc Networking and Computing, pp. 201–210 (2016)
12. Huang, Y.F., Yao, T.Y., Yang, H.J.: Performance of hand gesture recognition based on received signal strength with weighting signaling in wireless communications. In: International Conference on Network-Based Information Systems, pp. 596–600 (2015)
13. Wang, J., Katabi, D.: Dude, where's my card?: RFID positioning that works with multipath and non-line of sight. In: ACM SIGCOMM Conference on SIGCOMM, pp. 51–62 (2013)
14. Fortin-Simard, D., Bouchard, K., Gaboury, S., Bouchard, B., Bouzouane, A.: Accurate passive RFID localization system for smart homes. In: IEEE International Conference on Networked Embedded Systems for Every Application, pp. 1–8 (2013)

15. Chang, L., Chen, X., Meng, H., Fang, D.: Poster: HALL: High-accuracy and low-cost RFID localization in large-scale environment. In: International Conference on Mobile Systems, Applications, and Services Companion, p. 17 (2016)
16. He, W., Wu, K., Zou, Y., Ming, Z.: WiG: Wifi-based gesture recognition system. In: International Conference on Computer Communication and Networks, pp. 1–7 (2015)
17. Abdelnasser, H., Youssef, M., Harras, K.A.: WiGest: A ubiquitous wifi-based gesture recognition system. In: IEEE Conference on Computer Communications, pp. 1472–1480 (2015)
18. Ding, H., Shangguan, L., Yang, Z., Han, J., Zhou, Z., Yang, P., Xi, W., Zhao, J.: FEMO: a platform for free-weight exercise monitoring with RFIDs. In: ACM Conference on Embedded Networked Sensor Systems, pp. 141–154 (2015)
19. Zou, Y., Xiao, J., Han, J., Wu, K., Li, Y., Ni, L.M.: GRfid: a device-free RFID-based gesture recognition system. IEEE Trans. Mobile Comput. **16**(2), 381–393 (2017)
20. Joshi, K., Hong, S., Katti, S.: Pinpoint: localizing interfering radios. In: Usenix Conference on Networked Systems Design and Implementation, pp. 241–254 (2013)
21. Laxmikanth, P., Susruthababu, S., Surendra, L., Babu, S.S., Ratnam, D.V.: Enhancing the performance of AOA estimation in wireless communication using the music algorithm. In: International Conference on Signal Processing and Communication Engineering Systems, pp. 448–452 (2015)
22. Lavate, T.B., Kokate, V.K., Sapkal, A.M.: Performance analysis of MUSIC and ESPRIT DOA estimation algorithms for adaptive array smart antenna in mobile communication. In: Second International Conference on Computer and Network Technology, pp. 308–311 (2010)
23. Akbari, F., Moghaddam, S.S., Vakili, V.T.: MUSIC and ESPRIT DOA estimation algorithms with higher resolution and accuracy. In: International Symposium on Telecommunications, pp. 76–81 (2011)
24. Xiong, J., Jamieson, K.: ArrayTrack: a fine-grained indoor location system. In: Usenix Conference on Networked Systems Design and Implementation, pp. 71–84 (2013)

Understanding Data Partition for Applications on CPU-GPU Integrated Processors

Juan Fang[1,2(✉)], Huanhuan Chen[1,2], and Junjie Mao[1,2]

[1] Beijing University of Technology, 100 Ping Le Yuan,
Chaoyang District, Beijing, China
fangjuan@bjut.edu.cn, chenhuan@emails.bjut.edu.cn,
maojunjie@sina.com
[2] China Information Technology Security Evaluation Center, Beijing, China

Abstract. Integrating GPU with CPU on the same chip is increasingly common in current processor architectures for high performance. CPU and GPU share on-chip network, last level cache, memory. Do not need to copy data back and forth that a discrete GPU requires. Shared virtual memory, memory coherence, and system-wide atomics are introduced to heterogeneous architectures and programming models to enable fine-grained CPU and GPU collaboration. Programming model such as OpenCL 2.0, CUDA 8.0, and C++ AMP support these heterogeneous architecture features. Data partition is one of the collaboration patterns. It is essential for improving performance and energy-efficiency to balance the data processed between CPU and GPU. In this paper, we first demonstrate that the optimal allocation of data to the CPU and GPU can provide 20% higher performance than fixed ratio of 20% for one application. Second, we evaluate another 5 heterogeneous applications covering the latest architecture features, found the relation of the data partitioning with performance.

Keywords: Data partition · GPU · Heterogeneous architectures

1 Introduction

In many modern processors such as Intel's Kaby Lake, and AMD's Bristol Ridge, the GPU is resident on the same die as the CPU. CPU and GPU share the same physical memory, which can significantly reduce the cost of host-device data copying. Heterogeneous system architectures and programming models are moving to tighter integration [1, 2] by introducing features such as shared virtual memory (SVM), memory coherence, and system-wide atomics to enable fine-grained CPU and GPU collaboration. Some programming models have introduced support for the heterogeneous architecture features described above, including OpenCL 2.0 and CUDA 8.0 and C++ AMP.

Many works have been done to effectively leverage the power of the both CPU and GPU before the programming models mentioned above emerge. Many of them are focus on task allocation between CPU and GPU. Vilches et al. [3] dynamically adjust the size of the workload assigned to the GPU and CPU to maximize the GPU and CPU utilization while balancing the workload. Grewe et al. [4] propose a machine learning-based approach to determine the partition of OpenCL kernels while taking

© Springer Nature Singapore Pte Ltd. 2018
L. Zhu and S. Zhong (Eds.): MSN 2017, CCIS 747, pp. 426–434, 2018.
https://doi.org/10.1007/978-981-10-8890-2_32

GPU contention into account. Lang et al. [5] propose a method for dynamically balancing the workload of a parallel conjugate gradient method between CPU and GPU. Pérez et al. [6] design a library for OpenCL enabling a single data-parallel kernel to take full use of all the available computing devices on a heterogeneous system. However, they do not take advantage of features of modern architecture and programming models.

Applications on heterogeneous architectures have different collaboration patterns. Several general collaboration patterns have been investigated in [7]. Data partition is one of the main collaboration patterns between different processors performing the same operation concurrently on different data elements. Input and output data can be stored in SVM which helps avoid explicit copying of data between devices and merging of final result. Besides, system-wide atomics can be used in applications that requires atomic updates to an output value or synchronization flag. Recent studies demonstrate that data partition between the CPU and the GPU can improve the overall performance of a heterogeneous computing system. The main challenge with this pattern is find the optimal partition strategy to allocate data between CPU and GPU. Zhang et al. [8] rewrite programs from three GPU-only or CPU-only benchmark suites with the OpenCL framework. Eight of forty-two co-run programs can achieve higher performance over running on GPU or CPU alone. The programs do not have the-state-of-art features of heterogeneous architecture, which is essential to the implementation and performance.

Chai [7] is used in this work, a benchmark suite covers different computation behaviors to exercise different features of the architecture. We evaluate 6 data partitioning programs with various partitioning granularity from Chai. This paper tries to explore the new findings about data partitioning application with modern programming model executed on integrated architecture.

The remainder of this paper is organized as follows: Sect. 2 gives a brief introduction to the background and motivation. We describe the experimental settings and workflow in Sect. 3. In Sect. 4, analysis on the result is presented. In the end, Sect. 5 conclude this paper.

2 Background and Motivation

2.1 Data Partition

In data partition, different devices perform the same task on different parts of the input or output concurrently. Figure 1 shows an example application that consists of two coarse-grain sub-tasks. The second sub-task's execution depends on the first sub-task's result. Generally, a synchronization will follow a coarse-grain sub-task to ensure collaboration between different devices [9], memory consistency for SVM. The size of a collection can be changed in the next coarse-grain sub-task. As a result, the size of data processed on a device in this coarse-grain sub-task will be different from that in another. Each sub-task is divided into two data-parallel fine-grain task collections. The execution of each collection is on a single device such as CPU, GPU.

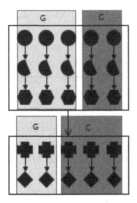

(a) Data Partition Application

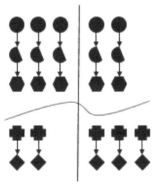

(b) Execution Flow

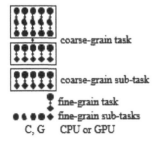

(c) Legends

Fig. 1. Data partition application execution

2.2   Heterogeneous Architecture Features

Heterogeneous architecture features described in this section are based on not only hardware architecture but programming models. Figure 2 shows an integrated architecture in which CPU and GPU share off-chip memory. In some modern processors, CPU and GPU share last level cache. Each CPU core has own L1 or L2 cache. Each GPU core has own L1 cache, and two or more SMs share a L2 cache. SVM allows CPU and GPU to share the same virtual address range. It is an OpenCL 2.0 terminology. Giving such sharing, the explicit data copy between CPU memory and GPU memory is not necessary anymore. Communication through the network-on-chip is more efficient than a dedicated high bandwidth interconnect, such as PCIe. CPU and GPU also can use the same pointer to access data structures. Furthermore, Fine-grain SVM and coarse-grain SVM help efficient data share and synchronization in different grain.

The Heterogeneous System Architecture (HSA) [9] is a programming model that is designed to easily and efficiently develop a wide assortment of data-parallel and task-parallel applications. An HSA-compliant system will require architecture features such as SVM, cache coherence, flat addressing of memory, atomic memory operations. OpenCL 2.0 also benefit the features that HSA requires.

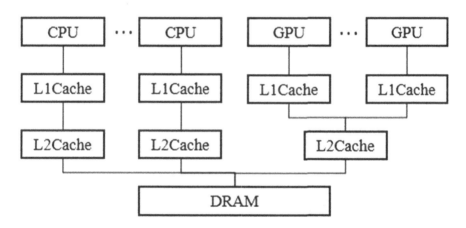

Fig. 2. Simulated heterogeneous architecture

2.3   Impact of Partition

Figure 3 plots the execution time of bézier tensor-product surface (BS) with different ratios of data processed on CPU. The implementation of BS from CHAI perform data partition on the output surface, dividing it into square tiles and assigning them to different CPU threads or GPU workgroups. The GPU workgroup size is chosen to be the same as the tile size. The input matrix of control points and the output surface points are stored in SVM. As we can see, the finish time grows as the data size of CPU increases. It is clear that the finish time is constant when the percent between 0% and 6%, while the CPU time significantly increased. The CPU execution time rises steadily as the percent is greater than 6%, while the GPU time varies slightly even no changes. A reasonable explanation as cited in many research is that the total execution time of a heterogeneous application on a heterogeneous system is the maximum of the CPU and GPU execution times. Although this assumption is simplistic, it can enable us to gain some insights into an optimal partition point.

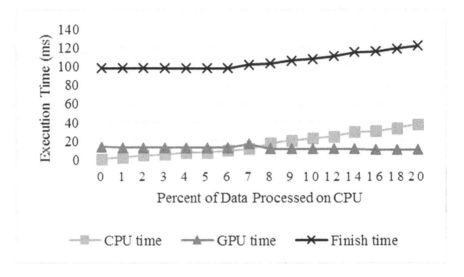

Fig. 3. BS execution time with different partition

3 Methodology

3.1 Simulation Settings

We use gem5-gpu [10] to simulate an integrated heterogeneous CPU-GPU system. Gem5-gpu is a cycle-level simulator that integrate gem5 [11] and GPGPU-Sim [12]. Gem5's full-system mode running the Linux operating system is used in our simulation.

The simulated system is depicted in Fig. 1 as described in Sect. 2. Gem5-gpu supports a shared virtual address space between the CPU and GPU. GPU accesses CPU's page table for virtual to physical translation. Ruby cache hierarchy with VI_hammer [10] coherence protocol is used in the configuration. All GPU cores and their L1caches are connected to one crossbar, which is also connected to the GPU L2cache. All CPU cores and their private L1caches, L2caches ate connected to another crossbar. These two crossbars are connected to another crossbar, which is also connected to the directory and memory. Table 1 lists the configurations of the system. We simulate a heterogeneous system composed of an 8 core CPU and an integrated GPU equipped with 8 Maxwell-like stream multiprocessors.

Table 1. Key configuration parameters

CPU	# of CPU cores	8
	CPU frequency	2 GHz
	L1D cache L1I cache	64 KB 32 KB
	L2 cache	512 KB
GPU	# of GPU cores	8
	L1 cache	64 KB
	L2 cache	1 MB
DRAM	DRAM size	3 GB

Table 2. Benchmarks, GPU configurations

Abbrev.	Benchmark	Configuration (#wi, #wg)
BS	Bézier surface	16, 32
HSTI	Image histogram (input partitioning)	256, 16
HSTO	Image histogram (output partitioning)	256, 16
PAD	Padding	256, 8
RSCD	Random sample consensus	256, 8
SC	Stream compaction	256, 8

3.2 Benchmarks

Table 2 lists the applications that we use for evaluation. The applications are come from Chai benchmarks suites. Chai provide 8 data partitioning applications cover different computation behaviors to exercise different features of the architecture. Chai encompasses a well-rounded combination of aspects such as partitioning granularity, use of system-wide atomics, inter-worker synchronization, and load balance. We select 6 data partitioning applications as our benchmarks. The parameters in last column specify the GPU configurations for each application including GPU threads per block (work item) and the number of blocks (workgroup). We do not adjust the configuration for each benchmark to exploit available resource in the simulated system. We assign 6 threads to each benchmark to complete the task, assign 1 thread to the benchmark when the GPU acquires all the data. The datasets for each application is default.

3.3 Workflow

We run the programmers 1 time. We only take GPU kernel time, CPU kernel time, finish time into statistics. The kernel time is the average of 10 runs after 5 warmup runs. We dump the statistics at the end of the CPU kernel and the GPU kernel, do not reset the statistics. So, the finish time is approximately the total simulation time divided by times of run.

4 Result Analysis

Figure 4 shows the results of execution time with variable ratios for each benchmark. For HSTI, HSTO, SC, PAD, the finish time is indifferent to the data partitioning. The execution time on CPU and GPU is not sensitive to data partitioning as well. Load balancing is not so important to improve the performance. We checked the implementation of HSTO, found that both CPU and GPU must go through the entire input. So the execution time on CPU and GPU are similar. It is clear that partitioning ratio has effect on only two applications. For RSCD, the GPU time do not change while the finish time rises as the CPU time grows as expected. The total execution time is determined by the last processor to complete the task.

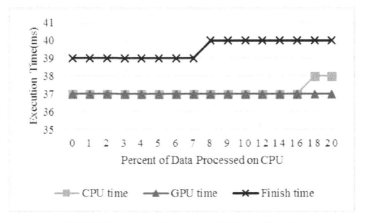

(a) HSTI Execution Time with Different Partitioning

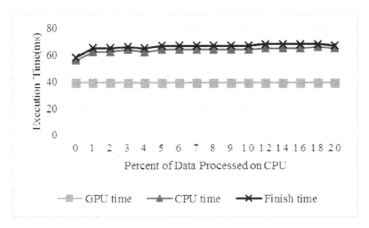

(b) HSTO Execution Time with Different Partitioning

Fig. 4. Execution time of benchmarks with different partition

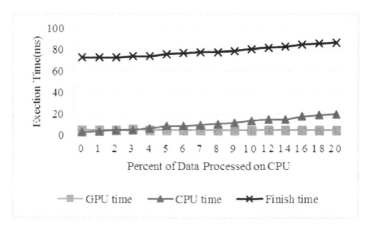

(c) RSCD Execution Time with Different Partitioning

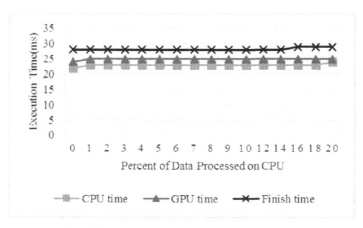

(d) SC Execution Time with Different Partitioning

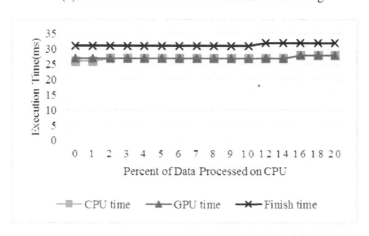

(e) PAD Execution Time with Different Partitioning

Fig. 4. (*continued*)

5 Conclusion

In this paper, we run the heterogeneous programs written in new programming model taking advantage of integrated architecture on integrated system. Some applications are sensitive to data partitioning, while others not. We still need load balancing on the architectures with such latest features. Elaborative distribution of workload should be taken to get best performance according to system's configuration. Data partitioning has little effect on the platform whose one of the processors is very powerful if the dataset is small.

Acknowledgement. This work is partially supported by the National Natural Science Foundation of China under Grant NO. 61202076 and NO. 61202062.

References

1. Khronos Group: The OpenCL specification, Version 2.0 (2015)
2. NVidia: CUDA C programming guide v. 8.0, September 2016
3. Vilches, A., Asenjo, R., Navarro, A., Corbera, F., Gran, R., Garzarán, M.: Adaptive partitioning for irregular applications on heterogeneous CPU-GPU chips. In: International Conference on Computational Science, vol. 51, pp. 271–350, pp. 140–149 (2015)
4. Grewe, D., Wang, Z., O'Boyle, M.F.P.: OpenCL task partitioning in the presence of GPU contention. In: Caşcaval, C., Montesinos, P. (eds.) LCPC 2013. LNCS, vol. 8664, pp. 87–101. Springer, Cham (2014). https://doi.org/10.1007/978-3-319-09967-5_5
5. Lang, J., Rünger, G.: Dynamic distribution of workload between CPU and GPU for a parallel conjugate gradient method in an adaptive FEM. Procedia Comput. Sci. **18**, 299–308 (2013)
6. Pérez, B., Bosque, J.L., Beivide, R.: Simplify programming and load balancing of data parallel applications on heterogeneous system. In: Proceedings of the 9th Annual Workshop on General Purpose Processing using Graphics Processing Unit, pp. 42–51 (2016)
7. Gómez-Luna, J., Hajj, I.E., Chang, L.-W., García-Flores, V., de Gonzalo, S.G., Jablin, T.B., Pena, A.J., Hwu, W.-M.: Chai: collaborative heterogeneous applications for integrated-architectures. In: IEEE International Symposium on Performance Analysis of Systems and Software (2017)
8. Zhang, F., Zhai, J., He, B., Zhang, S., Chen, W.: Understanding co-running behaviors on integrated CPU/GPU architectures. IEEE Trans. Parallel Distrib. Syst. **28**, 905–918 (2017)
9. Hwu, W.-M.W.: Heterogeneous System Architecture: A New Compute Platform Infrastructure. Morgan Kaufman (2015)
10. Power, J., Hestness, J., Orr, M.S., Hill, M.D., Wood, D.A.: gem5-gpu: a heterogeneous CPU-GPU simulator. IEEE Comput. Archit. Lett. **14**(1), 34–36 (2015)
11. Binkert, N., Beckmann, B., Black, G., Reinhardt, S.K., Saidi, A., Basu, A., Hestness, J., Hower, D.R., Krishna, T., Sardashti, S., Sen, R., Sewell, K., Shoaib, M., Vaish, N., Hill, M. D., Wood, D.A.: The gem5 simulator. SIGARCH Comput. Archit. News **39**(2), 1–7 (2011)
12. Bakhoda, A., Yuan, G., Fung, W., Wong, H., Aamodt, T.: Analyzing CUDA workloads using a detailed GPU simulator. In: International Symposium on Performance Analysis of Systems and Software (2009)

Privacy-Preserving and Traceable Data Aggregation in Energy Internet

Yue Zhang and Zhitao Guan$^{(\boxtimes)}$

North China Electric Power University, Beijing 102206, China
guan@ncepu.edu.cn

Abstract. Energy Internet is considered as a promising approach to solve the problems of energy crisis and carbon emission. It needs to collect user's real-time data for optimizing the energy utilization. Edge nodes like *GWs* (gateway) are used for data aggregation to improve the efficiency of the system. Due to a large number of *GWs* are widely distributed and difficult to be managed, which brings potential security threats for the Energy Internet. Existing data aggregation schemes fails in preventing the adversary from controlling or destroying *GWs*. In this paper, we propose an IBE-based Device Traceable Privacy-Preserving Aggregation Scheme, named IBE-DTPPA. Increasing the *RA* (Residential Area) users' data aggregation integrity verification by BGN Cryptosystem; using IBE Cryptosystem to encrypt aggregation data, calculating ciphertext based on *GW's* dynamic ID, realizing the target *GW* traceability; choosing *CC* (Control Center) dynamic identity information as public key to realize *CC* authentication, preventing adversary from using *CC*'s identity fraudulently. Through extensive analysis, we demonstrate that IBE-DTPPA resists various security threats, and can trace target *GW* efficiently.

Keywords: Device tracking · Authentication · Data aggregation
Energy Internet

1 Introduction

Energy Internet as a pluralistic energy network [1], as the issues of environmental pollution and energy crisis are becoming increasingly serious, Energy Internet supports the large-scale use of renewable energy sources, which has been given broad intensive attention. Energy Internet can be divided into energy network and information network. Energy generated from various users turns into electricity and interacts with the power plant through the energy transfer network and information network, as shown in Fig. 1. Compared with smart grid, the Energy Internet can make full use of the various types of distributed energy [2], so the energy management and real-time data analysis are important in Energy Internet [3, 4]. In the Energy Internet, the scope of system data collection will be expanded greatly, SMs and a variety of smart appliances will be used as collection devices to upload nearly real-time periodically, however, frequently electricity usage data collection may bring user sensitive information leakage and other issues, which threaten user privacy [5], and calculation cost and communication overhead bring much pressure to the system. Using data aggregation [6, 7] not only

© Springer Nature Singapore Pte Ltd. 2018
L. Zhu and S. Zhong (Eds.): MSN 2017, CCIS 747, pp. 435–449, 2018.
https://doi.org/10.1007/978-981-10-8890-2_33

reduces communication overhead but also protects individual data privacy. Most of the existing aggregation schemes use homomorphic encryption to encrypt users' data, device like SM (smart meter) encrypts data and aggregates in edge nodes in communication network without decryption, which can reduce the communication overhead and calculation cost for other entities, improving system efficiency, as show in Fig. 1.

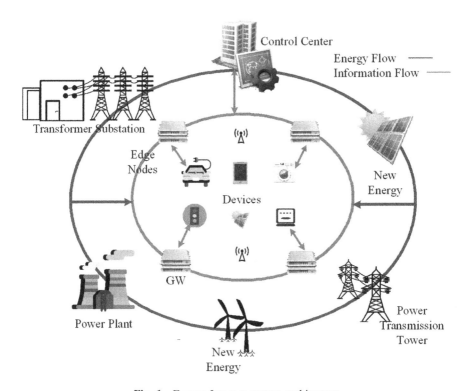

Fig. 1. Energy Internet system architecture

Due to a large number of GWs are widely distributed in the RA, it is difficult to manage, vulnerable to be destroyed or controlled by the adversary, resulting in the error aggregation data will be transmitted to CC, improper power generation plan or dynamic price will reduce system reliability, as shown in Fig. 2, then how to trace the target gateway in time to ensure Energy Internet reliability, which is still a problem. In addition, CC's identity is vulnerable to be used fraudulently by the adversary, which may cause user privacy disclosure. To solve above problems, in this paper, we propose IBE-based Device Traceable Privacy-Preserving Aggregation Scheme based on IBE (IBE-DTPPA).

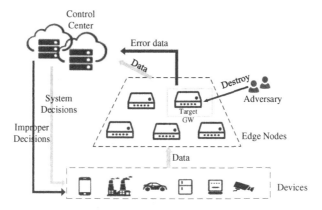

Fig. 2. Energy Internet edge equipment threat

A security-efficient, supporting target GW traceability. The main contributions of this paper are divided into three parts as follows:

(1) We add a random number in aggregation in BGN Cryptosystem to realize verification of aggregation data integrity. Choose CC's dynamic ID as public key IBE encryption, ID updates aperiodically in short period of time, ensuring the authenticity of CC's identity.

(2) We encrypt the RA aggregation data by IBE Cryptosystem, calculating ciphertext based on GW's dynamic ID, realizing the target GW traceability.

(3) We prove the security of our scheme, analyze the relevant parameters through detailed analysis, proving our scheme is secure against different attacks and can realize device traceability efficiently.

The rest of this paper is organized as follows. Section 2 introduces the related work. In Sect. 3, some preliminaries are given. In Sect. 4, showing the system model and design goals. In Sect. 5, our scheme is stated. In Sect. 6, security analysis is given. In Sect. 7, the paper is concluded.

2 Related Work

Existing data aggregation schemes have a common concern, individual user's privacy-sensitive data should not be exposed. The common solutions to realize data aggregation contain homomorphic encryption [8] and data obfuscation [9]. However, the selection of parameters in data obfuscation is a difficult task. Therefore, homomorphic encryption has been widely used. Existing schemes use a homomorphic encryption to encrypt user's privacy-sensitive data and the edge nodes like gateway in the Energy Internet can aggregate all user's data without decryption, Przydatek et al. propose a specific framework for secure data aggregation in distributed energy environment, although Przydatek et al.'s framework could provide efficient data aggregation, the data privacy still needs to be improved. To address the individual user privacy issue in data aggregation, Shi et al. [10] propose a scheme to aggregate time-series data, which allows a group of collection devices upload the encrypted user's data to the aggregator periodically, and aggregate the data without disclosing any information. Homomorphic hash function [11] has been used to authenticate SM and CC. In [12], Lu et al. proposes an efficient and privacy-preserving aggregation scheme by homomorphic multidimensional data encryption schemes (EPPA), which can realize the multidimensional data aggregation. On this basis Chen et al. [13] try to use third parties to achieve fault tolerance of data aggregation, but the obvious disadvantages is that third party security is difficult to guarantee. Shi et al. [14] proposes the DG-APED scheme, which can resolve the problems caused by malfunctioning SMs. it will aggregate the data by grouping, and drop the group which contains the damaged SM. However, because of error rate is not ideal and extra computational cost in searching the damaged member also needs to spend. Works [15] are committed to achieve the efficient data aggregation, but the cost of realizing fault tolerance is still too high, and there is still room for improvement. Works [16] are proposed to realize the differential privacy in aggregation schemes. Wang et al. [17] proposes an electric vehicle in the smart grid traceability of privacy protection and precision incentive scheme, using a restrictive partially blind signature technique and pseudonym in V2G (vehicle-to-grid) networks to achieve traceability of malicious users. Several other papers (e.g., [18–24]) have studied related security and network issues.

3 Preliminaries

3.1 Bilinear Maps

Let G_0 and G_1 be two multiplicative cyclic groups of prime order p and g be the generator of G_0. The bilinear map e is, $e : G_0 \times G_0 \rightarrow G_1$, for all $a, b \in \mathbb{Z}_p$:

Bilinearity: $\forall u, v \in G_1, e(u^a, v^b) = e(u, v)^{ab}$

Non-degeneracy: $e(g, g) \neq 1$

Symmetric: $e(g^a, g^b) = e(g, g)^{ab} = e(g^b, g^a)$

3.2 Elliptic Curve Cryptography (ECC)

Elliptic curve encryption (ECC) algorithm [25, 26], proposed by Koblitz and Miller in 1985, Define an elliptic curve E and a field $GF(q)$.Consider x, y Abel with a form of rational number $E(q)$, Elliptic curve equation E defined as

$$y^2 + a_1 xy + a_2 y = x^3 + a_3 x^2 + a_4 x + a_6$$

The point $E(K)$ on the elliptic curve that satisfies the equation plus the set of infinity points is expressed:

$$E(K) = \{(x, y) \in k^2 | y_2 + a_1 xy + a_2 y = x^3 + a_3 x^2 + a_4 x + a_6\} \cup \{0\}$$

3.3 Complexity Assumptions

Definition 1. ECC is based on the problem of finding elliptic curve discrete pairs (ECDLP) is difficult.

That is, for a base point on the elliptic curve, it is easy to give an integer test, but it is very difficult to derive the integer from the point and point, that is, there is no algorithm to solve the polynomial time, which is elliptic curve discrete Logarithmic problem, to provide security for ECC-based encryption algorithms.

Definition 2 Bilinear Diffie-Hellman (BDH) Problem. The Bilinear Diffie-Hellman (BDH) problem in G is as follows: Given $(P, aP, bP, cP)(a, b, c \in Z_q^*)$, calculate, $\omega = e(P, P)^{abc} \in G_2$, e is a bilinear mapping, P is the generator of G_1, G_1, G_2 is the order of prime numbers q of the two groups, Set the algorithm A to solve the BDH problem, The advantage of an adversary τ is defined as $\Pr|A(P, aP, bP, cP) = e(P, P)^{abc}| \geq \tau$.

There is no valid algorithm to solve the BDH problem, so it can be assumed that the BDH problem is a difficult problem.

3.4 Based on BDH IBE (Identity-Based Cryptosystem)

IBE [25] algorithm consists of four steps:

Step 1   System initialization:

Let $k \in Z^+$ be a safety parameter, run the BDH parameter generation algorithm g, Output prime number q, group orders of q, G_1, G_2, a bilinear mapping $e : G_1 \times G_1 \rightarrow G_2$. Select a random generator $P \in G_1$, random selection $s \in Z_q^*$, calculating $P_{pub} = sP$. Select a hash function $H_1 : \{0, 1\}^* \rightarrow G_1^*$, for n, Select another hash function $H_2 : G_2 \rightarrow \{0, 1\}^n$, the message space is $M = \{0, 1\}^n$ ciphertext space is $C = G_1^* \times \{0, 1\}^n$, System parameters are public: params $= <q, G_1, G_2, e, n, P, P_{pub}, H_1, H_2 >$, s is the master key, is confidential.

Step 2   Encryption:

The identity ID of the recipient is encrypted as a public key, $M \in M$, calculate $Q_{ID} = H_1(ID) \in G_1^*$, choosing random number $r \in Z_q^*$, generating ciphertext:

$$C = <rP, M \oplus H_2(g_{ID}^r) >, \quad g_{ID} = e(Q_{ID}, P_{pub}) \in G_2^* \tag{1}$$

Step 3   Key generation:

For a given bit string ID $= \{0, 1\}^*$, calculate $Q_{ID} = H_1(ID) \in G_1^*$, then calculate secret key $d_{ID} = sQ_{ID}$, master key is s.

Step 4 Decryption:

Set ciphertext is $C = <U, V> \in C$, then use d_{ID} calculate

$$V \oplus H_2(e(d_{ID}, U)) = M, \text{ Get the plaintext } M \tag{2}$$

3.5   BGN (Boneh-Goh-Nissim) Cryptosystem

Given the security parameter g, composite bilinear parameters $(p, q, \mathbb{G}, \mathbb{G}_1, e)$ are generated by $\varsigma(\kappa)$, where $n = pq$ and p, q are two k-bit prime numbers $g \in \mathbb{G}$ is a generator of order n. Set $h = g^q$, then h is a random generator of the subgroup of $\mathbb{G}$ order p. The public key is $PK = (N, \mathbb{G}, \mathbb{G}_1, e, g, h)$, and the corresponding private key is $SK = p$.

Step 2 Encryption:

We assume the message space consists of integers in the set $m = \{0, 1, \ldots \ldots W\}$ with $W \ll q$. To encrypt a message m, we choose a random number $r \in \mathbb{Z}_N$ and compute the ciphertext:

$$c = E(m, r) = g^m \cdot h^r \in \mathbb{G} \tag{3}$$

Step 3 Decryption:

Given the ciphertext $c = E(m, r) = g^m h^r \in \mathbb{G}$, the corresponding message can be recovered by the private key $SK = p$,

$$c^p = (g^m \cdot h^r)^p = (g^p)^m. \tag{4}$$

Let $g^* = g^p$, To recover m, it suffices to compute the discrete log of c^p base g^*. Since $0 \le m \le T$, the expected time is around $O(\sqrt{T})$ when using the Pollard's lambda method [26].

4   Models and Goals

4.1   System Model

In this section, we propose an IBE-based Device Traceable Privacy-Preserving Aggregation Scheme in the Energy Internet. The system model as Fig. 3 shows, mainly composed of CC, TCA (Trusted Third Party), edge nodes like GWs, and a varied of Users in the RA.

User: We divide all the users into distributed energy providers, energy consumers and electric vehicle users. They all need to upload their real-time data to the control center for the energy optimization through SMs. As the real-time data is related to user privacy, the data must be encrypted by the SM before sending to the CC.

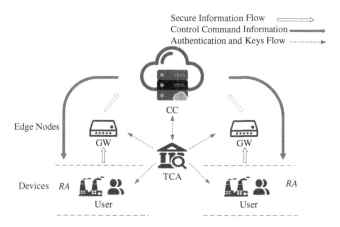

Fig. 3. System model

GW (gateway): is responsible for collecting the encrypted data sent by SMs in RA, calculating the aggregation of real-time data by running the homomorphic algorithm and uploading the sum to the control center. Responsible for data aggregation integrity verification and encryption of aggregated data by IBE. In order to improve the efficiency of the system, the user selects the nearest available GW in RA.

TCA (Trusted Third Party): responsible for the SM, GW and CC initialization to generate keys and system parameters, generating dynamic IDs for the GW in RA and CC, and CC authentication.

CC (Control Center): Can acquire the summary of real–time data from GW with these data, CC can get the trend of power consumption and create the power generation plan or dynamic price immediately. In order to improve efficiency of the Energy Internet, different regions set up different CCs.

4.2 IBE-DTPPA Scheme Procedure

The procedure of IBE-DTPPA Scheme has the following four steps:

Step 1   User data request and encryption:

(1) When the CC Sends a data request in RA, or Users' data is collected periodically (15 min), the TCA is initialized to generate the encryption parameters for SM and GW. (2) SM encrypts current data by BGN, and transfers to the nearest available GW in RA.

Step 2   Data aggregation and aggregation integrity verification:

(1) When GW receives encrypted data from users in RA, then GW aggregates data and user random numbers. (2) The aggregation integrity of the user data in RA is verified by the random number aggregation.

Step 3   Secondary Encryption:

If the data is successfully aggregated, the aggregation is re-encrypted by IBE encryption based on the dynamic ID of CC in GW, choosing CC's ID as public key, calculating ciphertext based on GW's ID. To realize the CC real-time authentication and traceability of malicious GW. The ciphertext is forwarded to CC.

Step 4   Decryption and GW traceability:

If the authentication of CC is successful, CC gets decrypt permission, getting the aggregation data in RA, if CC doubts the authenticity of the aggregation data, and wants to trace the source, then the GW which responsible for the data aggregation will be traced. If find the GW is destroyed or controlled by the adversary, the malicious GW will be isolated and replaced by other available GWs in RA in time.

4.3   Adversary Model

We assume that SM installed on the user side is a trusted device. The communication channel is not secure and adversary may eavesdrop on the channel. The GW is vulnerable to be controlled or destroyed by the adversary. CC is not fully credible, will not take the initiative to disclose user information, but the adversary will use CC's identity fraudulently to steal user's data, which will bring the privacy and security threats to users.

4.4   Design Goals

Considering the above mentioned, our design goals can be divided into three aspects.

(1) Privacy-preserving: users' data in RA is inaccessible to any other users. The outside adversary, GW or CC should not acquire the real-time data of users even if they try to conspire with each other.
(2) Target GW traceable: The aggregation data encrypted by IBE Cryptosystem, calculating the ciphertext by GW's dynamic ID. When CC wants to trace the source of the aggregation data, tracing the target GW efficiently.
(3) CC authentication and aggregation integrity verification: preventing the adversary from fraudulently using CC's identity, using CC's dynamic ID as IBE public key to realize real-time authentication of CC. In order to ensure the accuracy of data collection of RA, random number aggregation is used to verify the integrity of user data aggregation in RA by BGN Cryptosystem.

5   IBE-DTPPA Scheme

5.1   System Initialization

(1)   Device dynamic identity generation

In order to achieve CC real-time authentication, preventing the adversary tracing the data owner based on the fixed ID of GW, in our scheme, updating the dynamic ID of

GW and CC ID_{G_i} ID_{C_i} in a short period, updated ID_{G_i}, ID_{C_i} by TCA. The update period is bounded by the times of calculations of RA data collection. For example, the number of GW calculations $Times_{GW}(Times_{GW} \leq 50)$ and CC $Times_{CC}(Times_{CC} \leq 100)$, and the TCA updates the ID for the device when the threshold is reached.

(2) System parameter generation

Step 1. TCA runs $Gen_1(k)$, generating the parameters used for DBH-based IBE Cryptosystem: Given the security parameter $k \in Z^+$, calculating a prime number q_{IBE}, groups $G_1, G_2, G_1 \times G_1 \rightarrow G_2$ of order q_{IBE}. Select the random generate $P \in G_1$, selecting random number $s \in Z_q^*$, calculating $PK_{IBE} = sP$, selecting Hash Function $H_1 : \{0,1\}^* \rightarrow G_1^*$ $H_2 : G_2 \rightarrow \{0,1\}^n$. Public parameter is $par_{IBE} = \ <q_{IBE}, G_1, G_2, e, n, P, P_{pub}, H_1, H_2 >$.

Step 2. Run $Gen_2(k)$, generating the required parameters for BGN Cryptosystem, (p, q, G), p, q are two prime numbers, selecting random numbers $g \in G$, $x \in G$, calculating $h = x^q$, $PK_{BGN} = (N, G, g, h)$, $SK_{BGN} = p$.

Step 3. In order to achieve aggregation integrity verification, when RA users $U = \{U_1, U_2, ..., U_n\}$ data encrypted by BGN (assigned to the same GW), TCA will generates a system random number r_s for the RA users, calculating the random number of each user based on the system random number:

$$(r_1 + r_2 + ... + r_n) = r_s \bmod p \qquad (5)$$

Send the different random number r_i for each user to the user in RA for encryption. Parameter generation process as Fig. 4 shows.

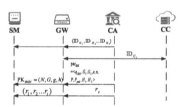

Fig. 4. System initialization

5.2   User Data Encryption

(1) SM (Smart Meter)

User U_i in RA_j collects user's data d_i periodically (15 min) by SM, encrypting d_i by BGN Cryptosystem, and based on the user's random number r_i, according to the formula (3), calculating $C_{BGNi} = g^{d_i} h^{r_i}$.

After the encryption process, in order to prevent the attacker from listening at the target GW, and increase the efficiency of the system. TCA choose the nearest available GW in RA_j for the users to aggregate data randomly. And then SM forwards C_{BGNi} to the chosen GW.

(2) GW (Gateway)

Upon receiving all the encrypted data from SMs, GW_a aggregates all the data by:

$$
\begin{aligned}
C_{Ua_j} &= \prod_{i=1}^{n} C_{BGNi} \\
&= g^{d_1} h^{r_1} \cdot g^{d_2} h^{r_2} \cdots g^{d_n} h^{r_n} \\
&= \left(g^{\sum_{i=1}^{n} d_i} h^{\sum_{i=1}^{n} r_i} \right) \\
&= g^{\sum_{i=1}^{n} d_i} h^{r_s'}
\end{aligned}
\tag{6}
$$

After aggregating data in GW_a, and then aggregates user random number r_i, compared with system random number r_s, $\sum_{i=1}^{n} r^i \overset{?}{=} r_s$ if it does hold, proved aggregation is successful, otherwise, directly abandon the data, sending a data request to CC again, which will increase system strategy reliability and reduce overhead of error aggregation data for the system.

5.3   Secondary Encryption

In order to achieve the traceability of the GW device and increase the security of the CC, we encrypts aggregation data by IBE Cryptosystem in IBE-DTPPA scheme. We use CC's dynamic ID as the public key, calculating ciphertext based on GW's dynamic ID as random number. Secondary aggregation data encryption, increasing the data security, CC real-time identity authentication to ensure that CC is not be used fraudulently and trace target GW efficiently. The process as:

When the GW requests the secondary encryption of the aggregated data, TCA generates the public parameters par_{IBE} for the IBE encryption, sending the GW dynamic ID, ID_{g_a} CC dynamic ID, ID_{C_i} and the public parameters par_{IBE} to the target GW. TCA calculates the public key based on ID_{C_i}, calculating ciphertext C' by IBE Encryption. The current time stamp. TS_t is set, in order to prevent replay attack. And in order to ensure the integrity of the message, we select the hash function $H_2 : G_2 \rightarrow \{0,1\}^n$, generating a message digest δ, and GW sends it with TS_t, C' to the CC.

Step 1. Calculate $Q_{ID_{C_i}} = H_1(ID_{C_i}) \in G_1^*$;

Step 2. The GW dynamic identity information $ID_{g_i} \in Z_q^*$ is taken as a random number.

Step 3. According to the formula (1), calculating the ciphertext:

$$C' = \, <\mathrm{ID}_{g_a}P, \; g^{\sum_{i=1}^{n} d_i} h^{r'} \oplus H_2(g_{\mathrm{ID}_{g_a}}^{\mathrm{ID}_{g_a}}) > \tag{7}$$

Step 4. Calculate $\delta = H_2(C')$, sending $\{\delta = H_2(C'), C', TS_t\}$ to the target CC.

5.4   Data Decryption and Devices Traceability

(1)   CC Authentication

After receiving $\{\delta = H_2(C'), C', TS_t\}$, and CC verifies whether $H_2(C') \overset{?}{=} \delta$, If it does hold, the message has not been tampered, otherwise the data request is sent again to the user in RA_j. Then verifies whether the aggregated data is available by checking TS_t then CC sends a decrypted data request to the TCA, following as:

Step 1   TCA authenticates the CC's current identity and generates the key: $Q_{\mathrm{ID}_{C_i}} = H_1(\mathrm{ID}_{C_i}) \in G_1^*$, $SK_{IBE} = d_{\mathrm{ID}_{C_i}} = sQ_{\mathrm{ID}_{C_i}}$, when the verification is successful, sending $sQ_{\mathrm{ID}_{C_i}}$ to CC.

Step 2   Decrypt $C' = \, <\mathrm{ID}_{g_i}P, \; g^{\sum_{i=1}^{n} d_i} h^{r'} \oplus H_2(g_{\mathrm{ID}_{g_i}}^{\mathrm{ID}_{g_i}}) >$ by IBE Cryptosystem. According to the formula (2), as:

$$\begin{aligned}
C_{Ua_j} &= g^{\sum_{i=1}^{n} d_i} h^{r'} \oplus H_2\left(g_{\mathrm{ID}_{g_i}}^{\mathrm{ID}_{g_i}}\right) \\
&\oplus H_2(e(sQ_{\mathrm{ID}}, \mathrm{ID}_{g_i}P)) \\
&= g^{\sum_{i=1}^{n} d_i} h^{r'}
\end{aligned} \tag{8}$$

Generate $\mathrm{ID}_{G_i}P$ and C_{Ua_j} by IBE Cryptosystem encryption.

Step 3   Decrypt C_{Ua_j} according to secret key $SK_{BGN} = p$ by BGN Cryptosystem, as:

$$\begin{aligned}
C^{SK_{BGN}} &= \left(g^{\sum_{i=1}^{n} d_i} h^{r'}\right)^p = g^{\sum_{i=1}^{n} d_i p} x^{nr'} \\
&= g^{\sum_{i=1}^{n} d_i p} e^{r'} \\
&= (g^p)^{\sum_{i=1}^{n} d_i}
\end{aligned} \tag{9}$$

To recover $\sum_{i=1}^{n} d_i$, which suffices to compute the discrete log of c^p base g^*. Since $0 \leq d \leq T$, CC can get the sum of users' data $\sum_{i=1}^{n} d_i$ in expected time $O(\sqrt{nT})$ using the Pollard's lambda method [26].

(2) Target GW Device Traceability

If CC doubts the authenticity of the aggregation data, and wants to trace the source, then the GW which responsible for the data aggregation will be traced, sending $ID_{G_i}P$ in the ciphertext C' by IBE Cryptosystem to TCA, CC send $ID_{G_i}P$ to TCA, calculating the target GW's dynamic ID, ID_{G_i} based on public parameter P, TCA trace the target GW by ID_{G_i}. If TCA finds the GW is destroyed or controlled by the adversary, the malicious GW will be isolated and replaced by other available GWs in RA in time.

6 Security Analysis

In this section, we analyze the security properties of the proposed IBE-DTPPA scheme. In particular, following the security requirements discussed earlier, our analysis will focus on how IBE-DTPPA scheme can achieve the privacy of individual user data in RA, the authentication of CC and the verification of data aggregation, and the suspicious GW traced efficiently.

(1) **The individual user's data is privacy-preserving in the proposed IBE-DTPPA scheme**

In the propose IBE-DTPPA scheme, user U_i's data in RA, $(d_1, d_2, \ldots, d_i)$ sensed by SMs are encrypted as $C_{BGNi} = g^{d_i}h^{r_i}$ by BGN cryptosystem. Since BGN cryptosystem is provably secure against chosen plaintext attack based on the subgroup decision assumption, the data $(d_1, d_2, \ldots, d_i)$ in C_{BGNi} is also semantic secure and privacy-preserving. Therefore, even though the adversary $\mathcal{A}$ eavesdrops C_{BGNi}, he still cannot identify the corresponding contents. After collecting all reports $(C_{BGN1}, C_{BGN2}, \ldots, C_{BGNi})$ from the RA, the GW will not recover each user's data, instead, it just computes $C_{Ua_j} = \prod_{i=1}^n C_{BGNi}$ to perform report aggregation. Therefore, even if the adversary $\mathcal{A}$ intrudes in the GW's database, he cannot get the individual report $(d_1, d_2, \ldots, d_i)$ either. Finally, after receiving $C_{Ua_j} = \prod_{i=1}^n C_{BGNi}$ from GW, the CC recovers C_{Ua_j} as $D_j = \sum_{i=1}^n d_i$. However, since D_j is an aggregated result, even if the adversary $\mathcal{A}$ steals the data, he still cannot get the individual user U_i's data $(d_1, d_2, \ldots, d_i)$ Therefore, from the above three aspects, the individual user's report is privacy-preserving in the proposed IBE-DTPPA scheme.

(2) **The authentication of CC and the security of aggregation data can be guaranteed in IBE-DTPPA scheme**

(1) In the propose IBE-DTPPA scheme, each individual user's data is encrypted by BGN cryptosystem and the aggregated report are encrypted by IBE Cryptosystem, choosing CC's dynamic ID, ID_{C_i} as public key and encrypt the aggregation data generate C'_{Ua_j} by IBE Cryptosystem, the CC's identity authentication can be realized. Since ID_{C_i} updates aperiodically by TCA, the adversary $\mathcal{A}$ cannot get CC's current ID, preventing the adversary $\mathcal{A}$ from using CC identity fraudulently.

(2) GW sends message $M = \{\delta, C', TS_t\}$, $\delta = H_2(C')$ to the CC, δ is the digest of hash function $H_2 : G_2 \to \{0, 1\}^n$ in random oracle model, C' and is a valid ciphertext

of IBE Cryptosystem. Since in IBE-DTPPA scheme, IBE Cryptosystem is based ECC (Elliptic curve cryptography) algorithm, which is under the assumption that ECDLP problem is hard, IBE is semantic secure against the chosen plaintext attack under the assumption that BDH problem is hard. Therefore, $M = \{\delta, C', TS_t\}$ is semantic secure against chosen-plaintext attack based on IBE Cryptosystem and random oracle model. As a result, the authentication of CC's identity can be realized, adversary $\mathcal{A}$ in the Energy Internet cannot fraudulently use CC identity to steal the user's data, the security of ciphertext encrypted by IBE Cryptosystem can be guaranteed in IBE-DTPPA scheme.

(3) **Target GW in the Energy Internet can be traced efficiently in IBE-DTPPA scheme**

After the CC's authentication is successful, CC recovers the aggregated data D_j in RA_i from C'_{Ua_j}. If CC doubts the authenticity of the aggregation data, and wants to trace the source, CC will send $ID_{G_i}P$ in C'_{Ua_j} to TCA, to trace the target GW which responsible for the data aggregation, TCA calculates GW's dynamic ID, ID_{G_i} based on public parameter P, GW will be traced efficiently. If find the GW is destroyed or controlled by the adversary, the malicious GW will be isolated and replaced by other available GWs in RA in time. As a result, the adversary $\mathcal{A}$ in the Energy Internet cannot control any GW to transmit error aggregated data, thus improving the CA's system strategic-making reliability.

7 Conclusion

This paper, we proposed IBE-DTPPA scheme, IBE-based Device Traceable Privacy-Preserving Aggregation Scheme. It can realize: (1) the traceability of target GW device; (2) CC real-time authentication to preventing the adversary from using CC identity fraudulently; (3) increase data aggregation integrity verification, to ensure the accuracy of system decision-making while creating the power generation plan or dynamic price immediately. We also provide security analysis to demonstrate its security.. For future work, we will work on resolving the fault-tolerant in GW, deepen the IBE-DTPPA scheme.

Acknowledgement. This work is partially supported by Natural Science Foundation of China under grant 61402171, the Fundamental Research Funds for the Central Universities under grant 2016MS29.

References

1. Wang, K., Yu, J., Yu, Y., et al.: A survey on Energy Internet: architecture, approach, and emerging technologies. IEEE Syst. J. **PP**(99), 1–14 (2017)
2. Guan, Z., Li, J., Zhu, L., Zhang, Z., Du, X., Guizani, M.: Towards delay-tolerant flexible data access control for smart grid with renewable energy resources. IEEE Trans. Ind. Inform. **13**(6), 3216–3225 (2017)

3. Wang, K., Ouyang, Z., Krishnan, R., et al.: A game theory-based energy management system using price elasticity for smart grids. IEEE Trans. Ind. Inform. **11**(6), 1607–1616 (2015)

4. Guan, Z., Li, J., Wu, L., Zhang, Y., Wu, J., Du, X.: Achieving efficient and secure data acquisition for cloud-supported Internet of Things in smart grid. IEEE Internet Things J. **4** (6), 1934–1944 (2017)

5. Davies, S.: Internet of energy [smart grid security]. Eng. Technol. **5**(1), 1–2 (2010)

6. Efthymiou, C., Kalogridis, G.: Smart grid privacy via anonymization of smart metering data In: First IEEE International Conference on Smart Grid Communications. IEEE, pp. 238–243 (2010)

7. Tan, X., Zheng, J., Zou, C., et al.: Pseudonym-based privacy-preserving scheme for data collection in smart grid. Int. J. Ad Hoc Ubiquitous Comput. **22**(2), 120 (2016)

8. Guan, Z., Si, G., Wu, J., et al.: Utility-privacy tradeoff based on random data obfuscation in internet of energy. IEEE Access **5**, 3250–3262 (2017)

9. Beussink, A., Akkaya, K., Senturk, I.F., Mahmoud, M.M.E.A.: Preserving consumer privacy on IEEE 802.11s-based smart grid AMI networks using data obfuscation. In: Proceedings of the IEEE Conference on Computer Communications Workshops (INFOCOM WKSHPS), pp. 658–663, April 2014

10. Shi, E., Chan, T.-H.H., Rieffel, E.G., Chow, R., Song, D.: Privacy-preserving aggregation of time-series data. In: NDSS, vol. 2, p. 4 (2011)

11. Kim, Y.S., Heo, J.: Device authentication protocol for smart grid systems using homomorphic hash. J. Commun. Netw. **14**(6), 606–613 (2012)

12. Lu, R., Liang, X., Li, X., et al.: EPPA: an efficient and privacy-preserving aggregation scheme for secure smart grid communications. IEEE Trans. Parallel Distrib. Syst. **23**(9), 1621–1631 (2012)

13. Chen, L., Lu, R., Cao, Z.: PDAFT: a privacy-preserving data aggregation scheme with fault tolerance for smart grid communications. PeerPeer Netw. Appl. **8**(6), 1122–1132 (2015)

14. Shi, Z., Sun, R., Lu, R., Chen, L., Chen, J., Shen, X.S.: Diverse grouping-based aggregation protocol with error detection for smart grid communications. IEEE Trans. Smart Grid **6**(6), 2856–2868 (2015)

15. Han, S., Zhao, S., Li, Q., Ju, C.-H., Zhou, W.: PPM-HDA: privacy-preserving and multifunctional health data aggregation with fault tolerance. IEEE Trans. Inf. Forensics Secur. **11**(9), 1940–1955 (2015)

16. Hua, J., Tang, A., Fang, Y., Shen, Z., Zhong, S.: Privacy-preserving utility verification of the data published by non-interactive differentially private mechanisms. IEEE Trans. Inf. Forensics Secur. **11**(10), 2298–2311 (2016)

17. Wang, H., Qin, B., Wu, Q., et al.: TPP: traceable privacy-preserving communication and precise reward for vehicle-to-grid networks in smart grids. IEEE Trans. Inf. Forensics Secur. **10**(11), 2340–2351 (2015)

18. Xiao, Y., Du, X., Zhang, J., Guizani, S.: Internet Protocol Television (IPTV): the killer application for the next generation internet. IEEE Commun. Mag. **45**(11), 126–134 (2007)

19. Du, X., Chen, H.H.: Security in wireless sensor networks. IEEE Wirel. Commun. Mag. **15** (4), 60–66 (2008)

20. Xiao, Y., Rayi, V., Sun, B., Du, X., Hu, F., Galloway, M.: A survey of key management schemes in wireless sensor networks. J. Comput. Commun. **30**(11–12), 2314–2341 (2007)

21. Du, X., Xiao, Y., Guizani, M., Chen, H.H.: An effective key management scheme for heterogeneous sensor networks. Ad Hoc Netw. **5**(1), 24–34 (2007)

22. Du, X., Guizani, M., Xiao, Y., Chen, H.H.: A routing-driven elliptic curve cryptography based key management scheme for heterogeneous sensor networks. IEEE Trans. Wirel. Commun. **8**(3), 1223–1229 (2009)

23. Du, X., Guizani, M., Xiao, Y., Chen, H.H.: Secure and efficient time synchronization in heterogeneous sensor networks. IEEE Trans. Veh. Technol. **57**(4), 2387–2394 (2008)
24. Du, X., Xiao, Y., Chen, H.H., Wu, Q.: Secure cell relay routing protocol for sensor networks. Wirel. Commun. Mob. Comput. **6**(3), 375–391 (2006)
25. Shamir, A.: Identity-based cryptosystems and signature schemes. In: Blakley, G.R., Chaum, D. (eds.) CRYPTO 1984. LNCS, vol. 196, pp. 47–53. Springer, Heidelberg (1985). https://doi.org/10.1007/3-540-39568-7_5
26. Gallant, R., Lambert, R., Vanstone, S.: Improving the parallelized pollard lambda search on anomalous binary curves. Math. Comput. Am. Math. Soc. **69**(232), 1699–1705 (2000)

Cloud Computing: Virtual Web Hosting on Infrastructure as a Service (IaaS)

Juan Fang[✉], Zeeshan Shaukat, Saqib Ali, and Abdul Ahad Zulfiqar

Faculty of Information Technology, Beijing University of Technology,
Pingleyuan No. 100, Chaoyang District, Beijing, China
fangjuan@bjut.edu.cn, wakeupzee@live.com,
saqibsaleem788@hotmail.com, abdul_ahad241@yahoo.com

Abstract. Cloud computing is an Information Technology (IT) model that provides convenient, on-demand network access to a shared pool of configurable computing resources (e.g., networks, servers, storage, applications, and services), which can be rapidly provisioned and released with minimal management effort and service provider interaction. Infrastructure as a Service (IaaS) is a new trend setter in the field of cloud computing which recently emerged as a new architype for hosting and delivering services on the internet. This study will discuss the characteristics and benefits of operating Virtual Web-Hosting together with Infrastructure as a Service (IaaS) model of cloud computing. Moreover, this study will also highlight the architectural principles, main concepts, and state of the art implementation and challenges of virtual web-hosting on Infrastructure as a service (IaaS).

Keywords: Component · Cloud computing · Web hosting · Virtualization
IaaS

1 Introduction

Cloud computing emerged as engine of enterprise technology innovation for delivering and hosting services on the internet. The end users of a cloud computing network usually have no idea where the servers are physically located, they just spin up their application and start working. One of the main advantage of cloud computing is that it allows anyone to deploy their services within few minutes and provides a service worldwide [1]. Cloud computing is considered as global network metaphor, previously telephone networks were considered as cloud but now cloud used in reference to represent the internet as a whole [2]. In short cloud computing is known as delivery model for often virtualized computing resources of various servers, applications, data and other resources that are integrated with each other and provided as a service on the Internet.

Supported by National Natural Science Foundation of China under (Grant NO. 61202076).

L. Zhu and S. Zhong (Eds.): MSN 2017, CCIS 747, pp. 450–460, 2018.
https://doi.org/10.1007/978-981-10-8890-2_34

Major Uses of Cloud Computing: Cloud computing has reshaped business models to gain benefit from this new IT paradigm. Indeed, cloud computing provides several compelling features that make it attractive to businesses. Probably everyone using cloud computing right now, even if they don't realize that. Using an online facility to send or receive emails, editing of online documents, watching television or movies online, listening online music, playing games on internet or storing pictures and other files on online drives, is likely made possible by cloud computing behind the scenes. The first ever cloud computing facilities are barely more than a decade old [3]. Cloud computing may be attributed being a recent research topic. Research on cloud structures, processes and qualification of businesses employees to govern cloud services is at infancy [4]. But already a variety of firms from tiny start-ups to global corporate, government organizations to non-profits are implementing the technology for all sorts of reasons. Here are a few of the uses of cloud computing (Fig. 1):

- Hosting websites and blogs
- Creation of new apps and services
- Streaming audio and video content
- Storing, backing up and recovering data
- Delivering software on demand services
- Analyses of data patterns to make predictions

Fig. 1. Logical explanation of cloud computing

Web-hosting is the process of acquiring remote servers that allows to post a website or web page on the Internet. A web host is a business responsible to provide the technologies and services required for the website to be viewed onto Internet. Traditional web-hosting provides cost efficient solution to host the website low-cost maintenance. But, along with these advantages, it also has downsides of performance degradation and single point of failure etc. Currently, cloud based web hosting is the most innovative hosting technology available to businesses that allows the website to be hosted on multiple virtual machines that act as one system [5].

2 Services Architecture

Cloud Computing services are generally divided into three broader categories which is also known as cloud computing stack, because these services are built on top of one another: (1) infrastructure as a service (IaaS), (2) platform as a service (PaaS) and (3) software as a service (SaaS). With the advantage of these three types of services, a cloud platform can provide highly scalable services for end-users.

Infrastructure-as-a-service (IaaS): IaaS is known as most basic building block of cloud computing services stack. Infrastructure-as-a-service is a form of hosting which includes routing services, network access, and storage. With IaaS, user rent IT infrastructure servers and virtual machines (VMs), storage, networks, operating systems from a cloud provider on a pay-as-you-go basis [6] ***Examples:*** *Microsoft Azure, GoGrid.*

Platform-as-a-service (PaaS): PaaS provide cloud computing services in an on-demand environment for developing, testing, delivering and managing software applications and for that it is also known as cloud-ware. Platform-as-a-Service is designed for developers to quickly and easily create web or mobile applications, without worrying about tedious process of installing or managing the software needed for development application. Normally developers select PaaS platforms to host their applications for administration and management tasks [7] ***Examples:*** *Google App Engine, ForceCom.*

Software-as-a-service (SaaS): SaaS is a method which referred to deliver software applications on demand and typically on a subscription basis over the Internet. With SaaS, cloud providers host and manage the software application and underlying infrastructure and handle any maintenance, like software upgrades and security patching. Users connect to the application over the Internet, usually with a web browser on their smartphone, tablet or PC [8] ***Examples:*** *SalesForce, RackSpace* (Fig. 2).

In this paper we will discuss about IaaS platform and the transformation of traditional web hosting solution to IaaS based hosting solution.

In a traditional web hosting environment host have to manage and take care of on-premise software and hardware services like Networking, Storage, Servers, Virtualization, Operating system, Middleware, Data and Application. The creation of hosting services on a virtual rather a physical version of a computing resources which include server hardware, operating system(OS), storage devices and so forth is known

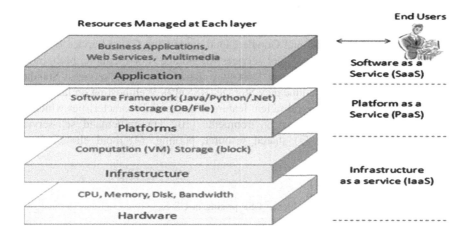

Fig. 2. Cloud services stack layers

Table 1. Traditional Vs hosting on IaaS

Traditional Hosting		Hosting on IaaS	
User Manages	Applications	**User Manage**	Applications
	Data		Data
	Middleware		Middleware
	Operating Systems		Operating Systems
	Virtualization	**Cloud Manage**	Virtualization
	Servers		Servers
	Storage		Storage
	Networking		Networking

as Virtual Web-Hosting. While using Infrastructure as a service(IaaS) model of cloud computing host can get rid of hardware infrastructure requirement and have to only mange soft services like Operating System, Middleware, Data and Application etc. *See Table* 1.

3 Characteristics and Benefits

Microsoft Azure, Amazon S3 and Google Cloud are leading Cloud Service Providers (CSP) which offers different types of services for storage (For Example: blob, block, file, etc.) with different prices for at least two classes of storage services: Standard Storage (SS) and Reduced Redundancy Storage (RSS) [9]. Web-hosting on IaaS model of Cloud Computing have several salient feature and essential characteristics which are different from traditional hosting environments [10]: (1) on-demand self-service, (2) broad network access, (3) shared resource pooling, (4) rapid elasticity, and (5) measured service (Table 2).

Table 2. CSP pricing in US $

Cloud pricing charged by CSP			
CSP	Amazon	Google cloud	Azure
SS (GB/Month)	0.0330	0.026	0.030
RRS (GB/Month)	0.0264	0.020	0.024
Out-network	0.08	0.12	0.087
Reduce out-network	0.02	0.12	0.087
Get (Per 100 K request)	4.4	10	3.6
Put (Per 1000 request)	5.5	10	0.036

Benefits of Hosting on IaaS:

- IaaS circumvents up-front investment of setting and maintaining an on-site datacenter.
- Hosting on IaaS provides much more flexibility than traditional web-hosting.
- Services hosted on IaaS are generally web-based. Therefore, they can be easily accessible through any smart device with Internet connection.
- With IaaS there is no need to worry about hardware failure, troubleshooting hardware problems or any system updates.
- IaaS allows to decoupling and separation of the business service from the IT infrastructure.
- IaaS normally use Geo-distribution and ubiquitous network access which eliminates single point of failure.
- Resources can be allocated or de-allocate easily so service providers can acquire resources only as per current demand.
- IaaS hosting operationally efficient, and allow more rapid deployment of new services which eventually reduce cost.

4 State of the Art Implementation and Challenges

In this section we will discuss dominant commercial competitors and state of the art implementation of virtual web hosting on infrastructure as a service (IaaS) with research challenges:

4.1 Commercial Competitors

Currently there are three major competitors in the cloud computing market such as Windows Azure, App Engine and Amazon.

A. Windows Azure Cloud Platform by Microsoft:

Microsoft Windows Azure is a comprehensive set of cloud computing services that IT professionals and developers use to build, deploy and manage applications through Microsoft network of global datacenters [11]. Microsoft Windows Azure have integrated tools, DevOps and an Azure marketplace which support IT professionals and developers in efficiently building web-scale solutions. Microsoft window azure provides a consistent and unique platform across clouds which can be further divided into four layers in terms of End-user experience, Unified Application Model, Services and Cloud Infrastructure [12].

Microsoft's Window Azure platform comprises of three major components and each component is responsible to provides a specific set of cloud services to users. Microsoft Azure offers a Windows based environment for running cloud based applications and storing application data on servers in global datacenters; Azure SQL offers cloud based data services on SQL Server. Distributed infrastructure services to cloud-based and local applications provided by .Net.

Azure cloud platform can be used by both applications on the cloud and applications on local systems. Fabric Controller Software is used to monitored all of the physical resources, Virtual Machines and applications in the datacenter. The users upload a configuration file with each of its application that provides an XML-based description of what the application needs. Fabric controller decides where new applications should run, choosing physical servers to optimize hardware utilization based on that XML configuration file [13].

B. App Engine Cloud Platform by Google:

Google App Engine is a fully managed cloud platform that completely abstracts away infrastructure requirement and usually used for traditional web based applications in google managed data centers. Google App-engine allows developers to build modern mobile and web applications on an open cloud platform managed by google, it allows users to bring their own language runtimes, third-party libraries and frameworks. Google App Engine goes out of the box to supports multiple languages including Node.js, Java, C#, Ruby, Go, Python, and PHP. Programmers from these languages can be immediately productive in a familiar environment [14].

Google App-Engine provide automatic scaling for web applications as the number of requests increases for an application, App-Engine automatically assigns more resources for that application to knob the additional demand [15]. Google app engine provide state of the art advantages like Automatic Scaling, Quickly Start and build faster, Automatic Security Scanning for applications hosted on Google Cloud datacenters.

C. AWS Cloud Platform by Amazon:

AWS (Amazon Web Services) is a platform which provides on-demand cloud computing services to end-users i.e. individuals and organizations. Amazon Web Services also own its own marketplace which offer free and paid software products that run on AWS tier [16]. Amazon Web Services (AWS) Cloud provides broad range of infrastructure services, such as compute power, storage services, networking and databases which are delivered as a utility: on-demand, available in seconds, with pay-as-you-go pricing model. From Directories to content delivery, data warehousing to deployment tools, around ninety AWS services are available to end-users.

AWS services can be provisioned quickly, without upfront expense. This allows enterprises, start-ups, businesses, and public sector customers to access the building blocks they need to meet business requirements [17]. Amazon Elastic Compute Cloud (aka: Amazon EC2) is a web based cloud service designed for developers to make web-scale computing easier. EC2 provides secure and resizable compute capacity in the cloud. AWS (Amazon Web Services) batch job dynamically provision optimal quantity and type of compute resources (e.g., CPU or memory-optimized instances) based on volume and specific resource requirements (Table 3).

Table 3. Representative commercial products comparison

CSPs	Microsoft	Google	Amazon
Target	General purpose Windows apps	Traditional web applications	General purpose apps
Compute	Microsoft CLR VM Predefined roles of app	Predefined web apps framework	OS Level on a Xen VM
Scaling	Automatic scaling based on configuration file specified by users	Automatic scaling transparent to users	Automatically scaling based on users specified parameters
Storage	Microsoft Azure storage service and SQL Data Services	Google Big Table and Mega Store	Amazon Simple DB Elastic Block Store; Amazon Simple (S3);

4.2 Implementation

In this section we will discuss state of the art implementation of Virtual Web-Hosting on Infrastructure as a Service model of Microsoft Windows Azure Cloud.

Infrastructure:
For running virtual web-hosting over Infrastructure as a Service(IaaS) model of Microsoft Windows Azure Cloud we need create a virtual machine on Azure Portal [18].

Table 4. Virtual machine configurations with parameters

Configuration:	Parameters
Package name	D3_V2 promo
Number of CPU cores	4 Cores
CPU core size	2.40 GHz × 4
RAM	14 GB
Data disks	8 Data disks
Max IOPS	12000 IOPS
SSD storage	200 GB SSD
Other features	Load balancing
Cost per/month	150 US$/Month

Microsoft offers wide range of Virtual Machine sizes with variety of feature. The virtual machine we use for this paper have the specifications mentioned in below table (Table 4):

After successful creation of virtual machine with above parameters we install Ubuntu [19] 14.04 LTS Operating System(OS) on our virtual machine. For running successful web hosting on VM we need to install different software such as HTTP server and Web-Hosting control panel. Details of software installed with their version is given below (Fig. 3 and Table 5):

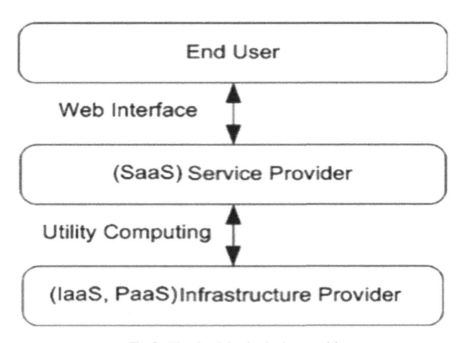

Fig. 3. Virtual web-hosting business model

Table 5. Software description

Name	Description	Version
Ubuntu	Operating system	14.04
Apache [20]	HTTP server	2.4.7
PHP [21]	Server scripting	5.5.9
MySQL [22]	Database	5.5.58
phpMyAdmin [23]	Database administration	4.0.10
Sentora [24]	Web hosting control panel	1.0.3

Tools:

For installation of above mentioned software's to successfully implement virtual web hosting business model with respect to a Computer System(PC) [25] following tools are used.

- Putty SSH [26]
- WinSCP [27]
- FileZilla [28]
- Adobe Photoshop CS6 [29]
- NetBeans [30]

Challenges:

IaaS is widely adopted in IT industry. But still there are some key challenges need to be addressed for Virtual web hosting on IaaS. Data security on IaaS is an important research topic along with novel architecture, Automated Provision of Services, Migration of Virtual Machine, Server Consolidation, Traffic analysis and management.

5   Conclusion

As per comparative analysis between traditional web hosting systems and IaaS based virtual web hosting systems we found that IaaS based virtual web hosting systems are more effective than traditional web hosting systems as for starting web- hosting business there is no up-front investment required. Virtual web hosting on IaaS is highly scalable as compared to traditional web hosting systems. The Operating cost of IaaS based virtual web hosting systems are around 30% less comparing to traditional web hosting systems as IaaS allows resources to be allocated and deallocated as per requirement and there is no need to spend extra money on training staff to manage traditional on premises hosting systems and also there is huge saving on electricity bills and network charges as well. However, despite the fact virtual web hosting offered significant benefits, the current technologies are not matured enough to realize its full potential. Key challenges like Data Security and resource provisioning got high attentions from research community and a lot of research work is going on in these domains.

References

1. Sreeramaneni, A., Seo, B., Chan, K.: A Business Driven Scalable Cloud Computing Service Platform (PaaSXpert). 한국정보기술학회논문지 **15**(1), 35–44 (2017)
2. Bhardwaj, S., Jain, L., Jain, S.: Cloud computing: a study of infrastructure as a service (IAAS). Int. J. Eng. Inf. Technol. **2**(1), 60–63 (2010)
3. Jadeja, Y., Modi, K.: Cloud computing - concepts, architecture and challenges. In: 2012 International Conference on Computing, Electronics and Electrical Technologies (ICCEET) (2012)
4. Hoberg, P., Wollersheim, J., Krcmar, H.: The business perspective on cloud computing-a literature review of research on cloud computing (2012)
5. Bhingarkar, S., Shah, D.: A survey: cloud hosted website protection using soft computing techniques. In: 2017 7th International Conference on Cloud Computing, Data Science & Engineering - Confluence (2017)
6. Chen, C.C., et al.: Efficient hybriding auto-scaling for openstack platforms. In: 2015 IEEE International Conference on Smart City/SocialCom/SustainCom (SmartCity) (2015)
7. Gesvindr, D., Buhnova, B.: Architectural tactics for the design of efficient PaaS cloud applications. In: 2016 13th Working IEEE/IFIP Conference on Software Architecture (WICSA). IEEE (2016)
8. Ladhe, T., et al.: Platform design considerations for transforming a SaaS solution to a PaaS offering. In: 2015 International Conference on Developments of E-Systems Engineering (DeSE). IEEE (2015)
9. Mansouri, Y., Toosi, A.N., Buyya, R.: Cost optimization for dynamic replication and migration of data in cloud data centers. IEEE Trans. Cloud Comput. (2017)
10. Mell, P., Grance, T.: The NIST definition of cloud computing (2011)
11. Microsoft: Microsoft Windows Azure (2017). https://azure.microsoft.com. Accessed 2017
12. Eijk, M.V.: Getting started with Azure Resource Manager (2016)
13. Zhang, Q., Cheng, L., Boutaba, R.: Cloud computing: state-of-the-art and research challenges. J. Internet Serv. Appl. **1**, 7–18 (2010)
14. Google: Google App Engine Cloud Platform (2017). https://cloud.google.com/appengine/. Accessed 2017
15. Tamboli, M.G., Patel, M.Y.: International Journal of Advance Research in Engineering, Science & Technology. Energy **3**(5) (2016)
16. Amazon: AWS (Amazon Web Services) (2017). https://aws.amazon.com. Accessed 2017
17. Mathew, S.: Overview of Amazon Web Services (2017)
18. Microsoft: Windows Azure Portal (2017). https://poratl.azure.com/
19. Ubantu: Leading operating system for PCs, IoT devices, servers (2017). https://www.ubuntu.com/
20. Apache: Apache open source HTTP Server (2017). https://www.apache.org/
21. PHP: Hypertext Preprocessor, Server-side scripting language (2017). http://www.php.net/
22. MySQL: Open-source relational database (2017). https://www.mysql.com/
23. phpMyAdmin: Open source administration tool for MySQL and MariaDB (2017). https://www.phpmyadmin.net/
24. Sentora: Open-source web hosting control panel (2017). http://www.sentora.org/
25. Wikipedia: Category: Computer systems on Wikipedia (2017). https://en.wikipedia.org/wiki/Category:Computer_systems
26. Putty: Open Source SSH and Telnet Client (2017). http://www.putty.org/

27. WinSCP: Open-source SFTP, FTP, WebDAV and SCP client (2017). https://winscp.net/eng/
28. FileZilla: Cross-platform FTP application (2017). https://filezilla-project.org/
29. Adobe: Photoshop graphics editor for macOS and Windows (2017). http://www.adobe.com/products/photoshop.html
30. Netbean: Intigrated Development Environment (IDE) (2017). https://netbeans.org/

Modeling and Evaluation of the Incentive Scheme in "E-photo"

Shijie Ni[✉], Zhuorui Yong, and Ruipeng Gao

School of Software Engineering, Beijing Jiaotong University, Beijing, China
{15301009,16301141,rpgao}@bjtu.edu.cn

Abstract. "E-photo" is to solve the inconvenient problem when users want some photos. It is a self-service model with the help of internet crowdsourcing. Users download "E-photo" and register as "E-photo" members, then they can get the task and earn the corresponding reward as incentives. The pricing task is the core problem in "E-photo". If the pricing is not reasonable, some tasks will not be cared, thus involving the failure of commodity inspection. In this paper, we fuse the logistic regression model and cohesive hierarchical model, and propose a better pricing method for "E-photo".

1 Introduction

Nowadays, with the popularization of mobile devices and the optimization of the network environment, everything becomes easier and more convenient in the daily life. For example, if users want to take photos or need photos but unfortunately can not do it by themselves, then they have to ask others for help, thus becoming a social issue as crowdsourcing.

"E-photo" is a self-service model for internet crowdsourcing applications. Users download "E-photo" and register as "E-photo" members, then they can get the task and earn the reward as incentives. "E-photo" provides enterprises with a variety of commercial inspections and information collections. Compared with traditional market research methods, it can significantly save the investigation cost and effectively ensure the authenticity of the survey data and shortening the survey cycle. As a result, "E-photo" software becomes a crucial the application platform, and its task pricing is the key module. If the pricing is not reasonable, some tasks will be cared by no one, causing the failure of commodity inspections. Thus, pricing scheme has become the biggest challenge.

The existing methods are the non-linear function fitting of BP neural network based on three factors related to geographic location, such as "task density of task" and "membership density of task". This method regards unknown system as a black box. Firstly, the BP neural network is trained by system's inputs and outputs to enable the

This work is supported in part by NSFC 61702035 and China Postdoctoral Science Foundation (Grant 2017M610759 and 2017T100033).

network expressing some unknown functions and then uses the trained network to predict future outputs, e.g., the price of the unfinished mission, and get the new pricing for the unfinished missions. In the establishment of this model, the influencing factors of the pricing scheme are mainly divided into two aspects, the influencing factors of geographical location and the influencing factors of non-geographical location. In the absence of data, the latitude and longitude of the task is taken as the location information and use the K-mean Clustering, so that the task price in each category is less relevant to the geographic location and more influenced by the non-geographic location factors, and then quantify the impact of non-geographic location on the basis of the pricing of each task in the same category. However, in the quantification of non-geographic location factors, there is a subjective scoring, prone to errors, then the evaluation could be unreasonable.

This paper argues that the completion of the task, the logarithm of the density of the ability to complete the task and the task of pricing logistic regression model can be established to improve the task completion rate. After modeling and data analysis, we found that raising the task pricing can improve the task completion rate, but we should also consider the issue of company cost and the gain and the loss, so we can not excessively increase it. Therefore, we choose to use a dichotomy of growth factors Price 67.5 yuan task, we will not raise prices. Considering that we need to distinguish the intensity of the tasks and package the tasks, we decided to set up a cohesive hierarchical clustering model using the position of the task (latitude and longitude) and the distance between two tasks as variables. We take samples to test the theoretical and practical values of the model to enhance the credibility of the results. Taking into account the combination of more models, we ensure the operability of the model and increase the accuracy. In data processing, multiple variables are merged to avoid the influence of multiple variables on event repetition, and we increase the feasibility of the model and the credibility of the correlation coefficient. We also leverage the clustering analysis to improve the fitting degree of the model.

The combination of clustering models and logistic models allows users to find their favorite tasks and pricing, and to make unpopular tasks packaged. In future, we will consider the benefits of the behavior, and the rewards should not be limited to money. For the use of this model, we will greatly improve the degree of task completion, reduce abnormal task retention time, and avoid abnormal pricing which caused by the abnormal location, thus reducing the company unplanned and unnecessary financial losses.

2   Related Work

2.1   PSM and VBSE

This study presents an application of the price-sensitivity measurement(PSM) method to the Value-Based Software Engineering(VBSE) process. The software development team needed customer-based pricing input to decide which of two software modules to develop first. The PSM method was used to provide an estimate of the prices potential buyers would be willing to pay for each module. [1]

2.2 Custom Software Price

Price of custom software is very essential for a user. However, there is little information to help users judge the effectiveness of custom software price. Therefore, one of our research goals is building price estimation model and showing its accuracy for the user's judgment to the validity of the custom software price. The other goal is how to get value for money custom software. First, the researchers analyzed relationships of unit price of effort, unit price of function point, and productivity. The analysis result showed productivity is more important variable than unit price of effort for the custom software price estimation. Next, relationships of other variables were analyzed to identify important variables for the price estimation. The result suggested some variables such as system architecture are essential. [2]

2.3 Value-Based Pricing Model [3]

This analysis helps to develop the software service-specific pricing models to incorporate variables capturing customer value. There are two typical models: SaaS pricing model and Sibson's Scheme of value pricing [4]. The key to develop the model is to understand the price that the client is able and willing to pay for the service [5]. So, the IT service provider needs a strategy that integrates the value driving parameters into a single model and narrows the gap between the service offerings and customer expectation. The solution is designing a service model that is in line with maintaining a 'client first culture'. Depending on the respective service's measures, variables can be attached with weights to derive a value based price. The description of the two selected software service pricing models can explain the existing technique and contribute to the construction of the new model.

2.4 The Current Situation

The existing methods are the non-linear function fitting of BP neural network based on three factors related to geographic location, such as "task density of task" and "membership density of task". This method regards unknown system as a black box. Firstly, BP neural network is trained by system input and output data to enable the network to express the unknown function and then use the trained network to predict the output of the system.

BP neural network without prior determination of the mathematical relationship between the input and output mapping, only through its own training to learn some rules, given the input value is closest to the desired output value of the results. As an intelligent information processing system, the core of artificial neural network to realize its function is the algorithm. BP neural network is a multi-layer feed-forward network trained by error back propagation (referred to as error back propagation). Its algorithm is called BP algorithm. Its basic idea is gradient descent method, using gradient search technology, in order to make network's mean square error of the actual output value and the expected output value is the minimum.

Make $out_j^{(i)}$ and $in_j^{(i)}$ as the output and the input of the ixj neuron, the relation of input and output in the each layer of the internet is:

The first layer (input layer):

$$out_j^{(1)} = in_j^{(1)} = x \ i = 1, 2, 3 \tag{1}$$

Where X is the result of a comprehensive digitization of all the factors.

The second layer (hidden layer):

$$\begin{cases} in_j^{(2)} = \sum_{i=1}^{3} w_{ij}^{(1)} out_j^1 \\ out_j^{(2)} = f(in_j^{(2)}) \end{cases} \tag{2}$$

The third layer (output layer):

$$out_j^{(3)} = in_j^{(3)} = \sum_{i=1}^{3} w_i^{(2)} out_i^{(2)} \tag{3}$$

Based on the above analysis, the actual establishment and training of pricing model based on BP neural network is completed by Matlab programming. Predicting the price of the unfinished mission, and get the new pricing for the unfinished mission. Using BP neural network to fit the new pricing of the unfinished task with the pricing of the originally completed task, to form a new pricing scheme.

In the establishment of this model, the influencing factors of the pricing scheme are mainly divided into two aspects, the influencing factors of geographical location and the influencing factors of non-geographical location. In the absence of data, the latitude and longitude of the task is taken as the location information and use the K-mean Clustering, so that the task price in each category is less relevant to the geographic location and more influenced by the non-geographic location factors, and then quantify the impact of non-geographic location on the basis of the pricing of each task in the same category. However, in the quantification of non-geographic location factors, there is a subjective scoring, prone to errors, then the evaluation could be unreasonable.

3 Methods

3.1 Pricing Rules

In order to find out the pricing rule, we need to analyze the data. According to the data, the precision and latitude of the task are imported into the API of the map. At the same time, the task completion conditions are respectively analyzed, and the task is completed as black dots on the map when uncompleted task expressed as green dots. The resulting figure below:

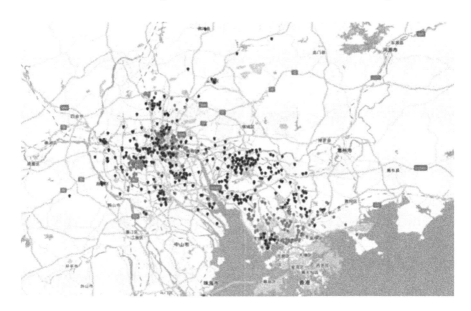

Fig. 1. The black pots mean that the task is completed while the green ones means uncompleted. (Color figure online)

In the Fig. 1 we can not intuitively find out the relationship of the pricing rules, because we think the intensity of the task is related to the location of the city. Therefore, we decided to process the membership data. We found that the member's density is positively correlated with the task density, taking into account the capacity of members to take over the task and not only reflected in the location of the members of the concentration, we take the latitude and longitude of members, the distribution of task limits and honor value combination of methods to define the ability of members to complete the task (*Abi*) concept.

We multiply each member's honor percentage (*Wi*) with each member's job limit (*NPi*) to compute the ability to accomplish each member's task:

$$Ab_i = w_i \times NP_i \tag{4}$$

So we combine two groups of data, then get the following figure:

According to the observation and analysis of the Fig. 2, we think the pricing and completion of the task can be done by comparing the blue-red points (the pricing and completion at a certain location, the uncompleted is the blue point and the completed is the red dots) and the ability of members to complete their tasks, thus we think there is a certain linear relationship between mission capabilities.

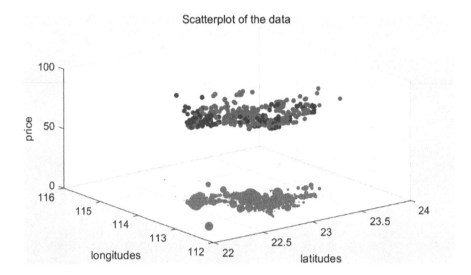

Fig. 2. The z-axis represents the price, the two horizontal axes represent the latitude and longitude, the price = 0 where the plane is the member's information, the specific coordinate of the point represents the position of the member. (Color figure online)

Here, we consider that all members are normal human beings in modern society. Therefore, we regard the living area of mankind in modern society as the unit area (*AH*), about 23 square kilometers. Therefore, we introduce the density of members' ability to accomplish their tasks (*AbDi*):

$$AbD_i = \frac{Ab_i}{A_H} \tag{5}$$

Then we use the density of completing the task (*AbDi*) and pricing (P) data, then we get the following Fig. 3 for analysis:

Through analysis of the ability to complete the task (*AbDi*), we found that after taking a logarithm (log (*AbDi*)). We can find out the linear correlation and get the following Fig. 4:

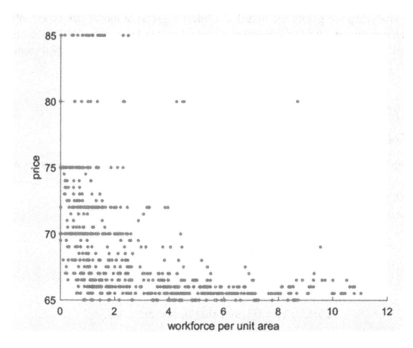

Fig. 3. The x-axis represents workforce per unit area, and the y-axis represents price.

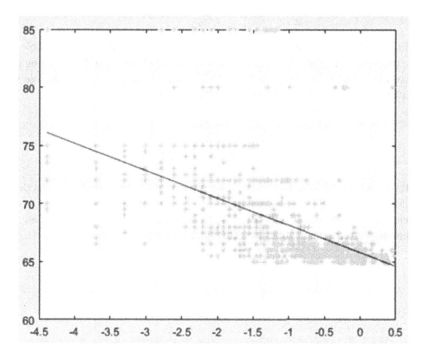

Fig. 4. log (*AbDi*)'s linear correlation

By analyzing the graph, we find that a linear regression model can be established between the pricing (P) and the logarithm of the density of tasks (log ($AbDi$)) to find the correlation. With the MATLAB tool, we set the price (Pi) fitting the ability to complete the task (log ($AbDi$)), then we get:

$$P_i = -2.53493 * \log(AbD_i) + 65.98933 \tag{6}$$

3.2 Logistic Regression Model

In order to improve the task completion rate, we consider a logistic regression model among task completion (Cdi), logarithm of the density of completed tasks (log ($AbDi$)) and task pricing (P).

The basic form of Logistic model is:

$$\mathrm{Cd}_i(Y = 1|p_i, \log(AbD_i)) = \frac{e^{(\beta0+\beta1\log(AbD_i)+\beta2p_i)}}{1 + e^{(\beta0+\beta1\log(AbD_i)+\beta2p_i)}} \tag{7}$$

Considering that Cdi can only take the value of 0 or 1, we assume:

$$\pi = \mathrm{Cd}_i(Y = 1|p_i\log(AbD_i)), \ 0 < \pi < 1 \tag{8}$$

Then the model is transformed into:

$$\ln\frac{\pi}{1-\pi} = \beta0 + \beta1\log(AbD_i) + \beta2p_i \tag{9}$$

Using the MATLAB tool, the regression coefficients and the data in the table (X1, X2) are processed into the glmval function to verify. We found that the matching probability of the model to the data reaches 72.8%, which is in our expectation. We think this model is effective pricing Model, the end result is:

$$\begin{aligned}
&Cd_i(y = 1|P_i\log(AbD_i)) \\
&= \frac{e^{(-4.873-0.143*X_1+0.071*X_2)}}{1 + e^{(-4.873-0.143*X_1+0.071*X_2)}}
\end{aligned} \tag{10}$$

After analyzing the model data in 4.2, we found that a logistic regression model can be established among the task completion (Cd), pricing (P), and the density of tasks to complete the task (log ($AbDi$)). If you want to improve the task completion Rate, then according to the formula (7), then we get (Fig. 5):

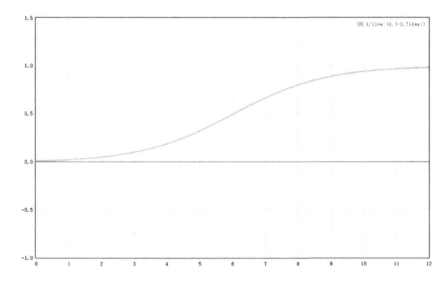

Fig. 5. The log (*AbDi*) which is after data processing.

For the analysis of this function, we find that after the second derivative, the point at which the independent variable is zero is a turning point in the growth rate of the function. By evaluating, we find that: When log(AbDi) = 67.34842934, the probability of mission completion begins to slow down.

After a large amount of the data analysis and attempts, we achieve the new pricing rules.

When pricing is less than 67.5:

$$PNew_i = -2.3650 * \log(AbDi) + 67.0367 \tag{11}$$

When pricing is more than 67.5:

$$PNew_i = -2.5350 * \log(AbDi) + 65.9893 \tag{12}$$

3.3 Cohesive Hierarchical Clustering Model

Considering that we need to differentiate the tasks and package the tasks, we decided to set up a cohesive hierarchical cluster model based on the task position (latitude and longitude) and the distance between two tasks. We assume that the task length (Lo), latitude (La).

1. We assume that there are i tasks to be clustered, we first classify them into I. Each task is a class, and each class represents its position in longitude (*Loi*) and latitude (Lai).
2. Then we find the two classes with the smallest distance among the m classes. For the "minimum distance" we use the following method (Ward's Linkage and Centroid Linkage method to calculate the weighted average) (Fig. 6):

Fig. 6. The log (*AbDi*) which is after data processing. Select all sets from two classes, then calculate the middle point in (Si, Sj).The distance between each point in the two classes and the center is summed to obtain the distance value between the two classes in this method.

(1) Ward's Linkage:

The formula is:

$$WD_{c_1 \cup c_2} = \sum_{x \in C_1 C_2} D(x, \mu_{C_1 C_2})^2 \tag{13}$$

(2) Centroid Linkage (Fig. 7):

Fig. 7. Select all sets from two classes, the center points of the two classes are calculated respectively on the average of longitude and latitude, and the distance between the two classes' center points is taken as the distance value between the two classes.

The formula is:

$$CD_{C_1 \cup C_2} = D(\frac{1}{|C_1|} \sum_{x \in C_1} \vec{x}, \frac{1}{|C_2|} \sum_{x \in C_2} \vec{x}) \tag{14}$$

3. After finding the two classes which have the smallest distance, we put two classes in one class, then we finish the clustering process once.
4. Repeat steps 2 and 3 until all the tasks are in one class.
5. At this point, we need to find a suitable class size. In the step 1, we artificially defined the number of classes is 31, but the analysis found that some classes contain up to a dozen of the tasks, not easy to package release. So we analyzed that each class contains the task number of 6 is the most appropriate.

We packaged the completion of the task to complete the density of capacity (Package$i$) into the pricing rules in 3.2., then we get a new pricing rules.

When pricing is less than 67.5:

$$PA_i = -2.3650 * Package_i + 67.0367 \tag{15}$$

When pricing is more than 67.5:

$$PA_i = -2.5350 * Package_i + 65.9893 \tag{16}$$

4   Discussion

This paper extracts samples to test the model theoretical results and the actual value, which enhances the credibility of the results. We take into account the combination of more models to ensure the operability of the model and increase the accuracy. In data processing, the combination of multiple variables to avoid the impact of multiple variables on an event repeat, increasing the feasibility of the model and increasing the credibility of the correlation coefficient. The use of cluster analysis improves the degree of fit to the model. Our approach provides a proper incentive scheme for crowdsourcing applications, e.g., indoor tracking and map construction [9–15].

The disadvantage is short of considering more model combinations, which has a certain impact on the accuracy of the model. And we don't consider the scheduled task start time's impact on the overall. Also lack of data noise reduction, and data mapping is not smooth. We have no accurate sieve to abnormal data points.

5   Conclusion

In this paper we introduce "E-photo", a self-service model for internet crowdsoucing applications. Task pricing in "E-photo" is the core problem. If the pricing is not reasonable, some tasks will be cared by no one, which causes the failure of commodity inspection. We introduce the way others used towards the pricing in current situation. We also use the logistic regression model and cohesive hierarchical cluster mode to discuss the pricing rules of the task in "E-photo". At last, we evaluate the results and discuss the limitations of our model.

References

1. Harmon, R., Raffo, D., Faulk, S.: Incorporating price sensitivity measurement into the software engineering process, National Science Foudation grant EEC-9905789
2. Tsunoda, M., Monden, A., Matsumoto, K., Ohiwa, S., Oshino, T.: Analysis of Attributes Relating to Custom Software Price. IEEE (2012)
3. Kamdar, A., Orsoni, A.: Development of Value-Based Pricing Model for Software Services. IEEE (2009)
4. Sibson, R.: 'A Service' in Creative Pricing (Elizabeth Marting, ed.), pp. 147–52. American Marketing Association, New York (1968). Cited in [5]
5. Gabor, A.: Pricing Principles and Practices. Cambridge University Press, New York (1985)
6. Wang, B.: Mathematical Modeling Concise Tutorial. Tsinghua University Press, Beijing (2012)
7. Giordano, F.R., Fox, W.P., Horton, S.B., Weir, M.D.: A First Course in Mathematical Modeling. Machinery Industry Press, China (2009)
8. Wang, B., Li, G., Li, X.: Matlab and Mathematics Experiment. China Railway Press, Beijing (2014)
9. Gao, R., Zhao, M., Ye, T., Ye, F., Luo, G., Wang, Y., Bian, K., Wang, T., Li, X.: Multi-story indoor floor plan reconstruction via mobile crowdsensing. IEEE Trans. Mob. Comput. **15**(6), 1427–1442 (2016)
10. Gao, R., Tian, Y., Ye, F., Luo, G., Bian, K., Wang, Y., Wang, T., Li, X.: Sextant: towards ubiquitous indoor localization service by photo-taking of the environment. IEEE Trans. Mob. Comput. **15**(2), 460–474 (2016)
11. Gao, R., Zhao, M., Ye, T., Ye, F., Wang, Y., Luo, G.: Smartphone-based real time vehicle tracking in indoor parking structures. IEEE Trans. Mob. Comput. **16**(7), 2023–2036 (2017)
12. Gao, R., Zhou, B., Ye, F., Wang, Y.: Knitter: fast, resilient single-user indoor floor plan construction. In: Proceedings of IEEE INFOCOM (2017)
13. Gao, R., Zhao, M., Ye, T., Ye, F., Wang, Y., Bian, K., Wang, T., Li, X.: Jigsaw: indoor floor plan reconstruction via mobile crowdsensing. In Proceedings of ACM MobiCom (2014)
14. Zhou, B., Elbadry, M., Gao, R., Ye, F.: BatMapper: acoustic sensing based indoor floor plan construction using smartphones. In: Proceedings of ACM MobiSys (2017)
15. Zhou, B., Elbadry, M., Gao, R., Ye, F.: BatTracker: high precision infrastructure-free mobile device tracking in indoor environments. In: Proceedings of ACM SenSys (2017)

Intelligent Environment Monitoring
and Control System for Plant Growth

Wenjuan Song[1,2(✉)], Bing Zhou[3], and Shijie Ni[4]

[1] Chinese Research Academy of Environmental Sciences, Beijing, China
943468968@qq.com
[2] Inner Mongolia Agricultural University, Huhhot, Inner Mongolia, China
[3] ECE Department, Stony Brook University, New York, USA
bing.zhou@stonybrook.edu
[4] School of Software Engineering, Beijing Jiaotong University, Beijing, China
15301009@bjtu.edu.cn

Abstract. Indoor planting can purify the air, beautify the environment, satisfy people by closing to the nature and farming. However, the plants are easy to stop growing or even to die due to the lack of proper environment situations, such as lack of water or sunlight. This paper leverages the Internet of Things (IoT) and cloud computing technology to monitor the light intensity, air temperature and soil humidity of indoor plants. The plant growth condition and environment situation are also reflected to the user's smartphone and stored in the cloud. Outdoor users can also control the water pump to irrigate the plants and LED to add light supply via their smartphones. With our prototype, our system accurately monitors the environment and intelligently controls the plant growth.

Keywords: Plant growth · Environmental conditions · Internet of Things
Cloud computing · Intelligent monitoring system

1 Introduction

With the rapid development of social economy and human life quality, the distance between people and natural environment are getting further and further. People's desire for green vegetation impel the tendency to indoor planting. Indoor plants not only relieve the visual fatigue caused by the computer, but also improve the air quality. Thus, indoor plant cultivation has become an indispensable element in our home and office environment. Nowadays, modern families can no longer be satisfied with simple flower planting, thus they start to plant a variety of plants and vegetables. However, due to the busy office work and long-time business travel, users are always absent from home and leaving the plants with water shortages. Additionally, due to inadequate indoor sun exposure, plant growth is also obstructed. Water, temperature and light are the major environment factors which have the most impacts on plant growth.

"Intelligent plant monitoring" refers to the application via IoT technology to monitor plant growth environment parameters (including light, temperature and soil moisture), and through the cloud computing technology, the growth situation is quickly reflected in users'

© Springer Nature Singapore Pte Ltd. 2018
L. Zhu and S. Zhong (Eds.): MSN 2017, CCIS 747, pp. 473–482, 2018.
https://doi.org/10.1007/978-981-10-8890-2_36

smartphones and stored in the cloud. In addition, it should timely take corresponding measures and controls to ensure the normal growth of plants. In this paper, we develop a plant growth environment monitoring system, which consists of a low-power microcontroller as the main control system module, a LCD screen, and humidity, temperature, light sensors to simulate the natural environment of soil humidity. Those data are packaged to the smartphone via Bluetooth communication, and then transferred to the cloud.

The plant growth environment monitoring system is small and inexpensive to user, which is suitable for home and office area applications. Through a simple human-computer interface on smartphone, users set a variety of environmental parameters for each selected plants, e.g., the required light, temperature, and soil humility. When the measured values exceed or under the thresholds, our system will automatically upload the reminder message to the user's smartphone. As the whole process is intelligent and eco-friendly, users can easily plant as well as enjoy a "natural oxygen bar" at the same time.

2   Background on Environmental Conditions for Plants Growth

Environment refers to the space in which plants live and the various natural factors that directly or indirectly affect the plant life and development [1]. Plant growth and development are directly affected by some natural factors, such as temperature, light, soil humidity [2] and so on.

2.1   Light

Light is an important ecological factor that affects the survival, growth and distribution of plants and it is also the energy source for photosynthesis of plants [3].

The plant can be divided into 3 types, including light-demanding plant, shade-demanding plant and mid-demanding plant according to different requirements for the light. Light-demanding plants are those plants that grow better in a strong light conditions and grow poorly in a shaded and weak light conditions, such as *Rosa chinensis* Jacq., etc.; Shade-demanding plants are those plants prefer to live in the weaker light conditions compare with light-demanding plant, such as *Phalaenopsis aphrodite* Rchb. F. and *Monstera deliciosa*, etc.; Mid-demanding plants are those plants live in light condition between the two types of plants. These plants grow best under the full sunlight, and also can tolerate the shade condition, such as *Hemerocallis fulva* (L.) L., *Mirabilis jalapa* L. and so on.

According to the influence of the light time on the growth and development, the plants are divided into three types, including long-day plants, short-day plants and mid-day plants [4]. A long-day plants are those plants which length of sunlight exceeds its critical day length required for flowering, such as *Brassica chinensis* L., *Raphanus sativus* L. and so on. Short-day plants are those plants which length of sunlight is shorter than the critical day length required for flowering, such as *Viola philippica* and so on. The mid-day plants are those plants which their flowering is less affected by the length of the light. They can bloom under any sunshine lengths, as long as other conditions are suitable, such as *Taraxacum mongolicum* Hand.-Mazz.

Figure 1 shows *Brassica chinensis* L., an example of long-day plants, with suitable environment by 25–30° C temperature and 75% Relative Humidity [5].

Fig. 1. *Brassica chinensis* L.

2.2 Water

Water is an important factor for plant survival. The physiological activity of plants can be carried out normally only with the proper water. Most plants absorb moisture from the soil rely on their roots [6]. Therefore, this paper measure the soil humidity as a key parameter to determine whether the plants are dehydrated.

According to the water requirement, the plants can be divided into xerophytes, aquatic plants, wet plants and mesophytes. The xerophytes grow in arid environment. They can maintain the balance of water themselves and keep growing under drought condition for a long time, such as *Opuntia stricta* and so on. Wet plants grow in humid environments. They cannot survive under water shortage condition for a long time. They are the least drought-tolerant terrestrial plantsa, such as *Begonia grandis* Dry and so on. Mesophytes are land plants that grow in moderation humidity conditions. Most plants fall into this category. Aquatic plants are plants that live in the water, such as *Nelumbo nucifera* and so on.

2.3 Temperature

Similar with the light, temperature is also a key factor that it influences the various physiological and biochemical activities of plant. Only if the plant lives in a certain temperature conditions can they grow. It is harmful for plant survival if the temperature is too high or too low.

3   Measurement Principle on Soil Humidity

The soil resistance value is related to humidity. For example, the resistance is small in humidity soil and the resistance is large in dry soil, thus the humidity size can be measured based on the soil resistance value. However, if we use the normal measurement method as-is, we cannot obtain the stable resistance measurement values. The reason is that the moisture in soil can be regarded as electrolyte, it will be polarized under the action of DC voltage, resulting in the separation and accumulation of anions and cations, so that the soil resistance cannot reflect the soil moisture.

This paper adopts a new measurement method. As shown in Fig. 2, the soil resistance constructs an electronic circle with two capacitances, and constructs an oscillating circuit with NE555. At the meantime, the output of NE555 is digital signals, thus can be connected with the digital control system to measure the circuit oscillation frequency. At last, we transform the circuit oscillation frequency into soil humility via numerical fitting of Eq. 1.

$$f = \frac{1}{0.00003 + 8.109E - 9R} \tag{1}$$

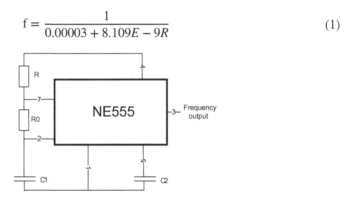

Fig. 2. Electric schematic diagram.

In order to evaluate the accuracy of our novel soil humility measurement method, we use the readings from a professional hygrometer as the ground truth, and Fig. 3 shows the CDF of our measurement errors. We measure the humility of a sample soil every

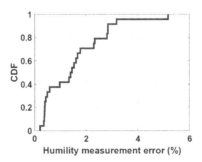

Fig. 3. CDF of soil humility measurement errors.

hour in a day. We observe that the 90-percentile measurement errors are around 3%, which shows the effectiveness of our method.

4   System Architecture

Based on the above soil humidity method, we propose an intelligent plant monitoring system, as Fig. 4 shows. It is comprised of the frontend, home smartphone, and the cloud. We also develop the Bluetooth communication for sensory data transmission between the frontend and the smartphone, and the WAN transmission between the smartphone in home and the cloud. In our system, the smartphone serves as the home control center, which transfers original data, and provide kind user interface for monitoring and control.

Below we introduce our plant monitoring system in details.

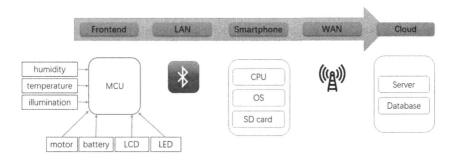

Fig. 4.   The architecture of plant monitoring system

4.1   Frontend Sensery System

In the frontend sensory system, we aim to measure the soil humility, the air temperature and the illumination period. As Fig. 4 shows, we build the humility sensor based on our own observations, and these three sensors are all attached to the MCU. We also attach a LCD for display, a LED for light supply, and a battery for energy supply.

In order to irrigate the plants when users are absent, our MCU also controls a motor as a water pump. Thus users can send the irrigation order with their smartphone even when they are out, and our system irrigate the amount of water just as the plant needs.

Finally, the MCU packages the data every second, and sends the data to the control center in home via Bluetooth communication, which is an energy efficient data transmission protocol and widely equipped on smartphones.

4.2   Home Control Center: Smartphone

The home control center receives the sensory data from frontend sensors, and store the data in local database. It also keeps a database for the environment requirements on the selected plants, thus can determine whether the environment is satisfied. In case the plant lacks of water, the control center will send an alert to the user via WAN, and send the irrigation request back to the frontend system when necessary.

4.3 Cloud Server and Database

We build the cloud on a tomcat server with fixed IP address, and use the JDBC to store the data in a MySQL database. In future we will transplant the server to a cloud server, e.g., on the Aliyun platform, thus providing the service to the public.

5 Frontend Sensery System

The working principle of our frontend sensory system is as follows: we combine the humidity, temperature and light intensity sensors to collect the humidity, temperature and light intensity information of the environment, and perform the A/D conversion to collect such signals via a single chip microcomputer for data processing. The system does not irrigate when the humility value is larger than the bound; it automatically turns on the watering pump when the humidity value is lower than the bound and the temperature value is lower than the set value. In case the humidity value is lower than the bound but the temperature value is higher than its set value, then only when the light intensity is lower than the set value, our system will automatically start the irrigation facilities. Users can also set different conditions to stop watering conditions in the above methods: e.g., humidity is higher than the set value, or watering time exceeds the set period. We employ a LCD screen to help users set the system in a menu way. We also leverage a solar powered battery for sustainable operation without additional power supply (Fig. 5).

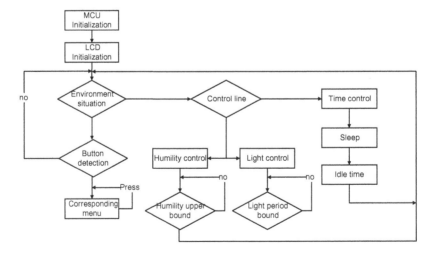

Fig. 5. Software work flow.

Our system waters the plants only at night during the summer, which prevents plants from being sunburn wounds while minimizing water loss due to evaporation. Watering the plants in the daytime in winter reduces the risk of frost damage.

Our frontend sensory system uses a MEGA8 high-end microcontroller as the processing unit for the frontend system. It has an 8 K flash program memory, 1 K RAM, 512 Bit EEPROM, four 10-bit AD conversion circuits with two 8-bit AD conversion circuits. It also has an independent built-in watchdog circuit, which is extremely simple and reliable. We also use a 48 × 84 pixel PCD 8544 LCD screen, which is of low price and easy to buy. The LCD display is connected to the microcontroller via the SPI synchronous serial interface.

Humidity detection. The soil resistance value is related to its humidity. When the humidity is low, the resistance value is small, and the resistance value is high when drying. Therefore, the soil resistance can be used to measure the soil humidity. However, direct measurement method by the conventional DC method cannot measure a stable resistance value. The reason is that: since the water in the soil can be regarded as the electrolyte, it will polarize under the action of the DC voltage, resulting in the separation and aggregation of the anions and cations, thus the soil resistance cannot reflect the soil moisture. Our system develops the original R-F conversion detection circuit to measure the soil humility: the NE555 oscillator circuit adds the AC to the two electrodes, transforms the soil resistance into a pulse signal to facilitate single-chip processing. The actual use of our method is reliable and practical.

We use an 8-bit A/D converter built-in microcontroller to sample and transform the temperature and light intensity information. Temperature probe is an ordinary thermistor, and the microcontroller only conducts a simple conversion for the results instead of using a look-up table. Although the accuracy is not very high, it works well and meets the system requirements. Light intensity are measured using a small photoelectric sensor, and the A/D built in the microcontroller directly samples and transforms the results of the sensor output voltages.

When the watering conditions are met, our system outputs a 12 V voltage at the output port, driving the water pump to start watering. In order to control the amount of water poured, we connect the pump outlet with the water control valve, thus control the amount of water well. In cloudy days, our system controls the LED to make up the light supply, thus keep the suitable environment for any plant.

The system uses the solar-powered battery, without additional power supplies. Although solar cells can also be used directly to power the system, such designs require larger and expensive solar cells. Regarding that our system requires high-current work for only a few minutes in one day, the average power consumption is relatively small, thus our system uses a small solar battery to charge the lithium battery pack, and pack the lithium battery for high-current work at night. The system uses lithium battery pack for its smart charge and discharge protection circuit, and convenient and reliable usage.

6   Control Interface on Smartphone

Humidity settings. Users can set the soil humidity according to the plant species and soil types, with the upper and lower bound. When the soil humidity value is larger than the humidity upper bound, regardless of temperature, light intensity, the system stops watering (at this time the soil humidity has been saturated). When the soil moisture value is smaller than the humidity lower bound (when the soil is dry, water the plant), the system then set the temperature and light intensity to decide whether to irrigate (Fig. 6).

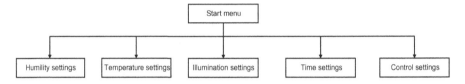

Fig. 6. Initialization process.

Temperature and illumination settings. When the soil humidity is smaller than the humidity lower bound (humidity meets the water conditions), if the soil temperature is lower than the temperature lower bound, the system starts watering the plant. For example, in summer, the soil temperature is too high (temperature is larger than the temperature upper bound), we implement the irrigation equipment with a water pump which is easy to burn plants, thus the system set the light intensity according to the decision whether to irrigate, when the light intensity is larger than the light intensity lower limit (such as during the day), the system does not water the plant. When the light

Fig. 7. Smartphone control interface.

intensity is smaller than the light intensity lower bound (such as night), our system starts the pump to water the plant (Fig. 7).

Time and control settings. In order to allow the soil to have a gradual process for absorbing water, users can set the watering time period. In this case, users set the watering mode to stop the system from watering based on the upper humidity bound or set to stop watering based on the length of time.

7 Conclusion

In this paper, we use the method of resistance-frequency (RF) conversion circuit to measure the soil humility, and develop an intelligent environment monitoring system for plant grows. In addition, the system can control the water pump to irrigate home plants when necessary, report the environment situation to users via smartphones, and store the sensory data in the cloud. From evaluation and our prototype, the method proposed in this paper costs low and is worth to be popularized. Our system can be connected with other indoor localization techniques [7–14] to help improve our daily life.

References

1. Deqin, L., Yunxia, D., Shuwen, Z., Xiaohang, W.: Quantifying parameter sensitivity and calibration in simulating soil temperature and moisture. Chin. J. Atmos. **39**(5), 991–1010 (2015)
2. Qiaosheng, G.: Environmental requirements for medicinal plant growth and development, China News of Traditional Chinese Medicine, 19 June 2002
3. Xiangzeng, X., Jinyan, Z., Guanghui, Z., Guangqiang, L.: Effects of light intensity on photosynthetic capacity and light energy allocation in Panax notoginseng. Chin. J. Appl. Ecol. 1–14 (2017)
4. Cong, L., Tian, T., Shan, L., Liang, Yu.: Growth response of Chineses woody plant seedlings to different lighy intensities. Acta Ecol. Sin. **38**(2), 1–8 (2018)
5. Beibei, G.: Study of crop growth environment simulation system, Tianjin University of Technology and Education (2013)
6. Juan, X., Yi, C., Fei, T., Chuntao, L.: The influence of environmental factors on flower growth and family flower - growing techniques. J. Anhui Agric. Sci. **31**(4), 656–658 (2003)
7. Gao, R., Zhao, M., Ye, T., Ye, F., Luo, G., Wang, Y., Bian, K., Wang, T., Li, X.: Multi-story Indoor floor plan reconstruction via mobile crowdsensing. IEEE Trans. Mob. Comput. **15**(6), 1427–1442 (2016)
8. Gao, R., Tian, Y., Ye, F., Luo, G., Bian, K., Wang, Y., Wang, T., Li, X.: Sextant: towards ubiquitous indoor localization service by photo-taking of the environment. IEEE Trans. Mob. Comput. **15**(2), 460–474 (2016)
9. Gao, R., Zhao, M., Ye, T., Ye, F., Wang, Y., Luo, G.: Smartphone-based real time vehicle tracking in indoor parking structures. IEEE Trans. Mob. Comput. **16**(7), 2023–2036 (2017)
10. Gao, R., Zhou, B., Ye, F., Wang, Y.: Knitter: fast, resilient single-user indoor floor plan construction. In: Proceedings of IEEE INFOCOM (2017)
11. Gao, R., Zhao, M., Ye, T., Ye, F., Wang, Y., Bian, K., Wang, T., Li, X.: Jigsaw: indoor floor plan reconstruction via mobile crowdsensing. In: Proceedings of ACM MobiCom (2014)

12. Zhou, B., Chen, X., Hu, X., Ren, R., Tan, X., Fang, X., Xia, S.: A Bluetooth low energy approach for monitoring electrocardiography and respiration. In: Proceedings of IEEE Healthcom (2013)
13. Zhou, B., Elbadry, M., Gao, R., Ye, F.: BatMapper: acoustic sensing based indoor floor plan construction using smartphones. In: Proceedings of ACM MobiSys (2017)
14. Zhou, B., Elbadry, M., Gao, R., Ye, F.: BatTracker: high precision infrastructure-free mobile device tracking in indoor environments. In: Proceedings of ACM SenSys (2017)

TSA: A Two-Phase Scheme Against Amplification DDoS Attack in SDN

Zheng Liu[1], Mingwei Xu[1(✉)], Jiahao Cao[1], and Qi Li[2]

[1] Department of Computer Science and Technology, Tsinghua University,
Beijing 100084, China
xmw@cernet.edu.cn
[2] Graduate School at Shenzhen, Tsinghua University, Shenzhen 518055, China

Abstract. Amplification attack, as a new kind of DDoS attack, is more destructive than traditional DDoS attack. Under the existing Internet architecture, it is difficult to find effective measures to deal with amplification attack. In this paper, we propose a two-phase reference detecting scheme by utilizing Software Defined Infrastructure capabilities: switch side is volume-based and controller side is feature-based. The proposed scheme is protocol-independent and lightweight, unlike most of the existing strategies. It can also detect amplification attack in the request phase for a small price, before these attacks cause actual harm. Upon the architecture, we design detection algorithms and a prototype system. Experimental results with both online and offline data sets show that the detection scheme is effective and efficient.

Keywords: Amplification DDoS attack · Software defined network
Two-phase detecting · Entropy

1 Introduction

Distributed Denial-of-Service (DDoS) attack is still a threat to the Internet security, though a lot of efforts have been put to deal with the attack. The headache gets worse when a new kind of DDoS attack, the amplification DDoS attack appears [1–3]. Amplification DDoS attack takes advantage of IP address spoofing and traffic amplification through reflectors to cause even more damage at a lower price than the traditional DDoS attack. Since the source IP addresses in the queries are forged into the target victim's, the amplified associated responses in much larger size from the resolvers are sent to the victim.

Many schemes [4–6] have been proposed to mitigate the harm from amplification DDoS attack, but the effect is not ideal enough. On one hand, they are proposed aiming at some certain protocol. This kind of defensive measures can be called protocol patched-up measures. As mentioned above, there are many protocols can be utilized in amplification DDoS attack [1] and many other protocols may be utilized in the future potentially. In the face of this fact, these protocol patched-up measures play limited roles. On the other hand, many other

© Springer Nature Singapore Pte Ltd. 2018
L. Zhu and S. Zhong (Eds.): MSN 2017, CCIS 747, pp. 483–496, 2018.
https://doi.org/10.1007/978-981-10-8890-2_37

measures are proposed to cope with amplification DDoS attack fundamentally, namely to stop address spoofing. For example, References BCP38 [7] and BCP84 [8] are designed to wipe out address spoofing. These measures are also not effective enough, since ISP providers do not have enough incentive to deploy them. Software Defined Networks (SDN) can conduct flow scheduling flexibly, and it can be utilized to resolve the DDoS attack problem [9–11].

What are the challenges to design a scheme that can detect and mitigate the amplification DDoS attack successfully? First, the scheme must come into effect as soon as possible. It makes no sense if the detecting system works after the attack has caused widespread damage; Second, the scheme should not cope with only one kind of amplification DDoS attack that utilizing a specific protocol. There are too many protocols can be utilized in amplification DDoS attack, which puts forward high requirements to scalability of the detecting scheme; Third, the scheme should be so lightweight that can be deployed to monitor traffic online. How to increase the efficiency of the system and reduce its cost simultaneously is a concern.

In this paper, the authors propose a **T**wo-phase detecting **S**cheme against **A**mplification DDoS attack (TSA) in software-defined networking (SDN). The first phase detection is volume-based realized on the data plane, and the second phase detection is feature-based realized on the control plane. Combining these two kinds of detection mechanisms contributes to considering efficiency and effectivity at the same time. With the help of SDN architecture, the detecting scheme can be strong in scalability and configure the network flexibly. The detecting scheme monitors all the traffic flows through switches and picks out the suspect flows in the first detecting phase, then report these suspect flows to the controller to judge further in the second detecting phase. The proposed detecting scheme conducts the detection on request traffic, so as to make effective defense before the attack causes large-scale damage. It is also protocol-independent and lightweight, which makes it can be deployed online to execute detection.

The main Contributions as follows:

- A detecting scheme against amplification DDoS attack in SDN is proposed. The proposed scheme has three bright spots: detecting in the request phase, protocol-independent and lightweight.
- Upon the proposed scheme, a two-phase detecting algorithm is designed based on both volume and feature.
- According to the algorithm, a prototype system is implemented. Abundant experiments are conducted based on it with both online and offline traffic.

The rest of paper is organized as follows. Section 2 introduces the background and motivation of this study. In Sect. 3, the framework of the detecting scheme is stated. According to the framework, the two-phase detecting algorithm is described in Sect. 4. After that, the authors implement a prototype system and evaluate the scheme with both online and offline traffic in Sect. 5. Finally, we conclude in Sect. 6.

2 Background and Motivation

The section will first provide an introduction into the characteristics of amplification and DDoS Attack. We can see the reason why such an attack is so destructive. We end the section by analyzing the challenges of the attack defense.

2.1 Amplification and DDoS Attack

Generally speaking, the research on conventional DDoS attack is close to saturation, and attackers have been devoting themselves into exploiting new variants of DDoS attack [12,13]. Amplification DDoS attack, a kind of DDoS attack, becomes more and more influential in recent years. In amplification DDoS attack, taking NTP amplification attack as an example, the attacker controls the botnet to repeatedly send the "Get Monlist" requests to NTP servers, meanwhile using the victim's IP address as source address of requests. NTP servers respond by sending the list to the victim. The bandwidth amplification factor can reach 556.9. Since UDP offers non-guaranteed datagram delivery, IP address spoofing can be realized more easily than TCP. Amplification DDoS attack refers to the attack launched with UDP-based protocols within the scope of this article.

Till now, the largest known DDoS attack ever on the Internet is amplification DDoS attack. In February 2014, hackers succeeded in targeting content-delivery and anti-DDoS protection firm "CloudFlare" with NTP amplification attack, making the attack volume size reach 400Gbps at its peak. In the attack, 4529 NTP servers were abused, run on 1298 different networks. In summary, two key characters of amplification DDoS attack should be pay attention to: First, attackers send requests to reflectors using spoofed IP address which is the address of victim as their source address; Second, the size of the responses returned from reflectors to the victim are much larger than that of the requests sent from botnet to reflectors.

2.2 Challenges of Attack Defense

From above, we can conclude that amplification DDoS attack is more destructive than conventional DDoS attack. What's worse is that it is quite difficult to defend against this kind of attack under the current Internet architecture. **On one hand**, there are three convenient conditions for attackers to make an amplification DDoS attack with small cost: (1). IP address spoofing still exists in plenty of networks. As much as 24.6% of networks allow IP address spoofing, which is obtained in "Spoofer Project" [14]; (2). There are abundant of servers can be utilized as reflectors in amplification DDoS attack to amplify the attack traffic to the victim. From the "Open Resolver Project" [15], 28 million DNS open resolvers pose significant threat; (3). It was discovered in [1], More than ten kinds of network protocols can be used in amplification DDoS attack. Even worse, many other network protocols may be added into the set of "troubled" protocols potentially. **On the other hand**, it is quite hard to detect malicious traffic and handle the attack timely: (1). The malicious requests sent from botnet to reflectors are difficult to distinguish from valid requests. From the perspective of the victim, responses are from valid servers; (2). Even if the detection is timely, how to tell relevant network nodes (e.g., routers or servers) to make effective strategies is another problematic issue under the current Internet architecture.

3   System Framework

As explained in Sect. 2, proposing a scheme to detect and mitigate amplification DDoS attack faces many challenges. In this paper, we propose a two-phase scheme named TSA based on SDN to solve the challenging problem.

3.1   Principles of Attack Detection

Volume-based approaches and feature-based approaches are two different kinds of mechanisms in the field of anomaly detection. They have their own advantages and disadvantages. In short, Volume-based approaches are often used for conventional traffic analysis at a relatively low cost. On the contrary, feature-based approaches provide more fine-grained insights than volume-based approaches at the cost of performance.

Our detecting system executes two-phase detection by using volume-based and feature-based methods together. In SDN architecture, data plane is non-intelligent and needs to forward network traffic immediately. The first-phase preliminary detection based on traffic volume can be conducted in the data plane. Control plane is intelligent and can make logical decisions. Then, the second-phase farther detection based on feature can be conducted in the control plane. The proposed detecting system has three principles:

3.1.1   Rapidity

It is insignificant that if attacks have caused damage before they are detected successfully. In order to avoid this, the proposed detecting system concentrates on attack launching phase. The traffic anomaly detection targeted at request traffic that sent from botnet to servers.

3.1.2   Protocol Independent

The detecting system is suitable for amplification DDoS attacks launched with different protocols. By constructing different flow tables, the proposed system can be applied to different protocols, including the existing and potential ones.

3.1.3   Lightweight

The cost brought by monitoring traffic needs to be controlled at a low level. Reporting suspect packets to the controller is triggered by attacks instead of polling by the controller, which protects throughput from sharp decrease.

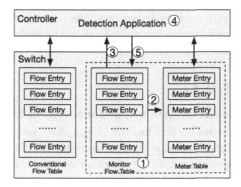

Fig. 1. The system framework of TSA

3.2 Framework of TSA

To meet the principles proposed above, the system is designed composed of two detecting phases. The first phase is executed on the switch side. In order to detect suspect traffic and to conduct volume-based detection, relevant traffic flows need to be converged together by constructing a new flow table. The new flow table is used for monitoring all the traffic through it. When the volume of some aggregated traffic flows exceeds the threshold that is adjusted dynamically, the aggregated traffic flow is judged as suspect traffic and sent to the controller to be judged further. The proposed system monitors the requests sent from botnet to servers instead of responses sent from servers to the victim. If the attack traffic can be detected in the request phase, the defense of the system is effective. The system needs to be applied to different amplification DDoS attacks with all kinds of protocols, which can be resolved by adjusting the source/destination port field of flow table. Few changes are made to OpenFlow except some modified information formats, which makes the system is lightweight.

The second detecting phase is executed on the controller side. After the first detecting phase, some suspect traffic flows have been sent to the controller. To guarantee the correctness of detection, feature-based method that can provide fine-grained insights is adopted on the controller side. Analyzing the distribution of source IP addresses of all the reported suspect traffic flows can reach a conclusion whether there is an amplification DDoS attack or not. Entropy-based method [16–18] is a kind of feature-based methods for traffic analysis and anomaly detection. Based on the conclusion, the controller makes further step to deal with these suspect traffic flows and adjust the volume threshold on the switch side.

The system framework of TSA is described in Fig. 1. A new flow table used for monitoring is built, ranking at the last of all the existing flow tables (the first step); All the traffic flow to the monitor flow table that monitored with the help of meter table (the second step); The suspect flow will be sent to the controller (the third step); The controller is collecting all the suspect flows until the total number of reported suspect flows is enough. Then, the controller makes the further detection with entropy-based methods (the fourth step); At last, the controller constitutes new forwarding rules to drop the malicious traffic (the last step).

3.3 Advantages of TSA

3.3.1 ISP Providers Have Abundant Incentive to Deploy the System
The distribution of network servers has the geographic concentration. The distribution matches the "Pareto principle" approximately. Generally speaking, abundant servers are gathered in a few autonomous domains. The ISP providers of these domains have incentive and duty to deploy the detecting system.

3.3.2 Two-Phase Detection Can Increase Accuracy
The first phase picks up suspect traffic flows with low possibility of false negative. Since if the rate of corresponding gathered flow does not reach the monitoring threshold, it can not cause fatal damage. The second phase feature-based detection act on suspect traffic can reduce the possibility of false positive.

3.3.3 Monitoring All the Flows Instead of Sampling
Monitoring all the flows and making preliminary decision, which obtains suspect traffic flows. What are sent to the controller are only the suspect flows. The influence on performances is evaluated in Sect. 5 and is acceptable.

4 Detection Procedure and Algorithm

4.1 First-Phase Based on Traffic Volume

The attack requests are sent from thousands of hosts in botnet, so that each attack flow may not present differences from normal flows. The key to this problem is to construct specific flow table. With the help of the specific flow table, attack flow can be gathered together as much as possible and present abnormal.

4.1.1 Flow Table Construction
To monitor all the flows pass through the switch, a new flow entry is created to each existing flow entry. All these new created flow entries compose a new flow table used for monitoring. The new flow table is put at last of all the flow tables to make all the flows pass through it. The 5-tuple of a flow including IP source and destination address, source and destination port, and protocol are chosen to make correlative flows get together for simplification. All the other fields of the new flow entry are filled with wildcards. In amplification DDoS attack, all the attack requests' source addresses are forged into the address of the victim. In consideration of further detection on the controller side focus on the distribution of source address, the source IP address field in new flow entry does not need to be chosen. These four chosen fields are designed as follows: destination IP address

(IP_dst) keeps the same with the correlative flow entry's IP_dst. Destination port (port_dst) is set to be the corresponding protocol number. For example, in DNS amplification attack, the port_dst in new flow entry is set to 53. Source port (port_src) keeps the same with the corresponding flow entry's port_src. Protocol is set to UDP. An extra flow entry with all the wildcards needs to be added into the new flow table. The extra entry is given the lowest priority to guarantee all the traffic that do not need to be monitored can be forwarded directly.

4.1.2   Meter Table Construction

Meter table is used to measure the rate of packets assigned to it. The flow entries of the new flow table direct to meter table entry by fill their instructions with relevant meter identifier. The monitoring rate can be set through counter field. We use meter table cooperated with the new flow table to monitor the rate of all flows and find suspect traffic flows to sent to the controller. The existing type of meter band does not include reporting to the controller. Some changes are made to add this reporting function. Except the adding function, the message format remains unchanged. The extension to meter table does not influence the performance of switches' throughput, and can be realized in hardware easily.

4.2   Second-Phase Based on Flow Feature Distribution

On the controller side, feature-based detection provides fine-grained insights. Based on the suspect traffic flows, the controller analyzes the distribution of source address of all suspect flows. Entropy is adopted as the metric to conduct the detection.

4.2.1   Entropy

All the amplification-attack traffic packets are filled with victims' address as the source address. Based on the fact that the majority of reported suspect traffic flows are indeed attack traffic, the distribution of source addresses of suspect traffic flows presents concentration. The entropy metric is used for measuring unpredictability, and utilized in the field of anomaly detection. The entropy in the amplification DDoS attack is quite low. The calculation formula of entropy is defined as:

$$H_M = \sum_{i=1}^{M} -p_i log_2 p_i \tag{1}$$

where M is the number of different IP address kinds, p_i represents the ratio of i_{th} of address from all kinds of address.

$$p_i = \frac{N_i}{N} \tag{2}$$

where N_i is the number of packets with i_{th} kind of address, N represents the number of all the packets. In order to compare the entropy values under different conditions, the entropy value need to be standardized as follows:

$$H = \frac{H_M}{log_2 M} \tag{3}$$

where the log_2^M is upper bound of the entropy value.

4.2.2 The Feature-Based Detection Algorithm

The algorithm procedure is presented in Algorithm 1. The controller is collecting suspect traffic flows until the quantity is sufficient. Then the controller launches the calculation of entropy value and compares the result with the threshold preset to judge whether there is an attack or not. If the entropy value is lower than the threshold, the controller makes the conclusion that there is an attack in progress. The controller considers the flow with highest ratio of source address as attack flow since there is only one or a few victims in amplification DDoS attack. After that, the controller creates new rules to discard the attack flow and calculates the new volume threshold on the switch side with a heuristic algorithm. Then, the controller sends the commands to switches to update the flow table and meter table.

Algorithm 1. Feature-based Detection

    Input: The pre-set number of suspect packets N_t and the pre-set entropy threshold E_t

    Output: Void

1   $n \leftarrow$ the number of collected suspect packets;

2   **if** $n \geq N_t$ **then**

3 | Compute the entropy value e;

4   **if** $e \leq E_t$ **then**

5 | Decide it is an attack and update flow table;

6   **else**

7 | Decide it is not an attack;

8   return 0;

4.2.3 Calculation of Monitoring Threshold Value of Switch

The threshold value on the switch side is used to judge whether the monitored flow is malicious or not. We propose a heuristic algorithm to update the threshold. The heuristic algorithm is executed when the controller verifies that there is an attack in progress. Then the controller judges the ratio of attack volume of all the suspect traffic volume. If the traffic volume of the attack flow exceeds 80% (according to the Pareto's Law) of all the suspect traffic volume, the threshold should be lower to decrease false negative. Else if the traffic volume of the attack flow less than 80% of all the suspect traffic volume, the threshold should be higher to decrease false positive.

5 Evaluation

5.1 Prototype System Implementation

The prototype system is implemented with Mininet plantform and RYU controller system. The Mininet environment is built in a server with the CPU type "Intel Xeon E5504" and 8 Gb memory to simulate large-scale network topology. The controller with RYU system is built in a PC with the CPU type "Intel Pentium Dual-core E5500" and 2 Gb memory.

5.1.1 Modification to OpenFlow Switch

The OpenFlow open vSwitches are realized with the software "Ofsoftswitch 13". This software is compatible with OpenFlow v1.3 protocol, and support Flow table structure and meter table structure. "Ofsoftswitch 13" is based on Linux user mode, realized with C language. To realize the automatically reporting function, the authors analyze and modify the source code of "Ofsoftswitch 13", and recompile the source code in the Linux system. The authors expand and modify reserve type "OFPMBT-EXPERIMENTER" that supported by OpenFlow protocol, to construct a new meter type and a new information type.

5.1.2 Application Developed on Controller

The authors develop an application on the controller with RYU system. To realize the defense function, the reported information "OFP-EXPERIMENTER-DETECT" is analyzed by the application. Based on the cookie of relevant flow entry, the application modifies the actions of that entry and adds a new action "output, controller", which makes each flow is copied and sent to the controller. When the received flows are enough, the application begins to launch the detecting algorithm based on entropy to conduct the defense function. If there is an attack, the application modifies the action set of relevant flow entries to drop attack traffic. Meanwhile, the meter table keeps monitoring all the flows. When the meter table does not report suspect flows, the application change actions to old situation to forward these flows normally.

5.2 Dataset

5.2.1 Topology

The adopted topology is the backbone network topology of Standford. We build the topology in Mininet environment by "python" scripts. For simplicity and without loss of generality, the number of hosts is set to 48 and the number of switches is set to 26. All the attackers forge their address as the victim's address and send requests to DNS servers. Other legal hosts send requests to DNS servers randomly.

5.2.2   Online Traffic

The online traffic includes background traffic and attack traffic. The background traffic are simulated by "poisson process" that is defined as $p_k(t) = \frac{(\lambda t)^k}{k!} e^{-\lambda t}$. The authors program with python to send packets based on the definition "poisson process". These packets act as background traffic. The authors program with "Scapy" to generate attack traffic. Meanwhile, to realize the amplification of request traffic, the authors program to simulate the DNS servers.

5.2.3   Offline Traffic

The authors adopt the "DoS-DNS-amplification-20130617" dataset as offline traffic. The dataset contains one DNS amplification attack, phased by researchers between two sites in US. The attack lasted for 10 min. In the attack scenario, there are 6 DNS servers, 1 attacker and 1 victim. The size of all the compressed traffic files is about 5.43 GB.

5.3   Experimental Method

Upon the proposed detecting architecture and two-phase detecting algorithms, a prototype system is implemented. To prove the proposed detecting scheme is effective and efficient in the face of amplification DDoS attack, several experiments are conducted in the prototype system with both online and offline traffic.

5.3.1   Validation of Entropy

It needs to be validated whether choosing entropy value as evaluation index in feature-based detection is effective. The validation is conducted with both the online and offline traffic. For online traffic part, experiments are executed with the prototype system. We can observe and compare the different entropy values in and not in attacks. Further, the authors change the rate of attack traffic to evaluate the entropy value in different situations. For offline traffic part, the traffic in the dataset "DoS_DNS_amplification-20130617" are almost response traffic, while the proposed detecting scheme concentrates on request traffic. The authors calculate the entropy of destination IP address to simulate the entropy of source address.

5.3.2   Influence on Performance

Throughput, CPU utilization and delay are chosen to evaluate the performance cost. (a). Some new information are exchanged between switches and the controller. The influence on the switch throughput should be evaluated; (b). On the controller side, how much overhead is introduced when the feature-based detection works should be evaluated with the help of CPU utilization; (c). For the whole system, the cost brought on performance can be evaluated with the change of transmission delay.

5.4   The Experiment Results

5.4.1   Validation of Entropy

Online measurement: With the prototype system, the entropy value of all the suspect traffic source address is calculated. The result is shown in Fig. 2(a). The average rate of normal DNS requests is 5pps, and the rate of attack DNS requests of each attacker is 20pps. The attack starts at 15 s and ends at 30s. We can state that the entropy value is lower obviously when there is an attack. The authors change the rate of attack request of each attacker and calculate the corresponding entropy value. The result is shown in Fig. 2(b). We can conclude that the entropy reduces when the rate of attack traffic rises. The detecting system will behave well with an appropriate entropy threshold.

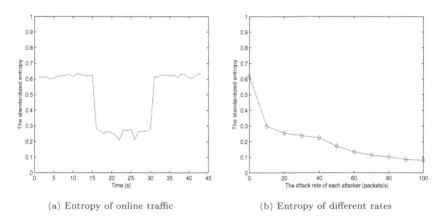

(a) Entropy of online traffic   (b) Entropy of different rates

Fig. 2. The validation of entropy with online measurement

Offline Measurement: Since the traffic in the offline dataset is almost response traffic, the entropy value of destination IP address is regarded as evaluation index and the entropy value of source IP address is regarded as reference index. From Fig. 3 we can conclude that the entropy value is quite low when there is an attack. The entropy metric works well in the feature-based detection.

5.4.2   Influence on Performance

Throughput: Some new information need to be sent to the controller for measurement. It can not be avoid that some cost is brought to switches. The authors evaluate the performance influence on the switch side with the throughput of switches. From Fig. 4, We can see that the difference throughput between using and not using the system is acceptable.

CPU utilization: The controller needs to collect the reported packets from switches and conduct the feature-based detecting algorithm. The authors evaluate the performance influence on the controller side with the cpu utilization

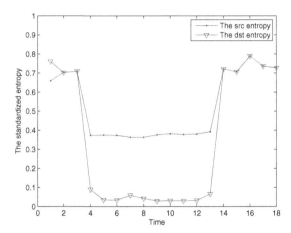

Fig. 3. The validation of entropy with offline measurement

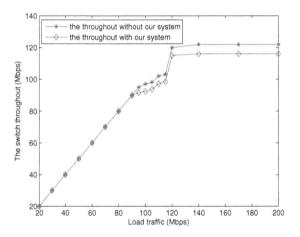

Fig. 4. The evaluation of performance influenced by switches' throughput

in Fig. 5. The CPU utilization is high in the initial phase, since the controller needs to make decisions for all the switches to route. After configuring all the switches, the controller's CPU utilization reduces and keeps at a low level when the detecting system does not work. Nevertheless, there is a peak value when the detecting system works. The high CPU utilization does not keeps for a long interval, and the difference can be accepted.

Delay: The authors adopt transmission delay as the evaluation index. The RTT values between two hosts are measured with "ping" command for hundreds of times and are recorded in Fig. 6. The RTT differences between using and not using the system are insignificant. It can be declared that the prototype system is lightweight in many aspects.

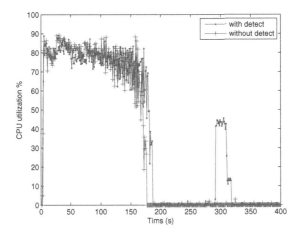

Fig. 5. The evaluation of performance influenced by controller's CPU utilization

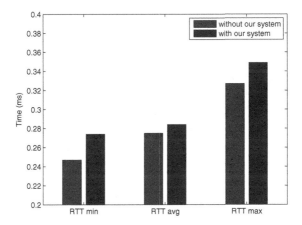

Fig. 6. The evaluation of performance influenced by transmission delay between hosts

6 Conclusion

This work presents a two-phase detecting scheme for amplification DDoS attack detection. One phase is volume-based and the other is feature-based. We show that the proposed scheme can deploy defense in attack initial phase with protocol-independent and lightweight characters. According to the scheme, a prototype system is designed and implemented. The experimental results with both online and offline traffic state that our detecting scheme is effective and efficient.

Ackowledgements. The research is supported by the National Natural Science Foundation of China under Grant 61625203, the National Key R&D Program of China under Grant 2016YFC0901605.

References

1. Rossow, C.: Amplification Hell: Revisiting Network Protocols for DDoS Abuse. In: NDSS (2014)
2. Ryba, F.J., Orlinski, M., Whlisch, M., et al.: Amplification and DRDoS Attack Defense-A Survey and New Perspectives. arXiv preprint arXiv:1505.07892 (2015)
3. Fachkha, C., Bou-Harb, E., Debbabi, M.: Fingerprinting internet DNS amplification DDoS activities. In: NTMS, pp. 1–5. IEEE (2014)
4. Tsunoda, H., Ohta, K., Yamamoto, A., et al.: Detecting DRDoS attacks by a simple response packet confirmation mechanism. Comput. Commun. **31**(14), 3299–3306 (2008)
5. Kambourakis, G., Moschos, T., Geneiatakis, D., et al.: A fair solution to DNS amplification attacks. In: WDFIA, pp. 38–47. IEEE (2007)
6. Khrer, M., Hupperich, T., Rossow, C., et al.: Exit from hell? reducing the impact of amplification DDoS attacks. In: Security Symposium, pp. 111–125. USENIX (2014)
7. BCP38. https://tools.ietf.org/html/bcp38
8. BCP84. https://tools.ietf.org/html/bcp84
9. Shin, S., Yegneswaran, V., Porras, P., et al.: Avant-guard: scalable and vigilant switch flow management in software-defined networks. In: SIGSAC, pp. 413–424. ACM (2013)
10. Zaalouk, A., Khondoker, R., Marx, R., et al.: Orchsec: an orchestrator-based architecture for enhancing network-security using network monitoring and SDN control functions. In: NOMS, pp. 1–9. IEEE (2014)
11. Shin, S., Porras, P.A., Yegneswaran, V., et al.: FRESCO: modular composable security services for software-defined networks. In: NDSS (2013)
12. Beitollahi, H., Deconinck, G.: Analyzing well-known countermeasures against distributed denial of service attacks. Comput. Commun. **35**(11), 1312–1332 (2012)
13. Xiang, Y., Li, K., Zhou, W.: Low-rate DDoS attacks detection and traceback by using new information metrics. Trans. Inf. Forensics Secur. **6**(2), 426–437 (2011)
14. Spoofer Project. https://www.caida.org/projects/spoofer/
15. Open Resolver Project. http://openresolverproject.org
16. Feinstein, L., Schnackenberg, D., Balupari, R., et al.: Statistical approaches to DDoS attack detection and response. In: DARPA Information Survivability Conference and Exposition, vol. 1, pp. 303–314. IEEE (2003)
17. Nychis, G., Sekar, V., Andersen, D.G., et al.: An empirical evaluation of entropy-based traffic anomaly detection. In: SIGCOMM, pp. 151–156. ACM (2008)
18. Lall, A., Sekar, V., Ogihara, M., et al.: Data streaming algorithms for estimating entropy of network traffic. In: SIGMETRICS, vol. 34, no. 1, pp. 145–156. ACM (2006)

Simulation Standardization: Current State and Cross-Platform System for Network Simulators

Zohaib Latif[1], Kashif Sharif[1,2]($\boxtimes$) , Maria K. Alvi[3], and Fan Li[1,2]($\boxtimes$)

[1] School of Computer Science, Beijing Institute of Technology, Beijing, China
{z.latif,kashif,fli}@bit.edu.cn
[2] Research Center of High Volume Language Information Processing and Cloud Computing Applications, Beijing, China
[3] School of Electrical Engineering and Computer Science,
National University of Sciences and Technology, Islamabad, Pakistan
13msitmkhalid@seecs.edu.pk

Abstract. The amount of research done in the field of mobile ad hoc networks is extraordinarily large. Evaluation of protocols designed for ad hoc networks is challenging as the cost of node deployment in terms of resources required is high, hence, most of the researchers use simulations for performance evaluation. In this paper we address the pitfalls of simulation studies in ad hoc routing protocols published in recent years. We have conducted a survey to evaluate the current state of simulation studies published in top conference/journals of the communication domain. In majority of the published papers (the way simulation results are reported) we have found design flaws, unrealistic assumptions, are non-reproducible, and statistically invalid results. We also propose a standardizing architecture for automating the reporting and replication process for network simulators. This platform independent architecture alleviates the challenge of simulation parameter reporting and facilitates in designing better network simulation experiments.

1 Introduction

Research papers are being published in every domain of studies whether its science or arts, and the credibility of a research is a major concern among researchers. To ensure the effectiveness of work done, the content of the publication should reflect all the factors which other researcher may need to reproduce or improve upon the idea. Since research is a chain of innovation in which one work leads to another, a research study published which damages the accuracy in anyway, is a serious threat to all the work that may follow. The issue of validity

The work of F. Li was supported by the National Natural Science Foundation of China (NSFC) under Grant 61772077, Grant 61370192, and Grant 61432015.

L. Zhu and S. Zhong (Eds.): MSN 2017, CCIS 747, pp. 497–508, 2018.
https://doi.org/10.1007/978-981-10-8890-2_38

and credibility has been repeatedly addressed by many studies in different fields of sciences [1–4]. It is important to note that previous studies have found little or no significant improvement in this problem.

Simulation being a powerful testing tool is very popular among the researchers worldwide. Its usage increases when it comes to computer and telecommunication research as it provides flexible model construction, cost effective, and simple verification mechanism(s). The actual purpose of simulation is to validate the methodology, so it is important that it produces accurate and credible results. The domain of computer networks (in general) has relied heavily on simulation based experimentation. To facilitate this, dozens of simulation software have been created (commercial and open source). However, most of the published research fails to report and document the simulation experiments, which in turn makes it (almost) impossible to replicate, compare to, and improve upon the proposed solution.

This paper presents the current state of simulation studies particularly for routing protocols in Mobile Ad hoc Networks (MANETs). We have used three factors in the evaluation criteria i.e. realistic simulation scenarios, statistical validity of results, and repeatability of experiment. The realistic scenario verifies whether the simulation is modeling real world situations, or just a collection of random nodes. The statistical validity verifies whether the methods opted to perform the analysis are rigorous enough. Repeatability verifies whether the researcher has provided enough information to public to reproduce or improve upon the same work. This study included published papers from 2010 to 2017 in the top tier conferences and journals sponsored by IEEE and ACM.

The second contribution of this paper is introduction of standardization mechanism of reporting methods for simulators. We have developed a tool as proof of concept, for NS2, which simplifies reporting of research work for easy repeatability.

2   Related Work

Studies done in this domain in the past are summarized in this section along with their recommendations. The main focus of these studies was credibility.

Kurkowski [5] reviewed 114 papers published in MobiHoc between 2000 and 2005 in terms of credibility and found less than 15% of the papers to be completely repeatable. Only 56 papers mentioned the simulation tool used to simulate. Out of those 56 papers, 87.9% did not state the version of simulation tool which is necessary to get the exact same results as reported in paper. Only 12% of the papers appeared to be statistically sound. Kurkowski did not consider the realistic-ness of simulation scenarios, rather considered reporting of Tx range and mobility of nodes only, which is not enough to define a real scenario [6].

In [7] authors question the validity of simulation studies, the working of simulation tools, and how they are producing misleading results. The research highlights that different packages available for simulation are prone to imprecision. It also addresses the repeatability issue due to lack of documentation of research work, simulation tool name, tool version and variable settings for simulation. Results should be accurate and statistically sound, which is possible by using pseudo random number generator (PRNG), optimal number of simulation runs and confidence interval. These studies have put emphasis on repeatability and statistical validity for a reliable simulation study, which is not sufficient for credible results. In [6] authors presents realistic scenarios as another aspect of valid simulation results. This study claims that the most important parameters for a realistic environment are mobility model and propagation model. It also conducted a survey on MobiHoc conference publications for realistic scenarios. Their results were quite distressing as only 2 out of 52 papers gave information about the mobility and the radio model used.

The number of papers which are reported in these studies were published in 2010 or earlier conferences and journals. Since then, no re-evaluation has been done on credibility of published work. The effort of this paper is not to undermine the credibility or authenticity of research work, but rather to highlight and focus the attention of researchers to follow some standard mechanism (or best practices) while evaluating their protocols and algorithms. Although some conferences/journals require availability of source code for evaluation by peer reviewers, but after publication the need of availability of such resources is almost negligible.

In this paper we have merged the methodology of three big contributions to do the analysis [5–7]. We took the recommendations from [5,7] for repeatability and statistical validity, and added realistic scenario as third criteria. We did the analysis on recent proceeding (2010 2017) of top tier conferences and journal for MANET studies. Moreover, we have developed a standardization architecture which will make the reporting easy in a way to ensure the credibility and repeatability of MANET studies.

3   Methodology

The three fundamental questions addresses in this paper are:

– How is the reported research tested against real world situation?
– Is the research done via simulation repeatable/reproducible by other researchers?
– Is the published work statistically valid?

3.1   Realistic Scenario

A method tested in unrealistic environment does not represent the solution required for the intended situation. Adhoc networks are highly dynamic, thus the movement of the nodes and the radio propagation patterns greatly vary. Using Random Way Point (RWP) as mobility pattern does not reflect the true nature of humans or vehicles. Moreover, effects of terrain and environmental obstacles on the radio propagation have to be as close to real world as possible.

Using unrealistic environmental variables or leaving them to default values of simulators do not give results that can be used in reality [8]. Due to the unpredictable patterns of mobility in ad-hoc networks, appropriate mobility model should never be omitted [9,10] from simulation studies. Mobile wireless nodes have a certain transmission range, coupled with obstacles, signal reflection, and other interferences; the radio propagation is never smooth [11]. In our survey we evaluate whether mobility and radio model are mentioned in the paper, even if they have used the default models provided by the simulator(s).

3.2   Repeatability

Repeatability is a major concern and a moral responsibility of a researcher. To make an effort available to other for testing and improvement, one must report their work properly to make it reproducible. It is important to mention the tool name because each simulation tool has its own working environment and produces different results for same method tested [7]. Each version may have a different process to evaluate the method it is important to state version of the tool. Also, if any of the parameter is missing or not addressed, it is almost impossible to repeat the work in exact same way [12]. Due to different constraints, it may not be possible to report all parameters, but the basic parameters or the ones which have been modified from their default values, should be reported.

3.3   Statistical Validity

The processes of data collection and data analysis are two of the most crucial steps of any simulation study. Modern discrete event network simulators have made the data collection easy. The challenge of data analysis still needs to be addressed. Statistical validity of any simulation is measured by the following parameters [5,7]:

- Number of Simulation Runs/Confidence Interval (CI): Once simulation is never enough. It has to be repeated enough number of times.
- Seed Value: Directly affects the Pseudo random Number Generation, which in turn determines the mobility, propagation, and overall simulation. Usually seed value is based on time by the simulator.
- Statistical Value (p-value): After analysis, statistical significance of the research should always be calculated.

This study included published papers from IEEE and ACM sponsored top conferences/journals (between 2010 and 2017) which included (but not limited to) INFOCOM, MobiHoc, MobiCom, SIGComm, SECON, ICNP, LCN, ICCCN, WCNC, Trans. on Mobile Computing, Trans. on Networking, Trans. on Communications. We have considered papers that addressed routing protocols in MANETs, and used simulators are a method of evaluation. It is important to note that there are other publications in these venues which use simulators, but we have restricted the scope to network layer protocols only and evaluated for the three criteria discussed in this section.

4   Results and Analysis

The results discussed in this section are solely based on the information reported in papers. The aim is to highlight the challenges of reporting simulation studies, and not to undermine the work/novelty/credibility of any researcher. The evaluation is of 38 research papers on MANET routing. We explain the finding in form of percentages, and their possible impact.

4.1   Realistic Scenario

All selected papers were analyzed to see, if mobility model and radio propagation model were discussed/described. The objective is not to evaluate the correctness of mobility or propagation model, but rather to see if any of these were used/reported in the simulation as shown in Table 1. We found that 47% of the papers did not mention any mobility model. 26% used Random Waypoint (RWP) model, which is an unrealistic and rudimentary mobility model [13]. 10% reported only node speed which is not enough to define the actual mobility pattern. Remaining 14% papers referred to other mobility models (some of which may be considered realistic e.g. RPGM, Gipps, etc.).

Table 1. Realistic scenario

Criteria		Value
Mobility model	Not reported	47%
	RWP	26%
	Incomplete information	10%
	Static	3%
	Other models	14%
Radio prop. model	Not reported	69%
	Incomplete information	13%
	Reported	18%
Overall	Complete information	5%
	Partial information	50%
	No information	45%

For the radio propagation model, 69% papers did not mention any information. It is unclear if Free Space Path Loss model was used or path loss. 13% studies gave incomplete information by only mentioning the transmission range of the signal. Only 18% studies mentioned the use of propagation models (two-ray ground, etc.). To summarize the outcomes, only 5% papers clearly mentioned both, mobility and propagation model. 45% of the research papers did not mention any of these parameters. 50% gave incomplete information. The results are surprising, as past studies have laid storing importance on both the parameters.

More over the nature of MANETs demands that mobility and propagation be considered while developing new protocols and algorithms. If these protocols are implemented in real world, the results will be drastically different than reported in the research paper.

4.2 Statistical Validity

For evaluation the statistical validity of the reported simulations, we have collected the following parameters: seed value, confidence interval, number of simulation iterations, and p-value significance (Table 2). Out of 38 papers 16% stated about the use of different seeds for testing the simulations. Rest may have left the value to the default simulator algorithm (usually based on system clock). Although it is safe to say that modern systems are intelligent enough to pick random seeds, but many times the researchers write their own simulators and overlook the importance of seed values.

Table 2. Statistical validity

Criteria		Value
Seed value	Reported	16%
	Not reported	84%
CI	Not reported	66%
	0.9	8%
	0.95	26%
No. of runs	Reported	39%
	Not reported	61%
Overall	Complete information	3%
	Partial information	37%
	No information	60%

66% did not report confidence interval used in their experiments. 61% of the research publish did not give any information about the number of runs of simulations. Surprisingly, none of the papers reported any p-value test for significant change in improvement. Although improvement is claimed, but whether it is significant enough is not clear from the papers. Following the criteria of these 3 parameters (excluding p-value), only 3% of the papers are statistically valid as they have reported all the three factors. 37% of the research papers reported partial parameters, while remaining 60% did not report any parameter in this category. The lack of statistical information puts the validity of paper in doubt.

4.3 Repeatability

Repeatability has been evaluated based on the following: (a) Simulation Tool (b) Simulation Tool version (c) Basic Simulation Parameters. 16% studies did not report the simulation tool name; although they do mention that they have obtained the result through simulation (Table 3). One can only assume if they have written their own simulators or not. Out of those 84% studies which reported the simulation tool, 45% mentioned the version of tool.

Table 3. Repeatability

Criteria		Value
Sim. tool	Reported (NS-2: 37%, NS-3, Matlab, SWAN, etc.)	84%
	Not reported	16%
Sim. tool version (of 84% above)	Reported	45%
	Not Reported	55%
Sim. basic param.	Reported	58%
	Partial information	32%
	Not reported	10%
Overall	Repeatable	26%
	Partial information (repeatable with assumptions)	53%
	Not repeatable	21%

The basic parameters considered for simulation repeatability are: No. of nodes, Network area, Tx range, Data rate, Packet size, MAC layer protocol, Bandwidth, Application, and Simulation time. 58% papers reported all the basic parameters, 10% did not mention any parameters, and remaining gave partial information. Taking three parameters for repeatability and their state in papers, 21% of the papers were not repeatable for not mentioning the tool name, version, and simulation parameters. 53% were not completely repeatable for skipping tool version, or giving incomplete simulation parameters. Remaining 26% are completely repeatable as they stated enough information to reproduce the experiment.

4.4   Conclusion: State of Adhoc Simulation Studies

Our findings about the current state of ad-hoc simulation studies are disconcerting. The survey by Kurkowski et al. claimed less than 15% of the research papers completely repeatable. After ten years of continuous emphasis on the importance of repeatability very little improvement has been observed by our survey, only 26% papers were found repeatable. Beside repeatability, the statistical validity and realistic scenarios state is more unpleasant. Since this situation is jeopardizing the integrity of research by publishing unrepeatable work, there is a necessity to improve upon the credibility of research. The challenge can have two dimensions:

– Problems in reporting of simulation studies: It can be assumed that the problems identified in the previous results are just due to exclusion of details from the papers in order to comply with the page limitations. Among a number of ways, best is to include a web link to the details of simulation scripts and the source code. This link should remain available to the research community for a sufficient period of time. Many online code sharing websites offer free services in this regard.

– Problems in design of simulation studies: This is a graver problem that can stem from either lack of knowledge about plethora of variable available in simulators for configuration, or just poor experimental design. In either case, it puts the whole research in doubt. This too can be remedied if a practice of simulator parameter sharing becomes more common in the research community. Even if most of the parameters are left to default values, knowledge of their existence will help researchers design better experiments.

In the next section we discuss the design and implementation of an architecture for standardization of reports in simulation based studies. Both of the problems highlighted above can benefit, if there is a standard, easy to use, and sharable format available for configuration files of simulators.

Table 4. Description of common simulators

Simulator	Description
NS2	C/C++ as core and Otcl for experiment setup
NS3	C++ as core and experimental setup. Python also used for scripting
OMNet++	C++ is class libraries, whereas eclipse and NED is used for designing and evaluation
OPNet	Uses C/C++ and provides GUI

5   Cross-Platform Architecture for Network Simulators

A number of discrete event network simulators are openly available (Table 4), and are commonly used by research community. They are designed in a way that decouples the core protocol implementation from the user interface. The user interface can be graphical or textual script file.

Most of the configuration is done via the interface or scripts. Modification in the core is done to change the behavior of the protocol. Both problems of simulation design and reporting can be addressed at the interface/script part, if the generation of input parameters to the core is done using a standardized interface. The output of such an interface will contain detailed parameters and can be shared easily with other researchers.

5.1   System Architecture

The system architecture (Fig. 1) is designed to be independent of simulation software, with modular components in order to facilitate the generation of script/configuration files for running simulations. Different modules of system architecture are;

- GUI (with XML Input & Script Importer): This module interacts with the user and provides options to import a preexisting XML file (generated by this software), scripts/programs written for tools mentioned in Table 4, or to input new parameters. Once the imported file is loaded, the parameters become configurable, and the user can change them to desired values. For a new experiment, the GUI is powered by the Experiment Designer module, which aids in converging different parts of simulation setup.
- Experiment Designer: This module is the main engine for the system having a default parameter database. It queries the user for required parameters, and invokes other modules in the system. It also verifies that the input given

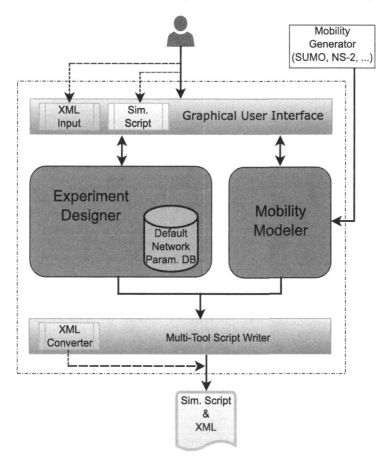

Fig. 1. System architecture.

by the user is within acceptable ranges (e.g. non-negative values, minimum connection pairs, etc.). Traffic pattern generation is also part of this engine. User can select from drop-down menu the type of traffic they wish to generate, and system provides them with set of input parameters required for that specify traffic type. The system facilitates by randomizing the connections, and allowing the user to alter based on their choice. Some of the basic parameters include, network area, node density, seed values for random number, simulation time, MAC layer details, protocol types, traffic types, node connections, etc.

– Mobility Generator: Unlike the traffic generation, the mobility generator is a separate module, which capitalizes on the availability of 3rd party mobility generation scripts. Once the mobility of simulation is generated it is converted into script for the target simulator.

– Script Writer (with XML Converter): This module generates the final executable script for different simulation tools, along with an XML version of it. The generated output in not just a collection of parameters provided by the user, but a complete list of variables required in the simulation. For example (Fig. 2), ns-default.tcl contains all possible configurable parameters and their default values. Information is borrowed from this file, and made part of the resulting script and XML file. XML file can be used to import same simulation again by the system for replication. It can also be used by other researchers to parse and extract desired configuration for their experimentation.

Fig. 2. Sample XML and TCL output files for NS-2.

5.2 Standardization

Our system is a basic tool for standardizing the way simulation studies are reported. With the availability of the detailed XML file for research community, the process to replicate the experiment will be seamless using this system. Moreover, with the added capability to interact with realistic mobility generation tools and real world traces, our system enables the users to create more realistic scenarios.

6 Conclusion

Scientific experiment is conducted to validate, accept or refute the hypothesis. If the experiment is flawed or not documented properly, it misinforms others who might make advancement in work by building upon unreliable foundations. This paper presents a survey to know the state of ad hoc simulation networks in terms of credibility and repeatability. The three aspects which were focused for credibility were how much of research published is repeatable, statistically valid and tested in a realistic scenario. We observed that only 26% papers were completely repeatable, only 3% of the papers mentioned the complete information required for the study to be statistically valid and only 5% of the papers have given complete details about mobility and radio propagation model, which directly affects the results reflecting the performance of solution. To address the challenge of reporting standardization and better design network simulation experiment, we have purposed a software system that enables the users to create simulation scripts, and publish them in globally acceptable formats. The loop back system can take the XML format reports and recreate the input script.

References

1. Jensen, J.D.: Scientific uncertainty in news coverage of cancer research: effects of hedging on scientists and journalists credibility. Hum. Commun. Res. **34**(3), 347–369 (2008)
2. Patton, M.Q.: Enhancing the quality and credibility of qualitative analysis. Health Serv. Res. **34**(5 Pt 2), 1189 (1999)
3. Metzger, M.J.: Making sense of credibility on the web: models for evaluating online information and recommendations for future research. J. Assoc. Inf. Sci. Technol. **58**(13), 2078–2091 (2007)
4. Riege, A.M.: Validity and reliability tests in case study research: a literature review with hands-on applications for each research phase. Qual. Mark. Res. Int. J. **6**(2), 75–86 (2003)
5. Kurkowski, S., Camp, T., Colagrosso, M.: MANET simulation studies: the incredibles. In: ACM SIGMOBILE Mobile Computing and Communications Review, vol. 9, no. 4, pp. 50–61 (2005)
6. Gunes, M., Wenig, M.: On the way to a more realistic simulation environment for mobile ad-hoc networks. In: International Workshop on Mobile Services and Personalized Environments, GI LNI (2006)

7. Andel, T.R., Yasinsac, A.: On the credibility of MANET simulations. Computer **39**(7), 48–54 (2006)
8. Peng, L., Bo, Z., Zhongyong, Z.: Simulation of VANET in a more realistic scenario. In: IEEE, ISSN, pp. 978–1000 (2011)
9. Feeley, M., Hutchinson, N., Ray, S.: Realistic mobility for mobile ad hoc network simulation. In: Nikolaidis, I., Barbeau, M., Kranakis, E. (eds.) ADHOC-NOW 2004. LNCS, vol. 3158, pp. 324–329. Springer, Heidelberg (2004). https://doi.org/10.1007/978-3-540-28634-9_28
10. Divecha, B., Abraham, A., Grosan, C., Sanyal, S.: Impact of node mobility on MANET routing protocols models. JDIM **5**(1), 19–23 (2007)
11. Martinez, F.J., Toh, C.-K., Cano, J.-C., Calafate, C.T., Manzoni, P.: Realistic radio propagation models (RPMs) for VANET simulations. In: Wireless Communications and Networking Conference, WCNC 2009, pp. 1–6. IEEE (2009)
12. Sandve, G.K., Nekrutenko, A., Taylor, J., Hovig, E.: Ten simple rules for reproducible computational research. PLoS Comput. Biol. **9**(10), e1003285 (2013)
13. Prabhakaran, P., Sankar, R.: Impact of realistic mobility models on wireless networks performance. In: IEEE International Conference on Wireless and Mobile Computing, Networking and Communications : WiMob 2006, pp. 329–334. IEEE (2006)

Task Offloading with Execution Cost Minimization in Heterogeneous Mobile Cloud Computing

Xing Liu[1], Songtao Guo[1(⊠)], and Yuanyuan Yang[2]

[1] College of Electronic and Information Engineering, Southwest University,
Chongqing 400715, China
songtao_guo@163.com
[2] Department of Electrical and Computer Engineering, Stony Brook University,
Stony Brook, NY 11794, USA

Abstract. Mobile cloud computing (MCC) can significantly enhance computation capability and save energy of smart mobile devices (SMDs) by offloading remoteable tasks from resources-constrained SMDs onto the resource-rich cloud. However, it remains a challenge issue how to appropriately partition applications and select the suitable cloud to offload the task under the constraints of execution cost including completion time of the application and energy consumption of SMDs. To address such a challenge, in this paper, we first formulate the partitioning and cloud selection problem into execution cost minimization problem. To solve the optimization problem, we then propose a system framework for adaptive partitioning and dynamic selective offloading. Based on the framework, we design an optimal cloud selection algorithm with execution cost minimization which consists of offloading judgement and cloud selection. Finally, our experimental results in a real testbed demonstrate that our framework can effectively reduce the execution cost compared with other frameworks.

Keywords: Mobile cloud computing · Application partition
Task offloading · Cloud selection · Execution cost minimization

1 Introduction

In recent years, smart mobile devices (SMDs) such as smartphones have become an indispensable part of modern life. The SMDs have been the preferred computing device to accommodate most up-to-date mobile applications, like interactive games, image/video applications and etc [16]. However, due to the physical size constraint, SMDs are in general resource-constrained [7], with limited energy supply and computation capacity. In particular, it is still a challenge how to run computing-intensive applications on resource constrained SMDs.

With the development of communication technology, cloud computing applied in the mobile industry has formed an emerging and promising method

© Springer Nature Singapore Pte Ltd. 2018
L. Zhu and S. Zhong (Eds.): MSN 2017, CCIS 747, pp. 509–522, 2018.
https://doi.org/10.1007/978-981-10-8890-2_39

to solve this challenge [7], which is mobile cloud computing (MCC). MCC allows mobile devices to take advantage of rich resources provided by the clouds. Thus, MCC not only extends battery lifetime but also utilizes the computation resource of cloud system. In recent years, a *computation offloading* [7,14] which migrates resource-intensive computations from SMDs to the cloud via wireless access, has been proposed as a way of implementing mobile cloud computing. Moreover, the suitable *computation partition* is precondition of computation offloading, which also is the hot research topic of MCC. The objective of computation partition and offloading is solving the problem which minimizes the execution cost of applications including completion time and energy consumption of SMDs.

Previous research works have proposed solutions to address the problem [5,6,8,12,14–16]. Chun et al. in [14] proposed a CloneCloud that automatically offloads an application from the mobile device to the smartphone clone in the cloud at a fine-granularity level while optimizing the execution time for a target computation. Based on CloneCloud, Yang et al. in [16] optimized the overall execution time by dynamically offloading a part of Android codes running on smart mobile device to the cloud. In practice, according to computing resources, the clouds can be divided into many categories. For different categories of clouds, the offloading cost of the same application is different. However, how to select an appropriate category of clouds to minimize the execution cost is not considered in the previous works.

This paper mainly focuses on how to appropriately partition application and dynamically select the best cloud to offload. First, we formulate the cloud selection problem into an optimization problem of minimizing execution cost, which includes the completion time of application and energy consumption of SMDs. In order to solve this problem, we then design a novel system framework which performs the method-level offloading with least transfer package size. This framework provides runtime support for the application partitioning and offloading, and consists of profiler, solver and communication module. According to the amount of local computation resource, the SMDs divide each thread of the application into some small tasks, named offloading tasks, and migrates the tasks to the best cloud to execute so as to achieve the minimum execution cost. Based on the framework, we propose a best cloud selection algorithm assigned into the solver of framework.

Compared with previous works, the contributions of this paper can be summarized as follows:

– We present an integrated and novel framework of code partitioning and offloading. The comments of our framework are highly modularized and easily extended.
– We propose an optimization model for the local execution time and energy consumption of SMDs by taking into account the execution time of the cloud.
– Based on the proposed optimization model, we provide a cloud selection algorithm to achieve the minimum execution cost.

The rest of this paper is organized as follows. In Sect. 2, we introduce the related work. In Sect. 3, we present the MCC system and optimization model.

Section 4 outlines the proposed framework and Sect. 5 presents the algorithms for optimal cloud selection. In Sect. 6, we evaluate the performance of the proposed algorithm. Section 7 concludes the paper.

2   Related Work

MCC focuses on solving the problems of *what* to offload and *how* to offload [10,11]. The primary objective of offloading and partitioning policies is to enhance the performance of mobile device in terms of execution/completion time and throughput by utilizing cloud resource [4,7,13–16]. Guo et al. in [7] proposed an energy-efficient dynamic offloading strategy that optimizes the performance of mobile devices through the dynamic voltage and frequency scaling (DVFS) in local computing. Yang et al. in [15] studied the computation partitioning in order to optimize the partition between the mobile devices and cloud such that the application has maximum throughput.

In addition, in [14], the Multi-User Computation Partitioning Problem (MCPP) was designed to achieve minimum average completion time for all the users. Compared with these works, we not only consider the cost of thread offloading, but also take into account the price of thread partition. On the basis of the partition technique in [16], we study how to judge whether an application thread is necessary to offloading. After that, we develop heterogeneous selection scheme for diverse remote cloud resources with the optimal size of the transmission packet.

There are a few works on the design of application frameworks in cloud computing [5,6,8,12,13,15]. The most popular one is MAUI [6], which describes a system which offloads fine-grained code to the cloud, while maximizing the potential of energy saving. However, it can't guarantee to satisfy the requirement of completion time. Actually, either completion time or energy consumption was only considered in previous works. Our work aims to develop systematic method to improve the time and energy efficiency of task offloading. Thus we utilize an online profiler to monitor the completion time of the application, and dynamically decide whether and where to offload tasks based on user requirements.

3   Network Architecture and Problem Formulation

3.1   Network Architecture

Our cloud system consists of a specific SMD and multiple types of mobile cloud systems that can provide different services, as shown in Fig. 1. The SMD accesses the Internet via base station or wireless access point, and then visits the cloud resources over the network.

In this paper, two kinds of cloud system would be considered, i.e., central cloud c_1 and cloudlets c_2. Furthermore, $c_k = \{c_k^1, c_k^2, \cdots, c_k^m\}$, $k = 1, 2$ denotes the cloud c_k has m cloud severs. However, the CPU frequencies of different servers in a cloud system are different. Thus, the CPU frequency of each sever in cloud c_k is $f_{c_k}^j$,

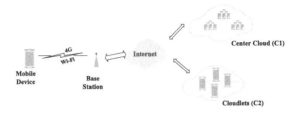

Fig. 1. Overview of mobile cloud computing system

where $j \in \{1, 2, \cdots, m\}$ represents the sever j of cloud c_k. Note that f_0 denotes the local CPU frequency of SMDs. In addition, we denote when the SMD accesses to cloud c_k via network access, the corresponding channel data transmission rate is $R_{c_k}, k = 1, 2$.

3.2   Problem Formulation

MCC aims to solve the problem of energy consumption and execution time of SMDs, which is the main research content of this paper.

In our system, a process is an Android application running on the Dalvik virtual machine (VM). An application process may comprise multiple threads, part of which are called as *remoteable threads*, which may contain multiple remotely executable methods (REMs) while others will be called as *un-remoteable threads*, which do not have REMs. MCC mainly focuses on the remoteable threads. Thus unless otherwise specified, the thread in this paper is considered as the migratable thread.

Next, we consider the execution cost of an application under the diversity condition. When the SMD runs an application, the solver in our framework will partition the application as primary heap objects (PHOs), which will be described in Sect. 4.2.1 in detail. We define the set of PHOs as $N = \{i | i = 1, 2, ..., n\}$. Moreover we leverage an indicator $x_{i,c_k}, k = 1, 2, \forall i \in N$, to represent the task allocation, i.e.,

$$x_{i,c_k} = \begin{cases} 1, & \text{if task } i \text{ is assigned to cloud } c_k, \\ 0, & \text{otherwise.} \end{cases}$$

where x_{i,c_k} is either 0 or 1, thus we can take $X = \{(x_{i,c_k}) | i \in N, k = 1, 2\}$ as task allocation matrix.

We use a tuple $\{\alpha_i, \omega_i\}$ to denote task i, for $i \in N$, in which α_i is the input data size (in bits) from SMDs to cloud, and ω_i is the number of CPU cycles that is required by task processing, respectively. For a task i, we consider whether offloading it or not from the aspect of completion time and energy consumption. Similar to the existing work [4], we ignore the download time and downlink energy consumption of the task. Therefore, the completion time of task

T_i includes the computing time T_i^{comp} and transmission time T_i^{trans}, formulated as (1).

$$T_i = T_i^{comp} + T_i^{trans} \quad = \frac{\omega_i}{f_{c_k}^j} + \frac{\alpha_i}{R_{c_k}} \tag{1}$$

where $k = 1, 2$, and $T_i^{loc} = \frac{\omega_i}{f_0}$ denotes the local execution time of task i.

The energy consumption of task i, denoted as E_i, consists of two parts, which are the energy consumption of waiting for remote execution E_i^{wait}, and the energy consumption of transferring task to clouds E_i^{trans}, described as

$$E_i = E_i^{wait} + E_i^{trans} \quad = P_{idle} \times \frac{\omega_i}{f_{c_k}^j} + P_s \frac{\alpha_i}{R_{c_k}} \tag{2}$$

where $k = 1, 2$, and P_{idle} indicates the waiting power of SMDs when task i is migrated to clouds. P_s denotes transfer power of SMDs. We let $E_i^{loc} = P_c \times \frac{\omega_i}{f_0}$ denote the local computing energy consumption when task i is executed locally, where P_c represents computation power of SMDs.

Furthermore, the execution time $T(X)$ of an application can be expressed as Eq. (3).

$$T(X) = \sum_{i \in N} x_{i,c_k} \times T_i$$
$$= \sum_{i \in N} x_{i,c_k} \times \left(\frac{\omega_i}{f_{c_k}^j} + \frac{\alpha_i}{R_{c_k}} \right) \quad = \sum_{i \in N} x_{i,c_k} \Theta_{i,c_k} \tag{3}$$

where $k = 1, 2$. The energy consumption $(E(X))$ can be given by Eq. (4)

$$E(X) = \sum_{i \in N} x_{i,c_k} \times E_i \quad = \sum_{i \in N} x_{i,c_k} \times \left(P_{idle} \frac{\omega_i}{f_{c_k}^j} + P_s \frac{\alpha_i}{R_{c_k}} \right)$$
$$= \sum_{i \in N} x_{i,c_k} \Phi_{i,c_k} \tag{4}$$

In particular, the local execution time and energy consumption of application are given by respectively

$$T^{loc}(X, f_0) = \sum_{i \in N} x_{i,0} \frac{\omega_i}{f_0} \tag{5}$$

$$E^{loc}(X, f_0) = \sum_{i \in N} x_{i,0} P_c \times \frac{\omega_i}{f_0} \tag{6}$$

We use the execution cost as the metric to measure whether to migrate to the cloud. Hence, execution cost $Cost(X)$ can be defined by the summation of makespan $T(X)$ and the energy consumption $E(X)$ of the application, for $k = 1, 2$, i.e.,

$$Cost(X) = \lambda_t T(X) + \lambda_e E(X)$$
$$= \lambda_t \sum_{i \in N} x_{i,c_k} \Theta_{i,c_k} + \lambda_e \sum_{i \in N} x_{i,c_k} \Phi_{i,c_k} \tag{7}$$

where $\lambda_t, \lambda_e \in [0,1]$ are scalar weights, and $\lambda_t + \lambda_e = 1$. These weights can be adjusted by the preference related with energy and delay deadline of users.

Overall, the optimization problem formulated is how to select the cloud to offload for minimizing the execution cost of the task. The optimization framework can be formulated as follows:

$$\min_{X,C,S} Cost(X) \tag{8}$$

$$s.t \begin{cases} \sum_{i \in N} T(X) \le t_{delay} & \text{(9a)} \\[2mm] \sum_{i \in N} E(X) \le e_{threshold} & \text{(9b)} \\[2mm] \sum_{k=1,2} x_{i,c_k} = 1, & \forall i \in N & \text{(9c)} \\[2mm] X = \{(x_{i,c_k}) | i \in N, k = 1, 2\} & \text{(9d)} \end{cases}$$

The constraint (9a) denotes the completion time constraint which ensures that the total completion time of all the tasks in an application executed on SMDs is bounded by the required maximum finish time (i.e., delay deadline), t_{delay}. Similarly, (9b) specifies that the total energy consumption is less than or equal to the maximum energy consumption $e_{threshold}$. Constraint (9c) demonstrates that a task can only be assigned to one device. (9d) represents the task allocation.

4   System Framework Design

To address the optimization problem (8), a system framework is proposed, which consists of three components: Profiler, Solver and Communication Module, shown in Fig. 2. First, the profiler is mainly responsible for analyzing and

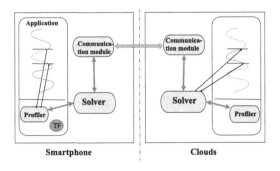

Fig. 2. The overview of system framework

detecting the network conditions, cloud conditions and mobile device performance, as well as transmitting correlative data to the solver. Then, based on the data provided by the profiler, the solver makes decision on partitioning and offloading. Finally, the communication module sends the task packages to the cloud, and receives the results returned from the cloud. In the following, we introduce the three components in details.

4.1 Profiler

The profiler is mainly deployed on the mobile device to detect and collect the parameters and configure resources of SMDs and clouds.

When SMD starts to execute an application, the system would create a temporary buffer (TF) in SMD's memory to store the information consisting of the device performance, such as P_{idle}, P_s, and P_c of SMDs, the network access, i.e., the channel data transmission rate R_{c_k}, and the cloud resource, that is, the types of clouds c_k, as well as the CPU frequency $f_{c_k}^j$. Moreover, this temporary buffer will be immediately released once the application is completed.

The solver can directly get data from cache TF, when it makes decision. What's more, the profiler is detecting the information in real-time, updating the data of TF at any time to ensure that the values obtained by solver are not expired.

Furthermore, the profiler also measures and analyzes whether the thread of the mobile application is remoteable. Here, we define three types of unremoteable codes: (1) the codes that implement the application's user interface; (2) the codes that interact with I/O devices where such interaction only makes sense on the mobile device; (3) the codes that interact with any external component that would be affected by re-execution [6]. If the thread is remoteable, which indicates that the thread doesn't include above three types of codes, the profiler will mark this thread as attribute [Remoteable], and transfer it to the solver.

4.2 Solver

The solver is mainly used to solve the problem of minimizing the execution cost $Cost(X)$ of an application, which consists of two modules in our system: the partition module and the migration module.

4.2.1 Partition Module

Partition module is used for code partition of application. When the profiler detects a remoteable thread, the partition module catches this thread. The state being transferred of remoteable thread includes stack, register and reachable heap object. Therefore, by using the partitioning technique in [16], the partition module determines the accessible heap objects (AHOs) by recursively chasing the reference links. Then the partition module deletes the super classes to make AHOs become the primary heap objects (PHOs), which is fewer than AOHs.

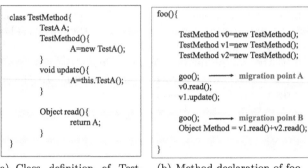

(a) Class definition of Test-
Method.

(b) Method declaration of foo.

Fig. 3. A example of Java code.

After that, we use the notion of dirty to further partition the PHOs. An example of code is shown in Fig. 3. Figure 3(a) defines the class $TestMethod$, and Fig. 3(b) declares the method $foo()$ and $goo()$ when these methods call the class $TestMethod$. The method $foo()$ calls method $goo()$ twice in Fig. 3(b), where we consider that two call points of the method $goo()$ are migration point A and migration point B, respectively. When there is the migration point A, class objects $V0, V1, V2$ are not invoked. While there is migration point B, class objects $V0, V1$ have been called, thus we label the objects, $V0, V1$, as dirty that have been invoked before call points. Other objects like $V2$ are un-dirty.

The dirty objects are identified by a famous compiler analysis technique, called *side-effect* [16]. For the un-dirty object, we do not migrate it rather than create a stub, and only migrate the stub. The stub consists of class name, object ID, and the address of an object which is necessary for the solver on the cloud to create new instance of un-dirty PHOs. After migrating stub to the cloud, we would use *on-the-fly* technique [3] to online instantiate un-dirty PHOs, named *on-cloud-copy*. Finally, we migrate the dirty objects and the stubs of un-dirty objects of PHOs, which is called offloading task.

4.2.2 Migration Module

The migration module mainly performs offloading decision for the task. In this module, we propose a best cloud selection algorithm (introducing in Sect. 5). According to transmission delay and energy saving required by the mobile user's preference for application execution, the module makes optimal offloading decision, i.e. selecting a best cloud to execute the migrated tasks, to minimize the cost $Cost(X)$.

We adopt t_{delay} to denote the tolerance of execution delay and $e_{threshold}$ to represent the tolerance of energy consumption. Different offloading strategies can be made by users based on their requirements for energy and delay as follows:

– When a mobile device is at low battery energy state, it can choose $\lambda_t < \lambda_e$, where $\lambda_t, \lambda_e \in [0, 1]$. Meanwhile $\sum_{i \in N} E(X)$ is bounded by $e_{threshold}$, i.e., $\sum_{i \in N} E(X) \leq e_{threshold}$.

- When a mobile device is running delay-sensitive applications (e.g., video streaming) that require to reduce as much as delay, it can set $\lambda_t > \lambda_e$, where $\lambda_t, \lambda_e \in [0,1]$. Simultaneously, $\sum_{i \in N} T(X) \le t_{delay}$.
- When a mobile device has low battery energy and runs the delay-sensitive applications, it can set $\lambda_t = \lambda_e$, where $\lambda_t, \lambda_e \in [0,1]$, so as to jointly optimize the energy consumption of mobile devices and the application completion time. Similarly, $\sum_{i \in N} E(X) \le e_{threshold}, \sum_{i \in N} T(X) \le t_{delay}$.

4.3   Communication Module

Communication module is responsible for the communication between local mobile device and clouds. When the solver has partitioned the thread and made offloading decision, the communication module serializes and packages the offloaded states and sent to cloud. When the cloud finishes the execution of a task, the communication module at cloud serializes the execution result, and sends it to mobile device. The local communication module receives the results from the cloud, and then compares it with source codes. The results from the cloud are merged with the local source codes and the SMD run the merged program again.

   In general, our system framework analyzes an application via profiler to determine whether each thread of the application can be offloaded. Furthermore, using the partition module of solver of the framework, these threads that need to be uploaded are partitioned as a smaller size of tasks, while the migration module calculates the execution time T_i, the energy consumption E_i, and the execution cost of each task $Cost_i$, according to the user's different preferences for time and energy consumption. We propose a best cloud selection algorithm on the migration module of solver based on the computation result of the partition module and obtain the cloud category with least cost, which will be given in Sect. 5. Finally, we offload the task to the selected cloud.

5   Best Cloud Selection Algorithm Design

In this section, we design a best cloud selection algorithm shown in Algorithm 1, which selects a cloud to transfer the task for achieving the minimum execution cost $Cost(X)$. The algorithm is applied to the migration module of our framework and consists of two parts: one is to decide whether the task can be offloaded, and the other is to migrate the remoteable task to which clouds.

   In the following, we describe the first part of our algorithm. When the solver captures a task execution thread, we need to determine whether the thread needs to be uploaded to the cloud. Except for the previous judgement of profiler, we also need to decide whether the partitioned task is offloaded or not according to T_i and E_i. The judgement condition is given as Eq. (10).

$$\begin{cases} \text{task } i \text{ is executed remotely,} & if \ \frac{T_i^{loc}}{T_i} > 1, and \ \frac{E_i^{loc}}{E_i} > 1 \\ \text{task } i \text{ is executed locally,} & otherwise. \end{cases} \tag{10}$$

For a given task i, if its local computation time T_i^{loc} is greater than the remote execution time T_i, and the local energy consumption E_i^{loc} is also larger than the offloading energy consumption E_i, then the task will be offloaded to the cloud; otherwise, the task will be executed on local device. If task i is considered to be migrated, then the algorithm labels the attribute $[Remoteable]$ to the task, as described in line 2–10 of Algorithm 1.

Besides, we will describe the second part of our algorithm. As described in line 14–15, the task i is determined to be uploaded to the cloud, and the cost $Cost_i$ of the task i for cloud c_1 and c_2 is calculated, as shown in line 14. Next, we compare all $Cost_i$ of task i by line 15, and obtain the minimum cost $Cost_i^{min}$. After that, we assign the cloud c_k with minimum cost $Cost_i$ of task i to the best cloud K. Finally, we select the cloud K as the best offloading cloud, and migrate the partitioned task to the cloud, as shown in line 16–18.

In addition, we analyze the time complexity of the algorithm. We consider n tasks and m clouds in the algorithm. For each task, the time complexity of calculating minimum cost of finding the best cloud among m clouds is $O(m)$, which is shown in Lines 12–20. Therefore, the time complexity of n tasks to calculate the minimum cost is denoted as $O(n \times m)$, from Lines 2 to 21.

Algorithm 1. Best Cloud Selection Algorithm.

Input: : λ_t, λ_e: user's preference;
    $i \in N$: execution tasks that had partitioned;
    $j = 1, 2, \cdots, m$: the number of severs of c_k;
Output: : best cloud selection K;
 1: set parameters: $f_{c_k}^j, R_{c_k}, P_{idle}, P_s, P_c$
    and $T_i, T_i^{loc}, E_i, E_i^{loc}, Cost_i, Cost_i^{min}$;
 2: **for** $i = 1$ to n **do**
 3:    compute T_i, T_i^{loc} and E_i, E_i^{loc} by (1), (2), (5) and (6) respectively;
 4:    /* offloading judging */
 5:    **if** $\frac{T_i^{loc}}{T_i} > 1$ and $\frac{E_i^{loc}}{E_i} > 1$ **then**
 6:        task i will be migrated to clouds;
 7:        label i as [Remoteable];
 8:    **else**
 9:        execute task i locally;
10:    **end if**
11:    /* cloud selection */;
12:    **if** task i is remoteable **then**
13:        **for** $j = 1$ to m **do**
14:            $Cost_i = \lambda_t T_i + \lambda_e E_i$; //$Cost_i$ is the execution cost of a task i on cloud c_k
15:            $Cost_i^{min} = \min_{c_k \in C}\{Cost_i\}$
16:            **if** $K = c_k$ **then**
17:                migrate task i to cloud c_k;
18:            **end if**
19:        **end for**
20:    **end if**
21: **end for**

---

6   Performance Evaluation

We implement our system module on the Android 4.1.2. The smart mobile device is a SAMSUNG Galaxy Nexus with dual-core 1.2 Ghz CPU and 1 GB of RAM. As for the cloud sever, we consider two categories of clouds, i.e., the central cloud and cloudlets. The central cloud consists of 3 IBM X3850X6 severs, each of which has 4 quad-core 3.4 Ghz Xeon CPUs and 128 GB of RAM running Ubuntu 14.0. Then we use 30 Android 4.1.2 SAMSUNG Nexus S5 smartphones with quad-core 2.5 GHz CPU and 2 GB RAM, as cloudlets. The experimental parameters are listed in Table 1.

Table 1. Default parameter setup

Parameter	Value
ω_i	$330\alpha_i$
$f_{c_k}^j$	$[10,\ 54.4]$ GHz
f_0	2.4 GHz
R_{s_v,c_k}^{UL}	$[10,\ 25]$ Mbps
R_{s_v,c_k}^{DL}	R_{s_v,c_k}^{UL}
P_s	1.5 W
P_c	2.4 W
P_{idle}	50 mW

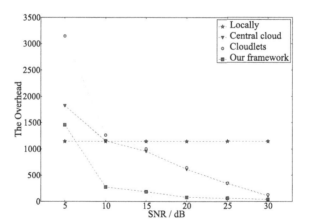

Fig. 4. Impact of wireless channel data transmission rate.

Figure 4 shows the effect of data transmission rate on task execution cost as well as the practicality of our framework. We use the *Face Detection* [1] as experimental application, which needs to identify 99 images and access the cloud via 4G. According to the *Shanon* theorem, we know that the data transmission rate is limited by channel bandwidth and Signal-Noise Ratio(SNR). Therefore, for the wireless access, we set the channel bandwidth $B = 5$ MHz. Theoretically, when the bandwidth B is fixed, the larger the SNR is, the greater the channel data transmission rate is. With the increasing of SNR, the execution cost of the application is decreasing. Compared with other three methods, i.e., all tasks are executed locally, on the central cloud and on the cloudlets, our proposed framework of application partition and optimal cloud selection is much shorter than other methods in term of execution cost. Furthermore, we find that our framework reduces about 80% compared with local execution, and is less about 60% and 65% than the execution in central cloud and cloudlets.

Figure 5 illustrates that the impact of user's preferences, λ_t and λ_e on the completion time and energy consumption of application with different number of tasks. Here, we implement the examination by solving the *N-Queens* problem [8], and give the comparison of execution time and energy consumption for different ratios of $\frac{\lambda_t}{\lambda_e}$. It can be observed from Fig. 5(a) that for a given task, the completion time decreases as λ_t increases, however, the changes of the energy consumption are opposite in Fig. 5(b). This is reasonable since a large λ_t will lead to the little tolerance for completion time for the user. Therefore, the proposed system framework will automatically set the weight value of λ_t to be larger than λ_e, which means that it mainly optimizes the completion time of the application to meet the needs of the user.

Figure 6 demonstrates the comparison of execution cost of our framework with the least context migration system in [9] called framework 1, and the multisite offloading framework using Markov decision process in [13] named framework 2 by the applications of *Face Detection* [1], *N-Queens* [8], *and Sudoku* [2]. We can observe from Fig. 6 that the average overhead in our framework is about 35% less than framework 1, and 30% less than framework 2 in application completion. The reason is that our framework transfers much less data and selects adaptively the optimal cloud.

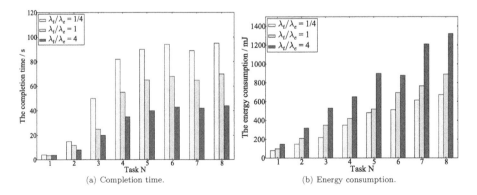

(a) Completion time.   (b) Energy consumption.

Fig. 5. The impact of user's preference $\frac{\lambda_t}{\lambda_e}$

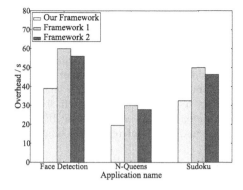

Fig. 6. Comparison of overhead of three framework for different applications.

7   Conclusion

In this paper, we study the execution cost minimization problem in mobile cloud computing. We design an application framework including profiler, solver, and communication module. This framework provides runtime support for adaptive partitioning and dynamic offloading selection in application execution. Under this framework, we propose a novel cloud selection algorithm which is composed of offloading judgement and cloud selection. We implement the framework in a real testbed and experimental results demonstrate that compared to the existing frameworks, our framework can effectively reduce the execution time and energy consumption.

Based on these, the future work will consider the task offloading allocation problem in the multiple network connection ways and variety mobile cloud system scenarios.

Acknowledgement. This work was supported by the National Natural Science Foundation of China (No. 61373178, 61373179, 61402381), Natural Science Key Foundation of Chongqing (cstc2015jcyjBX0094), the Fundamental Research Funds for the Central Universities (XDJK2013A018, XDJK2015C010, XDJK2015D023), and Natural Science Foundation of Chongqing (CSTC2016JCYJA0449), China Postdoctoral Science Foundation (2016M592619) and Chongqing Postdoctoral Science Foundation (XM2016002).

References

1. Face detection.https://facedetection.com/
2. Sudoku. https://play.google.com/store/apps/details?id=com.icenta.sudoku.ui
3. Chabrier, T., Tisserand, A.: On-the-fly multi-base recoding for ECC scalar multiplication without pre-computations. In: 2013 IEEE 21st Symposium on Computer Arithmetic, pp. 219–228 (2013)
4. Chen, X.: Decentralized computation offloading game for mobile cloud computing. IEEE Trans. Parallel Distrib. Syst. **26**, 974–983 (2015)

5. Chun, B.G., Ihm, S., Maniatis, P., Naik, M., Patti, A.: CloneCloud: elastic execution between mobile device and cloud. In: Conference on Computer Systems, pp. 301–314 (2011)
6. Cuervo, E., Balasubramanian, A., Cho, D.K., Wolman, A., Saroiu, S., Chandra, R., Bahl, P.: MAUI: making smartphones last longer with code offload. In: International Conference on Mobile Systems, Applications, and Services, pp. 49–62 (2010)
7. Guo, S., Xiao, B., Yang, Y., Yang, Y.: Energy-efficient dynamic offloading and resource scheduling in mobile cloud computing. In: IEEE INFOCOM 2016 - The 35th Annual IEEE International Conference on Computer Communications, pp. 1–9 (2016)
8. Kosta, S., Aucinas, A., Hui, P., Mortier, R., Zhang, X.: Thinkair: dynamic resource allocation and parallel execution in the cloud for mobile code offloading. In: 2012 Proceedings IEEE INFOCOM, pp. 945–953 (2012)
9. Li, Y., Gao, W.: Code offload with least context migration in the mobile cloud. In: 2015 IEEE Conference on Computer Communications (INFOCOM), pp. 1876–1884 (2015)
10. Liu, J., Ahmed, E., Shiraz, M., Gani, A., Buyya, R., Qureshi, A.: Application partitioning algorithms in mobile cloud computing: taxonomy, review and future directions. J. Netw. Comput. Appl. 48(C), 99–117 (2015)
11. Khan, A.R., Othman, M., Madani, S.A., Khan, S.U.: A survey of mobile cloud computing application models. IEEE Commun. Surv. Tutor. 16(1), 393–413 (2014)
12. Satyanarayanan, M., Bahl, P., Caceres, R., Davies, N.: The case for VM-based cloudlets in mobile computing. IEEE Pervasive Comput. 8(4), 14–23 (2009)
13. Terefe, M.B., Lee, H., Heo, N., Fox, G.C., Oh, S.: Energy-efficient multisite offloading policy using Markov decision process for mobile cloud computing. Pervasive Mob. Comput. 27(C), 75–89 (2016)
14. Yang, L., Cao, J., Cheng, H., Ji, Y.: Multi-user computation partitioning for latency sensitive mobile cloud applications. IEEE Trans. Comput. 64(8), 2253–2266 (2015)
15. Yang, L., Cao, J., Tang, S., Li, T., Chan, A.T.S.: A framework for partitioning and execution of data stream applications in mobile cloud computing. In: 2012 IEEE Fifth International Conference on Cloud Computing, pp. 794–802 (2012)
16. Yang, S., Kwon, D., Yi, H., Cho, Y., Kwon, Y., Paek, Y.: Techniques to minimize state transfer costs for dynamic execution offloading in mobile cloud computing. IEEE Trans. Mob. Comput. 13(11), 2648–2660 (2014)

Author Index

Printed in the United States
By Bookmasters